Harnessing the Internet of Everything (IoE) for Accelerated Innovation Opportunities

Pedro J.S. Cardoso
University of Algarve, Portugal

Jânio Monteiro
University of Algarve, Portugal

Jorge Semião
University of Algarve, Portugal

João M.F. Rodrigues
University of Algarve, Portugal

A volume in the Advances in Computer and
Electrical Engineering (ACEE) Book Series

Published in the United States of America by
    IGI Global
    Engineering Science Reference (an imprint of IGI Global)
    701 E. Chocolate Avenue
    Hershey PA, USA 17033
    Tel: 717-533-8845
    Fax: 717-533-8661
    E-mail: cust@igi-global.com
    Web site: http://www.igi-global.com

Library of Congress Cataloging-in-Publication Data

Names: Cardoso, Pedro J. S., editor. | Monteiro, Janio, editor. | Semiao,
    Jorge, editor. | Rodrigues, Joao M. F., editor.
Title: Harnessing the internet of everything (IoE) for accelerated innovation
    opportunities / Pedro J.S. Cardoso, Janio Monteiro, Jorge Semiao, and
    Joao M.F. Rodrigues, editors.
Description: Hershey, PA : Engineering Science Reference (an imprint of IGI
    Global), [2019] | Includes bibliographical references and index.
Identifiers: LCCN 2018024572| ISBN 9781522573326 (hardcover) | ISBN
    9781522573333 (ebook)
Subjects: LCSH: Internet of things.
Classification: LCC TK5105.8857 .H37 2019 | DDC 004.67/8--dc23 LC record available at https://lccn.loc.gov/2018024572

This book is published in the IGI Global book series Advances in Computer and Electrical Engineering (ACEE) (ISSN: 2327-039X; eISSN: 2327-0403)

British Cataloguing in Publication Data
A Cataloguing in Publication record for this book is available from the British Library.

For electronic access to this publication, please contact: eresources@igi-global.com.

Advances in Computer and Electrical Engineering (ACEE) Book Series

Srikanta Patnaik
SOA University, India

ISSN:2327-039X
EISSN:2327-0403

MISSION

The fields of computer engineering and electrical engineering encompass a broad range of interdisciplinary topics allowing for expansive research developments across multiple fields. Research in these areas continues to develop and become increasingly important as computer and electrical systems have become an integral part of everyday life.

The **Advances in Computer and Electrical Engineering (ACEE) Book Series** aims to publish research on diverse topics pertaining to computer engineering and electrical engineering. **ACEE** encourages scholarly discourse on the latest applications, tools, and methodologies being implemented in the field for the design and development of computer and electrical systems.

COVERAGE

- VLSI Design
- Microprocessor Design
- Circuit Analysis
- Optical Electronics
- Chip Design
- VLSI Fabrication
- Power Electronics
- Applied Electromagnetics
- Computer science
- Electrical Power Conversion

IGI Global is currently accepting manuscripts for publication within this series. To submit a proposal for a volume in this series, please contact our Acquisition Editors at Acquisitions@igi-global.com or visit: http://www.igi-global.com/publish/.

Titles in this Series

For a list of additional titles in this series, please visit: www.igi-global.com/book-series

Advancing Consumer-Centric Fog Computing Architectures
Kashif Munir (University of Hafr Al-Batin, Saudi Arabia)
Engineering Science Reference • copyright 2019 • 217pp • H/C (ISBN: 9781522571490) • US $210.00 (our price)

New Perspectives on Information Systems Modeling and Design
António Miguel Rosado da Cruz (Polytechnic Institute of Viana do Castelo, Portugal) and Maria Estrela Ferreira da Cruz (Polytechnic Institute of Viana do Castelo, Portugal)
Engineering Science Reference • copyright 2019 • 332pp • H/C (ISBN: 9781522572718) • US $235.00 (our price)

Advanced Methodologies and Technologies in Network Architecture, Mobile Computing, and Data Analytics
Mehdi Khosrow-Pour, D.B.A. (Information Resources Management Association, USA)
Engineering Science Reference • copyright 2019 • 1857pp • H/C (ISBN: 9781522575986) • US $595.00 (our price)

Emerging Innovations in Microwave and Antenna Engineering
Jamal Zbitou (University of Hassan 1st, Morocco) and Ahmed Errkik (University of Hassan 1st, Morocco)
Engineering Science Reference • copyright 2019 • 437pp • H/C (ISBN: 9781522575399) • US $245.00 (our price)

Advanced Methodologies and Technologies in Artificial Intelligence, Computer Simulation, and Human-Computer Interaction
Mehdi Khosrow-Pour, D.B.A. (Information Resources Management Association, USA)
Engineering Science Reference • copyright 2019 • 1221pp • H/C (ISBN: 9781522573685) • US $545.00 (our price)

Optimal Power Flow Using Evolutionary Algorithms
Provas Kumar Roy (Kalyani Government Engineering College, India) and Susanta Dutta (Dr. B. C. Roy Engineering College, India)
Engineering Science Reference • copyright 2019 • 323pp • H/C (ISBN: 9781522569718) • US $195.00 (our price)

Advanced Condition Monitoring and Fault Diagnosis of Electric Machines
Muhammad Irfan (Najran University, Saudi Arabia)
Engineering Science Reference • copyright 2019 • 307pp • H/C (ISBN: 9781522569893) • US $225.00 (our price)

The Rise of Fog Computing in the Digital Era
K.G. Srinivasa (Chaudhary Brahm Prakash Government Engineering College, India) Pankaj Lathar (Chaudhary Brahm Prakash Government Engineering College, India) and G.M. Siddesh (Ramaiah Institute of Technology, India)
Engineering Science Reference • copyright 2019 • 286pp • H/C (ISBN: 9781522560708) • US $215.00 (our price)

IGI Global
DISSEMINATOR OF KNOWLEDGE

701 East Chocolate Avenue, Hershey, PA 17033, USA
Tel: 717-533-8845 x100 • Fax: 717-533-8661
E-Mail: cust@igi-global.com • www.igi-global.com

Editorial Advisory Board

Table of Contents

Detailed Table of Contents

Chapter 1

    Ergin Dinc, University of Cambridge, UK
    Murat Kuscu, University of Cambridge, UK
    Bilgesu Arif Bilgin, University of Cambridge, UK
    Ozgur Baris Akan, University of Cambridge, UK

In this chapter, the authors put forward the notion of internet of everything (IoE) as an effort to maximally connect our communication infrastructure to the universe, which can itself be regarded as the real IoE, an interconnected network of physical phenomena (i.e., Everything we perceive as independent wholes that persist through time, such as molecules, light, waves, living organisms, and celestial objects, with the purpose of gaining better understanding of its mechanisms and manipulating them to enable novel technologies via a networked sensing, analysis, and actuation approach). The strategy to outline the IoE effort is by dissecting the vast IoE landscape into IoXs according to their various application domains (Xs), for each of which the authors give an up-to-date account of the state-of-the-art in related fields and point out the challenges in contemporary research faces. They also discuss a wide spectrum of challenges and future research directions (e.g., ubiquitous connectivity, security, big data, etc., which are common to many IoXs and penetrate into the IoE effort in general).

Chapter 2

    Pedro J. S. Cardoso, University of Algarve, Portugal
    Jânio Monteiro, University of Algarve, Portugal
    Nelson Pinto, University of Algarve, Portugal
    Dario Cruz, University of Algarve, Portugal
    João M. F. Rodrigues, University of Algarve, Portugal

The internet of everything is a network that connects people, data, process, and things, making it easier to understand that many subfields of knowledge are discussable while addressing this subject. This chapter makes a survey on the application of machine learning algorithms to the internet of everything. This survey is particularly focused in computational frameworks for the development of intelligent systems and applications of machine learning algorithms as possible engines of wealth creation. A final example shows how to develop a simple end-to-end system.

Chapter 3

Nelson Pinto, University of Algarve, Portugal
Dario Cruz, University of Algarve, Portugal
Jânio Monteiro, University of Algarve, Portugal
Cristiano Cabrita, University of Algarve, Portugal
Jorge Semião, University of Algarve, Portugal
Pedro J. S. Cardoso, University of Algarve, Portugal
Luís M. R. Oliveira, Universidade da Beira Interior, Portugal & Universidade do Algarve, Portugal
João M. F. Rodrigues, University of Algarve, Portugal

In many countries, renewable energy production already represents an important percentage of the total energy that is generated in electrical grids. In order to reach higher levels of integration, demand side management measures are yet required. In fact, different from the legacy electrical grids, where at any given instant the generation levels are adjusted to meet the demand, when using renewable energy sources, the demand must be adapted in accordance with the generation levels, since these cannot be controlled. In order to alleviate users from the burden of individual control of each appliance, energy management systems (EMSs) have to be developed to both monitor the generation and consumption patterns and to control electrical appliances. In this context, the main contribution of this chapter is to present the implementation of such an IoT-based monitoring and control system for microgrids, capable of supporting the development of an EMS.

Chapter 4

José Jasnau Caeiro, Instituto Politécnico de Beja, Portugal
João Carlos Martins, Instituto Politécnico de Beja, Portugal

Internet of Things (IoT) systems are starting to be developed for applications in the management of water quality monitoring systems. The chapter presents some of the work done in this area and also shows some systems being developed by the authors for the Alentejo region. A general architecture for water quality monitoring systems is discussed. The important issue of computer security is mentioned and connected to recent publications related to the blockchain technology. Web services, data transmission technology, micro web frameworks, and cloud IoT services are also discussed.

Chapter 5

Gonçalo Marques, Universidade da Beira Interior, Portugal

The study of systems and architectures for ambient assisted living (AAL) is undoubtedly a topic of great relevance given the ageing of the world population. On the one hand, AAL technologies are designed to meet the needs of the ageing population in order to maintain their independence as long as possible. On the other hand, internet of things (IoT) proposes that various "things," which include not only communication devices but also every other physical object on the planet, are going to be connected and will be controlled across the internet. The continuous technological advancements turn possible to build smart objects with great capabilities for sensing and connecting turn possible several advancements in AAL and IoT systems architectures. Advances in networking, sensors, and embedded devices have made it possible to monitor and provide assistance to people in their homes. This chapter reviews the state of art on AAL and IoT and their applications for enhanced indoor living environments and occupational health.

Developing IoT projects from scratch requires a lot of knowledge and expertise; moreover, it takes a very long time to be developed. It can be hard for starters and even senior developers to perfect every aspect of an IoT project in a timely manner. These aspects include hardware, communication, data storage, security, integration, application, data processing, and analysis. This chapter introduces a cloud-based platform that is concerned with data storage, device management, data processing, and integration with external systems, all while providing high level of security and allowing for future scaling. This platform should accelerate and simplify the development of IoT projects by lowering the entry barrier and offloading some of the burden off developers to give them more time to focus on other aspects such as hardware and applications. The authors discuss many implementation issues in the functional and design perspective that may guide others to make their own platforms from this insight view.

Home automation (HA) systems can be considered as an implementation of the internet of everything (IoE) where many devices are linked by intelligent connections in order to improve the quality of life at home. This chapter is dedicated to analyzing current trends and challenges in HA. Energy management, safer homes, and improved control over the house are some of the benefits of HA. However, privacy, security, social disruption, installation/maintenance issues, economic costs, market fragmentation, and low interoperability represent real problems of these IoE solutions. In this regard, the latest proposals in HA try to answer some of these needs with low-cost DIY solutions, wireless solutions, and IP-based HA systems. This chapter proposes a way to deal with the interoperability problem by means of the open-source platform openHAB. It is based on the concept of a home automation bus, an idea that enables the separation of the physical and the functional view of any device, allowing to create a technology-agnostic environment, which is perfect for addressing the interoperability problem.

The concept of internet of everything involves an intelligent connection of people, processes, data, and things. In this sense, shared spaces aimed to connect different users that collaborate following a common purpose are of relevance to the field. Many computer-based collaborative environments have been proposed in recent years. However, the design of mixed-platform collaborative spaces, in which different paradigms—such as augmented reality (AR) and virtual reality (VR)—are blended, is still uncommon. This chapter aims to analyze the benefits and features of these systems, reviewing existing related works and proposing a series of features for the design of effective mixed-platform collaborative shared spaces. In particular, the authors propose five setups with different levels of immersion/interaction, which are aligned to the current state of the art. These systems will be analyzed with respect to navigation, user representation, interaction, and annotation, among others. Finally, some applications are proposed within the given framework.

Panagiotis Kasnesis, University of West Attica, Greece
Dimitrios G. Kogias, University of West Attica, Greece
Lazaros Toumanidis, University of West Attica, Greece
Michael G. Xevgenis, University of West Attica, Greece
Charalampos Z. Patrikakis, University of West Attica, Greece
Gabriele Giunta, Engineering Ingegneria Informatica, Italy
Giuseppe Li Calsi, Engineering Ingegneria Informatica, Italy

Climatic changes and intensive industrialization have contributed to increasing the risk of damage of cultural heritage (CH) artefacts. On the other hand, small and medium-sized museums, as well as small CH sites struggle to fulfil international recommendations for protection and conservation, due to budget limitations. The constantly increasing potential of IoT-enabled devices and the establishment of cloud technologies as an enabling framework can help address this issue. In this chapter, the authors present an internet of everything (IoE) architecture, empowered by an easy-to-deploy cloud framework for the protection of CH. Particular use cases from CH sites are presented, as these have been identified in H2020 STORM project for safeguarding cultural heritage through technical and organizational resources management.

Janet L. Holland, Emporia State University, USA
Sungwoong Lee, Emporia State University, USA

The internet of everything (IoE) envelopes the internet of things (IoT) that was simply focusing primarily on machine-to-machine sensor-based smart device communications. The IoE expands to include people and processes in a much more comprehensive scope. The internet of everything is expanding our ability to collect massive amounts of data for comprehensive analysis to achieve a level of understanding not previously possible. Since the internet of everything (IoE) has such a strong focus on collecting and analyzing data using smart sensor-enabled devices, eye tracking data is a perfect match. Eye tracking and other biometric sensor-based data can be collected and analyzed locally in real time through fog/edge computing or cloud-based big data analytics.

Chapter 11

Jorge Semião, University of Algarve, Portugal
Ruben Cabral, University of Algarve, Portugal
Hugo Cavalaria, University of Algarve, Portugal
Marcelino Santos, University of Algarve, Portugal
Isabel C. Teixeira, University of Algarve, Portugal
J. Paulo Teixeira, University of Algarve, Portugal

Ultra-low-power strategies have a huge importance in today's integrated circuits designed for internet of everything (IoE) applications, as all portable devices quest for the never-ending battery life. Dynamic voltage and frequency scaling techniques can be rewarding, and the drastic power savings obtained in subthreshold voltage operation makes this an important technique to be used in battery-operated devices. However, unpredictability in nanoscale chips is high, and working at reduced supply voltages makes circuits more vulnerable to operational-induced delay-faults and transient-faults. The goal is to implement an adaptive voltage scaling (AVS) strategy, which can work at subthreshold voltages to considerably reduce power consumption. The proposed strategy uses aging-aware local and global performance sensors to enhance reliability and fault-tolerance and allows circuits to be dynamically optimized during their lifetime while prevents error occurrence. Spice simulations in 65nm CMOS technology demonstrate the results.

Chapter 12

Viacheslav Izosimov, Semcon Sweden AB, Sweden
Martin Törngren, KTH Royal Institute of Technology, Sweden

Our societal infrastructure is transforming into a connected cyber-physical system of systems, providing numerous opportunities and new capabilities, yet also posing new and reinforced risks that require explicit consideration. This chapter addresses risks specifically related to cyber-security. One contributing factor, often neglected, is the level of security education of the users. Another factor, often overlooked, concerns security-awareness of the engineers developing cyber-physical systems. Authors present results of interviews with developers and surveys showing that increase in security-awareness and understanding of security risks, evaluated as low, are the first steps to mitigate the risks. Authors also conducted practical evaluation investigating system connectivity and vulnerabilities in complex multi-step attack scenarios. This chapter advocates that security awareness of users and developers is the foundation to deployment of interconnected system of systems, and provides recommendations for steps forward highlighting the roles of people, organizations and authorities.

Chapter 13

Christian Wittke, Leibniz-Institut für innovative Mikroelektronik, Germany
Kai Lehniger, Leibniz-Institut für innovative Mikroelektronik, Germany
Stefan Weidling, Leibniz-Institut für innovative Mikroelektronik, Germany
Mario Schoelzel, Leibniz-Institut für innovative Mikroelektronik, Germany

With the growing number of wireless devices in the internet of things (IoT), maintenance and management of these devices has become a key issue. In particular, the ability to wirelessly update devices is a must in order to fix security issues and software bugs, or to extend firmware functionality. Code update mechanisms in wireless sensor networks (WSNs), a subset of IoT networks, must handle limited resources and strict constraints. Also, over-the-air (OTA) code updates in the context of an IoT ecosystem may open new security vulnerabilities. An IoT security framework should therefore be extended with additional mechanisms to secure the OTA code update functionality. The chapter presents an overview of various OTA code update techniques for WSNs and their security flaws along with some existing attacks and possible countermeasures. It is discussed which attacks can be used more easily with the code update functionality. Countermeasures are compared as to whether they secure the weakened security objectives, giving a guideline to choose the right combination of countermeasures.

Foreword

Recent advances in electronics, computing, networking and the internet have resulted to the development of millions of low-cost and yet powerful internet-connected devices. The Internet of Everything (IoE) is the latest internet evolution that incorporates billions of such devices (which we refer to as "things"). IoE devices are often owned by different organizations and individuals who may be deploying and using them for their own purposes but may also making them available to other internet users. IoE applications harness the data produced by federations of such IoE devices to address grant challenges that have been too difficult to address before, such as managing our energy and waters resources better, advancing health and age care to improve health outcomes and lower costs, increasing the productivity and product quality of our industry, achieving greater safety in our roads, and improving the quality of our lives.

More specifically, IoE applications provide unprecedented opportunities for monitoring, understanding/diagnosing, and improving human health and age care. These are accomplished by employing smart wearable devices that provide personalized monitoring of vital signs and by introducing digestible sensors embedded in smart pills that allow doctors to monitor when their patients take medication and how much they take. Smart meters for power, gas and water are well-established IoE devices that allow on demand reading and analysis of the resources consumed by individual dwellings, as well as individual supply circuits and corresponding appliances inside each dwelling, such as water heaters. IoE applications, such as demand side management, extend further the use of smart meters to individual electric, gas, water circuits, and appliances in the customer's premises and introduce additional functionality for controlling (e.g., remotely turning on and off) such "managed" circuits/appliances to meet power, gas, and water consumption targets set by distributors and/or the customers themselves. Such IoE applications also involve customer recommendation and decision-making that optimize the use of renewable and traditional power generation sources, appliances, weather conditions, as well as occupancy patterns and living preferences that are set by the customers via their smart phones and wearables. Smart cities, and more specifically traffic management and safety, is another IoE application domain where IoE roadside sensors and onboard devices are currently deployed. For example, roadside sensors, such as wireless MacID readers, are currently deployed in busy freeways for measuring the speed of traffic by tracking the mobile phones of the vehicle drivers. A multitude of on-board OBD-II devices are currently used to collect real-time information about vehicles and their drivers (e.g., the OBDLink MX WiFi device plugs into the OBD-II port of any vehicle and turns the smartphone of its driver to a sophisticated scantool, trip computer, and real-time car performance monitor that keeps track of individual driving habits). Driver alertness is also being monitored via eye tracking IoE devices that detect if the driver is watching the road whenever an obstacle appears. The IoE devices in industrial plants include large machines that produce data used to compute productivity and product quality KPIs. The scope of IoE applications that use these and other IoE devices is limited only by the imagination of application developers, and many new IoE devices are being develop and appear in the market every day.

There are currently billions of such IoE devices in use around the world and their number, capabilities, and the scope of their use keeps growing rapidly. For example, Gartner reported that $11.2 billion IoE devices were in use worldwide in 2018 (up 31 percent from 2017), and their number will reach $20.4 billion by 2020. Total spending on IoE devices and services reached almost $2 trillion in 2017. Estimates from other sources are more ambitious.

IoE applications that to use IoE devices and their data to provide novel IoE services and products perform all or a subset of the following steps in the IoE application lifecycle:

1. Deploy or (increasingly more frequently) discover the IoE devices that can provide the data each IoE application needs,
2. Integrate these IoE devices and their data,
3. Analyse the integrated data to provide the target IoE service/product, and
4. Repeat all the above when any of the devices currently used to provide the target service or product become unavailable or disappears (e.g., this may occur any time when the owner of an IoE devices has no longer use for it, or decides to block others from accessing it), or when a new, possibly more suitable, IoE devices becomes available.

IoE application development also involves performing (1)-(4) above securely, in the cloud, and on the move. IoE security and privacy are a major concern that IoE applications need to address, and major security and privacy challenges are due to the large number of IoE devices and their limited computing power. Using cloud computing resources to store and process IoE data permits IoT applications to provide services and products anywhere and without the need to own and maintain a server or a data centre. Mobile IoE solutions are needed when the devices used by an IoE application or their end users are mobile. Edge computing and microservices technologies allow the portability of IoE data analytics and actuation software close to the IoE devices to eliminate slow cloud response times. These are key capabilities in developing IoE applications aiming to provide high value information anywhere and in real-time.

This book first dissects the IoE landscape into various application-specific IoT enclaves, provides and overview of the state-of-the-art, and identifies research challenges (Chapter 1). It then specifically covers IoE opportunities and corresponding IoE applications in energy and water monitoring and management (Chapters 3 and 4, respectively), in improving age care and quality of life (Chapters 5 and 6, respectively), and preserving cultural heritage (Chapter 9). The book also deals with the computing, networking, security and user interface aspects that are needed to develop effective IoE solutions, and when grouped together comprise an IoE platform for developing IoE applications. Chapter 6 covers the data storage, data management, and data integration aspects of the IoE platform. Chapter 2 provides and overviews of data analytics, and more specifically machine learning solutions for IoE data analysis. Micro and web services for providing code portability, and the potential role of blockchain for IoE data management are covered in Chapter 4. Chapters 7, 12, and 13 focus on IoE security and privacy issues and outline corresponding solutions. Chapter 11 dives in low-power electronics and nanoscale integrated circuits with are so important for increasing number, sensing capability, and operation time of battery-powers IoE devices. Human-computer interaction for IoE, including augmented reality, virtual reality and eye tracking, are discussed in chapters 8 and 10.

Overall, this book brings together a variety of research activities from around the world that are centred on (1) the development of a wide range of IoE applications aiming to address emerging opportunities in the IoE space, and (2) the key technologies that are needed for the development of such IoE solutions and also to establish IoE platforms, which make IoE solution development faster and cheaper.

This combination of IoE applications with the key technologies that are needed for IoE application development makes this book useful to researchers and industry innovators in the IoE space, practitioners the IoE application domains covered in this book and beyond, and policy makers. Furthermore, this book helps building a common understanding of the principles, related theories, and technologies and their use in IoE applications that currently lacks in the IoE space that is comprised by technological stove-pipes guarded by competing commercial vendors. This book succeeds in highlighting common approaches and connections between the IoE solutions proposed by multiple authors and the use of these in addressing real IoE opportunities in several different applications areas.

Dimitrios Georgakopoulos
Swinburne University of Technology, Australia

Preface

As the reader may guess, ever since we decided to edit this book, our main objective is to invite people to delve into the Internet of Everything (IoE). The IoE makes the Internet connections more valuable than ever before, converting information into wise actions that create unprecedented capabilities, richer experiences, and economic opportunities to all players in this market. The truth is that the Internet is evolving at a remarkable rate to the IoE, many times in ways difficult to imagine in recent years. In its way, many phases were overpassed, from the digitizing access to information (connectivity), the digitization of business processes (e.g., e-commerce), the digitization of interactions (e.g., social or cloud), to the digitised world connecting people, data, process and things (the IoE).

Many overlapping fields of research cooperate to carry out this IoE venture. Artificial intelligence, computer science, informatics, electronics, mathematics, management, or social sciences are just a few examples. This vastness of fields brought together a set of international experts on the design, evaluation, implementation and use of innovative technologies which include computer scientists, electrical engineers, security experts, data scientists, business intelligence analysts, and managers.

As this book delves in to the theory and applications of the IoE, many chapters explore machine learning, Internet if Things (IoT), software, hardware, smart homes and cities, human computer interaction, management or economics sciences, touristic added value etc. On its grounds, the book emphasizes trending research fields, for which major companies (such as Microsoft, Google, Amazon, or Apple), technology leaders (e.g., Elon Musk or Mark Zuckerberg), universities, research centers, and media are constantly addressing in their speeches. Those entities put this book in an environment with rapid growth, a market of billions of dollars, and potentially billions of users.

The book's target include academicians, researchers, advanced-level students, technology developers, policy makers or simple curious, that are interested in the new trends of IoE. The book can help professors, engineers, policy makers, and investigators in the teaching and in the improvements of their systems and applications. In addition, for professors and professionals in IoE engineering, the book will help them to improve their knowledge about the contemporary theories, technologies and tools available, and in this way be more demanding and capable of improving their products or teaching.

IoE general concepts, practical application, platforms, physics/electronic and security are addressed in the present book being organized as follows. Chapter 1, "Internet of Everything: A Unifying Framework Beyond Internet of Things," analyses the IoE landscape according to various application domains, giving for each an up-to-date account of the state-of-the-art in related fields. The authors also discuss a wide spectrum of challenges and future research directions, including ubiquitous connectivity, security, big data, etc., which are common to many application domains and penetrate into the IoE effort in general. Machine Learning, applied in the last decades in a vast research fields (e.g., image recognition, speech recognition, medical diagnosis, recommendation engines, surveillance, autonomous vehicles or personal assistants), has also the potential to improve the IoE research by adding value to the sector's productivity chain. In that sense, the second chapter, "Application of Machine Learning Algorithms to the IoE," presents a survey on the application of machine learning algorithms to the Internet of Everything. The survey is particularly interested in computational frameworks for the development of intelligent system, including different types of storage and applications of machine learning. An example of a system, which includes the data acquisition device, the data communication and storage, and a machine learning application is also included in the chapter.

The number of IoE applications and variety is huge, as stressed in some of the following chapters. One of the fields of application of IoE includes Energy Management. In this area, Chapter 3, "IoE-Based Control and Monitoring of Electrical Grids: A Smart Grid Perspective," presents the implementation of an IoT based system for microgrids, that supports the development of an Energy Management System (EMS). These EMS enable not only the monitoring, but also the optimized control of microgrids that integrate renewable energy sources. After presenting and comparing the state-of-the-art solutions in wireless sensor networks that can be used to build such an EMS, the authors describe the implementation of a set of LoRaWAN devices that can be used to support the development of the EMS. In the natural environment area, managing and delivering water involves careful planning to ensure its quality and security, more easily accomplishable using the IoE. The fourth chapter, "Water Management for Rural Environments and IoT," presents a work being developed in the management of water quality monitoring systems. The discussion includes a general architecture for water quality monitoring systems, computer security (namely the one related to the blockchain technology), web services and data transmission technology, micro web frameworks, and cloud IoT services. Another topic of great relevance given the ageing of the world population and the need to maintain the people's independence as long as possible is addressed in the next chapter, "Ambient Assisted Living and Internet of Things." The chapter presents a study on ambient assisted living (AAL) and IoT with particular focus on the their applications for enhancing indoor living environments and occupational health. With its main focus on smart homes, wearables sensors and health systems, the chapter provides a transversal vision of IoT and AAL technologies.

The computational development of IoE platforms requires qualified workers and many working hours to be developed. Those platforms are many times similar in their core meaning that their usage can be somehow standardized or comum. The next chapters present two solution. Chapter 6, "Cloud-Based IoT Platform: Challenges and Applied Solutions," introduces a cloud-based platform for the IoT concerned with data storage, device management, data processing and the integration with external systems, while providing high level of security and scaling. The platform's objective is to accelerate and simplify the development of IoT projects by lowering the entry barrier and offloading some of the burden off developers, giving them more time to focus on other aspects such as hardware and applications. Implementation issues in the functional and design perspective are also discussed. Chapter 7, "Challenges and Trends in Home Automation: Addressing the Interoperability Problem With the Open-Source Platform openHAB," analyses current trends and challenges in home automations, by proposing a way to deal with the interoperability problem by means of the open-source platform openHAB. The system is based on the concept of a Home Automation Bus, an idea that enables the separation of the physical and the functional view of any device, allowing to create a technology-agnostic environment, which is perfect for addressing the interoperability problem.

As mentioned before, the concept of IoE involves an intelligent connection of people, processes, data and things. The following chapter, "Mixing Different Realities in a Single Shared Space: Analysis of Mixed-Platform Collaborative Shared Spaces," aims to analyze the benefits and features of Augmented, Virtual and Mixed Reality systems, reviewing related works and proposing a series of features for the design of effective mixed-platform collaborative shared spaces. In particular, the authors propose five setups with different levels of immersion/interaction. These systems were analyzed with respect to navigation, user representation, interaction and annotation, among others, including some applications proposed within the given framework. In addition, the constantly increasing potential of IoT enabled devices and the establishment of cloud technologies as an enabling framework which can help address damage of Cultural Heritage (CH) artefacts. In Chapter 9, "An IoE Architecture for the Preservation of the Cultural Heritage: The STORM Use Case," the authors present an IoE architecture, empowered by an easy to deploy cloud framework for the protection of CH. One Particular use cases from CH sites are presented. All this information (and more as can be seen in other chapters) is causing our ability to collect massive amounts of data for comprehensive analysis to achieve a level of understanding not previously possible. Since the IoE has such a strong focus on collecting and analyzing data using smart sensor enabled devices, eye tracking data is a perfect tool to retrieve information. Chapter 10, "Internet of Everything (IoE): Eye Tracking Data Analysis," focuses on eye tracking and other biometric sensor based data that can be collected and analyzed locally in real time through fog/edge computing or cloud based big data analytics.

IoE implementation is not possible without the hardware and the new technologies integrated circuits especially designed for sensors and ultra-low-power circuits. In "Ultra-Low-Power Strategy for Reliable IoE Nanoscale Integrated Circuits," an Adaptive Frequency and Voltage Scaling technique is used, based on aging-aware global and local performance sensors, to implement drastic power savings in circuits and cyber-physical systems for IoE. By working at subthreshold supply voltages and controlling the supply voltage according with the available environmental and working conditions, the proposed technique allows circuits to be dynamically optimized, during their lifetime, while prevents error occurrence.

The last two chapters focus in security in the field of IoE. "Security Awareness in the Internet of Everything" presents fictious stories to stress the problems and potential risks about security in IoE. One contributing factor of this chapter is the level of security education of users of IoE systems. Another factor concerns security-awareness of the engineers developing cyber-physical systems. Authors interviewed developers, did surveys and workshops showing that this and other stories can become a reality. Authors did practical evaluation looking at the connectivity of commercial vehicles, as representative for internet-of-things applications, and shared thoughts towards attacking not connected society-critical facilities. The chapter ends with countermeasures for dealing with cyber-security threats, highlighting the role of authorities. With the growing number of wireless devices in the Internet of Things, maintenance and management of these devices has become a key issue. In particular, the ability to wirelessly update devices is a must in order to fix security issues and software bugs, or to extend firmware functionality. In this field, Chapter 13, "Securing Over-the-Air Code Updates in Wireless Sensor Networks," presents an overview of various over-the-air code update techniques for WSNs and their security flaws along with some existing attacks and possible countermeasures. It also discusses which attacks can be used more easily with the code update functionality and gives a guideline to choose the right combination of countermeasures.

As a conclusion, the book brings together a comprehensive collection of research trends on the edge field of IoE from a set of international experts on the theoretical, design, evaluation, implementation and use of innovative technologies on the fields. This allows to join in a single document many points of view that usually are not integrated, as these subjects are scattered in many articles (e.g., proceedings, journals and Internet). Furthermore, many chapters are focused on applications, making it more compelling for a majority of potential readers. Scholars and/or practitioners of fields such as ML, IoT, management, engineering systems, among others can reference it as an information source. Each chapter brought state of the art research, complemented with applications, most of them not yet developed and published, except by the authors.

We hope you will enjoy reading *Harnessing the Internet of Everything (IoE) for Accelerated Innovation Opportunities.*

Pedro J. S. Cardoso
University of Algarve, Portugal

Jânio Monteiro
University of Algarve, Portugal

Jorge Semião
University of Algarve, Portugal

João M. F. Rodrigues
University of Algarve, Portugal

Acknowledgment

The editors would like to acknowledge the help of all the people involved in the project. A special thanks and gratitude is due to the chapters' authors and to the specialists that took part in the review process.

The editors would also like to acknowledge their research centers, LARSyS (Laboratory of Robotics and Engineering System – FCT: UID/EEA/50009/2013), ISR-Lisbon (Institute for Systems and Robotics, CIAC-UAlg (Center for Research in Communication Sciences and Arts), and INESC-ID (Instituto de Engenharia de Sistemas e Computadores - Investigação e Desenvolvimento).

Chapter 1
Internet of Everything:
A Unifying Framework Beyond Internet of Things

Ergin Dinc
University of Cambridge, UK

Murat Kuscu
University of Cambridge, UK

Bilgesu Arif Bilgin
University of Cambridge, UK

Ozgur Baris Akan
University of Cambridge, UK

ABSTRACT

In this chapter, the authors put forward the notion of internet of everything (IoE) as an effort to maximally connect our communication infrastructure to the universe, which can itself be regarded as the real IoE, an interconnected network of physical phenomena (i.e., Everything we perceive as independent wholes that persist through time, such as molecules, light, waves, living organisms, and celestial objects, with the purpose of gaining better understanding of its mechanisms and manipulating them to enable novel technologies via a networked sensing, analysis, and actuation approach). The strategy to outline the IoE effort is by dissecting the vast IoE landscape into IoXs according to their various application domains (Xs), for each of which the authors give an up-to-date account of the state-of-the-art in related fields and point out the challenges in contemporary research faces. They also discuss a wide spectrum of challenges and future research directions (e.g., ubiquitous connectivity, security, big data, etc., which are common to many IoXs and penetrate into the IoE effort in general).

DOI: 10.4018/978-1-5225-7332-6.ch001

INTRODUCTION

In this age of enlightenment, our understanding of the universe grows rapidly with an accelerating rate. We now understand that universe is a vast, but nevertheless connected, entity whose evolution is described by a set of rules, the laws of physics. It is empirically apparent that these rules give rise to recurrent, i.e., persisting through time, shapes within the universe, which we observe and label as entities such as light, electrons, nuclei, molecules, living creatures, planets, stars, galaxies etc, i.e., everything we distinguish as persistent carriers of information. These laws of physics we formulate, apart from trying to explain the existence of everything, serve at the same time as protocols of communication between these information carrying entities. Thus, our description of the universe can, and should, be regarded as a theory for an INTERconnected NETwork of EVERYTHING we perceive. In short, the universe from our perspective is the INTERNET of EVERYTHING (IoE). However, the quest for establishing a coherent understanding of this IoE requires, as is well known, the probing of it by means of methods within our grasp, i.e., our technology. In this regard, the technological term IoE, i.e., the concept of expanding our INTERNET, INTERconnected NETwork of computers, to EVERYTHING, actually stands for the effort of expanding our technology and infrastructure to match as much as possible to the IoE that is the universe and to gain control over it. This effort, the vision of IoE, therefore, is that of connecting our already developed infrastructure to all the various entities we observe within this universe, and now on we will mean by IoE our effort of connecting to everything there is.

For achieving this vision, we start by dissecting the vast IoE landscape into IoXs according to their various application domains (Xs), e.g., Nano Things (NT), People and Senses (PS), Sensors (S), Agricultural Things (AT), Money (M), Energy (En), Vehicles (V), Battlefield Things (BT), Industrial Things (IT), and Space (Sp), and analyze each IoX effort in itself. Careful observation and contemplation show that any IoX effort, or in general IoE, will have the four components that it relates to, namely people, things, processes and data. At its origin, as being a human effort IoE contains *people* at its center. People are observers of their surroundings, and from human cognitive perspective the first thing identified are the objects, referred mostly as *things*. By primitive empirical observation we see some things around us are in motion, and more careful analysis, called science, shows us that actually everything is in motion, according to some set of rules, which we try to decipher. We refer to isolated coherent motion of things distinguishable from their surrounding as *processes*. Finally, we translate our observations of various processes around us into our own language and call it *data*. Thus, naturally, each IoX will contain these four components. Each of these components have a natural relationship with each other, as symbolically depicted in Figure 1.

Realization of the IoE framework demands highly interdisciplinary approaches to overcome unique connectivity, interoperability and energy-efficiency challenges mainly resulting from the close interaction between cyber and physical worlds and the interaction between machines (e.g. machine-to-machine (M2M) communication), and the enormous number of interconnected entities. The things and the people are interconnected anytime and everywhere within the IoE framework, implying a challenge for ubiquitous connectivity. Heterogeneous characteristics of technologies and services connected to each other require a high level of interoperability for seamless operation, which in turn calls for the design of novel interfaces, including those between bio-cyber domains. Bandwidth scarcity stands as a major challenge due to the huge number of connected entities, and calls for novel solutions, such as the upgraded cognitive radio techniques and the use of new frequency bands. Devising communication techniques orthogonal to electromagnetic (EM) communication, such as molecular communications,

Figure 1. Components of the IoE framework

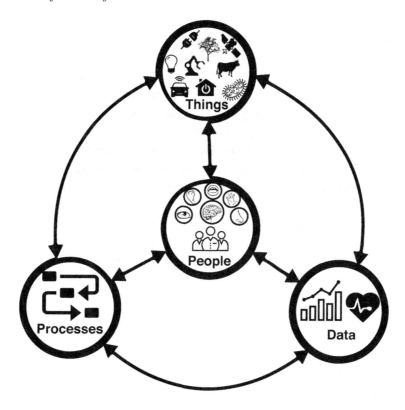

can also help effectively target the challenge for bandwidth. Miniaturization is another major challenge, which implies not only the requirement for scaling down the network nodes and transceivers, but also the communication links. This necessitates the design of novel communication techniques that can operate at nanoscale. The increased number of connected devices and ubiquitous connectivity requirement also imply substantial energy challenges, which can be targeted through devising energy-efficient systems and new energy harvesting methods for IoE nodes. The increasing number of interconnected entities continuously streaming huge amount of heterogeneous data requires devising new data analytics tools to handle the BIG data to provide useful services. Connected to this challenge, there are also increasing security and privacy risks, which can be targeted through designing fast and reliable encryption algorithms, new key distribution schemes, and developing comprehensive privacy regulations tailored to this novel framework. In this chapter, we will discuss these challenges in detail and provide a comprehensive review of possible solutions to realize IoXs from molecules to universe.

Inspired by the Universe, interconnected network of everything, having several natural internets, IoE concept can be categorized into many IoXs as illustrated in Figure 2. We categorize IoXs from molecular level to universal level. At the molecular level, Internet of Nano Things (IoNT) aims to provide connections with living entities such as bacteria, cells, neurons, that are communicating by means of molecular communication. This way, these entities become "things" that generate data to be processed to increase our understanding. Internet of Sensors (IoS) includes the deployment of massive number of sensors to interact with our surroundings at all dimensions. IoS concept is very similar with the current IoE applications. However, IoE concept stands for connecting everything there is. For example, neural interfaces will provide bridge between the Internet and human mind such that our minds will be also connected in the context of Internet of People (IoP). Cryptocurrencies have already revolutionized our understanding of money by removing the need for central ledger by creating a distributed ledger via blockchain, which outperforms the traditional central ledger approach by interconnected network of nodes. Money has already become a part of the Internet, and this new concept is denoted as Internet of Money (IoM). Internet of Agricultural Things (IoAT) and Internet of Industrial Things (IoIT) are application-based IoXs that gather data through sensor networks and exploit the collected data to increase efficiency in production and manufacturing. At the universal level, Internet of Space (IoSp) includes the future deployment of interplanetary internet and natural interactions between objects in the universe through gravitational waves. To sum up, this book chapter introduces our vision of IoE, INTERconnected NETwork of EVERYTHING, from molecules to the universe.

INTERNET OF Xs

Internet of Nano Things (IoNT)

One of the crucial building blocks of the IoE framework is IoNT, which defines artificial networks of nanoscale functional units, such as nano-biosensors, engineered bacteria, integrated into the Internet infrastructure (Akyildiz & Jornet, The Internet of nano-things, 2010). IoNT concept is positioned to exploit the unusual interactions with the physical environment stemming from the nanoscale dimensions and expected to greatly enhance the functionalities of nanomachines through cooperative nanonetworks and enable groundbreaking applications based on new methods of monitoring intricate and dynamic processes and interfering with them at unprecedented spatio-temporal resolutions as in Figure 3.

The progress in IoNT is mostly fueled by the advances in nanotechnology through the discovery of new nanomaterials, e.g., 2-d layered materials such as graphene and MoS_2 with exceptional optoelectrical and chemical properties (Ferrari, et al., 2005), and development of new nanoscale device architectures and processes for sensing, actuating, computing and energy harvesting. Moreover, continuously

Figure 2. Major IoXs within the IoE framework

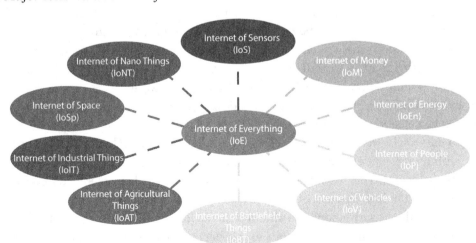

extended understanding and control of living cells through the advances in synthetic biology create new opportunities for IoNT. Depending on the physical properties and the size of network nodes, several technologies have been proposed within the larger IoNT scope. For example, Internet of Bio-Nano Things (IoBNT) has been coined to define the molecular communication networks of animate objects, such as engineered bacteria (Akyildiz, Pierobon, Balasubramaniam, & Koucheryavy, 2015). The optical networks of fluorophore-based single molecular devices have been termed the Internet of Molecular Things (IoMT) (Kuscu & Akan, 2016; Kuscu, Kiraz, & Akan, 2015).

Envisaged applications of IoNT are mostly centered around the medical domain. For example, implantation of IoNT inside human body can enable continuous health monitoring with nanoscale sensing agents transferring real-time health status to remote healthcare providers for early-stage disease diagnosis (Akan, Ramezani, Khan, Abbasi, & Kuscu, 2017). Moreover, actuation capabilities of nanomachines at single-cell and even single-molecular level can enable novel treatment techniques, such as smart drug delivery and artificial neurons (Felicetti, Femminella, Reali, & Liò, 2016; Malak & Akan, 2014). Furthermore, environmental toxic agent monitoring and military surveillance are envisioned to be enabled by this emerging framework.

Research in this field has so far focused on the physical layer, as the associated challenges resulting from the peculiarities of nanoscale physics are the most pressing. Extending connectivity of the IoE down to nanoscale requires developing new means of communications. Utilization of THz-band has been proposed to overcome the antenna size problems for wireless nanonetworks (Jornet & Akyildiz, 2011); however, technology in this field is still in its infancy. On the other hand, bio-inspired molecular communications (MC), which is already utilized by living cells stands as a more effective solution, especially for IoBNT. A large body of research has been devoted to developing reliable modulation and detection techniques for MC (Kilinc & Akan, 2013; Nakano, Moore, Wei, Vasilakos, & Shuai, 2012). However, the developed methods are still far away from being practical for resource-limited nanomachines. In addition to MC and THz-band EM, optical, acoustic and magneto-inductive communications are also considered for use in nanonetworks (Johari & Jornet, 2017).

Figure 3. (a) Conceptual drawing for a continuous health monitoring application of the IoNT. (b) Molecular Communications for nanonetworks. (c) Bio-cyber interface for IoNT based on field-effect-transistor biosensors.

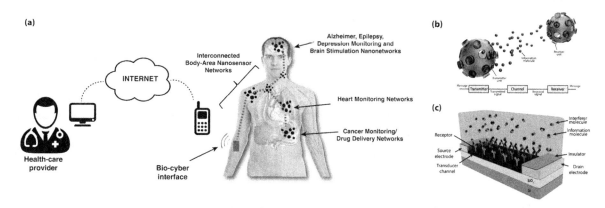

One of the major challenges of IoNT is the requirement of seamless interfaces between nanonetworks and macroscale networks which can facilitate the transfer of data in both ways with minimum intervention. In the case of IoBNT, the concept is translated into bio-cyber interfaces requiring transduction mechanisms between the molecular and electromagnetic signals (Akyildiz, Pierobon, Balasubramaniam, & Koucheryavy, 2015). Use of nano-biosensing methods and optogenetics are proposed to enable bio-cyber interfaces (Kuscu & Akan, 2016; Wirdatmadja, Barros, Koucheryavy, Jornet, & Balasubramaniam, 2017). Energy is another challenge for IoNT, as the conventional means of energy supply and storage are not feasible at nanoscale. Current research targets energy-efficient communication techniques for nanonetworks, as well as development of novel nanoscale energy harvesting methods exploiting the physical dynamics of the immediate environment, such as the chemical energy harvesting from glucose for IoBNT (Wang & Wu, 2012). IoNT will be the largest component of IoE in terms of number of network nodes. This requires handling of unprecedentedly big data produced by the networks of billions of nanomachines mostly in raw form due to the limited computational capabilities of envisioned nanomachines. Therefore, development of new BIG data analytics tools is imperative to enable the envisaged applications of IoNT (Balasubramaniam & Kangasharju, 2012). In parallel to the research activities, there is a continuous standardization effort which has yielded the IEEE Recommended Practice for Nanoscale and Molecular Communication Framework (IEEE 1906.1-2015) (Bush, et al., 2015). The research in this field is in its infancy, and still calls for fundamental research addressing the physical layer challenges, such as development of new noise-resilient communication methods, transceiver architectures, energy storage and harvesting methods, nano-macro and bio-cyber interfacing methods.

Internet of People and Senses (IoPS)

Internet of People and Senses (IoPS), defining the direct sharing of human cognitive functionalities and senses among different people, and between people and machines through the Internet, stands as the most radical technology within the IoE framework in terms of prospective applications. The technology consists in bio-cyber interfaces, including the so-called brain-machine interfaces between the human nervous system and electronic domain of machines; and in that sense, it is closely connected to the progress in IoNT, especially towards high-resolution cell stimulation and sensing technologies. The framework is expected to enable interconnection of brains, i.e., Brainets, sharing cognitive functionalities, and thus opening the door to higher level of consciousness and intelligence along with radically different forms of collaboration among people (Stocco, et al., 2015). Moreover, by allowing communication of touch, smell, taste, and vision digitally through the Internet, IoPS will create new business opportunities through novel forms of social networks with these non-verbal modalities of communication. It will enable the direct conceptual communication without the noise and data loss intrinsic to the conventional languages. A prospective application of this in the medical field will be towards restoring the communication functions of those with certain neural disorders, e.g., stroke. Real-time transmission of touch and actuation, i.e., the Tactile Internet, is expected to enable delivering of skills and labor globally (Aijaz, Dohler, Aghvami, Friderikos, & Frodigh, 2017). The technology will also transform the current augmented reality technologies and tactile applications for industry automation, transport, remote healthcare, education, and gaming.

Challenges of IoPS are mostly centered around the interface, i.e., transducing touch, smell, and taste patterns generated in the brain into digital signals, and recreating them in the receiver end (Spence, Obrist, Velasco, & Ranasinghe, 2017). The solution requires profound understanding of the human nervous system, which is currently being targeted by two major research projects, i.e., the White House BRAIN Initiative of the United States (US) (Jorgenson, et al., 2015), and the Human Brain Project of the European Union (EU) (Markram, et al., 2011). The other challenge is to develop noninvasive, biocompatible and high resolution interfacing technologies. Fortunately, the study of new nanomaterials with unprecedented chemical and electrical characteristics has greatly facilitated the research in this direction. For example, graphene proved to be a good candidate for high resolution neural interfacing without altering the neuronal growth (Fabbro, et al., 2016). There is also exciting progress towards realizing direct brain-to-brain communications using conventional electroencephalography (EEG) electrodes (Grau, et al., 2014). Haptic applications through digital touch communications are already widespread, especially in the medical domain, enabling surgeons to remotely control and operate medical robots (Simsek, Aijaz, Dohler, Sachs, & Fettweis, 2016). There are also initiatives, e.g., Neuralink, aiming to develop whole-brain interfaces, so called neural laces, consisting of billions of tiny electrodes that are able to detect and stimulate individual neurons, enabling the real-time digital representation of the entire brain, and neural functions and memories therein.

Internet of Sensors (IoS)

Sensing is the key to the IoE perspective, as a proper interaction with the Universe starts with understanding, or sensing, the physical realm. Sensing methods, size and operation of the sensing devices, and types of the sensed data are continuously evolving along with the advancements in spatio-temporal precision of the sensing operation, communication and processing of the sensed data, thus, we are now in a position to base our IoE vision in sensing the whole universe and building applications on top of the acquired knowledge.

The crucial role of sensing in understanding the universe renders the Internet of Sensors (IoS) the backbone and the largest component of this Universe-scale cyber-physical system. Our definition of Internet of Sensors comprises the wireless sensor networks, social sensor networks, body area sensor networks, intrabody nanosensor networks, and other orthogonal technologies, such as bacteria sensor networks and molecular sensor networks. As we elaborate on the bio-nanosensor networks before in detail, we limit our discussion here to the WSNs and social sensor networks, with a focus on their integration into the IoE framework.

WSNs are ad hoc networks consisting of a large number of low-power but intelligent sensors sharing their sensed information in a centralized or distributed manner. Advances in sensing and wireless networking technologies over the last 20 years, have led to a widespread deployment of WSNs with miniaturized sensor nodes in many application domains, such as, smart agriculture, weather forecasting, smart grid, healthcare monitoring, traffic management, forest fire monitoring (Rawat, Singh, Chaouchi, & Bonnin, 2014; Ojha, Misra, & Raghuwanshi, 2015). The transformation of current wireless sensor networks into an integrated part of the IoE can be envisioned along these four paths: (i) The software component of the WSNs implemented in each node and gateways should be tailored to accommodate additional middleware, APIs and other software components to support the IoS applications (Perera, Zaslavsky, Christen, & Georgakopoulos, 2014). This in turn would increase the energy demand of sensor networks, which can be addressed by developing passive or energy-harvesting sensor network architectures (Akan, Isik, & Baykal, 2009; Vullers, Van Schaijk, Visser, Penders, & Van Hoof, 2010) (ii) Current WSNs are mostly designed for specific application purposes. In contrast, IoS should consist of general purpose sensor networks, which can collect many types of data in different environments, and concurrently support different kinds of applications (Perera, Zaslavsky, Christen, & Georgakopoulos, 2014). Additionally, they should be scalable after first implementation, and integrable into other sensor networks within the broader IoS network, which can be supported through semantic interoperability. (iii) The local connectivity of current WSNs should be transformed to support the global connectivity of the IoS, requiring revisiting the current network topologies. The global connectivity demand brings further security and privacy challenges to WSNs, which is being addressed by new security and data privacy management methods (Li & Xiong, 2013), in parallel to the discussion that connecting every sensor node to the global network may not be needed for some applications (Alcaraz, Najera, Lopez, & Roman, 2010). (iv) The envisioned applications of IoE demand a substantial increase in the number of sensor nodes and in the amount of collected data with improved spatial and time resolution. This in turn brings big data challenges, which can be addressed by compressed sensing methods, like distributed source coding, context-aware big data analytics methods (Aktas, Kuscu, Dinc, & Akan, 2018; Li, Da Xu, & Wang, 2013). The high density of sensor nodes and the data demands of the applications will also bring a burden on the limited source of bandwidth, which can be tackled through cognitive radio methods (Akan, Karli, & Ergul, 2009).

Another component of the IoS is people, which, in fact, act as social sensors connected to the mobile Internet, and informing about certain societal events, traffic conditions, and emergency situations (Campbell, et al., 2008). Acquiring useful information from Mobile Big Data, i.e., data generated and shared by people with certain reliability, through social sensor networks, i.e., online social networks (OSNs), will require intense use of data analytics tools (Cepni, Ozger, & Akan, 2017). The research along this direction has already yielded many social sensing methods (Aggarwal & Abdelzaher, 2013) along with new application domains, such as vehicular social sensor networks (VSSNs) (Cepni, Ozger, & Akan, 2017), which can be readily adapted to the IoS framework.

Internet of Agricultural Things (IoAT)

The continuously increasing food demand, increasing food security and health concerns among people, and the need for a greener agriculture have led to the deployment of smart agriculture solutions based on terrestrial WSNs over the last decade (Barcelo-Ordinas, Chanet, Hou, & García-Vidal, 2013; Ojha, Misra, & Raghuwanshi, 2015). Supported by universal connectivity, scalability, heterogeneity, and big data analytics tools, the Internet of Agricultural Things (IoAT) is now taking a huge step forward to cover all ICT solutions in each step of agriculture from smart farming to smart food logistics and smart food processing (Sundmaeker, Verdouw, Wolfert, & Freire, 2016; Tzounis, Katsoulas, Bartzanas, & Kittas, 2017).

Application of the IoAT starts with the precision agriculture (PA) based on acquisition and sharing of weather forecasts with high spatiotemporal precision, real-time monitoring of ambient conditions and soil quality, cattle tracking and livestock health monitoring with wearable sensors (Barcelo-Ordinas, Chanet, Hou, & García-Vidal, 2013). On top of this information stream, with interoperable farm objects, IoAT enables automated and efficient irrigation systems, and accurate prediction of crop production quality and livestock health and growth. The fully automated and space/water/energy-optimized nature of IoAT will also enable urban farming with indoor food production, increasing the available farmland area, reducing the costs and increasing the speed of delivery of products to the consumers (Yang, et al., 2018).

IoAT will also have a huge impact on the food production and the supply chain, as it provides real-time tracking opportunities for individual products in terms of quantity and quality during production, storage and shipments (Sundmaeker, Verdouw, Wolfert, & Freire, 2016; Nukala, et al., 2016). By allowing precise planning of the production and supply chain with real-time data from market and automation among interoperable devices, IoAT can reduce the associated costs tremendously. The tracking of products and their quality will also enable the smart food awareness, allowing the consumers to trace back the production and shipment history of individual items.

Given the plethora of smart solutions already available in the market, IoAT now stands as the most technologically mature component of the IoE framework. The current research in IoAT is centered around generating value from heterogeneous big data with predictive analytics tools, and devising new applications for automating and optimizing the entire food supply chain (Wolfert, Ge, Verdouw, & Bogaardt, 2017). In this direction, one of the large scale research projects funded by European Commission is Internet of Food and Farm 2020, which is aimed at maintaining sufficient, safe and healthy food by IoT technologies, and increasing the competitiveness of food chains in Europe (Sundmaeker, Verdouw, Wolfert, & Freire, 2016). Within the broader IoE perspective, integration of individual IoX components into the IoAT can create greater value for each envisioned application. For example, IoNT could provide better monitoring of crop and livestock with nanosensor networks real-time tracking the health and quality with molecular precision. Moreover, the use of Internet of Drones is considered for enabling automated multimedia monitoring of the farms and tracking the cattle (Akyildiz & Jornet, 2010; Tripicchio, Satler, Dabisias, Ruffaldi, & Avizzano, 2015).

Internet of Money (IoM)

Money has also evolved over time from non-monetary exchange system, i.e., barter, to commodity money, which were produced from valuable metals, then to the printed banknotes, and now money has digitalized thanks to online banking services empowered by the proliferation of personal computers and Internet access. However, the banking system has been evolved to a highly bulky system that is not flexible and not easy-to-use. For example, opening a bank account can take up to a week and several eligibility constraints if you are not the citizen of the country, where you are trying to open the bank account. Furthermore, international money transfers require 3-4 days and can cost around 30-40$ due to the closed system banking with lots of intermediaries. To alleviate some of these problems, some internet services, e.g., PayPal, has been introduced as a solution early in the new Millennia. However, this still required connection with a bank account.

In 2009, the blockchain technology has been introduced by Satoshi Nakamoto's white paper (Nakamoto, 2009). Blockchain does not require any central ledger, and it allows users' computers, which are also denoted as cryptocurrency miners, act as distributed ledger to authorize the transactions. In this method, the transactions are approved if the transaction is approved by half of the users. Given that the total number of users are high, the distributed ledger is safer and more secure than the centralized approach, and the cost of operation is significantly lower. In exchange for the computations performed, cryptocurrency miners are awarded cryptocurrency coins, Money 4.0, such as Bitcoin. Cryptocurrency has become popular and its market capitalization reached above $600 billion in the last quarter of 2017 (Coinmarketcap.com, 2015). Cryptocurrency accounts, online wallets, can be opened in seconds and cryptocurrencies can be transferred without any cost. Cryptocurrencies can reach to everyone, and enable wire and transfer of funds anywhere on the world such as disaster areas with no banking available. Cryptocurrencies can be spent in some websites for buying goods/services and exchanged to Money 3.0, banknotes issued by governments. Cryptocurrencies are the money of the Internet. The value of

Cryptocurrencies is with the connectivity of their network and power of connection, this makes Money 4.0 as the Internet of Money (IoM) which is connected and free (Antonopoulos, 2016).

Evolution of Money is also in the IoM and the development of it also face with significant IoE challenges. First issue is increasing approval time of the transactions due to increasing number of cryptocurrency transactions and size of the blockchain file that keeps all of the transactions. More importantly, there is no standardization in cryptocurrencies, that is against their nature. Therefore, some governments see cryptocurrencies as the black money that is used by criminal organizations. That's why, some governments are trying to ban/restrict the use of cryptocurrencies. In addition, bandwidth scarcity may apply to the blockchain network when the number of small transactions increase and the response time of the network will increase. Except the standardization, the other challenges can be solved by improved connectivity.

Internet of Energy (IoEn)

Internet of Energy (IoEn) means the automation of both energy supply and demand in order to make the energy system more efficient, environmentally friendly and sustainable as seen in Figure 4. IoEn is enabled by the employment of IoT in the energy system and this is often referred as Smart Grid. The supply of the energy is required to be always greater than the demand. In order to provide enough energy supply, regulatory bodies often perform auction to determine the supply coming from different sources such as fossil fueled plants or renewable energy plants. The traditional system is bulky and cause the production of excess energy to guarantee energy supply. In addition, it is also challenging to add distributed renewable energy sources to the inflexible power grid.

Smart grid provides the automation and real-time monitoring of the energy system by the employment of IoT in the form of smart meters, actuators, wireless sensor networks to monitor both energy demand and supply. This way, smart grid enables intelligent power infrastructure that is more flexible, sustainable, efficient and environmentally friendly (Karnouskos & Terzidis, 2007). Energy production

Figure 4. Components of the Internet of energy

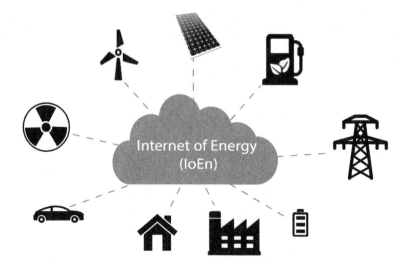

from renewable resources such as wind and solar can be performed by both big industrial companies via renewable power plants and private producers having small scale equipment in their house or field. In order to include different scale of renewable energy sources, decentralized power generation and monitoring are provided by IT infrastructure and connectivity provided by smart grid systems (European SmartGrids Technology Platform, 2016). At the end, deregulated intelligent energy system can optimally control the energy supply to be more reliable, cost-effective and environmentally friendly.

The benefits of decentralized and intelligent power system can be further exploited through service based IoEn applications (European SmartGrids Technology Platform, 2016). For example, adaptive energy pricing can be performed according to the demand for the energy and type of the energy supply. In such a system, IoT powered household devices such as washing machines and dishwashers can operate during the hours of the day with lowest electricity cost or with highest percentage of renewable energy supply to reduce the emissions. Furthermore, electric cars are expected to take over the fossil fueled ones. This will create a significant demand for energy. Energy companies can estimate the location and time of the energy demand by real-time monitoring of the electric cars' battery state and their location (Bedogni, et al., 2013). Renewable energy sources are often time-varying and storage of the energy is costly. To tackle this problem and maximize the usage of renewable energy sources, (Jaradat, Jarrah, Bousselham, Jararweh, & Al-Ayyoub, 2015) considers using the batteries of idle electric cars as storage in a fully connected city, specifically smart grid and smart cars.

The implementation of IoEn has many challenges. Integrating renewable energy production from small and large-scale players into decentralized and deregulated energy production increases the complexity of the power grid. Therefore, interoperability of the energy system and WSNs to monitor these systems is an important issue. More importantly, energy market is a massive market that may be targeted by cyber-attacks. In a fully autonomous power grid, any failure in IT technologies can results in billion-dollar losses (McDaniel & McLaughlin, 2009). Moreover, faulty data can be injected by hackers to the energy network in order to manipulate electricity cost or used amount. Along with the security problems, privacy of the customers can be exploited by analyzing the real-time electricity usage behavior. Although the transition from centralized to decentralized and autonomous power grid bears significant risks, it is a required transition in order to make the power grid more cost-effective, reliable and environmentally friendly.

Internet of Vehicles (IoV)

The concept of vehicular ad hoc networks, decentralized network of mobile nodes, has been around by many years (Hartenstein & Laberteaux, 2008). In spite of the significant research efforts, vehicular ad hoc networks (VANETs) have not found many applications to become a real thing. This concept is evolving to Internet of Vehicles (IoV), that considers decentralized network of multi-vehicles, intra-vehicle sensor network, connectivity with infrastructure in order to enable real-time monitoring, advanced situational awareness and efficiency. VANETs generally consider single type of vehicles, whereas IoV consists of all kinds of vehicles including ground vehicles: cars, cycles; naval vehicles" ships, submarines; flying vehicles: drones, flying taxis, aircraft. These vehicles will collect data about their condition and surroundings in order to share with other vehicles. The vehicles will form a social network between each other such that the ones going to the same place or coming from same place can share situational information and form social relationships between vehicles without human intervention (Cepni, Ozger, & Akan, 2017; Maglaras, Al-Bayatti, He, Wagner, & Janicke, 2016).

Figure 5. Energy neutral Internet of Drones (enIoD)

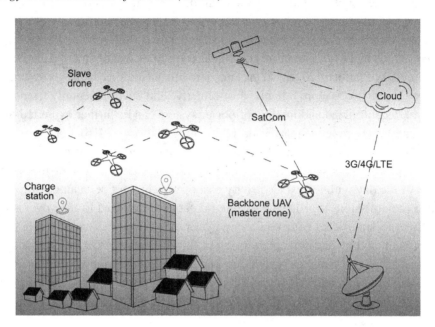

The concept of IoV can be divided into some sub-categories according to the type of the vehicles. We investigate some of these vehicles in order to summaries IoV. Internet of cars includes wireless sensor network to monitor condition of the car to early detection of component failures and enhanced safety. In addition, smart cars will collect information about the road safety and possible hazards to warn the neighboring roads or vehicles travelling that area. Advanced situational awareness is also paving way for the fully autonomous driving. Therefore, the optimal control of traffic may be possible by providing less congestion and fuel efficiency (Dandala, Krishnamurthy, & Alwan, 2017; Soylemezgiller, Kuscu, & Kilinc, 2013).

There is an increasing demand for drone applications in almost every industry for various purposes such as monitoring remote areas, providing cellular coverage, parcel delivery. Drones need to be connected to a control center or communicate with each other to avoid collisions and extended drone coverage. This gives rise to the Internet of Drones. In case of drones, battery life is an important constraint that limits the application areas of drones. To tackle this issue, the authors of (Long, Ozger, Cetinkaya, & Akan, 2018) introduced energy neutral internet of drones, where fully autonomous drones charge themselves by landing on a station with wireless power transfer capable charging station (see Figure 5), and the charging stations are solar powered, so there is no additional energy need to accommodate high number of drones that can be used for several applications.

Another important IoV venue is Internet of Aircraft, where huge amount of critical data about equipment can be generated via wireless avionics sensor networks (ITU-R, 2010). In addition to this, aircraft already transmit their course and speed to aircraft in the vicinity and ground receivers with the automatic dependent surveillance broadcasting (ADS-B) system. Although aircraft have several wireless communication systems on-board, they do not have broadband connectivity for delivering the data generated by wireless avionics sensor networks. For this purpose, there are significant research interest for providing broadband connectivity for aircrafts via direct air-to-ground communication (Dinc, et al., 2017; Vondra, et al., 2017; Dinc, Vondra, & Cavdar, 2017) and air-to-air communication (Medina, Hoffmann, Rossetto, & Rokitansky, 2012). At the end, Internet of Aircraft provides enhanced situational awareness, early fault detection and improved safety.

As in the other IoXs, the benefits of IoV also come with a price, several challenges to realize the concept. First, interoperability of various networks under different mobility conditions, i.e. different speeds for different vehicles types 1km/h up to 1000km/h. To this end, (Fangchun, Shangguang, Jinglin, Zhihan, & Qibo, 2014) includes a good summary of routing techniques for VANETs including store-and-forward and delay tolerant network techniques. Privacy becomes a significant issue considering the internet of cars as the generated data can be exploited to track users of smart cars. To alleviate this issue, Information Centric Networking, where only content of the transmitted data is considered rather than the sender, has been introduced (Gerla, Lee, Pau, & Lee, 2014). Almost all the IoV applications includes the collection of massive amount of data. Therefore, transmission of the collected data imposes new challenges considering the scarce wireless communication resources. Therefore, 5G networking techniques such as utilization of high frequency bands, edge-cloud computing, multi-tenancy and network virtualization will improve the system.

Internet of Battlefield Things (IoBT)

Internet of battlefield things (IoBT) defines the employment of IoT in modern warfare, network centric warfare, to provide improved surveillance and situational awareness (Suri, et al., 2016). Network centric warfare is associated with the utilization of information technology in warfare to provide competitive advantage: sharing data, managing units and effective command & control. For this purpose, IoBT includes several sensor networks to monitor military vehicles, soldiers, and terrain. Like in IoV, future military vehicles can be considered as a swarm of sensors creating data about the conditions of the vehicle and sharing the data with the military vehicles and control centers in the vicinity. In the same way, soldiers will be also monitored with various sensors, such as heart rate, body temperature, location of the soldiers. Moreover, tiny sensors that can sense the presence of hostile units can be placed on terrain to improve the situational awareness over large areas.

In order to realize IoBT, smart dust concept, placement of many sensors and robots in critical areas to collect data that can be processed to infer tactical information, has been proposed in 1997 by Kristofer S.J. Pister (Pister, 1997). Although this is a very old concept, we have not seen the employment of such sensor networks in modern warfare due to the specific challenges of military communication networks.

Ensuring information security is of utmost importance for military communication networks. For this reason, military communication networks generally use special frequency spectrums with end-to-end encryption. In addition, these networks mostly rely on intranets having little or no interconnection between them because ensuring security is getting harder as the connectivity of the system increases. This is one of the main reasons that IoT is expanding slowly in military. However, IoBT may offer competitive advantage by providing critical tactical information to improve situational awareness. Security in IoBT scenarios has started take significant research attention. In (Abuzainab & Saad, 2017), the authors model an attacker, that disrupts the connectivity of IoBT sensor nodes, as a multistage Stackelberg game. Furthermore, they proposed a method to decrease the number of expected disconnections by 46%. Another game theoretical approach is presented in (Xiao & Sun, 2018) for jamming. In (Xiao & Sun, 2018), the authors considered a scenario, where the attacker jams the channel to stop status updates.

Ubiquitous connectivity is also an important challenge for IoBT, where secure communication link is required anytime and anywhere. Therefore, network centric military networks are expected to utilize various communication methods to provide continuous connectivity. Alternative direct point-to-point communication links are required in places with low satellite coverage. To this end, troposcatter and ducting communication channels can be a promising alternative to maintain secure communication links (Dinc & Akan, 2014; Dinc & Akan, 2015). Troposcatter communication is provided by receiving scattered communication links at the lower troposphere and can be utilized as a communication up to 300km range with the carrier frequency of 4.7GHz (Dinc & Akan, 2015). Moreover, ducting effects of lower atmosphere can be used to connect naval units with the range of 500 km around 10 GHz carrier frequency with low detect and intercept probability (Dinc & Akan, 2014). In addition, quantum key distribution can be utilized to exchange encryption keys in a secure way from aircraft or satellites that are capable of quantum communication (Nauerth, et al., 2013).

Internet of Industrial Things (IoIT)

Historically, the first industrial revolution marks the first breakthrough in human manufacturing capabilities, where machinery operated with steam energy provided the means for automation. Second industrial revolution came about with electrification of the machinery and the mastering of moving assembly line pioneered by Henry Ford, which ushered the age of mass production. Finally, the advent of digital revolution and emergence of computers triggered the third industrial revolution by digitalization of machinery, i.e., robotics, in manufacturing plants, which significantly increased yield while simultaneously decreasing the cost of production (Drath & Horch, 2014).

The fourth industrial revolution, termed Industry 4.0, is a pre-announced revolution that is still under way, and it strives for the combination of Internet and future-oriented technologies with already electrified industrial machinery (Lasi, Fettke, Kemper, Feld, & Hoffmann, 2014), which is nothing but the introduction of IoE framework into industry (Shrouf, Ordieres, & Miragliotta, 2014). It aims to improve industry services via optimizing manufacturing process involved by means of increasing the effectiveness of collaboration between machinery (Wang, Wan, Zhang, Li, & Zhang, 2016), boosting yield and efficiency, as well as by improving product and service quality utilizing Big Data analytics (Lee, Kao, & Yang, 2014). To achieve this task, the whole connected system of physical entities such as factory equipment and products together with cyber-entities, collection of software collaborating to provide optimal control of the physical processes, referred to as Cyber Physical Systems (CPSs) (Lee, Bagheri, & Kao, 2015), are deployed into factories and industrial plants within the context of IoE (Jazdi, 2014; Jeschke, Brecher, Meisen, Ozdemir, & Eschert, 2017). Furthermore, issues such as safety, security and surveillance at industrial workplaces can be improved upon significantly by utilizing WSNs incorporated into the employed CPS (Bicen & Akan, 2012).

Even though industry is amongst the first to employ IoE paradigm, there are still many challenges facing the implementation of IoIT (Perera, Liu, Jayawardena, & Chen, 2014). The primary challenge arises in the design and integration of CPS to be used, which heavily depend on the type of industry and the processes involved in manufacturing (Zhou, Liu, & Zhou, 2015). Another major challenge lies in the integration of Big Data analytics into the operation, which again is very case-sensitive, and therefore requires customized solution for each industry and even for each workplace (Da, He, & Li, 2014).

Internet of Space (IoSp)

Two historically unrelated human endeavors, venture into space and development of Internet, are becoming increasingly correlated. Communications satellites (CSs) put into orbit around Earth are starting to play a more significant role in supporting the Internet and are expected to be the backbone of future IoE (Raman, Weigel, & Lee, 2016). On the other hand, the emerging CS infrastructure is envisioned to provide operational support for large scale space exploration and colonization efforts as part of IoSP.

All of the satellites utilized for communications purposes reside in Low Earth Orbit (LEO, 160 – 2,000 km), Medium Earth Orbit (MEO, 2,000 – 35,786 km) and Geosynchronous Orbit (GSO, at 35,786 km). Satellites in GSO rotate around the Earth synchronously with it having an inclination determined by the angle of intersection of the projection of the great circle drawn by the orbit with Earth's equator. The unique GSO with zero inclination, exactly 35,786 km above the Equator is called the Geostationary Orbit (GEO), and it is the most important one, as satellites in this orbit are stationary above a point in equator. Consequently, they provide temporally continuous coverage for non-polar regions, which renders a total coverage of Earth's non-polar regions by only few satellites possible. However, GEO satellite communication with ground suffers from high round trip time (RTT, ~ 250 ms, processing time overheads excluded) and path-loss. In contrast, LEO and MEO satellites are closer to Earth. Consequently, they suffer less path loss and RTT is significantly decreased. Especially in the case of LEO, the decreased distance enables RTT less than 40 ms. As another consequence of being close to Earth, satellites in LEO (MEO) orbits rotate faster than Earth, as a result of which a receiver on ground sees a given satellite only temporarily. To provide full coverage on Earth at all times one requires a strategically placed constellation of LEO satellites, in which satellites operate in a coordinated manner to provide continuous service (Draim, 1987). Growing demand on data rates has initiated plans for deployment of new LEO satellite constellations (Buchen, 2015), which has erupted rivalry between two space companies, SpaceX and OneWeb (Svitak, 2015), as well as, new GEO high troughput satellites (HTSs), supporting unprecedented data rates thanks to spotbeam technology, e.g., ViaSat-3 composed of three 1 Tbit/s capacity HTSs for global coverage, which in total exceeds rate provided by current CSs combined (Dankberg & Hudson, 2016).

Space is starting to contribute to the Internet, but what can Internet do for space? We are at an age, where interest in space missions have peaked. From asteroid mining to manned mission to Mars (SpaceX, 2018), companies with ambitious plans are preparing to undertake grand scale space missions. Due to atmospheric path-loss a message from ground cannot be directly sent to a distant spaceship, it has to be relayed via satellites. Existing communications infrastructure, barely supporting Earth, is unfit to satisfy the needs required (Burleigh, Cerf, Crowcroft, & Tsaoussidis, 2014). The new LEO satellite constellations by SpaceX and OneWeb, and the VIASAT CSs in GEO, besides supporting communications on Earth, will also have the potential to provide support for space mission communications, in particular the mission to Mars. Another issue is that space communications is inherently different because of the high latencies caused by large distances involved and disruptions of communications due line of sight obstructions by large objects such as planets and moons (Akan, Fang, & Akyildiz, 2002). Delay and disruption tolerant networking techniques and communication protocols are necessary and being developed (Silva, Burleigh, Hirata, & Obraczka, 2015). Finally, upon colonization of another planet, and establishing an Internet infrastructure on it, one can start talking about interplanetary Internet, the next milestone in IoSP (Akan, Fang, & Akyildiz, 2004).

IoE CHALLENGES AND FUTURE RESEARCH DIRECTIONS

Ubiquitous Connectivity and Interoperability

The fundamental objective of the IoE is to connect everything everywhere at any time, and this ambitious goal brings about challenges regarding ubiquitous connectivity and interoperability. Considering the diverse technologies involved in making up the devices to be connected, diverse environments in which these devices are aimed to operate, and the huge number of devices of various functionalities, satisfying the connectivity demand is highly challenging task. Addressing this challenge to provide a universe-scale connectivity from molecules to the planets requires developing new communication techniques for environments that have never been explored by conventional means before, such as the intrabody biochemical domain of envisaged molecular networks. Other challenging domains include underwater, underground and space. On the other hand, not all devices have the same connectivity requirements. Some of them may need low-latent and high-speed connectivity, as in industrial networks, some may tolerate delay and low communication rates. Moreover, most of the devices can be expected to need only intermittent connectivity for energy-efficiency and shared bandwidth purposes. Involvement of diverse technologies and applications from nanonetworks to interplanetary networks in the IoE framework also makes seamless interoperability a must, which should be addressed in all network layers (Bandyopadhyay & Sen, 2011). Nano-macro and bio-cyber interfaces will play a critical role in providing the necessary interoperability and seamless connectivity among different networks. For example, connection of molecular communication nanonetworks or intrabody networks to conventional wireless networks require developing lossless signal transduction mechanisms between the chemical and electromagnetic domains, which are fundamentally different in terms of signal propagation characteristics (Akyildiz, Pierobon, Balasubramaniam, & Koucheryavy, 2015). In the IoT domain, the interoperability challenge is currently being addressed through standards and protocols to cope especially with the diversity in requirements in the application layer, and the diversity of the data shared among different domains, based on the extension or adoption of the conventional Internet standards and protocols (Sheng, Yang, Yu, Vasilakos, & Mccann, 2013; Aloi, et al.; Derhamy, Eliasson, & Delsing, 2017). As IoE contains more diverse set of technologies, e.g., IoNT, IoPS, it requires revisiting these standardization efforts by adopting more inclusive approaches to accommodate the new services and applications brought about by the integration of these technologies. However, there is not much work in this direction, except some recent reviews of the prospective challenges (Dressler & Fischer, 2015; Balasubramaniam & Kangasharju, 2012).

Miniaturization

Miniaturization is one of the main driving forces of IoE, as the progress towards this vision is powered by the enablement of low-cost, energy- and size-efficient integrated circuits, sensors, and batteries that are able to be embedded into any object in a concealed way. The urge to interface with living systems at molecular resolution for unprecedentedly personalized biomedical applications with network agents invisible and noninvasive to the individuals is pushing the miniaturization efforts further down to the molecular scales. Driven by the advancements in nanotechnology, the miniaturization of integrated circuits has achieved to keep the pace with the anticipated shrinking rate by Moore's Law over the last 50 years. Development of tools to manipulate novel nanomaterials, like graphene, CNT, and heterostructures based on two-dimensional layered materials with extraordinary optoelectronic properties, has already led to the realization of nanotube radio prototypes (Rutherglen & Burke, 2007), flexible and patchable graphene-based RF/microwave antennas (Huang, et al., 2015), graphene plasmonic THz antennas (Jornet & Akyildiz, 2013), graphene RF receiver integrated circuits (Han, Garcia, Oida, Jenkins, & Haensch, 2014), single molecular optical transceivers (Kuscu, Kiraz, & Akan, 2015), and one and two dimensional chemical, biological and physical sensors (Hill, Vijayaragahvan, & Novoselov, 2011; Patolsky & Lieber, 2005), all with nanoscale dimensions. Single molecule transistors (Xiang, Wang, Jia, Lee, & Guo, 2016), enzyme and DNA origami-based chemical computing devices (Stojanovic, Stefanovic, & Rudchenko, 2014), and nanoscale spintronic devices (Torrejon, et al., 2017) are other orthogonal approaches driving miniaturization. Although miniaturization efforts have yielded highly promising laboratory prototypes, optimizing them from energy-efficiency, cost, and complexity perspectives, their integration into network nodes with miniaturized energy storage and harvesting units, and finally development of industrial-scale methods for manufacturing nanoscale components remain as open issues. As the network nodes become smaller, the constraints on energy storage and device functionality become more stringent, which, in turn, require revisiting the conventional communication technologies. Nanoscale and bio-inspired molecular communications within the IoNT framework, can bring important opportunities in this direction (Akyildiz & Jornet, 2010).

Big Data

"Data is the new oil!" as stated by many data experts. As much as it is for the oil, data needs to be plenty and processed to be of value. The former holds; the total amount of digital data created by human endeavor, the digital universe, expands with an ever-increasing rate, doubling itself every two years (Gantz & Reinsel, 2011). Accordingly, the size of the digital universe is estimated to ascent from 4.4 Zetabytes (ZB = 10^{21} bytes) in 2013 to 44 ZB in 2020 (Zwolenski & Weatherill, 2014). There is plenty of data and more is coming! The latter, the need to process the data, referred to as structured data, for it to be valuable, stems from the fact that data is consumed, much like an engine consumes processed oil, by cleverly designed learning algorithms, and for it to be consumable it needs to be structured. As an end product one obtains valuable information of specific interest compressed and juiced out from the initial raw data of gigantic amounts, which sums up the human effort termed as Big Data.

The need for processing raw data into structured data underlines the main challenge facing Big Data (Chen, Mao, & Liu, 2014). International Data Corporation (IDC) estimates that only 22% of the digital universe in 2013 was useful if it were tagged, a process of appending metadata to the original data to describe the content, and that only 5% of this data was actually analyzed (Turner, Reinsel, Gantz, & Minton, 2014). By 2020 the percentage of useful data is expected to rise above 35%, mainly due to the expected surge of data from embedded systems as a consequence of the **IoE** framework, which from a share of 2% of the digital universe in 2013 is expected to surge above 10% (Turner, Reinsel, Gantz, & Minton, 2014). Correspondingly, IoE related embedded system data is projected to grow from 88 Exabytes (EB = 10^{18} bytes) in 2013 to 4.4 ZB in 2020, a staggering 50-fold increase.

The second big challenge facing Big Data arises in the analysis of structured data in digital universe. Almost always the amount of that needs to be analyzed is so big that it needs to be stored across multiple devices, and in many cases this is intrinsically so as the desired data is generated by multiple sources, e.g., some specific information about Facebook users obtained from their online profiles. Moreover, the amount of computation required to analyze the massive data overweighs the capabilities of a single device, enforcing the distribution of computational work of a single task over many devices, termed as distributed computing (Peleg, 2000). One collection of open-source software, Hadoop Distributed File System, has been developed specifically for the purpose of accomplishing this task, allowing enterprises of all scales to undertake the difficult but rewarding endeavor of utilizing distributed computing (Shvachko, Kuang, Radia, & Chansler, 2010). Distributed computing also requires, or optimizes with, compatible storage systems, which, in the dawn of the IoE data explosion, is an important issue to keep in consideration with its own technical challenges (Cai, Xu, Jiang, & Vasilakos, 2017).

Scarcity of Resources

The IoE concept requires massive employment of sensor networks, which sense their surroundings and transmit data packages to a gateway or a server for further processing. The deployment of sensor networks in order to realize various IoXs is expected to add a significant traffic load to the communication networks, that have limited frequency spectrum. The scarcity of the spectrum resources necessitates both efficient use of frequency spectrum and expending the frequency spectrum, i.e., the utilization of millimeter wave frequencies, terahertz spectrum, as well as free-space optics and visible light communication systems (Ergul, Dinc, & Akan, 2015).

Low-power wide-area networks(LPWANs), especially Lora (Link-labs.com, 2018) and Sigfox (Sigfox.com, 2018) networks, has been the dominant solution in recent years to address the connectivity demands from various IoE applications such as smart metering, smart home, environmental monitoring and supply-chain & logistics. LPWAN enables sensor nodes to transmit their data from 0.3 kbps up to 50 kbps with low bandwidth, good battery life, low operational and deployment cost and high number of sensor node density. LPWAN market revenue is expected to reach $13.9 billion in 2022 (Grant, 2016). Although available LPWAN technologies has been successfully satisfied the demand and requirements from early IoE applications, emerging standards, Narrowband IoT (NB-IoT) (Grant, 2016) is expected to dominate the market by enabling deployment of LPWAN in the existing GSM networks, GPRS, and LTE networks. NB-IoT has extended coverage and supports sensor lifetime up to ten years with relatively low cost. That's why, mobile network operators are investing in realizing NB-IoT.

Cognitive radio, that enables usage of licensed spectrum by unlicensed users by dynamic spectrum sharing, can be also a solution for the ever-increasing spectrum demand (Akan, Karli, & Ergul, 2009). Especially IoE nodes with low reporting frequencies and low packet sizes can use licensed spectrum by spectrum sensing and transmit data when the spectrum is idle. To this end, the employment of cognitive radio in smart grid systems and public protection and disaster relief scenarios has been investigated in (Bicen, Gungor, & Akan, 2012) and (Ergul, Shah, Canberk, & Akan, 2016), respectively. However, standardization for cognitive radio networks is required due to additional interference to the licensed users.

Energy Efficiency and Energy Harvesting

Battery lifetime of sensor nodes is a significant limiting factor for IoE employments. Most sensors rely on batteries, which empower both nodal operations and data transmission. With the deployment of LPWANs, sensor nodes with battery lifetime up to 10 years has been commercialized. However, these sensors have limited processing power, data transmission capabilities and more importantly batteries may experience random depletions. Sensor batteries are cheap, but the cost of battery replacement may incur significant costs. For example, if a sensor that monitors a power generator runs out of battery, the power generator needs to be closed just for changing the battery of a simple sensor. In order to tackle this issue, energy harvesting techniques are promising to make sensor nodes no or little dependent on the battery lifetime.

There are various energy harvesting techniques: solar, thermal, airflow, mechanical, RF, magnetic-field (M-field) and electric-field (E-field). These techniques have advantages and disadvantages in different scenarios. In order to make harvested energy more stable and reliable, the current trend is to combine different energy harvesting techniques as proposed in (Ozger, Cetinkaya, & Akan, 2017; Akan, Cetinkaya, Koca, & Ozger, 2018). Furthermore, the authors of (Long, Ozger, Cetinkaya, & Akan, 2018) have proposed energy neutral Internet of Drones concept, in which solar powered charging station is utilized to charge fully autonomous drones with inductive wireless power transfer. This way, this concept is not consuming any energy from the grid and totally energy neutral.

The main challenge for energy efficiency and energy harvesting is to bring the cost and the size of the energy harvesters down. Thus, application domain of energy harvesting techniques can be extended. More importantly, to realize the proposed IoE vision, energy harvesting devices that can operate in nanoscale and microscale are required. In the IoNT concept, nanomachines, that can sense and perform certain tasks, will be injected to human body. These nanomachines cannot rely on batteries containing hazardous chemicals and limiting the lifetime of devices. For this purpose, the IoE concept necessitate novel biocompatible energy harvesting devices to empower nanomachines.

Privacy and Security

There are already billions of devices connected to the Internet under the IoE framework, and the numbers are increasing with an accelerating rate. These devices exhibit a wide spectrum of heterogeneity, which, besides interoperability issues, introduces vulnerabilities in the security of communication and privacy of the users (Abomhara & Koien, 2014). Moreover, IoE has a non-uniform and many-layered structure, which presents plentiful opportunities for various attacks such as unauthorized access to tags, tag cloning, denial of service attack, malicious code injection and man in middle attack (Ren, Liu, Ye, & Zhang, 2017). Ubiquitous connectivity under IoE implies communication pathways from arbitrary users to crucial IoE nodes such as industrial control systems and critical infrastructure, attaching physical consequences, even possibly threatening human lives, to successful cyber-attacks (Sadeghi, Wachsmann, & Waidner, 2015). Furthermore, achievement of ubiquitous connectivity requires a distributed IoE framework, where active participation of IoE nodes to establish relay links is necessary, which introduces new security challenges compared to a centralized approach, where the data nodes have no functionality other than transmitting contained data upon request (Roman, Zhou, & Lopez, 2013).

Another concerning issue, which is already showing problematic signs as portrayed by the Facebook trial for unlawful collection of data from customers, is the inevitable necessity of trust to third parties for data storage and manipulation. The magnitude of the threat this issue poses on client privacy can be appreciated from the fact that, in 2013 two-thirds of the digital universe data were created by consumers, yet enterprises had responsibility for 85% of the digital universe (Turner, Reinsel, Gantz, & Minton, 2014).

All the new and emerging privacy and security challenges being brought about by the novelties of the IoE paradigm gain more significance as one considers the consequences of the threat. Classical cyber-attacks had their disruptive power in means of data, may it be theft, ransoming, or pure vandalism. Permeation of the digital world into the real one via the IoE paradigm enables cyber-attacks to have physical consequences (Medaglia & Serbanati, 2010). Ranging from stealing smart cars, trespassing and disrupting industrial processes to hacking into personalized digital healthcare platforms the spectrum of possible cyber-attacks and their consequences rapidly expands.

CONCLUSION

In this chapter we have put forward the notion of IoE as an effort to communicate with the universe, i.e., the real IoE, with the purpose of expanding our understanding of its mechanisms and manipulating them to enable novel technologies via a networked sensing, analysis and actuation approach. In order to give a comprehensive outline of the IoE effort, we have divided the IoE landscape into IoXs according to their various application domains (Xs), namely, Nano Things (NT), People and Senses (PS), Sensors (S), Agricultural Things (AT), Money (M), Energy (En), Vehicles (V), Battlefield Things (BT), Industrial Things (IT), and Space (Sp). For each IoX, we have portrayed the state-of-the-art in related fields and pointed out the challenges contemporary research faces. Furthermore, we have delved deeper into various challenges and future research directions that are common to many IoXs and penetrate into the IoE effort in general, which included ubiquitous connectivity and interoperability, miniaturization, big data, scarcity of resources, energy efficiency and harvesting, and privacy and security.

As all IoXs deal with large amounts of data, and facilitation of many novel IoE applications rely on making use of this data, progress in big data research is correlated with advancements on all IoX fronts. Moreover, challenges in ubiquitous connectivity and interoperability permeate throughout the IoE landscape, as each IoX effort has its own repertoire of enabling IoE devices with different application specific requirements, which contribute to the heterogeneity of the overarching IoE network. This heterogeneity also introduces novel security threats specific to each IoX, where the increasing sensitivity of IoX application domains, such as intra-body applications under IoNT and IoPS, considerably magnifies the risks. On the other hand, issues such as energy efficiency and harvesting, miniaturization and scarcity of resources, pertain to only some of IoXs, e.g., to IoNT and IoPS in the prospect of intra-body applications, and to IoSp due to remoteness of operational regions and the cost of escaping gravity.

To conclude, in our quest of exploring the secrets of this universe, our urge to understand and tame it compels us to network with it in an ever more increasing complexity, which can be summarized as the effort IoE. With this chapter, we have tried to shed some light onto the vast IoE landscape by providing an accessible exposure to it.

REFERENCES

Abomhara, M., & Koien, G. M. (2014). Security and privacy in the Internet of Things: Current status and open issues. *International Conference on Privacy and Security in Mobile Systems (PRISMS)*, 1-8. 10.1109/PRISMS.2014.6970594

Abuzainab, N., & Saad, W. (2017). *Dynamic Connectivity Game for Adversarial Internet of Battlefield Things Systems*. arXiv:1708.05741v2 [cs.IT]

Aggarwal, C. C., & Abdelzaher, T. (2013). Social sensing. *Managing and mining sensor data*, 237-297.

Aijaz, A., Dohler, M., Aghvami, A. H., Friderikos, V., & Frodigh, M. (2017). Realizing the tactile internet: Haptic communications over next generation 5G cellular networks. *IEEE Wireless Communications*, *24*(2), 82–89. doi:10.1109/MWC.2016.1500157RP

Akan, O., Fang, J., & Akyildiz, I. (2004). TP-Planet: A reliable transport protocol for interplanetary internet. *IEEE Journal on Selected Areas in Communications*, *22*(2), 348–361. doi:10.1109/JSAC.2003.819985

Akan, O. B., Cetinkaya, O., Koca, C., & Ozger, M. (2018). Internet of Hybrid Energy Harvesting Things. *IEEE Internet of Things Journal*, *5*(2), 736–746. doi:10.1109/JIOT.2017.2742663

Akan, O. B., Fang, H., & Akyildiz, I. F. (2002). Performance of TCP protocols in deep space communication networks. *IEEE Communications Letters*, *11*(11), 478–480. doi:10.1109/LCOMM.2002.805549

Akan, O. B., Isik, M. T., & Baykal, B. (2009). Wireless Passive Sensor Networks. *IEEE Communications Magazine*, *47*(8), 92–99. doi:10.1109/MCOM.2009.5181898

Akan, O. B., Karli, O. B., & Ergul, O. (2009). Cognitive Radio Sensor Networks. *IEEE Network*, *23*(4), 34–40. doi:10.1109/MNET.2009.5191144

Akan, O. B., Ramezani, H., Khan, T., Abbasi, N. A., & Kuscu, M. (2017). Fundamentals of molecular information and communication science. *Proceedings of the IEEE*, *105*(2), 306–318. doi:10.1109/JPROC.2016.2537306

Aktas, M., Kuscu, M., Dinc, E., & Akan, O. (2018). D-DSC: Decoding Delay-based Distributed Source Coding for Internet of Sensing Things. *PLoS One*, *13*(3), e0193154. doi:10.1371/journal.pone.0193154 PMID:29538405

Akyildiz, I. F., & Jornet, J. M. (2010). The Internet of nano-things. *IEEE Wireless Communications*, *17*(6), 58–63. doi:10.1109/MWC.2010.5675779

Akyildiz, I. F., Pierobon, M., Balasubramaniam, S., & Koucheryavy, Y. (2015). The internet of bio-nano things. *IEEE Communications Magazine*, *53*(3), 32–40. doi:10.1109/MCOM.2015.7060516

Alcaraz, C., Najera, P., Lopez, J., & Roman, R. (2010). Wireless sensor networks and the internet of things: Do we need a complete integration? *1st International Workshop on the Security of the Internet of Things (SecIoT'10)*.

Aloi, G., Caliciuri, G., Fortino, G., Gravina, R., Pace, P., Russo, W., & Savaglio, C. (n.d.). Enabling IoT interoperability through opportunistic smartphone-based mobile gateways. *Journal of Network and Computer Applications, 81*, 74-84.

Antonopoulos, A. M. (2016). *The Internet of Money*. Merkle Bloom LLC.

Balasubramaniam, S., & Kangasharju, J. (2012). Realizing the internet of nano things: Challenges, solutions, and applications. *IEEE Computer*, *46*(2), 62–68. doi:10.1109/MC.2012.389

Bandyopadhyay, D., & Sen, J. (2011). Internet of things: Applications and challenges in technology and standardization. *Wireless Personal Communications*, *58*(1), 49–69. doi:10.100711277-011-0288-5

Barcelo-Ordinas, J. M., Chanet, J. P., Hou, K. M., & García-Vidal, J. (2013). A survey of wireless sensor technologies applied to precision agriculture. *Precision Agriculture*, 801–808.

Bedogni, L., Bononi, L., Di Felice, M., D'Elia, A., Mock, R., Montori, F., & Vergari, F. (2013). *An interoperable architecture for mobile smart services over the internet of energy. In World of Wireless, Mobile and Multimedia Networks (WoWMoM)* (pp. 1–6). IEEE.

Bicen, A. O., & Akan, O. B. (2012). Cognitive Radio Sensor Networks in Industrial Applications. In V. C. Gungor & G. P. Hancke (Eds.), *Industrial Wireless Sensor Networks: Applications, Protocols, and Standards*. CRC Press.

Bicen, A. O., Gungor, V. C., & Akan, O. B. (2012). Spectrum-Aware and Cognitive Sensor Networks for Smart Grid Applications. *IEEE Communications Magazine*, *50*(5), 158–165. doi:10.1109/MCOM.2012.6194397

Buchen, E. (2015). Small satellite market observations. *Small Satellite Conference*.

Burleigh, S., Cerf, V. G., Crowcroft, J., & Tsaoussidis, V. (2014). Space for Internet and Internet for space. *Ad Hoc Networks*, *23*, 80–86. doi:10.1016/j.adhoc.2014.06.005

Bush, S. F., Paluh, J. L., Piro, G., Rao, V., Prasad, R. V., & Eckford, A. (2015). Defining communication at the bottom. *IEEE Transactions on Molecular. Biological and Multi-Scale Communications*, *1*(1), 90–96.

Cai, H., Xu, B., Jiang, L., & Vasilakos, A. V. (2017). IoT-based big data storage systems in cloud computing: Perspectives and challenges. *IEEE Internet of Things Journal*, *4*(1), 75–87.

Campbell, A. T., Eisenman, S. B., Lane, N. D., Miluzzo, E., Peterson, R. A., Lu, H., & Ahn, G. S. (2008). The rise of people-centric sensing. *IEEE Internet Computing*, *12*(4), 12–21. doi:10.1109/MIC.2008.90

Cepni, K., Ozger, M., & Akan, O. B. (2017). Vehicular Social Sensor Networks. In Vehicular Social Networks. CRC Press.

Chen, M., Mao, S., & Liu, Y. (2014). Big data: A survey. *Mobile Networks and Applications*, *19*(2), 171–209. doi:10.100711036-013-0489-0

Coinmarketcap.com. (2015, May 25). *Cryptocurrencies by Market Capitalization*. Retrieved from https://coinmarketcap.com

Da, X. L., He, W., & Li, S. (2014). Internet of things in industries: A survey. *IEEE Transactions on Industrial Informatics*, *10*(4), 2233–2243. doi:10.1109/TII.2014.2300753

Dandala, T. T., Krishnamurthy, V., & Alwan, R. (2017). Internet of Vehicles (IoV) for traffic management. In *International Conference on Communication and Signal Processing (ICCCSP)* (pp. 1-4). IEEE. 10.1109/ICCCSP.2017.7944096

Dankberg, M., & Hudson, E. (2016). VIASAT: On a Mission to Deliver the World's Lowest-Cost Satellite Bandwidth. *Recent Successful Satellite Systems: Visions of the Future*.

Derhamy, H., Eliasson, J., & Delsing, J. (2017). IoT Interoperability - On-Demand and Low Latency Transparent Multiprotocol Translator. *IEEE Internet of Things Journal*, *4*(5), 1754–1763. doi:10.1109/JIOT.2017.2697718

Dinc, E., & Akan, O. B. (2014). Beyond-Line-of-Sight Communications with Ducting Layer. *IEEE Communications Magazine*, *52*(10), 37–43. doi:10.1109/MCOM.2014.6917399

Dinc, E., & Akan, O. B. (2015). More than the eye can see: Coherence time and coherence bandwidth of troposcatter links for mobile receivers. *IEEE Vehicular Technology Magazine, 10*(2), 86–92. doi:10.1109/MVT.2015.2410786

Dinc, E., Vondra, M., & Cavdar, C. (2017). Multi-user Beamforming and Ground Station Deployment Problem for 5G Direct Air-to-Ground Communications. *Proceedings of IEEE GLOBECOM.*

Dinc, E., Vondra, M., Hofmann, S., Schupke, D., Prytz, M., Bovelli, S., ... Cavdar, C. (2017). In-flight Broadband Connectivity: Architectures and Business Models for High Capacity Air-to-Ground Communications. *IEEE Communications Magazine, 55*(9), 142–149. doi:10.1109/MCOM.2017.1601181

Draim, J. E. (1987). A common-period four-satellite continuous global coverage constellation. *Journal of Guidance, Control, and Dynamics, 10*(5), 492–499. doi:10.2514/3.20244

Drath, R., & Horch, A. (2014). Industrie 4.0: Hit or hype? *IEEE Industrial Electronics Magazine, 8*(2), 56–58. doi:10.1109/MIE.2014.2312079

Dressler, F., & Fischer, S. (2015). Connecting in-body nano communication with body area networks: Challenges and opportunities of the internet of nano things. *Nano Communication Networks Journal, 6*(2), 29–38. doi:10.1016/j.nancom.2015.01.006

Ergul, O., Dinc, E., & Akan, O. B. (2015). Communicate to Illuminate: State-of-the-art and Research Challenges for Visible Light Communications. Physical Communication Journal, 72-85.

Ergul, O., Shah, G. A., Canberk, B., & Akan, O. B. (2016). Adaptive and Cognitive Communication Architecture for Next-generation PPDR Systems. *IEEE Communications Magazine, 54*(4), 92–100. doi:10.1109/MCOM.2016.7452272

European SmartGrids Technology Platform. (2016). *Vision and Strategy for Europe's Electricity Networks of the future.* European Commission.

Fabbro, A., Scaini, D., León, V., Vázquez, E., Cellot, G., Privitera, G., ... Bosi, S. (2016). Graphene-based interfaces do not alter target nerve cells. *ACS Nano, 10*(1), 615–623. doi:10.1021/acsnano.5b05647 PMID:26700626

Fangchun, Y., Shangguang, W., Jinglin, L., Zhihan, L., & Qibo, S. (2014). An overview of Internet of Vehicles. *China Communications, 11*(10), 1–15. doi:10.1109/CC.2014.6969789

Felicetti, L., Femminella, M., Reali, G., & Liò, P. (2016). Applications of molecular communications to medicine: A survey. *Nano Communication Networks, 7*, 27–45. doi:10.1016/j.nancom.2015.08.004

Ferrari, A. C., Bonaccorso, F., Fal'ko, V., Novoselov, K. S., Roche, S., Bøggild, P., ... Kinaret, J. (2005). Science and technology roadmap for graphene, related two-dimensional crystals, and hybrid systems. *Nanoscale, 7*(11), 4598–4810. doi:10.1039/C4NR01600A PMID:25707682

Gantz, J., & Reinsel, D. (2011). Extracting value from chaos. *IDC iview, 19*(1142), 1-12.

Gerla, M., Lee, E. K., Pau, G., & Lee, U. (2014). Internet of vehicles: From intelligent grid to autonomous cars and vehicular clouds. In *World Forum on Internet of Things (WF-IoT)*. IEEE.

Grant, S. (2016). *3GPP Low Power Wide Area Technologies - GSMA White Paper*. GSMA.

Grau, C., Ginhoux, R., Riera, A., Nguyen, T. L., Chauvat, H., Berg, M., ... Ruffini, G. (2014). Conscious brain-to-brain communication in humans using non-invasive technologies. *PLoS One*, *9*(8), 105225. doi:10.1371/journal.pone.0105225 PMID:25137064

Han, S. J., Garcia, A. V., Oida, S., Jenkins, K. A., & Haensch, W. (2014). Graphene radio frequency receiver integrated circuit. *Nature Communications*, *5*(1), 3086. doi:10.1038/ncomms4086 PMID:24477203

Hartenstein, H., & Laberteaux, L. P. (2008). A tutorial survey on vehicular ad hoc networks. *IEEE Communications Magazine*, *46*(6), 164–171. doi:10.1109/MCOM.2008.4539481

Hill, E. W., Vijayaragahvan, A., & Novoselov, K. (2011). Graphene sensors. *IEEE Sensors Journal*, *11*(12), 3161–3170. doi:10.1109/JSEN.2011.2167608

Huang, X., Leng, T., Zhu, M., Zhang, X., Chen, J., Chang, K., ... Hu, Z. (2015). Highly flexible and conductive printed graphene for wireless wearable communications applications. *Scientific Reports*, *5*(1), 18298. doi:10.1038rep18298 PMID:26673395

ITU-R. (2010). *Technical characteristics and operational objectives for wireless avionics intra-communications (WAIC)*. REPORT ITU-R M.2197.

Jaradat, M., Jarrah, M., Bousselham, A., Jararweh, Y., & Al-Ayyoub, M. (2015). The Internet of Energy: Smart Sensor Networks and Big Data Management for Smart Grid. *Procedia Computer Science*, *56*, 592–597. doi:10.1016/j.procs.2015.07.250

Jazdi, N. (2014). Cyber physical systems in the context of Industry 4.0. In *2014 IEEE International Conference on Automation, Quality and Testing, Robotics* (pp. 1-4). IEEE. 10.1109/AQTR.2014.6857843

Jeschke, S., Brecher, C., Meisen, T., Ozdemir, D., & Eschert, T. (2017). Industrial internet of things and cyber manufacturing systems. *Industrial Internet of Things*, *2017*, 3–19. doi:10.1007/978-3-319-42559-7_1

Johari, P., & Jornet, J. M. (2017). Nanoscale optical wireless channel model for intra-body communications: Geometrical, time, and frequency domain analyses. *IEEE Transactions on Communications*.

Jorgenson, L. A., Newsome, W. T., Anderson, D. J., Bargmann, C. I., Brown, E. N., Deisseroth, K., ... Marder, E. (2015). The BRAIN Initiative: developing technology to catalyse neuroscience discovery. *Phil. Trans. R. Soc. B*, *370*(1668), 20140164.

Jornet, J. M., & Akyildiz, I. F. (2011). Channel modeling and capacity analysis for electromagnetic wireless nanonetworks in the terahertz band. *IEEE Transactions on Wireless Communications*, *10*(10), 3211–3221. doi:10.1109/TWC.2011.081011.100545

Jornet, J. M., & Akyildiz, I. F. (2013). Graphene-based plasmonic nano-antenna for terahertz band communication in nanonetworks. *IEEE Journal on Selected Areas in Communications*, *31*(12), 685–694. doi:10.1109/JSAC.2013.SUP2.1213001

Karnouskos, S., & Terzidis, O. (2007). Towards an information infrastructure for the future Internet of energy. *ITG-GI Conference Communication in Distributed Systems (KiVS)*, 1-6.

Kilinc, D., & Akan, O. B. (2013). Receiver Design for Molecular Communication. *IEEE Journal on Selected Areas in Communications*, *31*(12), 705–714. doi:10.1109/JSAC.2013.SUP2.1213003

Kuscu, M., & Akan, O. (2016). The Internet of Molecular Things Based on FRET. *IEEE Internet of Things Journal,* (1), 4-17.

Kuscu, M., & Akan, O. B. (2016). On the Physical Design of Molecular Communication Receiver Based on Nanoscale Biosensors. *IEEE Sensors Journal, 16*(8), 2228–2243. doi:10.1109/JSEN.2016.2519150

Kuscu, M., Kiraz, A., & Akan, O. B. (2015). Fluorescent molecules as transceiver nanoantennas: The first practical and high-rate information transfer over a nanoscale communication channel based on FRET. *Scientific Reports, 5*(1), 7831. doi:10.1038rep07831 PMID:25591972

Lasi, H., Fettke, P., Kemper, H. G., Feld, T., & Hoffmann, M. (2014). Industry 4.0. *Business & Information Systems Engineering, 6*(4), 239–242. doi:10.100712599-014-0334-4

Lee, J., Bagheri, B., & Kao, H. A. (2015). A cyber-physical systems architecture for industry 4.0-based manufacturing systems. *Manufacturing Letters, 3,* 18–23. doi:10.1016/j.mfglet.2014.12.001

Lee, J., Kao, H., & Yang, S. (2014). Service innovation and smart analytics for industry 4.0 and big data environment. *Procedia Cirp, 16,* 3–8. doi:10.1016/j.procir.2014.02.001

Li, F., & Xiong, P. (2013). *Practical secure communication for integrating wireless sensor networks into the internet of things*. Academic Press.

Li, S., Da Xu, L., & Wang, X. (2013). Compressed sensing signal and data acquisition in wireless sensor networks and internet of things. *IEEE Transactions on Industrial Informatics, 9*(4), 2177–2186. doi:10.1109/TII.2012.2189222

Link-labs.com. (2018). *LoRa is groundbreaking physical layer (PHY) wireless technology*. Retrieved from Link-labs.com: https://www.link-labs.com/lora

Long, T., Ozger, M., Cetinkaya, O., & Akan, O. B. (2018). Energy Neutral Internet of Drones. *IEEE Communications Magazine, 56*(1), 22–28. doi:10.1109/MCOM.2017.1700454

Maglaras, L. A., Al-Bayatti, A. H., He, Y., Wagner, I., & Janicke, H. (2016). Social Internet of Vehicles for Smart Cities. *Journal of Sensor and Actuator Networks, 5*(1), 3. doi:10.3390/jsan5010003

Malak, D., & Akan, O. (2014). Communication theoretical understanding of intra-body nervous nanonetworks. *IEEE Communications Magazine, 52*(4), 129–135. doi:10.1109/MCOM.2014.6807957

Markram, H., Meier, K., Lippert, T., Grillner, S., Frackowiak, R., Dehaene, S., ... Grant, S. (2011). Introducing the Human Brain Project. *Procedia Computer Science, 7,* 39–42. doi:10.1016/j.procs.2011.12.015

McDaniel, P., & McLaughlin, S. (2009). Security and Privacy Challenges in the Smart Grid. *IEEE Security and Privacy, 7*(3), 75–77. doi:10.1109/MSP.2009.76

Medaglia, C. M., & Serbanati, A. (2010). An overview of privacy and security issues in the internet of things. *The Internet of Things,* 389-395.

Medina, D., Hoffmann, F., Rossetto, F., & Rokitansky, C. H. (2012). *A Geographic Routing Strategy for North Atlantic In-Flight Internet Access Via Airborne Mesh Networking*. Academic Press.

Nakamoto, S. (2009). *Bitcoin: A Peer-to-Peer Electronic Cash System.* Retrieved from https://bitcoin.org/ bitcoin.pdf

Nakano, T., Moore, M. J., Wei, F., Vasilakos, A. V., & Shuai, J. (2012). Molecular communication and networking: Opportunities and challenges. *IEEE Transactions on Nanobioscience, 11*(2), 135–148. doi:10.1109/TNB.2012.2191570 PMID:22665393

Nauerth, S., Moll, F., Rau, M., Fuchs, C., Horwath, J., Frick, S., & Weinfurter, H. (2013). Air-to-ground quantum communication. *Nature Photonics, 7*(5), 382–386. doi:10.1038/nphoton.2013.46

Nukala, R., Panduru, K., Shields, A., Riordan, D., Doody, P., & Walsh, J. (2016). Internet of Things: A review from 'Farm to Fork.' *Signals and Systems Conference (ISSC),* 1-6. 10.1109/ISSC.2016.7528456

Ojha, T., Misra, S., & Raghuwanshi, N. S. (2015). Wireless sensor networks for agriculture: The state-of-the-art in practice and future challenges. *Computers and Electronics in Agriculture, 118,* 66–84. doi:10.1016/j.compag.2015.08.011

Ojha, T., Misra, S., & Raghuwanshi, N. S. (2015). Wireless sensor networks for agriculture: The state-of-the-art in practice and future challenges. *Computers and Electronics in Agriculture, 118,* 66–84. doi:10.1016/j.compag.2015.08.011

Ozger, M., Cetinkaya, O., & Akan, O. B. (2017). *Energy Harvesting Cognitive Radio Networking for IoT-enabled Smart Grid. ACM/Springer Mobile Networks and Applications (MONET).*

Patolsky, F., & Lieber, C. M. (2005). Nanowire nanosensors. *Materials Today, 8*(4), 20–28. doi:10.1016/S1369-7021(05)00791-1

Peleg, D. (2000). Distributed computing. *SIAM Monographs on discrete mathematics and applications,* (5).

Perera, C., Liu, C. H., Jayawardena, S., & Chen, M. (2014). A survey on internet of things from industrial market perspective. *IEEE Access: Practical Innovations, Open Solutions, 2,* 1660–1679. doi:10.1109/ACCESS.2015.2389854

Perera, C., Zaslavsky, A., Christen, P., & Georgakopoulos, D. (2014). Context aware computing for the internet of things: A survey. *IEEE Communications Surveys and Tutorials, 16*(1), 414–454. doi:10.1109/SURV.2013.042313.00197

Pister, K. S. (1997). *Smart Dust: BAA97-43 Proposal Abstract.* Retrieved April 19, 2018, from berkeley.edu: http://www.eecs.berkeley.edu/~pister/SmartDust/SmartDustBAA97-43-Abstract.pdf

Raman, S., Weigel, R., & Lee, T. (2016, March 8). *The Internet of Space (IoS): A future backbone for the Internet of Things?* Retrieved August 29, 2018, from iot.ieee.org: https://iot.ieee.org/newsletter/march-2016/the-internet-of-space-ios-a-future-backbone-for-the-internet-of-things.html

Rawat, P., Singh, K. D., Chaouchi, H., & Bonnin, J. M. (2014). Wireless sensor networks: A survey on recent developments and potential synergies. *The Journal of Supercomputing, 68*(1), 1–48. doi:10.100711227-013-1021-9

Ren, Z., Liu, X., Ye, R., & Zhang, T. (2017). Security and privacy on internet of things. *7th IEEE International Conference on Electronics Information and Emergency Communication (ICEIEC)*, 140-144. 10.1109/ICEIEC.2017.8076530

Roman, R., Zhou, J., & Lopez, J. (2013). On the features and challenges of security and privacy in distributed internet of things. *Computer Networks, 57*(10), 2266–2279. doi:10.1016/j.comnet.2012.12.018

Rutherglen, C., & Burke, P. (2007). Carbon nanotube radio. *Nano Letters, 7*(11), 3296–3299. doi:10.1021/nl0714839 PMID:17941677

Sadeghi, A. R., Wachsmann, C., & Waidner, M. (2015). Security and privacy challenges in industrial internet of things. *Proceedings of the 52nd annual design automation conference*, 54. 10.1145/2744769.2747942

Sheng, Z., Yang, S., Yu, Y., Vasilakos, A., Mccann, J. L., & Leung, K. (2013). A survey on the ietf protocol suite for the internet of things: Standards, challenges, and opportunities. *IEEE Wireless Communications, 20*(6), 91–98. doi:10.1109/MWC.2013.6704479

Shrouf, F., Ordieres, J., & Miragliotta, G. (2014). Smart factories in Industry 4.0: A review of the concept and of energy management approached in production based on the Internet of Things paradigm. In *2014 IEEE International Conference on Industrial Engineering and Engineering Management (IEEM)* (pp. 697-701). IEEE. 10.1109/IEEM.2014.7058728

Shvachko, K., Kuang, H., Radia, S., & Chansler, R. (2010). The hadoop distributed file system. *IEEE 26th symposium on mass storage systems and technologies*, 1-10.

Sigfox.com. (2018). *Sigfox, the world's leading IoT services provider*. Retrieved from Sigfox: https://www.sigfox.com/en#!/technology

Silva, A. P., Burleigh, S., Hirata, C. M., & Obraczka, K. (2015). A survey on congestion control for delay and disruption tolerant networks. *Ad Hoc Networks, 25*, 480–494. doi:10.1016/j.adhoc.2014.07.032

Simsek, M., Aijaz, A., Dohler, M., Sachs, J., & Fettweis, G. (2016). 5G-enabled tactile internet. *IEEE Journal on Selected Areas in Communications, 34*(3), 460–473. doi:10.1109/JSAC.2016.2525398

Soylemezgiller, F., Kuscu, M., & Kilinc, D. (2013). A traffic congestion avoidance algorithm with dynamic road pricing for smart cities. In *International Symposium on Personal Indoor and Mobile Radio Communications (PIMRC)* (pp. 2571-2575). IEEE. 10.1109/PIMRC.2013.6666580

SpaceX. (2018). *SpaceX*. Retrieved from SpaceX: http://www.spacex.com/mars

Spence, C., Obrist, M., Velasco, C., & Ranasinghe, N. (2017). Digitizing the chemical senses: Possibilities & pitfalls. *International Journal of Human-Computer Studies, 107*, 62–74. doi:10.1016/j.ijhcs.2017.06.003

Stocco, A. P., Losey, D. M., Cronin, J. A., Wu, J., Abernethy, J. A., & Rao, R. P. (2015). Playing 20 questions with the mind: Collaborative problem solving by humans using a brain-to-brain interface. *PLoS One, 10*(9), 137303. doi:10.1371/journal.pone.0137303 PMID:26398267

Stojanovic, M. N., Stefanovic, D., & Rudchenko, S. (2014). Exercises in molecular computing. *Accounts of Chemical Research, 47*(6), 1845–1852. doi:10.1021/ar5000538 PMID:24873234

Sundmaeker, H., Verdouw, C., Wolfert, S., & Freire, L. P. (2016). Internet of food and farm 2020. *Digitising the Industry-Internet of Things Connecting Physical, Digital and Virtual Worlds*, 129-151.

Suri, N., Tortonesi, M., Michaelis, J., Budulas, P., Benincasa, G., Russell, S., ... Winkler, R. (2016). Analyzing the applicability of internet of things to the battlefield environment. In *International Conference on In Military Communications and Information Systems (ICMCIS)* (pp. 1-8). IEEE. 10.1109/ICMCIS.2016.7496574

Svitak, A. (2015). *SpaceX, OneWeb Unveil Rival Broadband Constellation Plans*. Retrieved from Aviation Week & Space Technology: http://aviationweek.com/space/spacex-oneweb-unveil-rival-broadband-constellation-plans

Torrejon, J., Riou, M., Araujo, F. A., Tsunegi, S., Khalsa, G., Querlioz, D., ... Kubota, H. (2017). Neuromorphic computing with nanoscale spintronic oscillators. *Nature*, *547*(7664), 7664. doi:10.1038/nature23011 PMID:28748930

Tripicchio, P., Satler, M., Dabisias, G., Ruffaldi, E., & Avizzano, C. A. (2015). Towards smart farming and sustainable agriculture with drones. In *IEEE International Conference on Intelligent Environments*, 140-143. 10.1109/IE.2015.29

Turner, V., Reinsel, D., Gantz, J., & Minton, S. (2014). *The Digital Universe of Opportunities: Rich Data and the Increasing Value of the Internet of Things*. IDC Whitepaper.

Tzounis, A., Katsoulas, N., Bartzanas, T., & Kittas, C. (2017). *Internet of Things in agriculture, recent advances and future challenges*. Academic Press.

Vondra, M., Dinc, E., Prytz, M., Frodigh, M., Schupke, D., Nilson, M., ... Cavdar, C. (2017). Performance Study on Seamless DA2GC for Aircraft Passengers toward 5G. *IEEE Communications Magazine*, *55*(11), 194–201. doi:10.1109/MCOM.2017.1700188

Vullers, R. J., Van Schaijk, R., Visser, H. J., Penders, J., & Van Hoof, C. (2010). Energy harvesting for autonomous wireless sensor networks. *IEEE Solid-State Circuits Magazine*, *2*(2), 29–38. doi:10.1109/MSSC.2010.936667

Wang, S., Wan, J., Zhang, D., Li, D., & Zhang, C. (2016). Towards smart factory for industry 4.0: A self-organized multi-agent system with big data based feedback and coordination. *Computer Networks*, *101*, 158–168. doi:10.1016/j.comnet.2015.12.017

Wang, Z. L., & Wu, W. (2012). Nanotechnology-enabled energy harvesting for self-powered micro-/nanosystems. *Angewandte Chemie International Edition*, *51*(47), 11700–11721. doi:10.1002/anie.201201656 PMID:23124936

Wirdatmadja, S. A., Barros, M. T., Koucheryavy, Y., Jornet, J. M., & Balasubramaniam, S. (2017). Wireless Optogenetic Nanonetworks for Brain Stimulation: Device Model and Charging Protocols. *IEEE Transactions on Nanobioscience*, *16*(8), 859–872. doi:10.1109/TNB.2017.2781150 PMID:29364130

Wolfert, S., Ge, L., Verdouw, C., & Bogaardt, M. J. (2017). Big data in smart farming–a review. *Agricultural Systems*, *153*, 69–80. doi:10.1016/j.agsy.2017.01.023

Xiang, D., Wang, X., Jia, C., Lee, T., & Guo, X. (2016). Molecular-scale electronics: From concept to function. *Chemical Reviews*, *116*(7), 4318–4440. doi:10.1021/acs.chemrev.5b00680 PMID:26979510

Xiao, Y., & Sun, Y. (2018). *A Dynamic Jamming Game for Real-Time Status Updates*. arXiv:1803.03616 [cs.IT]

Yang, J., Liu, M., Lu, J., Miao, Y., Hossain, M. A., & Alhamid, M. F. (2018). Botanical Internet of Things: Toward Smart Indoor Farming by Connecting People, Plant, Data and Clouds. *Mobile Networks and Applications*, *23*(2), 188–202. doi:10.100711036-017-0930-x

Zhou, K., Liu, T., & Zhou, L. (2015). Industry 4.0: Towards future industrial opportunities and challenges. *12th International Conference on Fuzzy Systems and Knowledge Discovery (FSKD)*, 2147-2152. 10.1109/FSKD.2015.7382284

Zwolenski, M., & Weatherill, L. (2014). The digital universe: Rich data and the increasing value of the internet of things. *Australian Journal of Telecommunications and the Digital Economy*, *2*(3), 47. doi:10.7790/ajtde.v2n3.47

ADDITIONAL READING

Akan, O. B., Cetinkaya, O., Koca, C., & Ozger, M. (2018). Internet of Hybrid Energy Harvesting Things. *IEEE Internet of Things Journal*, *5*(2), 736–746. doi:10.1109/JIOT.2017.2742663

Akan, O. B., Ramezani, H., Khan, T., Abbasi, N. A., & Kuscu, M. (2017). Fundamentals of molecular information and communication science. *Proceedings of the IEEE*, *105*(2), 306–318. doi:10.1109/ JPROC.2016.2537306

Akyildiz, I. F., & Jornet, J. M. (2010). The Internet of nano-things. *IEEE Wireless Communications*, *17*(6), 58–63. doi:10.1109/MWC.2010.5675779

Antonopoulos, A. M. (2016). *The Internet of Money*. Merkle Bloom LLC.

Grau, C., Ginhoux, R., Riera, A., Nguyen, T. L., Chauvat, H., Berg, M., ... Ruffini, G. (2014). Conscious brain-to-brain communication in humans using non-invasive technologies. *PLoS One*, *9*(8), 105225. doi:10.1371/journal.pone.0105225 PMID:25137064

Huang, A. Q., Crow, M. L., Heydt, G. T., Zheng, J. P., & Dale, S. J. (2011). The Future Renewable Electric Energy Delivery and Management (FREEDM) System: The Energy Internet. *Proceedings of the IEEE*, *99*(1), 133–148. doi:10.1109/JPROC.2010.2081330

Roman, R., Zhou, J., & Lopez, J. (2013). On the features and challenges of security and privacy in distributed internet of things. *Computer Networks*, *57*(10), 2266–2279. doi:10.1016/j.comnet.2012.12.018

Sheng, Z., Yang, S., Yu, Y., Vasilakos, A., Mccann, J. L., & Leung, K. (2013). A survey on the ietf protocol suite for the internet of things: Standards, challenges, and opportunities. *IEEE Wireless Communications*, *20*(6), 91–98. doi:10.1109/MWC.2013.6704479

KEY TERMS AND DEFINITIONS

Internet of Agricultural Things (IoAT): Networks of sensors, actuators, and computational devices functionalized for smart agriculture applications (e.g., precision agriculture, smart food logistics, livestock health monitoring).

Internet of Battlefield Things (IoBT): The employment of IoT in modern warfare, network-centric warfare, to provide improved surveillance and situational awareness.

Internet of Energy (IoEn): Automated and intelligent power grid, which monitors and optimizes supply and demand from small/medium/large-scale producers and consumers.

Internet of Industrial Things (IoIT): Automation and optimization of industrial processes via cyber physical systems for higher productivity, better product quality, and safer workplace.

Internet of Money (IoM): Fully connected monetary system, where the value of the currency is derived from the connectivity like cryptocurrencies.

Internet of Nano Things (IoNT): A networking framework comprising artificial networks of nanoscale functional units (e.g., nano-biosensors, engineered bacteria) integrated into the Internet infrastructure.

Internet of People and Senses (IoPS): Communication of human cognitive functionalities and senses among people, and between people and machines through the internet.

Internet of Sensors (IoS): Internet of sensor networks consisting of sensors differing in sensed data type, size, material properties, and connectivity and energy requirements. The definition covers the conventional wireless sensor networks, social sensor networks, body area sensor networks, intrabody nanosensor networks, and molecular sensor networks.

Internet of Space (IoSp): The effort of expanding our Internet infrastructure into outer space to support human space exploration and colonization of other planets (e.g., Mars).

Internet of Vehicles (IoV): Decentralized networking of all kinds of vehicles and infrastructure.

Chapter 2
Application of Machine Learning Algorithms to the IoE:
A Survey

Pedro J. S. Cardoso
iD https://orcid.org/0000-0003-4803-796
University of Algarve, Portugal

Jânio Monteiro
University of Algarve, Portugal

Nelson Pinto
iD https://orcid.org/0000-0002-8041-9199
University of Algarve, Portugal

Dario Cruz
iD https://orcid.org/0000-0001-9465-0845
University of Algarve, Portugal

João M. F. Rodrigues
University of Algarve, Portugal

ABSTRACT

The internet of everything is a network that connects people, data, process, and things, making it easier to understand that many subfields of knowledge are discussable while addressing this subject. This chapter makes a survey on the application of machine learning algorithms to the internet of everything. This survey is particularly focused in computational frameworks for the development of intelligent systems and applications of machine learning algorithms as possible engines of wealth creation. A final example shows how to develop a simple end-to-end system.

DOI: 10.4018/978-1-5225-7332-6.ch002

INTRODUCTION

The first steps toward the present Internet were made in the late 1950s, with the initial studies on packet switching. After that, the development of protocols for internetworking, by which multiple separate networks could be joined into a network of networks, were made. Later, in 1969, the first internetwork message was sent over the Advanced Research Projects Agency Network (ARPANET), from the University of California to a second network node at Stanford Research Institute. A definition came for the Internet as the worldwide interconnection of individual networks operated by government and other third parties. However, the very first commercial Internet Service Providers for the Internet we know and use today only appeared in the late 1980s, established in Australia and the United States. In the same decade, the earlier World Wide Web was devised with the linking documents conception, forming an information system reachable by any network node, consequence of the researches made at European Organization for Nuclear Research (CERN). Since then, the Internet usage has spread in such a way that the International Telecommunications Union estimates the number of world Internet users at 3.6 billion by end 2017, i.e., 48% of the world's population.

In the Internet context, several, many times overlapping concepts, appeared in the last decades (Lueth, 2015; Perera, 2017): Machine-to-Machine (M2M), Internet of Things (IoT), Internet (of People – IoP), Web of Things (WoT), Internet of Everything (IoE) etc. (see Figure 1). As the name suggests, M2M indicates the communication between machines over some mean and protocol. In the present, those communications many times are done using the Internet Protocol (IP). On the other hand, the IoP is the internet that connects people, delivering information generated by persons. The WoT has a narrower scope as it solely focuses on software architecture. IoT is more intricate to bound since many times it moves from the sensors, tags and actuators to the end users, passing through the deployment of electronics and firmware, communications, (embed, edge or datacenter) computation, data storage etc. (see Figure 2). Conjugating the characterizations presented in various works (Serpanos & Wolf, 2018; Tan & Wang, 2010; Vermesan & Friess, 2011), a long definition arises as: the IoT is the dynamic global network infrastructure, with self-configuring capabilities based on standard and interoperable communication protocols, where a massive number of physical and virtual things have identities, physical attributes, and virtual personalities. These things use intelligent interfaces, often over the same Internet Protocol that connects the Internet, to connect and communicate, without human-to-machine input, through wired and wireless networks within social, environment, and user contexts, being seamlessly integrated in smart spaces and into the information network. In other words, IoT allows people and things (physical devices, vehicles, buildings and other items embedded with electronics, software, sensors, tags, actuators, tags etc.) to be connected anywhere, anytime, with anything and anyone, enabling the collection and exchange of data. Extending the IoT concept, IoE aims to include all sorts of connections that one can envision as, the IoE is the networked connection of people, data, process, and things. In other words, IoE extends IoT by including intelligent and robust communication between machines-to-people (M2P), machine-to-machine, people-to-machines and people-to-people (P2P), i.e., the more expansive IoE concept includes M2M communications, machine-to-people and technology assisted people-to-people interactions.

It is expected that by 2020 between 20 and 30 billion devices will be interconnected in the IoT/IoE space. This rise in the quantity of apparatuses will also be accompanied by a growing diversity of distinct IoT/IoE device types, capable of directly gathering information from multiple sources, including health monitoring, asset tracking, environmental monitoring, predictive maintenance and home automation, computers, vehicles, smartphones, appliances, jewelry, toys, wearables, building automation systems, and much more, ranging from consumer devices to industrial assets.

As already stated, equipped with connectivity, electronics (including sensors, tags and actuators) and software (to capture, filter and exchange data about themselves and their environment), IoT/IoE devices are a source of endless data, which can be used for the improvement of the systems that they populate. The huge amount of data generated by sensors must therefore be analyzed using proper methodologies in the search for patterns, to make predictions, to classify the data, detect outliers, detect security problems etc. This is where Machine Learning (ML) will have an important role. In its pure form, ML is supported in mathematical and computer science techniques to build models from given data, which are then applied to new and unseen data, in order to predict new outcomes (Alpaydin, 2016; Domingos, 2015; Witten, Frank, Hall, & Pal, 2016).

ML algorithms ordinarily allow to save resources by automatically analyzing data, which produces an expectably better overview of the available information, to make decisions that are more reasoned. But, where is ML applied? Imagine you decide to go to the cinema. You go to Google, click the "Search by voice" link and are asked to "Speak now… Listening…". To which you reply, "films near me". Behind the scene, a ML algorithm starts to work, translating your speech to text (Schalkwyk et al., 2010). Another system receives your order and searches the information system for proper answers to your question: "But, where does he/she lives? What are his/her interests? What time is it? How far is he/she from the nearest cinema rooms?" The result is an advised list of films, supported in yours and others preferences and actions. You choose the first one from the list, after all, the algorithm has just guessed what you want to see, and you have one hour until the session begins. Just enough time. While you leave the house, you say "Ok Google, turn off the lights" – again your speech is transformed into a command, turning off all the lights in the house. When you arrive to your car, the navigation app is activated, and you wait for a few instants while algorithms, supported on your previous query, street maps, predicted and real traffic etc., decide the best directions to the cinema. Before arriving the cinema, you are pulled over by a policeman who asks for documents and proof of insurance, the one that a ML algorithm helped to decide the quote based in your profile (Roy & George, 2017). In the cinema parking, you use the assisted self-parking from your car, based on sensors' data and visual computing algorithms (Wang, Song, Zhang, & Deng, 2014). Finally, at the cinema you pay with your credit card, from a company that uses ML methods to attract new customers, drive up turnover, provide personalized recommendations, and detect frauds (Matsatsinis, 2002).

Focused on the described context, this chapter makes a survey on the application of ML algorithm in the IoE environment, mainly from the storage and machine learning point of views. The survey will be particularly interested in frameworks for the development of intelligent systems and ML applications. We should notice that other important issues are out of the scope of this chapter, such as cloud computing, cybersecurity, advanced analytics, connectivity and communication technologies, augmented and virtual reality, blockchain etc. Also out of the chapter's scope is edge computing (see Figure 2), which offers significant computational advantages such as real-time decision making through edge analytics, reduced data transfer cost through compression and cleansing, improved security and data continuity through local operations.

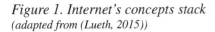

Figure 1. Internet's concepts stack
(adapted from (Lueth, 2015))

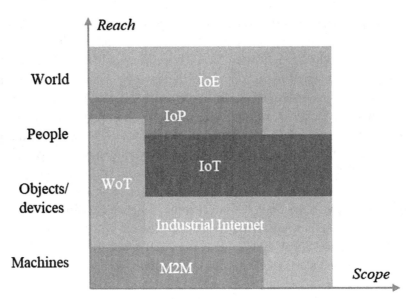

This chapter is structured as follows. The second section, "Data Storage Perspectives and Applications", will be devoted to the analysis of the information storing problematics. The section will start by analyzing different perspectives from local to global databases, with distinct storage systems (particular emphasis is given to relational and document oriented databases). A survey on publications about data storage in the IoT/IoE context will finalize the section. Next, the "Machine Learning Algorithms and Applications" section will address the ML problematics from an IoT/IoE perspective. A brief survey on the type of problems solved by ML is presented. Also addressed are the available tools to implement ML systems, finalizing with some applications of ML systems in the IoE context. The final sections draw some solutions, recommendations, future research directions and a conclusion.

Figure 2. IoT technology model

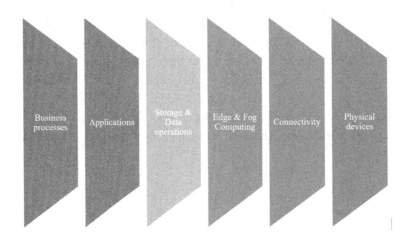

DATA STORAGE PERSPECTIVES AND APPLICATIONS

In general, sensors produce Boolean, single numerical data (integer or floating-point numbers), or more complex information, possibly containing several forms of data, that is grouped together. For example, temperature sensors produced integer/float values with different precisions, depending on the application and sensor's precision; Ambient sensors (can) read light intensity, temperature, humidity, and motion in a room; Global Positioning System (GPS) sensors return values such as latitude, longitude, altitude, or speed; and IP camera sensors produce arrays of values. The frequency of readings, the types of queries to be made on the data, and the quantity of data are also important factors, as they must be taken into consideration while deciding to store the data locally or globally. Therefore, the implementation of the database, i.e., the set of related data and the way it is organized, is an issue in the IoE field that should be carefully considered as it can deeply influence the performance of the system.

Storing data using the file system of local devices, such as a SD card, hard drive etc., can be difficult depending on what the data embodies. Therefore, many times the use of proper databases systems is highly recommendable, being those usually divided in two main types: relational and non-relational (or NoSQL) databases (Perkins, Redmond, & Wilson, 2018). The difference between the types of databases emerge in how they are built, the type of information they store, and how they store it. The software that implements the interactions with end-users, other software, and the database is called Database Management Systems (DBMS). Among its functions, the DBMS allows the administration of the database and the implementation of the basic create, read, update, and delete (CRUD) operations over the data.

In the case of relational databases, as main elements, they have entities/relations, many times seen as tables, and relationships between those entities. Each table's row contains a tuple of information, identified by the table's primary key. The relationships are maintained using a system of linked information from different tables through the use of primary and foreign keys, being divided in three types of relationships: one-to-one (exactly one record in the first table corresponds to none or one record in the related table), one-to-many (a primary table contains one record that relates to none, one, or many records in a secondary table), and many-to-many (each record in both tables can relate to any number of records in the other table). Examples of a one-to-one relationship, not very common as this case is usually solved by merging the two tables, would be between a sensor and its unique identification if they were placed in different relations; an one-to-many relationship example would be the link between a sensor and its readings; and a many-to-many relationship occurs between a set of mobile sensors and their location within a set of possible ones.

Structured Querying Language (SQL) is the common choice to communicate with relational DBMS (RDBMS), being implemented by the vast majority of those RDBMS programs. Storage can also be classified as local, global or hybrid, depending on the location of the data. Commercial and non-commercial application, among other, include PostgreSQL (2018), MySQL (2018), Microsoft SQLServer (Assaf, West, Aelterman, & Curnutt, 2018; Microsoft-SQL-Server, 2017), or SQLite (2018). SQLite distinguishes itself from the rest by being a server-less RDBMS, i.e., a database engine that runs within the same process, thread, and address space as the application, where there is no message passing or network activity.

Relational databases, in general satisfy, four properties, namely: Atomicity, Consistency, Isolation and Durability (ACID). Atomicity points that a transaction is a logical unit of work which must either perform all data modifications, or none; Consistency means that all data must be left in a consistent state at the end of the transaction; Isolation means that data modifications made by a transaction are independent of other transactions; and Durability implies that when a transaction is completed, effects of the modifications are permanent in the system. The DBMS that implement these four properties are termed as ACID compliant.

In our context, different sensors produce different forms of data, making it hard to create a well-structured database schema for that heterogeneous/dynamically structured set of data. In this sense, to store that unstructured information, it might be useful to use schema-less databases, making most of the adjustments to the database transparent and automatic. Furthermore, not all ACID properties are necessarily significant in the IoE context. In this sense, NoSQL systems have gained popularity for reasons such as the flexibility they provide in organizing data, obtained by relaxing the more rigid schemas stipulated by the relational model. The term NoSQL is used as an umbrella term for all databases and data storage that do not follow the RDBMS principles, being also often related to large data sets accessed and manipulated on a Web scale (Harrison, 2015; Perkins et al., 2018). We should notice that this flexibility does not mean that a schema should not be thought. On the contrary, the schema allows applications to know what and where is the information.

NoSQL databases are usually divided in four categories, namely: key-value pair storage, where every single item in the database is stored as a key and its value (e.g., Riak-KV (2018)); Wide column store, where data is stored in a columnar fashion (e.g., Cassandra (2018)); document store, where data is stored as semi-structured documents, typically in JSON (JavaScript Object Notation) or XML format (e.g., MongoDB (2018)): and graph databases, that use graph structures for semantic queries with nodes, edges and properties to represent and store data (e.g., Neo4j (2018)).

Among those databases, one of the most well-known schema-less database is, probably, the MongoDB database (Chodorow, 2013; Perkins et al., 2018). MongoDB presents a high performance, high reliability, easy scalability (vertically and horizontally through replication and auto-sharding, respectively) and map-reduce support. A MongoDB database is structured as a set of collections, which store documents. These documents are BSON objects (Bassett, 2015), a binary JSON document format supporting dynamic schemas, i.e., documents in the same collection are not forced to have the same structure.

Table 1 summarizes a comparison between relational databases and MongoDB terminology. Also, Figure 3 compares relational and document storage databases, and the main DBMS's features are summarized in Table 2 (see Appendix).

Recently, RDMS such as MySQL started to support a native JSON data type defined by the RFC 7159 that enables efficient access to data in JSON documents. Among other, MySQL automatically validates JSON documents, stored in JSON columns, producing an error upon the insertion of invalid documents, which would not happen when storing JSON-format strings in a common string column. Furthermore, the storage is optimized by converting the documents stored in the JSON columns to an internal binary format. That optimized format allows quick read access to document elements and look up sub-objects or nested values directly by key or array index, without reading all values, before or after them, in the document.

Data Storage in the IoT Context

Several works addressed the database problematics in the IoE context. For instance, Bell (2016) presents a full manual to prepare an IoT system, from the building of hardware devices for data acquisition to the data storage in a relational database (MySQL). A comparison between MySQL and a MongoDB instance for IoT application is made by Rautmare & Bhalerao (2016). The authors use a simplified relational

Figure 3. Comparing relational and document-oriented databases structures

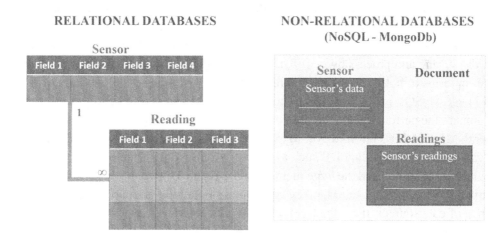

Table 1. Comparing (common) relational and MongoDB terminology

Relational Databases	MongoDB
ACID Transactions	ACID Transactions (on V 4.0)
Table	Collection
Row	Document
Column	Field
Secondary Index	Secondary Index
Join operations	Embedded documents, lookup etc.
Group by operations	Aggregation Pipeline

schema and compare the time taken to execute select and insert queries against a varying number of records and threads. Adiono et al. (2017) present a study on the selection and design of communication protocols, design of communication security, and database design for IoT based smart home systems. Applied to a smart system, the authors address the communication protocol and database design in order to be able to implement all the features of the smart home system, such as device's categorization, scenarios, scheduling, notification etc. Kang, Park, Rhee, & Lee (2016) devised a data repository schema over MongoDB that can integrate and store heterogeneous IoT data sources, such as RFID, sensor, and GPS. Their work takes into consideration the Fosstrak, an open source RFID software platform which provides electronic product code information services implementation based on MySQL. In a related work, Kang, Park, & Youm (2016) analyze traceability requirements and an event schema for storing traceability. In (Paethong, Sato, & Namiki, 2016) is explained how to construct a database server for IoT middleware that has data distribution and low-power consumption by using credit-card size computers, guarantying satisfactory performances and affordable price. In this sense, they use a Raspberry Pi 2 and compare the results (operation's time and power consumption) with the ones obtained with an x86 (namely an Intel Core i7), using MySQL and MongoDB as DBMS. The results show that the Raspberry Pi has a power consumption of about half of the x86 computer but is 80% slower than the x86 machine. Malić, Dobrilović, & Petrov (2016) present a solution for wireless security cameras, based on IoT enabled open-source hardware and a MongoDB database as the storage system. Their system uses an Arduino Yún with a webcam to capture images which are then stored in a MongoDB database. Kiraz & Toğay (2017) compare relational (MySQL) and non-relational (MongoDB) database management systems for the storing and processing of IoT data, concluding that MongoDB has better performance than MySQL in terms of both writing and reading operations. Similar to the previous work, Seo, Lee, & Lee (2017) use MySQL and MongoDB to compare RDBMS and NoSQL in the IoT context. They gradually compare the performance of create, read, update, and delete (CRUD) operations, concluding that, in general, MongoDB is preferred over MySQL for handling large amounts of data. They also point some disadvantages on using MongoDB such as the weak transaction capabilities when compared with the relational database system and the large memory space required. Strohbach, Ziekow, Gazis, & Akiva (2015) summarize what they consider the key components required for smart city application, namely: the abundance of data sources, the infrastructure, networks, interfaces and architectures being defined in the IoT community, the vast range of big data technologies available that support the processing of large data volumes, and the ample and wide knowledge about algorithms as well as toolboxes that can be used to mine the data. In the same work, a case study from the smart grid domain that illustrates the application of big data on smart home sensor data is discussed.

Comparing MySQL and MongoDB Schemas: An Example

To better illustrate the concepts previous explained, let us design a simple schema to store data acquired from sensors into a database. Figure 4 sketches the enhanced entity–relationship (EER) model for a relational database, designed to store that sensors' data. The model includes the *Sensor* entity, which will be placed in a *Location* and read values in a certain *Unit*. Each sensor *Reading* is associated to a sensor (using the idSensor foreign key, a collection of fields in one table that uniquely identifies a row of another table or the same table) stored with a corresponding timestamp. This schema allows each location (and *Unit*) to have associated multiple sensors and each sensor can have multiple readings. On the other hand, each reading corresponds to a single sensor and each sensor has a single location and unit.

In MongoDB, documents are stored as BSON (usually thought as JSON documents) and a direct correspondence to the EER model in Figure 4 would translate those entities to three documents (*Location*, *Sensor*, and *Reading*), such as the ones presented in Listing 1.

Figure 4. Enhanced entity–relationship (EER) model designed to store data from sensors in a relational database

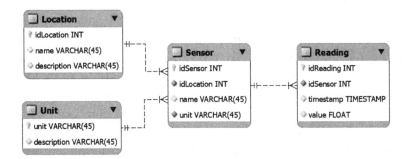

Listing 1. An initial model designed to store data from sensors in a JSON adequate database (e.g., MongoDB)

```
# Location document
{
  "_id": "1801",
  "name": "Prometheus Server",
  "description": "Prometheus Server @ lab. 163 / ISE / UAlg"
}
# Sensor document
{
  "_id": "s011",
  "location_id": "507...801",
  "sensor_name": "cpu_sensor",
  "unit": "percent"
}
# Reading document
{
  "_id": "r999",
  "sensor_id": "507...011",
  "timestamp": "2018-05-18T16:00:00Z",
  "value": 10.2
}
```

Employing any of these solutions implies that, for instance, a query to obtain the readings of the cpu_sensor requires costly join operations (either directly using the SQL join operator or doing it on the application side). However, document-oriented databases, such as MongoDB, allow embedding documents. Therefore, a solution would be to embed the information in a single document as presented in Listing 2.

The use of embedded documents, and the implementation of required secondary indexes, allows reaching readings from a location without doing join operations. However, there are some limitations. For instance, justified in the MongoDB documentation, it is important to ensure that a single document cannot use excessive amount of RAM or, during transmission, excessive amount of bandwidth. Furthermore, the maximum BSON document size is 16 megabytes, which can be a serious limitation when using embedded documents. To store documents larger than the maximum size, MongoDB provides the GridFS API (see MongoDB's documentation). As an alternative, the documents could be split when they reach the size limit, after a certain number of reading, by periods of time (probably a good solution when looking for readings in time windows), or some other adequate policy. The proposed MongoDB's embed solution has other problematics, such as, the need to first retrieve the document where the insertion is to be made and do its update before uploading it again (as an alternative, see MongoDB's $push operator).

To avoid that insertion overhead, a solution is to do the denormalization of the data, which can be done in any of the DBMS solutions. For instance, the MongoDB's solution could be the one presented in Listing 3, with the disadvantage of repeatedly storing the same data (e.g., location_name, description or sensor_name), which can represent a large waste of storage space and facilitate the occurrence of integrity issues.

Listing 2. An embedded document model designed to store data from sensors in a JSON liable database (e.g., MongoDB).

```
{
  "_id": "s011",
  "location_name": "Prometheus Server",
  "description": "Prometheus Server @ lab. 163 / ISE / UAlg",
  "sensors": [
    {
      "sensor_name": "mem_sensor",
      "values": [
        {
          "value": 35.4,
          "timestamp": "2018-05-09T17:10:00.273Z"
        },
        {
          "value": 35.4,
          "timestamp": "2018-05-09T17:10:01.276Z"
        }
      ],
      "units": "percent"
    },
    {
      "sensor_name": "cpu_sensor",
      "values": [
        {
          "value": 6.1,
          "timestamp": "2018-05-09T17:10:00.273Z"
        },
        {
          "value": 6.4,
          "timestamp": "2018-05-09T17:10:01.276Z"
        }
      ],
      "units": "percent"
    }
  ]
}
```

Listing 3. Denormalized schema to store a single reading by document.

```
{
  "_id": "s011",
  "location_name": "Prometheus Server",
  "description": "Prometheus Server @ lab. 163 / ISE / UAlg",
  "sensor_name": "cpu_sensor",
  "value": 35.4,
  "timestamp": "2018-05-09T17:10:00.273Z",
  "units": "percent"
}
```

MACHINE LEARNING ALGORITHMS AND APPLICATIONS

Supported in mathematical and computer science techniques, ML algorithms are mechanisms that use datasets to find patterns and correlations to build models. Those models are then applied to new data in order to predict its outcomes (Domingos, 2015; Witten et al., 2016).

ML are usually separated in two major classes, namely: supervised learning and unsupervised learning. Supervised learning has the task of inferring models/functions from labeled data, i.e., data that has an input vector and desirable target value. Those built models are then used to make predictions of the response values for new datasets. Supervised Learning is itself divided in classification and regression classes. The former one is used to make categorical predictions, i.e., to predict values where data can be separated into classes. Common classification algorithms include support vector machines (SVM) (Campbell & Ying, 2011; Suykens, Signoretto, & Argyriou, 2015), neural networks (Cartwright, 2015), decision trees (Hartshorn, 2016), logistic regression (Hosmer, Lemeshow, & Sturdivant, 2013) and k-nearest neighbor (kNN) (Shakhnarovich, Darrell, & Indyk, 2005). The latter, regression, is used to make predictions when continuous response values are desired. Common regression algorithms include linear regression, nonlinear regression, generalized linear models, decision trees, and neural networks. Some authors include other classes such as semi-supervised learning with the goal of employing a large collection of unlabeled data jointly with a few labeled examples for improving generalization performance, or reinforcement learning, which is used to support agents' decisions based on the notion of cumulative rewards.

On the other hand, unsupervised learning is a type of machine learning where inferences are to be drawn from datasets of unlabeled data (Celebi & Aydin, 2016), automatically discovering useful patterns in such data. Several kinds of applications can be found such as pattern recognition, market basket analysis, social network analysis, information retrieval, recommender systems or fraud detection. For instance, recommendation systems are used daily by information systems to expose intelligence, making search engines, social media, e-stores, digital music services etc. Recommender system algorithms are a class of information filtering system which have the job to predict the user's preferences, based on a given or guessed profile, i.e., companies apply learning algorithms on their huge datasets and let them oracle what customers want, instead of meticulously encoding the preferences of all consumers (Cardoso, Guerreiro, Monteiro, & Rodrigues, 2018; Rao & Rao, 2016; Ricci, Rokach, & Shapira, 2015).

As a consequence of this evolution, many agree that briefly most of the knowledge will be obtained and located in computers, i.e., as stated by Alpaydin (2016), "data starts to drive the operation; it is not the programmers anymore but the data itself that defines what to do next". This results in entire industries building themselves around ML, along with emergent research and academic specialties.

In general, the ML work-flow is divided in four large steps: (a) get (enough) data - collect data related to the problem; (b) clean, prepare, and manipulate data – converting the data into a form that computers can operate on (e.g., convert things to numerical data and categorize data); (c) define and train the selected model using test and validation data – build a mathematical model of the data depending on the type of problem being solved (e.g., regression, classification, clustering, or recommendations); and (d) predict outcomes over new and unseen data – apply the trained model to unseen data to, depending on the problem at hand, predict values, classify or associate the data, recommend other objects, etc.

Computational Tools

When delving into the ML world, many times, ML users/programmers no longer must implement a large number of the necessary methods, as they are included in several, free or payed, visual and programmable frameworks. In fact, frameworks, libraries, applications, and datasets are available and deeply simplify many ML implementation by roughly providing out of the box solutions. For instance, Tensorflow is an open source software library for high performance numerical computation using data flow graphs, with strong support for ML and deep learning (Abadi et al., 2016). Its flexible numerical computation core is used across many scientific domains, being easily deployable across a variety of computational platforms (e.g., CPU – Central Processing Unit, GPU – Graphics Processing Units, and TPU – Tensor Processing Unit). Caffe2 (2018), an improvement of Caffe 1.0 (Jia et al., 2014), is a deep learning framework that provides an easy and straightforward way to experiment with deep learning. The framework, using the Caffe2's cross-platform libraries, allows to scale applications from deployment using the power of GPUs in the cloud to mobile devices. The Amazon Machine Learning (AML, 2018) service provides visualization tools and assistants that guide all skill levels developers to use machine learning technology, allowing the creation of machine learning models without having to learn complex algorithms. The obtained models allow performing predictions in the users' applications using an API. Another advantage is the lack of need to manage any infrastructure, being the system scalable and serving those predictions in real-time. The Azure ML Studio (Microsoft, 2018) also provides Machine Learning as a Service (MLaaS). In its most pure form, no coding is required since a visual tool provides an end-to-end flow with a drag-and-drop environment used to build, test, and deploy predictive analytics solutions on your data. The Studio includes hundreds of built-in packages and support for custom code, namely in R and Python (Elston, 2015). Furthermore, the models can be published as web services, easily consumed by custom apps or other tools such as Excel. With the objective of making ML scalable and easy, MLlib (Meng et al., 2016) provides common learning algorithms (e.g., classification, regression, clustering, and collaborative filtering), featurization (e.g., feature extraction, transformation, dimensionality reduction, and selection), pipelines, persistence (e.g., saving and loading algorithms, models, and pipelines) and other utilities (e.g., linear algebra, statistics, data handling etc.). Being part of the Apache's Spark computing system, a unified analytics engine for large-scale data processing, MLlib provides high-level APIs in Java, Scala, Python and R. In the same context, data can be easily manipulated using Spark SQL which provides capabilities to operate on datasets and data frames with sources in data files (e.g., CSV, JSON, XML etc.), RDBMS, NoSQL DBMS etc. The Scikit-Learn

(Pedregosa et al., 2011) is an open source tools for data mining and data analysis. The library is built for the Python programming language and uses optimized libraries such as NumPy, SciPy, and matplotlib. The Scikit-Learn furnishes several ML algorithms in areas such as classification, regression, clustering, and dimension reduction. The Orange (2017) is an open-source data visualization, machine learning and data mining toolkit with a visual programming front-end. Furthermore, Orange can also be used as a Python library. WEKA (2017) is another graphical user interfaces (GUI) ML tool, written in Java and running on almost any platform. As many of the previous tools, WEKA is a collection of ML algorithms for solving data mining problems. The algorithms can either be applied directly to a dataset or called from your user's Java code. The KNIME: Konstanz Information Miner (Berthold et al., 2009; KNIME, 2017) is a modular environment, which enables easy visual assembly and interactive execution of a data pipeline. MLJAR (2017) implements several ML algorithms including built-in hyper-parameter search, parallel training of models, automatic selection of algorithms, a web programming interface, the deploy of the fitted models in the cloud or locally, and a Python wrapper over the MLJAR API. But many other visual and non-visual libraries exist, such as, VELES (2018) (a distributed platform, which provides machine learning and data processing services for a user), the Shogun-Toolbox (Soeren Sonnenburg et al., 2017) (an open-source machine learning library that offers a wide range of efficient and unified machine learning methods), Torch (Collobert, Kavukcuoglu, & Farabet, 2011) (a scientific computing framework with wide support for ML algorithms using GPUs), or the MLPACK (Curtin et al., 2013) (a scalable machine learning library, written in C++, that aims to provide fast, extensible implementations of machine learning algorithms).

We have already referred Python and Java as languages for which several libraries and ML tools exist (Müller & Guido, 2016). However, others languages also are frequently used in ML, such as R (Elston, 2015; James, Witten, Hastie, & Tibshirani, 2013; Lesmeister, 2015; Yu-Wei, 2015), F# (Mukherjee, 2016), Matlab (Kim, 2017), or Go (Whitenack, 2017).

Machine Learning in the IoE/IoT Context

An endless number of applications and usages are expected for the data collected by the IoE devices. Control and understand of complex environments or the improvement of efficiency, accuracy, and throughput of productive activities, are just a few envisioned effects in this context. For instance, Satish, Begum, & Shameena (2017) proposed an agricultural system to monitor and scan environmental parameters and plant growth. The collected data is then utilized by pest control sensors that are capable of predicting pest behavior, in order to reduce the damage done by pests on a large scale. The data is collected making use of an Arduino together with several sensors, including air temperature and humidity (using a DHT11), soil moisture, and pH. The devices are placed in different locations and the collected information is stored on a MongoDB database. Finally, a decision tree algorithm is used to predict damages and an advisable combination of pesticides is proposed, to reduce the harm caused by excessive usage of those chemicals at a later stage. Another agricultural production system based on IoE/IoT is proposed by Lee, Hwang, & Yoe (2013). The work defines a monitoring system that examines the crop environment and provides methods to improve the efficiency of decision making by analyzing previous harvesting statistics. Among other aspects, statistical predictions, and real time and historical environmental data from IoT services are used to do growth forecast. Alam, Mehmood, Katib, & Albeshri (2016) examined the applicability of eight well-known data mining algorithms for IoT data, namely SVM, kNN, Linear Discriminant Analysis, Naïve Bayes, C4.5, C5.0, Artificial Neural Networks (ANNs), and Deep Learning ANNs (DLANNs) algorithms. Their results on three IoT datasets show that C4.5 and C5.0 have better accuracy, are memory efficient and have relatively higher processing speeds, while ANNs and DLANNs can provide highly accurate results but are computationally expensive. Ahmed et al. (2017) studied the role of big data in IoT, discussing the big data processing and platforms, key requirements for big data processing, and analytics in an IoT environment. They also present a taxonomy of big data and analytics solutions that are designed for IoT systems, categorized as big data sources (e.g., city management, manufacturing), system components (e.g., data acquisition, data retention), big data enabling technologies (e.g., ML, commodity sensors), functional elements (e.g., data input, data output), and analytics type (e.g., descriptive, predictive or prescriptive). A complex of correlation-based methods for security incidents detection and the investigation in large-scale networks of heterogeneous devices such as IoT is proposed by Lavrova & Pechenkin (2015). The proposed approach was inspired by the SIEM (Security Information and Event Management) systems, which deploy multiple groups of agents to collect security related events from end-user devices, servers, network equipment, firewalls, antivirus, intrusion prevention systems etc. The decision about the existence of a security incident is supported in results of event correlation, by detecting interconnections between events from different devices. The authors also state that the complexity of security incidents detection in the IoT, among other things, is derived from the high heterogeneity of "things" and the low capacity of many of those "things", which does not allow integration of more complex protection means. Shanthamallu, Spanias, Tepedelenlioglu, & Stanley (2017) made a survey of ML methods, analyzing several of those methods (e.g., linear regression, logistic regression, SVM, k-NN, and deep learning) and many application in the IoT field. Another survey on data mining for the IoT was made by Chen et al. (2015). The work starts by doing an analysis on the data mining functionalities, followed by a brief analysis of several ML methods for classification, clustering, association analysis, and time series analysis, and finishes with a study on the use of data mining in several contexts (e.g., e-commerce, industry, health care, and governance) associated with IoE/IoT.

Building an ML/IoT System in Three Steps

This section proposes a simple example of ML/IoT system. As always, to implement a ML system, data is needed. So, let us start by implementing a web service which allows the collection of data from any device connected to the Internet, i.e., to receive data and store it on a database (a MongoDB database on this example). Stored data can then be accessed directly the applications (see an example below) or using the web service (not implemented in the presented example).

A solution to implement a web service is to use the Python programming language and, in particular, the Flask micro web framework (Grinberg, 2018). Listing 4 presents a snippet of the webservice's basic code. The route decorator is used to bind a function to an URL, in this case the new_reading function to the http://SERVER_IP:5000/iot/api/v1.0/reading URL, where the webservice is located at SERVER_IP IP address and 5000 is the Flask's default port.

We should notice that the webservice and MongoDB database are presumed to be running on the same location and data posted to the server in JSON format will be inserted into the MongoDB without any kind of further validation. Out of the scope of this chapter, it is recommendable to read more about several issues (e.g., security) in the Flask's documentation or in (Grinberg, 2018).

Listing 4. Example of webservice implemented in the Python's Flask framework.

```python
from flask import Flask, request, abort, jsonify
from pymongo import MongoClient
# create a connection to a MongoDB server running in your localhost
client = MongoClient('localhost', 27017)
# Set 'db' to use the IoT database
db = client.IoT
# create an instance of the Flask class -- see documentation
app = Flask(__name__)
@app.route('/iot/api/v1.0/reading', methods=['POST'])
def new_reading():
    # check if a valid json was posted
    if not request.json:
        abort(400)
    # insert data into the 'readings' collection
    db.readings.insert_one(request.json)
    # reply with an 'ok'/201 message
    return jsonify({'status': 'ok'}), 201
if __name__ == '__main__':
    # start the application in debug mode
    app.run(debug=True)
```

Two examples of how to post data to the webservice are given next. The first example gets the utilization percentages for the user's CPU time from a computer using Python and makes the posting of this data to the above implemented server (Listing 5). In this case, a JSON is posted to the webservice running on the server located at SERVER_IP IP(port 5000). Data includes information about the sensor's name, the acquired value (in this case, a float representing the current system-wide CPU utilization by normal processes executing in user mode, as a percentage), a timestamp, and the unit type of the posted value.

An environmental IoT device is proposed in the second example. This IoT sensor node can measure and transmit the temperature and humidity of a location to the Internet based webservice. The diagram of the projected IoT device is presented in Figure 5, being composed of an ESP8266 development board (NodeMCU) which is connected with a DHT22 (temperature and humidity) sensor. The ESP8266 microcontroller supports IEEE 802.11 communications and thus can be connected to any Wi-Fi network. Furthermore, the ESP8266 can be programmed in languages such as C++ or Python, and the microcontroller's programming framework includes several libraries, which support standard communication protocols like HTTP, TCP and IP (among many others).

Listing 6 presents an example of a Python code to run on the device that will to post JSON formatted data, similar to the ones in Listing 3, to the API's endpoint located at http://SERVER_IP:PORT/iot/api/v1.0/reading where, as before, SERVER_IP:PORT are the webservice's IP and corresponding port, WIFI_SSID is the wireless network service set identifier (SSID) and WIFI_PASSWD the corresponding authentication password. The temperature and humidity readings are sent every 30 seconds (30000 milliseconds) and the device's time is reset every one hour (3600000 milliseconds).

Listing 5. Example of the posting of CPU usage data to the webservice

```
import datetime, psutil, requests
# run forever
while True:
    response = requests.post('http://SERVER_IP:5000/iot/api/v1.0/reading',
                    json={
                            'location_name': 'Prometheus Server',
                            'sensor_name': 'cpu_user_sensor',
                            'value': psutil.cpu_times_percent(interval=1).user,
                            'timestamp': str(datetime.datetime.utcnow()),
                            'units': 'percent'
                        }
                )
```

Figure 5. Temperature and Humidity sensor connected with an ESP8266 development board

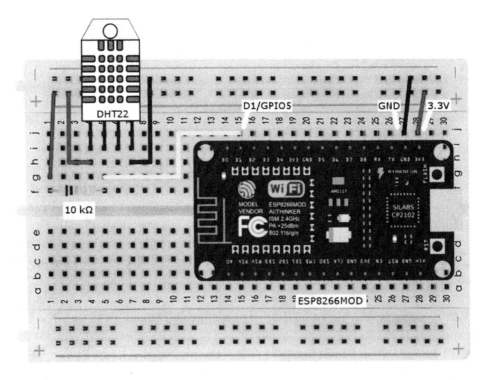

Finally, some ML can be done using the stored data. The code snippet in Listing 7 shows a basic script to train a model to predict the temperature given the humidity, month, day, hour, and minute. The proposed example starts by getting the data from the MongoDB database, filtering it to contain data from the sensor with location_name equal to "lab. 163 @ ise.ualg" and sensor_name equal to "Environment 1". Pandas library (McKinney, 2011) is used to do some data manipulation and then Scikit-learn package (Pedregosa et al., 2011) is used to split the dataset into training and test data, do a grid search

Listing 6. Python code used to program the IoT device in order to send the readings to the information system.

```python
import dht, machine, network, ntptime, urequests
def read_send(timer_read_send):
    """Post collected data to the webservice"""
    sensor.measure()
    datetime = rtc.datetime()
    urequests.post('http://SERVER_IP:5000/iot/api/v1.0/reading',
            json='''{"location_name": "lab. 163 @ ise.ualg",
                    "sensor_name": "Environment 1",
                    "temperature": {},
                    "humidity": {},
                    "timestamp": {}/{:02d}/{:02d} {:02d}:{:02d}:{:02d}}
                '''.format(sensor.temperature(), sensor.humidity(),
                        datetime[0], datetime[1], datetime[2],
                        datetime[4], datetime[5], datetime[6]))
def update_rtc(timer_update_rtc):
    """set device's time"""
    ntptime.settime()
wlan = network.WLAN(network.STA_IF)
wlan.connect(WIFI_SSID, WIFI_PASSWD)
while not wlan.isconnected():
    pass
rtc = machine.RTC()
ntptime.settime()
sensor = dht.DHT22(machine.Pin(5))
timer_read_send = machine.Timer(1).init(
        period=30000, mode=machine.Timer.PERIODIC, callback=read_send)
timer_update_rtc = machine.Timer(2).init(
        period=3600000, mode=machine.Timer.PERIODIC, callback=update_rtc)
```

with cross validation to find a good set of parameters for a Support Vector Regression (SVR) algorithm (Basak, Pal, & Patranabis, 2007), and store the model for future use.

The grid search with cross validation phase can be very time-consuming depending, for instance, on the number of observation feed to the model and the number of tested parameters. A solution might be the pruning of the number of observations using the PyMongo's limit method to specify the maximum number of documents the cursor will return (in the example, this number was limited to 10000). In this case, it might also be advisable to sort and filter the observation taking into consideration their timestamp. It is a good idea to observe the score value over the test set, which returns the coefficient of determination R^2 of the prediction, being the best possible score 1.

Finally, Listing 8 shows a snippet of code to predict the temperature for a humidity of 89% on a 5th of January, at midnight. The previously saved model is loaded and the predict method does the estimate.

Listing 7. Example of the training of a Support Vector Regression (SVR) model to predict temperatures given humidity, month, day, hour and minute.

```python
from sklearn.externals import joblib
from pymongo import MongoClient
import pandas as pd
from sklearn.model_selection import train_test_split
from sklearn.svm import SVR
from sklearn.model_selection import GridSearchCV
if __name__ == '__main__':
    # get data from the 'readings' collection into a pandas' dataframe - lim-
ited to 10000 observations
    readings_collection = MongoClient().IoT.readings
    df = pd.DataFrame(list(readings_collection.find({'sensor_name': 'Environ-
ment 1', 'location_name':'lab. 163 @ ise.ualg'},{'_id': False, 'temperature':
True, 'humidity': True, 'timestamp': True}).limit(10000)))
    # do necessary castings
    df['humidity'] = df['humidity'].astype(float)
    df['temperature'] = df['temperature'].astype(float)
    df['timestamp'] = pd.to_datetime(df['timestamp'])
    # split the dates into its components
    df['Ye'] = df['timestamp'].dt.strftime('%y')
    df['Mo'] = df['timestamp'].dt.strftime('%m')
    df['Da'] = df['timestamp'].dt.strftime('%d')
    df['Ho'] = df['timestamp'].dt.strftime('%H')
    df['Mi'] = df['timestamp'].dt.strftime('%M')
    # get an array of observation (X) and corresponding targets (y)
    X = df[['humidity', 'Mo', 'Da', 'Ho', 'Mi']].values
    y = df['temperature'].values
    # split the data set into training and testing sets
    X_train, X_test, y_train, y_test = \
        train_test_split(X, y, random_state=1)
    # train an SVR model, using grid search and cross-validation - see Grid-
SearchCV and SVR documentation - this step takes some time!
    param_grid = {'degree': [2, 3], 'kernel':['poly', 'rbf'],
                  'C': [0.0001, .001, 0.01, 0.1, 1, 10, 100, 1000]}
    model = GridSearchCV(estimator=SVR(), param_grid=param_grid, cv=5,
                        return_train_score=True, verbose=10, n_jobs=6)
    model.fit(X_train, y_train)
    print('''best score: {} \n best params: {} \n score over test: {} \n Best
estimator: {}'''.format(model.best_score_, model.best_params_, model.score(X_
test, y_test), model.best_estimator_))
    # store the model for future usage
    joblib.dump(model, 'model.joblib')
```

Listing 8. Load stored model and make a temperature prediction

```
from sklearn.externals import joblib
# load stored model
model = joblib.load('model.joblib')
# predict the temperature
print(model.predict([[.89, 1, 5, 0, 0]]))
```

SOLUTIONS, RECOMMENDATIONS, AND FUTURE RESEARCH DIRECTIONS

Within such a vast research field there is no single set of solutions, no definite recommendation. One thing is for sure: IoE, IoT and ML are here to stay. In such a massive environment, vertical specialization will be an asset as a "Jack of all trades, master of none" will not properly tackle the nuclear issues. Certainly, a general knowledge of all fields will be of interest, as it will allow the understanding of intrinsic limitations, enabling properly designed architectures from a macro perspective. This assumption also results from the observation of the huge number of research and development fields involved, which span far beyond algorithms and software to include sensors, tags and actuators, communications protocols, power feeding (e.g., consumption, use of renewal sources, batteries) etc. All these fields are passible of broad investigation, as easily found in many recent documents. Nevertheless, soft development, the main focus of this chapter, has also many things to improve. The longevity, the amount, and the type of generated data will require new storage techniques and new algorithms. On the storage side, deep research should be made in distributed databases, capable of locally storing and efficiently retrieving data on request. These distributed databases must be adequate to the data's type and size, and especially ready to synchronization, in some cases a major issue as data might be outdated in very short intervals of time. New ML algorithmic solutions, capable of reaching better accuracies but also in a more efficient way, are also a major research field. Once again, algorithms capable of returning answers in real-time, possibly in computational constrained environments, will certainly be of major interest. Therefore, mathematical optimization, new data structures, and new ML methods which take advantage of the particularities of the data, expected outcomes, and computational restrictions are of high interest. These restrictions will be even more visible when considering edge computing and edge storage as these edge environments are in general very limited on the available energy, communications and computational capacities (e.g., memory and CPU power). These limitations can make real-time solutions a possible nightmare but, when overcame, they can also significantly improve the overall performance of the systems, for instance, by doing pre-computation on the data (e.g., data aggregation or data filtering). Similarly, distributed computing on either edge nodes or on server farms will certainly be a field where improvements, possibly algorithmic dependent, will be of usage. Finally, we cannot skip cloud services as a way to use an infrastructure in a transparent manner, significantly reducing maintenance and, possibly, infrastructural costs.

CONCLUSION

Machine Learning applied to IoE is certainly more than a short-term trend. The applications to the users are steaming a flourishing field, where academies, private and public corporations, and all other entities will have key roles. The benefits will be reflected in many activities, including agriculture, financial services businesses, entertainment companies and mass media agencies, industrial manufacturers, real estate businesses, retailers, wholesalers and distributors, transportation businesses, utilities, services, among others. So, the use of the data collect by IoE devices will allow the understanding and control of complex environments around us. This understanding and control will enable better automation, better responses, and improved efficiency and accuracy. All in all, proper devices, data and ML methods will have a significant part in creating a smarter IoE.

ACKNOWLEDGMENT

This work was supported by project AGERAR (0076_AGERAR_6_E) financed by the European Union, under the scope of the FEDER program and Interreg initiative, by project M5SAR I&DT n. 3322 financed by CRESC ALGARVE2020, PORTUGAL2020 and FEDER, and by the Portuguese Foundation for Science and Technology (FCT), project LARSyS [UID/EEA/50009/2013], CIAC.

REFERENCES

Abadi, M., Agarwal, A., Barham, P., Brevdo, E., Chen, Z., Citro, C., … Zheng, X. (2016). *Tensorflow: Large-scale machine learning on heterogeneous distributed systems.* ArXiv Preprint ArXiv:1603.04467

Adiono, T., Marthensa, R., Muttaqin, R., Fuada, S., Harimurti, S., & Adijarto, W. (2017). Design of database and secure communication protocols for Internet-of-things-based smart home system. In TENCON 2017 - 2017 IEEE Region 10 Conference (pp. 1273–1278). IEEE. doi:10.1109/TENCON.2017.8228053

Ahmed, E., Yaqoob, I., Hashem, I. A. T., Khan, I., Ahmed, A. I. A., Imran, M., & Vasilakos, A. V. (2017). The role of big data analytics in Internet of Things. *Computer Networks*, *129*, 459–471. doi:10.1016/j.comnet.2017.06.013

Alam, F., Mehmood, R., Katib, I., & Albeshri, A. (2016). Analysis of Eight Data Mining Algorithms for Smarter Internet of Things (IoT). *Procedia Computer Science*, *98*, 437–442. doi:10.1016/j.procs.2016.09.068

Alpaydin, E. (2016). *Machine Learning: the New AI*. The MIT press.

AML. (2018). *Amazon Machine Learning*. Retrieved May 11, 2018, from http://aws.amazon.com/aml/

Assaf, W., West, R., Aelterman, S., & Curnutt, M. (2018). *SQL Server 2017 Administration Inside Out*. Microsoft.

Basak, D., Pal, S., & Patranabis, D. C. (2007). Support vector regression. *Neural Information Processing Letters and Reviews*, *11*(10), 203–224.

Bassett, L. (2015). *Introduction to JavaScript Object Notation: A To-the-Point Guide to JSON* (1st ed.). O'Reilly Media.

Bell, C. (2016). MySQL for the Internet of Things (W. Spahr, Ed.). Apress. doi:10.1007/978-1-4842-1293-6

Berthold, M. R., Cebron, N., Dill, F., Gabriel, T. R., Kötter, T., Meinl, T., ... Wiswedel, B. (2009). KNIME: The Konstanz Information Miner. *AcM SIGKDD Explorations Newsletter*, *11*(1), 26–31. doi:10.1145/1656274.1656280

Caffe2. (2018). *Caffe2*. Retrieved October 7, 2018, from https://caffe2.ai/

Campbell, C., & Ying, Y. (2011). *Learning with Support Vector Machines* (R. J. Brachman & T. Dietterich, Eds.). Morgan & Claypool. doi:10.2200/S00324ED1V01Y201102AIM010

Cardoso, P. J. S., Guerreiro, P., Monteiro, J., & Rodrigues, J. (2018). Applying an Implicit Recommender System in the Preparation of Visits to Cultural Heritage Places. In M. Antona & C. Stephanidis (Eds.), *Universal Access in Human--Computer Interaction. Design and Development Approaches and Methods: 12th International Conference, UAHCI 2018, Held as Part of HCI International 2018, Las Vegas, USA, July 15--20, 2018*. Springer International Publishing. 10.1007/978-3-319-92052-8_33

Cartwright, H. (Ed.). (2015). *Artificial Neural Networks* (Vol. 1260). New York, NY: Springer New York; doi:10.1007/978-1-4939-2239-0

Cassandra. (2018). *Cassandra*. Retrieved October 7, 2018, from http://cassandra.apache.org/

Celebi, M. E., & Aydin, K. (Eds.). (2016). *Unsupervised Learning Algorithms* (1st ed.). Springer International Publishing. doi:10.1007/978-3-319-24211-8

Chen, F., Deng, P., Wan, J., Zhang, D., Vasilakos, A. V., & Rong, X. (2015). Data Mining for the Internet of Things: Literature Review and Challenges. *International Journal of Distributed Sensor Networks*, *11*(8), 431047. doi:10.1155/2015/431047

Chodorow, K. (2013). *MongoDB: The Definitive Guide*. O'Reilly Media.

Collobert, R., Kavukcuoglu, K., & Farabet, C. (2011). Torch7: A Matlab-like Environment for Machine Learning. *BigLearn, NIPS Workshop*.

Curtin, R. R., Cline, J. R., Slagle, N. P., March, W. B., Ram, P., Mehta, N. A., & Gray, A. G. (2013). MLPACK: A Scalable C++ Machine Learning Library. *Journal of Machine Learning Research*, *14*, 801–805.

DB-Engines. (2018). *DB-Engines*. Retrieved October 7, 2018, from https://db-engines.com

Domingos, P. (2015). *The master algorithm: How the quest for the ultimate learning machine will remake our world*. Basic Books.

Elston, S. F. (2015). *Data Science in the Cloud: with Microsoft Azure Machine Learning and R*. O'Reilly Media.

Grinberg, M. (2018). *Flask Web Development: Developing Web Applications with Python*. O'Reilly Media, Inc.

Harrison, G. (2015). *Next Generation Databases: NoSQL, NewSQL, and Big Data.* Apress. doi:10.1007/978-1-4842-1329-2

Hartshorn, S. (2016). *Machine Learning With Random Forests And Decision Trees: A Visual Guide For Beginners.* Amazon Digital Services LLC.

Hosmer, D., Lemeshow, S., & Sturdivant, R. (2013). *Applied logistic regression.* Wiley. doi:10.1002/9781118548387

James, G., Witten, D., Hastie, T., & Tibshirani, R. (2013). *An Introduction to Statistical Learning with Applications in R.* Springer. doi:10.1007/978-1-4614-7138-7

Jia, Y., Shelhamer, E., Donahue, J., Karayev, S., Long, J., Girshick, R., ... Darrell, T. (2014). Caffe. In *Proceedings of the ACM International Conference on Multimedia - MM '14* (pp. 675–678). New York: ACM Press. 10.1145/2647868.2654889

Kang, Y.-S., Park, I.-H., Rhee, J., & Lee, Y.-H. (2016). MongoDB-Based Repository Design for IoT-Generated RFID/Sensor Big Data. *IEEE Sensors Journal, 16*(2), 485–497. doi:10.1109/JSEN.2015.2483499

Kang, Y.-S., Park, I.-H., & Youm, S. (2016). Performance Prediction of a MongoDB-Based Traceability System in Smart Factory Supply Chains. *Sensors (Basel), 16*(12), 2126. doi:10.339016122126 PMID:27983654

Kim, P. (2017). *MATLAB Deep Learning: With Machine Learning, Neural Networks and Artificial Intelligence* (1st ed.). Apress. doi:10.1007/978-1-4842-2845-6

Kiraz, G., & Toğay, C. (2017). IoT Data Storage: Relational & Non-Relational Database Management Systems Performance Comparison. In A. Yazici & C. Turhan (Eds.), *34. TBD National Informatics Symposium* (pp. 48–52). Ankara, Turkey: Academic Press.

KNIME. (2017). *KNIME.* Retrieved October 7, 2018, from https://www.knime.com/

Lavrova, D., & Pechenkin, A. (2015). Applying Correlation and Regression Analysis to Detect Security Incidents in the Internet of Things. *International Journal of Communication Networks and Information Security, 7*(3), 131–137.

Lee, M., Hwang, J., & Yoe, H. (2013). Agricultural Production System Based on IoT. In *2013 IEEE 16th International Conference on Computational Science and Engineering* (pp. 833–837). IEEE. 10.1109/CSE.2013.126

Lesmeister, C. (2015). *Mastering Machine Learning with R.* Packt Publishing.

Lueth, K. L. (2015). *IoT basics: Getting started with the Internet of Things.* IoT Analytics (White Paper).

Malić, M., Dobrilović, D., & Petrov, I. (2016). Example of IoT platform usage for wireless video surveillance with support of NoSQL and cloud systems. In Proceedings of the ICAIIT2016 (pp. 27–34). University "St. Kliment Ohridski". doi:10.20544/AIIT2016.04

Matsatsinis, N. F. (2002). An intelligent decision support system for credit card assessment based on a machine learning technique. *Operations Research, 2*(2), 243–260. doi:10.1007/BF02936329

McKinney, W. (2011). Data Structures for Statistical Computing in Python. In *9th Python in Science Conf. (SCIPY 2010)* (pp. 51–56). Academic Press.

Meng, X., Bradley, J., Yavuz, B., Sparks, E., Venkataraman, S., Liu, D., ... Talwalkar, A. (2016). MLlib: Machine Learning in Apache Spark. *Journal of Machine Learning Research, 17*(1), 1235–1241.

Microsoft. (2018). *Azure ML Studio*. Retrieved October 7, 2018, from https://studio.azureml.net

Microsoft-SQL-Server. (2017). *Microsoft SQL Server*. Retrieved from https://goo.gl/nTzmGr

MLJAR. (2017). *MLJAR*. Retrieved October 7, 2018, from https://mljar.com/

MongoDB. (2018). *MongoDB*. Retrieved September 1, 2015, from https://www.mongodb.org/

Mukherjee, S. (2016). *F# for Machine Learning Essentials: Get up and running with machine learning with F# in a fun and functional way*. Packt Publishing.

Müller, A. C., & Guido, S. (2016). Introduction to machine learning with Python: a guide for data scientists. O'Reilly Media.

MySQL. (2018). *MySQL*. Retrieved October 7, 2018, from https://www.mysql.com/

Neo4j. (2018). *Neo4j*. Retrieved October 7, 2018, from https://neo4j.com/

Orange. (2017). *Orange*. Retrieved September 1, 2018, from https://orange.biolab.si/

Paethong, P., Sato, M., & Namiki, M. (2016). Low-power distributed NoSQL database for IoT middleware. In *2016 Fifth ICT International Student Project Conference (ICT-ISPC)* (pp. 158–161). IEEE. 10.1109/ICT-ISPC.2016.7519260

Pedregosa, F., Varoquaux, G., Gramfort, A., Michel, V., Thirion, B., Grisel, O., ... Duchesnay, E. (2011). Scikit-learn: Machine Learning in Python. *Journal of Machine Learning Research, 12*, 2825–2830.

Perera, C. (2017). *Sensing as a Service for Internet of Things: A Roadmap*. Leanpub Publishers.

Perkins, L., Redmond, E., & Wilson, J. (2018). *Seven Databases in Seven Weeks: A Guide to Modern Databases and the NoSQL Movement*. O'Reilly UK Ltd.

PostgreSQL. (2018). *PostgreSQL*. Retrieved September 15, 2018, from https://www.postgresql.org/

Rao, R. R., & Rao, M. V. (2016). A Survey on Recommender System. *International Journal of Computer Science and Information Security, 14*(5), 265–271.

Rautmare, S., & Bhalerao, D. M. (2016). MySQL and NoSQL database comparison for IoT application. In *2016 IEEE International Conference on Advances in Computer Applications (ICACA)* (pp. 235–238). IEEE. 10.1109/ICACA.2016.7887957

Riak-KV. (2018). *Riak KV*. Retrieved from http://basho.com/products/riak-kv/

Ricci, F., Rokach, L., & Shapira, B. (Eds.). (2015). *Recommender Systems Handbook*. Springer-Verlag GmbH. doi:10.1007/978-1-4899-7637-6

Roy, R., & George, K. T. (2017). Detecting insurance claims fraud using machine learning techniques. In *2017 International Conference on Circuit, Power and Computing Technologies (ICCPCT)* (pp. 1–6). IEEE. 10.1109/ICCPCT.2017.8074258

Satish, T., Begum, T., & Shameena, B. (2017). Agriculture Productivity Enhancement System using IOT. *International Journal of Theoretical and Applied Mechanics, 12*(3), 543–554.

Schalkwyk, J., Beeferman, D., Beaufays, F., Byrne, B., Chelba, C., Cohen, M., … Strope, B. (2010). "Your Word is my Command": Google Search by Voice: A Case Study. In Advances in Speech Recognition (pp. 61–90). Boston, MA: Springer US. doi:10.1007/978-1-4419-5951-5_4

Seo, J. Y., Lee, D. W., & Lee, H. M. (2017). Performance Comparison of CRUD Operations in IoT based Big Data Computing. *International Journal on Advanced Science. Engineering and Information Technology, 7*(5), 1765. doi:10.18517/ijaseit.7.5.2674

Serpanos, D., & Wolf, M. (2018). *Internet-of-Things (IoT) Systems*. Cham: Springer International Publishing. doi:10.1007/978-3-319-69715-4

Shakhnarovich, G., Darrell, T., & Indyk, P. (Eds.). (2005). *Nearest-Neighbor Methods in Learning and Vision: Theory and Practice*. The MIT Press.

Shanthamallu, U. S., Spanias, A., Tepedelenlioglu, C., & Stanley, M. (2017). A brief survey of machine learning methods and their sensor and IoT applications. In *2017 8th International Conference on Information, Intelligence, Systems & Applications (IISA)* (pp. 1–8). IEEE. 10.1109/IISA.2017.8316459

Sonnenburg, S., Strathmann, H., Lisitsyn, S., Gal, V., García, F. J. I., Lin, W., … Esser. (2017). *Shogun-Toolbox/Shogun: Shogun 6.1.0*. Zenodo. doi:10.5281/zenodo.1067840

SQLite. (2018). *SQLite*. Retrieved October 7, 2018, from http://sqlite.org

Strohbach, M., Ziekow, H., Gazis, V., & Akiva, N. (2015). Towards a Big Data Analytics Framework for IoT and Smart City Applications. In Modeling and Optimization in Science and Technologies (pp. 257–282). Academic Press. doi:10.1007/978-3-319-09177-8_11

Suykens, J. A. K., Signoretto, M., & Argyriou, A. (Eds.). (2015). *Regularization, Optimization, Kernels, and Support Vector Machines*. CRC Press.

Tan, L., & Wang, N. (2010). Future internet: The Internet of Things. In *2010 3rd International Conference on Advanced Computer Theory and Engineering (ICACTE)* (pp. V5-376-V5-380). IEEE. 10.1109/ICACTE.2010.5579543

VELES. (2018). *VELES*. Retrieved September 16, 2018, from https://velesnet.ml

Vermesan, O., & Friess, P. (2011). *Internet of Things - Global Technological and Societal Trends From Smart Environments and Spaces to Green ICT*. River Publishers.

Wang, W., Song, Y., Zhang, J., & Deng, H. (2014). Automatic parking of vehicles: A review of literatures. *International Journal of Automotive Technology, 15*(6), 967–978. doi:10.100712239-014-0102-y

WEKA. (2017). *WEKA: Waikato Environment for Knowledge Analysis*. Retrieved September 18, 2018, from https://www.cs.waikato.ac.nz/ml/weka/

Whitenack, D. (2017). *Machine learning with Go*. Packt Publishing.

Witten, I. H., Frank, E., Hall, M. A., & Pal, C. J. (2016). *Data Mining: Practical Machine Learning Tools and Techniques*. Morgan Kaufmann.

Yu-Wei, D. C. (2015). *Machine Learning with R Cookbook: Explore over 110 recipes to analyze data and build predictive models with the simple and easy-to-use R code*. Packt Publishing.

ADDITIONAL READING

Batalla, J. M., Mastorakis, G., Mavromoustakis, C., & Pallis, E. (2017). *Beyond the Internet of Things: Everything Interconnected* (1st ed.). Springer. doi:10.1007/978-3-319-50758-3

Bhatt, C., Dey, N., & Ashour, A. S. (2017). *Internet of Things and Big Data Technologies for Next Generation Healthcare*. Springer. doi:10.1007/978-3-319-49736-5

Di-Martino, B., Li, K.-C., Yang, L. T., & Esposito, A. (2018). *Internet of Everything: Algorithms, Methodologies, Technologies and Perspectives* (1st ed.). Springer Singapore. doi:10.1007/978-981-10-5861-5

Hulten, G. (2018). *Building Intelligent Systems: A Guide to Machine Learning Engineering* (1st ed.). Apress. doi:10.1007/978-1-4842-3432-7

Hussain, F. (2017). *Internet of Things: Building Blocks and Business Models*. Cham: Springer International Publishing. doi:10.1007/978-3-319-55405-1

Minteer, A. (2017). *Analytics for the Internet of Things*. Packt.

Shark, A. (2015). *The Digital Revolution in HIgher Education: The How & Why the Internet of Everything is Changing Everything*. CreateSpace Independent Publishing Platform.

KEY TERMS AND DEFINITIONS

Internet of Things (IoT): Dynamic global network infrastructure, with self-configuring capabilities based on standard and interoperable communication protocols, where a massive number of physical and virtual things have identities, physical attributes, and virtual personalities.

Machine Learning: Mechanisms that use datasets to find patterns and correlations in order to build models which will be applied to new data in order to predict its outcomes.

NoSQL Databases: System which provides a mechanism to store data in other than tabular relations and relationships used in relational databases.

Relational Databases: System which provides a mechanism to store data in sets of tuples/tabular relations. Relationships between those sets are implemented through systems of primary and foreign keys.

APPENDIX

Table 2. Main features of the databases addressed in the chapter

	Primary Database Model	Secondary Database Models	Server Systems	Data Scheme	Typing	Secondary Indexes	Operations Language	Server-Side Scripts	Triggers	Partitioning Methods	Replication Methods	Transaction Concepts
Cassandra (V 3.11.2)	Wide column store	None	Linux, Windows, OS X, etc	No	Yes	restricted	Own protocol, Thrift	No	Yes	Sharding	selectable replication factor	No
Microsoft SQL Server (V 2017)	Relational	Document store, Key-value store, Graph DBMS	Linux, Windows	Yes	Yes	Yes	SQL	SQL	Yes	Horizontal partitioning, Sharding	Yes, version dependent	ACID
MongoDB (V 3.6.4)	Document store	Key-value store	Linux, Windows, OS X, etc	No	Yes	Yes	Own protocol	JavaScript	No	Sharding	Master-slave	No
MySQL (V 8.0.11)	Relational	Document store, Key-value store	Linux, Windows, OS X, etc	Yes	Yes	Yes	SQL	SQL	Yes	Horizontal partitioning, Sharding	Master-master, Master-slave	ACID
Neo4j (V 3.3.5)	Graph	None	Linux, Windows, OS X, etc	Optional	Yes	Yes	Neo4j-OGM, etc	Yes	Yes	None	Causal Clustering	ACID
PostgreSQL (V 10.3)	Relational	Document store, Key-value store	Linux, Windows, OS X, etc	Yes	Yes	Yes	SQL	SQL	Yes	Declarative partitioning	Master-slave	ACID
Riak KV (V 2.1.0)	Key-value	None	Linux, OS X	No	No	restricted	HTTP API, Erlang	JavaScript, Erlang	Yes	Sharding	selectable replication factor	No
SQLite (V 3.23.1)	Relational	Key-value store	Server-less	Yes	Yes	Yes	SQL	No	Yes	No	No	ACID

(Adapted from (DB-Engines, 2018))

Chapter 3
IoE–Based Control and Monitoring of Electrical Grids:
A Smart Grid's Perspective

Nelson Pinto
University of Algarve, Portugal

Dario Cruz
University of Algarve, Portugal

Jânio Monteiro
University of Algarve, Portugal

Cristiano Cabrita
University of Algarve, Portugal

Jorge Semião
University of Algarve, Portugal

Pedro J. S. Cardoso
University of Algarve, Portugal

Luís M. R. Oliveira
*Universidade da Beira Interior, Portugal &
Universidade do Algarve, Portugal*

João M. F. Rodrigues
University of Algarve, Portugal

ABSTRACT

In many countries, renewable energy production already represents an important percentage of the total energy that is generated in electrical grids. In order to reach higher levels of integration, demand side management measures are yet required. In fact, different from the legacy electrical grids, where at any given instant the generation levels are adjusted to meet the demand, when using renewable energy sources, the demand must be adapted in accordance with the generation levels, since these cannot be controlled. In order to alleviate users from the burden of individual control of each appliance, energy management systems (EMSs) have to be developed to both monitor the generation and consumption patterns and to control electrical appliances. In this context, the main contribution of this chapter is to present the implementation of such an IoT-based monitoring and control system for microgrids, capable of supporting the development of an EMS.

DOI: 10.4018/978-1-5225-7332-6.ch003

INTRODUCTION

At the end of the last century, a growing environmental concern led to the introduction of renewable energy sources throughout the electrical grids. The defined targets, such as a reduction of 80% (compared to 1990 levels) in CO_2 emissions until 2050 in Europe, has led countries, companies and public entities to search for solutions, that span from generating more renewable energy to reducing consumption.

In terms of generation, nuclear, solar, wind or biomass energy have become important sources of clean energy, allowing zero CO_2 emissions. As far as consumption is concerned, the fields where most of the reduction of consumption can happen are known and include buildings, transportation and electrical production (La Scala, Bruno, Nucci, Lamonaca & Stecchi, 2017). It is also known that cities consume 75% of the energy generated and produce 80% of CO_2, and therefore it is of great importance to act in improving their efficiency.

In order to promote the gradual replacement of outdated and inefficient equipment, the European Energy Efficiency Directive 2012/27/EU has defined that by 2020 energy savings should reach the 20% target, when compared with the estimated value for that same date without any actions.

The Mediterranean countries in particular, which have many annual hours of sunshine, can take advantage of this fact, to achieve the CO_2 reduction targets through solar electricity production. In Portugal, for instance, the average number of hours of sunshine per year varies between 2200 and 3000, depending on the region (Aiminho.pt, 2018). In addition, its geographic location, by the sea, leads to the existence of some regular and intense winds, which can be used profitably, both in coastal or mountainous regions (Costa, 2004). Wind already contributes to an electricity production ratio of 21.6% (of the total amount produced in Portugal), plus 1.6% that result from solar sources (Associação Portuguesa de Energias Renováveis APREN, 2017). Portugal has even managed to produce enough energy to feed the country for several days, using only renewable energy sources (REN, 2018).

Traditionally, the generation and distribution of electricity was done in a scheme that started in production plants, followed by transmission in high/medium voltage lines and distribution in low voltage to the final consumer. This scheme was implemented throughout the twentieth century and has remained until the present day. Although control and monitoring technologies or remote protection were included at the end of the century, they were not integrated into the entire grid, but only placed at important infrastructure points (stations, substations or high voltage) in order to allow some control and remote access (Sendin, Sanchez-Fornie, & Berganza, 2016). In general, the entire electrical grid had little automation and communication, in addition to the advanced age of many of the equipment, thus not being able to guarantee the reliability and efficiency that were intended to allow.

More recently, the introduction of renewable energy sources has created a set of new challenges for which the traditional grid had not been designed for. In this context the energy is injected by the producers at the distribution level, in parallel with the one conveyed by traditional sources, in a scheme known as Distributed Generation (DG). This trend was initially motivated by what was called microproduction, where traditional customers could also become producers, injecting the energy produced by them into the conventional grid. The concepts of micro and nanogrid were at this stage introduced, as small electrical grids, isolated or not from the main grid, that could be independently managed (La Scala, Bruno, Nucci, Lamonaca & Stecchi, 2017). In these networks, the distribution is usually done in alternating current (AC), but there are other direct current (DC) solutions that can be considered, or in some cases a mixture of the two.

The problem that results from the DG, comes from the fact that renewable energy sources are known as intermittent sources, i.e. the power generated by these sources is known to vary significantly over time and difficult to predict. In order to alleviate this burden, storage systems can be considered as a solution, that allows transferring power from the excessive production phases, to the high consumption ones, ensuring the proper balance of the system. Besides storage, and since it is not possible to control the generation, it is important to implement solutions that allow the adjustment of consumption levels in accordance with the generated power, in what is known as Demand Response (DR).

The ongoing modernization of the existing infrastructure, to support all these new realities, is making use of the latest communication technologies with the aim of creating a greener, safer, reliable, efficient and intelligent electrical grid. This is the basis of the so-called Smart Grid (SG), a concept that aims to integrate information and communication technologies with the electric distribution and production grids (Risteska Stojkoska, & Trivodaliev, 2017). Smart grids result from the massification of the Internet access and are in line with the development of the Internet of things (IoT), allowing any device to be connected to the Internet and thus to communicate with persons and/or other machines. Its adoption in electrical grids has, however, been slow. The still novelty of many solutions and their yet to proof reliability, still does not guarantee the requirements imposed by a critical infrastructure, such as the electrical grids (Borlase, 2017). One of the simplest and most common applications of IoT devices in Smart Grids is the advanced metering infrastructures (AMI), enabling the monitoring of the consumption of a building and the real time detection of problems. Electronic metering equipment has become commonplace and accessible, making it possible to measure consumption and productions in real time, thus being very useful in management, production and storage systems.

In terms of buildings, they also need to become more efficient, in order to meet the requirements of CO_2 reduction. Part of these requirements can be met with the use of building materials with better isolation properties, but the other part involves the utilization of more efficient equipment. In both cases the monitoring of consumption is a tool that can help diagnosis if, why and when, the building is consuming more than expected, correlating it with other variables like air temperature, solar radiation or occupancy, that influence it.

Besides monitoring, many automation solutions nowadays allow remote control of electric equipment, lighting, heating, ventilation, and air conditioning systems through Internet Protocol (IP) standards. This trend is being complemented by many software platforms in the cloud that currently allow storage and graphical representation of all this data. In this context, machine learning and optimization are being merged with these platforms to enable a maximization of efficiency. Machine learning can be used to perform anomaly detection, and optimization can be used to perform load scheduling in accordance with the tariff rates and renewable energy generation levels.

In terms of mobility, the current shift towards electric vehicles (EVs) will potentially reduce the dependency in fossil fuels and contribute to a reduction in CO_2 emissions. However, in order to meet this objective some changes are required, namely: (1) more renewable energy production; (2) an update of electrical grids to be able of accommodating higher currents (Saleem, Crespi, Rehmani, & Copeland, 2017) and (3) the development of energy management systems (EMSs) to support demand response of the charging processes.

One of the advantages of introducing EVs results from the fact that they can be used as storage units, whenever the generation surpasses consumption (known as grid to vehicle, G2V). Optionally, they can also re-supply this stored energy to the network (known as vehicle to grid, V2G). In any case, energy management systems are required and will play an important role in such control. EMSs usually monitor local variables like occupancy and control home/building devices according to an optimization algorithm that try to use as much as possible the energy generated locally while reducing electrical costs. To perform this task, they are also required to communicate with the devices they control, with users, using IP networks through Human Machine Interfaces, and with other devices/machines in the Internet to, for instance, obtain information about weather forecasts or subsequent tariff rates (Wang, Wu, Ekanayake, & Jenkins, 2017).

However, managing energy is a difficult task due to the unpredictability of both, demand and production that results from some renewable energy sources. Solar or wind energy are always dependent on uncontrollable environmental conditions, which creates a problem of intermittent availability.

In order to be able to make decisions about storage, consumption, energy exports and to forecast future generation levels, it is necessary to acquire information from the electrical grid and to monitor some environmental and structural parameters. The gathering of this data can be made based on a network of sensors. At this level, using a wireless sensor network simplifies the installation, because it does not impose a cabling infrastructure. However, it requires proper signal coverage as certain measurement points might be geographically distant, imposing a proper selection of the wireless sensor network technology.

Objectives

This chapter presents the development of a system capable of monitoring electrical and environmental variables, using the most recent technologies available in Low Power Wide Area networks (LPWAN) and applicable to micro grids. The aim of the developed network is the measurement of continuous and alternating currents and voltages, in a micro grid that integrates photovoltaic and or wind generation, as well as the measurement of the consumption and state of charge of storage units. An example of such electrical grid is shown in Figure 1. The systems comprises both DC and AC buses. The DC bus can be connected with the AC grid or work in an islanded mode. As part of the AGERAR project (2018), the sensing and monitoring system will be installed and operating in an experimental micro-grid of the National Institute of Aerospace Technology (INTA), in Spain.

When deciding the wireless technology to be used, several key objectives were defined, namely: (1) capacity to support the typical coverages of small to medium micro grids, (2) be cost affordable, (3) be modular, (4) be open source, and (5) be scalable.

In addition to these requirements, the developed system should ensure data collection, transmission, processing, storage and presentation to users. The components used should be chosen in such a way as to make the whole system economically accessible and include the certifications that are required for application in a Smart Grid. In terms of AC, given the fact that there are many types of certified products to measure the associated voltages and currents, the project opted to use commercial energy meters and to communicate with them via MODBUS protocol (Modbus IDA, 2006). Different from AC however, in the case of DC, it was considered relevant to develop some sensors specially tailored for the micro grid of INTA, that can still be used in other electrical grids. Finally, the system should also allow adding new components or modules, without imposing infrastructural changes.

Figure 1. General architecture of the elements that can comprise a Smart Grid's network

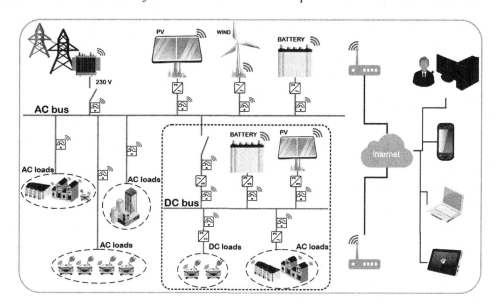

BACKGROUND

The monitoring and control of micro grids require the implementation of a Wireless Sensor Network (WSN) that can measure and transmit the associated electrical and environmental variables. These measurements can then be used by machine learning and optimization algorithms to automatically perform anomaly detection, or to control demand according with the forecasted generation. As some of these installations can be spread across large areas, the coverage of such a WSN is an important issue. There are a number of WSN technologies today, that can be used to accomplish such objective, some with quite a few years of existence and others more recent. Several applications of WSN are currently used in smarts grids. According to the intended specifications and focused in its scope, these technologies can be classified into 3 categories, namely: (1) short distances, with a range up to 250 meters, (2) medium distances, with ranges between 250 and 1000 meters and (3) long distances, for ranges above 1 km.

In the following we will describe each of these solutions, before comparing them and selecting the best solution for the AGERAR project.

Short Distance WSNs

In terms of short distances, solutions like Bluetooth (Bluetooth SIG, 2016), ANT (Dynastream, 2017), Zigbee (Zigbee Alliance, 2017), WirelessHART (Lennvall, Svensson, & Hekland, 2008; Phoenix Contact, 2015) and Enocean (EnOcean Alliance, 2016) can be used.

Bluetooth is a Body Area Network (BAN) or Personal Area Network (PAN) solution, on the market since the 1990s, and widely available. There are two variants, depending on the intended application, with the Basic Rate/Enhanced Data Rate (BR / EDR) for audio devices and Low Energy (BLE), adapted to devices with energy restrictions. It is currently in version 5, which was developed having in mind Internet of Things (IoT) applications, focusing even more on low energy consumption. This version introduces technical improvements in the protocols, when compared with the previous version 4, that allows data rates of up to 2 Mbps. The use of forward error detection and correction techniques (FEC) along with the reduction of transmission times support these data rates (Gilchrist, 2016; Ali, Shah, Farooq & Ghani, 2017). On July 13, 2017 the final specification of Bluetooth mesh 1.0 was published, a solution that will allow the implementation of the technology in an industrial environment with thousands of nodes, supporting the control and the monitoring. It only consists on the software definition of the mesh network, since BLE devices from version 4 onwards must support this operation (Bluetooth SIG, 2017; Ericsson, 2017).

ANT technology, similar to Bluetooth, was developed primarily for sports applications, although today the proprietary company (Dynastream) has created a version for IoT (Ant Blaze). The latter ensures reliable networks in environments that require easy installation and maintenance, thus allowing monitoring and control applications. ANT works in the 2.4 GHz ISM band, with 79 channels of 1MHz modulated in GFSK. It reaches 30 meters and allows connecting the various nodes (up to 500) in several topologies (Peer to Peer, star or mesh) with rates up to 60 kbps. It ensures broadcast, acknowledgment and works well with Wi-Fi and Bluetooth networks on the same frequencies. Data security is guaranteed with an AES-128 encryption (Dynastream, 2017).

ZigBee is a technology supported in the IEEE802.15.4 standard, which was designed for the transmission of small data packets over short distances, while consuming low energy levels. It defines a complete protocol stack, with the physical and medium access control layers coming from IEEE802.15.4, while the network and application layers are defined by the Zigbee Alliance. It is usually used in a mesh network, and a packet may pass through several devices until it reaches the gateway. It thus requires the use of routing algorithms (Gilchrist, 2016; Mahmood, Javaid, & Razzaq, 2015; Lennvall, Svensson, & Hekland, 2008; Koubaa, Alves, & Tovar, 2018). In Europe it can operate in the 2.4 GHz or 868 MHz ISM bands, using OQPSK or BPSK direct spectrum spread spectrum (DSSS) modulations. It allows 16 channels of 2 MHz and an emission power of up to 20 dBm. It applies Carrier Sense Multiple Access / Collision Avoidance (CSMA/CA) techniques to detect and minimize collisions and interferences in this widely used spectrum. It achieves ranges between nodes up to 150 meters in open environments and speeds of up to 250 kbps (2.4GHz) or 20 kbps (868 MHz) (Zigbee Alliance, 2014).

WirelessHART is a proprietary technology based on HART (an industrial automation protocol developed in the 1980s), which is designed primarily for industrial environments. The existing HART protocol was adapted to use the radio channel instead of a wired medium (Lennvall, Svensson, & Hekland, 2008; Phoenix Contact, 2015). Based on the physical layer defined by the IEEE 802.15.4 standard, it uses the 2.4 GHz ISM band. It defines a Time Division Multiple Access (TDMA) access scheme (which requires high temporal synchronization between nodes), as well as Frequency Hopping Spread Spectrum (FHSS), dividing the band into 15 channels of 2 MHz and modulating the signals in OQPSK. Each transmission takes place in a temporal window of 10 ms and the power can be adjusted according to the channel conditions up to a maximum of 10 dBm.

EnOcean is a closed technology that focuses in reducing consumption and capturing energy from the environment where it is applied. By using motion, light, heat, vibration and other converters, it can rule out the use of batteries to send data, as its sensors are self-powered. Its largest application is in residential home automation. The technology covers the first 3 layers of the OSI model (physical, data link and network), being standardized as ISO/IEC14543-3-10, thus ensuring interoperability between different manufacturers. The applications, and the form of interaction between these applications and the network layer, is defined by the EnOcean Alliance (2016). EnOcean uses the 868.3 MHz band, modulating the signals in Frequency Shift Keying (FSK) in a single channel. The data rate is 125 kbps, with a typical packet length of 14-byte, although the specification allows up to 255 bytes of data. The considered topologies are star, mesh and point to point, using self-powered sensors and gateways, powered externally (EnOcean, 2013, 2017, n.d.). It also allows the interconnection with other protocols used in home automation.

Medium Distance WSNs

For medium distances, the DASH7 (Weyn, Ergeerts, Berkvens, Wojciechowski, & Tabakov, 2015; Dash7 Alliance, 2017) Wi-Fi Halow (Jain & Taneeru, 2016; Baños-Gonzalez, Afaqui, Lopez-Aguilera & Garcia-Villegas, 2016) and White-Fi solutions can be considered.

DASH7 is an open protocol intended to support two-way communications using active RFID radio frequency technology in sub-GHz bands. It defines all end-to-end communications, based in a request response scheme, and uses an open source OSS-7 stack. One of the advantages is that it allows remote monitoring, (Gilchrist, 2016; Dash7 Alliance, 2017). It uses the 868 MHz ISM band on 25 or 200 kHz channels, modulated with 2GFSK. The normal ranges vary between 1 km and 5 km, with low latencies and data rates of 9, 6, 55.5 or 166.6 kbps (Dash7 Alliance, 2017; Tabakov, 2014; Weyn, Ergeerts, Berkvens, Wojciechowski, & Tabakov, 2015).

In terms of Wi-Fi, in order to adapt the traditional 802.11 networks, the IEEE proposed some changes in the physical and medium access layers to support higher coverages and lower power consumptions. It was designated as IEEE 802.11ah and was designed having in mind the typical IoT applications. One of the technical solutions used was to reduce the transmission frequency to 900 MHz. However, since it is not a free band worldwide, adaptations will be needed according to the region. It supports channels of 1, 2, 4, 8 or 16 MHz, modulated in BPSK, QPSK or n-QAM. However, due to the regional adaptation to ISM bands, Europe will only use 1 and 2 MHz channels. A range of up to 1 km in the line of sight is estimated.

Using various combinations of channels, encodings, modulations and streams, speeds between 150 kbps and 346.6 Mbps can be achieved, with packets that can contain up to 7991 bytes. As with traditional Wi-Fi, access points (AP) can be used to connect up to 8191 devices (Jain, & Taneeru, 2016; Baños-Gonzalez, Afaqui, Lopez-Aguilera, & Garcia-Villegas, 2016; Zemede, 2015; Domazetovic, Kocan, & Mihovska, 2016; Sun, Choi, & Choi, 2013).

Long Distance WSNs

Regarding long distances there are several solutions like LTE-M (Dawaliby, Bradai, and Pousset, 2016), Narrowband-IoT (GSMA 2017; Flore, 2016), EC-GSM-IOT (Olof Liberg, Sundberg, Eric Wang, Bergman, Sachs, 2018), RPMA (Ingenu, n.d.), Weightless (Webb, 2012), LoRa / LoRaWAN (Lora Alliance 2015; Augustin, Yi, Clausen and Townsley, 2016) and Sigfox (Sigfox, 2017a).

Starting from the 4G LTE cellular network, the Long Term Evolution-Machine (LTE-M) variant, also known as LTE CatM1 or simply LTE M1, was created by 3GPP, optimized for low-cost IoT devices requiring low throughputs and long coverages. The objective was to take advantage of the LTE structure in existing cellular networks, adding IoT functionality through software (Nokia, 2017; 3GPP, 2016). At the technical level the channel bandwidth was reduced to 1.4 MHz instead of the normal 20 MHz (depending on country and operator). The maximum transmission power was limited to 20 dBm and energy-saving procedures and discontinuous data reception (designated PSM and eDRX) were introduced, which do not exist in the LTE. The latter, aim to guarantee autonomy of up to 10 years using batteries. The throughput is 1 Mbps bidirectional. The topology is the same as the normal LTE cellular network, thus requiring a service provider (Gilchrist, 2016; Dawaliby, Bradai, & Pousset, 2016; GSMA, 2017). It allows roaming between cells, so it works on mobile devices. The latency is the same as LTE, in the order of milliseconds (Sequans, 2016).

NarrowBand-IoT technology, also known as LTE-NB, NB-IOT, or Cat-NB1 LTE, started from the need to further adapt the existing LTE M1 to an IoT usage, being specified by 3GPP in Release 13. The idea is to run parallel to the LTE network but in an integrated way, so that a software upgrade in the LTE network will suffice to allow its operation. The main point of development was the energy reduction, simplifying the structure of the modems and the operation of the network, allowing, this way, the minimization of the energy consumed, estimating autonomies higher than 10 years. At the same time this simplification support cheaper devices. It was also possible to ensure a good signal penetration, in order to allow the operation of the service in more inaccessible places, such as in basements (Ali, Shah, Farooq & Ghani, 2017; Nokia, 2017; 3GPP, 2016). It will operate on the same LTE bands (2100, 1800, 900 MHz depending on the operator) using a 200 kHz channel allocated on the guardband, or on a stand-alone carrier. It uses OFDMA as access schemes in the downlink and GMSK or SC-FDMA in the uplink. The maximum transmission power is 23 dBm.

NarrowBand-IoT achieves coverages up to 22 km, maximum data rates of 250 kbps downlink, 170 kbps in uplink and 200,000 subscribers per carrier. The modulations used are QPSK and BPSK. The topology is the same as a normal cellular network, requiring an associated service provider (Tabbane, 2016; GSMA, 2017; Flore, 2016; Rohde&Schwarze, 2016; Keysight, 2017). It does not allow roaming between cells, i.e. it will work well on fixed devices. In more adverse situations latency may be increased, to the order of the second (Sequans, 2016).

Although in Europe most operators use LTE, the GSM network is still active with many systems rely on it. Also, it is still prevalent in other regions of the world where LTE is not installed. Given this fact, it made sense to specify a GSM adaptation to IoT, in order to allow a globalization of the system. The cellular technology Extended Coverage GSM IoT (EC-GSM-IoT), also specified in Release 13 of 3GPP, aims to adapt existing GSM networks to an IoT context. The idea was to simplify the network and gain capacity and autonomy, without changing the existing infrastructures. Besides making the system compatible it allows parallel operation with the traditional GSM, after a software upgrade. This solution does not impose extra costs to the operators, thus allowing its easy adoption. It is expected, however, that GSM will gradually be switched off to free up spectrum for LTE.

At the technical level, new features were introduced, namely new coding schemes, new logical control and data channels, the possibility of keeping the terminals more time off (eDRX) and the possibility of sending data in a burst (Ali, Shah, Farooq & Ghani, 2017; Nokia, 2017; ABI Research, 2016). The frequency bands will be the GSM 900 MHz, using a 200 kHz channel. The data rates will be 70 or 240 kbps, depending on whether the modulation is GSMK or 8PSK. The maximum transmission power will be 23 dBm (Tabbane, 2016).

SigFox is a proprietary system developed by a French company with the same same, using a similar architecture and business model as the cellular network. Sigfox has created several partnerships with traditional telecom operators, implementing its base stations in the mobile infrastructure, thus trying to create a global network. It has an architecture that forces data to pass through its servers, where it is then made available to client applications. As such it requires a service subscription. The stack is proprietary and all of it is developed by the company, except for the case of the applications. The hardware is developed only by a set of partners (Gilchrist, 2016; Ali, Shah, Farooq & Ghani, 2017; Sanchez-Iborra & Cano, 2016; Agha, Pujolle & Yahiha, 2015).

SigFox supports long coverages and good penetrations using small data packets. It is mostly intended for uplink transmissions. It uses the 868 MHz band, with sub-channels of 192 kHz. In these, there are multiple 100 Hz channels called ultra narrowband (UNB), where the data is transmitted. The system applies a frequency hopping scheme to minimize collisions within the 192 kHz channel. They are modulated in the uplink using BPSK and in the downlink with GFSK. The maximum transmission power is 20 dBm (Quinnell, 2015; Sigfox, 2017; Disk91.com, 2015). The ranges can reach 50 km in open countryside or 10 km in urban environments. The throughput is quite low, only 100 bps, which means that the transmission time of a packet is in the order of seconds. This makes it possible to detect the signal at greater distances or in places of worse coverage. The size of the packets is only 12 bytes in uplink and 8 in downlink. European regulations limit the duty cycle, limiting the maximum number of messages per day to 140 in uplink and 4 in downlink. Decreasing the data size and simplifying the frame headers made the whole protocol light so as not to require large processing of the devices, thus contributing to autonomies of up to 20 years. Similarly the cost of the devices is relatively low, due to its technical simplicity. There is no limit for the number of nodes in the network, with a maximum in the order of millions (Centenaro, Vangelista, Zanella, & Zorzi, 2016; Morin, Maman, Guizzetti, & Duda, 2017; Hernandez, Peralta, Manero, Gomez, Bilbao, & Zubia, 2017; Krupka, Vojtech, & Neruda, 2016; Sigfox, 2017).

Weightless is an open cell type technology, developed for Machine-to-Machine (M2M) communications and managed by Weightless SIG. It has been developed to be low cost, reliable, with good coverage and autonomy, safe and to allow millions of connected devices. The respective protocol architecture defines the operation of the Physical, MAC and Network layers, and the applications are defined by the user.

There are 3 Weightless variants (Gilchrist, 2016; Ali, Shah, Farooq & Ghani, 2017; Sanchez-Iborra, & Cano, 2016; Quinnell, 2015; Disk91.com, 2015; Webb, 2012), namely Weightless-W, Weightless-N and Weightless-P.

Weightless-W, was initially developed by NEUL (Quinnell, 2015) to take advantage of the bandwidth resulting from the release of the analog TV and radio channels. It uses 5MHz channels modulated in QAM. This variant is flexible in terms of supported speeds, which can range from 1 kbps to 10 Mbps, as well as packet size, allowing data length from 10 bytes. It ensures a reliable delivery of packages with acknowledgment mechanisms. The estimated range in urban environment is 5 km.

Weightless-N, was used by the nWave company (Sanchez-Iborra, & Cano, 2016) and was only meant for unidirectional transmissions in the uplink. It uses very narrowband channels of 200 Hz, modulated in DBPSK, and small packets of up to 20 bytes with rates of 100 bps. It has an estimated range of 3 km and allows devices with maximum autonomies of 10 years.

Weightless-P, was developed by M2 Communications (Sanchez-Iborra, & Cano, 2016) supports reliable bidirectional transmissions, using acknowledgments. It uses 12.5 kHz channels, modulated in OQPSK, being flexible in the size of the allowed packets. The data rates vary between 200 bps and 100 kbps with an estimated coverage of 2 km in urban environments. This solution is currently the most adopted one. It allows the adaptation of power and data rates, synchronous medium access mechanisms based on temporal or frequency (TDMA, FDMA) or asynchronous (ALOHA), inter-cell roaming, bidirectionality and is low cost.

All the variants of Weightless implement Advanced Encryption Standard (AES128) encryption on data, network authentication, and frequency hopping spread spectrum (FHSS) techniques to minimize interference. The architecture consists of a base station, a network manager that controls the network, and a database with user information or available frequencies.

RPMA is a proprietary technology developed by Ingenu (formerly On-Ramp) for M2M applications, proposed as a complete bi-directional alternative, without the restrictions of LoRa or Sigfox technologies. The entire stack was developed by the company in order to guarantee the desired specifications. Similarly to Sigfox, it follows a business model based on selling RPMA chips and charging its end users for the use of the network infrastructure, setup on a global scale. (Gilchrist, 2016; Quinnell, 2015; Centenaro, Vangelista, Zanella, & Zorzi, 2016). The 2.4 GHz band is open worldwide and is therefore widely used. Wi-Fi or Bluetooth, occupy this area of the spectrum causing enough interference. However, the regulations make it possible to use a band of 80 MHz and 27 dBm of transmission power. These values are much higher than those allowed for 868 MHz and do not impose duty cycle limitations. At the same time, when compared with other solutions in lower ISM bands, the 2.4 GHz band suffers from higher propagation losses as it is more difficult to penetrate into buildings. Ingenu applied spatial diversity to compensate for propagation losses, while maximizing transmission power. This way it is able of reaching 10 km in urban environments, resulting from a high link budget. In line of sight (LoS), the company claims reaching distances of 200 km. It uses channels of 1MHz (there are 40) with direct spectrum spread spectrum modulated in FSK. The medium access is done within time slots, where each sender sends its data encoded in a specific code. This way, the receiver can simultaneously distinguish between up to 1200 different signals on the same channel. The estimated capacity of each access point is 380,000 nodes. The maximum data rates are 624 kbps in the uplink and 156 kbps in the downlink, using packets between 6 and 10 kBytes. It supports network authentication, uses 256-bit encryption and allows roaming (Margelis, Piechocki, Kaleshi, & Thomas, 2015; Ingenu, n.d., 2016).

LoRa is a physical layer radio technology owned by Semtech, which manufactures chips and licenses the technology to other manufacturers. This technology delivers low-cost, high-power, high-range devices running on ISM bands. Supported in the physical layer, LoRa Alliance created an open access layer, LoRaWAN. The latter specifies a star-of-stars architecture composed of the following components (Gilchrist, 2016; Ali, Shah, Farooq & Ghani, 2017; Sanchez-Iborra, & Cano, 2016): (1) end nodes, (2) gateways; (3) network servers; and (4) client applications. One of the biggest advantages of this technology is that it is possible to implement a long-range private network by simply purchasing the equipment. It does not require external operators like Sigfox, RPMA or traditional cellular services. However, there are also operators that implement LoRa networks, either private (e.g. Orange) or public (e.g. TTN). In these, anyone can use their nodes and connect them to the gateway of the operator. The operation of the physical layer also guarantees good coverages and penetration, being robust against noise, Doppler and multipath effects (Lora Alliance, 2015; Agha, Pujolle, & Yahiha, 2015; Augustin, Clausen, & Townsley, 2016; Microchip, 2015; Filho, Filho, & Moreli, 2016).

Requirements and Comparative Analysis Between WSNs

One important requirement of the AGERAR project was to select a solution that could constitute a private network, i.e. not relying in public infrastructures or other parties. In order to select the type of WSN that better fits in the requirements of a medium size Micro Grid, we started by characterizing each of these solutions, including the evaluation of their strengths and weaknesses, when facing the requirements imposed by the project.

In particular, each and all of the above mentioned WSN solutions was analyzed according to: (1) theoretical range in both line of sight and in urban environments; (2) maximum bit rates in uplink, downlink and two-way communications; (3) network topology; (4) maximum payload size allowed; (5) number of devices allowed on the network; (6) expected power consumption and battery implications; (7) frequency bands and channels used; (8) other characteristics of the technology that may impact in its performance; and finally (9) availability in the market, cost of acquisition and operation.

In terms of features (1) to (4), table 1 summarizes the data obtained from the analysis of these technologies. In some cases, the urban ranges of some networks were not available (n.a.).

Resulting from the above-mentioned analysis, the LoRaWAN technology was selected to develop the WSN for Micro Grids. The main reasons for choosing this technology result from the fact that it supports coverages up to several kilometers, and the implementation of a private and scalable network using relatively inexpensive components. Additionally, the LoRaWAN technology already considers several mechanisms for data protection that are a fundamental feature in micro grids. The weaker point of this technology is associated with the duty cycle impositions (Lora Alliance, 2015), a legal constraint to avoid saturating the spectrum of the ISM band used (868 MHz). This limits the total time of transmission of a device to only 36 seconds per hour, in each of the channels used. The downlink transmission of data (i.e. from the gateways to the end device) also has some restrictions, which can translate into high latencies or unreliability. Although not a critical factor in our specifications, the low consumption of these solutions in which the batteries can last up to 10 years is a strong advantage to consider.

Finally, since the LoRaWAN technology does not allow high data rates, Wi-Fi was considered as an alternative to be used when real-time measurements are required. Thus the two technologies can coexist in the final architecture.

LoRa and LoRaWAN

In order to understand the various mechanisms and operation of LoRaWAN, in the following we proceed to describe in more detail the LoRa physical layer and the LoRaWAN medium access control layer.

Physical Layer

At the physical level, the LoRa model is based on a spread spectrum technique where the frequency of the signal is linearly changed over the duration of the signal, called chirp. This signal is transmitted in the channel using a bandwidth that is much higher than the one that would be required, for the associated data rate. In fact, given its low rate of transmission, the required bandwidth could be much lower. The advantage that results from this spread spectrum solution, is that it enables the decoding of the transmitted signal, even when the received signal strength is well below the noise level. In practice this enables higher coverages.

There are several spreading levels, which translates the number of bits in each chirp symbol. They are identified in LoRa by the Spreading Factor (SF). The chirp is cyclic, starting at a minimum frequency and rising linearly up to a maximum frequency, where it jumps back to the minimum frequency. The data to be sent, sets the place where this jump takes place. Figure 2 (upper image) represents a base chirp (in blue) comparing it to a chirp that translates the decimal value "10" (in red).

Table 1. Summary of the main features of the wireless sensor networks evaluated capable of being used to monitor a micro grid

	Frequency Band	Range		Data Rate		Network Topology	Maximum Payload Size	
		Urban	Rural or LOS	UpLink	DownLink		Down Link	Up Link
Short Range Networks								
Bluetooth 5	2.4 GHz	40 m	200 m	2 Mbps		Point-to-point, Mesh	From 31 to 255 bytes	
Bluetooth 4	2.4 GHz	10 m	50 m	1 Mbps		Point-to-point, Mesh	From 17 to 20 bytes	
ANT	2.4 GHz	n.a.	30 m	60 kbps		Point-to-point, Star, Mesh	n.a.	
Zigbee	2.4 GHz, 868 MHz	30 m	250 m	250 kbps, or 20 kbps @ 868 MHz		Mesh	From 73 to 100 bytes	
WirelessHART	2.4 GHz	n.a.	250 m	250 kbps		Mesh, Star or Star-Mesh	127 bytes	
EnOcean	868 MHz	30 m	300 m	125 kbps		Point-to-point, Mesh, Star	14 bytes	
Medium Range								
WiFi Halow	900 MHz (868 MHz)	n.a.	1 km	Between 150 kbps and 346.6 Mbps		Star or Tree	7991 bytes (optionally can reach 65535 bytes)	
DASH7	868 MHz ISM	n.a.	5 km	9.6 kbps, 55.5 kbps and 166.6 kbps		Star, Tree, Point-to-point	256 bytes	
Long Range								
NB-IoT	LTE	n.a.	22 km	250 kbps	170 kbps	Star	1000 bits (per TBS)	680 bits (per TBS)
LTE M	LTE	n.a.	22 km	1 Mbps		Star	From 100 to 1000 bytes	
EC-GSM-iot	GSM	n.a.	n.a.	From 70 to 240 kbps		Star	n.a.	n.a.
Weightless N	Sub GHz ISM	n.a.	3 km	100 bps	Non existent	Estrela	20 bytes	
Weightless P	Sub GHz ISM	n.a.	2 km	From 200bps to 100kbps		Star	≥ 10 bytes	
Weightless W	400-800 MHz (TV band)	n.a.	5 km	From 1kbps to 10Mbps		Star	≥ 10 bytes	
Sigfox	868 MHz ISM	n.a.	50 km	100 bps (maximum of 140|4 messages in DL|UL per day)		Star	12 bytes	
RPMA	2.4 GHz	n.a.	200 km	624 kbps	156 kbps	Star or Tree	From 6 to 10 kbytes	
LoRaWAN	868 MHz ISM	n.a.	30 km	300 bps a 50 kbps		Star or Tree	From 8 to 250 bytes	

Figure 2. LoRa physical layer, comprising: (upper image) two different chirps illustrate the encoding of the signals at the jump point between the maximum and minimum frequency (bottom image) impact of various LoRa parameters in the range, bit rate, receiver sensitivity and time on air
(adapted from (LoRa Alliance, 2017))

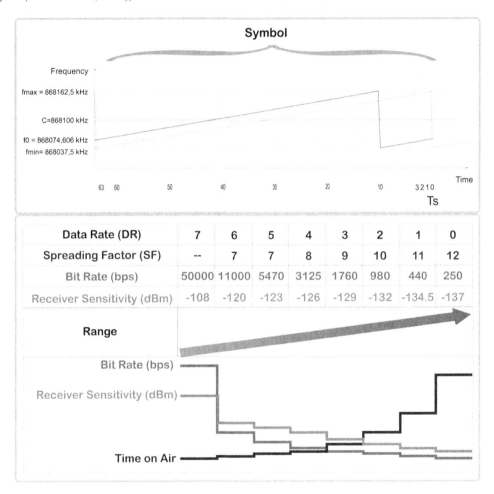

The allowed spreading factor values vary between 6 and 12. The larger the spreading factor, the larger is the range, but the smaller will be the data rate achieved. At the same time the higher the SF, the longer a transmission takes, with data rates varying between 292 to 50,000 bits per second.

Two other important factors in this modulation are the LoRa Signal-to-Noise Ratio (LSNR) and the sensitivity of the receiver, which translates the ability to decode a signal with a certain power. These are by default low, respectively -20 dB for the LSNR and -137 dBm for a receiver sensitivity. These capabilities make LoRa a viable solution in environments with noise and long transmission distances. Figure 2, bottom image, presents the relationship between all these LoRa factors.

Since modulations use the 868 MHz bands (which is unlicensed in Europe) LoRa has to meet certain legal constraints of spectral occupation; it defines that the maximum transmission power must be 14 dBm (25mW) and that a channel can only be used during 1% of the time (the so-called duty cycle of 1%). Thus during one hour, one terminal can only transmit in one channel during a total of 36 seconds. This restriction, is a strong setback when using LoRa for applications that require sending data in real time, since this would require much more than the allowed 36 seconds. However, regular transmissions that only require a periodicity between transmissions, of minutes, hours, or even days, with the correct SFs, are the best applications of LoRa. In any situation, it is always necessary to ensure compliance with the standards, keeping in mind that a transmission with different SFs, has different durations.

LoRaWAN Medium Access Control

In order to guarantee fair access to the medium between LoRa devices, both, a network architecture and a series of network management mechanisms were defined. The architecture (Lora Alliance, 2015) is a star-topology, and is composed of nodes, gateways, network servers and application servers. Specifically:

- Single-hop nodes represent the sensor nodes, which send/receive data asynchronously to/from one or more Gateways, using the LoRa RF.
- Gateways are responsible for receiving LoRaWAN data and forwarding it to a Network Server through a backhaul network. This is usually an IP network and packets are conveyed using UDP/IP packets.
- Network Servers are responsible for managing the entire network, communicating with nodes and gateways. They also forward the received data to the destination applications using TCP/IP SSL connections.
- Applications, use and process data received from the network server with which the user normally interacts.

The LoRaWAN specification defines several classes of nodes in terms of transmission and reception, with implications in their energy consumption. These are:

- Class A end devices, send data to the network when they need or periodically, in an asynchronous way. They do not listen to the medium before sending. They also do not know if there is a collision during the transmission. After each transmission, they open two temporal windows where they listen to the medium to receive data. Besides these two periods of time, they never listen, or receive data. This simple mechanism allows the device to consume very low amounts of energy, since it only needs to be awake when transmitting. However, this behavior results in a very high latency for downlink transmissions, since they can only happen after an uplink transmission.
- Class B end devices can receive data at certain moments, which are scheduled by the gateways. This allows the reception of data without having to transmit. However it requires a high synchronization between devices. The resulting consumption level is medium, as is latency.
- Class C end devices are always listening, except when sending data. They guarantee the lowest latency for data reception, with a possible application in actuators nodes. However they are the ones that consume more energy, and thus are not suitable for battery powered devices.

One of the most important mechanisms of this standard is adaptive data rate (ADR), which guarantees the adaptation of the rates and transmission power automatically, according with the quality of the data received. The data rates result from the LoRa SF values being used. Six variations exist, all using 125 kHz channels. In Europe they range between SF 7 and 12, with a bandwidth of 125 kHz, allowing bit rates between 5470 and 250 bits per second.

For a node to be able to connect to a network, some security keys must be configured, that allow the network server to assess whether a certain node is allowed to enter the network. In the initial phase there is an information exchange process, which associates the node with the network. This is called activation. Activation can occur by two methods: Activation by Personalization (ABP) or Over the Air Activation (OTAA). In the first one, there are 3 security keys that are statically configured on the network server and nodes. These allow encryption and decryption of user data or network commands. In the second method, the security keys are generated automatically at the time of the initial activation request and are then stored by the terminal devices for subsequent encryption operations. The existence of separate keys allows the encryption of different parts of the frame with different keys, thus isolating user data from the MAC network management commands. In addition to these encryptions, integrity check messages are always generated, which ensure that the data has not changed in the path, or was affected by errors.

Network management is done transparently to users, by the exchange of information between nodes and the network server, using MAC commands. These commands support all the network operations, including the activation, ADR and power changes, channel frequency changes, confirmation of message delivery (optional), adjustment of necessary timings, among others.

IoE BASED CONTROL AND MONITORING OF ELECTRICAL GRIDS

In this section we present the developed system for the monitoring and control of a Micro Grid. Figure 3 summarizes all the elements that are expected to collaborate in such a system.

Given the background knowledge of the technology, in order to build such architecture we started by selecting the electronic modules that can be found in the market, comparing their basic characteristics. Since the LoRaWAN architecture requires the utilization of various hardware elements, namely the gateway and the nodes, a selection was made in accordance to the requirements imposed by the project's objectives.

Figure 3. General architecture of the elements that support the monitoring and control of a Smart Grid

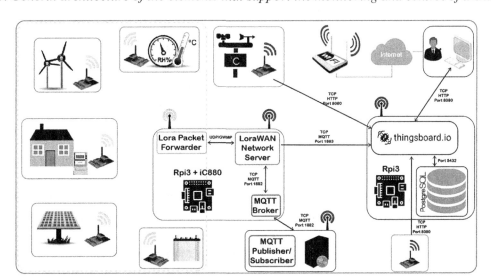

In terms of the WSN nodes, the selection fell on the Pycom LoPy (The Things Network, n.d.) micro-controller module which integrates LoRaWAN, WiFi and Bluetooth transceivers. The integration of the three technologies gives some versatility in the implementation of the network, in terms of communication options. At the same time, the 8 analog inputs and 2 outputs, the 24 General Purpose Input/Output (GPIOs), the Serial Peripheral Interface (SPI) and Inter-Integrated Circuit (I2C) communication ports, the LoRaWAN certification, the MicroPython programming facility and the reduced cost were important features that led to the selection of this platform. This solution also allows the use of an expansion card for USB programming, together with a Global Positioning System (GPS) expansion card (Pytrack), as shown in figure 4 (top, left image). Despite this choice, the system remains open to other modules.

Regarding the gateway, we decided to build it based on Raspberry Pi (RPI) and the IMST ic880-SPI concentrator. This setup guarantees the simultaneous decoding of 8 LoRaWAN channels, as well as the flexibility in the configuration and programming of the gateway. We can also run the LoRaWAN network server, central for the operation of this technology, in the same equipment, thus being simultaneously a gateway and a network server.

Development of the Gateway and of the Network Server

In the initial phase we started by assembling the proposed network, through the initial construction and configuration of the LoRaWAN gateway, in the Raspberry Pi version 3 (RPI3) device, followed by the installation of the LoRaWAN network server (also in the RPI3). A connecting shield was initially built to connect the two, using a perforated PCB plate, as shown in figure 4 (top, right image). This allowed the execution of the first tests. The gateway was then placed in a plastic enclosure to assure a better protection.

In the RPI3 a Raspbian operating system was installed, followed by the basic configuration and removal of unnecessary programs. Next, the Semtech reference packet routing software, manufacturer of the LoRa chips, was installed and tested. This allows for proper communication with the concentrator, using the SPI protocol. It also allows the configuration of the radio channel parameters, such as the frequencies of the channels. The inclusion of test programs, in the packet forwarder software, ensures that the module can be accessed via SPI and that data can be sent.

In the following step the LoRaWAN network services were installed in the RPI3. Then, the network configurations, together with the configurations supporting the nodes associated with the server were made. This server will also decrypt the data received and forward it to the associated applications. At this stage, the Message Queuing Telemetry Transport (MQTT) protocol was used for the data communications, in order to verify that data were routed correctly. An MQTT broker was installed on this RPI, and a client was used in another computer, allowing the reception of the data from the LoRaWAN server. This way, the data sent by the nodes can be viewed in the MQTT client.

Implementation of the LoRaWAN Sensor Nodes

After some initial tests that allowed the verification of the LoPy functionalities (in terms of inputs, outputs and I2C communications) the first implementation focused in the communications between the LoPy module and MODBUS devices, using the TCP and RS-485 interfaces. This is an important feature, required for the communication with many types of industrial devices. In fact, in the particular field of Smart Grids, it allows getting data from many types of energy meters, or also from PLC (Programmable Logic Controller) devices.

Figure 4, on the bottom images, shows the results of the communication with an energy meter through the MODBUS/RS-485 interface. The obtained data was then sent through the LoRaWAN network and displayed locally. Figure 4 (bottom, right image) illustrates the data obtained from the meter, as shown in an OLED display, connected to the LoPy module through an I2C interface.

Besides measuring consumption, the MODBUS over TCP functionality was used to obtain data from a PLC. The data comprised the level of generation and consumption of a photovoltaic array. This data was later integrated in the Thingsboard platform.

In the following step, the LoRaWAN communication was tested, adjusting the basic parameters involved, namely: SFs, frequencies, data frames and network activation of nodes. In this phase, the basic configurations were tested in both network server and nodes, using only one channel. During this process, each tested configuration was evaluated in terms of packet losses and coverage. After this step, with the assurance of functional modules, we proceeded to test the ADR mechanism, considering: 8 channels, uplink and downlink transmissions and different types of nodes (A and C).

Figure 4. The top left image shows the LoPy microcontroller with antenna (left), expansion board (center) and Lopy with Pytrack GPS expansion board (right). The top right image shows the perforated PCB plate connecting the LoRaWAN gateway with the Raspberry Pi. The bottom image presents the reading and display of data from an energy meter through an MODBUS/RS485 interface. The top right image presents the first version of the LoRaWAN gateway.

Setup of an Application Server

In order to simplify the analysis of the data, a Thingsboard platform was installed to work as application server. This platform allows the graphical visualization of the measurements, but also the quality of the signals received by the LoRaWAN network.

The application server was built on a separate RPI, in order to work independently from the network server. A PostgreSQL database was installed over a Raspbian operating system, to store all the data received. After the installation and configuration of the server, users were added, so they can access the system and the associated dashboards.

Figure 5. Site survey of the developed system, carried out at the INTA premises (top image) and developed charging station (bottom images)

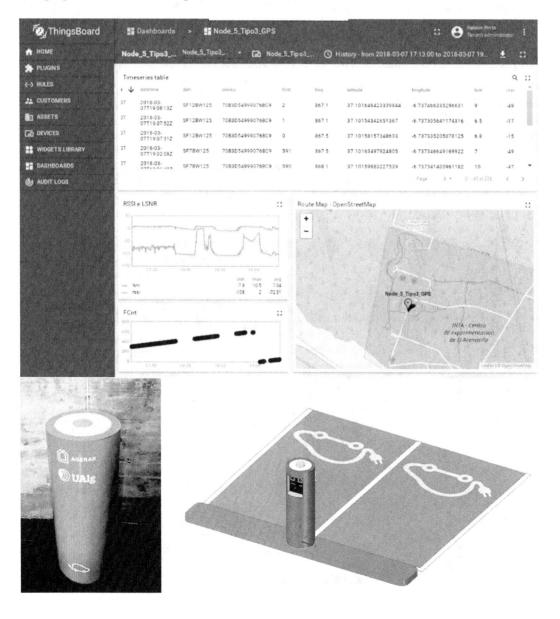

On this platform, each node has a unique identifier (called a token) which is configured on the device page. The network server, or any other device that wants to send data to Thingsboard, must also have the same token configured so that, when sending data, it is included in the message and thus recognized and associated with the respective node. Without this token, the data is not considered by the platform.

The system was tested at the premises of INTA, as shown in Figure 5 (upper image).

Communication and Storage of Meteorological Data

As shown in Figure 3, the system should be able to obtain and log data from a meteorological station. In a Smart Girds context, meteorological data is important for the scheduling of electric charges, including electric vehicles, and to predict consumption levels. In fact meteorological data gives us the knowledge about current and yet to come generation levels, but also can help predict the consumption levels, as it depends on the air temperature, solar radiation and humidity. It is thus critical in a Smart Grid to measure and store meteorological data.

We thus proceeded to incorporate in the system a weather station that is currently connected to a DataTaker datalogger (model DT85). The data logger is powered by a battery, and is connected to an Ethernet network. Its data can be accessed via a web page.

In order to extract the data from the data logger's web page, a Python script was created that, running in an existing Linux server, periodically retrieves and parses the content of the web page. It then sends and stores the temperature, humidity, radiation, wind speed and direction, rainfall, atmospheric pressure and battery voltage data, to an emoncms (n.d.) platform running on a local server, and at the same time stores it in an sqlite database, on the same machine.

Additionally, in order to continuously check the proper operation of the station, the Linux server has been programmed to send alerts to some email addresses, in particular: whenever the connection to the device fails; when it reads invalid values; or when the battery level drops beneath a certain level (8 V). After performing the tests and correcting the errors in the code, the obtained data was also made available to the local Thingsboard platform.

Development of an Electric Vehicles Charging Station

In addition to monitoring, an Electric Vehicle Supply Equipment (EVSE), or charging station was developed for AC charging (see Figure 5, bottom images). The station includes several electrical components (circuit breakers, contactors, EVSE charge controllers) to handle the high currents involved in the charging process.

Given the project's goal for demand control, the charging station must endure real time adjustment of electric current as requested by the electric vehicle (EV). This adjustment is made by the charge controller, which communicates with the vehicle, to inform it about the current that can be drawn from the electrical grid.

To develop this system, a charging process in mode 3 was selected (connection of the EV to mains supply at 250 V AC voltage or 400 V 3-phase at a maximum current of 32 A). An electronic circuit was implemented that communicates with the charge controller at the EVSE.

As the current is selected, the EVSE charge controller module informs the vehicle of the available current, using a control line between the two (called the Control Pilot and included in the charging cable). This communication mechanism is based on a Pulse Width Modulation (PWM) modulation, where the current that the vehicle can request is determined by the duty cycle of the square wave.

After several tests and simulations, a test was carried out with a real electric vehicle (Nissan Leaf at INTA), in order to confirm the correct operation of the system.

In the future, this control will be implemented in a LoPy module that besides the current adjustment will read the electrical parameters of a current meter, in order to send them to a remote server.

The architecture will constitute a smart charging system, that will schedules EV's charging, taking into consideration: (1) the driver's needs, (2) the energy that is being produced plus the energy that is expected to be produced by renewable energy sources, (3) the present/future tariff rates and (4) the limitations from the electrical grid.

CONCLUSION

In this chapter we describe the implementation of a monitoring and control system for electrical Micro Grids.

After analyzing several WSN solutions, a LoRaWAN solution was selected, trying to meet the requirements imposed by the AGERAR project. The LoRAWAN solution supports long range coverages, with the drawback of restricting the duty cycle (or time on air) of each device.

In accordance with this architecture the system comprises: (1) a set of wireless sensor nodes that measure electrical variables or retrieve data from MODBUS devices; (2) a gateway that relays data sent from nodes to a network server; (3) a network server that is responsible for managing the entire network, communicating with both nodes and gateways and forwarding data to (4) an application server that uses the ThingsBoard platform.

Field tests have shown that the implemented system is able to cover a radius of nearly one kilometer.

FUTURE RESEARCH DIRECTIONS

The next steps of the project comprise the full implementation of the DC current and voltage sensing modules, which will be installed in the experimental micro-grid. In addition, some sensor nodes will be placed in a pilot installation to be deployed at the University of Algarve.

The intelligence of the system will result from the integration of both machine learning and optimization algorithms. Machine learning algorithms will be used to predict the yet to come consumption levels. These results will be used by the optimization algorithms, that will employ a predictive based control of loads.

ACKNOWLEDGMENT

This work was supported by project AGERAR (0076_AGERAR_6_E) financed by the European Union, under the scope of the FEDER program and INTERREG initiative, and by the by the Portuguese Foundation for Science and Technology (FCT), project LARSyS (UID/EEA/50009/2013).

REFERENCES

ABI Research. (2016). *Best fit use Cases for LPWANs*. Whitepaper. Retrieved from https://www.ingenu. com/portfolio/best-fit-use-cases-for-lpwans/

AGERAR Project. (2018). *Armazenamento e gestão de Energia renovável em aplicações comerciais e residenciais*. Retrieved from http://institucional.us.es/agerar/pt

Agha, K., Pujolle, G., & Yahiha, T. (2015). *Mobile and Wireless Networks*. Somerset: Wiley.

Aiminho.pt. (2018). *Guia de Orientação para a utilização das Energias Renováveis*. Retrieved from http://www.aiminho.pt/imgAll/file/Sustentar/Guia_de_Orientacao_para_a_utilizacao_das_Energias_ Renovaveis.pdf in 6 Jun. 2018.

Ali, A., Shah, G. A., Farooq, M. O., & Ghani, U. (2017). Technologies and challenges in developing Machine-to-Machine applications: A survey. *Journal of Network and Computer Applications*, *83*, 124–139. doi:10.1016/j.jnca.2017.02.002

Associação Portuguesa de Energias Renováveis. (2017). Retrieved from http://www.apren.pt/pt/dadostecnicos/index.php?id=1147&cat=266

Augustin, A., Yi, J., Clausen, T., & Townsley, W. (2016). A Study of LoRa: Long Range & Low Power Networks for the Internet of Things. *Sensors (Basel)*, *16*(9), 1466. doi:10.339016091466 PMID:27618064

Baños-Gonzalez, V., Afaqui, M., Lopez-Aguilera, E., & Garcia-Villegas, E. (2016). IEEE 802.11ah: A Technology to Face the IoT Challenge. *Sensors (Basel)*, *16*(11), 1960. doi:10.339016111960 PMID:27879688

Bluetooth SIG. (2016). *Master Table of Contents & Compliance Requirements: Bluetooth core specification V5.0*. Author.

Bluetooth SIG. (2017). *Bluetooth technology*. Retrieved from https://www.bluetooth.com/bluetoothtechnology

Borlase, S. (2017). *Smart Grids: Advanced Technologies and Solutions* (2nd ed.). Taylor & Francis Group. doi:10.1201/9781351228480

Centenaro, M., Vangelista, L., Zanella, A., & Zorzi, M. (2016). Long-range communications in unlicensed bands: The rising stars in the IoT and smart city scenarios. *IEEE Wireless Communications*, *23*(5), 60–67. doi:10.1109/MWC.2016.7721743

Costa, P. A. S. (2004). *Atlas do potencial eólico para Portugal continental.* Lisbon: Faculdade de Ciências da Universidade de Lisboa.

Dash7 Alliance. (2017). *DASH7 Alliance Protocol Specification v1.1.* Retrieved from http://www.dash7-alliance.org/product/d7ap1-1/

Dawaliby, S., Bradai, A., & Pousset, Y. (2016). In depth performance evaluation of LTE-M for M2M communications. In *2016 IEEE 12th International Conference on Wireless and Mobile Computing, Networking and Communications (WiMob).* IEEE.

Disk91.com. (2015). *One day at Sigfox.* Retrieved from https://www.disk91.com/2015/news/technologies/one-day-at-sigfox/

Domazetovic, B., Kocan, E., & Mihovska, A. (2016). Performance evaluation of IEEE 802.11ah systems. In *2016 24th Telecommunications Forum (TELFOR).* IEEE.

Dynastream. (2017). *Ant Blaze Product Brief.* Retrieved from https://www.dynastream.com/assets/D52/Dynastream.ANT_BLAZE.Product.Brief.pdf

Emoncms. (n.d.). *Emoncms platform.* Retrieved from emoncms.org

EnOcean. (2013). *EnOcean Radio Protocol 1.* Retrieved from https://www.enocean.com/fileadmin/redaktion/pdf/tec_docs/EnOceanRadioProtocol1.pdf, in 13/06/2018.

EnOcean. (2017). *EnOcean Radio Protocol 2.* Retrieved from https://www.enocean.com/fileadmin/redaktion/pdf/tec_docs/EnOcean_Radio_Protocol_2.pdf, in 13/06/2018.

EnOcean. (n.d.). *868 MHz EnOCean for Europe.* Retrieved from https://www.enocean.com/en/enocean_modules/

EnOcean Alliance. (2016). *Introducing the EnOcean Eco-System.* Retrieved from https://www.enocean-alliance.org/wp-content/uploads/2016/11/Whitepaper_Introducing_the_EnOcean_Ecosystem.pdf

Ericsson. (2017). *Bluetooth mesh networking.* Whitepaper. Retrieved from https://www.ericsson.com/en/publications/white-papers/bluetooth-mesh-networking

Filho, H. G. S., Filho, J. P., & Moreli, V. L. (2016). The adequacy of LoRaWAN on smart grids: A comparison with RF mesh technology. In *2016 IEEE International Smart Cities Conference* (ISC2). IEEE. 10.1109/ISC2.2016.7580783

Flore, D. (2016). *3GPP Standards for the Internet-of-Things.* 3GPP. Retrieved from http://www.3gpp.org/images/presentations/3GPP_Standards_for_IoT.pdf

Gilchrist, A. (2016). *Industry 4.0: the industrial internet of things.* Apress. doi:10.1007/978-1-4842-2047-4

3. GPP. (2016). *Low Power Wide Area Technologies.* Whitepaper. Retrieved from https://www.gsma.com/iot/3gpp-low-power-wide-area-technologies-white-paper/

GSMA. (2017a). *LTE_M Deployment Guide, 2017.* Retrieved from https://www.gsma.com/iot/wp-content/uploads/2017/09/LTE-M-Deployment-Guide-CLP.29-v1.0.pdf

GSMA. (2017b). *NB-IoT Deployment Guide*. Retrieved from https://www.gsma.com/iot/wp-content/uploads/2017/08/CLP.28-v1.0.pdf

Hernandez, D. M., Peralta, G., Manero, L., Gomez, R., Bilbao, J., & Zubia, C. (2017). Energy and coverage study of LPWAN schemes for Industry 4.0. In *2017 IEEE International Workshop of Electronics, Control, Measurement, Signals and their Application to Mechatronics* (ECMSM). IEEE. 10.1109/ecmsm.2017.7945893

Ingenu. (2016). *Ingenu webinar: How RPMA works*. Retrieved from https://www.youtube.com/watch?v=4beoZapuBXw

Ingenu. (n.d.). *How RPMA works: an educational guide*. Whitepaper. Retrieved from https://www.ingenu.com/portfolio/how-rpma-works-white-paper/

Instituto Nacional de Técnica Aeroespacial. (2018). *INTA Web site*. Retrieved from http://www.inta.es

Jain, P. C., & Taneeru, S. (2016). Performance Evaluation of IEEE 802.11ah Protocol in Wireless Area Network. In *2016 International Conference on Micro-Electronics and Telecommunication Engineering (ICMETE)*. IEEE. 10.1109/ICMETE.2016.23

Keysight. (2017). *NB-Iot Technical Fundamentals*. Whitepaper. Retrieved from http://www.keysight.com/upload/cmc_upload/All/20170612-A4-JianHuaWu-updated.pdf

Koubaa, A., Alves, M. & Tovar, E. (2018). *IEEE 802.15.4: a Federating Communication Protocol for Time-Sensitive Wireless Sensor Networks*. IEEE.

Krupka, L., Vojtech, L., & Neruda, M. (2016). The issue of LPWAN technology coexistence in IoT environment. *17th International Conference on Mechatronics-Mechatronika*, 1–8.

La Scala, M., Bruno, S., Nucci, C. A., Lamonaca, S., & Stecchi, U. (2017). *From Smart Grids to Smart Cities: New Challenges in Optimizing Energy Grids*. John Wiley & Sons.

Lennvall, T., Svensson, S., & Hekland, F. (2008). A comparison of WirelessHART and ZigBee for industrial applications. In *2008 IEEE International Workshop on Factory Communication Systems*. IEEE. 10.1109/WFCS.2008.4638746

LoRa Alliance. (2015). *A technical overview of LoRa and LoRaWAN*. White paper. Author.

LoRa Alliance. (2017). *LoRaWAN 101 A technical introduction*. Retrieved from https://eleven-x.com/wp-content/uploads/2018/04/LoRaWAN-101-A-Technical-Introduction.pdf

Mahmood, A., Javaid, N., & Razzaq, S. (2015). A review of wireless communications for smart grid. *Renewable & Sustainable Energy Reviews*, *41*, 248–260. doi:10.1016/j.rser.2014.08.036

Margelis, G., Piechocki, R., Kaleshi, D., & Thomas, P. (2015). Low Throughput Networks for the IoT: Lessons learned from industrial implementations. In *2015 IEEE 2nd World Forum on Internet of Things (WF-IoT)*. IEEE.

Microchip. (2015). *LoRaWAN 101 Class*. Presentation. Retrieved from http://www.spincraft.com/hackers/wp-content/uploads/2017/01/LoRaWAN-101-Class-v2-MARCOM-1.pdf

Modbus, I. D. A. (2006). *Modbus Application Protocol Specification, V1.1b, December 28.* Retrieved from http://www.modbus.org/docs/Modbus_Application_Protocol_V1_1b.pdf

Morin, E., Maman, M., Guizzetti, R., & Duda, A. (2017). Comparison of the Device Lifetime in Wireless Networks for the Internet of Things. *IEEE Access: Practical Innovations, Open Solutions, 5,* 7097–7114. doi:10.1109/ACCESS.2017.2688279

Nokia. (2017). *LTE Evolution for IoT connectivity.* Retrieved from https://resources.ext.nokia.com/asset/200178

Olof Liberg, O., Sundberg, M., Eric Wang, Y.-P., Bergman, J., & Sachs, J. (2018). EC-GSM-IoT. In Cellular Internet of Things. Academic Press.

Phoenix Contact. (2015). *Getting the Most Out of Your WirelessHART® System.* Whitepaper. Retrieved from https://www.phoenixcontact.com/assets/downloads_ed/global/web_dwl_promotion/EN_Whitepaper_IE_WirelessHART_LoRes.pdf

Quinnell, R. (2015). *Low power wide-area networking alternatives for the IoT.* Retrieved from https://www.edn.com/design/systems-design/4440343/Low-power-wide-area-networking-alternatives-for-the-IoT

REN. (2018). *Produção renovável suficiente para abastecer o consumo de eletricidade em Portugal durante 63 horas.* Retrieved from https://www.ren.pt/pt-PT/media/comunicados/detalhe/producao_renovavel_suficiente_para_abastecer_o_consumo_de_eletricidade_em_portugal_durante_63_horas_2/

Risteska Stojkoska, B., & Trivodaliev, K. (2017). A review of Internet of Things for smart home: Challenges and solutions. *Journal of Cleaner Production, 140,* 1454–1464. doi:10.1016/j.jclepro.2016.10.006

Rohde&Schwarze. (2016). *Narrowband Internet of Things.* Whitepaper. Retrieved from https://www.rohde-schwarz.com/pt/applications/narrowband-internet-of-things-white-paper_230854-314242.html

Saleem, Y., Crespi, N., Rehmani, M. H., & Copeland, R. (2017). *Internet of things-aided smart grid: Technologies, architectures, applications, prototypes, and future research directions.* ArXiv.

Sanchez-Iborra, R., & Cano, M.-D. (2016). State of the Art in LP-WAN Solutions for Industrial IoT Services. *Sensors (Basel), 16*(5), 708. doi:10.339016050708 PMID:27196909

Sendin, A., Sanchez-Fornie, M., & Berganza, I. (2016). *Telecommunication networks for the smart grid.* Boston: Artech House.

Sequans. (2016). *Narrowband LTE: Which apps need Cat M1 and which need Cat NB1?* Retrieved from http://www.sequans.com/narrowband-lte-which-apps-need-cat-m1-and-which-need-cat-nb1/

Sigfox. (2017a). *Sigfox technical overview.* Retrieved from https://www.disk91.com/wp-content/uploads/2017/05/4967675830228422064.pdf

Sigfox. (2017b). *Sigfox technology overview.* Retrieved from https://www.sigfox.com/en/sigfox-iot-technology-overview in 06/06/2018

Sun, W., Choi, M., & Choi, S. (2013). IEEE 802.11 ah: A long range 802.11 WLAN at sub 1 GHz. *Journal of ICT Standardization*, *1*(1), 83–108. doi:10.13052/jicts2245-800X.115

Tabakov, Y. (2014). *DASH7 Alliance Protocol, DASH7 Alliance*. Retrieved from http://dash7-alliance. org/wp-content/uploads/2014/08/005-Dash7-Alliance-Mode-technical-presentation.pdf

Tabbane, S. (2016). *IoT Network Planning*. ITU. Retrieved from https://www.itu.int/en/ITU-D/Regional-Presence/AsiaPacific/SiteAssets/Pages/Events/2016/Dec-2016-IoT/IoTtraining/IoT%20network%20 planning%20ST%2015122016.pdf in 10/06/2018.

The Things Network. (n.d.). *LoPy Module*. Retrieved from https://www.thethingsnetwork.org/docs/ devices/lopy/

Wang, C., Wu, J., Ekanayake, J., & Jenkins, N. (2017). *Smart electricity distribution networks*. CRC Press.

Webb, W. (2012). *Understanding Weightless: Technology, Equipment, and Network Deployment for M2M Communications in White Space*. Cambridge University Press. doi:10.1017/CBO9781139208857

Weyn, M., Ergeerts, G., Berkvens, R., Wojciechowski, B., & Tabakov, Y. (2015). DASH7 alliance protocol 1.0: Low-power, mid-range sensor and actuator communication. In *2015 IEEE Conference on Standards for Communications and Networking (CSCN)*. IEEE. 10.1109/CSCN.2015.7390420

Zemede, M. (2015). *Explosion of the Internet of Things: What does it mean for wireless devices*. Keisight. Retrieved from http://www.keysight.com/upload/cmc_upload/All/IoT_Seminar_Session1_Explosion_ of_the_Internet_of_Things.pdf, in 18/06/2018.

Zigbee Alliance. (2014). *Webinar presentation: Introducing ZigBee 3.0*. Retrieved from http://www. zigbee.org/download/introducing-zigbee-3-0-webinar-presentation/

Zigbee Alliance. (2017). *Zigbee 3.0 Base Device Behavior Specification*. Retrieved from http://www. zigbee.org/download/paper-zigbee-3-0-base-device-behavior-specification/

ADDITIONAL READING

Ekanayake, J., Liyanage, K., Wu, J., Yokoyama, A., & Jenkins, N. (2012). *Smart Grid - Technology And Applications*. John Wiley & Sons. doi:10.1002/9781119968696

Jean-Philippe Vasseur & Adam Dunkels. (2010). *Interconnecting Smart Objects with IP: The Next Internet*. Morgan Kaufmann Publishers.

Qiu, R. C., & Antonik, P. (2017). *Smart Grid using Big Data Analytics: A Random Matrix Theory Approach*. Wiley Edts. doi:10.1002/9781118716779

KEY TERMS AND DEFINITIONS

Demand Response (DR): A set of solutions that allow the adjustment of consumption levels in accordance with the generated levels.

Distributed Energy Resources (DER): A type of distributed energy generation that results from renewable energy sources and is located at the distribution grid (i.e., at the consumer level).

Long Range Wide Area Network (LoRAWAN): A media access control layer protocol and system architecture that manages the exchange of data between LoRa capable end-node devices and applications. It is maintained by the LoRa Alliance.

Low-Power Wide-Area Network (LPWAN): A type of wide area wireless sensor network designed to allow low rate and long-range communication between sensor nodes.

Smart Charging: An optimized process of charging EVs that schedules their periods of charging, taking into consideration the driver's needs, the energy that is being, or is going to be, produced by renewable energy sources, the present/future tariff rates and the limitations from the electrical grid.

Smart Grid: An electrical grid that incorporates ICT to enable both machine-to-machine and human-to-machine communications and the optimization of the managed resources.

Wireless Sensor Networks: A protocol and network architecture that enables a wireless transmission of data between sensor nodes, or between them and a gateway.

Chapter 4
Water Management for Rural Environments and IoT

José Jasnau Caeiro
Instituto Politécnico de Beja, Portugal

João Carlos Martins
Instituto Politécnico de Beja, Portugal

ABSTRACT

Internet of Things (IoT) systems are starting to be developed for applications in the management of water quality monitoring systems. The chapter presents some of the work done in this area and also shows some systems being developed by the authors for the Alentejo region. A general architecture for water quality monitoring systems is discussed. The important issue of computer security is mentioned and connected to recent publications related to the blockchain technology. Web services, data transmission technology, micro web frameworks, and cloud IoT services are also discussed.

INTRODUCTION

Water is the main component of Earth's oceans, rivers and lakes. It is found in liquid, solid and gaseous states and is the major constituent of most living organisms. It is vital for all forms of life that are known to humanity.

The Alentejo region in Portugal is home to one of the largest dams and artificial lakes in western Europe---the Alqueva dam---, that constitutes a strategic water reserve. It guarantees the water supply to the population, agriculture and industry. It is a very important component of the irrigation system network of the Alentejo. Water is a critical resource and will become even more important because of the pressure exerted by climate change.

Water management systems may benefit from Internet of Things (IoT) systems in several ways. This chapter will describe how IoT can be used for several aspects of water management, namely starting from sensor networks dedicated to the acquisition of data related to water quality and quantity, to aggregator microcomputer systems, security issues and centralization of the information with further high-level

DOI: 10.4018/978-1-5225-7332-6.ch004

processing. The importance of novel technologies such as the blockchain and machine intelligence for the IoT area is also addressed.

The definition of IoT can be found across a large number of publications and Internet sites. The Institute of Electrical and Electronics Engineers created a dedicated site to the theme (https://iot.ieee.org) and in 2015 published a report trying to define what IoT is (IEEE Internet Initiative, 2015).

A short definition attributed to IEEE in March 2014, and mentioned in the report, is that IoT is "A network of items, each embedded with sensors, which are connected to the Internet". It can be included under the broader definition of ubiquitous computing and sometimes we may consider the definitions indistinguishable.

The water quality and resources monitoring systems described are limited to those that mention themselves as IoT proposals. The engineering aspects are favored in the chapter and the system proposals reflect such a choice.

The chapter starts with this introduction followed by a section with an overview of water management IoT applications described in the literature. Based upon the approaches in the literature a general water quality monitoring architecture is presented in the section with this title. The types of sensors, the communication network, the data storage and data processing subsystems are shown in a systems diagram and discussed.

After the general water quality monitoring architecture presentation some general relevant additional topics are discussed, namely: computer security; data transmission protocols; micro web frameworks; cloud IoT platforms and machine intelligence. These are very short sections destined only to give the reader some sense of the importance of these topics for the design of real world IoT systems.

Before the final conclusion two sections present two examples: a water quality monitoring system and an irrigation and drainage network monitoring system. Each is designed using an IoT approach including: low cost sensors and hardware; some sort of Internet connection and data storage.

The chapter ends with a short conclusion collecting some of the main aspects of the sections.

WATER MANAGEMENT IOT APPLICATIONS

IoT applications for water management in rural environments address two questions: irrigation water quality management and water resources management.

In Portugal, information about the water quality and water resources is presented online at the (http://snirh.pt/) Internet site. This data is collected using traditional chemical and physical analysis from samples collected in the field. Unfortunately, due to cost issues, the data at many sites is not collected anymore. IoT systems are typically low cost and could present an alternative for the problem of updating old networks of water quality monitoring systems.

During the last few years some proposals for IoT based water quality monitoring systems have appeared in scientific literature. A short review follows.

An architecture using web services for real time water quality data acquisition is presented by Wong and Kerkez (2016). The proposal is centered around the web services concept, namely tackling the transmission of data collected by the hardware developed by the authors--- a water quality sensor node using the NeoMote wireless sensing platform. A set of three different web services were implemented on three separate devices and programmed using three different programming languages. The web services are developed for the Xively IoT platform (https://www.xively.com/).

A real-time water quality monitoring system using IoT is described in Das and Jain (2017). The system is designed with data collected from three different types of sensors: pH; electrical water conductivity and temperature. The sensors collect analog signals and use ADCs to convert the signals to digital format. Zigbee communication modules send the data to a processing module microcontroller (LPC2148). After some processing the data is sent to a central server managed by The MathWorks, Inc., (the same company that owns MATLAB), dedicated to IoT applications: ThingsSpeak (https://thingspeak.com).

An online measurement and reporting system for the quality of water based on a wireless sensor network is authored by (Parameswari and Moses, 2017). The objective is the implementation of a low cost, IoT based system, measuring temperature; electrical conductivity; acidity (pH) and turbidity. An Arduino Uno microcontroller is used for data acquisition and sending the processed data to a server using a Wi-Fi connection. Afterwards, the data is sent to a cloud-based server using a Google Drive spreadsheet.

Another proposal of an IoT platform with sensing, data processing and wireless communications, for remote aquatic environmental monitoring is presented by Li et al. (2017). The quality of water is evaluated on its physical, chemical and biological parameters, namely: temperature, pH, dissolved oxygen, electrical water conductivity and oxidation-reduction potential. The conversion of sensor signals to sensor readings is carried out by a system designated by mote (Waspmote with the ATmega1281, manufactured by Libelium Comunicaciones Distribuidas S.L.). The collected data is processed by a Raspberry Pi 3 and then transmitted by Wi-Fi or Zigbee radio transmitter. The Base Station (BS) is built around a Linux based router. The authors present algorithms for the characterization of a study area that they call a Hexagonal Grid-Based Survey Planner. The sampling locations are generated by adoption of a hexagonal cell decomposition and a spanning-tree based path planning algorithm is used to travel between the sampling location of interest. A normalized Online Water Quality Index is produced by the system.

A surface water IoT system for measurement and monitoring of sensor data is presented by Kafli (2017). It uses an ARM microcontroller (LPC1768) with several sensors that measure temperature and humidity; carbon monoxide; pH and water level. The data is saved into a data logger and sent to an Internet cloud system (IBM IoT Watson platform) for processing and analysis.

An Intel Galileo Gen2 is used as the core controller for a water quality monitoring system, in the proposal of Salunke and Kate (2017). An Arduino microcontroller is connected to sensors for measurement of temperature; pH and turbidity. The data collected is observed by connecting to the core controller.

An implementation of a real-time water quality monitoring system is described by Pranata, Lee and Kim (2017). It measures temperature, acidity and dissolved oxygen. The sensors are placed underwater and data is sent using a wireless Zigbee communications to a central system. The system adopts MQ Telemetry Transport (MQTT) which is a lightweight, ISO-standard publish-subscribe protocol, intentionally developed for open and simple device communication at a premium network bandwidth and/or small code footprint. The communication nodes are built with Arduino boards. The public MQTT broker adopted for this implementation is HiveMQ (https://www.hivemq.com/).

Another real time water quality monitoring system is proposed by (Menon, Ramesh and Divya, 2017). The system measures the most typical parameters: temperature; turbidity; acidity (pH); dissolved oxygen and electrical conductivity, and also some chemical parameters, such as sulphate; ammonia and nitrate. The sensors are supported by a WaspMote board. The system is powered by a solar panel and supports the communication of data with: LoRaWan; 4G; Wi-Fi and Zigbee protocols. The data from the WaspMote boards is transmitted to the base stations and afterwards sent from these base stations to Water Quality Monitoring stations where the concerned water authorities analyses the data and issue alerts. The IoT Azure platform, (https://azure.microsoft.com/en-us/services/iot-hub), was chosen for the storage of data and ASP.NET for the web application.

An efficient water quality monitoring system built using Field Programmable Gate Arrays (FPGA) is presented by (Myint, Gopal and Aung, 2017). An ADC is connected between the FPGA and a set of sensors that measure acidity (pH); temperature; carbon dioxide; turbidity and water level. A Zigbee communications module sends the data from the FPGA system to a base station where the user can observe the acquired information. The next section will address the design of a generic system architecture that encompasses most of the systems reviewed in the literature that was reviewed in this section.

SYSTEM ARCHITECTURE FOR WATER QUALITY MONITORING

The majority of the systems described in the water quality monitoring literature follow the architecture in the diagram shown in Figure 1.

The system is divided into four major subsystems: data acquisition; data aggregator; data server and cloud server.

The data acquisition subsystem incorporates the sensors, which may communicate to the microcontroller the physical and chemical parameters of water under the form of electrical signals. These may be analogue or digital. In the case of analog electrical signals, the microcontroller must have some data acquisition and conditioning electronics. The signals may be filtered and scaled and afterwards converted to a digital format by sampling with an analog to digital converter (ADC). Many sensors have an associated circuitry that converts the analog signal into a digital signal and permit an easy communication with the microcontroller via I2C (Inter Integrated Circuit) which is a synchronous, single ended computer bus, via SPI (Serial Peripheral Interface bus) or UART (Universal Asynchronous Receiver-Transmitter) protocol.

The micro controller unit is a low power processing device that collects the sensor data, provides the first level of signal processing and sends the information to a data aggregator subsystem. The communication module is commonly wireless since the distance between the data acquisition subsystem and the data aggregator subsystem is usually high. Low power consumption is a concern for the data acquisition subsystem and it is common to use low power microcontrollers and low power long range communication protocols such as LoRaWan or SigFox or low power small range communication protocols such as Bluetooth Low Energy (BLE) or ZigBee.

Figure 1. Generic architecture for water quality monitoring systems using an IoT approach. The sensor set is chosen according to the specific monitoring needs of each system.

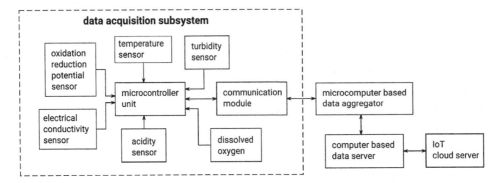

The data aggregator provides another layer of computer processing power. It is composed of a low power microcomputer designed for IoT applications. It usually runs a Linux based operating system with low RAM requirements and some sort of flash memory storage. The most typical example is the Raspberry Pi family of microcomputer boards. Most of the Raspberry PI deployments adopt Raspbian operating system version that is based on the Debian Linux distribution. Ubuntu also has an IoT version (https://www.ubuntu.com/internet-of-things) with support for a diverse set of hardware. The data aggregator may perform some sort of signal processing and pattern recognition, data encryption and temporary local storage. This subsystem will have an increasingly important role in what concerns computer security since it has enough processing power and software resources for this purpose. These microcomputers usually receive data using serial communication protocols from the microcontroller-based data acquisition subsystem and send data to central data servers using the Internet. Sometimes the data aggregator subsystem sends directly the information to cloud based IoT services. It is common to use web services to send the data. Central data servers may use traditional relational databases or NoSQL databases, such as MongoDB, to store the information. In a very shortly foreseeable future, new types of databases, using some sort of blockchain technology representation, are to be expected.

COMPUTER SECURITY IN WATER MONITORING SYSTEMS

One major concern on the IoT area is related to the computer security issues for IoT systems. Due to the connections to the Internet or to the wireless sensor networks, these systems are subject to attacks that usually plague other network-connected computer-based systems. The large number of IoT devices and the low energy and low-cost requirements pose a challenge in terms of hardware protection and computer security policies.

Water is one of the most valuable and critical resources available to mankind and is usually included in the definition of strategic resources. Information security is thus one major concern in terms of water quality monitoring systems.

For a secure IoT system deployment some aspects must be considered: information privacy, confidentiality and integrity; authentication, authorization and accounting; service availability; *etc.*.

The blockchain technology is emerging as one of the main constituents of computer security and the IoT area will certainly benefit from it (Khan & Salah, 2018). Blockchain is a technology that uses community validation to maintain the content of data, represented by a chain of blocks replicated across multiple users. A minimal block is typically constituted by: an index; a traditional Unix timestamp; some data; a hash representation of block and a hash representation of the previous block. The hash representation of the previous block effectively constitutes a cryptographic link between blocks resulting in the secure blockchain. The hash representation of the block is usually constructed using a proof-of-work system. This prevents hackers from altering the data in the blockchain thus ensuring data integrity. Data is typically stored using a peer-to-peer network eliminating the risks associated with centrally held data. A traditional approach to data security is focused on the implementation of computer security management policies for the database servers and the data transmission channels. The blockchain technology is focused, instead, on the security of the data itself. Each block of data is guaranteed not to be subject of attack therefore assuring that a large set of computer security requirements are fulfilled, namely: privacy; confidentiality and integrity, to mention a few. Since IoT devices have low computational power and storage, the blockchain validation is a difficult problem.

A model of the impact on blockchain synchronization and wireless connectivity is studied by Danzi et. al. (2017). The authors define two protocol variants and build a numerical simulation based on a traffic model. This is used to extract measures of interest: the time needed for the blockchain synchronization or the minimal bandwidths requirements to stay synchronized. The major contribution is the explicit modelling of the impact that wireless connectivity has on the blockchain synchronization and smart contract execution. The numerical results are based on the Ethereum protocol statistics and for the wireless LTE Cat M1 and Bluetooth Low Energy (BLE) technologies. An important conclusion is that the blockchain protocols require the allocation of a considerable set of downlink resources vs. typical IoT systems that usually generate uplink traffic.

Another proposal for the application of the blockchain technology to IoT is presented by Dorri, Kanhere and Jurdak (2017). Again, the low computing power available to IoT devices is seen as a challenge to the adoption of the blockchain technology. Central to the security of the blockchain is the Proof Of Work (POW) since it is this mechanism that typically prevents the hacking of the data in the blockchain. The authors replace the POW with a distributed trust mechanism thus eliminating the high computational demand of the blockchain.

The problem of control and configuration of IoT devices is studied by Huh, Cho and Kim (2017) and they propose using the Ethereum (https://www.ethereum.org/) blockchain platform for the device management. Smart contracts are used to write code that defines the behavior of IoT devices. The proof of concept is presented with Raspberry Pi microcomputers.

Traditional computer security approaches are also a valuable tool in IoT systems and there is a large amount of literature on the subject.

DATA TRANSMISSION PROTOCOLS

IoT systems may support one or more data transmission protocols. High latency, low energy resources and long transmission distances are typical for water quality management systems. These specialized data protocols are designed for, or adequately support, machine-to-machine (M2M) applications.

The first example of such a data transmission protocol, and perhaps the most widely adopted, is Message Queuing Telemetry Transport (MQTT) that enables a publish/subscribe messaging model (https://mqtt.org). A system called the "broker" intermediates the communication between client machines. A client may be either a "subscriber" or a "publisher" and information is organized using a hierarchy of topics. When new data is generated the "publisher" t sends a message with the new data to the broker system. This system then sends the data to the clients that have subscribed to that topic. MQTT is easy to use and well adapted to the needs of IoT systems. A widely used implementation is the Eclipse Foundation Paho MQTT (https://www.eclipse.org/paho/). Systems such as the Raspberry PI, Arduino or Pycom support MQTT. The latter is an easy to use microcontroller system that can be programmed in dialect of Python specifically adapted for microcontrollers: MicroPython (https://micropython.org/).

Alternatives to MQTT are available using other models for communication between machines.

The Constrained Application Protocol (CoAP) is an application layer protocol that is intended for use in resource-constrained internet devices (http://coap.technology). CoAP is used in the same constrained network (e.g., low-power, lossy networks), between devices and general nodes on the Internet, and between devices on different constrained networks both joined by an internet. CoAP is also being used via other mechanisms, such as SMS on mobile communication networks. With CoAP the server is installed at the end node, the sensor. The client node is installed at the controller which addresses several servers.

The Simple (or Streaming) Text Oriented Messaging Protocol (STOMP) provides an interoperable wire format enabling the communication from STOMP clients with any STOMP message broker, providing easy and widespread messaging interoperability among programming languages, computational platforms and brokers (http://stomp.github.io).

Another free and open standard is the Extensible Messaging and Presence Protocol (XMPP) available since 1999 and claims security features interesting for IoT (https://xmpp.org).

Other protocols worth mentioning are: Mihini/M3DA; the Advanced Message Queuing Protocol (AMQP); the Data-Distribution Service for Real-Time Systems (DDS); the Lightweight Local Automation Protocol (LLAP); the Lightweight M2M (LWM2M); the Simple Sensor Interface (SSI); Representational State Transfer (REST); Hypertext Transfer Protocol Version 2 (HTTP/2); Simple Object Access Protocol (SOAP); Websocket, developed as part of the HTML5 initiative; etc.

A large set of communication protocols are available addressing different needs for IoT. Many different details must be considered when choosing a particular protocol. Namely the most usual is the software implementation for a particular hardware.

MICRO WEB FRAMEWORKS AND PROGRAMMING TOOLS

The designer may choose a traditional web framework such as Django (https://www.djangoproject.com/) to build web apps and services for IoT applications. A very rich ecosystem is built around this traditional web framework and full usage of the Python programming language is possible. It is a good choice for the computer-based data server since all the major databases (SQL and NOSQL) have some sort of integration with Django. Django follows a traditional Model-Template-View (MTV is Model View Controller under a Django nomenclature) approach to software development. The Model (database representation) is done using an ORM (Object Relational Model) for SQL databases, the View is where the system logic lies, and the Template is where the user interface lies.

Micro web frameworks such as the Python programming language-based Flask web framework, provide an example of a software development platform for the creation of a web services server that runs in low power machines such as the Raspberry Pi (http://flask.pocoo.org). Web sockets are implemented with the Flask-SocketIO package (https://flask-socketio.readthedocs.io/en/latest). A MQTT package for Flask is available at (https://github.com/neubatengog/FlaskMqtt) supporting the Eclipse PAHO implementation for the IoT (https://www.eclipse.org/paho). The Raspberry Pi microcomputer and the Flask micro web framework integrate easily. The Raspberry Pi provides strong support to the Python programming language development tools and packages. Flask is very light on resources and thus widely adopted in IoT systems. It is much lighter than Django although it follows a similar MVC based approach.

Node-RED (https://nodered.org/) is a node.js (https://nodejs.org/en/) based programming tool for IoT. JavaScript is the programming language used for the node.js application. Node-RED presents a browser-based editor that makes it easy to build IoT applications. A node is a function block available to the Node-RED programmer and presently there are more than 200 000 nodes available. The Raspberry PI Raspbian OS comes with Node-RED. It is very easy to build a prototype encompassing data acquisition and transmission, database storage or to present data through HTTP using the dashboard palette of nodes (https://github.com/node-red/node-red-dashboard). The designer can build prototypes using a visual programing approach that greatly reduces the development time.

CLOUD IOT PLATFORMS

Cloud IoT platforms provide a centralized storage for the information acquired from the water quality sensors. Several options are available with different services provided (https://www.postscapes.com/internet-of-things-platforms/). Some cloud IoT providers have System Development Kits available for several different programming languages whilst others only provide means to store and retrieve the data. Most support HTTP and MQTT protocols.

IBM Watson and Google Cloud provide machine learning services that in a foreseeable future will become very important for water quality monitoring systems. Relevant for the choice of IoT cloud services is whether one has an open source license or not.

Cloud IoT providers will soon face the challenge of blockchain technology and the InterPlanetary File System (IPFS) is an example for a distributed peer to peer method of storing data (https://github.com/ipfs/ipfs).

MACHINE INTELLIGENCE AND IOT

The large amount of data that may be generated by the sensors used in IoT systems provides useful information for machine intelligence-based systems. Machine learning will be a major factor in the next few years in terms of computing systems. An explosion of applications is seen during the last few years and a Google's TensorFlow package (http://www.tensorflow.org) contributed to the momentum seen in this area. There are several APIs available for different programming languages but only the Python API is considered stable. It is an open source symbolic math library for dataflow programming and used for neural networks-based machine learning approach. TensorFlow runs on multiple CPUs and GPUs and supports massive parallel programming with GPUs. It is computationally efficient and destined for usage with very large data sets.

Another package used for the same purpose as TensorFlow is provide by Facebook: PyTorch (https://pytorch.org/). It is a machine learning library for the Python programming language based on Torch (http://torch.ch), which is a scientific computing framework with support for machine learning algorithms that profit from using a parallel programming approach with GPUs.

Both TensorFlow and PyTorch are N-dimensional array based libraries with very efficient implementations. A full stack IoT application will therefore start at the bottom with the sensors and microcontrollers collecting huge amounts of data and end at the machine intelligence level where automated decisions and analyses are provided to the end user.

Programming languages such as Python, MATLAB are major players in the machine intelligence community and simultaneously in the IoT community with many packages available to the developer.

It is worth mentioning the increasing importance of computer vision in machine intelligence systems and the correlation between crop development, assessed through images, and water quality is foreseeable. The OpenCV (http://opencv.org) set of libraries and packages is increasingly used within the pattern recognition community and also the IoT community.

Any discussion of machine intelligence packages is incomplete if scikit-learn (https://github.com/scikit-learn/scikit-learn) is not presented. This package is one of the most complete that is available for Python and therefore for the Raspberry PI.

The designer of IoT applications will be presented with several challenges in terms of systems integration. It will have to consider the hardware side of IoT up to the user interface that will increasingly be based upon machine intelligence.

IRRIGATION AND DRAINAGE NETWORK MONITORING SYSTEM

In the context of IoT applications for the Alentejo region a system is presented that monitors water drainage networks for monitoring irrigation channels in agriculture, or for monitoring an urban drainage network. The system detects the rise of water levels within the channels due to obstruction or due to heavy rainfall.

Irrigation and drainage channels may become clogged, which can result in serious damages and incur into a large monetary loss. In the case of wastewater, when the regular drainage channel becomes obstructed, contaminated water is normally directed to alternative bypass channels or, in more extreme situations, it can expose the drainage system, invading open-air areas, with the resultant problems with the inhabitants, in addition to the public health problems that this situation may raise.

Particularly, with the increasingly frequent occurrences of extreme climatic phenomena, which include high precipitation over a short period of time, it is important to have a way to get real-time information on the state and levels of water in the drainage channels. This data can also be useful in the monitoring of irrigation channels and water streams since appropriate decisions can be taken for civil protection and to follow prevention measures to minimize the impact of these phenomena on populations or in cultures. It is known that the sooner a flood alert is issued, the less damage it will cause (Pappenberger et al., 2015).

The usual solution for monitoring the channels is to inspect them, which in many situations implies the allocation of teams to inspect the channels on a regular basis, and in the case of sudden rainfall it is frequent to have no information at all.

Therefore, a system that collects and sends information on the status of the channels allows acting in a timely and informed way, which can avoid serious material damages, safeguards the people and crops and, at the same time, allows the reduction of operational maintenance costs of these channels.

The system presented in Figure 2 is a subset of the general architecture presented in Figure 1 and is composed of two distinct modules. A remote module, based on a microcontroller, to which level sensors and a communications module are attached, which sends the information to a server. The second component of the system is the server application, which receives the information sent by the remote modules

Figure 2. Architecture for water drainage monitoring systems using an IoT approach

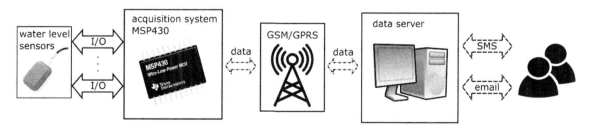

installed in the various critical points of the drainage channels, compiles and treats the information and makes its presentation. It will also send the alerts.

The remote module is intended to monitor the drainage channels and report changes in the water level. The system presents the following constraints: since the modules can be installed in underground channels, the system needs to be exclusively powered by a battery and it is not possible to charge it by means of a solar panel, for example. Therefore, the energy consumption of the system must be low to preserve the battery charge and reduce maintenance costs.

Due to the aforementioned restrictions the remote module is based on a low-power Texas Instruments microcontroller of the MSP430 family. The MSP430 is a 16-bit microcontroller family with limited processing capacity but with extremely low power consumption and versatile at the same time. The microcontroller is responsible for analyzing changes in the sensor states and communicating with the server via SMS messages using a GSM/GPRS module. The set of sensors used are switch level sensors.

For the communications module, an ITEAD's GPRS /GSM platform is used, based on the SIMCOM's SIM900 integrated circuit. Communication with this module is done using AT commands. The drawback of this module is that in the process of sending SMS messages, the current may reach peaks of 2 A, which is quite high for a system that in many situations should be autonomous in terms of energy. However, there are more suitable solutions in terms of energy efficiency, such as those offered by SIGFOX and LoRaWAN, that allow communications over long distances with a reduced energy consumption, but which have the problem of not covering part of the territory and need access to local hubs. Therefore GSM / GPRS communications are used in this particular system since the deployment is more widespread.

The remote module software is programmed in the C language and implements several independent state machines, one for detecting changes in water levels that are triggered by interruptions sent by level switches, a state machine for management and reporting information, and another state machine that deals with communications. The various state machines place the system in a low power mode, which typically consumes a current of 0.9 μA at a frequency of 1 MHz, which corresponds to one of the lowest energy consumptions among microcontrollers on the market.

The main goal of the server module is to receive and process the gathered data from the remote modules, and to notify specific user groups about change in the water levels. A full stack web framework built with the Python programming language: Django (https://www.djangoproject.com) is used for the data presentation. Django follows the traditional Model-View-Controller software paradigm and allows a flexible approach in terms of choice of the underlying database because it adopts an Object Relational Model (ORM) for dealing with the persistent data. The robustness, scalability, type of open source license, and a high level of reliability and availability, led to the selection of the PostgreSQL database (https://www.postgresql.org).

The server module can use a GSM modem with a SIM card, or in the case of a great volume of SMS messages the stakeholder can subscribe a SMS service from a mobile communications operator. In the case of direct use of a modem to receive SMS, a software package, like SMSTools (http://smstools3. kekekasvi.com), can be used to read the incoming SMS and send notifications by SMS to users.

The main functions of the server application are: reception and processing of data about the channels' water level received by SMS using the GSM communication technology; register and track the channels being monitored. A mapping of the positioning of the remote monitoring modules is done and the number of alerts that occurred on each channel is displayed in a map using the Google Maps API, which is available at (https://developers.google.com/maps). It registers and manages the remote modules: battery state, module version, communication modules, SIM cards, etc., as well as the recording and visualization of installations and maintenance performed on them. Also, the maintenance interventions made to the modules and to the channels to eliminate the flood warnings are registered and managed. Reports with the statistical information about floods, water levels, for example, and channels visited and directly intervened are generated. These reports can be personalized to display only the selected information, where the user selects the data that intended to export and select the time intervals.

The server application also permits users to send messages between each other and schedule interventions, via email of by SMS. The server can also be connected to a weather forecast server so that it can predict the rainfall for the next five days and, based on history, it can also predict the channels that will flood with a given likelihood, that are shown with a red pin on the map. This forecast uses statistical data about the correlation between precipitation volume and previous flood occurrences.

Due to its open source adoption, other modules can easily be added to the server application, namely the mapping of critical geographical areas in terms of floods, planning maintenance interventions and channels cleaning, a module to provide information to citizens in a city, including the sending of alerts, and the configuration and sending of automatically generated reports of several kinds.

SYSTEM FOR WATER QUALITY MONITORING

An IoT system for monitoring the water quality of dams, lakes and ponds is presented. The monitoring of water quality is very important, especially if it is used for human and animal consumption, but also when it is used for agriculture or aquaculture. To measure the water quality parameters traditionally it is common to send a human operator to the specific location where the parameters should be acquired and measure directly, possibly in several different places and with specific instrumentation, the values relevant to assess the water quality, and then return to the laboratory, download all the data to a computer and process the gathered information. Since this is a laborious procedure, the water quality is not measured with the desirable frequency, and it can happen that certain physical and chemical parameters--- for example, optimal for the emergence of certain harmful algae, that demand to take a certain set of measures--- are not detected on time.

Again, IoT has opened up the possibility to have systems that are real-time and can uninterruptedly monitor the water quality, sending the acquired data to a server that manages and processes information and extract patterns so that supervisors can take the necessary actions.

This system also follows the general architecture shown in Figure 1 but presents another subset of distinct modules as can be perceived by looking at Figure 3.

The remote microcontroller-based module acquires data from different types of sensors for each relevant physical and chemical parameter, that is sent to the server by the communications system. The server application retrieves the information sent by the remote modules located along the water mass and processes the information that is made available for analysis and visualization.

The main functions of the remote system are the collection and transmission of the sensor data to a server where it is analyzed. The sampling periodicity is flexible and adaptable to application needs. A higher sampling rate may increase the power consumption significantly. The system collects the following signals relevant to water quality: temperature of water (DS1820 waterproof sensor); pH (Atlas Scientific pH sensor); dissolved oxygen (O2) (Atlas Scientific Dissolved Oxygen sensor); dissolved carbon dioxide (CO2) (SKU: SEN0219); electrical conductivity (Atlas Scientific Conductivity Probe K 1.0 sensor); turbidity (Atlas Scientific Embedded NDIR CO2 Meter) and pressure (to measure depth)

Figure 3. Architecture for the water quality monitoring systems following an IoT approach

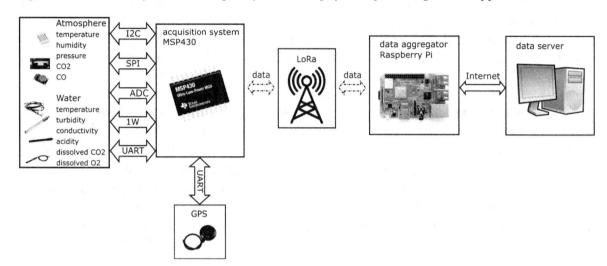

(SKU: SEN0257). Although less costly sensors are available, these offer a good trade-off between cost, performance, and accuracy.

The remote module is complemented with sensors to measure air quality, like temperature (DHT22), humidity (DHT22), carbon monoxide (MQ-7 sensor). In many situations, it is useful to have a GPS module thus providing the module with geographical positioning data.

In dams and in deep water reservoirs, the water parameters are frequently measured at different depths, therefore the system can be equipped with a motor to lower and raise the sensors platform. Alternatively, one could opt to have several sensor groups positioned at different depths, however, since the sensors can be quite expensive, the first configuration would be preferred. The sampling interval can go from several minutes, to twice or three times a day, according to literature. This remote system is more demanding in terms of the number of sensors and interfaces than the previous one described. The microcontroller chosen to be used for this platform is again a MSP430 family microcontroller. These microcontrollers come in different varieties, and several types and number of peripherals are available, it is possible to choose the most adequate for the application with the necessary number of I/O pins, and the change between microcontrollers of the MSP430 family can be done with a minimum effort.

The communications module should be chosen depending on the amount of data to be transmitted and on the terrain. Because of the amount of data to be transmitted, a low bandwidth technology, like SIGFOX, is not appropriate. Therefore, LoRa or a mobile communications operator that provides data communications is chosen. The LoRa system is particularly suited for a place where several locations are being simultaneously monitored and the installation cost of a LoRa gateway base station is justified. This communication base station is associated with the aggregation system, based on a more powerful computational platform, like the Raspberry Pi 3, that forms part of the blockchain processing system, and sends the processed data to a cloud server using a wired Internet connection or through a large bandwidth wireless mobile communications technology, like the 3G/4G mobile communications network.

Another important issue to consider for this system is the power supply. Normally, these kinds of systems are installed in anchored floating platforms and they need considerable power, especially if a motor is used to measure water quality at different depths. The most appropriate power source is the use of a battery complemented by a solar panel, that powers the system and charges the battery at the same time.

The server gathers all the data from the remote modules and saves it on a database for further processing and analysis. Besides information processing and analysis, the server can also provide a framework to manage the installation and maintenance of the remote stations. Again, a web framework to take into consideration is Django, based on the Python programming language, and for the database management system the scalability and availability of the open source database PostgreSQL is a convenient solution. The association of the blockchain with a conventional database improves the processing times.

The web server application provides the following capabilities: the immediate geographically referenced visualization of the collected data in different formats like graphs but also as lists and tables for further study by external experts, with an easy tool to export those lists to different file formats like CSV, XML, JSON and PDF, for example. The server application is also able to configure alerts based on different threshold values for the relevant parameters and send it automatically to several recipients.

FUTURE RESEARCH DIRECTIONS

Research in IoT water quality monitoring systems will address topics also found in research of other IoT systems that gather critical data, namely: information security and system availability. A very active research thread is found in the usage of blockchain technology to address information security issues.

Artificial intelligence is another area of knowledge that will be increasingly important for IoT systems. A very interesting example of application is found in Xiao *et al.* (2018), where machine learning techniques are studied for usage in the realm of IoT devices.

Associated problems that are always present in the IoT area, and even more for the distributed type of systems used for water quality monitoring are communications and energy. Low power and long-range communications and low power computing devices are demanded for this kind of applications, and further technological developments should be focused on these issues. Another topic of research, that could provide valuable contributions to the IoT, is on energy harvesting devices that can collect energy from wind, heat, sun, from vibrations, *etc.*, and transform it to electrical energy capable of feeding a power grid isolated IoT system.

CONCLUSION

Water quality and water resource monitoring and management IoT based systems present a viable low-cost alternative to traditional monitoring and management methods.

The chapter presents an overview of some of the most recent work in this area in order to familiarize the reader with the available proposals found in the literature. There are no standard commercial solutions that address all the challenges in the field. The most popular solution is presented by the Libelium company (http://www.libelium.com/smart-water-sensors-to-monitor-water-quality-in-rivers-lakes-and-the-sea/) and is essentially a hardware solution.

A general architecture encompassing most of the systems presented in the IoT water quality monitoring systems literature is presented in this chapter. An example of a system being developed for the Alentejo region is described in the context of this general architecture. Another example of a system devoted to water resources management, namely flood monitoring, is also presented.

The introduction of the blockchain technology to IoT solves a large number of computer security issues, namely those related to data tampering that is critical to water quality and resources management since it is a critical infrastructure. The acknowledgement of the general importance of blockchain technology is leading to a revolution in terms of data storage that will have a very strong impact in all areas and namely in IoT applications. Some examples of the research done in the blockchain technology for IoT are presented in the chapter.

The chapter briefly addressed the communication protocols that may be used in water quality monitoring systems. Also, micro web frameworks such as Flask and a visual programming tool such as Node-RED where presented as a solution for rapid deployment of IoT solutions.

Machine learning based on the sensor data produced was briefly described along with two of the major libraries available for this purpose: TensorFlow and PyTorch.

A general overview of the water quality and resources monitoring and management is presented in this chapter together with some examples of systems.

ACKNOWLEDGMENT

This research was supported by the ENGAGE SKA Project, [POCI-01-0145-FEDER-022217], financed by the Programa Operacional Competitividade e Internacionalização (COMPETE 2020), under the FEDER component, and by the Fundação para a Ciência e Tecnologia, I.P., under its national component.

REFERENCES

Aste, T., Tasca, P., & Di Matteo, T. (2017). Blockchain Technologies: The Foreseeable Impact on Society and Industry. *IEEE Computer Magazin*, *50*(9), 18–28. doi:10.1109/MC.2017.3571064

Danzi, P., Kalør, A. E., Stefanović, Č., & Popovski, P. (2017). *Analysis of the communication traffic for blockchain synchronization of IoT devices*. Retrieved from http://arxiv.org/abs/1711.00540

Das, B., & Jain, P. C. (2017). Real-time water quality monitoring system using Internet of Things. *2017 International Conference on Computer, Communications and Electronics (COMPTELIX)*, 78–82. 10.1109/COMPTELIX.2017.8003942

Dorri, A., Kanhere, S. S., & Jurdak, R. (2017). Towards an optimized blockchain for IoT. *2017 IEEE/ACM Second International Conference on Internet-of-Things design and implementation (IoTDI)*, 173–178. doi:10.1145/3054977.3055003

Huh, S., Cho, S., & Kim, S. (2017). Managing IoT devices using blockchain platform. *2017 19th International Conference on Advanced Communication Technology (ICACT) IEEE*. doi:10.23919/icact.2017.7890132

Kafli, N., & Isa, K. (2017). Internet of Things (IoT) for measuring and monitoring sensors data of water surface platform. *2017 IEEE 7th International Conference on Underwater System Technology: theory and applications (USYS)*, 1–6. doi:10.1109/USYS.2017.8309441

Khan, M. A., & Salah, K. (2018). IoT security: Review, blockchain solutions, and open challenges. *Future Generation Computer Systems*, *82*, 395–411. doi:10.1016/j.future.2017.11.022

Li, T., Xia, M., Chen, J., Zhao, Y., & de Silva, C. (2017). Automated water quality survey and evaluation using an IoT platform with mobile sensor nodes. *Sensors (Basel)*, *17*(8), 1735. doi:10.339017081735 PMID:28788098

Menon, G. S., Ramesh, M. V., & Divya, P. (2017). A low cost wireless sensor network for water quality monitoring in natural water bodies. *2017 IEEE Global Humanitarian Technology Conference (GHTC)*, 1–8. 10.1109/GHTC.2017.8239341

Minerva, R., Biru, A., & Rotondi, D. (2015). Towards a definition of the Internet of Things (IoT). *IEEE IoT Initiative*. Retrieved from https://iot.ieee.org

Myint, C. Z., Gopal, L., & Aung, Y. L. (2017). Reconfigurable smart water quality monitoring system in IoT environment. *2017 IEEE/ACIS 16th International Conference on Computer and Information Science (ICIS)*, 435–440. doi:10.1109/ICIS.2017.7960032

Pappenberger, F., Cloke, H. L., Parker, D. J., Wetterhall, F., Richardson, D. S., & Thielen, J. (2015). The monetary benefit of early flood warnings in europe. *Environmental Science & Policy*, *51*, 278–291. doi:10.1016/j.envsci.2015.04.016

Parameswari, M., & Moses, M. B. (2017). Online measurement of water quality and reporting system using prominent rule controller based on aqua care-IOT. *Design Automation for Embedded Systems*. doi:10.100710617-017-9187-7

Pranata, A. A., Lee, J. M., & Kim, D. S. (2017). Towards an IoT-based water quality monitoring system with brokerless pub/sub architecture. *2017 IEEE International Symposium on Local and Metropolitan Area Networks (LANMAN)*, 1–6. 10.1109/LANMAN.2017.7972166

Salunke, P., & Kate, J. (2017). Advanced smart sensor interface in Internet of Things for water quality monitoring. *2017 International Conference on Data Management, Analytics and Innovation (ICDMAI)*, 298–302. 10.1109/ICDMAI.2017.8073529

Wong, B. P., & Kerkez, B. (2016). Real-time environmental sensor data: An application to water quality using web services. *Environmental Modelling & Software*, *84*, 505–517. doi:10.1016/j.envsoft.2016.07.020

Xiao, L., Wan, X., Lu, X., Zhang, Y., & Wu, D. (2018). IoT Security Techniques Based on Machine Learning: How do IoT Devices Use AI to Enhance Security? *IEEE Signal Processing Magazine*, *35*(5), 41–49. doi:10.1109/MSP.2018.2825478

ADDITIONAL READING

Alaba, F. A., Othman, M., Hashem, I. A. T., & Alotaibi, F. (2017). Internet of Things security: A survey. *Journal of Network and Computer Applications*, *88*, 10–28. doi:10.1016/j.jnca.2017.04.002

Chen, Y., Kar, S., & Moura, J. M. F. (2018). The Internet of Things: Secure distributed inference. *IEEE Signal Processing Magazine*, *35*(5), 64–75. doi:10.1109/MSP.2018.2842097

Hammi, M. T., Hammi, B., Bellot, P., & Serhrouchni, A. (2018). Bubbles of Trust: A decentralized blockchain-based authentication system for IoT. *Computers & Security*, *78*, 126–142. doi:10.1016/j.cose.2018.06.004

Hanes, D., Salgueiro, G., Grossetete, P., Barton, R., & Henry, J. (2017). *IoT Fundamentals: Networking Technologies, Protocols, and Use Cases for the Internet of Things*. Indianapolis, USA: Cisco Press.

Kouicem, D. E., Bouabdallah A., & Lakhlef H. (2018). Internet of things security: A top-down survey. *Computer Networks*, *141*, 199-221, doi:1016/j.comnet.2018.03.012.

Lopez, J., Rios, R., Bao, F., & Wang, G. (2017). Evolving privacy: From sensors to the Internet of Things. *Future Generation Computer Systems*, *75*, 46-57, doi:1016/j.future.2017.04.045.

Raj, A., & Raman, A. C. (2017). *The Internet of Things: Enabling Technologies, Platforms, and Use Cases*. London, England: CRCPress.

Unsalan, C., & Gurhan, H. D. (2014). *Programmable Microcontrollers with Applications: MSP430 LaunchPad with CCS and Grace*. New York: McGraw-Hill Professional.

KEY TERMS AND DEFINITIONS

Blockchain Technology: A decentralized and public digital ledger used to register transactions and other data, guaranteeing thrust on the recorded information, through a cryptographically secured chain of blocks.

Chemical Sensors: A chemical sensor measures the change in composition of a substance like the PH or the quantity of a substance in mole.

Cloud: A shared set of computing resources, with easy access and management, usually through the Internet. It may provide a very large and configurable set of resources: network, CPU, data storage, message brokerage, etc.

Computer Security: Area of study related to the protection of computer systems from harmful interference, potentially damaging to hardware, software or other data, eventually leading to information theft, misdirection of services or other unlawful events.

Data Transmission Protocols: A set of rules that define the way data is transferred between different agents. A data transmission protocol defines the physical media to the composition of the message itself, possible going through error detection and correction.

Internet of Things: A set of technologies, like microcomputers, communications networks and sensors combined and integrated to provide insight about different physical and chemical processes remotely.

Machine Learning: The field of science where algorithms that learn from data are studied and used for the purpose of object classification. These algorithms are applied to data analysis and used for the construction of models applied to prediction.

Physical Sensors: A sensor that measures the change in a physical parameter, like temperature or electric current, of a body or substance.

Water Quality Management Systems: Electronic systems that automatically collect data about physical and chemical properties of water. These systems may provide only raw data about the water characteristics, present this data as charts and other graphical view, or apply machine learning techniques to further enhance the water quality analysis.

Web Framework: Software providing a standard way to develop web applications, such as web services, web resources or application interface protocols. Web frameworks are usually developed for a single programming language.

Chapter 5
Ambient Assisted Living and Internet of Things

Gonçalo Marques
Universidade da Beira Interior, Portugal

ABSTRACT

The study of systems and architectures for ambient assisted living (AAL) is undoubtedly a topic of great relevance given the ageing of the world population. On the one hand, AAL technologies are designed to meet the needs of the ageing population in order to maintain their independence as long as possible. On the other hand, internet of things (IoT) proposes that various "things," which include not only communication devices but also every other physical object on the planet, are going to be connected and will be controlled across the internet. The continuous technological advancements turn possible to build smart objects with great capabilities for sensing and connecting turn possible several advancements in AAL and IoT systems architectures. Advances in networking, sensors, and embedded devices have made it possible to monitor and provide assistance to people in their homes. This chapter reviews the state of art on AAL and IoT and their applications for enhanced indoor living environments and occupational health.

INTRODUCTION

Ambient Assisted Living (AAL) is an emerging multi-disciplinary field aiming at providing an ecosystem of different types of sensors, computers, mobile devices, wireless networks and software applications for personal healthcare monitoring and telehealth systems ("Universal Open Platform and Reference Specification for Ambient Assisted Living: http://www.universaal.org/.," n.d.). AAL aims to addresses the technologies that can be used to increase the quality of life of elders or disabled by providing a secure and protected living environment (Bacciu, Barsocchi, Chessa, Gallicchio, & Micheli, 2014). A great diversity of scientific research groups from multiple areas merge efforts to create solutions to help people to stay at home as long as possible (Fuchsberger, 2008). AAL delivers significant opportunities in the progress of advanced Information and Communication Technology (ICT) solutions, services and systems with the aim to increase the quality of life, autonomy, social life participation and employability, reducing the costs of health and social care (Botia, Villa, & Palma, 2012). Ambient intelligence (AmI)

DOI: 10.4018/978-1-5225-7332-6.ch005

represents a generation of intelligence computing where a great diversity of sensors and computers stand everywhere and for everyone, AAL is a variety of AmI systems (Cubo, Nieto, & Pimentel, 2014). AAL solutions aim to assist the elderly people independently and actively living should leverage the efforts from both the technical side and social side. Currently, there are a divert of efforts done by the government side focusing on the social connections (Sun, Florio, Gui, & Blondia, 2009). AAL need to supply both those who are presently ageing and are more probable to be technology averse, and those who will be elderly in the next decade but who may be technology friendly (O'Grady, Muldoon, Dragone, Tynan, & O'Hare, 2010). AAL systems will lead to positive impacts on different dimensions of health and quality of life. The needs and problems of the elderly can be addressed by applying appropriate solutions which influence the physical, mental and social dimensions of quality of life (Siegel, Hochgatterer, & Dorner, 2014). Currently, there are different AAL projects based on several sensors for measuring weight, blood pressure, glucose, oxygen, temperature, location and position and which use wireless technologies such as ZigBee, Bluetooth, Ethernet and Wi-Fi. There's a lot of challenges in the design and implementation of an effective AAL system such as information architecture, interaction design, human-computer interaction, ergonomics, usability and accessibility (Koleva, Tonchev, Balabanov, Manolova, & Poulkov, 2015). There are also social and ethical problems such as the acceptance by the older adults and the privacy and confidentiality that should be a requisite of AAL devices. In fact, it is also important to ensure that technology does not replace the human care and should be used as an important complement. At 2050 20% of the world population will be age 60 or older ("UN,'Worldpopulationageing:1950–2050,'2001,pp.11–13.," n.d.) that will result in an increase of diseases, health care costs, shortage of caregivers, dependency and brutal social impact. The is a fact that 87% of people prefer to stay in their homes and support the enormous cost of nursing care ("Centers for Disease Control and Prevention, n.d.). The indoor living environments should be monitored in real time as typically people spend about 90% of their time in indoor environments. In the case of older people and new-borns who are most likely affected may spend all their time in indoor environments (Walsh, Dudney, & Copenhaver, 1983). In particular, indoor air quality (IAQ) is a significant determinant of personal exposure to pollutants. The assessment that indoor air quality indicators must thereby determine how well indoor air (a) satisfies thermal and respiratory requirements, (b) prevents unhealthy accumulation of pollutants, and (c) allows for a sense of well-being as proposed by (Gold, 1992). The Internet of Things (IoT) concept states that numerous "things", which include not only communication devices but also every other physical object on the planet, are going to be connected and will be controlled across the Internet (Atzori, Iera, & Morabito, 2010). IoT will increase the ubiquity of the Internet by integrating every object for interaction via embedded systems, which leads to a highly distributed network of devices communicating with human beings as well as other devices (Xia, Yang, Wang, & Vinel, 2012). Advances in low-cost sensor manufacturing, communication protocols, embedded systems, actuators and hardware miniaturization have contributed turn possible to create intelligent IoT architectures (Pattar, Buyya, Venugopal, Iyengar, & Patnaik, 2018). Physical objects are embedded in technology and connected to the Internet in order to turn them smart. Therefore the "smart things" linked with middleware services helps to address the challenges of day-to-day life. IoT offers ubiquitous connectivity provided by intelligent, automatic, smart, and context-aware physical objects that think and act intelligently, without explicit human involvement (Agiwal, Saxena, & Roy, 2018). IBM's studies reveal how new technologies support the development of the IoT to provides the foundational infrastructure for a smarter planet (van den Dam, 2013). IoT and AAL should continue side by side, mutually contributing with scientific advances in technologies for enhanced living environments and occupational health. As people typically spend more than 90% of their time in indoor environments, the indoor living environments must be perceived as an imperative variable to be controlled for the inhabitants' wellbeing and occupational health (Walsh et al., 1983). Recently, several new systems have been developed for monitoring environmental parameters, always with the aim of improving the indoor air quality efficiency and occupational health (Marques & Pitarma, 2016a, 2016b, 2017, 2018; Pitarma, Marques, & Ferreira, 2017). The availability of cheap, low power, and miniature embedded processors, radios, sensors, and actuators, often integrated on a single chip, is leading to the use of wireless communications and computing for interacting with the physical world in applications such as air quality control and healthcare ICT systems. Considerable research is being carried out on building intelligent environments around people and on "smart homes" in order to improve the independence of the elderly people and reduced the required manual work. Devices such as RFID, motion detector and wearable sensors are used to assist the daily lives of the elderly people (Sun et al., 2009). In this paper, the topic of smart homes, wearables sensors and the IoT and AAL related projects will be discussed.

BACKGROUND

Several technologies such as smart homes, assistive robots, e-textile and mobile and wearable technologies combined with IoT technologies and many algorithms such as activity recognition, context modelling, location identification, planning, and anomaly detection have conduct to the development of important systems for enhanced living environments and occupational health (Rashidi & Mihailidis, 2013). As people spend most of his time indoors smart homes are undoubtedly an important domain for AAL. The wearables sensors are closely related to IoT as they are used as a ubiquitous and pervasive way to collect medical data and offer connectivity for data communication and storage. In this section, the smart homes and wearables are analyzed.

Smart Homes

Smart homes have been researched for decades, the first project of Smart Rooms is implemented by the MIT Media Lab (Moukas, Zacharia, Guttman, & Maes, 2000), today exist three major categories of smart homes. The first category detects and recognizes the actions of its residents to determine their health. The second aims at storing and retrieving of multi-media captured within the smart home, in different levels from photos to experiences. The third category is surveillance, where the data captured in the environment are processed to obtain information that can help to raise alarms, in order to protect the home and the residents. Although, there is also a type of smart homes that have the objective to reduce the energy consumption by monitoring and controlling electric devices (De Silva, Morikawa, & Petra, 2012) (Figure 1).

Recent advances in information technology allowed lower prices of smart homes but provide them intelligence environments to make complex decisions remains a challenge. In the future smart home, the number will increase with the use of sensors that will put the data acquired in monitoring databases in real time.

Three broad views are introduced by (Wilson, Hargreaves, & Hauxwell-Baldwin, 2015): a functional view; an instrumental view; and a socio-technical view. The functional view sees smart homes as a way of better managing the demands of daily living through technology. The instrumental view emphasizes

Figure 1. Smart homes main functionalities

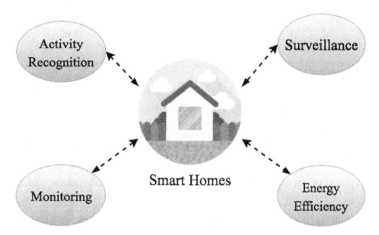

smart homes' potential for managing and reducing energy demand in households as part of a wider transition to a low-carbon future. The socio-technical view sees the smart home as the next wave of development in the ongoing electrification and digitalization of everyday life.

Smart home facilities are studied as one of the greatest promising markets since the infrastructure of mobile network environments and home security products are largely increasing (Park, Kim, Kim, & Kwon, 2018).

A smart home application is introduced by (Adib, Mao, Kabelac, Katabi, & Miller, 2015) called Vital-Radio, a wireless sensing technology that monitors breathing and heart rate without body contact, this demonstrates through a user study that it can track users' breathing and heart rates with a median accuracy of 99%. In Europe, some smart home projects include iDorm (Pounds-Cornish & Holmes, 2002), Gloucester Smart Home (Orpwood, Gibbs, Adlam, Faulkner, & Meegahawatte, 2004), CareLab (Henkemans, Caine, Rogers, & Fisk, 2007) and others. IoT brings significant advantages over traditional communication technologies for smart grid and smart home applications, however, these implementations are still very rare (Risteska Stojkoska & Trivodaliev, 2017). The IoT industry is directly related with smart homes as today homes incorporate intelligent objects that are connected to the Internet such as computers, tablets and smartphones (Decuir, 2015). In the near future developments in the IoT are related to data and on extracting actionable knowledge and providing value-added services. Smart homes should incorporate intelligent systems for data collection such as air quality monitoring and temperature monitoring for enhanced living environments and occupational health.

Smart homes are designed fundamentally for the elderly people in order to provide reliable care and to ensure safety and proper diagnosis by supervising the daily living, medicinal condition of the occupant and delivering feedback to the caregiver. An important feature of a smart home is the location detection. An IoT voice-based location detection system which can be integrated into a smart home and incorporates Amazon Echo as the voice interface and HC-SR04 ultrasonic sensor to detect the location of specific occupants is proposed by (Nath, Bajpai, & Thapliyal, 2018).

Security and privacy are the main problems for the practical purpose of smart home technologies. Scientific advances continue to be conducted in order to solve these problems. For instance, a secure data uploading scheme, which ensures that the cloud validates the data integrity while avoiding malicious home gateways that monitor and modify the data is proposed by (Shen et al., 2018). A Blockchain implementation for enhanced security and privacy for smart homes was presented by (Dorri, Kanhere, Jurdak, & Gauravaram, 2017).

Wearables

Wearable sensors are used in a large scale for AAL. The use of wearable sensors along with data treatment algorithms and visualization tools allow to better measure and describe real-life environments, mobility, physical activity, and physiological responses. A project that uses wearable sensors to collect real-life data among pediatric patients with cardiometabolic risk factors is proposed by Yan et al. (2014).

In AAL domains there are also notable projects that use a wearable headband for electroencephalogram (EEG) based detection of emotions allowing the evaluation of the quality of life of assisted people (Matiko et al., 2015).

Currently, the smartwatch incorporates a wide range of sensors and wireless communication technologies that can be used to create ubiquitous and pervasive health monitoring solutions. Therefore, smartwatches have excellent processing and storage capabilities that make possible to the end user a ubiquitous, a quick, easy and intuitive access to important physiological information (Figure 2).

Wearable motion sensors can help to detect behavioral anomaly situation in smart AAL by collected motion data combined with locational context (Zhu, Sheng, & Liu, 2015).

Wearable technologies can be used to reduce the expenditure on health care by enabling people to be monitored in their own homes, rather than in hospitals, for a fraction of the cost (López, Corno, & Russis, 2015). Wristbands are used as non-invasive sensors for measuring and monitoring various physiological parameters such as ECG, EEG, EDA, respiration, and even biochemical processes such as wound healing (Acampora, Cook, Rashidi, & Vasilakos, 2013).

Figure 2. Smartwatch

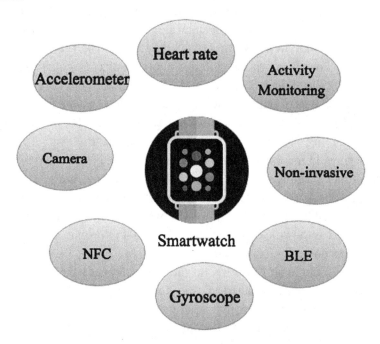

Today systems can take advantage of wearable computing devices with embedded camera by determining the user position and orientation by using visual odometry and SLAM (simultaneous localization and mapping) techniques to design assisted living systems capable to offer such guidance with on-site augmented reality, without introducing changes in the environment and using off-the-shelf equipment (Saracchini & Catalina, 2015).

There are also systems for promoting an active and healthy lifestyle for people and to recommend with guidelines and valuable information about their habits that incorporate wearable bio-signals sensors and machine learning algorithms (Páez, de Buenaga Rodríguez, Sánz, Villalba, & Gil, 2015).

HealthMon is a framework towards accessible mobile health that repurposes an affordable, retail wristband to clinical monitoring scenarios e.g. dementia, Parkinson's or ageing and it's used to real-time health monitoring and contextualized alerts proposed by (Stavropoulos, Meditskos, Andreadis, & Kompatsiaris, 2015).

Non-invasive wearable sensors for health monitoring are expected to provide low-cost solutions for remote monitoring of elderly people at home or in nursing homes and lead to major improvements in patient monitoring and care (Bandodkar & Wang, 2014).

Nowadays wearable sensors are used to predict and monitoring patients by combining clinical observations, identification of "abnormal" physiological data arising due to patient deterioration (Clifton, Clifton, Pimentel, Watkinson, & Tarassenko, 2014).

Wearable sensors are also used for recognizing academic performance, sleep quality, stress level, and mental health using personality traits, wearable sensors and mobile phones with a classification accuracies ranged from 67-92% (Sano et al., 2015). A new method for predicting depression using passive sensing data from students' smartphones and wearables are proposed by (Wang et al., 2018).

Rehabilitation programs are critical for stroke patients to regain daily living skills. Using wearable sensors is possible to provide an accurate and objective assessment of the motor function that is indispensable to plan the clinical treatment (Tseng, Liu, Hsieh, Hsu, & Chan, 2018).

The review of the state of art shows us intelligent systems and very interesting projects that lead us to the assertion of wearable sensors as having an extremely important role in the future and presents of the AAL systems.

IOT AND AAL

The IoT and AAL are closely related themes not only in terms of objectives but also in terms of technologies used. These two domains should be developed working side-by-side aiming at the creation of efficient systems for enhanced living environments and occupational health.

IoT is a paradigm where objects are connected to the internet and have sense capabilities. AAL combined with the IoT is a promising solution for the elderly public, promoting more autonomy, security, and quality of life (de Podestá Gaspar, Bonacin, & Gonçalves, 2018). Tendentiously IoT devices should be ubiquitous, context-aware and will enable ambient intelligence features directly related to AAL. IoT systems incorporate RFID, NFC and Sensor Networks at hardware level working with standards and protocols to support machine-to-machine communication such as those envisioned for the semantic web. IoT holds the promise of improving people's lives through both automation and augmentation at low cost (Whitmore, Agarwal, & Da Xu, 2015).

IoT devices are typically wireless and exposed to the public range, the ownership of data collected from IoT devices must be clearly established. In fact, IoT devices should use encryption methods and be equipped with privacy policies.

In order to address privacy issues AmbLEDs project, an ambient sensing system, proposes the use of LEDs instead of other types of more invasive sensors such as cameras and microphones for interact with people in AAL environments (Cunha & Fuks, 2014).

Humans will often be the integral parts of the IoT system and therefore IoT will affect every aspect of human lives (Stankovic, 2014). An example of IoT combined with AAL is proposed by (Suryadevara, Kelly, & Mukhopadhyay, 2014) where are we reported an integrated platform for monitoring and controlling of household that uses ZigBee Wireless network. SPHERE Project (Ni Zhu et al., 2015) aim to build a generic platform that fuses complementary sensor data to generate rich datasets that support the detection and management of various health conditions. This project uses three sensing technologies: environment, video, and wearable sensing. SPHERE is a really amazing Project that makes a very good bridge between IoT and AAL.

A cloud-based IoT platform for AAL is proposed by (Cubo et al., 2014), where the main objective is to manage the integration and behaviour-aware orchestration of devices as services stored and accessed via the cloud in AAL applications.

Technologies with a few years such as RFID are still used today in IoT and AAL domains in the development of intelligent systems that can detect user-object interactions via a supervised machine learning algorithm with a 86% accuracy (Parada, Segui, Cinos, Carreras, & Pous, 2015).

Home Health Hub Internet of Things (H3IoT) is a novel architectural framework for monitoring the health of elderly people at home and is an interesting IoT and AAL combination (Ray, 2014).

An unobtrusive sleep monitoring pillow that monitors breathing patterns and overall sleep quality quantifying five variables whose thresholds can be varied by medical staff based on IoT is proposed by (Veiga, Garcia, Parra, Lloret, & Augele, 2018). This system employs an intelligent algorithm that utilizes the gathered information to make decisions to improve the sleep quality of the user.

A smart-home IoT infrastructure for the support and extension of the independent living of older adults in their living environments that respond also to real needs of caregivers and public authorities was proposed by (Stavrotheodoros, Kaklanis, Votis, & Tzovaras, 2018).

A personal diabetes management device based on IoT that aims to provide a new mobile assistance service for insulin therapy and reduce the number of the patient hyperglycemia and hypoglycemia incidents and consequently their risks is proposed by (Jara, Zamora, & Skarmeta, 2011). Elderly Monitoring service is an IoT module of the SOCIALIZE platform, whose aim is to collect environmental and physical user data so that they can be supervised by medical and caregiver staffs was proposed by (Miori & Russo, 2017). With the quick development of the IoT and cloud computing, emerging trends and applications of cloud-based IoT in healthcare become evident. As described earlier there are several projects that show how the combination of the IoT paradigm combined with AAL systems allow the creation of important solutions that aim to solve common problems to both areas and reduce the cost of implementation.

IOT AND AAL: CHALLENGES

In spite of all enhancements done by IoT and AAL systems several challenges still exist in the implementation and design of ubiquitous and pervasive systems for enhanced living environments.

Research in AAL and IoT domains conclude that IoT systems not only fit most of AAL requirement and characteristics, but it also provides a significant coverage to empower the AAL real-life system chances to sustain and succeed face the dynamic and continuously requests for changes, adaption and extension add to the hardware related issues (Ben Hmida & Braun, 2017). IoT and AAL projects for elderly people require special attention because of their cognitive and physical limitations, therefore, AAL has several challenges. At the design level, the AAL systems must be as simple as possible and the wearable sensors must be compatible with body size. Therefore, the energy consumption is also very important, these systems must have a considerable battery lifespan in order to permit convenient use. The interaction must be made using objects such as smartphone and TV with which you are familiar in order to avoid stigma.

The provision of housing suited to their needs and their health status or of adequate support for adapting their housing, healthcare and services according to their physical state and measures must guarantee elderly persons to have appropriate support in terms of privacy and participation in setting minimum requirement for their comfort in the society and must be assumed as an important challenge (Geman et al., 2015).

If older adults perceive the value of having AAL systems installed in their homes, then they are prone to assume them as part of their lives and in other hand notification badges and audio-enhanced user interfaces, can be used to persuade the elderly to approach the system and eventually use it (Muñoz, Gutierrez, & Ochoa, 2015).

The integration of AAL services relates to interoperability, dynamic configuration, communication, context awareness (cognitive architectures) and the future AAL systems should have great security methods based on biometric and physiological features to safeguard user privacy (Li, Lu, & McDonald-Maier, 2015).

Smart connectivity in an AAL context relates to the availability of a reliable data channel between devices and between the human and devices and enabling an interface to the cloud/network where information gets personalized (Mihovska & Sarkar, 2018).

Important considerations about designing user interfaces and mechanisms for enhanced living environments for elderly people are considered by (Grguric, Gil, Huljenic, Car, & Podobnik, 2016).

Improving dependability, reliability, increasing standardization and interoperability stand as another important challenge of AAL systems (Monekosso, Florez-Revuelta, & Remagnino, 2015). Assistive robotics and socially interactive robotics raise privacy, the safety of the end user and wider social impact of the augmentation or replacement by human care through robots as great ethical issues (Felzmann, Murphy, Casey, & Beyan, 2015). The smart homes based on IoT not only require a framework for secure communication between internal and external entities but also a standardized key management to deliver confidentiality, tempering or reverse in smart meter and legal and strong framework for the privacy of user (Ali, Dustgeer, Awais, & Shah, 2017). Regarding the wearables sensors, there are also several challenges to be overcome such as communication reliability, transmission infrastructure, energy availability versus communication requirements, power interruptions and interoperability (Balsamo et al., 2017).

All described challenges must be considered in the design and architecture of IoT and AAL systems since it depends on the success and practical accomplishment of the developed systems.

CONCLUSION AND FUTURE DIRECTIONS

IoT is a paradigm that aims to improve the quality of human life. The main elements of IoT are identification, sensing, communication, computation, services and semantic. IoT systems and AAL will continue side by side mutually contributing scientific advances in assisted living allowing also lower the cost of assisted living systems.

This chapter presented an overview of IoT and AAL concepts focus on smart homes, wearables sensors and health systems and should provide a good transversal vision of IoT and AAL technologies. Currently, exist several IoT platforms and in spite of the technological evolution, several open issues continue to exist such as standardization, security and privacy, power and energy efficiency, intelligence, integration methodology, Big data, pricing, storage, network communications, scalability and flexibility.

AAL is an important domain to solve the independence problems of older adults and combined with smart homes, smartphones, wearable technology and IoT technologies offer several opportunities to answer emergency problems, disabilities and diseases. In despite of AAL systems benefits and technology advancements, human care never should be replaced.

IoT stands as a significant concept to enhance our day to day activities in several domains such as buildings, industry, healthcare, agriculture and education. IoT will enable smart cities, smart homes, smart agriculture, smart industrial and manufacturing process. In the near future, new research methods and technologies will increase the number of intelligent systems installed in the regular people houses. IoT and AAL will provide the base to create medical systems that could be bought by the regular user in a supermarket and be easily installed in their homes. Furthermore, the majority of living environments will be supervised in real-time providing notifications to alert the user in case of poor ambient quality. Our habitat will be constantly monitored and the data collected will be shared with the medical expert to correlate health complications with bad behaviors of the patient and support clinical evaluation.

REFERENCES

Acampora, G., Cook, D. J., Rashidi, P., & Vasilakos, A. V. (2013). A Survey on Ambient Intelligence in Health Care. *Proceedings of the IEEE*, *101*(12), 2470–2494. 10.1109/JPROC.2013.2262913

Aced López, S., Corno, F., & De Russis, L. (2015). Supporting caregivers in assisted living facilities for persons with disabilities: A user study. *Universal Access in the Information Society*, *14*(1), 133–144. doi:10.100710209-014-0400-1

Adib, F., Mao, H., Kabelac, Z., Katabi, D., & Miller, R. C. (2015). Smart Homes that Monitor Breathing and Heart Rate. In *Proceedings of the 33rd Annual ACM Conference on Human Factors in Computing Systems* (pp. 837–846). Seoul, Republic of Korea: ACM. 10.1145/2702123.2702200

Agiwal, M., Saxena, N., & Roy, A. (2018). Towards Connected Living: 5G Enabled Internet of Things (IoT). *IETE Technical Review*, 1–13. doi:10.1080/02564602.2018.1444516

Ali, W., Dustgeer, G., Awais, M., & Shah, M. A. (2017). IoT based smart home: Security challenges, security requirements and solutions. In *2017 23rd International Conference on Automation and Computing (ICAC)* (pp. 1–6). Huddersfield, UK: IEEE. 10.23919/IConAC.2017.8082057

Atzori, L., Iera, A., & Morabito, G. (2010). The Internet of Things: A survey. *Computer Networks*, *54*(15), 2787–2805. doi:10.1016/j.comnet.2010.05.010

Bacciu, D., Barsocchi, P., Chessa, S., Gallicchio, C., & Micheli, A. (2014). An experimental characterization of reservoir computing in ambient assisted living applications. *Neural Computing & Applications*, *24*(6), 1451–1464. doi:10.100700521-013-1364-4

Balsamo, D., Merrett, G. V., Zaghari, B., Wei, Y., Ramchurn, S., Stein, S., … Beeby, S. (2017). Wearable and autonomous computing for future smart cities: Open challenges. In *2017 25th International Conference on Software, Telecommunications and Computer Networks (SoftCOM)* (pp. 1–5). IEEE. 10.23919/SOFTCOM.2017.8115596

Bandodkar, A. J., & Wang, J. (2014). Non-invasive wearable electrochemical sensors: A review. *Trends in Biotechnology*, *32*(7), 363–371. doi:10.1016/j.tibtech.2014.04.005 PMID:24853270

Ben Hmida, H., & Braun, A. (2017). Enabling an Internet of Things Framework for Ambient Assisted Living. In R. Wichert & B. Mand (Eds.), *Ambient Assisted Living* (pp. 181–196). Cham: Springer International Publishing. doi:10.1007/978-3-319-52322-4_13

Botia, J. A., Villa, A., & Palma, J. (2012). Ambient Assisted Living system for in-home monitoring of healthy independent elders. *Expert Systems with Applications*, *39*(9), 8136–8148. doi:10.1016/j.eswa.2012.01.153

Centers for Disease Control and Prevention. (n.d.). *The state of aging and health in America 2007.* Available: https://www.cdc.gov/aging/pdf/saha_2007.pdf

Clifton, L., Clifton, D. A., Pimentel, M. A. F., Watkinson, P. J., & Tarassenko, L. (2014). Predictive Monitoring of Mobile Patients by Combining Clinical Observations With Data From Wearable Sensors. *Biomedical and Health Informatics. IEEE Journal of*, *18*(3), 722–730. doi:10.1109/JBHI.2013.2293059 PMID:24808218

Cubo, J., Nieto, A., & Pimentel, E. (2014). A Cloud-Based Internet of Things Platform for Ambient Assisted Living. *Sensors (Basel)*, *14*(8), 14070–14105. doi:10.3390140814070 PMID:25093343

Cunha, M., & Fuks, H. (2014). AmbLEDs para ambientes de moradia assistidos em cidades inteligentes. In *Proceedings of the 13th Brazilian Symposium on Human Factors in Computing Systems* (pp. 409–412). Foz do Iguaçu, Brazil: Sociedade Brasileira de Computação.

de Podestá Gaspar, R., Bonacin, R., & Gonçalves, V. P. (2018). Designing IoT Solutions for Elderly Home Care: A Systematic Study of Participatory Design, Personas and Semiotics. In M. Antona & C. Stephanidis (Eds.), *Universal Access in Human-Computer Interaction. Virtual, Augmented, and Intelligent Environments* (Vol. 10908, pp. 226–245). Cham: Springer International Publishing; doi:10.1007/978-3-319-92052-8_18

De Silva, L. C., Morikawa, C., & Petra, I. M. (2012). State of the art of smart homes. *Advanced Issues in Artificial Intelligence and Pattern Recognition for Intelligent Surveillance System in Smart Home Environment, 25*(7), 1313–1321. doi:10.1016/j.engappai.2012.05.002

Decuir, J. (2015). The Story of the Internet of Things: Issues in utility, connectivity, and security. *IEEE Consumer Electronics Magazine, 4*(4), 54–61. doi:10.1109/MCE.2015.2463292

Dorri, A., Kanhere, S. S., Jurdak, R., & Gauravaram, P. (2017). Blockchain for IoT security and privacy: The case study of a smart home. In *2017 IEEE International Conference on Pervasive Computing and Communications Workshops (PerCom Workshops)* (pp. 618–623). Kona, HI: IEEE. 10.1109/PERCOMW.2017.7917634

Felzmann, H., Murphy, K., Casey, D., & Beyan, O. (2015). *Robot-assisted care for elderly with dementia: is there a potential for genuine end-user empowerment?* Academic Press. doi:10.130258sg6q

Fuchsberger, V. (2008). Ambient assisted living: elderly people's needs and how to face them. In *Proceeding of the 1st ACM international workshop on Semantic ambient media experiences - SAME '08* (p. 21). Vancouver, Canada: ACM Press. 10.1145/1461912.1461917

Geman, O., Sanei, S., Costin, H.-N., Eftaxias, K., Vysata, O., Prochazka, A., & Lhotska, L. (2015). Challenges and trends in Ambient Assisted Living and intelligent tools for disabled and elderly people. *Computational Intelligence for Multimedia Understanding (IWCIM), 2015 International Workshop on*, 1–5. 10.1109/IWCIM.2015.7347088

Gold, D. R. (1992). Indoor air pollution. *Clinics in Chest Medicine, 13*(2), 215–229. PMID:1511550

Grguric, A., Gil, A. M., Huljenic, D., Car, Z., & Podobnik, V. (2016). A Survey on User Interaction Mechanisms for Enhanced Living Environments. In S. Loshkovska & S. Koceski (Eds.), *ICT Innovations 2015* (Vol. 399, pp. 131–141). Springer International Publishing; doi:10.1007/978-3-319-25733-4_14

Henkemans, O. B., Caine, K. E., Rogers, W. A., & Fisk, A. D. (2007). Medical monitoring for independent living: user-centered design of smart home technologies for older adults. *Proc. Med-e-Tel Conf. eHealth, Telemedicine and Health Information and Communication Technologies*, 18–20.

Jara, A. J., Zamora, M. A., & Skarmeta, A. F. G. (2011). An internet of things–based personal device for diabetes therapy management in ambient assisted living (AAL). *Personal and Ubiquitous Computing, 15*(4), 431–440. doi:10.100700779-010-0353-1

Koleva, P., Tonchev, K., Balabanov, G., Manolova, A., & Poulkov, V. (2015). Challenges in designing and implementation of an effective Ambient Assisted Living system. *Telecommunication in Modern Satellite, Cable and Broadcasting Services (TELSIKS), 2015 12th International Conference on*, 305–308. 10.1109/TELSKS.2015.7357793

Li, R., Lu, B., & McDonald-Maier, K. D. (2015). Cognitive assisted living ambient system: A survey. *Digital Communications and Networks, 1*(4), 229–252. doi:10.1016/j.dcan.2015.10.003

Marques, G., & Pitarma, R. (2016a). An indoor monitoring system for ambient assisted living based on internet of things architecture. *International Journal of Environmental Research and Public Health*, *13*(11), 1152. doi:10.3390/ijerph13111152 PMID:27869682

Marques, G., & Pitarma, R. (2016b). Health informatics for indoor air quality monitoring. In *Information Systems and Technologies (CISTI), 2016 11th Iberian Conference on* (pp. 1–6). AISTI. 10.1109/CISTI.2016.7521375

Marques, G., & Pitarma, R. (2017). Monitoring Health Factors in Indoor Living Environments Using Internet of Things. In Á. Rocha, A. M. Correia, H. Adeli, L. P. Reis, & S. Costanzo (Eds.), *Recent Advances in Information Systems and Technologies* (Vol. 570, pp. 785–794). Cham: Springer International Publishing; doi:10.1007/978-3-319-56538-5_79

Marques, G., & Pitarma, R. (2018). IAQ Evaluation Using an IoT CO2 Monitoring System for Enhanced Living Environments. In Á. Rocha, H. Adeli, L. P. Reis, & S. Costanzo (Eds.), *Trends and Advances in Information Systems and Technologies* (Vol. 746, pp. 1169–1177). Cham: Springer International Publishing; doi:10.1007/978-3-319-77712-2_112

Matiko, J. W., Wei, Y., Torah, R., Grabham, N., Paul, G., Beeby, S., & Tudor, J. (2015). Wearable EEG headband using printed electrodes and powered by energy harvesting for emotion monitoring in ambient assisted living. *Smart Materials and Structures*, *24*(12), 125028. doi:10.1088/0964-1726/24/12/125028

Mihovska, A., & Sarkar, M. (2018). Smart Connectivity for Internet of Things (IoT) Applications. In R. R. Yager & J. Pascual Espada (Eds.), *New Advances in the Internet of Things* (Vol. 715, pp. 105–118). Cham: Springer International Publishing; doi:10.1007/978-3-319-58190-3_7

Miori, V., & Russo, D. (2017). *Improving life quality for the elderly through the Social Internet of Things (SIoT). In 2017 Global Internet of Things Summit (GIoTS)* (pp. 1–6). Geneva, Switzerland: IEEE. doi:10.1109/GIOTS.2017.8016215

Monekosso, D. N., Florez-Revuelta, F., & Remagnino, P. (2015). Guest Editorial Special Issue on Ambient-Assisted Living: Sensors, Methods, and Applications. *Human-Machine Systems. IEEE Transactions On*, *45*(5), 545–549. doi:10.1109/THMS.2015.2458019

Moukas, A., Zacharia, G., Guttman, R., & Maes, P. (2000). Agent-Mediated Electronic Commerce: An MIT Media Laboratory Perspective. *International Journal of Electronic Commerce*, *4*(3), 5–21. doi:10.1080/10864415.2000.11518369

Muñoz, D., Gutierrez, F., & Ochoa, S. (2015). Introducing Ambient Assisted Living Technology at the Home of the Elderly: Challenges and Lessons Learned. In I. Cleland, L. Guerrero, & J. Bravo (Eds.), Ambient Assisted Living. ICT-based Solutions in Real Life Situations (Vol. 9455, pp. 125–136). Springer International Publishing. Retrieved from doi:10.1007/978-3-319-26410-3_12

Nath, R. K., Bajpai, R., & Thapliyal, H. (2018). IoT based indoor location detection system for smart home environment. In *2018 IEEE International Conference on Consumer Electronics (ICCE)* (pp. 1–3). Las Vegas, NV: IEEE. 10.1109/ICCE.2018.8326225

O'Grady, M. J., Muldoon, C., Dragone, M., Tynan, R., & O'Hare, G. M. P. (2010). Towards evolutionary ambient assisted living systems. *Journal of Ambient Intelligence and Humanized Computing*, *1*(1), 15–29. doi:10.100712652-009-0003-5

Orpwood, R., Gibbs, C., Adlam, T., Faulkner, R., & Meegahawatte, D. (2004). The Gloucester Smart House for People with Dementia — User-Interface Aspects. In S. Keates, J. Clarkson, P. Langdon, & P. Robinson (Eds.), *Designing a More Inclusive World* (pp. 237–245). Springer London; doi:10.1007/978-0-85729-372-5_24

Páez, D., de Buenaga Rodríguez, M., Sánz, E., Villalba, M., & Gil, R. (2015). Big Data Processing Using Wearable Devices for Wellbeing and Healthy Activities Promotion. In I. Cleland, L. Guerrero, & J. Bravo (Eds.), Ambient Assisted Living. ICT-based Solutions in Real Life Situations (Vol. 9455, pp. 196–205). Springer International Publishing. Retrieved from doi:10.1007/978-3-319-26410-3_19

Parada, R., Melia-Segui, J., Morenza-Cinos, M., Carreras, A., & Pous, R. (2015). Using RFID to Detect Interactions in Ambient Assisted Living Environments. *IEEE Intelligent Systems*, *30*(4), 16–22. doi:10.1109/MIS.2015.43

Park, E., Kim, S., Kim, Y., & Kwon, S. J. (2018). Smart home services as the next mainstream of the ICT industry: Determinants of the adoption of smart home services. *Universal Access in the Information Society*, *17*(1), 175–190. doi:10.100710209-017-0533-0

Pattar, S., Buyya, R., Venugopal, K. R., Iyengar, S. S., & Patnaik, L. M. (2018). Searching for the IoT Resources: Fundamentals, Requirements, Comprehensive Review and Future Directions. *IEEE Communications Surveys and Tutorials*, 1–1. doi:10.1109/COMST.2018.2825231

Pitarma, R., Marques, G., & Ferreira, B. R. (2017). Monitoring Indoor Air Quality for Enhanced Occupational Health. *Journal of Medical Systems*, *41*(2), 23. doi:10.100710916-016-0667-2 PMID:28000117

Pounds-Cornish, A., & Holmes, A. (2002). The iDorm - A Practical Deployment of Grid Technology. In *Cluster Computing and the Grid, 2002. 2nd IEEE/ACM International Symposium on* (pp. 470–470). IEEE. 10.1109/CCGRID.2002.1017192

Rashidi, P., & Mihailidis, A. (2013). A Survey on Ambient-Assisted Living Tools for Older Adults. *Biomedical and Health Informatics. IEEE Journal of*, *17*(3), 579–590. doi:10.1109/JBHI.2012.2234129

Ray, P. P. (2014). Home Health Hub Internet of Things (H3IoT): An architectural framework for monitoring health of elderly people. In *Science Engineering and Management Research (ICSEMR), 2014 International Conference on* (pp. 1–3). Academic Press. 10.1109/ICSEMR.2014.7043542

Risteska Stojkoska, B. L., & Trivodaliev, K. V. (2017). A review of Internet of Things for smart home: Challenges and solutions. *Journal of Cleaner Production*, *140*, 1454–1464. doi:10.1016/j.jclepro.2016.10.006

Sano, A., Phillips, A. J., Yu, A. Z., McHill, A. W., Taylor, S., Jaques, N., … Picard, R. W. (2015). Recognizing academic performance, sleep quality, stress level, and mental health using personality traits, wearable sensors and mobile phones. In *Wearable and Implantable Body Sensor Networks (BSN), 2015 IEEE 12th International Conference on* (pp. 1–6). IEEE. 10.1109/BSN.2015.7299420

Saracchini, R. F. V., & Catalina, C. A. (2015). An augmented reality platform for wearable assisted living systems. *Journal of Theoretical and Applied Computer Science*, *9*(1), 56–79.

Shen, J., Wang, C., Li, T., Chen, X., Huang, X., & Zhan, Z.-H. (2018). Secure data uploading scheme for a smart home system. *Information Sciences*, *453*, 186–197. doi:10.1016/j.ins.2018.04.048

Siegel, C., Hochgatterer, A., & Dorner, T. E. (2014). Contributions of ambient assisted living for health and quality of life in the elderly and care services - a qualitative analysis from the experts' perspective of care service professionals. *BMC Geriatrics*, *14*(1), 112. doi:10.1186/1471-2318-14-112 PMID:25326149

Stankovic, J. A. (2014). Research Directions for the Internet of Things. *Internet of Things Journal, IEEE*, *1*(1), 3–9. doi:10.1109/JIOT.2014.2312291

Stavropoulos, T. G., Meditskos, G., Andreadis, S., & Kompatsiaris, I. (2015). Real-time health monitoring and contextualised alerts using wearables. In *Interactive Mobile Communication Technologies and Learning (IMCL), 2015 International Conference on* (pp. 358–363). Academic Press. 10.1109/IMCTL.2015.7359619

Stavrotheodoros, S., Kaklanis, N., Votis, K., & Tzovaras, D. (2018). A Smart-Home IoT Infrastructure for the Support of Independent Living of Older Adults. In L. Iliadis, I. Maglogiannis, & V. Plagianakos (Eds.), *Artificial Intelligence Applications and Innovations* (Vol. 520, pp. 238–249). Cham: Springer International Publishing; doi:10.1007/978-3-319-92016-0_22

Sun, H., Florio, V. D., Gui, N., & Blondia, C. (2009). Promises and Challenges of Ambient Assisted Living Systems. In *2009 Sixth International Conference on Information Technology: New Generations* (pp. 1201–1207). Las Vegas, NV: IEEE. 10.1109/ITNG.2009.169

Suryadevara, N. K., Kelly, S., & Mukhopadhyay, S. C. (2014). Ambient Assisted Living Environment Towards Internet of Things Using Multifarious Sensors Integrated with XBee Platform. In S. C. Mukhopadhyay (Ed.), *Internet of Things* (Vol. 9, pp. 217–231). Springer International Publishing. doi:10.1007/978-3-319-04223-7_9

Tseng, M.-C., Liu, K.-C., Hsieh, C.-Y., Hsu, S. J., & Chan, C.-T. (2018). Gesture spotting algorithm for door opening using single wearable sensor. In *2018 IEEE International Conference on Applied System Invention (ICASI)* (pp. 854–856). Chiba: IEEE. 10.1109/ICASI.2018.8394398

UN. (n.d.). *World population ageing: 1950–2050*. UN.

Universal Open Platform and Reference Specification for Ambient Assisted Living. (n.d.). Retrieved from http://www.universaal.org/

van den Dam, R. (2013). Internet of Things: The Foundational Infrastructure for a Smarter Planet. In S. Balandin, S. Andreev, & Y. Koucheryavy (Eds.), *Internet of Things, Smart Spaces, and Next Generation Networking* (Vol. 8121, pp. 1–12). Berlin: Springer Berlin Heidelberg. doi:10.1007/978-3-642-40316-3_1

Veiga, A., Garcia, L., Parra, L., Lloret, J., & Augele, V. (2018). An IoT-based smart pillow for sleep quality monitoring in AAL environments. In *2018 Third International Conference on Fog and Mobile Edge Computing (FMEC)* (pp. 175–180). Barcelona: IEEE. 10.1109/FMEC.2018.8364061

Walsh, P. J., Dudney, C. S., & Copenhaver, E. D. (1983). *Indoor air quality*. CRC Press.

Wang, R., Wang, W., daSilva, A., Huckins, J. F., Kelley, W. M., Heatherton, T. F., & Campbell, A. T. (2018). Tracking Depression Dynamics in College Students Using Mobile Phone and Wearable Sensing. *Proceedings of the ACM on Interactive, Mobile, Wearable and Ubiquitous Technologies, 2*(1), 1–26. 10.1145/3191775

Whitmore, A., Agarwal, A., & Da Xu, L. (2015). The Internet of Things—A survey of topics and trends. *Information Systems Frontiers, 17*(2), 261–274. doi:10.100710796-014-9489-2

Wilson, C., Hargreaves, T., & Hauxwell-Baldwin, R. (2015). Smart homes and their users: A systematic analysis and key challenges. *Personal and Ubiquitous Computing, 19*(2), 463–476. doi:10.100700779-014-0813-0

Xia, F., Yang, L. T., Wang, L., & Vinel, A. (2012). Internet of Things. *International Journal of Communication Systems, 25*(9), 1101–1102. doi:10.1002/dac.2417

Yan, K., Tracie, B., Marie, M., Melanie, H., Jean-Luc, B., Benoit, T., & Marie, L. (2014). Innovation through Wearable Sensors to Collect Real-Life Data among Pediatric Patients with Cardiometabolic Risk Factors. *International Journal of Pediatrics, 2014*, 9. doi:10.1155/2014/328076 PMID:24678323

Zhu, C., Sheng, W., & Liu, M. (2015). Wearable Sensor-Based Behavioral Anomaly Detection in Smart Assisted Living Systems. *Automation Science and Engineering. IEEE Transactions on, 12*(4), 1225–1234. doi:10.1109/TASE.2015.2474743

Zhu, N., Diethe, T., Camplani, M., Tao, L., Burrows, A., Twomey, N., ... Craddock, I. (2015). Bridging e-Health and the Internet of Things: The SPHERE Project. *IEEE Intelligent Systems, 30*(4), 39–46. doi:10.1109/MIS.2015.57

ADDITIONAL READING

Aced López, S., Corno, F., & De Russis, L. (2015). Supporting caregivers in assisted living facilities for persons with disabilities: A user study. *Universal Access in the Information Society, 14*(1), 133–144. doi:10.100710209-014-0400-1

Atzori, L., Iera, A., & Morabito, G. (2010). The Internet of Things: A survey. *Computer Networks, 54*(15), 2787–2805. doi:10.1016/j.comnet.2010.05.010

Miori, V., & Russo, D. (2017). *Improving life quality for the elderly through the Social Internet of Things (SIoT). In 2017 Global Internet of Things Summit (GIoTS)* (pp. 1–6). Geneva, Switzerland: IEEE; doi:10.1109/GIOTS.2017.8016215

Park, E., Kim, S., Kim, Y., & Kwon, S. J. (2018). Smart home services as the next mainstream of the ICT industry: Determinants of the adoption of smart home services. *Universal Access in the Information Society, 17*(1), 175–190. doi:10.100710209-017-0533-0

Pattar, S., Buyya, R., Venugopal, K. R., Iyengar, S. S., & Patnaik, L. M. (2018). Searching for the IoT Resources: Fundamentals, Requirements, Comprehensive Review and Future Directions. *IEEE Communications Surveys and Tutorials*, 1–1. doi:10.1109/COMST.2018.2825231

Wearable and autonomous computing for future smart cities: Open challenges. In *2017 25th International Conference on Software, Telecommunications and Computer Networks (SoftCOM)* (pp. 1–5). Split: IEEE. doi:10.23919/SOFTCOM.2017.8115596

Wilson, C., Hargreaves, T., & Hauxwell-Baldwin, R. (2015). Smart homes and their users: A systematic analysis and key challenges. *Personal and Ubiquitous Computing*, *19*(2), 463–476. doi:10.100700779-014-0813-0

Xia, F., Yang, L. T., Wang, L., & Vinel, A. (2012). Internet of Things. *International Journal of Communication Systems*, *25*(9), 1101–1102. doi:10.1002/dac.2417

KEY TERMS AND DEFINITIONS

Ambient Assisted Living: An emerging multi-disciplinary field aiming at providing an ecosystem of different types of sensors, computers, mobile devices, wireless networks and software applications for personal healthcare monitoring and telehealth systems.

Ambient Intelligence: A concept that deals with a new world where computing devices are spread everywhere, allowing the human being to interact in physical world environments in an intelligent and unobtrusive way.

Internet of Things: The concept that refers numerous "things," which include not only communication devices but also every other physical object on the planet, are going to be connected and will be controlled across the Internet.

Personal Healthcare: Healthcare centered on the patient and provided anytime, anywhere, inside and outside the institutional points of care.

Smart Cities: Cities who adopt scalable solutions and computer science solutions to increase efficiencies, reduce costs, and enhance the quality of life.

Smart Homes: A smart home is a residence that uses Internet-connected devices to enable the remote monitoring and management of appliances and systems, such as lighting and heating.

Wearables: Computing devices that are worn under, with, or on top of clothing.

Chapter 6
Cloud–Based IoT Platform:
Challenges and Applied Solutions

Amany Sarhan
Tanta University, Egypt

ABSTRACT

Developing IoT projects from scratch requires a lot of knowledge and expertise; moreover, it takes a very long time to be developed. It can be hard for starters and even senior developers to perfect every aspect of an IoT project in a timely manner. These aspects include hardware, communication, data storage, security, integration, application, data processing, and analysis. This chapter introduces a cloud-based platform that is concerned with data storage, device management, data processing, and integration with external systems, all while providing high level of security and allowing for future scaling. This platform should accelerate and simplify the development of IoT projects by lowering the entry barrier and offloading some of the burden off developers to give them more time to focus on other aspects such as hardware and applications. The authors discuss many implementation issues in the functional and design perspective that may guide others to make their own platforms from this insight view.

INTRODUCTION

The term "Internet of Things" (IoT) was first used in 1999 by British technology pioneer Kevin Ashton to describe a system in which objects in the physical world could be connected to the Internet by sensors. Ashton coined the term to illustrate the power of connecting Radio-Frequency Identification (RFID) tags used in corporate supply chains to the Internet in order to count and track goods without the need for human intervention. Today, the Internet of Things has become a popular term for describing scenarios in which Internet connectivity and computing capability extend to a variety of objects, devices, sensors, and everyday items (Internet society, 2018).

The IoT market has started to move towards action and companies are realizing that building end-to-end IoT systems from scratch is a tedious task and a big risk with many business cases still shaky and not clearly validated (IoT Analytics, 2015). With so much re-inventing the wheel happening at the same time in different organizations, the market has responded by generating a wave of companies that

DOI: 10.4018/978-1-5225-7332-6.ch006

deliver out-of-the box solutions that encapsulate major parts of an end-to-end IoT system in repeatable and replicable building blocks that can be used in different areas in the market. These solutions are known as IoT platforms. IoT platforms enable companies to bring IoT solutions more rapidly to the market by cutting development time and expenses for IoT systems (Internet of Things Research, 2016).

Generally, IoT platforms can be classified into 4 main categories:

1. **Device Centric IoT Platforms**: These are developed as hardware-specific software platforms pushed by companies that commercialize IoT device components and have built a software backend that is referred to as an IoT platform. These backends are often reference implementations to ease the development of end-to-end IoT solutions, which are made available as starting points to other ecosystem partners. Examples - INTEL IoT platform (Internet of Things Research, 2016) and (Intel, 2018), ARM mbed IoT platform (Internet of Things Research, 2016) and (ARM, 2018).

2. **Communication/Connectivity Centric IoT Platforms**: They address the connectivity of connected IoT devices via communication networks. Connectivity based platforms primarily focus on providing innovative solutions for device/product manufacturers, which they can drop into their existing products to make them connected. Recent development provides specified analytics for extracting reports about the performance of connected devices. Examples - CISCO/Jasper (Internet of Things Research, 2016) and (Cisco, 2018), Ayla Networks (Internet of Things Research, 2016).

3. **Cloud Centric IoT Platforms**: These are offerings from larger cloud providers, which aim to extend their cloud business into the IoT as in Botta et al.'s (2016) and Razzaque et al.'s (2016). They offer different solutions with for example Infrastructure as-a-service (IaaS) backend that provide hosting space and processing power for applications and services. The backend is optimized for other applications that have been updated and integrated into IoT platforms. Examples - Microsoft Azure IoT (Microsoft, 2018), IBM Watson IoT platform (Internet of Things Research, 2016).

4. **Industrial Centric IoT Platforms:** These are the platforms designed to address the challenges of industrial IoT and integrate extensive features compared with the IoT consumer and business solutions (i.e. strong integrated IT and better end-to-end security framework). IoT connectivity extends to machines, sensors, devices and processes in the industrial sectors, and business outcomes produce increased manufacturing efficiencies, better resource utilization, and transformed support models that are driving adoption. In this context, the development of Industrial IoT platforms is driven by large manufacturing companies. Examples - Bosch IoT Platform (Internet of Things Research, 2016) and (Bosch, 2018), GE Predix (GE Predix, 2018).

As we have seen with the classification, not all IoT platforms are the same. The platform providers create IoT ecosystems that involve close partnerships with stakeholders, other vendors and service providers. IoT platforms (with their different classification) are addressing and handling the complex data and events integration, protocol translations, and connectivity issues, so that the developers can have more time for the IoT application and business requirements as mentioned in Internet of Things Research (2016) and (Perera, Liu, & Jayawardena, 2015).

Most of the available platforms are described as black boxes and not informative for researchers that would like to add improvements to the field. This will detour their research directions to developing specific IoT applications rather than working in generic platforms due to the lack of visibility of the whole platform building process. In this paper, we present the design and implementations issues of a cloud-based IoT platform we called "Galliot". Throughout the next sections, a deep insight is introduced for the functional components of the Galliot platform enabling other researchers to build on and enhance them with their different design decisions. The details of the components are intended to be thorough and extensive to guide the other researches in their IoT platform development. The functionality and cooperation of the platform components are clear and solid giving each component specific role which enables for further design chan1ges in similar platforms or in ours if new ideas appear in the literature. The interaction between the components are explained and the implementation precautions are given for each part. Also a proposed hierarchical model is used for organizing the project parts (devices, services) logically instead of the flat model currently used which helps grouping these parts and performing actions on groups which is also a proposed approach. Moreover, security is a major design issue almost in all components of the platform which is highlighted in each component discussion.

LITERATURE REVIEW

IoT systems are being widely developed due to the continuous efforts of the interested community and researchers. For casual users, building IoT applications from scratch is very hard and error prone. Therefore, users have been building their applications using open platforms. Many IoT platforms have been introduced in the literature in the last few years to simplify and speed up the process of application development. These platforms provide many services to the application builders starting from programming frameworks, data and device management, security and storage, to protocol translation. Many surveys have been presented to collect the most famous IoT platforms and viewing them from different views. In this paper, we will summarize these famous IoT platforms focusing on their similarities and dissimilarities to our proposed platform. The selected open-source platforms are OpenMTC, SiteWhere, FIWARE, and Webinos. The solutions are IBM's Watson, AWS, and Microsoft's Azure IoT Hub (Internet of Things Research, 2016).

OpenMTC is an open-source cloud-enabled IoT platform that contains important components that enable to connect to other platforms through the Back-End. The Core Features and Connectivity components of the Front-End, the connectivity between the Front- and Back-End, as well as the Connectivity component of the Back-End provide all necessary functionality to communicate between a device and the middleware. The OpenEPC component, that connects the Front- and Back-End components, also provides rules and filters functionality which encourages the developer to change the rules and filters easily through this component. The Connectivity, Core Features, and Application Enablement components are the main functions in the platform and are encapsulated in the Integration Middleware. The Application Enablement components provide all functionality to connect further applications to the middleware.

SiteWhere is an open-source IoT platform that complies to the IoT reference architecture. A gateway is used to enable the devices to communicate via diverse protocols with the platform (Internet of Things Research, 2016). The main functionality of the platform is provided by the SiteWhereTenant Engine, including the Device Management and the Communication Engine. It uses REST APIs (REpresentational State Transfer Application Programming interface) and Integration component to connect to further Applications to the platform.

FIWARE is an open-source cloud-based platform built on the IoT reference architecture and funded by the European Union and the European Commission. It contains a rich library of components and devices such as sensors and actuators can be integrated in the built application. Devices can communicate directly with the IoT Back-End or via a Gateway, which is positioned within the IoT Edge. Both the IoT

Gateway and the IoT NGSI Gateway enable and manage the communication of devices with the IoT Back-End. The main functionality of FIWARE is provided by the Data Context Broker upon which the application component is positioned. However, the definition of the device component differs from ours and, hence, the Sensor, Actuator, and Device components partly overlap. Nevertheless, there is still an appropriate mapping to our definition.

Webinos is an open-source middleware for the IoT and mobile devices, sponsored by the European Union FP7 project. The main focus of this platform is the security for the devices during communication. Moreover, it enables the users to send data to third-parties and to other users in a secure manner. The main components of this architecture are the Personal Zone Hub (PZH), which acts as a gateway to connect the devices, and the Personal Zone Proxy (PZP), which is a local component found at each device that aggregates sensor data and actuator commands and communicates with PZH. The PZH also provides local communications between devices by acting as a messaging hub but does not support any Applications to run locally, however, it just provides the APIs that allow third-party applications to be built and to communicate with devices. If we connect multiple PZPs (on multiple devices) to the same PZH, they can communicate as peer-to-peer via synchronizing PZP and PZH.

IBM Watson IoT Platform is a cloud-based platform. The most interesting components of this platform are Connect component that provides event handling functionality, the Analytics, Risk Management, and Information Management components that provide the core functionality of the platform, the IoT Industry Solutions and Third Party Apps components enable the connection of other applications.

AWS (Amazon Web Services) IoT (Guth et al.'s, 2018) is a cloud platform that aims to let smart devices easily connect and securely interact with the AWS cloud and other connected devices. Through AWS IoT, it is easy to use and utilize various AWS services like Amazon DynamoDB, Amazon S3, Amazon Machine Learning, and others (Guth et al.'s, 2018). Furthermore, AWS IoT allows applications to talk with devices even when they are offline. There are no restrictions on the used programming languages of developing smart applications or operating systems running them as they interact via REST APIs. AWS IoT provides an open-source client libraries and device SDKs that make the framework easily used for several embedded operating systems and microcontroller platforms. Any IoT device can connect to the AWS IoT cloud if it has the ability to be configured using one of the programming languages. The platform has a multi-layer security architecture; the security is applied at every level of the technology stack. First, authentication is required for each new device to be connected to the AWS IoT Cloud using one of many methods and as chosen by the end-user. It also supports mutual authentication at all points of connection. AWS IoT provides three ways of verifying identity: X.509 certificates, AWS IAM users, groups, and roles, and AWS Cognito identities (Guth et al.'s, 2018). HTTP (Hypertext Transfer Protocol) and WebSockets requests sent to the AWS IoT are authenticated using either AWS Identity and Access Management (AWS IAM) or AWS Cognito (Guth et al.'s, 2018). Second level of security is authorization and access control which can be applied by either mapping authored rules and policies to each certificate or applying IAM policies. This means that only devices or applications specified in these rules can have access to the corresponding device, that this certificate belongs to. The Rules Engine is used to do that as it has the responsibility of access management. The owner of a cloud-connected device can write a list of rules in the Rules Engine to authorize some devices or applications to access his device and prevent others. Finally, a secure communication is provided by this platform where all traffic to and from AWS IoT is encrypted over SSL/TLS protocol. All private data are stored encrypted using symmetric key cryptography (e.g. AES128).

Microsoft Azure platform composes of a set of services that enable end-users to interact with their IoT devices, receive data from them, perform various operations over data (e.g. aggregation, multidimensional analysis, transformation, etc.), and visualize it in a suitable way for business. This platform addresses the challenge of three different sub-problems: scaling, telemetry patterns, and big data. It supports a wide range of hardware devices, operating systems, and programming languages. IoT devices interact with Azure cloud through a predefined cloud gateway. The incoming data from these devices is either stored in the cloud for further processing and analytics by Azure cloud services (e.g. Azure Machine Learning and Azure, Stream Analytics) or offered immediately to some services for real-time analytics. The output of both tracks is presented and visualized in a customized way that fits the desires of customers and suites their business. The core functionality of the platform is provided by the Subscription Processing and the Application Management System, including the SmartApp Management & Execution components. Azure IoT Hub is a web service that enables bi-directional communication between devices and the cloud backend services in a secure manner. Azure IoT hub has an identity registry for holding the identity and authentication related information of each device. It also has device identity management unit to manage all connected and authenticated devices. Smart application specifications Microsoft provides various SDKs to support different IoT devices and platforms. IoT device SDKs along with IoT service SDKs are provided in order to make developers able to connect to Azure IoT Hub and let users manage their devices. The IoT device SDKs enable developers to implement client applications for a wide variety of devices ranging from simple network-connected sensors to a powerful standalone computing devices. Up to now, C, Node.js, Java, Python, and .NET programming languages are supported in such SDKs (Guth et al.'s, 2018). It uses many methods for securing the data in every layer such as mutual authentication for establishing a connection between devices and hub, TLS for secure communication by encrypting the handshaking process, SHA-256 support for authentication purposes. Each device is given a unique device identity key at deployment time then it authenticates itself to the IoT Hub by sending a token contains an HMAC-SHA256 signature string which is a combination of the generated key and a user-selected device Id. The IoT Hub allows a set of access control rules to grant or deny permissions to IoT devices and smart apps. The access control policies include activation and dis-activation of any IoT device. Data is stored in either DocumentDB or in SQL (Structured Query Language) databases, ensuring a high level of privacy. This platform is compatible with many operating systems and platforms include Windows, Android, Debian, mbed OS, Windows IoT Core, Arduino, TI-RTOS, and many others (Guth et al.'s, 2018).

PLATFORM FUNCTIONAL COMPONENTS OVERVIEW

Galliot platform tries to collect the main features provided by the current platforms with a major focus on flexibility and security of the devices and data. Some of the components found in the proposed platform are similar to the previous platforms with several changes made to enable connecting it to the newly added components, and others were developed from scratch to achieve our flexibility and security goals. Galliot platform is based on the architecture shown in Figure 1. The highlighted blue and red components are the components of concern which will be discussed along with their design and implementation issues. The services offered in each functional components briefly are:

- **Data Storage:** A NoSQL database is used for the purposes of data storage. This database includes every possible data needed by the platform, moreover, it is used to store data originating from the IoT devices.

- **Security and Privacy:** This is not a single component rather it is an implementation through all the components. We will explain how the security is applied across the various components in next sections.

- **Device Management:** A basic functionality is offered through a logical hierarchy (which will be proposed and explained later). This hierarchy consists of Projects, Services, Groups and Devices, respectively. All the hierarchy entities can be added, removed, edited and disabled. Information about each device status is automatically managed and actions can be taken depending on its operational status changes.

- **Processing and Action Management:** Here, an event-based IF-THEN rule engine is used along with a rule editor to write the code executed by the rule engine (i.e. tasks). The rule engine data is the received IoT data streams from the devices.

- **Additional Tools:** A Node.js client library is offered to ease the integration with the platform. It can be downloaded from the NPM (Node Package Manager) repository using with the name **"Galliot-client"**.

- **External Interfaces:** An Application Programming Interface (API) is provided to allow devices to exchange data, and to enable the platform user to easily develop applications based on the platform data.

Given these components and the services they provide; we can summarize the user view of the system as in Figure 2 which shows the system from the user perspective. REST part in "REST API" implies that this API is HTTP based. The design of the web application (the front-end) is what provides the user point of view of the system.

Internally, the system is separated into many processes, as shown in Figure 3, each process acting as a server. The only server that a user can interact with is the API and Front-End Server. All the other servers are used internally by the platform to realize the functional components. The API and Front-End Server is what serves the web application (Front-End) and any API user request with the help of the Database Server. The Timer Server is responsible for executing time-based actions. Mainly, these actions are concerned with managing devices status and data forwarding. The remaining servers (Task Manager, Task Handlers, and Resource Manager) constitute the Galliot platform rule engine.

Figure 1. General architecture of Galliot platform including the implemented functional components

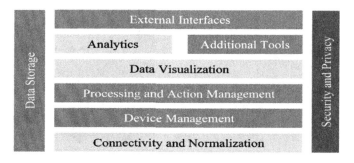

GALLIOT PLATFORM MANAGEMENT: DESIGN AND IMPLEMENTATION ISSUES

Given the previous overview, we can now understand how the user is enabled to manage his IoT project. In this section, the design and implementation of the user input forms will be discussed, explaining why the constraints exist, and why some design decisions were taken. We start by explaining the choice for NoSQL database, how to solve mutual access to the data, then the security measures used to protect both the platform and the data are declared, finally how user, project and devices are managed.

Using NoSQL Database

The first decision was made is to use NoSQL database instead of the relational database. NoSQL, which refers to Not Only SQL, is a major shift from traditional SQL databases that complements relational database. With the grow of the Internet, data became dynamic and exploding. Data are needed to be clustered to be stored on different storage media. As the relational databases cannot be clustered, NoSQL are thought of to store data. Moreover, it provides a mechanism for storing and retrieving data modeled

Figure 2. User view of the system

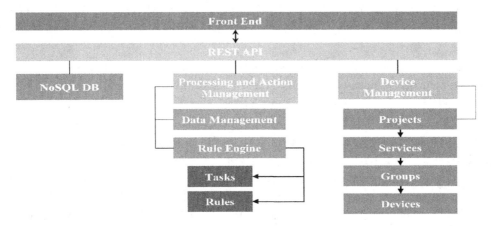

Figure 3. The internal working of the platform

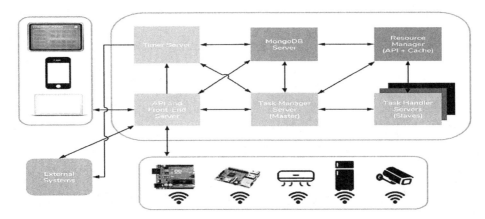

in a way other than the tabular relations. Since IoT field is not yet standardized, the device data will vary from a device to another. This enables using NoSQL to cope with such variable data length. With this note in mind, the differences between SQL and NoSQL are listed as:

1. **Data Integrity**: Most of the SQL databases allow enforcing the data integrity rules by using the foreign key constraints, while the same data integrity enforcement option is not available with NoSQL database.
2. **Scaling:** As the data in any enterprise grows rapidly, so as the data grows need to distribute the load among the multiple servers. With SQL, this can be tricky, while NoSQL's simple data models can make this process much easier and many are built with the scaling function from the very start.
3. **Performance:** NoSQL can be faster than SQL due to the former's simple and de-normalized store that allows the user to retrieve more and sometimes all information in a single request without the need for complex SQL queries (join). However, relational databases are still a better option for the purpose they are designed for, and implementing the same functionality with NoSQL for relational data has its challenges. If it is done wrong, it will yield a much worse performance.
4. **Data Storage:** In SQL, data is being stored in a relational model with rows and columns. Rows basically contain all the information of one specific entity while columns are all separate data points. In NoSQL, it encompasses a host of various databases each with the different data storage model. Some main are graph, columnar, document and key-value.
5. **Schemas and the Flexibility:** In SQL each record confirms to a fixed schema, which means that each column must be decided and should be locked before the data entry and each of the rows must have data for each column. This can also be improved, but it requires alerting the full database and going to offline. In NoSQL, schemas are the dynamic part, data can be easily added and there is no need that each row must contain data of each column as in the relational database.

The most important gain by NoSQL was schema flexibility and scalability. This allows for dynamic schemas with minimal effort.

Solving Database Conflicts

Data conflicts occur when more than one client reads and/or writes the same data item concurrently as found in Tanenbaum and Van Steen (2013). These conflicts may be read-write conflict - when one client reads inconsistent data in the middle of another client's write or write-write conflict – when two people updating the same data item at the same time. If the server serializes them, one is applied and immediately overwritten by the other (lost update).

To solve this issue, two major approaches as mentioned in Menascé and Nakanishi (1982) that can be used. The first approach is pessimistic concurrency control (or pessimistic locking) in which the system assumes the worst; two or more users want to update the same record at the same time. To solve this conflict, it simply locks the record, no matter how unlikely conflicts actually are. This makes it impossible for two or more users to update the row at the same time. Depending on the lock mode (shared, exclusive, or update), other users might be able to read the data even though a lock has been placed. The second is the optimistic concurrency control (or optimistic locking) approach which assumes that although conflicts are possible, they will be very rare. Instead of locking every record every time it is used, the system just looks for indications that two users actually did try to update the same record at the same time. If that evidence is found, then one user's update is discarded and the user is informed. The optimistic approach was chosen as the probability of the user editing the same resource from two different browsers is very low and to avoid locking unnecessary data that may not be concurrently accessed.

Security Layers

In Galliot platform, several layers of security were used to protect the platform, the stored data and the data in and out to/from devices. The first layer is user authentication while the second layer is protecting communication data between the devices and the platform, the API requests are also validated in three different methods.

User Authentication

To authenticate and secure user's session, JSON Web Token (JWT) is used as suggested by Jones, Bradley and Sakimura (2015). JSON is an acronym for JavaScript Object Notation which is a minimal, readable format for structuring data which was mentioned in and Bray (2013). It is used primarily to transmit data between a server and web application as an alternative to XML. JSON is more compact than XML and most programming languages and tools have good support for JSON which makes it a clearly better choice. JWT is an open standard (RFC 7519) that defines a compact and self-contained way for securely transmitting information between parties as a JSON object. This information can be verified and trusted because it is digitally signed. JWTs can be signed using a secret (with the HMAC algorithm) or a public/ private key pair using RSA (Rivest–Shamir–Adleman) encryption algorithm. Figure 4 illustrates how JWT is used for user login and management of his project through the platform.

The signature is unique and allows the server to detect any tampering with the JWT. But the JWT is sent in base64 encoding in the request, which means it is not encrypted by default. To encrypt it, JWTs can be sent over HTTPS which encrypts the traffic or use X.509 certificates. In general, it is always advised to not put sensitive data in a JWT as a good security practice as discussed in Jones, Bradley and Sakimura (2015) and Bray (2013).

An important note here is that JWT is not limited to authentication, as it is compact and self-contained way for securely transmitting information between parties as a JSON object. It can be used for other purposes like activating the user account using his email, and confirming an email change if the user changes his email. However, there still is a drawback of using JWT as means for authentication. It has

Figure 4. How an application use JWT to authenticate the user

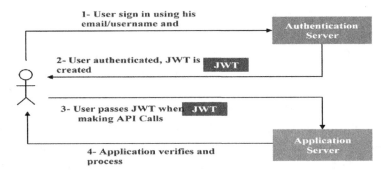

to be sent with every request, which - when compared to a session id - is larger in size. So, there is a tradeoff between more header size with easier scaling vs small header size with harder scaling.

In total, four tokens are used for each user. These are:

1. **Activation Token:** Used to verify the user email and activate his account. It expires after a certain time (we have chosen 24 hours). This token is used only once.
2. **Confirmation Token:** Used to verify new emails if the user decided to change his email. It expires after a certain time (we have chosen 24 hours). This is token is used only once.
3. **Login Token:** Used to allow the user login through the front-end to the control panel and manage his resources (e.g. hierarchy entities, tasks, etc.). This token is constantly expiring and refreshed as a security measure to limit account theft. The user's client (the browser) checks if the expiration date is almost reached (the lifetime of this token is 15 minutes) and requests a refresh token to use as long as the user is active. If the user is idle, the token will expire and he will have to login again. If an attacker changed the expiration date in the token, it will fail the signature matching step on the server side and the user will be asked to login again. Thus, this token ensures the security of online access to the system.
4. **Master API Key:** This is a token generated for each user account. Its main purpose is to be used with devices and user developed applications to connect with our API. It is called a Master Key because it has full permissions to manage user resources (e.g. hierarchy entities, tasks, etc.) except for his profile (for changing password and email). The user has the ability to disable this token or revoke it and generate a new Master API Key when needed. This should be done with care as any device or application using that Master API Key will lose access once it is revoked. This is for security purpose.

Looking at the available tokens, we can see that there is a very important limitation as the user does not have the ability to make custom tokens with custom capabilities (e.g. a token for sending data only for a specific device). More practical and useful API keys require the creation of an access control system, which is out of the scope of this project. Still, JWTs can serve as means of implementing such an access control system.

API Requests Validation

In order for a device or a user-made application to connect with the platform, two important headers have to be provided: Content-Type - which is always set to (application/json) and Authorization - where the user sends his token in Bearer format as in Jones, Bradley and Sakimura (2015) and Bray (2013). Given that the users of the platform will use the API to send and receive any data to/from devices, it is critical to treat all user inputs as untrusted data and apply strict validation of the input data on many levels.

The first level of validation is performed by the database which offers validation for input data types and regular expressions. The second level of validation is implemented in the API by only accepting input data that is defined in the database schema and ignoring any other data. All database data is identified by its owner field where it represents the username. A user will only have access to data containing his username as an owner. A username is verified in the API through the JWT. If an attacker somehow managed to change the user field in the token, the token will fail in signature matching resulting in a denied access to other users' data.

A third layer of input validation exists on the client-side, but this is only effective when the user is using the front-end. It is useless when a device or user developed application is connecting to the API. Whenever a user creates or updates a resource, the API timestamps this action using two data fields: (createdAt, and updatedAt). The API uses Coordinated Universal Time (UTC), as it does not change with daylight saving. Displaying this information in local time for each user becomes just a matter of adding an offset. Any other process that depends on scheduling or countdown timers (timer process and rule engine which we will discuss later) are based on UTC for the same reason.

Securing Data in Transition

An effective and simple approach to secure data exchanged with the platform is to use SSL/TLS certificates. HTTPS is used as means of exchanging data such as username and password (before granting a token) and data from/to devices. However, not all devices have the ability to communicate using HTTPS, as the SSL/TLS layer requires more processing power. An embedded device with 16 or 8-bit microprocessor may not have the necessary processing power to use HTTPS. This is a tradeoff for security, it introduces overhead in network traffic and processing. As a result, some data cannot be encrypted. For these types of situations, HTTP is also provided as a fallback. As a future work, simple encryption techniques could be used to solve such problem.

User Management

User management functionalities facilitate the platform users to collaborate, and manage enterprises users (group policy, add users, remove users, etc.) as mentioned in Razzaque et al.'s (2016) and in Li, Xu, and Zhao (2015). They include: user registration and mail activation and manage user profile that allows the user to manage his Master API Key (disable, revoke and regenerate), change his first name, last name, email and password. However, the user is not allowed to change his username as it is used to differentiate users' data from each other. It is also used to restrict user access to his data only and to generate user's Master API Key. The user's password is not stored in the database as it is. Instead, the password is salted then hashed. This is to prevent dictionary and pre-computed rainbow table attacks. The user can check and manage his Master API Key by navigating to his profile. There, he can disable the Master API Key, which means that any device that uses the Master API Key loses access until the Master API Key is enabled again. He can revoke the Master API Key and generate a new one which will require the user to reenter his password.

Project Management

Project and device management is accomplished using a logical hierarchy model that consists of: Projects, Services, Groups and Devices. To explain why this design decision was made, let us consider the traditional model that uses a flat device management approach. This means that the devices are added, and the action are specified for each device individually. There is no kind of grouping of these devices which can enable the user to easily take actions on a group of devices which may be needed in applications that uses large number of devices (such as sensors). This approach is the simplest to implement but when there are many devices, it becomes very difficult to take bulk-actions (e.g. to disable a group of devices, in this way, the user will have to disable them individually).

A hierarchical approach is thus considered which helps the users to group devices and take bulk-actions by assigning this action to the group instead of the individual devices which can reduce time and avoid error of repeating the same action for each device. Figure 4 illustrates the generalized hierarchy for any IoT project in Galliot platform. The higher level of the hierarchy is the project from which services originate. For each service, devices are defined and can then be grouped into groups.

The model may look simple, but it is organized and efficient specially when managing large number of services and devices and it will enable to make groups of devices for which the same actions may be applied easily. For simple systems containing only one device, the user will have to create one project, one service, one group and finally, one device.

Taking a closer look at the implementation level of the hierarchy model, there are some common implementation aspects to be considered:

- Each entity is identified by its owner (through username) and its name. This provides the separation of users' data in the database (the combination of owner and name makes the identity of an entity).
- Each entity is timestamped when it is created and updated, so the user can always know when the entity was created and last updated.
- Each entity (except for the Project entity which is the root of the hierarchy) has the name of all its ancestors (e.g. a group will contain the name of the service and project it belongs to). This is critical to achieve the hierarchical model.
- Since the entity name cannot be updated, the user is forced to delete the entity and create a new one. The user is unable to delete an entity if it has any children. This will prevent the scenario where a whole project, service or a group of devices get deleted by mistake or via an attacker. This makes deleting a whole project a harder process specially when the project contains many children. We can think of this procedure as one of the security approaches used to protect the system.

Figure 5. Generalized hierarchy

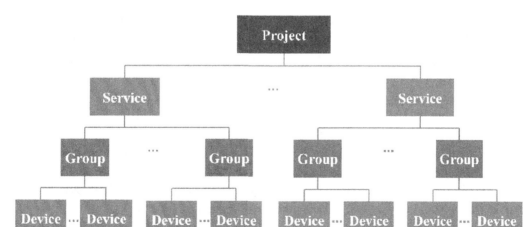

Devices Management

Devices are the most important entities in the hierarchy, since they are what send data and take actions. Devices entities can be thought of as virtual identities for any web connected device. This virtual identity facilitates offering services (such as rule engine, device status management ... etc) for many devices despite their heterogeneity. This is because once the device is web connected, this web connectivity acts as a layer of abstraction which unifies the interfacing with devices (i.e. HTTP protocol).

The device virtual identity is composed of the owner and the device name so that a device is known on the platform as device_name@owner. Any physical device that sends data has to state what device name it is using. The owner is automatically extracted from the token sent with the data (remember that the Master API Key is required with each request so that devices can send data).

Several device fields have been added to help manipulating device throughout the system. These fields are:

- **pEnable, sEnable, gEnable, enable:** These are the fields that allow for bulk enable/disable. The levels of enables are project, service, group and device, respectively. If - for example - a service called (sv1) was disabled, then all the devices under this service will be disabled. This disable action prevents any physical device from sending data using that platform's disabled device (e.g. device1@owner).
- **pName, sName, gName:** These fields are the names of the device ancestors in the hierarchy, namely project, service, and group name, respectively. These fields while they might seem redundant and a waste of space from a relational perspective, they make the bulk-actions faster if it requires a database operation (e.g. disabling all devices in a project requires a single database query that updates devices with the pName of that project and the correct owner). This also gives the user a quick information about what might be disabling his devices without the need to query the database multiple times to offer this information.
- **Longitude, Latitude:** These are optional fields that give the possibility for building and applying location based services (e.g. knowing the devices on the map for maintenance purposes).
- **Properties:** This is a special field that is an object of dynamic key-value pair. The user has the flexibility to add, remove and edit these pairs. It can be used in either of two ways:
  - **Hold Device Latest Data Stream Values:** If the data stream has a field name that is identical (case sensitive) to a property key name (e.g. data stream has a field named **my_temp**, and a property key is named **my_temp**). The value of that property key will be updated with the value of the same field from the data stream.
  - **User Purposes:** There is a possibility that a user may not want this default behavior, and prefer to use these properties for other purposes. In this case, he can either send data with fields different than the properties, or make a rule (as will be discussed in the rule engine section) that prevent the update, and do not worry about the names at all.
- **Type:** This is a field that determines the device type (sensor, actuator, sensor/actuator). This can be used for statistical purposes (e.g. how much sensors in a project, etc.).
- **activityTimeOut, aliveTimeOut, Status:** Two types of data have defined that a device can send: data stream and alive signal. The data stream is the data sent by the device while the alive signal telling if the device is still connected to the platform or not (i.e. the device can be connected to the platform but is not doing anything). Based on these two types of data, we define three device

status: disconnected, active, and idle. The activityTimeOut defines the expected time to receive the data stream. The aliveTimeOut defines the expected time to receive the alive signal. Both timeouts are user defined in seconds. The management of the device status is based on the defined data types and the time defined in activityTimeOut and aliveTimeOut which will be explained in a later section as it is a separate process (the timer process) that is private to the internal working of the platform (i.e. the process is not reachable by the user and it operates only on trusted data).

PROCESSING AND ACTION MANAGEMENT

Processing and Action management component can be considered as an essential component in any IoT platform. We have previously mentioned that this component represents the functions that operate on top of the received IoT data streams from the different IoT devices. In this section, the explanation of how data stream, alive signal, and other action management are achieved is given. However, the details of the execution of these actions is discussed later in the rule engine processes section.

Data Streaming

The user can access the API using his Master API Key which is used to send data. All data are time-stamped once they are received by the API. The server adds a UTC timestamp on the "createdAt" field. The user is only granted the send and receive data operations; he cannot modify or delete any device data on the platform. These restrictions are meant to prevent any tampering with the data (i.e. another level of data security). The user can obtain the history of the data stream either through the front-end or directly from the API, although the front-end offers him some filtering capabilities

Alive Signal

This signal is periodically sent by the device to indicate it is still connected to the application. It is almost identical to data streaming except that it includes no data; it just contains the name (or ID) of the device. The server puts a UTC timestamp on this request when received.

Data Forwarding

The goal of this feature is to allow the user to group some of the data collected by the platform and forward it to another RESTful service (HTTP based) for a further usage. We have two choices when considering what data to forward; either forward a single data stream or forward a group of data streams collected across the time defined by the forwarding frequency (Batches). We have chosen the latter. This is still not a complete feature, as the complete feature will allow the user to filter the data (e.g. if a device is measuring humidity and temperature, the user may want to only forward the temperature readings), assign this feature for any hierarchy level (i.e. it is still only limited for devices only), allow more than one data forwarder per device, and support for other protocols. This complete feature remains as a future work. For now, only forwarding device data streams using HTTP or HTTPS is implemented. The execution of the data forwarding action is done by a separate process (the same timer process that is used to manage the device status which is later explained).

Tasks and Rules

Tasks are user written code (JavaScript in our platform's case) and is executed by the rule engine. Code writing and its assignment are separated; the code is written as a task and is later assigned to an entity in the form of IF-THEN rule. This is mainly done through the front-end which offers a text editor with syntax highlighting and analyzer. The user can still send the code directly through the API. The user can perform platform's specific actions through these tasks (e.g. change device properties, send emails, etc.).

Rules are event based actions. To make use of the hierarchy, these rules should be able to be assigned to any hierarchy entity. We have prepared a set of predefined events for some important conditions as shown in Table 1.

The user can define his own condition (If expression) for the rule and assign a task to this condition (Then task). The action to be taken in case the condition is not satisfied is optional (Else task). When an event is fired, the matching IF condition is checked and the task specified after THEN is applied. Otherwise, if the condition is not satisfied and another task is specified after ELSE, this task is executed. Moreover, we have implemented the rules to be disabled and enabled. If a rule is disabled, it is not executed when the event is fired. Note that the device can have many rules, and a group of rules can be assigned for the same event.

THE TIMER PROCESS

Time-related actions are separated from the main API process. The reason for implementing them as separate processes is to not overload the main API process which gives us the benefit of scaling the overloaded parts of the applications. Each created timer has an expected execution date, and an actual execution date. These two dates provide information about the process overloading. The timer process handles two time-related actions: Device Status Management and Data Forward Execution.

Device Status Management

There are three possible device statuses while the device is enabled as shown in Figure 5:

Table 1. Predefined events and their firing conditions

Event	Firing Condition
data received	each time the platform receives a data stream from the device that is assigned this event fired rule.
alive received	each time the platform receives an alive signal from the device that is assigned this event fired rule
status changed	this event is fired whenever a device status is changed. In this case, the user has the information of what was the old status, and what is the new status.
device activated	whenever the device status is changed to active, which means the device is sending data streams.
device idled	whenever the device status is changed to idle, which means the device is no longer sending data streams (i.e. activeTimeOut is reached) but is still sending alive signals.
device disconnected	whenever the device status is changed to disconnected, which means the device is no longer sending data streams (i.e. activeTimeOut is reached) nor alive signals (i.e. aliveTimeOut is reached).

1. **Disconnected:** This is the default status once the device entity is created. This status either means that the device has never sent any data or alive signals, or the timeouts (activityTimeOut and alive-TimeOut) are reached.
2. **Active:** This status means that the device is sending data streams and the activityTimeOut is not reached. The device is considered active as long it is sending data streams, even if it is not sending alive signals.
3. **Idle:** This status means that the device is connected to the platform but is not sending data streams and is only sending alive signals. The device is thus connected to the platform but is not doing anything useful to the application. A good example of this is to imagine an air conditioner that can be turned on remotely. If it is idle, this means that it can be turned on remotely. However, if it is disconnected, the air conditioner is not connected to the platform, hence it cannot be remotely controlled.

The switching between these three statuses is illustrated in Figure 6. To implement this state machine, there are different approaches each with its tradeoff in memory consumption, execution delay (e.g. in the range of 1 or 2 seconds or in the range of minutes, etc.), and processing required.

The first approach is polling. For every data stream or alive signal received, a future date is set equal to the timeout plus the current date (depending on whether it is acitvityTimeOut or aliveTimeOut) and stored in a file or in the database. Then a process will run periodically to poll and check if that date is reached. If the date is reached, the device status is changed as illustrated in the state machine, depending on the current device status. This might seem as memory efficient but there is a tradeoff between memory consumption and execution delay. In order to achieve a small delay, (e.g. in the range of a 10 seconds), the polling should run very often (e.g. every second), and query a fast storage medium (i.e. RAM instead of mechanical storage). However, polling is not guaranteed to achieve small delay when there are many devices.

The second approach - which we preferred - is to use a countdown timer instead of polling. A timer is set for each device once the device sends any data stream or alive signal. As long as the device is sending data streams or alive signals, this timer is reset. Once the device stops sending data streams or alive signals, the countdown will reach zero and the device status is changed as illustrated in the state machine. Finally, the timer is cleared and the actual execution date is set.

Figure 6. Device status state machine

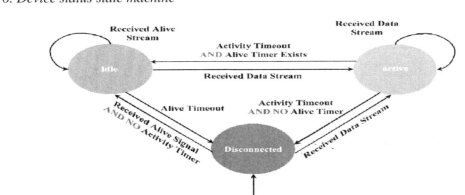

Figure 7 illustrates how the second approach of device status state machine is implemented. The timers are triggered by either data streams or alive signals. Note that the timer has to know the type of the received request (i.e. data stream or alive signal), the device name, and the owner.

Data Forwarding Execution

Since data forwarding has a frequency, which is based on time, the timer process is used to handle its execution. Managing and executing data forwarding is simpler than the device status management, as it only queries the database to get the necessary data and forwards it once the countdown is reached. Each device can have a single data forwarder.

The timer for data forwarding needs the following information: device name, device owner, data forwarder name, forwarding frequency, forwarding options (i.e. Host, Port, Path, Method, Headers), and forwarding data (body). Unlike the device status management, the rule engine is not notified about data forwarding as there is no such event is defined.

THE RULE ENGINE

The rule engine gives the user the ability to write a code and execute it on the server once an event is fired. The action management is centralized on the server and offloads some of the processing from the devices. The rule engine facilitates the addition of new platform features and allows the user to use them for his purposes. The rule engine requires two entities to run: the task to be executed and the rule upon which the task should be executed. However, developing a rule engine brings many challenges that we have chosen to solve as follows:

Figure 7. Status timer request handler

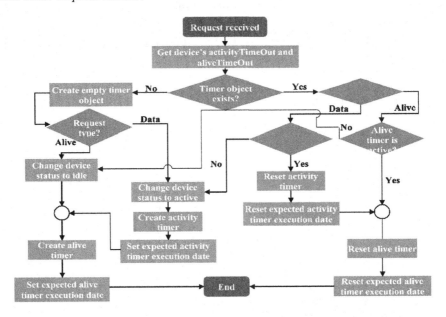

Figure 8. Execution after countdown is finished (right is for activity, left is for alive)

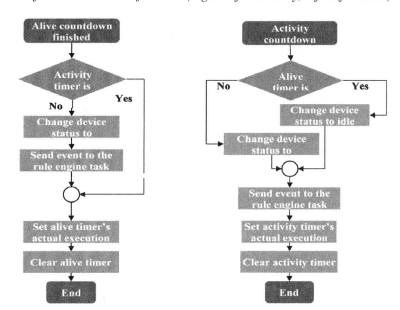

Concurrency Control

The rule engine provides a custom library of functions that can be used to read/write some platform resources (this is currently limited to device's data and properties). The conflicts arise when the user defined tasks require accessing the same resource at the same time for read/write operations. The solution to the concurrency issues is explained in the resource manager subsection.

Safe Code Execution

Giving the user the capability of running a code on the server can be a major security risk. If somehow there was a bug in the used tools or in the systems implementation, an attacker can exploit such feature (the server side code execution) for unauthorized access. To reduce the risk of such bugs, the task execution is isolated down into two levels.

The first level of isolation is by using code containers. The containers can be thought of as lightweight virtual machines from the perspective of our platform. The containers allow us to provide an environment that is similar to an operating system but isolated from the host operating system. Thus, what is inside the container cannot access the host system resources (file systems, network, system processes) unless they are defined. The container provides the bare minimum requirements (e.g. system tools and libraries) to run any application.

The second level of isolation is by using sandbox approach. The sandbox allows controlling the libraries and variables injected into it as required for a process to run. Sandboxes differ by their programming language and the runtime environment. Moreover, the sandbox allows setting a timeout for the process (e.g. a timeout of **1** second for the IF Expression and 2.5 seconds for task execution). These timeouts should be based on real monitored performance data.

Rule Engine Components

The rule engine consists of three main components: Task Manager, Task Handler and Resource Manager. Each rule engine component is implemented as a separate process. Figure 9 gives a simplified view of the three components interconnection. These processes communicate with each other using HTTP protocol. A more optimized inter-process communication would utilize a model with less overhead than server-client HTTP model. However, this remains as a future work. The role of each component is discussed in the next subsections.

Task Manager (Master)

This component can be thought of as the master as it is responsible for the following tasks are:

- **Handling Fired Event Requests:** Once a device event is fired, the task manager receives a request containing the event type, the device name, the owner, and any required data (data streams are provided if "data received" event is fired. In the case of "status changed" event, the old and the new status are provided). According to this, the task manager queries the database to get all the rules for that fired event. There exist six types of events for a device as mentioned before. Each event can have any number of rules where each rule consists of a condition and the task to be executed. The task manager then prepares and schedules the tasks for execution. The flowchart that shows the flow of this task is given in Figure 10.
- **Preparing Tasks for Execution:** There is a "meta" field for the tasks which is constructed after the code preprocessing performed during the creation of the task and provides the following information:
  - **Noop Flag:** Short for **No Operation,** which determines if the task script has actions to be taken or not (e.g. if the user declares some variables only, there is no actions to be taken and the flag is true).
  - **readArray:** A list of devices that the task will need to read their properties.
  - **writeArray:** A list of devices that the task will need to update their properties.

Figure 9. Simplified view of the rule engine processes

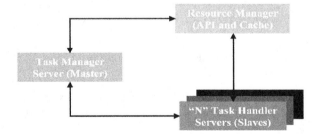

These metadata are required to prepare the tasks for execution. Once the event rules are acquired, the task manager prioritizes the rules according to the user priorities. When the rules have equal priorities, they are prioritized by their creation date. The task manager also evaluates the rules' IF-Expressions. The prioritization and evaluation determine what tasks to execute and in what order. Once the tasks are determined, the task manager queries the database to get their code. The Resource Manager is contacted to prepare the resources (i.e. send the readArray and writeArray to prepare the devices' properties). Finally, the task manager adds the acquired tasks as one group of tasks to the waiting list. An example of task group is given in Figure 11 which shows three task groups at different times.

- **Managing Tasks Waiting List:** The task manager checks for the ready task groups in the waiting list and dispatches them to the free slaves. A group of tasks is considered ready if all its required resources are unlocked. This operation is triggered in three cases: a new group of tasks is added (i.e. a new event is fired), a slave sends done signal, or a new resource is unlocked (provided by the resource manager). The flowchart that shows the flow of this task is given in Figure 10.

Figure 10. Task manager process (event received and waiting list checking)

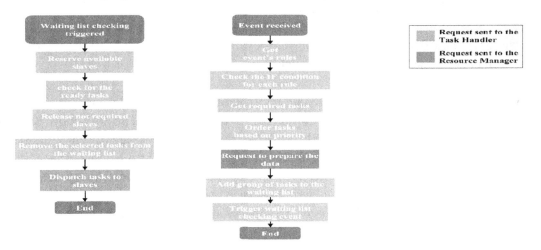

Figure 11. Example of tasks groups

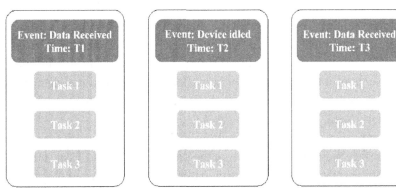

Task Handler (SLAVE)

This component is responsible for executing a group of tasks under the control of the task manager that is why it is referred to as a SALVE. Many instances can be made of the task handler. For the scope of this project, the number of slaves is predefined and constant (i.e. they are not dynamically created or removed). When the task manager dispatches a group of tasks to the task handler, the task handler iterates on that group of tasks. It fetches the data for each task through the resource manager and executes the code inside a sandboxed process inside a container.

The execution result of a task may contain:

- **Data to Be Saved:** This data is sent to the resource manager to update the device properties.
- **Emails to Be Sent:** If the user has specified an email to be sent, then it is returned to the task handler after code execution and sent. The sandbox inside the container is not allowed to send data outside the handler which will require returning to the task handler to send the emails.
- **End Flag Setting:** This flag is used to force the end of task execution due to a certain condition occurrence. The user can set this flag to prevent the execution of the remaining tasks by specifying the condition to be checked.
- **Store Flag Setting:** This flag is set to true by default and it enables the task handler to update the device properties with the data stream values. The update procedure is canceled, if this flag is set to false. The Store flag facilitate preventing the default behavior of a task to update device properties with their corresponding data stream fields.

On the end of task execution, the results are returned and the task handler informs the resource manager to unlock the writing devices (i.e. allow access to these devices but do not remove them from the cache if any other task is waiting to use them). When the group of tasks are executed, all the writing devices will be unlocked. The release of the reading devices is managed by the resource manager based on each read operation. However, when the End Flag is set to true, an unlock request and release request are sent to unlock the unused locked writing devices and release the reading devices (the cache is free to remove it as it is not needed anymore). The operation of the task handler is summarized in the flowchart in Figure 12.

Resource Manager

This component is responsible for handling the concurrency issues by preventing conflicts for parallel read/write operations, and thus ensuring that the different groups of tasks (i.e. the rules assigned to each device event) are executed in a chronological order. The resource manager consists of an interface (API) and key/value in-memory database (Redis). Redis is an in-memory key-value pair database. Being an in-memory database gives it the advantage of being faster than traditional databases. This makes it suitable for caching purposes and explains why it is used as a Time-Based cache in the rule engine for concurrency control purposes.

The resource manager offers six database operations in the form of database scripts (using Lua scripting language). The interface maps the requests from the Task Manager and Task Handlers to the internal database operations. These operations are self-explanatory. They are: prepare – to prepare the required resources for read/write operations. Some optimization is done to improve the performance (minimize

Figure 12. Task handler process

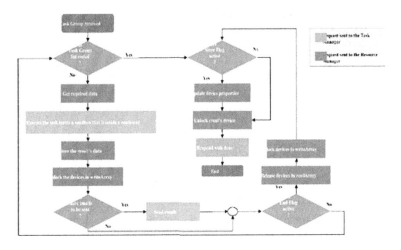

the duplicated data entries and shorten the query time), getValue – to get a resource value, setValue to set a resource value, isLocked – to check if a resource is locked, unlock – to unlock a resource and make it free for read, and release – to mark the resource as no longer required and it can be removed.

Given the goals we have mentioned, we set 5 rules to achieve them goals as follows:

1. The resource manager has to be informed about the events' operations to be made (read, write, read and write), and the timestamp of these fired events.
2. The chronological execution of operations, based on their event firing time, should be preserved without having any conflicts in their order.
3. Before a read operation is executed, all the data modifications preceding that read operation in time should be finished, so that the read operation gets the correct version of the data.
4. The writing operations should not overwrite any data that is still to be read by other events' operations preceding that writing operations in time.
5. When storing the data in the database (i.e. the platform database, not the in-memory database used for caching), the data should be in a final form. This means that there should be no events (preceding this final data in time) in the waiting list that wants to modify the data (i.e. writing operation).

There are three possibilities of operations done in parallel (Coulouris & Dollimore, 2011). Based on the previous rules, conflicts can be resolved. These possibilities are:

1. **Parallel Read Operations:** In this case, there is no conflict of operations given that the data are not modified during the read operations.
2. **Parallel Write Operations:** In this case, the conflict is resolved by saving the different field value versions. Then, these changes are merged (i.e. if the values of any field changes many times, choose the most recent value).
3. **Parallel Read and Write Operations:** Here we have two cases:
    a. **The Read Operation Belongs to an Event Preceding the Writing Operation:** In this case, there is no resource locking and the data can be read. because the old version of data is kept.

b. **Writing Operation Belongs to an Event Preceding the Reading Operation:** In this case, the resource is locked and the read operation is held back until all its preceding write operations are finished

The parallel Writing and Reading operations belong to different events. These events cannot have the same firing time as the Task Manager handling events requests is single threaded. So, each event has a unique firing time.

Cache Model

A key/value pair in-memory database is used for caching. The key is a string while the value can be of many types (e.g. string, list, hashtable, sets, sorted sets, etc.). We used hashtable as a value type for our cache model. In total, we have 2 hashtables for each device. Each key of these hashtables starts with a prefix, followed by the device ID, which is used as identifier. These hashtables are as follows:

1. **Data Hashtable:** Its key has the form "prefix:DeviceID" where prefix is set to "Device". The field name is a time stamp in the Unix epoch format. This field name represents the firing time of the event that requires the corresponding value. The purpose of each attribute in the value field is:
   a. **Data:** Holds the device properties values at the event firing time.
   b. **Change:** Holds the name of changed device properties.
   c. **nUsers:** Holds the number of operations requiring this resource.
   d. **Locked:** Determines if writing operations are still locking this record or not.
   e. **Dirty:** Determines if the changes in this record data has been saved to the database or not.
2. **Time Hashtable:** Its key has the form "prefix:DeviceID" where prefix is set to "Time". This table is used for optimizing the read operation. When an event operation requires the data at time (Tr), it will require the data with the maximum time (Tm) such that: [$Max(Tm) <= (Tr)$]. This means that if we have times: T1, T2, T3, T7, and T9, and an event requires the data at time T5, T5 will be mapped to the value in T3.

The implementation details of performing the operations on the cache are as follows:

- **Prepare:** This operation is broken down into three cases:
  - **Prepare Read:** It prepares the data to be used in a reading operation. First, the data is loaded if it does not exist in cache. Second, the value of nUsers is increased by one for the selected record in Data Hashtable. Finally, the selected record time is mapped to the event firing time in Time Hashtable
  - **Prepare Write:** It prepares the data to be used in a writing operation. First, the data is loaded if it does not exist in cache. Otherwise, the data attribute is copied from the most recent record and nUsers is set to one, dirty is set to false, and locked is set to false. Finally, a new record is created with the event firing time as the identifier (i.e. its key). If the record data was copied from an existing record in the cache, that existing record **nUsers** is increased by one.
  - **Prepare Read and Write:** It prepares the data be used in both operations. First, prepare write action is performed followed by the prepare read.

- **getValue:** First, the event firing time is mapped to the record using Time Hashtable. Second, the data is read from the record identified by the mapped time. Third, the record nUsers is decreased by one. Finally, when nUsers reaches zero, the record is removed.
- **setValue:** First, the record identified by the event firing time is selected and its data is updated with the new value. Finally, the changed properties names are added to the changed attribute with value of true.
- **isLocked -** First, the event firing time is mapped to the record using Time Hashtable. Then, the **dirty** attribute is checked. If it is true, the resource is locked.
- **Unlock:** This operation involves unlocking the device and storing the changes to the database. First, the locked field is checked for all the records of time less than the event firing time. If any of their locked attribute is true, then the locked attribute of the record identified by the event firing time is unset. Otherwise, all the changes in records with time less than the event firing time is merged. In such way, the last record data are merged with the current record data. We continue merging with the newer records as long as their locked attribute is false. Finally, the last updated record is stored in the database. The merge operation involves copying the values of the changed properties from the old record to the new record. Then, the name of changed properties is stored in the changed attribute. The number of users, nUsers, is decreased by one in the old and the new records. Finally, the dirty and locked attributes of the new record are unset.
- **Release:** First, the event firing time is mapped to the record using Time Hashtable. Second, nUsers is decreased by one for the record identified by the mapped time. Finally, when nUsers reaches zero, the record is removed.

EXPERIMENTAL USAGE OF THE PLATFORM

In this section, an illustrative scenario is presented that makes use of the platform features as shown in Figures 13 to 24. The goal of this scenario is show the platform in action and the operations it can perform. The scenario consists of device sending data streams of an ON/OFF controllable actuator. These data streams are forwarded to a Facebook page using the data forwarding feature. An email notification for when the load status is changed is sent through tasks and rules. A very simple mobile app is used to control the load through the platform.

FUTURE RESEARCH DIRECTIONS

Discuss future and emerging trends. Provide insight about the future of the book's theme from the perspective of the chapter focus. Viability of a paradigm, model, implementation issues of proposed programs, etc., may be included in this section. If appropriate, suggest future research opportunities within the domain of the topic.

Figure 13. Screenshot of registration form and email activation message

Figure 14. Screenshot of user dashboard

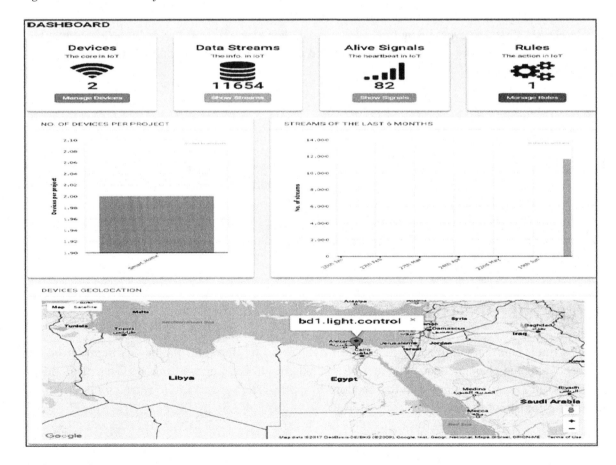

CONCLUSION

Figure 15. Screenshot of creating new project and new service

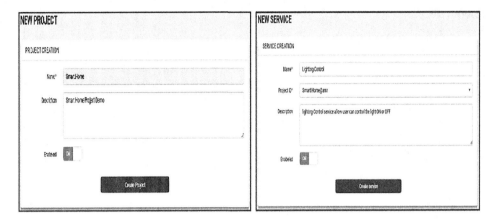

Figure 16. Screenshot of creating new group and new model

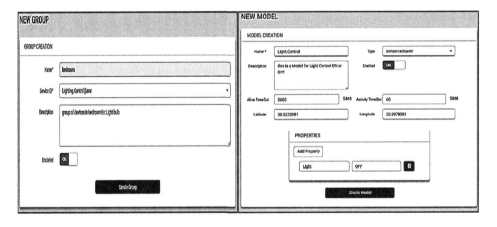

Figure 17. Screenshot of creating new device

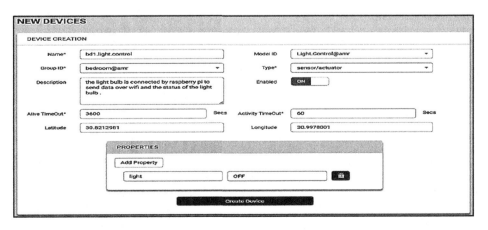

Figure 18. Screenshot of viewing all data streams in a datatable with advanced search filter

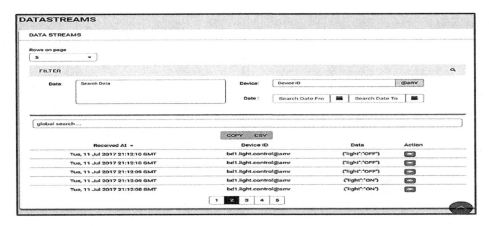

Figure 19. Screenshot of viewing all alive signals in a datatable with advanced search filter

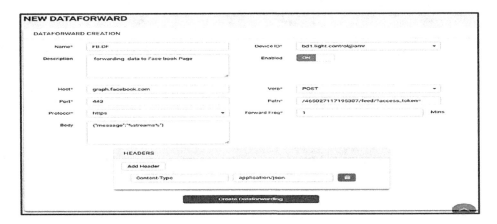

Figure 20. Screenshot of creating new data forward

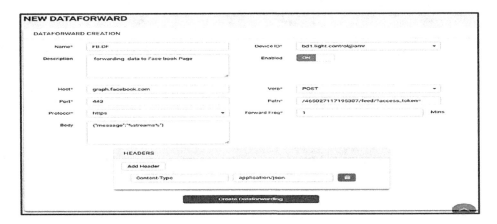

Figure 21. Screenshot of data forwarding to Facebook

Figure 22. Screenshot of creating new task

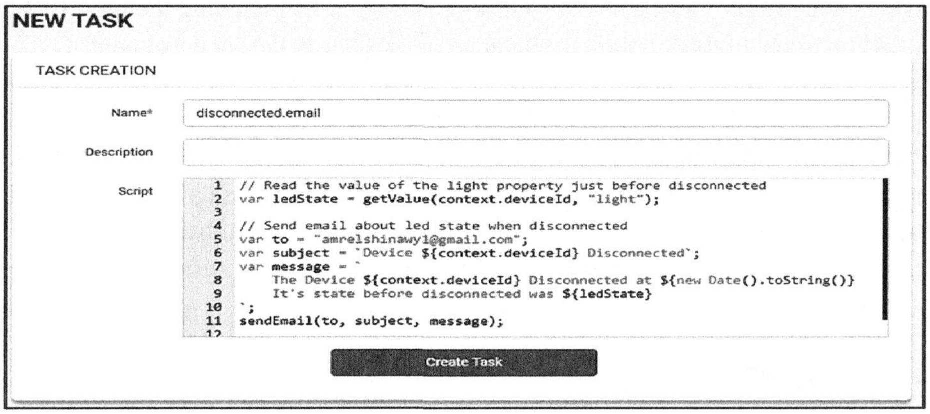

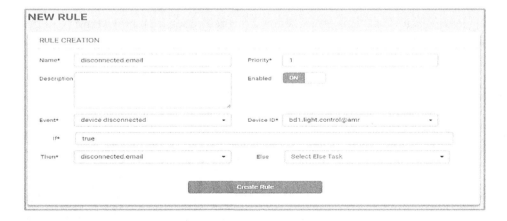

Figure 23. Screenshot of creating new rule

Figure 24. Screenshot of receiving email after device is disconnected

In this paper, we have presented a Cloud-Based IoT platform we called Galliot. Several design and implementation issues were revealed and discussed throughout the paper including the representation of the platform structure, the concurrency issues, the database issues, the device management and handling and finally the event and task management. We hope other researchers make use and benefit of these issues. We urge others to go on the same steps to enable the creation of such platform. This platform is the first Cloud IoT Platform to be developed in Egypt and North Africa. This paper is also the first version of the platform which we aim to improve upon. Things like better error messages and debugging features, better integration with other services, more lightweight protocols, more bulk actions support, collaboration features, an SDK based on the rule engine. and better access control system are set as future work.

ACKNOWLEDGMENT

I would like to acknowledge the student group who worked on this project as a part of their graduation project at computer and control engineering department, faculty of engineering, Tanta university: Amr El-Shinawy, Basma Ashraf, Dina El-Agder, Fouad Faid, Mohamed Seada, Mohamed Abu-Elgheit, Mohamed Sallam, and Norhan Gad. This project earned the best graduation project award in the Egyptian Engineer Day and the best software project on 2017.

REFERENCES

Al-Fuqaha, A., Guizani, M., Mohammadi, M., Aledhari, M., & Ayyash, M. (2015). Internet of Things: A survey on enabling technologies, protocols, and applications. *IEEE Communications Surveys and Tutorials, 17*(4), 2347–2376. doi:10.1109/COMST.2015.2444095

ARM. (2018). *ARM mbed*. Retrieved at October 24 2018, from http://www.mbed.com/en/platform/

Atzori, L., Iera, A., & Morabito, G. (2010). The Internet of Things: A survey. *Computer Networks, 54*(15), 2787-2805.

Bosch. (2018). *IoT Platform,* Retrieved at October 24 2018, from http://www.bosch-si.com/iot-platform/iot-platform/iot-platform.html

Botta, A., de Donato, W., Persico, V., & Pescap, A. (2016). Integration of Cloud computing and Internet of Things: A survey. Future Generation Computer Systems, 56, 684-700.

Bray, T. (2013). *The JSON Data Interchange Standard*. IETF.

Cisco. (2018). *Jasper*. Retrieved at October 24 2018, from http://www.jasper.com/

Coulouris, G., & Dollimore, J. (2011). *Distributed Systems: Concepts and Design*. Addison-Wesley.

Guth, J., Breitenbücher, U., Falkenthal, M., Fremantle, P., Kopp, O., Leymann, F., & Reinfurt, L. (2018). A detailed analysis of IoT platform architectures: concepts, similarities, and differences. Internet of Everything: Algorithms, Methodologies, Technologies and Perspectives, 81-101.

Intel. (2018). *Intel IoT*. Retrieved at October 24 2018, from http://www.intel.com/content/www/us/en/internet-of-things/overview.html

Internet of Things Research – European Union (2016). *Report on IoT Platform Activity*. Author.

Internet Society. (2001). *The Internet of Things: An Overview*. Retrieved at January 1, 2016, from https://www.internetsociety.org/resources/doc/2015/iot-overview

IoT Analytics. (2015). *IoT platforms: The central backbone for the Internet of Things*. Retrieved at October 24 2018, from http://www.iot-analytics.com

Jones, M., Bradley, J., & Sakimura, N. (2015). *Introduction to JSON Web Tokens*. IETF.

Li, S., Xu, L. D., & Zhao, S. (2015). The Internet of Things: A survey. *Information Systems Frontiers, Springer Publisher*, *17*(2), 243–259. doi:10.100710796-014-9492-7

Menascé, D. A., & Nakanishi, T. (1982). Optimistic versus pessimistic concurrency control mechanisms in database management systems. *Information Systems, 7*(1), 13-27.

Microsoft. (2018). *Microsoft Azure IoT*. Retrieved at October 24 2018, from http://www.microsoft.com/en-gb/internet-of-things/azure-iot-suite

Perera, C., Liu, C. H., & Jayawardena, S. (2015). The emerging Internet of Things marketplace from an industrial perspective: A survey. *IEEE Transactions on Emerging Topics in Computing*, *3*(4), 585–598. doi:10.1109/TETC.2015.2390034

Predix, G. E. (2018). *Predix: The World's First Industrial Internet Platform*. Retrieved at October 24 2018, from http://www.ge.com/uk/b2b/digital/predix

Razzaque, M. A., Milojevic-Jevric, M., Palade, A., & Clarke, S. (2016). Middleware for Internet of Things: A survey. *IEEE Internet of Things Journal*, *3*(1), 70–95. doi:10.1109/JIOT.2015.2498900

Tanenbaum, A. S., & Van Steen, M. (2013). *Distributed Systems: Principles and Paradigms*. Pearson Education Limited.

Xu, L. D., He, W., & Li, S. (2014). Internet of Things in industries: A survey. *IEEE Transactions on Industrial Informatics*, *10*(4), 2233–2243. doi:10.1109/TII.2014.2300753

ADDITIONAL READING

Afzal, B., Umair, M., Shah, G. A., & Ahmed, E. (2017). *Enabling IoT platforms for social IoT applications: Vision, feature mapping, and challenges. Future Generation Computer Systems*. Elsevier.

Bertino, E., & Islam, N. (2017). Botnets and Internet of Things Security. *IEEE Computer Society, 50*(2), 76–79. doi:10.1109/MC.2017.62

Farris, I., Taleb, T., Khettab, Y., & Song, J. S. (2018). A survey on emerging SDN and NFV security mechanisms for IoT systems. *IEEE Communications Surveys and Tutorials*.

Heimes, P., & Senel, S. (2018). *IoT Platforms for the Internet of Production*. IEEE Internet of Things Journal.

Li, Y., Orgeriea, A., Rodero, I., Amersho, B. L., Parashar, M., & Menaud, J. M. (2018). End-to-end energy models for Edge Cloud-based IoT platforms: Application to data stream analysis in IoT. *Future Generation Computer Systems, Elsevier, 87*, 667–678. doi:10.1016/j.future.2017.12.048

Shim, J. P., Sharda, R., French, A. M., Syler, R. A., & Patten, K. (2017). The Internet of Things (IoT): Platforms, Analytics, Security, Business Model, and Human Interaction. *Proceedings of the Twenty-Third Americas Conference on Information Systems*, Boston, MA.

Singh, K. J., & Kapoo, D. S. (2017). Create Your Own Internet of Things: A survey of IoT platforms. *IEEE Consumer Electronics Magazine, 6*(2), 57–68. doi:10.1109/MCE.2016.2640718

Thota, C., Sundarasekar, R., Manogaran, G., Varatharajan, R., & Priyan, M. K. (2017). *Centralized Fog Computing Security Platform for IoT and Cloud in Healthcare System. Exploring the Convergence of Big Data and the Internet of Things* (pp. 141–154). IGI Global.

KEY TERMS AND DEFINITIONS

API: An application program interface (API) is a set of functions, protocols, and tools for building software applications. It specifies and simplifies how software components should interact specially when programming graphical user interface (GUI) components.

Cloud: A global network of servers around the globe connected logically together to appear as a single system. These servers can either store and manage data, run applications, or deliver content or a service.

Concurrency Control: A database management systems (DBMS) concept that is used to solves the conflicts that occur with the simultaneous accessing or altering of data that can occur with a multi-user system. It prevents two or more users from editing the same record at the same time and also serializes transactions for backup and recovery.

IoT: A system of connected computing devices, machines, objects, people or sensors that have unique identifiers (UIDs). They have the ability to transfer data over a network which are then utilized to make decisions or actions.

IoT Platform: A high level support software that connects edge hardware, access points, and data networks to other parts of the value chain (which are generally the end-user applications). IoT platforms typically handle ongoing management tasks and data visualization, which allow users to automate their environment.

JSON: JavaScript object notation is a lightweight data-interchange format which is easy for humans to read and write and for machines to parse and generate. It is based on a subset of the JavaScript programming language.

Rule Engine: A sophisticated if/then statement interpreter that is used to specify a set of rules and the corresponding actions taken.

Chapter 7
Challenges and Trends in Home Automation:
Addressing the Interoperability Problem With the Open–Source Platform OpenHAB

Cristina Portalés
University of Valencia, Spain

Sergio Casas
 https://orcid.org/0000-0002-0396-4628
University of Valencia, Spain

Kai Kreuzer
openHAB Foundation e.V., Germany

ABSTRACT

Home automation (HA) systems can be considered as an implementation of the internet of everything (IoE) where many devices are linked by intelligent connections in order to improve the quality of life at home. This chapter is dedicated to analyzing current trends and challenges in HA. Energy management, safer homes, and improved control over the house are some of the benefits of HA. However, privacy, security, social disruption, installation/maintenance issues, economic costs, market fragmentation, and low interoperability represent real problems of these IoE solutions. In this regard, the latest proposals in HA try to answer some of these needs with low-cost DIY solutions, wireless solutions, and IP-based HA systems. This chapter proposes a way to deal with the interoperability problem by means of the open-source platform openHAB. It is based on the concept of a home automation bus, an idea that enables the separation of the physical and the functional view of any device, allowing to create a technology-agnostic environment, which is perfect for addressing the interoperability problem.

DOI: 10.4018/978-1-5225-7332-6.ch007

INTRODUCTION

The vision of a smart home that takes advantage of the latest advances in digital and information technologies - being able to anticipate our actions and satisfy our needs through intelligent or automatic actions - has been around for decades. The idea of bringing computers to our background in a *ubiquitous computing* paradigm was forecasted in 1991 by Weiser (Weiser, 1991), so that computers would increasingly enable the integration of simple objects, such as clothing labels, key fobs, light bulbs, etc. in an unobtrusive way in the user's life (Toschi, Campos, & Cugnasca, 2017). This vision is indeed very appealing and seductive, since it has an enormous potential in improving our daily life, saving time, money and energy, improving home comfort, safety, security, health care, weather-awareness and many other aspects.

With homes implementing Internet of Things (IoT) scenarios, this smart home vision is closer to reality than ever. The IoT is envisioned as a network that allows everyone and everyday objects to be connected anytime and anyplace. Smart homes can be seen as an interactive people-centric application of IoT, which is aimed at improving the quality of life (Feng, Setoodeh, & Haykin, 2017). The decrease in electronic hardware production costs is causing the number of IoT-capable devices to grow at astonishing rates. In fact, the number of IoT devices has already well exceeded the number of human beings living in our planet (Swan, 2012). Therefore, home automation is expected to benefit from this new digital revolution. Although not all smart home technologies provide direct communication between their devices and the Internet - gateways are needed in most systems -, smart home networks are considered IoT applications.

However, a smart home is much more than a building with connected digital components. Since many devices are connected together for a common purpose, in an orchestrated, convergent way, this smart home vision clearly represents an example of the Internet of Everything (IoE) paradigm, where individual devices are meaningful only in the context of the intelligent network in which they work, connecting data, processes, things and people.

There is not a standard or fixed definition of the term *smart home*. In fact the concept of *home* has many different connotations and meanings, as opposed to house/building (Gram-Hanssen & Darby, 2018). Nevertheless, it is widely accepted that a smart home is one (leaving aside the sociological connotations about the word home) that incorporates automation systems to provide its inhabitants with remote control and sophisticated monitoring over the building. A possible definition is "a dwelling incorporating a communications network that connects the key electrical appliances and services, and allows them to be remotely controlled, monitored or accessed."(Ye & Huang, 2011). This definition does not include an intelligent/smart behavior or even automations, but it is understood that a smart home is able to perform automatic programmable actions on behalf of their inhabitants and without human intervention. This ability is known as *home automation* (HA) and opens the possibility to treat the house as a digital system where all computer science paradigms can be applied, including artificial intelligence, machine learning, data mining, automatic reasoning or even big data. Although home automation and smart home do not refer to the exact same thing, they are often considered as synonyms (Stojkoska & Trivodaliev, 2017).

History on HA can be traced back to the final decades of the 19th century. Although no digital technology was involved, the comfort increase provided by the introduction of electricity at home in the late 1800s was significant. Of course, the concept of highly-automated digital home available for a mass market that we identify today as a smart home came only in the final quarter of the 20th century (Gram-Hanssen & Darby, 2018).

Despite the appealing futuristic visions of smart homes, the truth is that HA technologies have not been massively adopted (Brush et al., 2011). Although prospective users apparently have rather positive views about HA, (Hargreaves & Wilson, 2017) and a few systems have experimented some market success lately, worries about loss of independency, privacy, cost, interoperability and some other socio-technical risks (Wilson, Hargreaves, & Hauxwell-Baldwin, 2017) represent barriers that hinder the evolution and adoption of this technology. This shows the necessity of performing further research in the smart home field.

This chapter is dedicated to analyzing the current situation of the HA field, identifying strengths, weaknesses, opportunities, threats, trends and the many challenges this technology faces. One of these challenges is how to deal with the problem of interoperability in a fragmented market. We propose a way to overcome this issue by using the open-source software platform openHAB.

The chapter is structured as follows. Section 1 has already introduced the topic. Section 2 reviews the different features, technologies and applications of home automation. Section 3 deals with the strengths, weakness, challenges, opportunities and trends in home automation. Section 4 is dedicated to explain the openHAB platform. Section 5 explains how to use this software platform to deal with the interoperability problem. Finally, section 6 draws the conclusions and outlines possible future research lines.

SMART HOMES: FEATURES, APPLICATIONS AND TECHNOLOGIES

Different types of devices can be identified in home automation solutions: sensors, actuators, controllers, network-support devices, gateways and user interfaces. These devices are usually arranged in a network with different topologies (bus, ring, mesh, etc.) and different communication protocols, in order for the devices to communicate information between them and with the outside world. The communication networks used in smart home devices are called Home Area Networks (HANs). Of course, particular devices could act simultaneously as different types of devices. As consumer electronics can be in most cases miniaturized, it is not unusual that sensors and actuators act also as network-support devices, especially in wireless HANs (WHANs). There are also sensors that can play the role of actuators, and controllers that have gateway functionalities.

Sensors are used to collect information about the environment (both inside and outside home). Temperature, light, humidity, presence, motion, smoke, water, carbon monoxide, wind, atmospheric pressure, rain, sound, acceleration or vibration are some of the physical variables that can be measured used in a smart homes. Battery state, signal range, connection status can also be measured to perform self-diagnostics of the HAN.

Actuators allow to modify the environment in which the home inhabitants live. Relays, switches, dimmers, roller shutters, blinds, heaters, air conditioners, ventilation systems, garage doors, water/gas supply valves or irrigation systems are examples of actuators that can be remotely and automatically controlled by smart homes.

Controllers are special devices meant to manage, command and supervise the devices of the HAN, so they can be added to and removed from the network, setup and create intelligent and automatic actions based on their information. In most home automation systems, there is a single controller, or at least a single controller per network, if several HANs are simultaneously used.

Network-support devices are elements that allow a HAN to work properly or enhance their reliability. Depending on the network type, topology and physical communication technology employed, these devices could be signal repeaters, transducers, multiplexers, data routers, hubs, etc.

Gateways are devices that allow a HAN to receive and send information to other networks that do not use the same communication protocol. The foreign network could also be a HAN, or may be a different kind of network, like Ethernet or a mobile-phone network. Gateways to the Internet are especially important in IoT/IoE scenarios.

Finally, *user interfaces* are devices or means that are used to communicate information to and from the user, so that they can control the operation of the smart home and monitor its status. User interfaces can be tangible or intangible. Examples of tangible interfaces include tablets, smart phones, buttons, panels, rocker switches, contact breakers or key fobs. Intangible interfaces represent more natural interaction paradigms, like voice, gestures, looks, or body motion.

IoT devices can be applied for home automation in several different ways and for many different applications: light control, ventilation and air conditioning, security (door/window sensing, security cameras), safety (water/gas/carbon monoxide leak detection), entertainment (TV, music, games), presence and motion detection, economy (appliance control, electric metering), energy management, irrigation systems and gardening, comfort (roller shutters, heating), health care (children monitoring, elderly or disabled support), cleaning (vacuum cleaning, connection with home appliances), weather awareness, etc. Almost any application of digital and information technologies to the home environment can be considered home automation.

HA systems are based on different technologies. Although wired solutions are much more secure, reliable, robust and efficient, wireless home automation networks are becoming increasingly common, due to the difficulty or reluctance of wiring an existing home. New buildings are easier to adapt to wired HANs. However, a wireless HAN is easier to install, replace or update. For this reason, given the pace and the uncertainty at which home automation technology evolves, wired solutions represent a higher risk than wireless solutions and most homeowners choose WHANs. In addition, some technologies are able to operate through different physical mediums like Konnex (KNX), X10, LonWorks or Insteon (Stojkoska & Trivodaliev, 2017; Toschi et al., 2017; Withanage, Ashok, Yuen, & Otto, 2014) providing great flexibility.

Examples of wired technologies are KNX (twisted pair, power line and Ethernet), X10 (power line), Insteon (power line), LonWorks (twisted pair, optical fiber and power line) and HomePlug (power line). Examples of wireless home automation technologies are ZigBee, Z-Wave (Figure 1), Bluetooth, Wi-Fi, 6LoWPAN, EnOcean, UWB, Wavenis (Rathnayaka, Potdar, & Kuruppu, 2011) and also the radio-frequency versions of wired systems: KNX-RF, X10-RF, Insteon-RF and LonWorks-RF.

SMART HOMES: CHALLENGES AND TRENDS

Strengths and opportunities in HA are almost countless. With an increasing population demanding more and more energy - with its corresponding carbon footprint and contribution to global warming - an effective use of energy is crucial for the survival of our planet. Home automation should play a vital role in creating energy-efficient and energy-aware environments.

The concept of IoE has the potential to transform residential houses and offices making them more ecologically friendly. In fact, prospective users see energy management as the main purpose and ben-

Figure 1. Some Z-Wave devices. From left to right, top to bottom: a door/window sensor, a Z-Wave controller, a dimmer, a flood sensor, a motion sensor, a smoke sensor, a temperature chip and a relay switch (Fibar Group S.A., 2018)

efit of HA (Wilson et al., 2017). However, IT solutions do indeed need energy to operate and there are sometimes "hidden energy costs" (Hargreaves, Wilson, & Hauxwell-Baldwin, 2018). Energy savings by means of HA is explored through a well-established research line (Friedli, Kaufmann, Paganini, & Kyburz, 2016; Jahn et al., 2010; Louis, Caló, Leiviskä, & Pongrácz, 2015; Mehdi & Roshchin, 2015), which connects with the widely studied topic of smart grids (Lobaccaro, Carlucci, & Löfström, 2016; Zhou et al., 2016). One of the conclusions of this research body is that, although, smart homes could be energy-aware environments and are expected to reduce energy consumption, HA could also create a demand for previously unwanted products and services, causing an increase in energy consumption and environmental damage (Darby, 2018). Therefore, it is important that the HA system needs less energy to operate than it saves (Hargreaves et al., 2018). In this regard, home automation systems based on energetically efficient exploitation of resources represent the most promising trend in HA technology. EnOcean (Ploennigs, Ryssel, & Kabitzsch, 2010), an energy-harvesting HA solution is an example of how the IoE paradigm could be used in a sustainable way. Its energy-aware design has an impact in performance and throughput (Ploennigs et al., 2010). Nevertheless, this paradigm represents what a smart home should really be, and the authors hope this kind of solutions become a trend in the near future, although we are aware that market is driven by many factors and energy is just one of them.

Safer homes, both in terms of safety against accidents (A. Jose & Malekian, 2017; Lee & Lee, 2004) - such as fire, gas leaks, water leaks and especially the deadly and silent carbon monoxide poisoning -, health care (Laamarti & El Saddik, 2017; Moraitou, Pateli, & Fotiou, 2017) and security/protection against crime (Gibbs, 2016; Prasad, Mahalakshmi, Sunder, & Swathi, 2014) can be expected through the use of HA. Some of the projected uses of HA in this area are starting to be a reality (Friedewald, Da Costa, Punie, Alahuhta, & Heinonen, 2005; Korhonen, Parkka, & Van Gils, 2003), although we are still far from houses that detect medical conditions and avoid criminal activities. When this vision is completed, it would fulfill one of the expected features of the term home, which is perceived as a safe haven where its inhabitants can rest and live protected from the dangers of the outside world (Gram-Hanssen & Darby, 2018). In fact, security is still one of the main marketing arguments of HA vendors.

In this regard, and related with health care, Ambient Assisted Living (AAL) (Schmidt & Obermaisser, 2017; Suryadevara, Kelly, & Mukhopadhyay, 2014) is a new trend that overlaps with HA. AAL focuses on using concepts, methods, devices, systems, products and services in the home environment to support people, mostly elderly or disabled, in living independently (but monitored) for as long as possible. One of the strengths of IoT applications, and HA in particular, is that they can provide additional benefits to the concept of AAL (Ben Hmida & Braun, 2017) in order to improve the quality of life of the elderly and the disabled, who are often physically challenged by obstacles at home. With current demographic projections, especially in Europe (Geman et al., 2015), this research line is expected to become more and more important.

However, HA can do much more for home inhabitants. It allows to remotely monitor and modify the state of our home (heating, ventilation, blinds, water supply, etc.), it can improve the way we take care of our children, it allows also to perform presence simulation, it could make entertainment and multimedia devices easier to interconnect and it can provide our home with weather-awareness, allowing, for instance, to anticipate actions in reaction to weather changes (increase heating power before a winter storm starts, close windows and roller shutters on windy days, etc.).

Despite the incredible potential of the application of IoE to the smart home field, this application area still faces many challenges and problems. Security risks (A. C. Jose & Malekian, 2015) are one of the most worrisome problems of HA technologies. Some HA solutions have proven to be vulnerable to hacker attacks (Sivaraman, Chan, Earl, & Boreli, 2016) (Jacobsson, Boldt, & Carlsson, 2016). This is especially true in wireless networks (Knight, 2006) where information is not confined within a cable. In addition, privacy concerns are one of the most challenging problems that this technology should overcome to convince some hesitant users. As IoE devices are able to communicate with almost any other device, there is the risk that our private information be shared and monetized. As devices are designed to be very easy to use, obscuring almost everything that goes on at the 'back end' (Burgess, Mitchell, & Highfield, 2018), we cannot be sure that our intimacy is not being compromised.

Unlike traditional security concerns by traditional burglars, digital criminals can attack a home from almost any place in the world and they can do it whenever they like. Moreover, their attacks could remain unnoticed or cause severe damage, not only physical damage but also financial, emotional or reputational damage. Security in smart homes have many peculiar connotations that make good solutions especially harder to implement (A. C. Jose & Malekian, 2015). First, almost all data stored at home is completely personal. Thus, it could be particularly attractive for criminals. Second, HA systems usually consist of devices from different manufacturers. Each one comes with different features, problems and vulnerabilities. Third, HANs do not typically have a dedicated network administrator. Fourth, HANs are typically constantly changing, with the addition or removal of devices. From an engineer perspective, it is a nightmare to provide security to a network whose topology and content is unknown. Last, but not least, home automation environments are meant to be easily used. Security always introduces a degree of complication. Therefore, security procedures that reduce the convenience of using the HA may be rejected by users.

In this regard, social disruption represents a very important problem in smart homes. Technology is meant to make life easier. Home automation solutions that are too hard to understand, too complicated, too difficult to maintain or make users change their lifestyle may be rejected by them. It is important that machines fit the human environment instead of forcing humans to enter theirs. As Weiser cleverly pointed out "the most profound technologies are those that disappear. They weave themselves into the fabric of everyday life until they are indistinguishable from them" (Weiser, 1991). Seamless integration is therefore crucial to avoid social disruption.

However, the research community seems to have paid little attention to the evaluation of smart home initiatives in terms of real end-users' acceptability. Indeed, there is a striking contrast between the many research papers that deal with network technologies and estimate potential benefits of smart homes by means of simulations, compared to the relatively few works that report on measured efficiency and acceptability in real conditions (Darby, 2018). The authors believe this situation should change and this research direction should become a trend in home automation.

Another important social aspect is the impact of installing an HA ecosystem at home. Wired systems are often too invasive and sometimes require architectural or building changes in the house. Wireless devices are easier to install but suffer from the problems of interference, signal range and battery life. A system in which devices fail due to poor signal or in which the user needs to constantly change batteries, would be inacceptable if a true IoE paradigm is used with tens or hundreds of devices at home. The increasing complexity of HA solutions due to the large number of devices that may be installed, makes maintenance a problem that should not be overlooked.

The economic cost is also a problem. Some of the home automation solutions are expensive. Thus, they need to prove that this money is worth spending, saving energy bills, or providing a level of comfort that users feel important to pay for. IoE devices should not be expensive, since mass production is causing a reduction in production costs. Nevertheless, as home automation is usually linked to upper-class householders, prices are typically high. We believe market will find a way to solve this problem without any scientific or technological input.

Market fragmentation is also a big problem. Due to protocol incompatibility and lack of standardization, customers can find themselves locked in a vertical solution, where vendors claim to provide the whole chain of products from sensors and actuators to gateways and servers (Jacobsson et al., 2016), but do not offer customers the possibility and freedom of choosing products from different vendors when theirs do no offer the features users want. In such cases, potential users may feel disoriented and may refuse to enter the home automation market. This market fragmentation generates one of the main problems of smart home technologies: interoperability, which will be addressed later.

New trends are trying to offer answers to these problems. In response to the high price of some home automation technologies, low cost Do-It-Yourself (DIY) solutions are being proposed in recent years. This is an interesting trend in home automation, with many scientific works proposing DIY HA solutions, especially in newly industrialized and developing countries. Raspberry Pi (Chavan, Patil, & Naik, 2017; Kulkarni, Joshi, Jadhav, & Dhamange, 2017; Pampattiwar, Lakhani, Marar, & Menon, 2017; A. Patil, Shaikh, Ghorpade, Pawar, & Memane, 2017; S. A. Patil & Pinki, 2017; Prasad et al., 2014; Younis, Ijaz, Randhawa, & Ijaz, 2018), Arduino boards (Bolaji, Kamaldeen, Samson, Abdullahi, & Abubakar, 2017; Chandramohan et al., 2017; ElShafee & Hamed, 2012; Kannapiran & Chakrapani, 2017; More, Gai, Sardar, Rupareliya, & Talole, 2017; Piyare & Tazil, 2011; Soliman, Dwairi, Sulayman, & Almalki, 2017) and many others (Patel & Kanawade, 2017; Vikram et al., 2017) have been used to propose low-cost DIY HA systems. Most of these solutions have been proposed in the last three years, reflecting the fact that this idea is a clear trend in HA.

The problem with these solutions is that they are typically not interoperable with other DIY solutions, unless a common software is used, increasing market fragmentation. In addition, in most cases they are usually not compliant with an easy installation and maintenance. Nevertheless, some of the proposed systems provide functions and services similar to those of market products. Therefore DIY HA solutions are important to show that home automation is not necessarily an expensive business.

In response to market fragmentation, IP-based home automation is also starting to be explored. Although the Internet Protocol (IP) was not specially designed for home automation, IP-based home automation solutions are being proposed lately, despite the initial skepticism of scientists and researchers (Mainetti, Patrono, & Vilei, 2011). They are an emerging and promising trend in HA since IP-based solutions have the advantage that IP is a very common protocol with many services and protocols already implemented. In fact, many protocols used in other related areas, such as Modbus, have also IP versions of the protocols, in order to make them widely available. In addition, IP allows identifying devices with a unique worldwide accessible address for each device and it is the "language" of the Internet. This represents the ideal case for the IoT/IoE paradigm, since non-IP-based HANs need gateways to allow their nodes to be addressable and accessible to the outside world (see Figure 2). IP-based HANs could dramatically increase the capillarity of the Internet (Gomez & Paradells, 2010). However, this could come at a cost, since having several devices connected to the Internet, from different vendors (with different security policies and possibly connecting to private corporate cloud systems), increases the vulnerability of your home. In addition, these devices could jeopardize privacy as they could store private data in remote locations. Solutions are needed for these problems (Kreuzer, 2014).

IP-based HA can be provided by using 802.11.x (Wi-Fi) networks (ElShafee & Hamed, 2012; Jakovljev, Subotić, & Papp, 2017), which is not particularly efficient in terms of energy consumption, or by the recently proposed IPv6 over Low-Power Wireless Personal Area Networks (6LoWPAN), which was specifically designed for home automation and IoT scenarios (Arndt, Krause, Wunderlich, & Heinen, 2017; Dorge & Scheffler, 2011; Huang & Yuan, 2015; Tudose et al., 2011).

Wi-Fi solutions have the advantage that Wi-Fi infrastructure is present in almost every home (surely in houses that want to be "smart" by using HA), most of them using Wi-Fi routers giving direct access to the Internet. However, previous standards of the 802.11 family (802.11.a/b/g/n/ac) were not designed for home automation and the complexity, efficiency, power consumption and latency of Wi-Fi solutions are not in line with the needs of HA. For instance, both Z-Wave and ZigBee are by definition mesh networks, while Wi-Fi has a star topology. Only very recently, Wi-Fi Mesh (802.11s specification) has become available and might solve range issues of Wi-Fi for HA. The rest of the problems are also expected to change with the arrival of the 802.11.ah protocol (known as *HaLow*), which is designed for the IoT (Ahmed, Rahman, & Hussain, 2016; Banos, Afaqui, Lopez, & Garcia, 2017; Del Carpio et al., 2016).

The 6LoWPAN concept is based on the idea that "the Internet Protocol could and should be applied to even the smallest of devices" (Mulligan, 2007). This vision is fully compliant with IoT/IoE scenarios. 6LoWPAN allows IPv6 packets to be sent over IEEE 802.15.4 networks. 6LoWPAN shares the same physical and MAC layer with ZigBee, but upper layers make them incompatible (as seen in Figure 2). A tough battle between 6LoWPAN, 802.11.ah, Z-Wave, ZigBee and even Bluetooth LE can be expected in the following years (Del Carpio, Di Marco, Skillermark, Chirikov, & Lagergren, 2017).

In this regard, WHANs are gaining importance in the HA sector, with respect to wired solutions. As soon as battery-problems are solved, the authors expect that wired technologies will be reserved for of-

Figure 2. Interoperability problems in WHANs. Solid lines represent feasible connections. Dashed lines represent unfeasible direct communication.

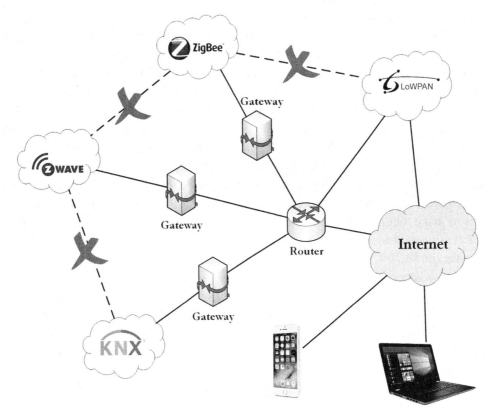

fices and new buildings whereas wireless solutions are going to be the preferred choice for mainstream residential customers. This tendency is already starting to take root.

Different IT companies compete to provide smart home capabilities. The result is a fragmented field with many different smart home ecosystems: Apple HomeKit, Google Home, Fibaro, EnOcean, Amazon Echo-Alexa, Nest, etc. Most of these ecosystems are not interoperable, although in some cases they share the same underlying physical technology. The vision of IoE is very appealing, since hundreds of devices in our homes have the ability to communicate creating a common intelligent ecosystem. However, if devices do not share a common language, this vision could be completely ruined. Users face a difficult decision: bet all their money on a single technology, with the risk of betting on the wrong product line, or just refuse to enter the home automation environment.

This challenge represents also an opportunity to create standard mechanisms in order to make the different solutions interoperable. We believe that interoperability is one of the most important requirements that the HA industry should fulfill in the near future.

This chapter deals with the interoperability problem in HANs - arguably the most important problem in HA - by proposing a way to make different smart home technologies work together through the use of the open-source platform openHAB. Several open-source home-automation platforms have been proposed in recent years, such as Home Assistant, Calaos, OpenMotics, MisterHouse, Domoticz, ioBroker, OpenNetHome, Jeedom, Smarthomatic, EventGhost, LinuxMCE, etc. However, openHAB stands out as a platform with a big community, with a huge list of supported technologies, mature enough to be used in complex scenarios, vendor-agnostic, extendable, multi-platform and fairly easy to learn. In the next sections this home automation platform is explained. We will show how to use it in order to solve the interoperability problem and make several HANs work together. Nevertheless, it is important to emphasize that some of the issues addressed in this chapter and solved with openHAB platform may be addressed with other open-source solutions. It is not in the aim of this chapter, however, to compare the different open-source solutions available in the market and in the academic community.

THE OPENHAB SYSTEM

openHAB (spelled with an initial lower case "o") is a technology-agnostic software platform that covers all the aspects of home automation (openHAB Foundation e.V., 2018) devices, protocols, automatic and intelligent actions, user interfaces, data logging, administration, configuration, remote monitoring, etc. It is based on the concept of a "Home Automation Bus", a vendor-agnostic asynchronous communication bus where all the HA information can be shared between the IoE devices that form the home automation network. This common language/platform is essential to provide interoperability between IoE devices from different vendors or even different technologies. A key point to provide this interoperability is that openHAB distinguishes between the physical and the functional view of the system. Whereas the physical view is required for setup, the functional view represents the information that matters to HA applications, such as user interfaces and automation logic.

openHAB 2.2 is the latest release of this HA platform. All openHAB releases are implemented in Java. Therefore, they can be run on almost any computer architecture and operating system (anyone that is able to run the Java Virtual Machine) such as Windows, Linux or macOS. Much effort has been done to provide support for low-cost computers, such as *openHABian*, a Linux distribution for ARM single-board computers like the Raspberry Pi and the PINE64, with all the bundles and packages necessary to run openHAB already pre-installed. For this reason, DIY implementations can be implemented with openHAB at a very small cost.

openHAB 2 uses Apache Karaf and Eclipse Equinox for a modular OSGi runtime environment (OSGi Alliance, 2018). Each component in openHAB is therefore an OSGi bundle. Jetty is used as an HTTP server, so that a REST service is provided to access and set-up the system, and web-based user interfaces can provide remote control and supervision of the home.

In addition, the former openHAB 1.x architecture has served as the base upon which the *Eclipse SmartHome* (ESH) framework (Smirek, Zimmermann, & Beigl, 2016) has been built, which in turn became the core component of openHAB 2. Both openHAB and ESH are open-source platforms available under the terms of the Eclipse Public License.

Five fundamental concepts are used in openHAB: things, channels, items, events and links. A *thing* is an entity that is able to provide HA capabilities. Although things are often associated with physical devices like sensors or actuators, a thing can also represent a web service or any other source/recipient of information that could be meaningful for the HA system. Things can potentially provide many smart home functionalities at once by means of one or several channels. A *channel* represents the information and functionality that things can provide to the system. In this regard, channels are passive and can be seen as just a declaration of what a thing can offer. Although a thing could provide many channels, users can choose which channels are effectively used by their openHAB instance. Channels are activated by linking them to items. An *item* represents the exact functionality that can be used by applications. There are several types of items: Switch, Dimmer, Contact, Number, Color, DateTime, Location, Rollershutter, Image, Player, String and Group. Each type represents one particular smart home functionality. Depending on the type, items can have different states, which can be read, sent or modified through the openHAB bus by means of *events*. Events in openHAB are significant occurrences that represent either changes or commands in the home. Events are sent through the openHAB bus and are typically associated with items. The state of items is kept in a data structure called the *item repository*. The item repository is updated when state changes are received from the event bus and can be queried by automation logic, persistence services and user interfaces. Things and items are bound by means of links. A *link* is an association between one channel and one item. Channels can be linked to multiple items and items can be linked to multiple channels. From a user perspective, things need to be set-up before the system is used, and channels should be linked to items so that their functionality becomes available. openHAB offers also a special type of thing called bridge. A *bridge* is a thing that provides openHAB with access to other things, like a gateway or an authentication server.

In order to separate the physical view and the functional view of devices and services, a thing represents the physical view, whereas items represent the functional view. The whole openHAB system is built around this idea. Items represent a virtual HA layer that encapsulates the functionality used by applications, hiding the physical details, so that interoperability between different technologies is possible. However, items do not necessarily refer to physical actions performed by devices. Items that represent parameters of the system or any other information whose value is not obtained from things, can be defined too (see Figure 3). The values of these items can be modified directly by the user via user interfaces or can be used as flags or system variables updated and modified by openHAB by means of rules. An example of this is an item that enables or disables an alarm system. This item would be either directly controlled by the user or set to on and off by the system by means of automatic rules.

It is important to emphasize that openHAB is not designed to be executed by the hardware devices that form the HAN. Instead, openHAB serves as an integration hub between different devices and acts as a broker between different protocols and services. Therefore, an openHAB installation is typically composed of a single instance of this software platform running on a single computer, which acts, in turn, as a global home automation controller.

Another important advantage of openHAB is that it is completely modular thanks to its OSGi-based architecture. There is a base functionality that implements the core concepts and data-types necessary to make the home automation bus work, but the particular capabilities that depend on specific technologies are offered by *add-ons*. Add-ons provide openHAB with different functionalities: bindings, user interfaces, persistence, actions, transformation services, voice services and third party integration (see Figure 4).

Bindings connect different device types and technologies to the openHAB system. By adding a particular binding to the system, openHAB is able to translate the signals from that particular protocol/ service/technology to openHAB. More specifically, bindings translate event bus events to and from external devices, services or systems. The fact that bindings communicate information through the event bus ensures that software coupling remains low. A binding can implement one direction or both. Therefore, bindings can be classified as "In-", "Out-" or "InOut-Bindings". There are more than 150 bindings, which allow to interconnect technologies and services like KNX, Z-Wave, ZigBee, DMX, EnOcean, Philips Hue, Homematic, NTP, Yahoo Weather, Wake-on-LAN, Belkin WeMo, Samsung TV, LG TV, Nest, Modbus, and many others. The number of bindings is expected to increase since openHAB is not

Figure 3. Physical and virtual layers in openHAB

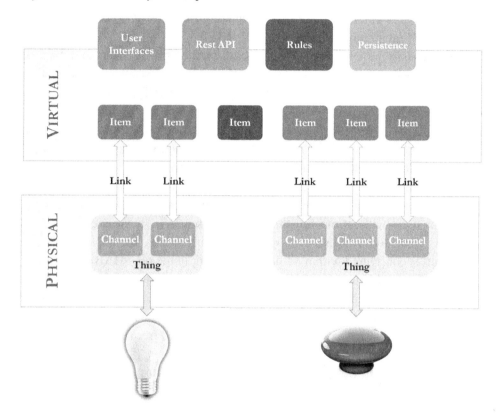

just a software platform. It is also a home automation open-source community devoted to improving the smart home experience and building an ecosystem around it.

User interfaces offer a front-end for user remote control, configuration and complex monitoring of home automation systems. System administration is performed through a web dashboard called *Paper UI*. Remote control and monitoring can be performed by several web interfaces or by smartphones apps (Android, iOS and Windows 10 versions are available). Two predefined user interfaces are provided with openHAB: *Basic UI* and *Classic UI*, both being web front-ends.

Persistence add-ons offer the possibility of storing time-series of states for items. Persistence services are necessary to build graphs showing the evolution of the items of a HA system. They can also be used to create automatic rules based on historic states, to achieve a better use of energy (avoiding repeated queries to the status of different sensors), to calculate average values and to recover the status of an item when a physical problem occurs. Multiple persistence services with different technologies are provided through several add-ons: MySQL, rrd4j, MQTT, JDBC, mapDB, Java Persistence API and InfluxDB. Many others can be added.

Actions are predefined operations that can be executed when a custom rule is defined in order to implement some kind of automatic behavior. openHAB offers a set of core actions that are always available, and a set of actions that can be installed through add-ons. The set of core actions available in openHAB include the modification/update of the state of an item (by sending the new state through the event bus), actions related with the audio system (change volume, play a sound or even say a given text through a text-to-speech engine), logging actions, timers or HTTP requests. Installable actions include: e-mail sending (through SMTP), Twitter integration, Telegram notifications, iOS and Android notifications, XMPP messages, KODI integration and many others.

Transformation services are used to translate raw information from sensors and devices to human-readable messages, by means of predefined JSON, XSLT, regular expressions and many other processes.

Voice services provide text-to-speech (TTS) and speech-to-text (STT) features. Several APIs and web services are available for that purpose.

Third party integration is performed to support the integration of technologies and ecosystems to which openHAB must be made available as a sub-system. openHAB has support for Apple HomeKit, Amazon Echo/Alexa, Google Calendar, Dropbox and many others.

openHAB is set-up by a series of configuration files. In openHAB 2 there is also the possibility of performing most of the set-up actions by means of the intuitive web interface *Paper UI*, so that the steps can be completed by users without much technological background. There are five main elements to configure in order to create a HA system with openHAB: things, items, sitemaps, persistence and rules. Each of these aspects is configured within a folder called *conf* in the openHAB installation.

The *things* subfolder (within the *conf* folder) is used for the configuration of things. Any thing that is used in openHAB is configured by means of a file with *.things* extension. For instance, to configure an NTP service, a file called *ntp.things* can be added to that folder. The following example represents a possible content for this file, so that a thing called *TimeUK* is defined from an NTP service, implemented in the NTP binding, to get the official time in the UK:

```
Thing ntp:ntp:TimeUK [hostname="uk.pool.ntp", refreshInterval=60, re-
freshNtp=30]
```

Figure 4. openHAB 2 architecture

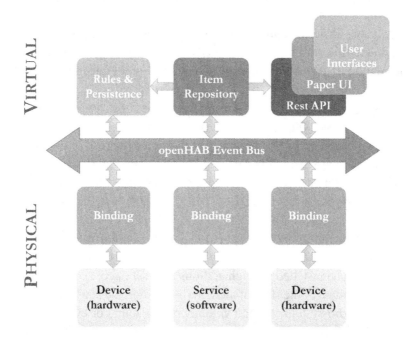

It is important to point out and emphasize that the *.things* file contains physical details for this element to work (in the example, an Internet host name).

An *items* subfolder is reserved for defining items. Although many item files can be created, a single file could be used to list and define all the items used by our system. Let us assume we name it *mySmartHome.items*. Following the NTP example, an item can be defined in this file to account for the date and time provided by the NTP server configured in the *ntp.things* file. This line would serve for that purpose:

```
DateTime dtOfficialDateTime {channel="ntp:ntp:TimeUK:dateTime"}
```

Note that this links the *dateTime* channel of the *TimeUK* thing with an item called *dtOfficialDateTime* of type *DateTime*. *dateTime* is one of the channels provided by the NTP binding. More lines can be added to the *mySmartHome.items* file in order to define and link all the items users need for their home automation system.

A *sitemaps* subfolder exists in order to configure *.sitemaps* files. A sitemap is used by openHAB to select what items can be presented in user interfaces in order to compose a user-oriented presentation of the HA system. User interfaces, including the openHAB mobile apps, take the information about the structure of the HA system from this file. A file called *mySmartHome.sitemap* could be setup for our previous simple example with the following content:

```
sitemap mySmartHome label="My openHAB Smart Home"
{
    Frame label="Time Information"
    {
        Text label="Date and Time in the UK" icon="calendar"
        {
            Text item= dtOfficialDateTime icon="calendar"
                    label="Official date and time: [%1$tA, %1$td.%1$tm.%1$tY]"
        }
    }
}
```

Similarly, persistence services are configured by *.persist* files in a *persistence* subfolder. These files describe what items need to be persisted, configuring also the frequency and some other properties. An example of a *mySmartHome.persist* file that configures openHAB to persist the *dtDateTime* item once in an hour, restoring also its value on start-up, could be like this:

```
Items
{
    dtOfficialDateTime: strategy = everyHour, restoreOnStartup
}
```

Last but definitely not least, openHAB offers the possibility to create predefined scripts that can be executed whenever a particular event occurs or a condition is met. These scripts are known as rules and are configured through *.rules* files in a *rules* folder. They are programmed in Xtend language, which is a dialect of Java. Existing Java library and code can be used seamlessly, and Java programmers should have no difficulties in creating rules with this programming language. In addition, simple rules can be defined from the openHAB 2 web administration front-end, so that less experienced users can also benefit from the possibility of creating custom rules.

An example of a *.rules* file with two rules, one for sending an e-mail when the system starts and one for sending a Telegram message when the main door is open, is presented next. For the second rule, it is assumed that three items exist in the system: *ctMainDoor*, representing a door contact sensor, *swAlarmEnabled*, representing a way to enable or disable the alarm of the house and *swAlarmSound*, which represents a siren actuator that emits a loud sound whenever it is turned on. For a detailed explanation of the rules syntax and other technical details, readers should refer to (openHAB Foundation e.V., 2018).

```
rule Start
when
    System started
then
    sendMail("myAccount@gmail.com", "openHAB message", "openHAB is starting")
end
rule DoorIsOpen
when
    Item ctMainDoor changed to OPEN
then
    sendTelegram("myTelegramId", "Main door is open!")
    if (swAlarmEnabled.state == ON)
       swAlarmSound.sendCommand(ON)
end
```

There are other elements that can be configured in openHAB, like icons, transformation services and actions. In addition, most of the add-ons that are part of openHAB can be configured by *.cfg* files in a *services* subfolder. Each add-on, like mail action, Twitter and Telegram actions, Apple HomeKit integration, KNX binding, smart TV bindings, etc. have their own *.cfg* so that particular hardware elements can be set-up.

ADDRESSING THE INTEROPERABILITY PROBLEM WITH OPENHAB

openHAB can be used to address the interoperability problem. In fact, openHAB has been successfully used in several projects at different scales. openHAB modular and technology-agnostic architecture makes it perfect for a variety of scenarios (Guimarães, Henriques, Pereira, & da Silva Silveira, 2018; Heimgaertner, Hettich, Kohlbacher, & Menth, 2017) and it can be used for almost any IoT/IoE application.

Solving the interoperability problem with openHAB is actually very simple. These are roughly the steps needed to integrate different services, products, protocols or devices and make them work together with openHAB. First, of course it is necessary to download, install and set-up openHAB. Next, search for the appropriate bindings that provide the functionality of the technologies you want to use, and setup the bindings with the right configurations. This step depends on the technologies you are using, but the process requires typically to setup a *.cfg* file for each binding. Next, add and configure things representing the devices/services you want to use, create items that represent the functionality you need from these devices, and link the items with the devices/services by means of links. With the *Paper UI* interface these steps are quite simple and can be performed with a visual front-end. (openHAB Foundation e.V., 2018). Optionally you may want to create rules to perform automatic actions (based on the defined items) or even store information by means of persistence services.

This procedure is better explained by showing an example. As a use case, we will show how to use openHAB to integrate four different technologies and ecosystems: KNX, Z-Wave, NTP and Samsung TV. Let us imagine that we have the following elements:

- 1 personal computer and a router providing LAN and Internet connection.
- 1 heating system controlled by a water boiler fueled by gas, with no thermostat.
- 1 KNX power supply.
- 1 KNX 8-channel actuator. One channel is connected to the water boiler and it is used to switch the gas burner on/off. The rest of the channels are used for lighting.
- 1 KNX-IP gateway connected to the router.
- 1 Z-Wave USB controller, connected to the PC.
- 1 Z-Wave 3-in-1 sensor, able to monitor motion (presence), temperature and light.
- 1 Samsung smart TV, connected to the router.
- 1 mobile phone (either iPhone, Android or Windows 10) with access to the router (either locally or via Internet) and the openHAB app installed.

Let us assume that we want to use the Z-Wave temperature sensor to serve as thermostat for the heating system and the motion and light sensor to turn the lights off when there is no human presence or there is enough natural light (more than 100 lumens). Let us also assume that we want to automatically turn off the TV at midnight and that the KNX device can also perform automatic actions on the lights and the heater based on the time of day. To do so, it needs a clock input, which we want to get from an NTP server in Spain.

For this simple but multi-technology scenario, we need to install the following openHAB bindings: KNX, Z-Wave, NTP and Samsung TV. Let us assume that the KNX endpoint for the clock input is 1/0/1, the KNX endpoint of the channel controlling the water boiler is 1/0/2, the KNX endpoint for the lights we want to control is 1/0/3, the local IP address of the KNX gateway is 192.168.1.2, the IP address of the PC is 192.168.1.3, the IP address of the smart TV is 192.168.1.4 and the device id for the Z-Wave sensor is 5f923bca:node2. With these requirements, we only need to create the following items:

```
DateTime dtDateTime    {channel="ntp:ntp:TimeES:dateTime", knx="1/0/1"}
Number nbSetPointTemp    "Desired Temperature"
Contact ctMotion    "Motion"    {channel="zwave:device: 5f923bca:node2:sensor_
binary"}
Number nbTemp    "Temp."    {channel="zwave:device:5f923bca:node2:sensor_ tem-
perature "}
Number nbLight    "Light"    {channel="zwave:device: 5f923bca:node2:sensor_ lu-
minance "}
Switch swHeater    {knx="1/0/2"}
Switch swLights    {knx="1/0/3"}
```

```
Switch swTvPower    "Television On/Off"   {channel="samsungtv:tv:myTv:power"}
Switch swTvMute     "Television Mute"     {channel="samsungtv:tv:myTv:mute"}
```

We assume that we have a thing called *TimeES*, which provides us with the time in peninsular Spain and a thing called *myTV* representing the Samsung smart TV (see Appendix).

The *dtDateTime* item will receive the time from the NTP service and feed the KNX input so that KNX knows the correct time of day. This way, both technologies become interoperable. As simple as that! Note that the syntax of the KNX binding does not use channels, since it is a legacy openHAB 1.x binding.

The item *nbSetPointTemp* is not linked to any channel. It will be included in a sitemap so that the user decides the target temperature for the room. Using any of the available user interfaces, the user will be able to control the heating system and many other aspects of this home with his/her phone, by means of the openHAB mobile app.

The items *ctMotion*, *nbTemp* and *nbLight* represent the information about motion (presence), temperature and light, provided by the Z-Wave sensor.

The item *swHeater* is linked to the KNX channel of the heater. It allows to switch it on/off from the KNX network. To perform the thermostat operation, we will need to create a very simple rule to toggle this item depending on the values of *nbSetPointTemp* and *nbTemp*.

The items *swTvPower* and *swTvMute* allow to monitor and control the state of the smart TV. With *swTvPower* we can switch it on/off, and with *swTvMute* we can mute/unmute the TV. To switch it off at midnight, we will need to create a rule in order to send an OFF command whenever the clock reaches midnight.

The Appendix shows the rules (*example.rules*) and some other configuration files needed to understand this example. It is important to note that this is a very simple example, yet much more impressing features could be added to this simple system without needing additional hardware: Apple HomeKit integration, presence simulation, notifications, etc.

As it can be seen, the open-source technology-agnostic philosophy of openHAB is perfect for HAN interoperability, and it is actually very simple to make different devices from different vendors, technologies and protocols work together. Although we have explained how to setup the most important configuration files, the example previously shown can also be configured with *Paper UI* instead. There is hence no need to be a technician to setup openHAB and most bindings are very easy to use. Nevertheless, there are potential security risks that should be taken into account when using bindings from untrusted sources. Due to its open and modular architecture, it is feasible to design a binding to expose system protected data over the REST interface (Ramljak, 2017). To solve this problem, openHAB 2 offers a repository binding where trustworthy bindings – supervised by the openHAB community - are uploaded.

CONCLUSION

The interconnection of computing elements have evolved very rapidly in the last 30 years. At first, when computers were tools used only for engineers and scientists, computers were interconnected to share data and processing power. This was the era of the *Internet of Computers* (Moser, Harder, & Koo, 2014). Later, computers became familiar objects used also for leisure and social interaction and almost every person owned a computer. When people started to use computers and Internet to access social media (Twitter, Facebook, etc.) the era of the *Internet of People* began. At the same time, computing elements different than desktop or laptop computers (mobile phones, tablets, sensors, single-board computers etc.), started to be very common. With all these devices connected, the idea of the *Internet of Things* was fulfilled. Now, researchers are focused on finding ways to create intelligent networks in which the elements are not just connected but serve a common meaningful purpose. This is the *Internet of Everything*.

Home automation is a perfect example of an IoE scenario. The goal is to create a network of interconnected elements at home, designed and placed to serve a common purpose: improve the quality of life. Therefore, its potential benefits are enormous. Smart energy consumption, safety, security, health-care, assisted living, entertainment, and a boost in home comfort are some of the few strengths and opportunities to apply HA. Nevertheless, as a human-centric technology, smart homes have to deal also with many challenges and problems such as digital security, social disruption, market fragmentation, economic, installation and maintenance costs.

Several trends have emerged to address some of these problems. AAL, low-cost DIY solutions, IP-based and wireless HA systems are some of the current trends in the smart home sector.

Market fragmentation has caused a really serious interoperability problem in smart homes. With several HA technologies and ecosystems, it is necessary to find a way to avoid any kind of vendor lock-in and make the different HA services and networks interoperable. This chapter proposes to use openHAB, an open-source vendor-agnostic software platform, to address this problem. openHAB has been specifically designed to separate the physical and the functional views of HA devices. Therefore, interoperability in HA could be easily handled by using openHAB, as it is explained in the chapter, until a standardized smart home protocol is proposed and accepted by the industry, the research community and of course, smart home users. IP-based HANs seem a natural solution for both reaching a standardized solution and also fully exploiting the benefits of IoE by means of worldwide addressable home devices.

As a people-centric IoE application, HA should be completely dedicated to fulfill the user needs. More frequently than would be desired, technology-focused HA systems have been designed, forgetting about what users really demand. One important question that HA engineers should ask is: What is a smart home? In the authors' opinions, home automation is whatever their smart home users want it to be!

REFERENCES

Ahmed, N., Rahman, H., & Hussain, M. I. (2016). A comparison of 802.11 AH and 802.15. 4 for IoT. *ICT Express*, 2(3), 100–102. doi:10.1016/j.icte.2016.07.003

Arndt, J., Krause, F., Wunderlich, R., & Heinen, S. (2017). *Development of a 6LoWPAN sensor node for IoT based home automation networks.* Paper presented at the Research and Education in Mechatronics (REM), 2017 International Conference on. 10.1109/REM.2017.8075226

Banos, V., Afaqui, M. S., Lopez, E., & Garcia, E. (2017). Throughput and Range Characterization of IEEE 802.11 ah. *IEEE Latin America Transactions*, 15(9), 1621–1628. doi:10.1109/TLA.2017.8015044

Ben Hmida, H., & Braun, A. (2017). Enabling an Internet of Things Framework for Ambient Assisted Living. In R. Wichert & B. Mand (Eds.), *Ambient Assisted Living: 9. AAL-Kongress, Frankfurt/M, Germany, April 20 - 21, 2016* (pp. 181-196). Cham: Springer International Publishing. 10.1007/978-3-319-52322-4_13

Bolaji, A. Q., Kamaldeen, R. A., Samson, O. F., Abdullahi, A. T., & Abubakar, S. K. (2017). A Digitalized Smart Mobile Home Automation and Security System via Bluetooth/Wi-Fi Using Android Platform. *International Journal of Information and Communication Sciences*, *2*(6), 93. doi:10.11648/j.ijics.20170206.11

Brush, A., Lee, B., Mahajan, R., Agarwal, S., Saroiu, S., & Dixon, C. (2011). Home automation in the wild: challenges and opportunities. *Proceedings of the SIGCHI Conference on Human Factors in Computing Systems*. 10.1145/1978942.1979249

Burgess, J., Mitchell, P., & Highfield, T. (2018). Automating the digital everyday: An introduction. *Media International Australia*, *166*(1), 6–10. doi:10.1177/1329878X17739020

Chandramohan, J., Nagarajan, R., Satheeshkumar, K., Ajithkumar, N., Gopinath, P., & Ranjithkumar, S. (2017). Intelligent Smart Home Automation and Security System Using Arduino and Wi-fi. *International Journal of Engineering And Computer Science*, *6*(3), 20694–20698.

Chavan, J., Patil, P., & Naik, P. (2017). Advanced Control Web Based Home Automation with Raspberry Pi. *International Journal of Advance Research. Ideas and Innovations in Technology*, *3*(2), 221–223.

Darby, S. J. (2018). Smart technology in the home: Time for more clarity. *Building Research and Information*, *46*(1), 140–147. doi:10.1080/09613218.2017.1301707

Del Carpio, L. F., Di Marco, P., Skillermark, P., Chirikov, R., & Lagergren, K. (2017). Comparison of 802.11ah, BLE and 802.15.4 for a Home Automation Use Case. *International Journal of Wireless Information Networks*, *24*(3), 243–253. doi:10.100710776-017-0355-2

Del Carpio, L. F., Di Marco, P., Skillermark, P., Chirikov, R., Lagergren, K., & Amin, P. (2016). *Comparison of 802.11 ah and BLE for a home automation use case*. Paper presented at the Personal, Indoor, and Mobile Radio Communications (PIMRC), 2016 IEEE 27th Annual International Symposium on.

Dorge, B. M., & Scheffler, T. (2011). *Using IPv6 and 6LoWPAN for home automation networks*. Paper presented at the Consumer Electronics-Berlin (ICCE-Berlin), 2011 IEEE International Conference on.

ElShafee, A., & Hamed, K. A. (2012). Design and implementation of a WIFI based home automation system. *World Academy of Science, Engineering and Technology*, *68*, 2177–2180.

Feng, S., Setoodeh, P., & Haykin, S. (2017). Smart Home: Cognitive Interactive People-Centric Internet of Things. *IEEE Communications Magazine*, *55*(2), 34–39. doi:10.1109/MCOM.2017.1600682CM

Fibar Group S.A. (2018). *Fibaro*. Retrieved 02/03/2018, 2018, from http://www.fibaro.com

Friedewald, M., Da Costa, O., Punie, Y., Alahuhta, P., & Heinonen, S. (2005). Perspectives of ambient intelligence in the home environment. *Telematics and Informatics*, *22*(3), 221–238. doi:10.1016/j.tele.2004.11.001

Friedli, M., Kaufmann, L., Paganini, F., & Kyburz, R. (2016). *Energy efficiency of the Internet of Things. Technology and Energy Assessment Report prepared for IEA 4E EDNA*. Lucerne University of Applied Sciences.

Geman, O., Sanei, S., Costin, H.-N., Eftaxias, K., Vyšata, O., Procházka, A., & Lhotská, L. (2015). *Challenges and trends in Ambient Assisted Living and intelligent tools for disabled and elderly people.* Paper presented at the Computational Intelligence for Multimedia Understanding (IWCIM), 2015 International Workshop on. 10.1109/IWCIM.2015.7347088

Gibbs, W. W. (2016). DIY Home Security. Deter Intruders with an Extra Loud Alarm. *IEEE Spectrum*, 20–21.

Gomez, C., & Paradells, J. (2010). Wireless home automation networks: A survey of architectures and technologies. *IEEE Communications Magazine*, *48*(6), 92–101. doi:10.1109/MCOM.2010.5473869

Gram-Hanssen, K., & Darby, S. J. (2018). "Home is where the smart is"? Evaluating smart home research and approaches against the concept of home. *Energy Research & Social Science*, *37*, 94–101. doi:10.1016/j.erss.2017.09.037

Guimarães, C. S. S., Henriques, R. V. B., Pereira, C. E., & da Silva Silveira, W. (2018). *Proposal IoT Architecture for Macro and Microscale Applied in Assistive Technology. In Online Engineering & Internet of Things* (pp. 36–43). Springer.

Hargreaves, T., & Wilson, C. (2017). *Perceived Benefits and Risks of Smart Home Technologies. In Smart Homes and Their Users* (pp. 35–53). Springer. doi:10.1007/978-3-319-68018-7_3

Hargreaves, T., Wilson, C., & Hauxwell-Baldwin, R. (2018). Learning to live in a smart home. *Building Research and Information*, *46*(1), 127–139. doi:10.1080/09613218.2017.1286882

Heimgaertner, F., Hettich, S., Kohlbacher, O., & Menth, M. (2017). *Scaling home automation to public buildings: A distributed multiuser setup for OpenHAB 2.* Paper presented at the Global Internet of Things Summit (GIoTS). 10.1109/GIOTS.2017.8016235

Huang, Z., & Yuan, F. (2015). Implementation of 6LoWPAN and its application in smart lighting. *Journal of Computer and Communications*, *3*(03), 80–85. doi:10.4236/jcc.2015.33014

Jacobsson, A., Boldt, M., & Carlsson, B. (2016). A risk analysis of a smart home automation system. *Future Generation Computer Systems*, *56*, 719–733. doi:10.1016/j.future.2015.09.003

Jahn, M., Jentsch, M., Prause, C. R., Pramudianto, F., Al-Akkad, A., & Reiners, R. (2010). *The energy aware smart home.* Paper presented at the Future Information Technology (FutureTech), 2010 5th International Conference on. 10.1109/FUTURETECH.2010.5482712

Jakovljev, S., Subotić, M., & Papp, I. (2017). *Realisation of a Smart Plug device based on Wi-Fi technology for use in home automation systems.* Paper presented at the Consumer Electronics (ICCE), 2017 IEEE International Conference on. 10.1109/ICCE.2017.7889340

Jose, A., & Malekian, R. (2017). Improving Smart Home Security; Integrating Logical Sensing into Smart Home. *IEEE Sensors Journal*, *17*(13), 4269–4286. doi:10.1109/JSEN.2017.2705045

Jose, A. C., & Malekian, R. (2015). Smart home automation security. *SmartCR*, *5*(4), 269–285.

Kannapiran, S., & Chakrapani, A. (2017). A Novel Home Automation System using Bluetooth and Arduino. *International Journal of Advances in Computer and Electronics Engineering*, *2*(2), 41–44.

Knight, M. (2006). How safe is Z-Wave? *Computing and Control Engineering, 17*(6), 18–23. doi:10.1049/cce:20060601

Korhonen, I., Parkka, J., & Van Gils, M. (2003). Health monitoring in the home of the future. *IEEE Engineering in Medicine and Biology Magazine, 22*(3), 66–73. doi:10.1109/MEMB.2003.1213628 PMID:12845821

Kreuzer, K. (2014). *Privacy in the Smart Home - Why we need an Intranet of Things.* Retrieved 02/03/2018, from http://www.kaikreuzer.de/2014/02/10/privacy-in-smart-home-why-we-need/

Kulkarni, B. P., Joshi, A. V., Jadhav, V. V., & Dhamange, A. T. (2017). IoT Based Home Automation Using Raspberry PI. *International Journal of Innovative Studies in Sciences and Engineering Technology, 3*(4), 13–16.

Laamarti, F., & El Saddik, A. (2017). *Home automation serving a healthier lifestyle.* Paper presented at the Medical Measurements and Applications (MeMeA), 2017 IEEE International Symposium on. 10.1109/MeMeA.2017.7985846

Lee, K. C., & Lee, H.-H. (2004). Network-based fire-detection system via controller area network for smart home automation. *IEEE Transactions on Consumer Electronics, 50*(4), 1093–1100. doi:10.1109/TCE.2004.1362504

Lobaccaro, G., Carlucci, S., & Löfström, E. (2016). A review of systems and technologies for smart homes and smart grids. *Energies, 9*(5), 348. doi:10.3390/en9050348

Louis, J.-N., Caló, A., Leiviskä, K., & Pongrácz, E. (2015). Environmental impacts and benefits of smart home automation: Life cycle assessment of home energy management system. *IFAC-PapersOnLine, 48*(1), 880–885. doi:10.1016/j.ifacol.2015.05.158

Mainetti, L., Patrono, L., & Vilei, A. (2011). *Evolution of wireless sensor networks towards the internet of things: A survey.* Paper presented at the Software, Telecommunications and Computer Networks (SoftCOM), 2011 19th International Conference on.

Mehdi, G., & Roshchin, M. (2015). Electricity consumption constraints for smart-home automation: An overview of models and applications. *Energy Procedia, 83*, 60–68. doi:10.1016/j.egypro.2015.12.196

Moraitou, M., Pateli, A., & Fotiou, S. (2017). Smart Health Caring Home: A Systematic Review of Smart Home Care for Elders and Chronic Disease Patients. In P. Vlamos (Ed.), *GeNeDis 2016: Geriatrics* (pp. 255–264). Cham: Springer International Publishing. doi:10.1007/978-3-319-57348-9_22

More, S. S., Gai, A. A., Sardar, V. S., Rupareliya, C. S., & Talole, P. T. (2017). Home Automation on Android Using Arduino. *Journal of Android and IOS Applications and Testing, 2*(1).

Moser, K., Harder, J., & Koo, S. G. (2014). *Internet of things in home automation and energy efficient smart home technologies.* Paper presented at the Systems, Man and Cybernetics (SMC), 2014 IEEE International Conference on. 10.1109/SMC.2014.6974087

Mulligan, G. (2007). The 6LoWPAN architecture. *Proceedings of the 4th workshop on Embedded networked sensors.* 10.1145/1278972.1278992 openHAB Foundation e.V. (2018). openHAB - a Vendor and Technology Agnostic Open Source Automation Software for Your Home. Retrieved 02/03/2018, 2018, from https://www.openhab.org

OSGi Alliance. (2018). *OSGi -The Dynamic Module System for Java.* Retrieved 02/03/2018, 2018, from www.osgi.org

Pampattiwar, K., Lakhani, M., Marar, R., & Menon, R. (2017). Home Automation using Raspberry Pi controlled via an Android Application. *International Journal of Current Engineering and Technology, 7*(3), 962–967.

Patel, S. M., & Kanawade, S. Y. (2017). Internet of Things Based Smart Home with Intel Edison. *Proceedings of International Conference on Communication and Networks.* 10.1007/978-981-10-2750-5_40

Patil, A., Shaikh, I. S., Ghorpade, V. P., Pawar, V. D., & Memane, P. S. (2017). Home Automation using Raspberry Pi & Windows 10 IOT. *Imperial Journal of Interdisciplinary Research, 3*(3).

Patil, S. A., & Pinki, V. (2017). Home Automation Using Single Board Computing as an Internet of Things Application. *Proceedings of International Conference on Communication and Networks.* 10.1007/978-981-10-2750-5_26

Piyare, R., & Tazil, M. (2011). *Bluetooth based home automation system using cell phone.* Paper presented at the Consumer Electronics (ISCE), 2011 IEEE 15th International Symposium on. 10.1109/ISCE.2011.5973811

Ploennigs, J., Ryssel, U., & Kabitzsch, K. (2010). *Performance analysis of the EnOcean wireless sensor network protocol.* Paper presented at the Emerging Technologies and Factory Automation (ETFA), 2010 IEEE Conference on. 10.1109/ETFA.2010.5641313

Prasad, S., Mahalakshmi, P., Sunder, A. J. C., & Swathi, R. (2014). Smart Surveillance Monitoring System Using Raspberry PI and PIR Sensor. *Int. J. Comput. Sci. Inf. Technol, 5*(6), 7107–7109.

Ramljak, M. (2017). *Security analysis of Open Home Automation Bus system.* Paper presented at the Information and Communication Technology, Electronics and Microelectronics (MIPRO), 2017 40th International Convention on. 10.23919/MIPRO.2017.7973614

Rathnayaka, A. D., Potdar, V. M., & Kuruppu, S. J. (2011). Evaluation of wireless home automation technologies. *Digital Ecosystems and Technologies Conference (DEST), 2011 Proceedings of the 5th IEEE International Conference on.* 10.1109/DEST.2011.5936601

Schmidt, M., & Obermaisser, R. (2017). Adaptive and technology-independent architecture for fault-tolerant distributed AAL solutions. *Computers in Biology and Medicine.* doi:10.1016/j.compbiomed.2017.11.002 PMID:29157726

Sivaraman, V., Chan, D., Earl, D., & Boreli, R. (2016). Smart-phones attacking smart-homes. *Proceedings of the 9th ACM Conference on Security & Privacy in Wireless and Mobile Networks.* 10.1145/2939918.2939925

Smirek, L., Zimmermann, G., & Beigl, M. (2016). Just a Smart Home or Your Smart Home–A Framework for Personalized User Interfaces Based on Eclipse Smart Home and Universal Remote Console. *Procedia Computer Science, 98,* 107–116. doi:10.1016/j.procs.2016.09.018

Soliman, M. S., Dwairi, M. O., Sulayman, I. I. A., & Almalki, S. H. (2017). Towards the Design and Implementation a Smart Home Automation System Based on Internet of Things Approach. *International Journal of Applied Engineering Research*, *12*(11), 2731–2737.

Stojkoska, B. L. R., & Trivodaliev, K. V. (2017). A review of Internet of Things for smart home: Challenges and solutions. *Journal of Cleaner Production*, *140*, 1454–1464. doi:10.1016/j.jclepro.2016.10.006

Suryadevara, N. K., Kelly, S., & Mukhopadhyay, S. C. (2014). Ambient Assisted Living Environment Towards Internet of Things Using Multifarious Sensors Integrated with XBee Platform. In S. C. Mukhopadhyay (Ed.), *Internet of Things: Challenges and Opportunities* (pp. 217–231). Cham: Springer International Publishing. doi:10.1007/978-3-319-04223-7_9

Swan, M. (2012). Sensor mania! the internet of things, wearable computing, objective metrics, and the quantified self 2.0. *Journal of Sensor and Actuator Networks*, *1*(3), 217–253. doi:10.3390/jsan1030217

Toschi, G. M., Campos, L. B., & Cugnasca, C. E. (2017). Home automation networks: A survey. *Computer Standards & Interfaces*, *50*, 42–54. doi:10.1016/j.csi.2016.08.008

Tudose, D. Ş., Voinescu, A., Petrăreanu, M.-T., Bucur, A., Loghin, D., Bostan, A., & Ţăpuş, N. (2011). *Home automation design using 6LoWPAN wireless sensor networks*. Paper presented at the Distributed Computing in Sensor Systems and Workshops (DCOSS), 2011 International Conference on. 10.1109/DCOSS.2011.5982181

Vikram, N., Harish, K., Nihaal, M., Umesh, R., Shetty, A., & Kumar, A. (2017). *A low cost home automation system using wi-fi based wireless sensor network incorporating Internet of Things (IoT)*. Paper presented at the Advance Computing Conference (IACC), 2017 IEEE 7th International.

Weiser, M. (1991). The computer for the 21st century. *Scientific American*, *265*(3), 94–104. doi:10.1038cientificamerican0991-94 PMID:1675486

Wilson, C., Hargreaves, T., & Hauxwell-Baldwin, R. (2017). Benefits and risks of smart home technologies. *Energy Policy*, *103*, 72–83. doi:10.1016/j.enpol.2016.12.047

Withanage, C., Ashok, R., Yuen, C., & Otto, K. (2014). *A comparison of the popular home automation technologies*. Paper presented at the Innovative Smart Grid Technologies-Asia (ISGT Asia), 2014 IEEE. 10.1109/ISGT-Asia.2014.6873860

Ye, X., & Huang, J. (2011). *A framework for cloud-based smart home*. Paper presented at the Computer Science and Network Technology (ICCSNT), 2011 International Conference on.

Younis, S. A., Ijaz, U., Randhawa, I. A., & Ijaz, A. (2018). Speech Recognition Based Home Automation System using Raspberry Pi and Zigbee. *NFC IEFR Journal of Engineering and Scientific Research, 5*.

Zhou, B., Li, W., Chan, K. W., Cao, Y., Kuang, Y., Liu, X., & Wang, X. (2016). Smart home energy management systems: Concept, configurations, and scheduling strategies. *Renewable & Sustainable Energy Reviews*, *61*, 30–40. doi:10.1016/j.rser.2016.03.047

ADDITIONAL READING

Apthorpe, N., Reisman, D., Sundaresan, S., Narayanan, A., & Feamster, N. (2017). Spying on the smart home: Privacy attacks and defenses on encrypted iot traffic. *arXiv preprint arXiv:1708.05044.*

Bojanova, I., Hurlburt, G., & Voas, J. (2014). Imagineering an internet of anything. *Computer, 47*(6), 72–77. doi:10.1109/MC.2014.150

Do, H. M., Pham, M., Sheng, W., Yang, D., & Liu, M. (2018). RiSH: A robot-integrated smart home for elderly care. *Robotics and Autonomous Systems, 101,* 74–92. doi:10.1016/j.robot.2017.12.008

Dorri, A., Kanhere, S. S., Jurdak, R., & Gauravaram, P. (2017). *Blockchain for IoT security and privacy: The case study of a smart home.* Paper presented at the Pervasive Computing and Communications Workshops (PerCom Workshops), 2017 IEEE International Conference on. 10.1109/PERCOMW.2017.7917634

García-Pereira, I., Gimeno, J., Pérez, M., Portalés, C., & Casas, S. (2018). *MIME: A Mixed-Space Collaborative System with Three Levels of Immersion and Multiple Users.* Paper presented at the IEEE and ACM International Symposium for Mixed and Augmented Reality 2018 (ISMAR 2018).

Gill, K., Yang, S.-H., Yao, F., & Lu, X. (2009). A zigbee-based home automation system. *IEEE Transactions on Consumer Electronics, 55*(2), 422–430. doi:10.1109/TCE.2009.5174403

Herrero, S. T., Nicholls, L., & Strengers, Y. (2018). Smart home technologies in everyday life: Do they address key energy challenges in households? *Current Opinion in Environmental Sustainability, 31,* 65–70. doi:10.1016/j.cosust.2017.12.001

Jain, S., Vaibhav, A., & Goyal, L. (2014). *Raspberry Pi based interactive home automation system through E-mail.* Paper presented at the Optimization, Reliabilty, and Information Technology (ICROIT), 2014 International Conference on. 10.1109/ICROIT.2014.6798330

Miraz, M. H., Ali, M., Excell, P. S., & Picking, R. (2015). *A review on Internet of Things (IoT), Internet of everything (IoE) and Internet of nano things (IoNT).* Paper presented at the 2015 Internet Technologies and Applications (ITA). 10.1109/ITechA.2015.7317398

Pavithra, D., & Balakrishnan, R. (2015). *IoT based monitoring and control system for home automation.* Paper presented at the Communication Technologies (GCCT), 2015 Global Conference on. 10.1109/GCCT.2015.7342646

Strengers, Y., & Nicholls, L. (2017). Convenience and energy consumption in the smart home of the future: Industry visions from australia and beyond. *Energy Research & Social Science, 32,* 86–93. doi:10.1016/j.erss.2017.02.008

Vujović, V., & Maksimović, M. (2015). Raspberry Pi as a Sensor Web node for home automation. *Computers & Electrical Engineering, 44,* 153–171. doi:10.1016/j.compeleceng.2015.01.019

Yeo, K. S., Chian, M. C., & Ng, T. C. W. (2014). *Internet of Things: Trends, challenges and applications.* Paper presented at the Integrated Circuits (ISIC), 2014 14th International Symposium on. 10.1109/ISICIR.2014.7029523

KEY TERMS AND DEFINITIONS

Automation: The technique of making an apparatus, process, device, or system operate automatically.

Internet of Everything (IoE): The intelligent connection of people, process, data, and things. The IoE builds on the foundation of the IoT by adding network intelligence that allows convergence, orchestration, and visibility across previously disparate systems.

Internet of Things (IoT): The interconnection via Internet of computing devices embedded in everyday objects, enabling them to send and receive data.

Interoperability: The ability of a system or device to work with or use the parts or equipment of another system.

Open-Source: A decentralized collaborative software-development paradigm based on peer-production. The code is accessible and available for the general public. Therefore, everyone can use and modify it without licensing restrictions.

openHAB: A vendor and technology agnostic open-source automation software for the home. It is a platform for integrating different home automation systems and technologies into one single solution that allows overarching automation rules and offers uniform user interfaces.

Smart Home: A home that incorporates automation systems to provide its inhabitants with remote control and sophisticated monitoring over the building.

APPENDIX: OPENHAB FILES FOR THE INTEROPERABILITY EXAMPLE

File **knx.cfg:**
```
# KNX gateway IP address
ip=192.168.1.2
# KNX IP connection type. Could be either TUNNEL or ROUTER
type=TUNNEL
# KNX gateway port
port=3671
# Timeout in milliseconds to wait for a response from the KNX bus
timeout=2000
# Use NAT (Network Address Translation)
useNAT=true
```
File **ntp.things:**
```
Thing ntp:ntp:TimeES [hostname="hora.roa.es", refreshInterval=60, refreshNtp=30
]
```
File **samsungtv.things:**
```
Thing samsungtv:tv:myTv [hostName="192.168.1.4", port=55000, refreshInter-
val=1000]
```
File **example.rules:**
```
rule Thermostat
when
    Item nbTemp changed or
    Item nbSetPointTemp changed
then
    var float temp = (nbTemp.state as DecimalType).floatValue()
    var float setPointTemp = (nbSetPointTemp.state as DecimalType).floatVal-
ue()
    if (setPointTemp > nbTemp)
        swHeater.sendCommand(ON)
    else
        swHeater.sendCommand(OFF)
end
rule LightsOff
when
    Item ctMotion changed or
    Item nbLight changed
then
    var float lum = (nbLight.state as DecimalType).floatValue()
    if ((ctMotion.state == CLOSED) || (lum > 100))
        swLights.sendCommand(OFF)
end
```

```
rule TvOff
when
    Time cron "0 0 0 * * ?"
then
    swTvPower.sendCommand(OFF)
end
```

Chapter 8
Mixing Different Realities in a Single Shared Space:
Analysis of Mixed-Platform Collaborative Shared Spaces

Sergio Casas

https://orcid.org/0000-0002-0396-4628

University of Valencia, Spain

Cristina Portalés

University of Valencia, Spain

Inma García-Pereira

University of Valencia, Spain

Jesús Gimeno

University of Valencia, Spain

ABSTRACT

The concept of internet of everything involves an intelligent connection of people, processes, data, and things. In this sense, shared spaces aimed to connect different users that collaborate following a common purpose are of relevance to the field. Many computer-based collaborative environments have been proposed in recent years. However, the design of mixed-platform collaborative spaces, in which different paradigms—such as augmented reality (AR) and virtual reality (VR)—are blended, is still uncommon. This chapter aims to analyze the benefits and features of these systems, reviewing existing related works and proposing a series of features for the design of effective mixed-platform collaborative shared spaces. In particular, the authors propose five setups with different levels of immersion/interaction, which are aligned to the current state of the art. These systems will be analyzed with respect to navigation, user representation, interaction, and annotation, among others. Finally, some applications are proposed within the given framework.

DOI: 10.4018/978-1-5225-7332-6.ch008

INTRODUCTION

Virtual Reality (VR) and Mixed Reality (MR) technologies are increasingly used in a variety of applications, such as education (Dunleavy & Dede, 2014), entertainment (Olanda, Pérez, Morillo, Fernández, & Casas, 2006), edutainment (Vera, Gimeno, Casas, García-Pereira, & Portalés, 2017), medicine (Dickey et al., 2016), cultural heritage (Tscheu & Buhalis, 2016), manufacturing (Caudell & Mizell, 1992), engineering (Lau, Chan, & Wong, 2007), vehicle simulation (Casas, Rueda, Riera, & Fernández, 2012), retail (Bonetti, Warnaby, & Quinn, 2018), construction (Gimeno, Morillo, Casas, & Fernández, 2011), artistic expression (Portalés & Perales, 2009), home automation and assisted living (Ullah, Islam, Aktar, & Hossain, 2012), awareness (Casas, Portalés, García-Pereira, & Fernández, 2017), and many others. Therefore, VR and MR can be considered transversal technologies, covering a wide range of applications and areas of knowledge. These technologies include both hardware and software, involving a variety of sensors and displays, among others.

Because of their nature and features, these technologies provide different benefits, which are sometimes complementary. For instance, VR allows the generation of safe environments in which different situations, potentially dangerous in real life, can be simulated; it can be used to perform virtual time travels and provide access to remote distant locations; etc. On the other hand, the MR technology, which includes both the Augmented Reality (AR) and Augmented Virtuality (AV) technologies, provides the presence of spatial cues for remote collaboration; allows that different virtual elements generated by a computer be spatially distributed; allows a seamless interaction between virtual and real objects, etc. However, the simultaneous use of these technologies within the context of the Internet of Everything (IoE) has been explored only by a few researchers.

While the Internet of Things (IoT) refers to a network of a variety of physical devices, embedded with electronics, software, sensors, actuators, and connectivity which enables these things to connect and exchange data, the concept of IoE goes further, in a sense that it involves an intelligent connection of people, processes, data and things. In this regard, the concept of IoE in the context of the VR and MR technologies, implies providing greater levels of connectivity. It is possible to think of these paradigms (MR and VR) as *things* within the IoE, so that collaborative shared spaces, in which different users use different immersive technologies but with the aim to collaborate with each other, can be proposed in order for users to be able to cooperate to achieve a common purpose. Therefore, in shared spaces the MR and VR technologies expand their capabilities to the level that not only machine-to-machine (M2M) connections are possible, but also machine-to-people (M2P) and technology-assisted people-to-people (P2P) interactions.

The unstoppable globalization of our society is also a force that drives this collaboration necessity. The need to work with people living in different parts of the world, something increasingly common in modern companies, which seek talent whenever this might be, makes remote collaboration an essential part of communication systems. Remote desktop applications, videoconferences and virtual blackboards are some of the mechanisms used to provide remote or local collaboration enhanced or provided by computer technology. This field is known as Computer Supported Cooperative Work (CSCW) and includes all sorts of computer-supported spaces where users can share ideas, procedures or knowledge. However, with the use of immersive technologies, such as VR or MR, this collaboration can potentially be as real as sharing a real space.

The concept of *shared space* can be applied in several ways. The most common one is by using the Collaborative Virtual Environment (CVE) paradigm (Snowdon, Churchill, & Munro, 2001), sometimes referred as Distributed Virtual Environment (DVE) paradigm (Casas, Morillo, Gimeno, & Fernández, 2009), where several users share a common virtual space by means of the VR paradigm. These CVE/DVE systems have been largely explored and they will not be revised in this chapter.

Telepresence and teleoperation are also forms of CSCW. The idea of *telepresence* involves allowing users to experience an existing remote physical space through communication and information technologies. The user can view, navigate through the remote space and sometimes even interact with remote objects by means of some kind of proxy entity (either a remote person or a robot). This latter scenario is referred as *teleoperation*.

Differently from VR-based and telepresence/teleoperation systems, there are also Augmented Reality (AR) systems designed to be used by several simultaneous individuals that can collaborate locally. However, to date, there are very few systems that combine two or more of the aforementioned interaction paradigms to create a shared collaborative space. For this reason, we focus in this chapter on mixed-platform collaborative systems, such as the one presented in (Piumsomboon, Dey, Ens, Lee, & Billinghurst, 2017), in which the use of different simultaneous technologies is proposed to share a common shared space. These systems are fundamentally different from those who focus on the same technology, in which all of the users have usually similar roles, interaction and navigation capabilities.

A *shared space* can be defined as "one where participants can create, see, share and manipulate objects within a bounded space" (Huang, Alem, & Albasri, 2011). The use of different technologies make possible that some users be co-located and some others be in remote places. Therefore, the shared space could be both virtual and real. For this reason, the complexity of these systems could be significantly high. Nevertheless, the use of different platforms allows harnessing the different available resources.

This chapter is aimed at describing the endless possibilities that can be provided if different immersive technologies are applied in a single shared space. Mixing several realities into a single collaborative shared space fulfils the ultimate goal of IoE, allowing people and things to be connected in several ways. We will describe the different setups that can be provided, reviewing the few existing proposals. In this regard, this chapter will classify the different collaborative setups (with or without mixed platforms) with respect to several features, and then some considerations regarding user representation, interaction, navigation, annotation and possible applications of mixed-platform shared spaces would be proposed.

The chapter is organized as follows. In a first section, the concept of mixed reality is introduced, and the technologies and paradigms related to VR and AR are explained in the context of the state of the art. Then, a section of mixed-platform collaborative spaces is given, paying special attention to both the state of the art and the advantages and disadvantages of such systems. In the next section, our proposed system is presented, where we deal with five setups with different levels of immersion/interaction. These setups are proposed following the current state of the art, so they are completely feasible with the current technologies. Finally, we propose some applications and give the conclusions of the chapter.

TECHNOLOGIES AND PARADIGMS

Mixed Reality is the result of blending the physical world with the digital world. Although different researchers use different terms to refer to this kind of systems, the term Mixed Reality was introduced by Milgram (Milgram & Colquhoun, 1999) who classifies the different Mixed Reality systems in which is called the Milgram virtuality continuum (see Figure 1). The amount of real or virtual elements can be different, which leads to the edges of the Milgram continuum (VR if everything is virtual and "reality"

Figure 1. The Milgram virtuality continuum (adapted from (Milgram & Colquhoun, 1999)). The left image represents a real scenario (in this case an archaeological site). The AR image augments this real scenario with virtual buildings that represent the original state of the site. In the AV image, everything is virtual except from the sky. Finally, the VR image shows a completely virtual reconstruction.

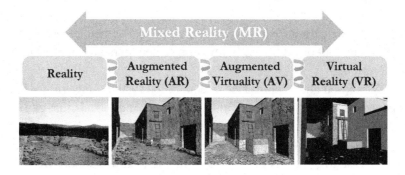

if everything is real; both edges are not, strictly speaking, MR systems because they do not blend physical and virtual elements). The concepts of AR and Augmented Virtuality (AV) lie in between, being the former the most commonly used, although the line separating AR and AV can be sometimes very thin.

Virtual Reality

VR can be defined as the technology by which a user, stimulated with computer-generated perceptual cues, experiences an alternative reality that is different from the one he/she actually lives in. The goal of VR is, thus, to teleport a user into a different virtual world, which is synthetically created by a computer. To achieve that, real perceptual cues are substituted by virtual perceptual cues.

The use of VR provides several benefits (Casas, Fernández, & Riera, 2017; Parsons & Cobb, 2011):

- It provides a safe environment in which different situations, potentially dangerous in real life, can be simulated, reducing risks and accidents.
- It brings the possibility to recreate a variety of situations, which can or cannot occur in the real world, without having to wait for them to happen.
- It can be used to perform virtual time travels and provide access to remote distant locations, which can be possibly inaccessible. This can be very important for the creation of collaborative remote shared spaces.
- It enables users to explore new actions and ideas, since the virtual environment offers a virtual playground in which anything is possible, without having to worry about irreversible consequences.
- It can be used for training, with a reduction of costs, because it reduces the need for having scarce and expensive training materials and resources.
- It can be used for therapy in different medical conditions.
- Different, possibly complex, situations can be simplified and also repeated and analyzed objectively, performing debriefings to explain users why or why not the expected behavior was accomplished.

The use of VR in shared spaces is important when users are in different, possibly very distant, locations. In such cases, VR can provide a virtual shared space in which all these users can meet.

Augmented Reality

AR is not a new paradigm. The term "Augmented Reality" was first coined in 1992 (Caudell & Mizell, 1992), and later defined in 1997 (Azuma, 1997) as the technology that simultaneously combines real and virtual objects which are interactive in real-time and are registered in 3D.

The advantages of AR are different from those of VR. To name a few, AR provides (Bimber & Raskar, 2005):

- An intrinsic ability to enhance reality, so that physical objects and entities can be augmented with additional virtual elements, such as images, sounds, 3D models, etc. that are not present in the real scene. This feature is precisely the one that provides the name to the technology and is key for the creation of augmented shared spaces.
- The presence of spatial cues for remote collaboration. AR allows that different virtual elements generated by a computer be spatially distributed throughout the shared space, so that users can use them as reference points for them to obtain a coherent shared vision of the collaborative space.
- A seamless interaction between virtual and real objects. Interfaces are said to have seams (Ishii, Kobayashi, & Arita, 1994) if there are functional, spatial, temporal, or even cognitive elements that compel users to change the way in which they interact with the interface. This ability to transition from real to virtual elements is crucial for the creation of collaborative shared spaces in which virtual and real elements need to be seamlessly blended.
- A tangible interface. In AR applications, the relationship between virtual objects and real objects is very strong. In this regard, physical objects can be used to manipulate virtual elements, and virtual objects can be used to create annotations and highlight real elements. The use of tangible interfaces and natural interaction metaphors that are quickly identifiable is also very important to create an easy-to-use way to communicate information to other users of the shared space.

The use of AR in shared spaces is especially important when users are co-located in the same physical space. With AR, it is possible that several concurrent users create, manipulate and share, on real-time, virtual information throughout this shared real world.

MIXED-PLATFORM COLLABORATIVE SPACES

A Brief Review of Existing VR/MR-Based Shared Spaces

The construction of shared spaces with MR technologies was studied in detail by Benford in 1998, abstracting out the key principles that define these systems and classifying the different technologies. Benford classifies the different CSCW with respect to three dimensions: transportation, artificiality and spatiality (Benford, Greenhalgh, Reynard, Brown, & Koleva, 1998). The concept of *transportation* "concerns the extent to which a group of participants and objects leave behind their local space and enter into some new remote space in order to meet with others, versus the extent to which they remain in their local space and the remote participants and objects are brought to them". In this regard, Benford distinguishes between local or remote systems. On the other hand, the concept of *artificiality* "concerns the extent to which a space is either synthetic or is based on the physical world", which is equivalent to the Milgram virtuality continuum where there are real, virtual and mixed-reality systems. Finally, spatiality "concerns their level of support for fundamental physical spatial properties such as containment, topology, distance, orientation, and movement". This latter concept applies only to those CSCW where a notion of space is provided, which can be as simple as a common place or much more complex such as shared spatial frame with consistent Cartesian space movement and distances.

The dimensions of transportation and artificiality allows creating a 2D plot where the different CSCW could be classified (see Figure 2). At the edges of this taxonomy we can find face-to-face physical meeting (local and physical), CVE/DVE (remote and synthetic), telepresence (remote and physical) and co-located AR/AV (local and mostly synthetic). Other CSCW, such as video-conferences, desktop shared virtual environments or ClearBoard (Ishii & Kobayashi, 1992) lie in-between these edges.

As we can see, when users are co-located in the same real space, AR seems the natural choice to enhance a physical meeting. On the contrary, if users are in different locations, VR can make possible that remote users work together. However, Benford did not explicitly consider that a combination of AR and VR systems could connect co-located and remote users, so they can collaborate. This allows also classifying the different MR-based CSCW in three major cases: only AR, only VR or a combination of AR and VR). This classification can also be extended if the different kinds of AR and VR hardware devices are considered.

Figure 2. Benford's transportation-artificiality classification (adapted from (Benford et al., 1998))

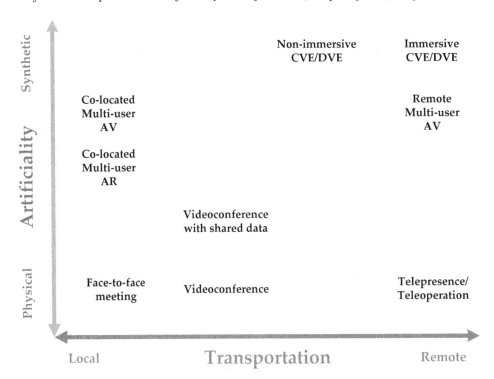

Several collaborative systems involving AR, VR or a combination of both have been proposed after Benford's study. There is also a wide variety of user representations, interaction modes, navigation paradigms, hardware devices, etc.

Examples of co-located collaboration using AR can be found in (Sugimoto, Hosoi, & Hashizume, 2004), where a system called *Caretta* is proposed, which provides a personal and a shared spaced supporting face-to-face collaboration by means of augmented PDAs and a multi-input sensing board. Caretta is a general system applicable to different co-located collaborative tasks and it was tested in urban planning tasks. Another example of this type can be found in (Billinghurst, Poupyrev, Kato, & May, 2000), where co-located users can see and interact with virtual and physical objects and at the same time see the rest of the participants. To achieve that, users wear a Head-Mounted Display (HMD) connected to a camera and to a computer, which is able to identified selected fiducial markers, so that virtual objects and virtual images are triggered. These virtual elements are used for different tasks.

A different co-located collaborative system is *ShareVR* (Gugenheimer, Stemasov, Frommel, & Rukzio, 2017). This system is designed to enable co-located asymmetric interaction between users wearing a HMD and users not wearing one. Unlike previous approaches, which use AR, this is an example of a collaborative VR system designed for co-located users.

Not surprisingly, remote collaboration is much more common, than co-located collaboration, since the need to share information and knowledge with co-located people can be fulfilled with traditional communication. Examples of remote collaboration are (Huang & Alem, 2013; Huang et al., 2011; Huang, Alem, & Tecchia, 2013a, 2013b; Le Chénéchal, Duval, Gouranton, Royan, & Arnaldi, 2016; Lee, Teo, Kim, & Billinghurst, 2017a, 2017b; Piumsomboon, Day, et al., 2017; Robert, Zhu, Huang, Alem, & Gedeon, 2013). In addition to this, the field of CVE/DVE represents also remote collaboration, where many examples can be found (Felnhofer et al., 2014; Passos, da Silva, Mol, & Carvalho, 2017). This is a mature field, where the major challenges, like the awareness problem, have been widely studied (Morillo, Moncho, Orduna, & Duato, 2006).

Another important factor is the technology and hardware used to create the shared space and the different users/roles that there might be within the shared environment. Different platforms (VR, AR, AV, etc.) provide different immersion and interaction capabilities, which in turn determine the type and number of users that may be supported. Most of the works proposed in the literature consider similar users. In (Billinghurst et al., 2000; Le Chénéchal et al., 2016; Lee et al., 2017a; Piumsomboon, Day, et al., 2017) all users wear an HMD. Much in the same way, in (Sodhi, Jones, Forsyth, Bailey, & Maciocci, 2013; Sugimoto et al., 2004) all users participate in the shared environment through similar hand-held devices. On the contrary, in (Duval et al., 2014) two different users with different immersion levels share the same space. One user uses a multiscreen system, whereas the second user uses a regular PC. Both users participate in the shared space by means of the VR paradigm. In (Gurevich, Lanir, Cohen, & Stone, 2012), a robotic arm is controlled by a remote user who sees the remote space by means of camera mounted on this robotic device. Heterogeneous users can also be found in *CoVAR* (Piumsomboon, Day, et al., 2017), a work that will be explained next.

The combination of AR and VR to form a shared space has been also explored, although not many researchers propose the seamless integration of both paradigms. One of the first approaches is (Kiyokawa, Takemura, & Yokoya, 1999), in which the *seamless view-mode switching* technique is proposed. This technique allows enjoying a shared space in two modes: a see-through mode and a blind mode. The former corresponds to AR, whereas the latter corresponds to VR. Unlike more recent approaches, both users are assumed to be co-located. One of the most interesting examples of AR/VR integration is CoVAR (Piumsomboon, Day, et al., 2017; Piumsomboon, Dey, et al., 2017). CoVAR supports collaboration between AR and VR users by sharing a 3D reconstruction of the AR user's environment. In this system, two distant users collaborate using immersive displays. The user in the real work wears an optical see-through AR device (HoloLens), whereas the remote user wears an HMD (HTC Vive). Both users have independent points of view, and they can move freely. A remarkable feature of CoVAR is that both eye-gaze (capturing the position of the pupil) and head-gaze are tracked. This setup is very interesting and contrasts with many other that use the same point of view for local and remote users, such as in (Huang & Alem, 2013; Lee et al., 2017a; Robert et al., 2013). Another example of AR/VR collaboration is the work presented in (Elvezio, Sukan, Oda, Feiner, & Tversky, 2017; Oda, Elvezio, Sukan, Feiner, & Tversky, 2015), in which two users wearing a Head-Worn Display (HWD) collaborate using virtual replicas. The remote expert employs either a VR or an AR system, whereas the local user employs an AR system. The disadvantage of this approach is that virtual proxies of all the objects used for the collaborative task are needed. Another example of mixed-platform collaboration is presented in (Stafford, Piekarski, & Thomas, 2006), where users located indoors working on tabletop projected displays and users located outdoors using mobile AR systems can communicate information. In this case, the indoor part does not use an immersive VR system.

Another important aspect of these CSCW systems is how the different participants see the rest of users in the shared space. This could have a great impact in the perception of a believable shared space. In systems where users are co-located, this need is not as intense, since users are sharing a real space. Nevertheless, virtual tools or hands could be depicted. On the contrary, those systems designed to be used by distant users need to be able to depict users in a consistent and believable way. It is widely understood, as demonstrated in (Piumsomboon, Day, et al., 2017) that showing where the other participants are looking at, helps and improves the desire for collaboration in the shared space. In (Huang et al., 2013a; Robert et al., 2013), only the hands of the expert are virtually depicted to the non-expert user. In these cases, both users share the same point of view, which simplifies user representation. In more general cases where the point of view is not shared and there is partial or complete navigation freedom, more sophisticated solutions are needed. For instance, in CoVAR (Piumsomboon, Day, et al., 2017), users are represented by a 3D model that is enhanced with two types of, so called, *awareness cues*, such as a pyramid showing the Field of View (FoV) and a ray showing the user's gaze. A similar approach is employed in (Sodhi et al., 2013) and in (Lee et al., 2017a, 2017b) where visual aids are depicted showing what other users view in the shared environment. In (Duval et al., 2014), not only a virtual representation of the user is depicted, but also the hardware they use to participate in the shared environment. This allows other users to know the interaction capabilities and the physical limitations of their counterparts.

Regarding user interaction, the different shared spaces proposed in the literature offer several paradigms, since different collaborative tasks entail different interaction capabilities. The most common interaction method is the *pointing paradigm*, by which a user indicates a specific action/object to a different user (Huang et al., 2013a; Robert et al., 2013; Sodhi et al., 2013). Gaze can also be used as a pointing interface, such as in (Piumsomboon, Day, et al., 2017). Object manipulation, and object annotation, such as in (Oda et al., 2015) are also natural interfaces for this kind of systems, although its implementation is complex.

Advantages and Disadvantages of Mixed-Platform CSCW Systems

Unlike other CSCW, mixed-platform collaborative setups offer a series of important advantages that should be highlighted.

In the first place, they allow that both co-located and remote users share the same space. The number of co-located or remote users could be changed and adjusted to the collaboration needs. With this approach, different technologies can be used depending on the location/resources of the user. AR is the preferred choice for co-located collaboration, whereas VR is the simplest option for remote users.

Second, by using mixed-platform and mixed-hardware CSCW, computational resources can be harnessed and optimized. Whether the user owns a sophisticated HMD, a see-through display or just a regular PC, if proper integration of technologies is applied, all of them could collaborate in a shared task. The amount of interaction and capabilities would be, obviously, limited by the hardware, but this should not be an obstacle to, at least, participate in the shared environment.

Although those CSCW not using mixed platforms can provide also different users and roles to the shared space, mixed-platform collaborative systems provide heterogeneous users in a natural manner, as they have to adapt to different users and technologies. This leads to different levels of immersion and different interaction, navigation and annotation capabilities.

On the other hand, the implementation of mixed-platform collaborative systems is not easy, since the integration of different technologies and paradigms imply restrictions that could be hard to overcome. In this regard, a minimum set of shared and awareness cues should be provided. This minimum set is essential for providing a meaningful application in which asymmetric collaboration not be a problem but an opportunity.

In this same line, the use of different technologies could be also hidden to the participants of the system, so that a consistent and transparent environment is provided for everyone. The opposite approach, by which the different devices that users use are explicitly shown, can also be considered so that participants have more information about their counterparts.

MIXED-PLATFORM PROPOSED SYSTEM

Having reviewed some of the works published in the academic literature, we hypothesize about the features that would be desired for a mixed-platform generic collaborative shared environment.

We propose five setups with different levels of immersion/interaction:

1. Immersive HMD with motion and hand gesture tracking. This can be implemented, for instance with an HTC Vive display and a Leap Motion gesture tracking device.
2. See-through display with motion and hand gesture tracking. This can be implemented, for instance with a HoloLens display and a Leap Motion gesture tracking device.
3. Immersive HMD with motion tracking.
4. A non-immersive mobile display with SLAM (Simultaneous Location And Mapping), so that the mobile device could be tracked in a controlled environment.
5. A desktop system with a PC.

Setup A and setup C are designed for VR systems. Setup B is conceived for AR use. Setup D could represent a mobile phone or a tablet, where AR could be implemented. However, a non-immersive VR system can also be implemented with this setup. Finally, setup E suits the non-immersive paradigm. Setups A, B and C can also be improved with gaze tracking if pupil detection is applied.

We propose that a real scenario be used as a *reference stage*, where the AR users would be co-located sharing a real space. Users using setup B and setup D will use this real scenario to (physically) navigate within this real environment. A few AR markers will be necessary to act as reference starting points for the SLAM tracking system (for setup D).

On the other hand, users using setups A, C and E need a virtual reproduction of the physical shared stage. In order for these users to collaborate with the co-located (local) users, a virtual reproduction of the stage is necessary. Years ago, a tedious ad-hoc modelling process was the only alternative. Today, it is possible to perform automatic modelling of complex scenarios with 3D scanning devices like Occipital's Structure Sensor. Although the resolution of this virtual scenarios is still not comparable to ad-hoc (human-designed) 3D models, these devices are likely to improve and already offer sufficient realism for them to be used in shared spaces without losing a great deal of spatial information. For this reason, we propose to use one of these 3D sensors to create a virtual reproduction of the actual stage, so that virtual and real users can collaborate in shared space.

Navigation

Unlike other systems, in which remote and local users share the same point of view, we propose that the user decides about this feature. This means that the system should provide independent navigation methods and independent points of view. However, at any given moment, any user could decide to observe the shared space through the eyes of other participants. Additional restrictions could be included, so that some users would need credentials or privileges to share their point of view or to observe someone else's. Finally, a god mode in which a third person general view is offered should also be a possibility, as in (Kiyokawa et al., 1999).

Navigation within the shared space depends heavily on the hardware used to participate in the system. Participants using setups A and C move through the remote space and their navigation is translated to the virtual shared space. Participants using setup B move through the real space since the AR display allows them seeing the existing real space. Participants using setup D carry a tablet or a similar mobile device, so that they also move freely around the real space. SLAM techniques are used for the system to track their movements and provide location awareness for the rest of the participants. Finally, users from setup E would use a keyboard or a mouse to navigate through the virtual shared space.

User Representation

User representation can be provided in several ways. We believe that providing different representations for the different users is beneficial. In this regard, if there are expert and non-expert users in the system they should be represented in a different way. Similarly, the depiction of the different users may be different for the different setups/hardware they use to enter the shared space. For instance, participants using setups A and B should be represented by an avatar with a virtual HMD and virtual hands that move like the user's hands. Setup C could be represented by an avatar with a virtual HMD, whereas setup D could be depicted as an avatar with a tablet. Finally, setup E could be depicted as a simple avatar with no additional elements.

As we propose free navigation and separated points of view, it is also important to represent the participant's gaze and fields of view. A line showing the gaze direction and a pyramid showing the extent of the field of view seem a proper way to represent these concepts.

Interaction

Many different interaction paradigms can be applied. This feature is heavily dependent on the application the systems is designed for. However, some general actions can be defined. In the first place, users should be able to point with their hands (or even with their eye-gaze if eye tracking is performed). Users with gesture tracking (setups A and B) can do it naturally. The rest should simulate it with a button, joystick or by touching a tactile screen. The position of the virtual hand can be inferred from the position of the tracked user.

Another interesting action is to cast rays. Again, users with gesture tracking could use a particular hand gesture to achieve this, whereas the rest should simulate it with interface elements. It is also possible to cast rays that follow the gaze direction, something that a few works use (Piumsomboon, Day, et al., 2017).

More complex actions, such the creation of virtual objects by means of predefined gestures or object manipulation, require complex setups such as setups A and B or specific applications with virtual replicas, such as in (Elvezio et al., 2017).

Annotation

Annotation is an important part of collaborative shared spaces, especially for distant users, since they need a way to communicate non-verbal information. This can be accomplished by means of gestures (Chang, Nuernberger, Luan, & Höllerer, 2017) or with specialized tools. As with interaction, the amount of possibilities is huge. We propose to use two different types of annotations: free drawings and virtual text. For free drawings, participants using setups A and B can use their hands. The rest need to use a touch screen (setup D), a mouse click (setup E) or some kind of joystick/pad (setup C). Regarding text, the simplest solution is to include a speech-to-text system, so that all users are able to place virtual texts in the location where their avatars are. Participants using setups D and E could also type the text with a keyboard (either virtual or real).

PROPOSED APPLICATIONS

The most obvious application of MR-based collaborative systems is for learning environments or similar uses, such as instruction, skill transference or procedure teaching. The typical setup involves two different users with different roles: an expert and an on-site operator. The expert is usually at a remote location and wants to help the operator perform a particular task. This can be done by sharing the operator's point of view, so that the expert can point out different objects or give advices based on this view, or it can be done with different points of view. Examples of this application use are (Huang & Alem, 2013; Le Chénéchal et al., 2016; Robert et al., 2013). Mixed-platform shared spaces can provide additional value here since the expert and the operator could have different computational resources.

A similar application is computer-enhanced co-working, where shared workspaces are provided so that remote workers can collaborate and share information as if they were in the same room. This eases the decision-making process. The main difference with the previous application is that, in this case, the different workers could have either equal or different roles, and there is not an expert helper and a helped person. An example of this type of use is (Sugimoto et al., 2004). This general co-working concept can be extended to medicine, construction, manufacturing, engineering, etc. providing endless possibilities. In this regard, the use of mixed-platform setups would be very important so that all computer resources (computers, tablets, mobile phones, HMD, etc.) can be applied in a common task and workers from different cities and countries can provide all their expertise into the shared task.

Another use of MR-based collaborative systems is military training. The most common setup is a CVE/DVE where the participants share a virtual battlefield or a military training site. The entertainment industry has provided very realistic CVE/DVE sagas like *Medal of Honor* or *Call of Duty*, where users can compete or collaborate in different military scenarios. Recent navigation systems such as walking treadmills (Jetly et al., 2017) can make these applications very immersive. Mixed-platform setups have not been explored for this application, to the best of our knowledge, but a combination of AR and VR could be possible in the future so that soldiers in a battlefield could receive vital information that comes from virtual soldiers/commanders that are not physically fighting the battle but have virtual access to the battlefield.

A different use that, to the best of our knowledge, has also not been explored yet is home automation. Most of us spend more time at the office than at home and we need homes that have some kind of intelligent behavior. The IoE paradigm allows the introduction of multiple internet-connected sensors and actuators so that home automation and remote monitoring/control of the home is possible. However, controlling our home with a 2D web interface in our mobile phones is not quite as being there. With MR-based shared spaces, it would be possible to virtually replicate our home and monitor/control all of our home appliances. In this regard, with mixed-platform shared spaces remote users could collaborate with Artificial Intelligent agents that control our home or with local inhabitants, fulfilling both the IoE paradigm and the concept of shared space.

CONCLUSION

Cooperative and collaborative tasks are increasingly needed in a globalized world where home-based workers and outsourcing are not just a transient trend. Computer-based and computer-supported collaboration systems are of the utmost importance to support the need for remote and co-located users working together in a productive fashion. Videoconference, telepresence, teleoperation, co-located AR applications or CVE/DVE systems have been proven beneficial for this goal. However, much more than using a single interaction/immersion paradigm could be done.

In this regard, this chapter has reviewed the need for designing mixed-platform shared spaces for collaborative tasks. Different paradigms such as VR and AR could be used together, in a complimentary way. The reason for this is that VR and AR offer different advantages for co-located users (AR) or remote users (VR), and much will be missing if these technologies are not combined in a meaningful way to provide shared spaces.

After reviewing the different solutions and analyzing these systems with respect to navigation, user representation, hardware technology, interaction and annotation, we have proposed a generic system for the design of mixed-platform shared spaces with five different setups. This system provides heterogeneous users with free navigation and independent points of views, allowing harnessing the computer resources available, since different technologies (tablet, PC, HMD, etc.) can be used to participate in the shared space. The proposed system is feasible and can be constructed with existing state-of-the-art technology, although its implementation could be complex, especially if all the features and interaction options are applied.

Much work can be done in this field, since not many mixed-platform shared spaces have been proposed to date. The aim of this chapter is to wake up and open a research avenue in this area, so different shared-spaces are proposed and implemented in the following years. Although the implementation is challenging, a great deal of effort should be invested in assessing the effectiveness of the collaborative work that can be performed with these systems, an aspect that has been somehow overlooked in previous works. Another important aspect for possible future work is annotation, which is currently a hot research topic.

ACKNOWLEDGMENT

This paper has been elaborated in the scope of the SIRAE project (RTC-2015-4203-7), which is supported by the Spanish *Plan Estatal de Investigación Científica y Técnica de Innovación* 2013–2016 and by the European Commission by means of FEDER funds.

REFERENCES

Azuma, R. T. (1997). A survey of augmented reality. *Presence (Cambridge, Mass.)*, *6*(4), 355–385. doi:10.1162/pres.1997.6.4.355

Benford, S., Greenhalgh, C., Reynard, G., Brown, C., & Koleva, B. (1998). Understanding and constructing shared spaces with mixed-reality boundaries. *ACM Transactions on Computer-Human Interaction*, *5*(3), 185-223.

Billinghurst, M., Poupyrev, I., Kato, H., & May, R. (2000). *Mixing realities in shared space: An augmented reality interface for collaborative computing.* Paper presented at the Multimedia and Expo, 2000. ICME 2000. 2000 IEEE International Conference on. 10.1109/ICME.2000.871085

Bimber, O., & Raskar, R. (2005). *Spatial augmented reality: merging real and virtual worlds.* CRC Press. doi:10.1201/b10624

Bonetti, F., Warnaby, G., & Quinn, L. (2018). *Augmented Reality and Virtual Reality in Physical and Online Retailing: A Review, Synthesis and Research Agenda. In Augmented Reality and Virtual Reality* (pp. 119–132). Springer. doi:10.1007/978-3-319-64027-3_9

Casas, S., Fernández, M., & Riera, J. V. (2017). Four Different Multimodal Setups for Non-Aerial Vehicle Simulations—A Case Study with a Speedboat Simulator. *Multimodal Technologies and Interaction, 1*(2), 10. doi:10.3390/mti1020010

Casas, S., Morillo, P., Gimeno, J., & Fernández, M. (2009). *SUED: An extensible framework for the development of low-cost DVE systems.* Paper presented at the In Proceedings of the IEEE Virtual Reality 2009 (IEEE-VR'09). Workshop on Software Engineering and Architectures for Realtime Interactive Systems (SEARIS).

Casas, S., Portalés, C., García-Pereira, I., & Fernández, M. (2017). On a First Evaluation of ROMOT—A RObotic 3D MOvie Theatre—For Driving Safety Awareness. *Multimodal Technologies and Interaction, 1*(2), 6. doi:10.3390/mti1020006

Casas, S., Rueda, S., Riera, J. V., & Fernández, M. (2012). *On the Real-time Physics Simulation of a Speed-boat Motion.* Paper presented at the GRAPP/IVAPP.

Caudell, T. P., & Mizell, D. W. (1992). Augmented reality: An application of heads-up display technology to manual manufacturing processes. *Proceedings of the Twenty-Fifth Hawaii International Conference.* 10.1109/HICSS.1992.183317

Chang, Y. S., Nuernberger, B., Luan, B., & Höllerer, T. (2017). *Evaluating gesture-based augmented reality annotation.* Paper presented at the 3D User Interfaces (3DUI), 2017 IEEE Symposium on. 10.1109/3DUI.2017.7893337

Dickey, R. M., Srikishen, N., Lipshultz, L. I., Spiess, P. E., Carrion, R. E., & Hakky, T. S. (2016). Augmented reality assisted surgery: A urologic training tool. *Asian Journal of Andrology, 18*(5), 732. doi:10.4103/1008-682X.166436 PMID:26620455

Dunleavy, M., & Dede, C. (2014). *Augmented reality teaching and learning. In Handbook of research on educational communications and technology* (pp. 735–745). Springer. doi:10.1007/978-1-4614-3185-5_59

Duval, T., Nguyen, T. T. H., Fleury, C., Chauffaut, A., Dumont, G., & Gouranton, V. (2014). Improving awareness for 3D virtual collaboration by embedding the features of users' physical environments and by augmenting interaction tools with cognitive feedback cues. *Journal on Multimodal User Interfaces, 8*(2), 187–197. doi:10.100712193-013-0134-z

Elvezio, C., Sukan, M., Oda, O., Feiner, S., & Tversky, B. (2017). *Remote collaboration in AR and VR using virtual replicas.* Paper presented at the ACM SIGGRAPH 2017 VR Village. 10.1145/3089269.3089281

Felnhofer, A., Kothgassner, O. D., Hauk, N., Beutl, L., Hlavacs, H., & Kryspin-Exner, I. (2014). Physical and social presence in collaborative virtual environments: Exploring age and gender differences with respect to empathy. *Computers in Human Behavior, 31*, 272–279. doi:10.1016/j.chb.2013.10.045

Gimeno, J., Morillo, P., Casas, S., & Fernández, M. (2011). An augmented reality (AR) CAD system at construction sites. In *Augmented Reality-Some Emerging Application Areas.* InTech.

Gugenheimer, J., Stemasov, E., Frommel, J., & Rukzio, E. (2017). Sharevr: Enabling co-located experiences for virtual reality between hmd and non-hmd users. *Proceedings of the 2017 CHI Conference on Human Factors in Computing Systems.* 10.1145/3025453.3025683

Gurevich, P., Lanir, J., Cohen, B., & Stone, R. (2012). TeleAdvisor: a versatile augmented reality tool for remote assistance. *Proceedings of the SIGCHI Conference on Human Factors in Computing Systems*. 10.1145/2207676.2207763

Huang, W., & Alem, L. (2013). HandsinAir: a wearable system for remote collaboration on physical tasks. *Proceedings of the 2013 conference on Computer supported cooperative work companion*. 10.1145/2441955.2441994

Huang, W., Alem, L., & Albasri, J. (2011). *HandsInAir: a wearable system for remote collaboration*. arXiv preprint arXiv:1112.1742

Huang, W., Alem, L., & Tecchia, F. (2013a). *HandsIn3d: augmenting the shared 3d visual space with unmediated hand gestures*. Paper presented at the SIGGRAPH Asia 2013 Emerging Technologies. 10.1145/2542284.2542294

Huang, W., Alem, L., & Tecchia, F. (2013b). *HandsIn3D: supporting remote guidance with immersive virtual environments*. Paper presented at the IFIP Conference on Human-Computer Interaction. 10.1007/978-3-642-40483-2_5

Ishii, H., & Kobayashi, M. (1992). ClearBoard: a seamless medium for shared drawing and conversation with eye contact. *Proceedings of the SIGCHI conference on Human factors in computing systems*. 10.1145/142750.142977

Ishii, H., Kobayashi, M., & Arita, K. (1994). Iterative design of seamless collaboration media. *Communications of the ACM, 37*(8), 83–97. doi:10.1145/179606.179687

Jetly, C. R., Meakin, L. C., Sinitski, E. H., Blackburn, L., Menard, J., Vincent, M., & Antwi, M. (2017). *Multi-Modal virtual-reality based treatment for members with combat related posttraumatic stress disorder: Canadian Armed Forces pilot study*. Paper presented at the Virtual Rehabilitation (ICVR), 2017 International Conference on. 10.1109/ICVR.2017.8007474

Kiyokawa, K., Takemura, H., & Yokoya, N. (1999). A collaboration support technique by integrating a shared virtual reality and a shared augmented reality. *Systems, Man, and Cybernetics, 1999. IEEE SMC'99 Conference Proceedings. 1999 IEEE International Conference on*. 10.1109/ICSMC.1999.816444

Lau, H., Chan, L., & Wong, R. (2007). A virtual container terminal simulator for the design of terminal operation. *International Journal on Interactive Design and Manufacturing, 1*(2), 107–113. doi:10.100712008-007-0013-5

Le Chénéchal, M., Duval, T., Gouranton, V., Royan, J., & Arnaldi, B. (2016). *Vishnu: virtual immersive support for helping users an interaction paradigm for collaborative remote guiding in mixed reality*. Paper presented at the Collaborative Virtual Environments (3DCVE), 2016 IEEE Third VR International Workshop on. 10.1109/3DCVE.2016.7563559

Lee, G. A., Teo, T., Kim, S., & Billinghurst, M. (2017a). *Mixed reality collaboration through sharing a live panorama*. Paper presented at the SIGGRAPH Asia 2017 Mobile Graphics & Interactive Applications. 10.1145/3132787.3139203

Lee, G. A., Teo, T., Kim, S., & Billinghurst, M. (2017b). *Sharedsphere: MR collaboration through shared live panorama.* Paper presented at the SIGGRAPH Asia 2017 Emerging Technologies. 10.1145/3132818.3132827

Milgram, P., & Colquhoun, H. (1999). A taxonomy of real and virtual world display integration. *Mixed reality: Merging real and virtual worlds, 1,* 1-26.

Morillo, P., Moncho, W., Orduna, J. M., & Duato, J. (2006). *Providing full awareness to distributed virtual environments based on peer-to-peer architectures. In Advances in Computer Graphics* (pp. 336–347). Springer.

Oda, O., Elvezio, C., Sukan, M., Feiner, S., & Tversky, B. (2015). Virtual replicas for remote assistance in virtual and augmented reality. *Proceedings of the 28th Annual ACM Symposium on User Interface Software & Technology.* 10.1145/2807442.2807497

Olanda, R., Pérez, M., Morillo, P., Fernández, M., & Casas, S. (2006). Entertainment virtual reality system for simulation of spaceflights over the surface of the planet Mars. *Proceedings of the ACM symposium on Virtual reality software and technology.* 10.1145/1180495.1180522

Parsons, S., & Cobb, S. (2011). State-of-the-art of virtual reality technologies for children on the autism spectrum. *European Journal of Special Needs Education, 26*(3), 355–366. doi:10.1080/08856257.201 1.593831

Passos, C., da Silva, M. H., Mol, A. C., & Carvalho, P. V. (2017). Design of a collaborative virtual environment for training security agents in big events. *Cognition Technology and Work, 19*(2-3), 315–328. doi:10.100710111-017-0407-5

Piumsomboon, T., Day, A., Ens, B., Lee, Y., Lee, G., & Billinghurst, M. (2017). *Exploring enhancements for remote mixed reality collaboration.* Paper presented at the SIGGRAPH Asia 2017 Mobile Graphics & Interactive Applications. 10.1145/3132787.3139200

Piumsomboon, T., Dey, A., Ens, B., Lee, G., & Billinghurst, M. (2017). *CoVAR: Mixed-Platform Remote Collaborative Augmented and Virtual Realities System with Shared Collaboration Cues.* Paper presented at the Mixed and Augmented Reality (ISMAR-Adjunct), 2017 IEEE International Symposium on.

Portalés, C., & Perales, C. D. (2009). *Sound and movement visualization in the AR-Jazz scenario.* Paper presented at the International Conference on Entertainment Computing. 10.1007/978-3-642-04052-8_15

Robert, K., Zhu, D., Huang, W., Alem, L., & Gedeon, T. (2013). *MobileHelper: remote guiding using smart mobile devices, hand gestures and augmented reality.* Paper presented at the SIGGRAPH Asia 2013 Symposium on Mobile Graphics and Interactive Applications. 10.1145/2543651.2543664

Snowdon, D., Churchill, E. F., & Munro, A. J. (2001). *Collaborative virtual environments: Digital spaces and places for CSCW: An introduction.* Paper presented at the Collaborative virtual environments. 10.1007/978-1-4471-0685-2_1

Sodhi, R. S., Jones, B. R., Forsyth, D., Bailey, B. P., & Maciocci, G. (2013). BeThere: 3D mobile collaboration with spatial input. *Proceedings of the SIGCHI Conference on Human Factors in Computing Systems.* 10.1145/2470654.2470679

Stafford, A., Piekarski, W., & Thomas, B. (2006). Implementation of god-like interaction techniques for supporting collaboration between outdoor AR and indoor tabletop users. *Proceedings of the 5th IEEE and ACM International Symposium on Mixed and Augmented Reality.* 10.1109/ISMAR.2006.297809

Sugimoto, M., Hosoi, K., & Hashizume, H. (2004). Caretta: a system for supporting face-to-face collaboration by integrating personal and shared spaces. *Proceedings of the SIGCHI conference on Human factors in computing systems.* 10.1145/985692.985698

Tscheu, F., & Buhalis, D. (2016). *Augmented reality at cultural heritage sites. In Information and Communication Technologies in Tourism 2016* (pp. 607–619). Springer. doi:10.1007/978-3-319-28231-2_44

Ullah, A. M., Islam, M. R., Aktar, S. F., & Hossain, S. A. (2012). *Remote-touch: Augmented reality based marker tracking for smart home control.* Paper presented at the Computer and Information Technology (ICCIT), 2012 15th International Conference on. 10.1109/ICCITechn.2012.6509774

Vera, L., Gimeno, J., Casas, S., García-Pereira, I., & Portalés, C. (2017). *A Hybrid Virtual-Augmented Serious Game to Improve Driving Safety Awareness.* Paper presented at the 14th International Conference on Advances in Computer Entertainment Technology - ACE 2017, London, UK.

ADDITIONAL READING

Billinghurst, M., & Kato, H. (1999). *Collaborative mixed reality.* Paper presented at the Proceedings of the First International Symposium on Mixed Reality. 10.1007/978-3-642-87512-0_15

Billinghurst, M., & Kato, H. (2002). Collaborative augmented reality. *Communications of the ACM, 45*(7), 64–70. doi:10.1145/514236.514265

Billinghurst, M., Kato, H., & Poupyrev, I. (2001a). The magicbook-moving seamlessly between reality and virtuality. *IEEE Computer Graphics and Applications, 21*(3), 6–8.

Billinghurst, M., Kato, H., & Poupyrev, I. (2001b). The MagicBook: A transitional AR interface. *Computers & Graphics, 25*(5), 745–753. doi:10.1016/S0097-8493(01)00117-0

Cowan, K., & Ketron, S. (2018). A dual model of product involvement for effective virtual reality: The roles of imagination, co-creation, telepresence, and interactivity. *Journal of Business Research.* doi:10.1016/j.jbusres.2018.10.063

Ekström, M. (2017). Communication tool in virtual reality–A telepresence alternative: An alternative to telepresence–bringing the shared space to a virtual environment in virtual reality.

García-Pereira, I., Gimeno, J., Pérez, M., Portalés, C., & Casas, S. (2018). *MIME: A Mixed-Space Collaborative System with Three Levels of Immersion and Multiple Users.* Paper presented at the IEEE and ACM International Symposium for Mixed and Augmented Reality 2018 (ISMAR 2018).

Gimeno, J., Casas, S., Portalés, C., & Fernández, M. (2018). *Addressing the Occlusion Problem in Augmented Reality Environments with Phantom Hollow Objects.* Paper presented at the IEEE and ACM International Symposium for Mixed and Augmented Reality 2018 (ISMAR 2018).

Greenwald, S., Kulik, A., Kunert, A., Beck, S., Frohlich, B., Cobb, S., et al. (2017). Technology and applications for collaborative learning in virtual reality.

Hoppe, A. H., Reeb, R., van de Camp, F., & Stiefelhagen, R. (2018). *Interaction of Distant and Local Users in a Collaborative Virtual Environment.* Paper presented at the International Conference on Virtual, Augmented and Mixed Reality. 10.1007/978-3-319-91581-4_24

Kolkmeier, J., Vroon, J., & Heylen, D. (2016). *Interacting with virtual agents in shared space: Single and joint effects of gaze and proxemics.* Paper presented at the International Conference on Intelligent Virtual Agents. 10.1007/978-3-319-47665-0_1

Piumsomboon, T., Lee, G. A., & Billinghurst, M. (2018). *Snow Dome: A Multi-Scale Interaction in Mixed Reality Remote Collaboration.* Paper presented at the Extended Abstracts of the 2018 CHI Conference on Human Factors in Computing Systems. 10.1145/3170427.3186495

Smets, G. J. (2018). *Designing for Telepresence: The Delft Virtual Window System. Local applications of the ecological approach to human-machine systems* (pp. 200–225). CRC Press.

Stoll, B., Reig, S., He, L., Kaplan, I., Jung, M. F., & Fussell, S. R. (2018). *Wait, Can You Move the Robot?: Examining Telepresence Robot Use in Collaborative Teams.* Paper presented at the Proceedings of the 2018 ACM/IEEE International Conference on Human-Robot Interaction. 10.1145/3171221.3171243

KEY TERMS AND DEFINITIONS

Augmented Reality: The technology that simultaneously combines real and virtual objects that are interactive in real-time and are registered in a three-dimensional space.

Interaction: A kind of action that occurs as two or more objects have an effect upon one another.

Internet of Everything (IoE): The intelligent connection of people, processes, data, and things. The IoE builds on the foundation of the IoT by adding network intelligence that allows convergence, orchestration and visibility across previously disparate systems.

Internet of Things (IoT): The interconnection via Internet of computing devices embedded in everyday objects, enabling them to send and receive data.

Mixed Reality: The result of blending the physical world with a synthetic one, including the paradigms of augmented reality and augmented virtuality.

Shared Space: In the context of mixed reality technologies, a common space where users (remotely or not) can collaborate.

Virtual Reality: The technology by which a user, stimulated with computer-generated perceptual cues, experiences an alternative reality that is different from the one he/she actually lives in.

Chapter 9
An IoE Architecture for the Preservation of the Cultural Heritage:
The STORM Use Case

Panagiotis Kasnesis
University of West Attica, Greece

Michael G. Xevgenis
University of West Attica, Greece

Dimitrios G. Kogias
University of West Attica, Greece

Charalampos Z. Patrikakis
University of West Attica, Greece

Lazaros Toumanidis
University of West Attica, Greece

Gabriele Giunta
Engineering Ingegneria Informatica, Italy

Giuseppe Li Calsi
Engineering Ingegneria Informatica, Italy

ABSTRACT

Climatic changes and intensive industrialization have contributed to increasing the risk of damage of cultural heritage (CH) artefacts. On the other hand, small and medium-sized museums, as well as small CH sites struggle to fulfil international recommendations for protection and conservation, due to budget limitations. The constantly increasing potential of IoT-enabled devices and the establishment of cloud technologies as an enabling framework can help address this issue. In this chapter, the authors present an internet of everything (IoE) architecture, empowered by an easy-to-deploy cloud framework for the protection of CH. Particular use cases from CH sites are presented, as these have been identified in H2020 STORM project for safeguarding cultural heritage through technical and organizational resources management.

DOI: 10.4018/978-1-5225-7332-6.ch009

INTRODUCTION

Preservation and protection of *Cultural Heritage (CH)* have always attracted the attention and interest of many parties (e.g., academics, researchers, local or domestic communities or private companies and the public sector) due to its historical, touristic and economic potentials. Recent advances in areas of computer science, especially the rapid growth of Cloud Computing and the Internet of Things (IoT), has been the driving force behind great developments and applied techniques, while the solutions proposed in this paper can be considered as equally efficient, for the preservation and protection of our Cultural Heritage. The use of (many kinds of) sensors can facilitate communications through their collected data to a database that can be located locally (i.e., edge of the network) or in the cloud (i.e., core of the network), where it can be accessed by various registered individual experts, is considered as a potential basic scenario in a modern Cultural Heritage data IoE use case. To perform efficiently, such solutions should follow a well-documented structure, in the form of an architecture, that describes the performance of each entity in a smart ecosystem. The structure of the system will depend on its intended functionality, since there is not a global solution that is adopted generally, but rather referenced ones that are applied with small changes depending on use cases and their needs.

To this end, Figure 1 presents the basic entities of an *Internet of Everything (IoE)* smart ecosystem, specialized with the goal of safeguarding our Cultural Heritage. In particular, the IoE entities are the following:

- **Things:** IoT devices (e.g., sensors) used for weather (e.g., air temperature), environmental (e.g., audio signals) and structural monitoring (e.g., material degradation) of the parameters linked to the risks that the cultural heritage sites face.
- **People:** Human-beings (e.g., experts) connected to each other through social networks or crowdsourcing applications.
- **Data:** Incoming data (from IoT devices or people) processed to extract useful information and detect hazardous events, in order to make cognitive decisions.
- **Process:** The stakeholders are informed in real-time about hazardous events through an emergency management system.

Delving deeper into the CH domain, and not only be limited on preservation efforts but also pointing out its social characteristics and how they can be affected by IoE solutions, currently there is an effort from the official personnel of modern museums, monuments and CH sites and experts to digitize the available artifacts. This digitization of the artifacts is considered to serve multiple reasons. First, to provide the opportunity to share info and digital (or virtual) view of artifacts, available to all the visitors even if those artifacts have been destroyed at some point from natural events or human actions or being deformed by the time. Secondly, artifacts digitization aims at recording an increase on the interest of visitors by offering (virtual) interactions with the artifact or its virtual representation, to provide for a better entertainment for the avid and not so interested visitor and, finally, to provide simple gamification features that could attract a wider range of visitors to experience a different kind of visit to a CH site. It is also important, that many of these features (or their combination) can provide a more personalized experience, allowing the memories (and knowledge) to last long after the end of the visit. To this end, recently the use of crowdsourcing and crowdsensing techniques is also being promoted in CH sites for enhancing the participation of the tourist in a more active way, rather than passively passing-by the arti-

Figure 1. Internet of Everything for safeguarding cultural heritage

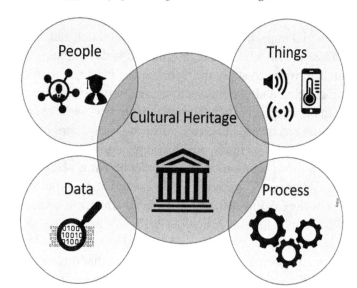

facts. But most importantly, for the preservation of CH sites, there is a possibility of using the data that can be uploaded by the users (e.g., videos, photos) as a mean to study for any deterioration or cracks on the exhibits. The latter is especially useful in CH sites where the available financial budget is very sparse to cover the needs for this critical operation by acquiring specialized, and possibly expensive, equipment.

As a result, this chapter provides the presentation of a logical architecture for an Internet of Everything (IoE) system that can be used to increase the preservation and protection of our Cultural Heritage (CH), as this is the case in STORM, an HORIZON 2020 funded European Project on Cultural Heritage. To design the system for STORM, five CH sites placed all-over Europe (e.g., Great Britain, Italy, Greece, Portugal and Turkey) have cooperated to provide detailed use-cases that highlight their needs, while out-of-the-shelf, modern technical equipment was selected to be used to address them. The communication of the technical equipment and the use of cloud computing to process and store the data form a complete system that will be described in the following sections.

To this end, the rest of the chapter is structured as follows: the following section provides a background study of various IoE (and IoT) solutions that aim to serve the preservation and enrich the experience from a visit to a CH site. Afterwards, the requirements and specifications of the proposed IoE architecture for the preservation of CH sites, as this has been designed to serve the STORM project, are described in detail. A complete guide from the needs of the sites to their translation in user requirements and the technical requirements/ solutions that address them will take place in this section. At the following section, a detailed description of the cloud infrastructure that is necessary for the functionality and efficient performance of the IoE system is provided with focus on the description of the necessary communication flaws while, on the final section, a description of how crowdsensing and crowdsourcing techniques can be used to enhance the preservation of CH sites focusing on their use on STORM project. Finally, future enhancements and conclusions are presented.

BACKGROUND

Given the importance and social impact on the protection, preservation and conservation of humanity's CH and modern communities, recent advances in Information and Communication Technologies (ICT) and current evolving trends have led to study the technologies playing a significant role in this effort. Especially, the rise of monitoring and communication capabilities of modern low-power, high usage sensors, plus their ability to interconnect (often through the Internet) while operating under any physical conditions and at any location can be used to create advanced ecosystems of smart things. From those ecosystems, potential solutions with so many possible applications in the CH field can be extracted. In this section, we describe various solutions where Internet of Things (IoT) or Internet of Everything (IoE) architectures and/or systems are considered for the preservation, protection or promotion of CH.

The use of digitization of the existing artifacts as a preservation action has been thoroughly studied in the literature (Green, 2017; Belhi, Bouras & Foufou, 2017; Gordon & Chaczko, 2017). All these studies encourage the fact that digitization is reliable as a form of protection and preservation of the CH's wealth but, at the same time, opens new possibilities on the way that this wealth is presented, attended and accepted by the visitors. Especially, in Shishido, Ito, Kawamura, Matsui, Morishima and Kitahara (2017) the use of crowdsourcing is studied as an effort to collect multiple images from the exhibits that would allow a 3D reconstruction of it and, therefore, its virtual representation. The idea of the virtual representation of objects has been presented in Minerva (2014). There, the author introduces the meaning of Servitization, as the result of virtualization in an IoT environment. Servitization allows the transformation of real-life objects and products into services that can be delivered by a programmable platform. Especially, the idea of the Virtual Continuum that is the digital representation of almost any real-life object has attracted the attention of the researchers in the Cultural Heritage domain that studied solutions where this notion is placed in motion, basically by proposing methods for visitors to use digital artifact interactions. Building on the notion of servitization, in Vassos, Malliaraki, Dal Falco, Di Maggio, Massimetti, Giulia Nocentini and Testa (2016), the authors provide an idea about how the virtual continuum can be served as an entertaining feature that would attract more visitors in the form of a chatbot, which interacts with them.

All the aforementioned solutions are based on an IoE architecture in order to be able to perform as described. But, as was discussed in Introduction, there is no common solution for an IoE (or IoT) architecture, rather, there are several proposed as referenced ones. With this in mind, an idea for the architecture of a platform that is powered by IoT capabilities is presented in Chianese, Piccialli & Jung (2016) where the researchers described, also, a possible use case demonstrating how IoT characteristics can enhance the experience of visitors in an archaeological site. In more detail, the authors described how, based on the proposed architecture, they developed an application for mobile phones (i.e., named TolkArt) allowing visitors to receive multimedia content on their phones, containing images of near-by exhibits, descriptions of the exhibition from their selection and multimedia files with artwork simulating one-way interaction with each artifact. Finally, visitors can use the application to describe their feelings about the visit while watching presentations posted to forum pages on the application or learning management systems.

In Chianese and Piccialli (2015) the authors build upon previous ideas and present an updated version of the application along with more details on the sensor network needed for the expected system performance. In addition, deeper analysis of the visitors' behavior is provided, where the results demonstrate how the overall experience is better rated and the overall time spent on the tour has been significantly increased, showing that the use of IoT solutions can enhance the visitor's experience. A similar approach was described by Chianese, Marulli, Moscato and Piccialli, (2013), where the authors proposed a location-based mechanism integrating mobile applications used to provide details, in the form of images and/or text, of the nearest exhibits.

Another referenced IoT architecture, aiming to prevent conservation of Cultural Heritage artifacts focusing on the use of sensing for this purpose is presented in Perles (2018). More specifically, a solution including the deployment of LoRa (Low Range) sensors is proposed that will communicate with Sigfox technologies (Sigfox, 2018). The authors studied the performance of this solution aiming to acquire optimal results regarding the avoidance of detrimental effects on the artwork of the exhibits in a Cultural Heritage site. The combination of LoRa with Sigfox was inspired by their use of many tourism applications in smart cities domain, an area that has also been highly benefited from IoT applications.

Finally, the authors in Ott and Pozzi (2011) studied how the role of ICT and the recent improvements in the field, manage to change and affect the teaching and learning of the CH. Digitization of artifacts is regarded as a very important step towards strongly involving ICT solutions for improving CH, since it is considered as an initial step to provide personalized experiences for visitors through mobile applications and gamification techniques. Finally, the authors propose that ICT could improve interdisciplinary learning approaches since it facilitates access to data from different sources combined in a way to provide general remarks used in different sites under similar weather or natural conditions.

DESIGNING AN IOE PLATFORM ARCHITECTURE FOR CULTURAL HERITAGE

This section deals with the necessary design decisions for the proposed IoE architecture, starting from specification of user requirements leading to the decision of the system requirements. For better understanding, the user requirements have been divided into two different categories: Functional requirements that are closely related to the system requirements (depending on the project CH site's needs) and Non-Functional requirements that are closely related to the user needs. After describing the user requirements, a translation to system requirements takes place, where these system requirements describe the specification of the technical modules and the connection between them.

Definition of Functional and Non-Functional Requirements

The first step taken towards the design of the STORM platform's architecture, was the identification of the use case requirements. In particular, we identified the use case scenarios, based on a detailed analysis of the regulatory framework, standards and classification work for Cultural Heritage sites, and the particular profiles, needs and expectations of participants sites.

Each pilot site in STORM (i.e., Mellor Heritage Project, Historical Centre of Rethymno, Baths of Diocletian, Roman Ruins of Troia and Ephesus) produced from two to five use cases for covering their needs and hazards in terms of both natural hazard protection and climate change effects mitigation. Table 1 presents all the parameters selected to define a use case.

During the definition of use cases, the preliminary (non-technical) user requirements were recorded; they were used to guide the formulation of functional and non-functional requirements. The parameters that define a preliminary user requirement are the following

Table 1. Description of the parameters that define a use case

Parameter		Definition
Name		Specifies the name of the scenario, which provides an abstract idea on what it addresses.
Identifier		A unique identifier for each scenario, consisting of letters referring to the site and a unique number per scenario per site.
Description	What	Describes the artifact or structure to be protected, restored or intervened.
	Where	Describes the location and particular conditions where the artifact, structure is located or stored.
	Why	Describes the particular reasons/risks for selecting this use case.
Scope		Defines all the means that will be used to achieve the goal.
Goal		The goal to be achieved.
Requirement		Preliminary user requirements for the use cases listed.
Assumptions		Specifies what is needed in order to achieve the use-case goal in terms of technical assumption (e.g., existing sensors and infrastructure) and organizational assumptions (e.g., existing techniques, processes, policies, regulations, etc.).
Post Conditions		The final conditions and linked results expected.
Technical Dependencies		Presents the technological solutions, already existing and to be developed, that will be needed for this use case.
Human Actors		Presents the human actors involved in this use case (i.e., firefighters).
Exceptions		Defines any exceptions influencing the good execution of scenarios related to the use case.

- **Req_ID:** A unique identifier per requirement using the schema *REQ-<pilot site>-<process action>-<sequential number>*. The field *pilot site* is referred by three letters (e.g., BOD for Baths of Diocletian), the field *process action* is referred by another three letters (MON for monitoring, MAN for management, INT for intervention) and the *sequential number* is the index of the requirement.
- **Relevance:** Defined by using MUST (for mandatory requirements), SHOULD (for desirable requirements) and COULD (for optional requirements).
- **Owner:** Involved in the requirement definition (matching with project objectives and needs) and implementation (matching with system functionalities and components).
- **Description:** Where a short explanation of the requirement is provided.

For example, the use case *Halls I, II and IV* placed in Baths of Diocletian produced the requirement that the environmental information must be collected by capturing sounds (Table 2).

Table 2. Preliminary requirement for capturing environmental sounds

Req_ID	Relevance2	Owner	Description
REQ-BOD-MON-02	M	TEIP	Information about the environmental conditions MUST be collected by capturing characteristic sounds accompanying corresponding events (e.g., local storm pattern, lightning and thunder).

As a result, the aforementioned requirement led, for example, to the formation of the functional requirement that describes how the classification techniques should be adopted to define the source of the sensor signals (e.g., thunderstorm) and the non-functional requirement of sensor reliability (Table 3).

In Table 3, the column Req_ID provides a unique reference identifier per requirement using the following format: *<type of requirement>-<requirement's acronym>-<sequential number>*. The type of requirement is indicated by FR for functional requirements and NFR for non-functional requirements. The requirement's acronym is indicated by two or three letters, usually the first letter of the requirement's name. For example, for the information extraction requirement we selected IE. Finally, the sequential number denotes the index. It should be noted, that the same requirement may apply to more than one use case.

For giving a short description of the requirements the verbs MUST, SHOULD, COULD defined the degree of necessity (IEEE, 1998). MUST verb (Essential) is used to indicate the platform will not be acceptable unless these requirements are provided in an agreed manner; SHOULD verb (Conditional) is used to imply that these requirements could enhance the software product, but it is not unacceptable if they are absent; COULD verb (Optional) is used to indicate a desirable requirement.

Finally, in order to respond to the collected system and user requirements defined we specified the system architecture for the STORM platform. For example, the *FR-IE-02 requirement* is addressed by the raw Data Pre-Processing, Feature Extraction and Data Processing modules.

The whole process for designing the system architecture (Figure 2), follows the recommendations of IEEE (IEEE, 1998), by ensuring the traceability of the specified requirements, covering both backward and forward traceability, as follows:

- Backward traceability (i.e., to preliminary user requirements), since each requirement refers the list of its source in earlier documents.
- Forward traceability (i.e., to platform architecture), since all the defined requirements have a unique name and can be referred to without ambiguity in the following documents.

Platform Architecture

Having discussed the Functional and Non-Functional user requirements, an architecture structure is designed to efficiently address those requirements. The architectural style that has been chosen to represent the STORM system architecture is the layered style. This style offers benefits in terms of interoperability, understandability and reuse. In this style, each layer exposes an interface (API) to be used by the layer above and below it. Specifically, each layer acts, at the same time, as a server and as

Table 3. Example of functional and non-functional requirements

Req_ID	Description	Preliminary Req_ID
FR-IE-02	Classification techniques MUST be performed on **sensor** signals to define its source.	REQ-BOD-MON-03
NFR-Rel-02	Reliable sensors SHOULD be used to measure the environmental parameters.	REQ-BOD-MON-03

Figure 2. Design process of STORM platform architecture

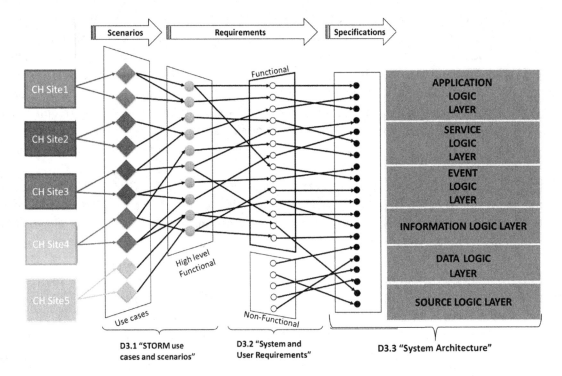

a client, respectively providing and consuming functionalities and services. In an ordered sequence of layers, each layer contains a set of modules or components that are logically related among each other through software connectors. A software connector is an architectural building block which aims an effective and regular interaction among the software components. Moreover, these layers allow a clear separation of concepts and functionalities, which in turn ensures flexibility, scalability, and maintainability of the entire architecture.

To this end, the proposed architecture in STORM is designed with respect to the IoE entities (i.e., People, Data, Process, and Things) and consists of 6 logical layers: Application, Service, Event, Information, Data and Source Logical layer (seen in Figure 2 at the last column).

The *Source Logic Layer* is the lower layer and consists of online and offline data originated from IoT devices (e.g., sensors), human and social networks. Each information source provides raw data (as structured and not structured data) that will be sent to the STORM cloud infrastructure to be stored and to be used to extract the relevant data for the cultural heritage domain.

The *Data Logic Layer* contains functional modules to gather and process the data collected from heterogeneous information sources in the STORM system. All the pre-processed data (also those from offline, human and social sources) are then validated and elaborated again using data validation, processing, classification and enrichment techniques to produce useful information.

The *Information Logic Layer* contains information processing and fusion modules dealing with the processing of useful information, produced by the data analysis modules, to extract classified events. To perform efficiently, several techniques of data analysis (e.g., patter recognition, data enrichment) are applied on the data collected from the above multimodal sources to maximize its accuracy and minimize loss function.

The *Event Logic Layer* defines a set of modules able to analyze and process (e.g., validate, aggregate and correlate) the classified events received as input from the Information Logic Layer, applying Complex Event Processing techniques. Moreover, the events will be elaborated using services such as Threats Analysis and Risk Assessment that allow for a valid Decision Support Mechanisms considering the better action to mitigate the critical situation.

The *Service Logic Layer* contains the service categories used by the STORM users to prevent, manage and mitigate the risk associated with natural hazards in the cultural heritage domain. The most important service categories include:

- Surveillance and Monitoring services that allow the CH operator to be aware on a detected critical situation and manage information retrieved from the field by physical sensors and human evaluators, exploiting both human cognitive ability and machine inference;
- Quick Damage Assessment services allow the CH operator to predict the possible consequences of the observed situation and select the best actions of the response process to mitigate the emergency considering the known risks;
- Surveying and Diagnosis services provide a set of innovative, cost-effective and non-invasive methods and processes for evaluating the efficacy and durability of protective and consolidating treatments, based on the historical and technological context as well as on the study of the properties of materials;
- Risk Assessment and Management services allow the assessment of all potential vulnerabilities and risks to specific cultural sites and the derivation of risk management strategies and definition of actions;
- Data Analytics services are defined and developed to enhance the understanding of the end users early, during or in the afterwards of a critical situation to enable an effective and efficient response to it; these services can interoperate by sharing common knowledge and results through the knowledge base;

The *Application Logic Layer* allows for the users/experts to interact with the STORM services and tools using Web application technologies, GIS services and mobile apps for tablet and smartphone devices as well as crowdsourcing and gamification applications. In this layer, the GUI functionalities are implemented to have an easy and intuitive access using a simple http browser to the operational and collaborative working environment for making decisions and sharing the cultural heritage knowledge. Collaboration between users is a very important aspect of this tier.

CLOUD-BASED INFRASTRUCTURE

With the basic components of the platform architecture being presented in the previous section, here we describe the adopted cloud infrastructure and the components that are used for integration and intercommunication purposes Cloud infrastructure plays an important role (as in most of the modern IoE systems) since it hosts all the needed services and is compliant with the non-functional requirements, such as scalability, availability and high maintenance. As a result, in this section, a detailed description of the

STORM's cloud-based infrastructure takes place, to fill in the structure of the proposed IoE architecture and complete its performance characteristics.

STORM Cloud Architecture

STORM Cloud's architecture is based on a tree approach; it consists of one Core cloud and several Edge clouds. The Core cloud can be described as a brokering system while the edge clouds are cloud environments located near the sites of interest. The role of the STORM Edge cloud is the collection, storage and processing of data gathered by sensors. This data can be raw or pre-processed and are gathered by services operating inside the virtual instances running on the Edge cloud. In order to achieve low latency, regarding data transfer, in network-constrained environments (e.g., Roman Ruins of Troia) Edge clouds should be located near each STORM site. However, if the site's workstations are not able to offer enough computational power for the support of an Edge cloud, then it can be served by the Edge cloud of a different site. Inside the Edge cloud, custom data processing services are deployed according to the needs of the site.

The STORM Core cloud is responsible for the collection of extracted information from the Edge clouds, the generation of events, the complex event processing, the communication with the STORM Edge clouds and the hosting of visualization tools and other services. Additionally, the Core cloud is also responsible for monitoring the status of the Edge clouds and their services running on virtual instances. Therefore, the Core cloud can be described as a brokering system, indicating which type of data each Edge cloud offers. Furthermore, several software services can be hosted in the Core cloud which may interact with the Edge clouds and retrieve data and information related to the existing sensors. This type of communication between the Core cloud and the Edge clouds can be accomplished with the use of APIs (e.g., RESTful APIs some of which are described later in this section).

Figure 3 presents the cloud-based architecture followed in STORM. The STORM Core cloud communicates with each STORM Edge cloud through the use of REST APIs. The STORM Edge clouds are able to communicate with the Core cloud and with the other Edge clouds via APIs. Each STORM Edge cloud has its own data gathering mechanisms and stores raw, processed or pre-processed data. These data can be offered as Open data and can be used for the extraction of information to be sent to the STORM Core cloud. Then, the STORM Core cloud will store and process the information to produce events using the required services and tools.

Additionally, the Core cloud hosts services which are able to communicate with the Edge clouds via the use of APIs and present information related to data and state of specific sensors in several sites. Finally, as it was mentioned earlier, the STORM Core cloud is able to act as a brokering system for the data sharing between the Edge clouds.

INTRA-CLOUD COMMUNICATION

One of the key functionalities of the STORM cloud infrastructure architecture is the communication between:

- The Sensors and the Edge clouds
- The Core and the Edge clouds

Figure 3. STORM cloud architecture

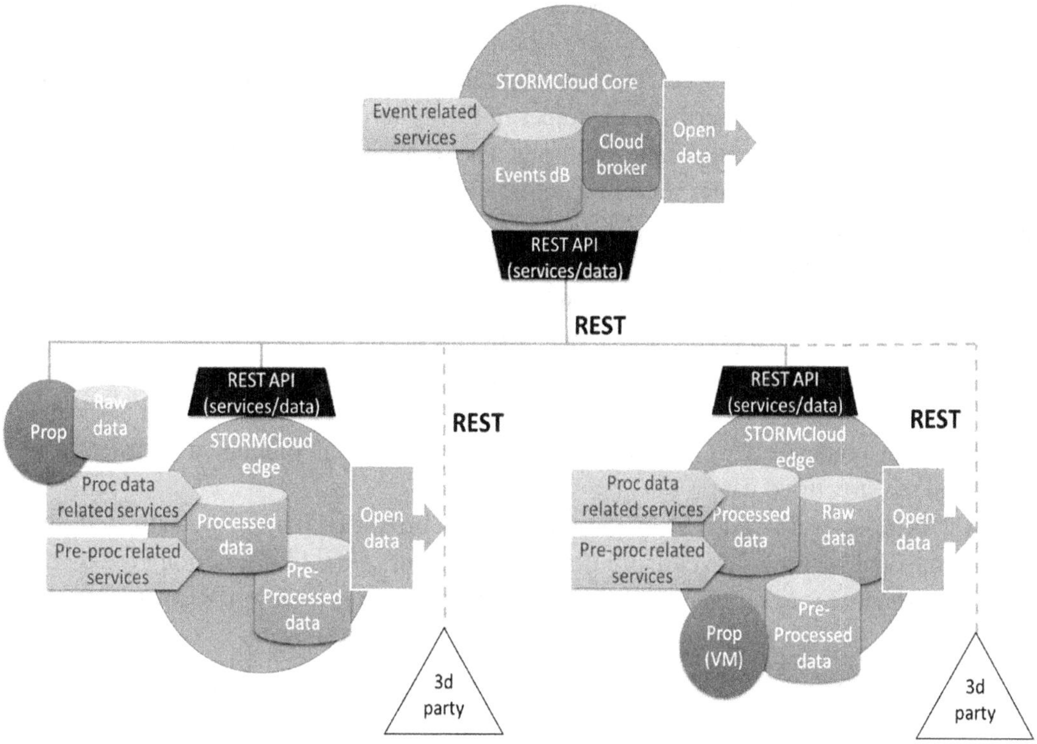

- Inside the Core cloud (intra-Core communication)
- The Edge clouds
- The Edge clouds and third-party providers

These communication flows can be fulfilled by taking advantage of the STORM cloud components:

- Edge Cloud Connector
- Core Cloud Connector
- Cloud Broker

These are based on RESTful services (e.g., communication between Core and Edge cloud) and the Publish-Subscribe pattern (e.g., communication between Edge and Core cloud or for intra-Core cloud communication).

The RESTful services are triggered when a REST call has been initiated. It is worth mentioning that the server - client model is followed in this technology, nevertheless the server is not concerned about the status of the client and vice versa. Therefore, the RESTful services are characterized as stateless. For example, if a REST call is performed by the client and the server status is down then the server will not answer and the client should perform another call later and, if the status is up, the server will respond.

On the other hand, the Publish – Subscribe (Pub/Sub) pattern is ideal for instant and asynchronous messaging. In this messaging pattern, the senders of messages are called publishers (producers) and the receivers of the messages are called subscribers (consumers). Moreover, the publishers do not send the messages directly to the subscribers, but, instead, they categorize the messages into classes called topics. Consequently, the consumers subscribe to the topics of their interest (i.e., topic-based filtering) in order to acquire the information provided by the publisher. The usage of the Pub/Sub technique increases the scalability of the system and enables real-time notifications.

Figure 4 illustrates the STORM cloud infrastructure and communication architecture, focusing on the communication flows between the STORM clouds. In particular, the sources (e.g., sensors) produce data to be collected by the Data Gathering Framework and are validated and/or pre-processed by the relevant components, deployed to the Edge cloud. Afterwards, the structured data are sent to the Edge Cloud Connector (ECC) and to the Data Processing components. The ECC is a RESTful service storing the real-time data to a NoSQL database and sends them (e.g., the last measurement of a sensor) directly to the Core Cloud Connector (CCC), as well as the Data Processing components extracting useful information from the structured data.

Since CCC is based on the Pub/Sub pattern, it acts as a broker and offers the extracted information and the real-time data via topics. In case of information, the subscribed Information Processing component generates from them classified events, which can be stored to the relevant repository or can be sent

Figure 4. STORM cloud infrastructure

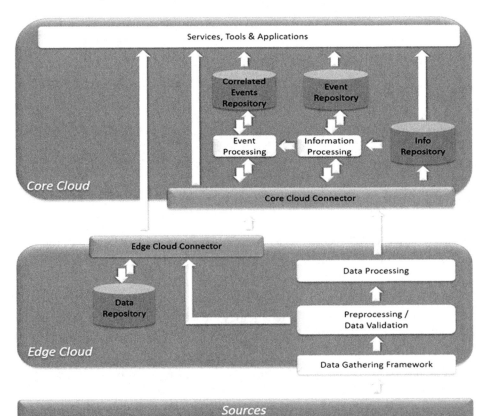

directly to the Event Processing components and to the CCC. Moreover, the Event Processing component that receives the generated events applies Complex Event Processing techniques to identify the correlated events (in terms of time and space), which can be, also, stored to a database or sent to the CCC. Finally, STORM services, tools, and applications have the ability to receive all kind of historical or real-time data (structured data/information/event/correlated events) utilizing REST APIs or the Pub/Sub pattern.

The following subsections explain in detail the mechanisms of the ECC and the CCC, and introduce the Cloud Broker, which is responsible for monitoring the cloud resources.

Edge Cloud Connector

The ECC component is a RESTful web service responsible for handling the structured data and runs at the STORM Edge cloud. In STORM, there can be two kinds of structured data: the data regarding the last measurement of a sensor (i.e., almost real-time data) and historical data (i.e., values covering a longer time period in the past). The former are forwarded to the CCC, while the latter are stored in a NoSQL database (e.g., MongoDB).

Figure 5 illustrates the RESTful interactions of the ECC. In particular, the ECC receives via a POST method (e.g., http://{DomainName}/storm/rest/manage/edgecloudconnector/data) by the Data Validator / Pre-processor components, all the incoming structured data and stores them to the NoSQL database. The data can be offered, afterwards, to the STORM consumers. The initiator of the communication should define the kind of data expected, by making the right calls (e.g., http://{DomainName}/storm/rest/manage/edgecloudconnector/site/{site}/nodes/sensors/list) and define the time period of the requested historical data (e.g., http://{DomainName}/storm/rest/manage/edgecloudconnector/nodes/{node}/sensor/{sensor}/data/date/{start}/{end}/limit/{limit}).

There are three kinds of entities that consume the services of the ECC, 1) the Core cloud, 2) the Edge clouds, and 3) third-party providers, initiating the following communication flows:

Figure 5. Abstract representation of the RESTful service offered by the Edge Cloud Connector

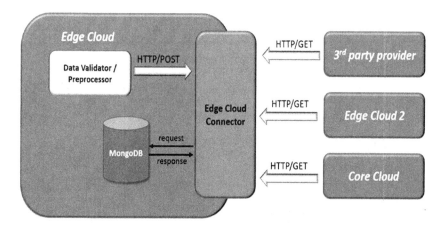

1. **Core to Edge Cloud Communication**: This communication flow deals with the transfer of data between RESTful services hosted in an Edge cloud and applications or services running at the Core cloud. The transferred data are retrieved, by the RESTful services running at the Edge cloud, from the existing structured data repository. Then, they are forwarded to the service or application at the Core cloud to initiate communications.

2. **Edge to Edge Cloud Communication**: As depicted in Figure 3, the communication between the Edge clouds will, also, be achieved through the use of the RESTful services. For example, if a data processing service deployed to an Edge cloud needs data stored in another Edge cloud, then it will have to make an HTTP request to the ECC, to retrieve these data.

3. **Third-Party Providers to Edge Cloud Communication**: For the communication between a third-party provider and an Edge cloud (preferably in the form of open data) REST APIs will be used, once more.

It should be noted that in any of the aforementioned cases the consumers will be firstly authenticated, in order to get the required API token from the ECC.

Core Cloud Connector

The transfer of real-time data and useful information from the Data Processing components to the CCC is based on the Pub/Sub pattern. Figure 6 presents the communication between the Edge cloud and the Core cloud, and the intra-Core cloud communication. The proposed mechanism provides many-to-many, real-time, asynchronous messaging decoupling senders and receivers. Moreover, it allows for secure and highly available communications between independently written applications. In this way, notifications will be triggered at the subscribed to the topic Core cloud services (e.g., the Event Processor) and/ or applications about any updates, originating from the Edge clouds.

1. **Edge to Core Cloud Communication:** The CCC receives messages from the ECC containing real-time data (i.e., last measurement) originated by sensors and from the Data Processing components

Figure 6. The Pub/Sub mechanism of the core cloud connector component

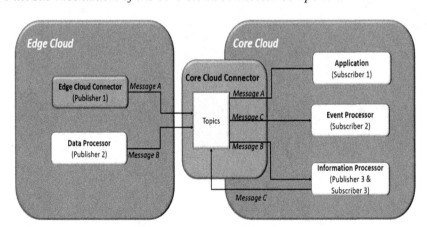

containing useful information. The messages will be using a JSON format. An example of such a data format is given in Figure 7.

2. **Intra-Core Communication:** In the Core cloud, the Pub/Sub method is, also, used by the CCC for the sharing of event/situations between the hosted components (i.e., Event Processor, services and applications). This kind of messages will, also, be using a JSON format.

Cloud Broker

The Cloud Broker is a component hosted inside the Core cloud, to provide a directory of services and a dashboard for monitoring the resources of STORM clouds. In addition, when a new service or new dataset is available through the STORM Cloud REST API, a notification to the Broker is provided through the use of CCC, so that, at each time, the Broker is aware of all of the available services and data at the cloud instance (Figure 8).

The interface of the Cloud Broker component was specified to interact with the Edge clouds through the usage of OpenStack RESTful APIs (OpenStack, 2018). The RESTful services (authentication and monitoring) are described in Table 4.

Implicit Mobile Crowdsensing: How It Is Used in STORM

To enhance the performance of the system, the use of mobile crowdsensing in the platform has, also, been studied in STORM. More specific, the implicit use of the human factor inside an IoE system is

Figure 7. Example of the information message in JSON format

```
[ { "type": "AirTemperature",
    "topic": "AirTempBoD1",
    "unitMeasurement": "Celsius",
    "value": 24,
    "nodeId": "eiciji43424i",
    "datetime": {
      "created": "2018-02-19 13:40:23.234",
      "transmited": "2018-02-19 13:40:23.334",
      "received": "2018-02-19 13:40:24.334"
    },
    "site": {
      "siteName": "Baths of Diocletian",
      "heritageAsset": "Michelangelo's Cloister"
    },
    "location": {
      "point": {"latitude": 41.321, "longitude": 12.4984
      }
    },
    "status": 1
  }
]
```

Figure 8. Representation of the cloud broker component

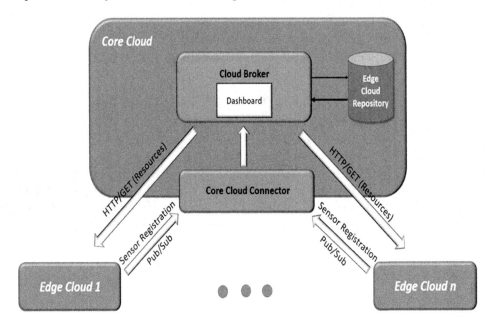

Table 4. Cloud broker's RESTful API

Method	Explanation
cloudBrokerAuth	The registered Edge cloud owners are authorized by the Core cloud.
os-simple-tenant-usage/{tenant_id} *(OpenStack API 2018)*	The Cloud Broker will consume the web services of the OpenStack Edge clouds in order to get updated about their status.
requestData	Each component running at the Core cloud will receive data using the methods of ECC and CCC as mentioned before.

studied, in order to help the protection and preservation of cultural heritage objects and assets. Mobile CrowdSensing (MCS) is a large-scale sensing paradigm where individuals with sensing and computing devices collectively share data and extract information to measure and map phenomena of common interest (Raghu, 2011). The complementary use of both machine and human intelligence aims to fill the gaps and resolve the limitations that each one may have standalone, like computing speed and power or perception and task understanding.

In order to collect sufficient data to process and extract meaningful results, there is the need of user motivation and engagement. For the implicit mobile crowdsensing STORM's module, the use of gamification techniques was adopted. The term gamification is used to describe *the use of elements of game design in non-game contexts* (Deterning et al. 2011). This use of such elements aims to gain or improve motivation and engagement in the applied domain. Gamification techniques apply in many different domains from research and education to software engineering (García et al. 2017) and industry. In cultural heritage, the goals of gamification techniques include the preservation and protection of cultural assets, the improvement of the visitors' satisfaction and awareness and the increase of conservation performance through crowdsourced useful information collection. Following the above definition, we design scavenger-hunt game scenarios in a playful manner, to be used in the context of hybrid human-machine data and information collection and processing for cultural heritage preservation. Visitors of an archaeological site, by making use of their mobile devices, can download and play a game, providing the same time useful information for the site. The game involves the completion of a series of tasks in the form of riddles. For each task, the user may be asked to answer a question relevant to the task, or maybe upload some media files, in order to continue. Furthermore, some annotation tasks may be included, like classifying a series of image or audio files. While the primary use of the collected data and information coming from the user and his/her mobile device is the game's tasks completion, a second implicit use of them is their processing and analysis, aiming to extract valuable information that can help in preserving the cultural heritage. In this scope of user participation awareness, mobile crowdsensing using gamification techniques can be characterized as implicit.

In the scope of the logical architecture of STORM, implicit mobile crowdsensing makes use of all the previously mentioned IoE layers. Starting from the *source logic layer*, site experts, collect media and any other interesting information about each archeological site's points of interests (POIs). Then, using a web application on the *application layer*, they provide information about these POIs, along with the relevant media (image, audio or video) resources. Each POI consists of the location of the point, a name, a short description and the area around it (a list of location coordinates). With these POIs as input, game creators construct a series of tasks for the players to complete. Each task may include the use of the user's location, media uploading, answering a question or classifying a series of images. Once the creation of the game is ready, visitors of each site can download the mobile application and start completing the tasks. While the players follow the instructions of each game's task, (s)he also provides both raw and many times enhanced with own submitted metadata, resources. The collected data through the *data gathering framework* are validated and processed, and the results are then forwarded to the *information logic layer*. The extracted information is then processed using machine learning, and any useful information is forwarder to the *event logic layer*. Event processing and management triggers the relevant service on the service layer and site managers can view, analyze the results on the STORM collaborative decision-making dashboard and take any further actions.

The collected and produced data are audio samples, images or videos, environmental measurements and GPS coordinates (Figure 9). Since the users are not aware of the threat evidence that these data may indicate, collected data need to be processed and properly analyzed in order to increase situation awareness. Audio signal and images need processing to be exploited by the STORM platform. In order to extract useful information from these types of data, Deep Learning methods are considered to be the most suitable, since they have revolutionized the fields of computer vision (Krizhevsky et al. 2012) and audio signal processing (Piczak 2015a). In particular, audio classification techniques will be applied in STORM to recognize sounds of interest at pilot sites (e.g., thunderstorm or heavy rain), while object detection techniques should be applied to identify the existence of structural hazards (e.g. cracks on a wall).

The extracted information is sent to the Core cloud, utilizing the Core Cloud Connector (Figure 6) that is based on the Publish-Subscribe (Pub/Sub) pattern. The CCC component is based on the Apache Kafka framework (2018), which consists of the following components:

- Producers (i.e., Publishers)
- Consumers (i.e., Subscribers)
- Topics
- Broker

Figure 9. Data flow from implicit mobile crowdsourcing to STORM Edge cloud

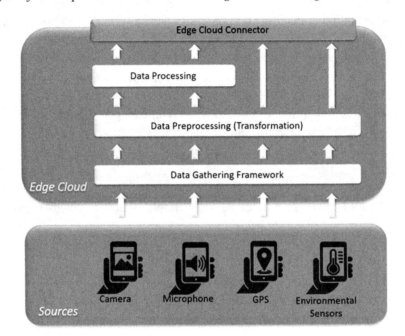

In particular, the Kafka Producer produces streams of data records (such as extracted information), which are clustered in a Topic (e.g., *ExtractedAudioInformation* topic), and are served by the Kafka Broker to the Kafka Consumer in order to be consumed. It should be noted that in order to achieve low latency, the CCC utilizes the Kafka Cluster (consisted of several Brokers), which is featured to enable the use of more than one Broker for handling the incoming request in parallel. Moreover, Kafka uses the Apache ZooKeeper framework (2018) to manage the Cluster and coordinate the topology of the Brokers.

Figure 10 presents how the extracted audio information from the Audio Data Processing component (*Audio Classifier*) is forwarded to the Audio Information Processing component exploiting the Kafka and the Zookeper frameworks. Subsequently, audio information is transformed into Events based on predefined semantic rules, that are designed with respect to the possible hazards that each pilot site faces. Semantic rules are used in order to apply deductive reasoning to extracted information from audio signals combined with spatiotemporal information.

FUTURE ENHANCEMENTS

One of the goals of the STORM project was to be considered as a source of information by Cultural Heritage experts. The information is designed to be shared with suggestions about the methodologies applied. In case a disastrous event occurs at a Cultural Heritage site, the details about the deployment of state-of-the-art equipment and the implementation of a robust, resilient, efficient system architecture can be of assistance.

Figure 10. Communication between audio data processor and audio information processor

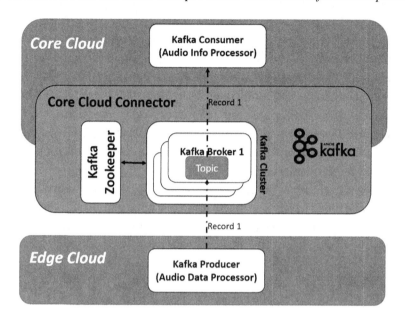

To this end, one of the possible enhancements of the proposed IoE system, which is produced for STORM project, is to include the notion of the *Digital Twin*, meaning the virtual identical sibling of a natural exhibit or artifact, which will be located on a Cultural Heritage site. This virtual sibling can be used, under the STORM logic, to provide for information regarding the effects (detrimental or not) that certain natural or human-related conditions have to the artifacts health and condition. At the same time, the digital twin can take part in simulations, where the conditions might change to simulate either the transfer of the physical object to a different environment or the behavior of similar objects that can be found at different sites. Through these simulations that will take place on cloud or at the edge using fog computing, researchers can share details about their findings and contribute strongly to the preservation of techniques needed to apply to different situations based on the (natural) conditions while, also, describing the warnings that could trigger the alarms for the prevention of detrimental actions at the exhibits.

Finally, having in mind the notion of the digital twin that was described above, an expansion to the provided infrastructure is, also, expected. This expansion will be focusing on the use of (virtual) containers as a means to serve the described simulations and to contribute to the overall minimization of the risks by cyber-attacks. Containers are more and more considered as a very good technique that can help with increasing the system's performance, while managing the available resources in a more efficient (both regarding the performance and the energy consumption) way and can play a significant role in the described IoE architecture.

CONCLUSION

In this article, we discussed the use of IoE and cloud technologies for enabling efficient protection and preservation of Cultural Heritage sites and artifacts, having in mind the need for using low cost solutions, easy to be deployed. The described framework can be considered as the basis over which future and emerging concepts, combining the results in different domains where IoE can be applied (i.e. smart cities), may be exploited. The use of a scalable, easy to deploy framework as the one presented here, makes use of heterogeneous infrastructures to provide the ground work for successful concepts such as the Digital Twin (a virtual representation of a tangible item, enabled through APIs introducing the concept of servitization rather than the traditional digitization) can be introduced. Links to solutions enabling intelligence towards the improvement of quality of life in cities can further enhance the benefits from the use of the IoE and cloud technologies, creating new opportunities for the economy and tourism, through the parallel exploitation (with respect to the preservation) of Cultural Heritage.

ACKNOWLEDGMENT

Work presented in this paper has received funding from the European Union's Horizon 2020 research and innovation programme under STORM project, grant agreement n°700191.

REFERENCES

Apache Zookeeper. (2018). Retrieved from https://zookeeper.apache.org/

Belhi, A., Bouras, A., & Foufou, S. (2017). Digitization and preservation of cultural heritage: The CEPROQHA approach. *2017 11th International Conference on Software, Knowledge, Information Management and Applications (SKIMA)*, 1-7. 10.1109/SKIMA.2017.8294117

Chianese, A., Marulli, F., Moscato, V., & Piccialli, F. (2013). Smartweet: A location-based smart application for exhibits and museums. *International Conference on Signal Image Technology and Internet Based Systems*, 408–415. 10.1109/SITIS.2013.73

Chianese, A., & Piccialli, F. (2015). Improving User Experience of Cultural Environment Through IoT: The Beauty or the Truth Case Study. In *Intelligent Interactive Multimedia Systems and Services. Smart Innovation, Systems and Technologies* (Vol. 40). Cham: Springer. doi:10.1007/978-3-319-19830-9_2

Chianese, A., Piccialli, F., & Jung, J. E. (2016). The Internet of Cultural Things: Towards a Smart Cultural Heritage. *12th International Conference on Signal-Image Technology & Internet-Based Systems (SITIS)*. 10.1109/SITIS.2016.83

Deterding, S., Khaled, R., Nacke, L.E., & Dixon, D. (2011). *Gamification: Toward a Definition*. In CHI 2011 Gamification Workshop Proceedings, Vancouver, BC, Canada.

Ganti, R. K., Ye, F., & Lei, H. (2011). Mobile Crowdsensing: Current State and Future Challenges. *IEEE Communications Magazine*, *49*(11), 32–39. doi:10.1109/MCOM.2011.6069707

García, F., Pedreira, O., Piattini, M., Cerdeira-Pena, A., & Penabad, M. (2017). A framework for gamification in software engineering. *Journal of Systems and Software*, *132*, 21–40. doi:10.1016/j.jss.2017.06.021

Gordon, L., & Chaczko, Z. (2017). Ontological Metamodel for Consistency of Data Heritage Preservation (DHP). *2017 25th International Conference on Systems Engineering (ICSEng)*, 438-442. 10.1109/ICSEng.2017.67

Green, I. (2017). *Digitisation as a preservation strategy of national heritage — A case of the Owela Museum. In 2017 IST-Africa Week Conference* (pp. 1–5). Windhoek: IST-Africa. doi:10.23919/ISTAFRICA.2017.8102283

IEEE. (1998). *IEEE Std 830: Recommended Practice for Software Requirements Specifications*. IEEE.

Kafka, A. (2018). *Distributed streaming platform*. Retrieved from https://kafka.apache.org/

Krizhevsky, A., Sutskever, I., & Hinton, G. E. (2012). Imagenet Classification with Deep Convolutional Neural Networks. *Advances in Neural Information Processing Systems*, 1–9.

Minerva, R. (2014). From Internet of Things to the Virtual Continuum: An architectural view. *IEEE Euro Med Telco Conference (EMTC)*. 10.1109/EMTC.2014.6996633

OpenStack. (2018). *OpenStack Installation Guide for Ubuntu*. Retrieved from https://docs.openstack.org/mitaka/install-guide-ubuntu/

Ott, M., & Pozzi, F. (2011). Towards a new era for Cultural Heritage Education: Discussing the role of ICT. *Computers in Human Behavior*, *27*(4), 1365–1371. doi:10.1016/j.chb.2010.07.031

Perles, A., Pérez-Marín, E., Mercado, R., Segrelles, J. D., Blanquer, I., Zarzo, M., & Garcia-Diego, F. J. (2018). An energy-efficient internet of things (IoT) architecture for preventive conservation of cultural heritage. *Future Generation Computer Systems*, *81*, 566–581. doi:10.1016/j.future.2017.06.030

Piczak, K. J. (2015a). Environmental sound classification with convolutional neural networks. *25th International Workshop on Machine Learning for Signal Processing (MLSP)*, 1–6.

Shishido, H., Ito, Y., Kawamura, Y., Matsui, T., Morishima, A., & Kitahara, I. (2017). Proactive preservation of world heritage by crowdsourcing and 3D reconstruction technology. *2017 IEEE International Conference on Big Data (Big Data)*, 4426-4428. 10.1109/BigData.2017.8258479

Sigfox. (2017). *SIGFOX - The Global Communications Service provider for the Internet of Things (IoT)*. Retrieved from https://www.sigfox.com/en

Sun, Y., Song, H., Jara, A. J., & Bie, R. (2016). Internet of Things and Big Data Analytics for Smart and Connected Communities. *IEEE Access: Practical Innovations, Open Solutions*, *4*, 766–773. doi:10.1109/ACCESS.2016.2529723

Vassos, S., Malliaraki, E., Dal Falco, F., Di Maggio, J., Massimetti, M., Giulia Nocentini, M., & Testa, A. (2016). *Art-Bots: Toward Chat-Based Conversational Experiences in Museums*. Academic Press. . doi:10.1007/978-3-319-48279-8_43

KEY TERMS AND DEFINITIONS

API: A programmable interface that describes how the communication between two ends (applications) will take place.

Broker: Middleware software responsible of matching requests to offers.

Chatbot: Smart digital discussion partners or discussion interfaces.

Crowdsensing: The technique where humans equipped with sensors (usually smart-phones) generate data (i.e., pictures or videos) during their visit in the area.

Cultural Heritage: The archaeological sites that promote and preserve the culture of a civilization.

Sensors: The devices that manage to observe and measure physical characteristics and provide a digital representation of the measurement.

Servitization: The process of digitizing an artifact, creating a digital representation that could be provided as a service to other software or platforms.

Chapter 10
Internet of Everything (IoE):
Eye Tracking Data Analysis

Janet L. Holland
Emporia State University, USA

Sungwoong Lee
Emporia State University, USA

ABSTRACT

The internet of everything (IoE) envelopes the internet of things (IoT) that was simply focusing primarily on machine-to-machine sensor-based smart device communications. The IoE expands to include people and processes in a much more comprehensive scope. The internet of everything is expanding our ability to collect massive amounts of data for comprehensive analysis to achieve a level of understanding not previously possible. Since the internet of everything (IoE) has such a strong focus on collecting and analyzing data using smart sensor-enabled devices, eye tracking data is a perfect match. Eye tracking and other biometric sensor-based data can be collected and analyzed locally in real time through fog/edge computing or cloud-based big data analytics.

INTRODUCTION

Defining the Internet of Things and the Internet of Everything

The slightly older "Internet of Things quite literally means *things* or *objects* connecting to the Internet – and each other" (Greengard, 2015, p. 15). The connected devices each have a Unique Identification Number (UID) and Internet Protocol (IP) address to identify them. The devices were typically connected via built in Radio Frequency Identification (RFID) or Near- Field Communications (NFC) using chips and tags. Newer systems integrate Bluetooth and Wi-Fi wireless technologies connected to the Internet of Everything.

DOI: 10.4018/978-1-5225-7332-6.ch010

The current Internet of Everything is a term coined by Cisco Systems. In one Cisco Systems article titled "Internet of Everything: The Value of Connections" (Hall, 2015), the author refers to four stages in the evolution of the Internet. Stage one, connectivity digitized access to information such as using email, browsers, and searching. Two, networked the economy to digitize processes using e-commerce, digital supply chains, and collaboration. Three, created immersive experiences to digitize interactions through social, mobile, cloud, and video media. Four, the Internet of Everything is digitizing the world by connecting people, processes, data, and things for more intelligent connections with a higher level of society impact. Cisco wants to "make the networked connections more relevant and valuable than ever before-turning information into actions that create new capabilities, richer experiences, and unprecedented economic opportunity for businesses, individuals, and countries" (Cisco Newsroom, 2018).

Dave Evan's article titled "Internet of Everything: How More Relevant and Valuable Connections Will Change the World (2012)", defines the IoE as things, processes, data, and people in the following way. "Things" are made up of physical items like sensors and devices, connected to the Internet and each other. "Process" provides the connections to deliver the information. "Data" gathered is streamed over the Internet to a central source, where it is analyzed and processed and can even send higher-level information back to machines, computers, and people for further evaluation and decision making. "People" connect to the Internet through their devices such as computers, tablets, smartphones and social networking sites. The people themselves can be sensor enabled to become nodes on the Internet, providing both static information and data for constantly emitting activity systems.

Figure 1 is an example of Cisco's IoE architectures (2015). On the left, you can see the author (Holland, 2018) added eye tracking to demonstrate how it can fit in. In addition, in the lower portion examples have been added. For example, below *things* the items listed represent the devices currently being used for collecting eye tracking data for analysis. At this time, not all aspects of Cisco's architecture are used for all processes, data, and people but the option is there for future expansion to more fully embrace the IoE.

The Internet of Everything includes "The 7 layers of the Open System Interconnection (OSI) Model" (Beal, 2018). It represents a conceptual networking framework for implementing the communication protocols between those seven layers. It was developed by the International Standards Organization (ISO). Each layer performs a specific function then passes the data on to the next layer. Layers 1-4 generally move the data around while 5-7 are application interaction levels. As seen in Figure 2, layer 1) provides the physical connections, 2) is for data links, 3) networks the data, 4) transports data, 5) session manages

Figure 1. Eye tracking within the IoE architectures
(Cisco, 2015; Holland, 2018)

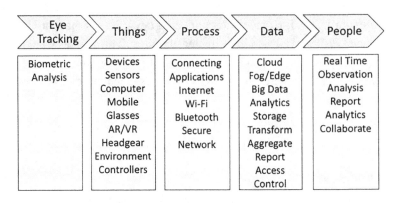

applications interactions, 6) presentation of data, and 7) application to achieve results. Some systems combine two or three layers. The different technical layer functions are defined in greater detail below.

Layer 1, is the physical layer and uses the network of electrical and mechanical hardware to send and receive data.

Layer 2, is the data link that encodes/ decodes data packets into bits. It furnishes transmission protocol knowledge while managing and handling errors in the physical layer, flow control and frame synchronization. The data link layer is divided into two sub layers: The Media Access Control (MAC) layer and Logical Link Control (LLC) layer. The MAC sub layer controls how a computer on the network gains access to the data and permission to transmit it. The LLC layer controls frame synchronization, flow control and error checking.

Layer 3, network provides switching and routing technologies, creating logical paths known as virtual circuits for transmitting data from node to node. Routing and forwarding are primary functions of this layer, while also addressing, Internet working, error handling, congestion control and packet sequencing.

Layer 4, transport provides transparent transfer of data between end systems or hosts, and is responsible for end-to-end error recovery and flow control, while ensuring complete data transfer.

Layer 5, session manages and terminates connections between applications. The session layer sets up, coordinates, and terminates conversations, exchanges, and dialogues between the applications at each end, dealing with session and connection coordination.

Layer 6, presentation provides independence from differences in data representation (e.g., encryption) by translating from application to network format, and vice versa. The presentation layer works to transform data into a form the application layer can accept. This layer formats and encrypts data to be sent across a network, providing freedom from compatibility problems. It is sometimes called the syntax layer.

Layer 7, application layer supports application and end-user processes. Communication partners are identified, quality of service is identified, user authentication and privacy are considered, and any constraints on data syntax are identified. Everything at this layer is application-specific. This layer provides application services for file transfers, and other network software services. Telnet and FTP are applications existing entirely in the application level. Tiered application architectures are part of this layer.

Cisco Systems (2015) has its own 7 Layers for the Internet of Everything as seen in Figure 3. Their levels represent the technology foundation and processes enabling distributed computing networks. Layer 1) The physical devices and controllers, 2) connectivity through communication and processing units, 3) edge computing through data element analysis and transformation, 4) data accumulation and storage, 5) data abstraction through aggregation and access, 6) application including reporting, analytics, and control, and 7) collaboration and processes involving people and business processes.

Cisco System's (2015) intelligent network architecture addresses end-to-end cybersecurity as an ongoing concern for the Internet of Everything. It is important to protect implementation before launching by putting controls in place to enforce and harden the system. During implementation, malicious attacks need to be detected, blocked, and defended against. After implementation, the scope, containment, and remediation can be addressed, including network, endpoint, mobile, virtual, and cloud connection points. The intelligent network includes a secure network fabric of intercloud, branching using Software Defined Network (SDN), Application Centric Infrastructure (ACI), access switching Power Over Ethernet (PoE). Secure identification may include fingerprint or face recognition mapping and wireless access. These features provide the intelligent network end-to-end security, management, and automation for the system.

The Cisco Systems (2015) Internet of Everything end-to-end architecture of connected devices include 1) Machine to Machine (M2M). Operational technologies referred to as 2) Machine to Human (M2H).

Figure 2. The 7 layers of the open system interconnection (OSI) model (Beal, 2018)

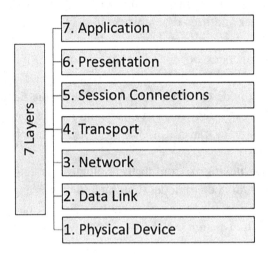

Figure 3. Cisco's 7 layers of the Internet of Everything model (2015)

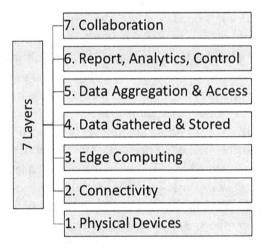

Mobile, Desktop and Rooms are considered 3) Human to Human (H2H). These are all part of connected devices in regards to analytics, decision making, productivity, and mission success.

Big data tends to be centralized, as found in cloud computing. An article on Fog computing (Noble, 2015) states how the cloud and fog/edge computing can be complimentary and combined. Fog computing provides distributed processing power on the devices themselves. This process compliments cloud computing by having individual devices take care of some of the data and processing. It has the side benefit of relieving network stress and congestion by allowing some analysis to take place on the network's edge, saving time and bandwidth to optimize performance and results.

According to Cisco white paper (2015) fog applications can analyze real-time data from network-connected things and then initiating an action. The action can involve machine-to-machine (M2M) communications or human-machine interaction (HMI).

In a Cisco article (2015) on fog computing they define the fog as extending the cloud to be closer to the things producing and acting on IoT data. The devices called fog nodes, can be deployed with a network connection. Any device with computing, storage, and network connectivity can be a fog node. Developers can port or write IoT applications for the fog nodes at the network edge. The fog nodes closest to the network edge take in the data from IoT devices. It is crucial the fog IoT application directs different types of data to the optimal place for analysis. The most time-sensitive data analyzed on the fog node closest to the things generating the data. The fog nodes closest to the grid sensors can look for signs of problems and then prevent them by sending control commands to actuators. Data waiting for seconds or minutes for action can be passed along to an aggregation node for analysis and action. In the Smart Grid example, each substation might have its own aggregation node reporting the operational status of each downstream feeder and lateral. Less time sensitive data is sent to the cloud for analysis, big data analytics, and long-term storage. The fog nodes can be set to send periodic summaries of grid data to the cloud for analysis and storage. Fog computing eliminates trips to the cloud for analysis. It reduces costs by offloading network traffic from the core network. It can also protect sensitive data by analyzing it in house, within the business. Fog computing is used to gain insights faster, improve service, and provide an additional layer of security. We now shift our focus to an examination of eye tracking using the IoE platform.

Eye Tracking Defined

The goal of eye tracking analysis is to provide an in-depth understanding of the devices/ materials/ things used, how effective our interactions are, emotional engagement, patterns, behaviors, conditions, trends, areas of confusion, and more. Using sensor enabled intelligent devices for data collection assists in providing deeper insights. Eye tracking data collection and analysis can include screen-based materials, objects, and authentic environments. Eye tracking analysis can be conducted in a lab setting with screen-based materials, or by using specialized devices to analyze objects such as smartphones and tablets, or by capturing virtual/augmented reality experiences using smart headgear, or in authentic environments in the field using mobile eye tracking glasses to examine actual use. One key feature of the IoT has been "about data and extracting value from it" (Greengard, 2015, p.54). After collecting the eye tracking data, the underlying sophisticated algorithms are applied. The feedback from the analysis allows us to then improve our products and interactions with them. The Internet of Everything now expands on this perspective by including people and processes.

Here you will learn more about how eye tracking and other biometric data collection and analysis techniques can be used effectively. Eye tracking devices include the sensors needed to know exactly where the research participants' eyes are focused. It determines their attention, focus, drowsiness, and additional mental states. This information provides deeper insights into behavior to improve interfaces, products, and design.

Smart connected devices are now being used for exchanging data over the Internet. The Internet of Everything now makes it possible to collect eye tracking data from individual's devices and other biometric sensor-enabled devices for analysis, applying algorithms to its large data sets to gain comprehensive insights. As one can imagine, these insights are very valuable to every field of study. In the business setting it represents "Billions of sensors! Trillions of dollars!" (Sinclair, 2017, p.xi). Silicon Valley's data-driven mindset is being applied to the products we now buy, use, and how they are being evaluated. The tremendous growth in the IoE is directly attributed to the Internet of connected devices, interfaced with sensors, allowing for increased data collection points used for analysis to improve consumer driven products and interaction outcomes. Using better, real world data, enterprises are able to perfect their products at ever increasing rates. The current focus is on using smart devices to gather data to improve outcomes in regards to products, services, and functionality.

Eye tracking data is a way to get Science-based hard data evidence on user behaviors, usability, what people are looking at and paying attention to in an effort to improve design or outcomes. Some of the eye tracking data collected is taken from what people look at, how long they dwell on it, in what order they view items, and what they miss seeing. Eye tracking research studies are based on measurements of eye position and movement. The data collected is based on corneal reflections to indicate areas of visual interest. It is referred to as Pupil Center Corneal Reflection (PCCR). PCCR is accomplished by illuminating the eye with near infrared light, not perceived by the human eye. The light enters the pupil and reflects from the iris in the cornea to track eye movement and direction of gaze. Using a high-resolution camera, the gaze direction can be tracked. The data collected can inform us what the study participants look at and actually see, thereby reflecting their attention. To collect better data available and enhance the functionality of IoE, which involves digital sensors, computing devices, and the internet, eye tracking technology and biometric data collection are attracting attention as a solution to address it in these days. For example, at the 51th International Consumer Electronics Show (CES) 2018, 7invensun introduced various eye tracking technologies and biometric data collection methods: VR eye tracking solution (e.g., aGlass DK II), AR eye tracking solution, cell phone unlocking technology through visual attention, eye alarm solution for people with mobility impairments, remote eye tracker (e.g., aSee Pro), and eye tracker for patients with Lou Gehrig's disease. Next, you will learn about the connections between eye tracking to the field of human computer interaction, its quality standards, the history, terms and techniques. Having a good foundation in the related fields of study can assist your own research efforts.

The Field of Human Computer Interaction (HCI)

Eye tracking falls within the field of Human Computer Interaction (HCI) research. Human computer interaction deals with how computers are designed and used. The field is built on "contributions from psychology, design, human factors, and ergonomics" (Myers, p. 1, 1996). Government funded research labs in HCI have made significant contributions with easy to use interfaces. In addition, it provided the "intellectual capital and trained the research teams for pioneer systems that, over a period of 25 years, revolutionized how people interact with computers" (Myers, p. 2, 1996). The research collected and analyzed has led to better products and better-informed HCI research.

Human Computer Interaction Quality Standard Principles

You may be wondering, what type of qualities are considered in human computer interaction research? One will often find guidelines over four-hundred pages in length. The problem with very large documents is how they can become unwieldy and not be consulted during a design and development process. The best guidelines tend to be short, simple, and usable. "Any system designed for people to use should be easy to learn and remember, effective, and pleasant to use" (Molich & Nielsen, p. 338, 1990).

International standards for Human Computer Interaction (HCI) and Usability are available to help define general principles of user-centered design and good practice. These standards are considered the authoritative statements of leading edge professional practice. The standards provide international consistency of practice. Their resources provide valuable references for professionals currently working in the field and for those new to the practice. In addition, it provides credibility through the use of internationally accepted user-centered practices. Examples of usability standards include the items listed below.

1. The use of the product (objective for the product effectiveness, efficiency and satisfaction in a particular context of use).
2. The user interface and interaction with the product.
3. The process used to develop a quality product.
4. The capability of an organization to apply user-centered design.

The International Organization for Standardization (ISO) and the International Electro-Technical Commission (IEC) comprise standardization bodies for HCI and usability. Technical work is completed by groups of experts in the field nominated by national standards committees with each acting as independent experts. They began working on the drafts over several years and periodically drafts are published, but often they change significantly before a consensus is reached. Then, formal voting by national member bodies takes place before it becomes official. They are also reviewed at least every five years in case updates need to be made. Nigel Bevan's article on International standards for HCI and usability is very helpful, providing a good foundation on how they work (Bevan, 2001). Table 1 provides some additional website resources for locating more information on Human Computer Interaction (HCI) and Usability standards.

Eye Tracking Usability

Examining human computer eye movements in regards to interactions with various hardware and software interfaces can be used to determine its usability. "For usability analysis, the user's eye movements while using the system are recorded and later analyzed retrospectively" (Jacob & Karn, p. 573, 2003). Real time data can be more challenging to interpret since it is going beyond performance, speed, or error data.

Table 1. Website resources for standards

Resources	Websites
International Organization for Standardization (ISO)	https://www.iso.org/home.html
British Standards Institution (BSI)	https://www.iso.org/member/2064.html
American National Standards (ANSI)	https://www.ansi.org
Cost Effective User-Centered Design Standards	http://www.usabilitynet.org/trump/resources/standards.htm

BACKGROUND

Eye-Based Human Computer Interaction (HCI) History

Visual observations of human eye movements started about 100 years before computers even came on the scene (Javal, 1878/1879). Early eye tracking devices were very invasive with direct mechanical contact with the cornea. The first non-invasive eye tracking used light reflected from the cornea, recording horizontal eye positions on a photographic plate with no head movement (Dodge & Cline, 1901). Motion picture photography was then applied to eye tracking to record movements in two dimensions by inserting a white speck into the eye (Judd & McAllister & Steel, 1905). Additional advances were made by combining corneal reflection and motion picture techniques (Mackworth & Mackworth 1958). During the 1930's, photographic techniques were applied to a study of typeface legibility, print size, page layout, etc. to the effects of reading speed and patterns of eye movements (Tinker, 1930). Motion picture cameras were used to study pilot's eye movements when using cockpit control instruments for landing (Fitts, Jones, Milton, 1950). This was considered to be the first application of usability engineering to improve product design. The first head mounted eye tracker provided more movement to users (Hartridge & Thompson, 1948). A new system was devised to superimpose the visual scene with the eye tracking data (Mackworth & Mackworth 1958). Additional advances were made to head mounted eye tracking devices to increase movement (Shackel, 1960) and (Mackworth, & Thomas 1962). Engineers and cognitive psychologists continued their investigations with the use of eye tracking.

Along with the advance in eye tracking technology, the application of a very important theoretical background and rationale for eye tracking studies emerged at that time: eye-mind assumption. The researchers Just and Carpenter (1980) claimed: "there is no appreciable lag between what is being fixated and what is being processed" (p. 331). This claim implies if a man is seeing a certain object, that means the man is thinking about the object. Thus, researchers have started to pay attention to eye tracking methodology as a good research tool for investigating people's cognitive processes.

The 80's were the start of Human Computer Interaction eye tracking research using real time data collection. Initially, disabled users were the primary focus of the studies (Hutchinson, Martin, Reichert, & Frey, 1989), (Levine, 1981; Levine, 1984). Flight simulator studies were conducted using ultra high-resolution to determine where the user was fixating then lower resolution was used in the periphery area (Tong & Fisher, 1984). Research was conducted by combining real-time eye movements with more traditional user-computer communications during the 80's (Bolt, 1981, 1982; Levine 1984; Glenn, Lavecchia, Ross, Stokes, Weiland, Weiss, & Zaklad, 1986; Ware & Mikaelian, 1987). With communication technology advances during the 90's and beyond, attention was then directed towards eye tracking usability research (Benel, Ottens & Horst, 1991; Ellis, 1998; Cowen, 2001) and the eyes as an input device (Starker & Bolt, 1990; Vertegaal, 1999; Jacob, 1991; Zhai, Morimoto & Ihde, 1999).

Eye tracking continues to expand to mobile devices both in the lab and within authentic settings for both research and commercial applications. Eye tracking technologies continue to improve the quality of data collection, analysis, and miniaturization of devices making them even more portable across a wide range of disciplines in natural settings.

Stationary eye-based research efforts have comprised the bulk of the known HCI data to date. The later mobile HCI enabled devices and current trends toward mobile and wearable devices, drives a whole new area of eye-based research efforts. As devices become smaller and more portable, within authentic settings, it may require some additional modifications to the processes.

Dynamic "Gaze Gestures" consist of a sequence of consecutive eye movements requiring more cognitive effort. They hold promise for researchers due to the increased accuracy demonstrated through consistent patterns.

The early commercial eye-trackers included bulky headgear to record video-based data. The equipment included; video recorders, and laptops to store and process video streams ranging on average from two to four hours in length. The main consideration was the massive amount of processing power needed to handle the large files. Over time, the gear keeps getting smaller and more portable. By searching online one can find many open source eye tracking hardware and software solutions for less money, making the research more accessible and personalized for the needed applications.

Electrooculography (EOG) uses lightweight electrodes attached to the skin around the eyes to measure changes in relative eye movements. The benefits of this approach rather than the traditional eye-tracking method is a reduction in power and the amount of data stored, processed, and transmitted. The recording time is extended to about seven hours of data collection.

Many tasks require a combination of both eye and hand movements like visual screens and gesture-based computer keyboard input. This has led to new research methods using multimodal interfaces for dual measurements.

Mobile devices often have built in cameras which can be used to capture eye-tracking data. If the device does not have it included, a webcam can be used. Videos can capture the user's face, eye, and iris movements.

Eye-movement patterns can reveal much about observed activities. Eye-gaze can demonstrate attention indicators. And, users eye fixations can point to attentional triggers. Eye contact and gaze direction in people can also provide cues to communications for regulating interactions, social-emotional connections, and the target of interest (Majaranta & Bulling, 2014).

All of this information can be used to help HCIs move towards the development of intuitive natural interfaces easy for the individual to use effectively.

Eye Tracking Terms Defined

To view an object, we have to fix our gaze on it long enough for our brains to process and perceive it. Fixations are pauses of about 100 ms, and typically 200 to 600 ms. During one fixation, we only see a narrow area with high acuity inside of the fovea as the details decrease rapidly towards the periphery of the eye. The fovea contains rods with cells sensitive to color and provide acuity. The periphery contains cells sensitive to light, shade, and motion. The rest of the periphery provide cues on where to look next and information from movement or changes in the scene. The eyes can follow a moving target, known as a smooth pursuit target. To view an object accurately we constantly scan it with rapid eye movements called saccades. Saccades are quick ballistic jumps of two degrees taking 30-120 ms each (Jacob, 1995). Eye data can then be collected recording gaze direction, movement patterns, pupil size, and saccades to communicate the user's state.

Three Eye Tracking Techniques

Three common eye tracking techniques are:

Video-based videooculography (VOG) using a head-mounted tracker or remote visible light video cameras for attentive user interfaces. It is not as accurate as the other methods, that follow. It is normally selected when the exact point of gaze is important, such as a point and select task.

Video-based infrared (IR) pupil-corneal reflection (PCR) with highly accurate point of gaze is acceptable for scientific studies, usability studies, gaze based interaction, commercial use, and marketing research. It provides head movement without much loss in accuracy. The infrared light is used to brighten the eye without disturbing the view and does not cause dilation since it is invisible to the participant. However, it does not work as well with outdoor lighting (Duchowski, 2003).

Electrooculography (EOG) is an invasive method used for ophthalmological studies of eye movement with high temporal accuracy (Marjaranta & Bulling, 2014). This method requires the use of sensors placed on the skin around the eye. It can be used in low light environments, for sleep studies, and lengthy low power recordings.

Gaze Controlled Interactions

The eyes can be set up to control movement on a computer screen to open up programs, activate menus, select tools and other functions. Eye movement commands are faster than traditional input media since individuals look at the items on the screen before manually clicking or tapping the cursor on it. Therefore, the eye movement can indicate the user's goals before acting upon any of them. Since most people have not controlled devices with their eyes only, it can be tricky to learn, and difficult to avoid activating undesired items. When eye movement control is working well, it seems to act on ones' intentions before expressing them.

Gaze interaction allows for eye input for command and control, hands free. Most gaze controlled systems use video and infrared illumination eye trackers. Gaze based interactions can be used in mobile settings, control assistive robots and wheelchairs, all by using eye motor skills. Gaze based interactions are providing the next generation of intelligent user interfaces complimenting natural and enhanced communications. This gaze controlled interaction makes eye tracking technology a potential input/output part of an IoE system. In an IoE system, interaction between human and things could be made noninvasively.

Multimodal Interactions

Combining modalities can extend eye controlled interactions. For example, voice activated commands can provide automated searching and translations that can then be combined with other tasks. Eye-contact detection can be used to activate appliance options. Sensors can be used in conjunction with eye tracking.

Physical gestures can be used to activate devices. These are all examples of multimodal physiological computing. In this case, the eye control is a secondary method of control.

It is possible to combine any number of stimuli with eye tracking. Some additional biometric data collection includes the use of facial expressions, electrical activity in the brain (EEG), respiration, electrical activity in the heart (ECG), muscles and nerves (EMG), emotional arousal (GSR), and stress.

This is effectively where the Internet of Things becomes the Internet of Everything. When the sensors simply stop collecting data and start feeding back into the system to help make changes, with the goal of improving products and services. Like Facebook found, there are going to be conflicts between the collection of the personal data and the potential for abuse causing road blocks and social barriers hindering further study and development of what could become safe and effective interactions.

Gaming, Virtual Reality, and Augmented Reality

Gaming, virtual reality, and augmented reality are excellent platforms for eye tracking studies. Since the participant is already wearing head gear, it is easy to attach an eye tracking camera and infrared light. Eye gaze interaction works best at a distance, much like you would find in a virtual world. The use of pervasive attention-aware systems and interfaces is a growing field and a perfect match for alpha and beta testing on product(s) and application(s) use(s).

Eye Tracking Sequence

Eye tracking works by measuring eye activity; where we look, what we ignore, or overlook, blink frequency, and the pupil reacting to stimulus. To track eye data requires a near infrared light to provide a non-visible light directed towards the eye for illumination without disturbing the participant. The eye tracker must be able to find the pupil using either a bright pupil or dark pupil (moving the light further away from the lens) technique. The eyes are used for pupil/cornea tracking, and range of eye movement tracking. The reflections are recorded by the eye tracker video camera. The software is used for the image processing algorithms, filters, and calculations to locate the details in the eyes and reflection patterns.

The data collected can record the size of the pupil, changes in pupil position, rotation of the eye, speed, direction of gaze, fixations, saccades, duration, and regressions. The visual data coordinates are collected and processed through the eye tracking software to analyze the results and export the information to be presented.

The hardware and software can be calibrated with the eyes in advance of the test to improve accuracy. The eye tracker measures how the eyes reflect light. The calibration process is then completed by having the participant's eyes visually follow a point across a screen.

The eye tracking sampling rate refers to how many times per second the eye positions are measured. The accuracy refers to how well the calculated eye fixation location matches the actual fixation location as represented as degrees of visual angle. Head movement is the allowable head movement for the eye tracker system used. Many eye trackers today use head gear or glasses that are not so limited by movement.

Some additional external influencing factors can include the stimulus presented, prior experience, age, fatigue, etc.

ISSUES

Eye Tracking Issues

Eye tracking issues have historically been caused by technical challenges, slow labor-intensive data extractions, and interpretation. Since our technologies have changed and evolved so much over time, it has allowed for better, more accurate, reliable, faster, and mobile eye tracking methods. As technology changes over time, it requires new approaches for eye tracking data collection. Innovations like smart glasses did not exist early on so traditional methods of eye tracking may not be appropriate or work effectively. In addition, about ten to twenty percent of the eyes studied can't be tracked reliably. Some of the problems with eye tracking result from lighting conditions, reflections, interference from eye glasses, glasses with photo-gray lenses turning dark in bright light, contact lenses, dry eyes, lazy eyes, corneas with a dim glint when illuminated below the eye, droopy eyelids, squinting, and even heavy makeup (Goldberg & Wichansky, 2003).

Physiological measurements such as EMG sensors placed around the eye on the face can be used as a way to collect additional data. This method of data collection is more invasive to the user. It can also be difficult to interpret the data. However, by combining or triangulating eye tracking and sensor data, the overall validity can be increased.

Determining the Appropriate Eye Tracking Devices

Stationary eye tracking cameras can be attached to the computer monitor or laptop. Or, custom stationary solutions can be integrated. Remotely mounted eye trackers result in some restrictions on the participant's range and speed of head motion of about a cubic foot, with a frequent loss of tracking. Head mounted eye trackers are attached to the participant's head to allow for freedom of movement without restrictions for portable computing. One potential problem is the decrease in precision from integrating two signals, one from the eye, and other from the environment.

There are three main types of eye tracking systems, all serving different purposes depending on your research objectives. Starting with the objectives first assists in guiding one to locate the appropriate equipment needed. Below, you will find three different setups using stationary screen based research, portable eye tracking glasses to use on location, and head gear often used for virtual and augmented reality.

Stationary screen based desktop eye tracking records eye movements from a distance. Normally it is mounted close to the computer under the screen. The participant is seated to view websites, printed materials, or other small objects. The head movement allowed is restricted by the tracker's range called the head box.

Mobile portable eye tracking glasses are often used in the field for recording the eye from the close range of the glasses worn. Participants are not required to be seated and can move about freely. Participants do not have restricted head movements since it is mounted to the head. It is used to record authentic environments such as task performance, usability, and product testing.

Eye tracking head gear are primarily used for virtual reality like you would find in gaming, augmented reality, and simulation testing. Below you will find a list of companies offering eye tracking devices and software to assist your search efforts.

IMOTIONS (https://imotions.com/) offers desktop screen based, special devices, wearable eye tracker glasses for out in the field, and AR/VR headgear. They offer data analytics for heat maps, areas of interest, object recognition, eye tracking metrics such as time spent, fixation, ratio, revisits, and mouse clicks. They examine gaze path, fixations, pupil size, distance metrics, and raw data output. They have just released educational packages and training materials as well.

The company Tobii (https://www.tobii.com/) offers wearable eye trackers for use in authentic real world environments. In addition, they offer a variety of screen based in-lab and out-of-lab eye trackers, along with a virtual reality headset. Their sensors are built into the HTC Vive headset. Their software allows for testing, recording, observation, interpretation, and presentation of results. Tobii has acquired Sticky, which focuses on video emotion analytics to measure the micro-expressions of viewers using facial coding technology to determine the feelings and perceptions of the audience relating to media, websites, commerce, advertising, products, and products on the shelf. In addition, they offer eye tracking heat maps to show the areas of interest, reading metrics, and other tools. They are well known for assistive technologies, research, gaming, virtual reality, and developer kits.

Gazepoint (https://www.gazept.com/) is a stationary screen based device. It is used for usability studies, behavior research, eye controlled assistive communications technology, and advertising efforts. They offer both hardware and software solutions.

EyeTech (https://www.eyetechds.com/), has a stationary screen based eye tracker. In addition, they have the ability to provide customize embedding of their smart tracker into a customer's device, and offers assistive device control.

SensoMotoric Instruments (SMI), (https://www.smivision.com/), has both a stationary screen based and wearable eye trackers to signal attention. Their wearable tracker is capable of recording a person's natural gaze behavior in real-time and in real world situations. It is used for a variety of settings including; remote, mobile, virtual reality, augmented reality, and multimodal research when combined with additional input methods such as sensors. They also provide their own software solutions, confirmed to have been purchased by Apple.

Mirametrix Glance (http://www.mirametrix.com/)are wearable eye tracker glasses. Their eye tracking is designed to collect information from the face, eyes, and gaze. It is designed for consumer electronics, academic research, usability testing, and software development.

Oculus (https://www.oculus.com/), bought The Eye Tribe company who developed head gear allowing the eye to control consumer devices. It can be used to control mobile devices and virtual reality. In the central viewing area, it is rendered in a higher quality image. Their product includes identification verification for security, games, and other devices all controlled by eye movements.

Google bought Eyefluence, who uses eye gesture cues for navigating menus and making selections. Users wearing head mounted virtual reality or augmented reality glasses use their eyes to control selections. It uses foveated rendering to allow for high-density displays on the central area viewed.

Fove (https://www.getfove.com/), uses a consumer virtual reality headset with eye tracking sensors and gaze control. It is designed for developers, creators, and researchers. The high-resolution image is in the foveal region. It has been used in healthcare, playing music with eyes, attending a distant wedding using a robot, and allows for faster and more authentic gaming.

MangoldVision (https://www.mangold-international.com/en/products/software/eye-tracking-with-mangoldvision), offers an out of the box eye tracking with both the hardware and software included. In addition, it includes information gathering on facial expressions, mouse actions, and keyboard entries.

Applied Science Laboratories (ASL), (http://host.web-print-design.com/asl/), offers a head mounted or desktop remote eye tracker. The video head tracking camera uses face recognition software to compensate for head movement, and analysis software.

The Eyetracking company offers hardware and EyeWorks software (http://www.eyetracking.com/Software/EyeWorks), to set up eye tracking, face tracking and cognitive state detection. It allows for multiple displays, mobile devices, physical objects, laptops and desktops. They offer sensors to measure heart rate, respiration, (GSR) and skin temperature, (EEG) neuroheadset, bio signal amplifier, and mobility. The hardware devices include head gear, glasses, and stationary screen based trackers from a variety of vendors. The EyeWorks software is used to collect gaze spots, traces, stats, clusters, clips, video, bee swarm, and spotlight videos. It is accomplished by looking at fixations, blinks, cognitive workload, pupil size, timing, mouse clicks, key presses, scrolling, interview responses, and questionnaire results. Software is available for the cognitive workload, head and eyelid tracking, server to synchronize, store, visualize, distribute data, and custom license bundle.

SR Research EyeLink (http://www.sr-research.com/), offers eye tracking for screen based, portable laptops, MRI/MEG eye tracking and other brain imaging methods, head mounted gear, and software for research.

7invensun (https://www.7invensun.com/), a Glass Eye Tracking for HTC Vive headset with plastic overlays having an array of infra-red lights and sensors to track eye and eyelid movements. It hooks to the headset through the USB port. In addition, they offer myopic lenses at 200, 400, 600 with the ability to change it on the fly for multiple users. The company uses eye tracking with foveated high quality rendering in the line of sight.

As you can see there are many different vendors offering a wide variety of eye tracking hardware and software choices to select from depending on your needs. Be sure to check the longevity of the devices, upgrades, training materials, level of difficulty, device integration with other biometrics, level of detail in data collection for validity and reliability, analysis software expenses, and support to protect your investment. Screen based hardware tends to be lower in cost. The price increases with mobile glasses and even more for virtual reality and augmented reality head gear. Some vendors include the analysis software and others charge a subscription fee. The analysis software is currently very costly. Some of the eye tracking set ups require the use of a PC computer with dual screens, one for the study participant and another for the researcher to view live results. To finance this research, many small universities are applying for grants to be able to secure funding. Sometimes partnerships with industry are formed for mutual benefit. And, sometimes a university department no longer uses the equipment as much due to external changes and is willing to share or turn it over to departments with a growing need.

SOLUTIONS

Eye Tracking Applications

Some of the fields currently using eye tracking include computing, mobile, wearables, gaming, entertainment, virtual reality, augmented reality, aviation, simulators, drones, military, defense, safety, security, automotive, fatigue, drowsiness, special needs, psychology, crime, cognitive, linguistics, neuroscience, bio mechanics, infant/child, education learning behaviors, universities, marketing, software companies, package design, signage, printed materials, television, film, shopping, vision, reading, primate research, human factors research, user experiences, emotion, interaction, sports performance, physical training, diseases, sleep studies, medical and clinical research. As you can see, almost every field is a potential candidate for eye tracking applications.

Eye Tracking Research Objectives

Here are some examples of how different fields are using eye tracking for research study objectives. Market research and advertising studies often examine products, product message, performance, design, user experience, navigation, search ability, and buying behaviors. Simulations can use eye tracking to evaluate the layout, design, user friendly, navigation, and training effectiveness. Website testing, gaming, and user experience design (UX) design looks at the usability, user experience, advertising effectiveness, locating products, examining what is ignored, overlooked, or attended to, ease of use, ease of learning, and pleasant experience. Neuroscience & psychology use eye tracking to look at the sequence of gaze patterns to better understanding cognition, attention, learning, and memory. Learning and education uses eye tracking to analyze attention, acquiring content, distractions, instructional environment, and designing instructional materials. Medical, including neurological and psychiatric, studies and practices include using eye tracking to diagnose diseases such as Attention Deficit Hyperactivity Disorder (ADHD), Autism Spectrum Disorder (ASD), Obsessive Compulsive Disorder (OCD), Schizophrenia, Parkinson's, Alzheimer's, and other medical needs (iMotions, 2017). As one can see, there are many field dependent research objectives with some overlapping cross disciplines.

Now, applying the Internet of Everything, the possibilities exist to start making diagnoses from observed responses of those affected, including their patients' observations of their environments, collecting data from multiple media and environmental sensors surrounding the individual patients. The patient data can be collected, processed, then fed back to assist individual patients to cope and to live more normal lives. The IoE could then allow feedback to be tailored to the individuals, to be adjusted with collective and personalized data to ever improve patient treatments. The same concerns raised under Multi-Modal Interactions apply here.

Eye Tracking Fighter Jet Example

Why do we care about eye tracking technology? It is simple, eye tracking shows where we are looking and even has the ability to control devices with our eyes.

Eye tracking is already in heavy use and has the potential for so much more.

Eye tracking helmets are being used in modern U.S. fighter jets. Instead of the heads up displays on the canopy in front of the pilot and co-pilot, the newer technology provides an adaptation to display controls inside of the visor.

With small, high resolution cameras mounted everywhere inside the cockpit, on the helmet, on the outside of the fighter, such as the F-35, the pilot has the ability to look everywhere and anywhere. How are commands made? By triggering the eye-tracking helmet functions through eye and head movements. Want to see what is coming from behind or below you? Look down, look back, eye track click the external cameras and .... there it is, one bogey on your butt, one screaming upward from below… activate counter measures, activate weapons, target bogeys, lock radar, fire antiaircraft missiles, computer takes it from there. Missile coming at you… trigger countermeasures, flares and exploding balls of metal foil. Multiple explosions… near and far. Mission back on track… recede back into stealth mode.

Eye Tracking in Education and Instructional Design Research Example

In education, one can conduct classroom research on instructional materials. Knowing what grabs each students' attention and what keeps it will help the instructor to improve instructional materials and has the potential for tailoring each individual students' lesson to keep them on task, on track to meet learning goals and objectives.

Gamification and simulations in education is also a great way to make learning fun and engaging for students. With eye-tracking controlled virtual reality educational games, you will be able to let students experience learning in a dynamic and exciting way. How cool to be able to take a virtual trip to the Pyramids, or other important sites.

Perhaps the instructors will even be able to monitor student engagement. Just short of knowing what learners are really thinking, short of reading their minds explicitly, one could see where their eyes are looking, giving you, the instructor, an indication of assurance the student is actually paying attention to and following along with the lesson. You could learn if the students are reading the textbook, watching your demonstration at the front of the class or staring out the window. In time, the instructor will come to know what grabs learner's attention and what keeps it. With the help of additional software, perhaps, eventually, embedded images and short story lines will draw the students back into learning.

Additional examples of educational eye tracking research include data collection on; information gathering, problem solving skills, learning strategies, social interaction patterns from teacher to student and between students, and how different educational materials work. The results of these studies can help us to tailor lessons to keep learners on task and on track to meet the learning goals and objectives.

Eye Tracking Future Imagined

For a more futuristic example, let's say you live in rural Kansas, where a large number of hospitals have closed due to a lack of demographics and political will to keep them open. You are driving through the countryside on rocky rolling gravel roads. A deer jumps out in front of you and you realize it would be safer to hit the deer but, you automatically attempt to swerve to miss it. You fail to miss the deer, but swerving and hitting it puts your car into a spin off into the ditch, then a tree. You are lucky to survive, and you are lucky your OnStar registers your accident with apparent survivable injuries. If you were in the city, the ambulance would be on the scene in 5 minutes then to a hospital with you on board within another 10, to 20 minutes from the time of the accident. Out here on the dusty plains, you are waiting 20-30 minutes for your rescue to arrive. If you don't get help soon, you will be dead. Lucky for you, a trooper, a volunteer firefighter EMT, and a helicopter arrive at about the same time. They pry you out of your battered car in 5 minutes, load you on the chopper, chart your flight to the nearest trauma center, note your condition is very serious. They divert the helicopter to the nearest mobile surgical unit. They agree to a nearby truck stop on the Interstate. You get there in 5 minutes, and then get transferred to one heck of an ambulance with a multi-armed robot inside. The two paramedics load you onboard to administer MRI/ CAT Scans on your injuries, feeding the status back to the University Hospital ER 200 miles away. An on-call doctor has donned their own version of the eye tracking medically equipped helmet and grabbed the controls to the WIFI enabled DaVinci surgical unit. Quickly assessing your internal injuries, orders plasma and saline drips to be initiated… antibiotics to be administered. You've been floating between consciousness and unconsciousness, wondering what has happened, why it all hurts so much, whether you will make it. They administer anesthesia, putting you to sleep to start the surgery as the tech enabled ambulance slowly begins the careful drive to the nearest hospital. By the time you make it to the nearest brick and mortar trauma center, the worst bleeders have been successfully sealed off, bones are starting to be put back where they belong, sutures for a few of the wounds are being completed. You are carefully transferred in the surgical vehicle to the land based center where all systems and your condition are cross-checked. They move you to a more sterile environment where the last of the emergency surgeries are completed. It was bad, a second surgeon had to be called into assist, but luckily your mobile DaVinci operating unit is a new model allowing two surgeons to act together or independently, as needed. Shortly, you will be air-lifted to the nearest hospital to begin your recuperation from your injuries. A bit far-fetched? Maybe today, but it is necessary if rural America is to survive.

If you want something a bit more realistic for today, for your life, your family's life? How about Driver's Ed? Driver's Ed, as we have known it these last few years has consisted of a day or so of reading, watching films or YouTube videos. Maybe, a simulator, watching the screen on your computer then reacting to what is happening. All of this is like driving with blinders on, not quite real enough. So, we take it to the next step. We provide enhanced Virtual Reality Glasses with eye-tracking technology and a steering wheel. Why do we bother, if cars are going to be self-driving? Our family is a bit old-fashioned and on a budget, maybe we are into NASCAR or INDY racing so we plan to maintain our human driving skills. With the eye tracking helmet on, we train our progeny to keep their eyes open, looking everywhere all the time while monitoring the car's gauges and monitors, and, of course, driving at unprecedented speeds. All of this happens before learners ever set one foot in a real car. Maybe, if we start sooner than later, we can teach them to drive safely, having experienced so much virtually. Using eye-tracking technology, we can make sure learners are seeing what they need to and reacting as they should. All of this in the safe confines of the classroom, not while out there driving a ton or more of metal at high speeds on crowded highways and byways.

In another scenario, such as a natural disaster earthquake hitting the city. Buildings collapse and people are trapped. A crew of rescuers arrive with an assortment of mechanical devices. One is a mechanical snake towing a series of what look like small match boxes. One of the crew members dons an eye tracking helmet and gloves, he prefers the gloves though they aren't normally needed, as they keep his hands busy. Otherwise, the snake can normally be controlled from within the helmet and heads up displays on the visor. The snake disappears into the pile of rubble tracking what sounds like heartbeats, breathing, or just a rhythmic rapping on something deep in the bowels of this destruction. Shortly after arriving a survivor is found and a matchbox is dropped off noting the exact location within the pile. The snake resumes its chase down into the rubble, looking for more survivors, leaving more little matchboxes. Following the snake a number of different types of mechanical devices are dispatched to each survivor to check their actual physical condition then to dispense a bit of liquid nutrition to help them. Various additional mechanical devices start plotting ways to either tunnel their way to each, to prop up unstable debris or move it to get the people and animals out. This rescue team has seen so many fires, quakes, bomb sites, and other disasters.

What about the pilot mentioned earlier? Is he really needed? No! With remote controlled or artificially intelligent drones, the human pilot can be safely miles away, flying a device now no longer encumbered by the weaker human link. No longer limited by what the human can bear, the drone can turn on an airborne dime, contort in a manner humans could not endure. The entire dogfight could be occurring with the eye-tracking helmet sitting quietly on the pilot's head, miles away.

Is this it? No. Think remote dentistry, veterinarians, the return of the remote house call, and so much more.

Preparing Instructional Eye Tracking Research Materials

To assist you in preparing specific eye tracking materials like one would find in education used for learning, the following best design practices based on past research are summarized for you.

When working with complex dynamic visual presentations, used for eye tracking studies, you will find differences in learners perceiving, interpreting, and performing. When comparing novices to experts, the experts attend to more relevant information, use better approaches, are faster, and use knowledge-based shortcuts. For this reason, the novice may benefit from some attentional guidance to know what to observe to acquire the knowledge (Jarodzka, Scheiter, Gerjets, & Gog, 2010).

One way to control the effective graphic design of the display media presented is by eliminating information not needed for the task at hand. Task-irrelevant information can impair learning and performance (Canham & Hegarty, 2010).

In a research study by Koning, Tabbers, Rikers & Paas, they used spotlight-cues to point out key content in an effort to reduce extraneous cognitive load and enhance the learning. They found the cues can guide attention to specific areas but it does not guarantee productive cognitive processing to learn from complex visualizations. There can be other factors influencing the effectiveness of learning (Koning, Tabbers, Rikers & Paas, 2010).

Another study found color spreading cues to be more effective than arrow cues when viewing complex animations. When using a synchronized version with high thematic relevance to the learning task the comprehension was improved. The spreading-color cue provided attention to causal chains. The researchers found this approach supported learners during the first phases of processing complex animations (Boucheix & Lowe, 2010).

One study examined the impact of animation speed on cognitive processing. They found the speed of the animation's presentation had an impact on comprehension of micro- and macro-events. Having user-controlled animation speeds can cause them to miss relevant educational information, better observed at specific speeds. Low speeds prior to high speeds resulted in a better processing match. It moved learners from slower micro-events to building a mental model which can later be integrated into a more global model (Meyer, Rasch, Schnotz, 2010).

Two studies found learners spending more time studying visualizations with spoken text added than those with written text. When using written text, learners begin reading before alternating between text and visualizations. Study participants spent the majority of their time reading text. So, for multimedia learning, changing the text into an aural format is more beneficial for learning (Schmidt-Weigand, Kohnert, Glowalla, 2010).

Consideration of other researchers' best practices with instructional design is a good way to begin preparing materials for your own eye tracking study using a good solid foundation.

Eye Tracking Lab Setup

A dedicated lab is preferred to maintain a consistent setup. For screen based lab equipment, a simple solid steady table is needed. Direct sunlight needs to be blocked out since it can have a negative impact on eye tracking data collection. Low ambient light works the best. Many of the products require specific computer setups and often use the PC platform. Two screens are needed, one for the study participant, and one for the researcher. Turn off anti-virus software, disable the screen saver, and turn off the Internet if it is not being used so it does not disturb the study with possible interruptions. Clean the computer to remove any possible distractions. All lab workers need to be trained to follow simple written protocols, to have consistency and maintain the validity of the study data collected (iMotions, 2017). Figure 4 shows an example of how an eye tracking lab can be set up.

Figure 4. Eye tracking lab and eye tracker (Ryu & Lee, 2017)

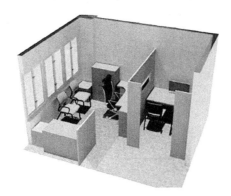 

Eye Tracking Measurement

To provide a little background on how eye tracking works we begin with how the eyes are operating when tracking and recording data. To view an object clearly, the eyeball moves the fovea, the small area in the center of the retina. As a result, it provides a good indication of within one-degree of the visual line of gaze to the area viewed (Jacob, 1990).

The eyes are rarely still because in order to see clearly the eyes dart from one fixation to another in a saccade. Saccades are the ballistic jittery movements of the eye from one point to another generally less than one degree in size. The fovea is the high-acuity region of the retina in the center area of the point of view. There are both high frequency tremors and drifts with the slow random eye movement away from a fixation corrected with a micro saccade. Micro saccades improve visibility since a stationary image on the retina soon fades away so it serves the purpose of keeping it in focus. It is hard to maintain an eye position without a visual stimulus to direct the fixation. The gaze duration refers to the cumulative time and average spatial location of a series of consecutive fixations within an area of interest. Gaze duration often includes several fixations and can include a relatively small amount of time for the short jittery eye movement saccades between these fixations. A fixation outside of the area of interest marks the end of the gaze. The goal is to look for higher-level intentions which are separated from the noisy, jittery saccades. This determines the area of interest or attention. The area of interest can relate to a variety of tasks such as; object selection and movement, data retrieval, menu scrolling and menu selection, as well as others. The scan path refers to the spatial arrangement of a sequence of fixations (Sibert, Jacob, 2000).

Areas of interest (AOI) are used to select sub-regions of the stimuli on the screen. The metrics can be separated for each region. When looking at the time elapsed between the scene presented and respondents looking at the region is called the time to first fixation (TTFF). It reflects the time spent in the region, how many fixations were counted, how many people looked away and back or revisits. The measurements are especially helpful when two or more areas need to be examined.

The ratio shows how many people looked at a specific area of interest. Optimizing the scene can direct attention towards a specific region on the scene. A higher ratio indicates fixations and gaze points are driven by external aspects of the stimulus or the target group is consistent in looking towards a specific area of interest while ignoring others. Figure 5 provides an example of a fixation, the ballistic saccade movements, and the area of interest.

Figure 5. Eye tracking illustration of a fixation, saccade, and area of interest (Lee, Ryu, & Ke, 2017)

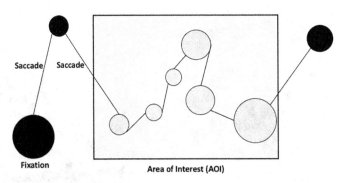

To measure gaze point, eye movement eye tracking is needed. Eye control is almost an unconscious act resulting in good quantitative metric data. The resulting processes and decisions of the participant helps the researcher to know what draws attention, cognitive workload, and emotional responses. Individual preferences and decision strategies of the target audience then becomes known. Next, you will learn about common metrics and terms used in eye tracking data collection.

Gaze points show the visual stimulus presented to the eyes looking at it. If the eye tracker collects data with a sampling rate of 60 Hz, you end up with 60 individual gaze points per second. If a series of gaze points are close in time and space, the gaze cluster shows where the eye is fixed on an object.

The term visual span refers to how much content can be taken in before fixations. Individuals with prior experience tend to have a higher visual span, allowing them to cover more information presented with less fixations. By contrast, if we have an animated object moving across the screen, the eye movements are different. With the animation, we fixate constantly to track the moving object, without any obvious saccades referred to as a smooth pursuit. Fixations and saccades demonstrate the visual attention and interest.

Heat maps are visualizations showing the distribution of fixations and gaze points to indicate attention. The red areas suggesting a high number of gaze points or an increased level of attention, followed by yellow and green. Areas without color were not attended to. Heat maps can be used to visualize the elements attracting more attention as viewed in Figure 6.

Time to First Fixation (TFF) indicates the time for response or all respondents on average to look at a specific area of interest. TFF can indicate both bottom-up stimulus driven searches or top-down attention driven searches. To see an example of TFF it is shown in Figure 7.

Fixation Time (FT) is the amount of time spent viewing the AOI. Time spent indicates motivation and attention with longer views indicating a higher level of interest. Fixation Count (FC) refers to the amount of fixation points in the AOI.

Fixation Sequences (FS) are position and timing information to generate a fixation sequence. As your eyes view an environment, they move around to where attention is drawn. Depending on where participants look and how much time is spent there, an order of attention is used to mark eye tracking data. This information reflects the areas of interest the respondents look at first. Figure 8 demonstrates the fixation sequence.

Figure 6. Eye tracking illustration of a heat map (Lee, Ryu, & Ke, 2017)

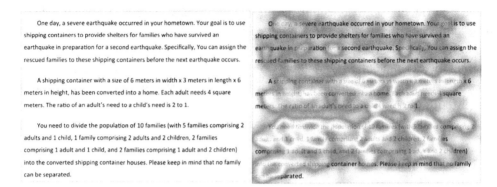

Figure 7. Eye tracking illustration of The Time to First Fixation (Lee, Ryu, & Ke, 2017)

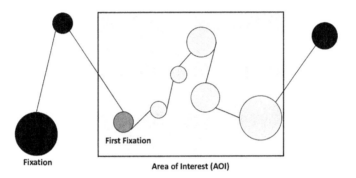

Figure 8. Eye tracking illustration of the fixation sequence (Lee, Ryu, & Ke, 2017)

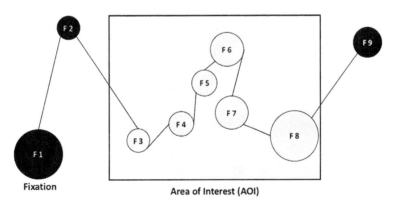

Figure 9 demonstrates actual eye tracking data from an unpublished study. In the study, the authors compared math word problem comprehension and solving process between expert (i.e., on the left side) and novice (i.e., on the right side) using eye tracking data. Specifically, they investigated whether the problem solver's visual fixations differ across Mayer's problem representation process (1985) when problem solving hints including two formats of information representation, symbolic and iconic formats, are provided side by side. The study found a problem solver tends to fixate a longer time and make more fixation spots on symbolic formats compared to iconic formats. Further, problem solvers increased fixation time and fixation counts on the symbolic formats while they were representing a given math problem (Lee, Ryu, & Ke, 2017).

Eye tracking metrics quantify visual attention driven by cognitive, emotional, and object viewing processes. Eye tracking is often combined with other biometric measurements for a more comprehensive perspective (iMotions, 2015).

Three challenges for stationary gaze-based systems include.

1. Eye-tracking accuracy
2. Calibration drift
3. Midas touch, or distinguishing the intentional eye movement from other eye movements.

Figure 9. Eye tracking comparison between expert (left) and novice (right) (Lee, Ryu, & Ke, 2017)

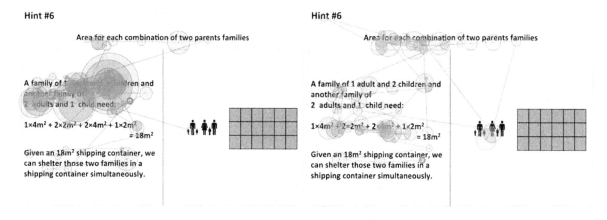

Figure 10. Output data is converted to numerical data for each family type (Lee, Ryu, & Ke, 2017)

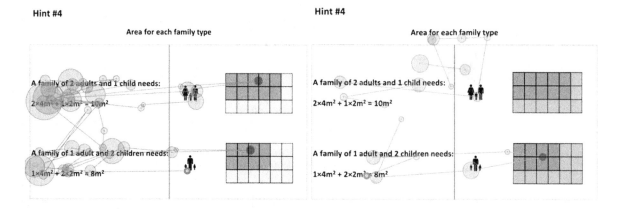

To get an idea of what type of items researchers are examining from eye tracking data, Jacob and Karn found some common trends in current research studies. Below you will find their list of eye tracking evaluation metrics (Jacob & Karn, 2003).

1. Number of fixations, overall
2. Gaze % (proportion of time) on each area of interest
3. Fixation duration mean, overall
4. Number of fixation on each area of interest
5. Gaze duration mean, on each area of interest
6. Fixation rate overall (fixation/s)

Figure 11. The what, how, and why of biometric measurements (iMotions, 2017)

IMOTIONS	What is measured?	How is it measured?	Which metrics can be derived?	How can the data be interpreted?
Eye tracking (infrared)	Corneal reflection & pupil dilation	Infrared camera point towards eyes	Eye moments (gaze, fixations, saccades), blinks, pupil dilation	Visual attention, engagement, drowsiness & fatigue, emotional arousal
GSR (galvanic skin response)	Changes in skin conductance due to sweating	Electrodes attached to fingers, palms or soles	Skin conductance response (SCR)	Emotional arousal, engagement, congruency of self-reports
Facial Expression Analysis	Activity of facial muscles & muscle groups	(Web-)cam point towards face along with computer algorithms for feature extraction	Postion and orientation of head & facial landmarks, activation of action units (AUs) & emotion channels	Emotional valence, engagement, congruency of self-reports
(Facial) EMG (electromyogram)	Changes in electrical activity caused by muscle contraction	Electrodes attached to the skin (above muscles)	Muscle contraction onset, offset & duration, AU activity	Emotional valence, responsiveness to stimuli
ECG / EKG (electrocardiogram)	Changes in electrical activity caused by heart contraction	Electrodes attached to chest or limbs	Heart rate (HR, BPM), interbeat interval (IBI), heart rate variability (HRV)	Emotional arousal, stress, physiological activity
PPG (photoplethysmogram)	Changes in light absorption of blood vessels	Optical sensor attached to finger, toe or earlobe	Optical heart rate (HR)	Emotional arousal, stress, physiological activity
EEG (electroencephalogram)	Changes in electrical activity of the brain	Electrodes places on scalp	Frequency band power (delta, theta, alpha, beta, gamma bands), frontal lateralization & asymmetry index event-related potentials, wavelets	Attention, emotional arousal, motivation, cognitive states, mental workload, drowsiness & fatigue,

FUTURE RESEARCH

Combining eye tracking results with other forms of data collection, provides a good way to triangulate the data for even stronger research results. iMotions (2017) has a blog titled "7 Ways to Measure Human Behavior" providing an excellent illustration of the options available for biometric testing, as shown in Figure 8. The chart can also be found at https://imotions.com/blog/sensor-chart/

The biometric data collected can be used to increase the validity and reliability of the testing results. Another, less costly secondary source of data collection can be gathered from participant surveys. Depending on the study goals and objectives the appropriate measurements of human behavior metrics can be selected.

CONCLUSION

Traditional Internet applications have primarily focused on publishing and retrieving information (Luigi, & Antonio, 2010). "The Internet of Things (IoT) and its relevant technologies can seamlessly integrate classical networks with networked instruments and devices" (Chen, Deng, Wan, Zhang, Vasilakos, & Rong, 2015, p.1). One of the underlying goals is to easily control, automate, and monitor, the "things", in regards to communicating with each other through the Internet, then making smart decisions through data mining. Data mining is used to gain useful information from the subsequent, not easily observed, data patterns. It includes decision making support and optimization for increased knowledge, techniques, and applications (Chen, Deng, Wan, Zhang, Vasilakos, & Rong, 2015).

The "Internet of the Future" is shifting towards the use of data-centric networks equipped with a variety of sensors, chips, and tags, to be used for data collection (Luigi, & Antonio, 2010, p. 2803). This Internet of the future is now the IoE; things, process, data, and people.

Eye tracking and other biometric data collection devices loaded with sensors are gathering the information then running it through specific computer algorithms to learn more about human attention, behavior, mental states, and patterns. In addition, the IoT objects loaded with "sensing, actuation, communication, control, and in creating knowledge from vast amounts of data" are furthering our understanding of how products are being used with an eye towards future improvements (Stankovic, 2014, p. 6). The data is being used both professionally and personally to improve human computer interactions with interfaces, products, and designs used. It will result in a qualitative shift in how we live, work, and interact with the products in our environment. "The vision of future Internet based on standard communication protocols considers the merging of computer networks, Internet of Media (IoM), Internet of Services (IoS), and Internet of Things (IoT) into a common global IT platform of seamless networks and networked things" (A de Saint-Exupery, 2009, p. 7). According to authors Gigli and Koo, they view "the future is the Internet of Things (IoT), which aims to unify everything in our world under a common infrastructure, giving us not only control of the things around us, but also keeping us informed of the state of the things around us" (Gigli & Koo, 2011, p. 1). The author Swan states, "There could be an adjustment period as humans adapt to an IoT landscape with more kinds of data and different mindsets, activities, behaviors, and perspectives when interacting with these data. Whole fields of study previously limited to self-reported information such as psychology could be radically supplemented and transformed with objective metrics obtained from the IoT" (Swan, 2012, p.217).

Eye tracking and other biometric data collection is a perfect match to the new IoE. We have been observing the increasing use of eye tracking metrics in all fields. With this trend, eye tracking devices continue to reduce in size to convenient miniaturized portable non-invasive devices, making them more user-friendly. Eye trackers have historically increased in ability, performance, and cost over time. Thereby, allowing for wider use across multiple fields of study. Eye tracking equipment needs to continue to advance as the IoE continues to grow and new technologies surface. This will increase opportunities for both prior product testing and later specific consumer applications. Considerations for selecting eye tracking equipment should include the quality, ease of use, non-invasive devices, shorter setup times, support, teaching/training, increased validity/reliability, good alignment to the specific environment, whether stationary or portable, lower cost, better output data, clearly identified goals/objectives, meets the target audience needs, and more.

In an article by iScoop (2018) on the Internet of Everything, they communicate the new vision for the IoE as one of a distributed decentralized hybrid network with a growing focus on edge computing. Edge computing allows for quicker real time analysis of the data. In addition, sensitive data can be protected by analyzing it in house. Benefits include leveraging the data to gain insights and improve quality of products and services offered. The Internet of Everything is moving beyond just gathering data from sensors. The IoE is using the sensor data collected to lead to actionable outcomes. The Internet of Everything framework requires an on-going high degree of standardization and interoperability to work effectively across platforms to improve communications. One challenge will be to keep secure the private data as it is collected and stored. Another challenge is the anticipated increase from the about 10 million sensors enabled smart devices currently to an anticipated 50 billion in the near future, each needing a unique IP address.

In a YouTube video, featuring Eli the computer guy, titled the "Introduction to the Internet of Everything", Eli explains the difference between the IoT vs the IoE. The IoT's deal with one way communications between devices using RFID chips and sensors. In contrast, the IoE uses two-way communications on the TCPIP network. The two-way communications can then send and receive information while acting on it based on programmed processes without human intervention, as desired. In this manner, the IoE is adding connectivity to create additional value. Therefore, the data collection and analysis can be used with programmed applications to act on it automatically. As with all of the growing IoE, it will be fun to see how new developments in eye tracking technologies are implemented within the IoE.

REFERENCES

Beal, V. (2018). *The 7 layers of the OSI model*. Retrieved July 19, 2018 from: https://www.webopedia.com/quick_ref/OSI_Layers.asp

Benel, D. C. R., Ottens, D., & Horst, R. (1991). Use of an eye tracking system in the usability laboratory. In *Proceedings of the Human Factors Society 35th Annual Meeting (pp. 461-465)*. Santa Monica, CA: Human Factors and Ergonomics Society.

Bevan N. (2001). International standards for hci and usability. *Int. J. Human-Computer Studies, 55*, 533-552. doi:10:1006/ijhc.2001.0483

Bolt, R. A. (1981). Gaze-orchestrated dynamic windows. *Computer Graphics*, *15*(3), 109–199. doi:10.1145/965161.806796

Bolt, R. A. (1982). Eyes at the interface. In *Proceedings of the ACM Human Factors in Computer Systems Conference* (pp. 360-362). ACM.

Boucheix, J. M., & Lowe, R. K. (2010). An eye tracking comparison of external pointing cues and internal continuous cues in learning with complex animations. *Learning and Instruction*, *20*(2), 123–135. doi:10.1016/j.learninstruc.2009.02.015

Bulling, A., & Gellersen, H. (2010, October). *Toward mobile eye-based human-computer interaction. IEEE Pervasive Computing.*

Canham, M., & Hegarty, M. (2010). Effects of knowledge and display design on comprehension of complex graphics. *Learning and Instruction*, *20*(2), 155–166. doi:10.1016/j.learninstruc.2009.02.014

Chen F., Deng P., Wan J., Zhang D., Vasilakos A, & Rong X., (2015). Data mining for the internet of things: Literature review and challenges. *International Journal of Distributed Sensor Networks*.

Cisco. (2012). *The Internet of everything: How more relevant and valuable connections will change the world.* Retrieved July 27, 2018 from: https://www.cisco.com/c/dam/global/en_my/assets/ciscoinnovate/pdfs/IoE.pdf

Cisco. (2015). *Fog computing and the internet of things: Extend the cloud to where the things are.* Retrieved July 21, 2018 from: https://www.cisco.com/c/dam/en_us/solutions/trends/iot/docs/computing-overview.pdf

Cisco Newsroom. (2018). *Cisco's technology news site.* Retrieved July 26, 2018 from: https://newsroom.cisco.com/ioe

Cowen, L. (2001). *An eye movement analysis of web-page usability* (Unpublished Masters' thesis). Lancaster University, UK.

De Koning, B. B., Tabbers, H. K., Rikers, R. M. J. P., & Paas, F. (2010). Attention guidance in learning from a complex animation: Seeing is understanding? *Learning and Instruction*, *20*(2), 111–122. doi:10.1016/j.learninstruc.2009.02.010

de Saint-Exupery, A. (2009). Internet of things: Strategic research roadmap. *IERC-European.* Retrieved March 11, 2018 from: http://www.internet-of-things-research.eu/pdf/IoT_Cluster_Strategic_Research_Agenda_2009.pdf

Dodge, R., & Cline, T. S. (1901). The angle velocity of eye movements. *Psychological Review*, *8*(2), 145–167. doi:10.1037/h0076100

Duchowski, A. T. (2003). *Eye tracking methodology: theory and practice.* London: Springer. doi:10.1007/978-1-4471-3750-4

Ellis, S., Candrea, R., Misner, J., Craig, C. S., Lankford, C. P., & Hutshinson, T. E. 1998). Windows to the soul? What eye movements tell us about software usability. In *Proceedings of the Usability Professionals' Association Conference 1998* (pp. 151-178). Academic Press.

Evans, D. (2012). The Internet of everything: How more relevant and valuable connections will change the world. *Cisco*. Retrieved July 19, 2018 from: https://www.cisco.com/c/dam/global/en_my/assets/ciscoinnovate/pdfs/IoE.pdf

Fitts, P. M., Jones, R. E., & Milton, J. L. (1950). Eye movements of aircraft pilots during instrument-landing approaches. *Aeronautical Engineering Review*, *9*(2), 24–29.

Gigli, M., & Koo, S. (2011). Internet of things: Services and applications categorization. *Advances in Internet of Things*. Retrieved March 11, 2018 from: https://pdfs.semanticscholar.org/17b6/b29ab24732 98315b92d8451d87336472d87f.pdf

Glenn, F., Lavecchia, H., Ross, L., Stokes, J., Weiland, W., Weiss, D., & Zaklad, A. (1986). Eye-voice controlled interface. In *Proceedings of the 30th Annual Meeting of the Human Factors Society* (pp. 322-326). Santa Monica, CA: Human Factors Society.

Goldberg, J. H., & Wichansky, A. M. (2003). Eye tracking in usability evaluation: A practitioner's guide. In J. Hyona, R. Radach, & H. Deubel (Eds.), *The mind's eye: cognitive and applied aspects of eye movement research* (pp. 493–516). Amsterdam: North-Holland. doi:10.1016/B978-044451020-4/50027-X

Greengard, S. (2015). *The internet of things*. MIT Press.

Hall, G. (2015). *Internet of everything: The value of connections*. Cisco Systems. Retrieved July 19, 2018 from: http://danto.info/InfoComm2015_Hall.pdf

Hartridge, H., & Thompson, L. C. (1948). Methods of investigating eye movements. *The British Journal of Ophthalmology*, *32*(9), 581–591. doi:10.1136/bjo.32.9.581 PMID:18170495

Holland, J., & Lee, S. (2018). *Internet of everything (IoE): Eye tracking data analysis. In Harnessing the Internet of Everything (IoE) for Accelerated Innovation Opportunities*. Hershey, PA: IGI Global.

Hutchinson, T. E., White, K. P., Martin, W. N., Reichert, K. C., & Frey, L. A. (1989). Human-computer interaction using eye-gaze input. *IEEE Transactions on Systems, Man, and Cybernetics*, *19*(6), 1527–1534. doi:10.1109/21.44068

IMOTIONS. (2015). *7 most used eye tracking metrics and terms*. Retrieved September 25, 2017 from: https://imotions.com/blog/7-terms-metrics-eye-tracking/

IMOTIONS. (2017). *Eye tracking: The complete pocket guide*. Retrieved Dec. 2, 2017 from: https://imotions.com/blog/eye-tracking/

iScoop. (2018). *What the Internet of everything really is – a deep dive*. Retrieved July 25, 2018 from: https://www.i-scoop.eu/internet-of-things-guide/internet-of-everything/

Jacob, R. J., & Karn, K. S. (2003). Eye tracking in human-computer interaction and usability research: Ready to deliver the promises. In The Mind's Eye: Cognitive and Applied Aspects of Eye Movement Research. Academic Press.

Jacob, R. J. K. (1990). *What you look at is what you get: Eye movement-based interaction techniques*. Washington, DC: Naval Research Laboratory.

Jacob, R. J. K. (1991). The use of eye movement in human-computer interaction techniques: What you look at is what you get. *ACM Transactions on Information Systems, 9*(2), 152–169. doi:10.1145/123078.128728

Jacob, R. J. K. (1995). Eye tracking in advanced interface design. In W. Barfield & T. A. Furness (Eds.), *Virtual environments and advanced interface design* (pp. 258–288). New York, NY: Oxford University Press.

Jarodzka, H., Scheiter, K., Gerjets, P., & Van Gog, T. (2010). In the eyes of the beholder: How experts and novices interpret dynamic stimuli. *Learning and Instruction, 20*(2), 146–154. doi:10.1016/j.learninstruc.2009.02.019

Javal, E. (1878). Essai sur la physiologie de la lecture. *Annales d'Oculistique, 79,* 97-117.

Judd, C. H., McAllister, C. N., & Steel, W. M. (1905). General introduction to a series of studies of eye movements by means of kinetoscopic photographs. Psychological Review, Monograph Supplements, 7, 1-16.

Just, M. A., & Carpenter, P. A. (1980). A theory of reading: From eye fixations to comprehension. *Psychological Review, 87*(4), 329–354. doi:10.1037/0033-295X.87.4.329 PMID:7413885

Lee, S., Ryu, J., & Ke, F. (2017). *Effects of Representation Format on Eye Movements in Math Problem Solving: Does Iconic Make a Difference?* Paper presented at the annual meeting of Association for Educational Communication and Technology, Jacksonville, FL.

Levine, J. L. (1981). *An eye-controlled computer.* Research Report RC-8857. New York: IBM Thomas J. Watson Research Center.

Levine, J. L. (1984). Performance of an eye tracker for office use. *Computers in Biology and Medicine, 14*(1), 77–89. doi:10.1016/0010-4825(84)90022-2 PMID:6713833

Longbottom, C. (2016). *A reference architecture for the IoE.* Retrieved July 19, 2018 from: https://www.whitepapers.em360tech.com/wp-content/uploads/A-reference-architecture-for-IoE.pdf

Luigi, A., & Antonio, I. (2010). The Internet of things: A survey. *Computer Networks.* Retrieved March 11, 2018 from https://www.cs.mun.ca/courses/cs6910/IoT-Survey-Atzori-2010.pdf

Mackworth, J. F., & Mackworth, N. H. (1958). Eye fixations recorded on changing visual scenes by the television eye-market. *Journal of the Optical Society of America, 48*(7), 439–445. doi:10.1364/JOSA.48.000439 PMID:13564324

Mackworth, N. H., & Thomas, E. L. (1962). Head-mounted eye-marker camera. *Journal of the Optical Society of America, 52*(6), 713–716. doi:10.1364/JOSA.52.000713 PMID:14467994

Majaranta, P., & Bulling, A. (2014). Advances in physiological computing. In Eye tracking and eye-based human-computer interaction (vol. 3, pp. 39-65). Academic Press.

Majaranta, P., & Raiha, K. J. (2002). Twenty Years of Eye Typing: Systems and Design Issues. *Proc. 2002 Symp. Eye Tracking Research and Applications*, 15-22. 10.1145/507072.507076

Mayer, R. E. (1985). Mathematical ability. In R. J. Sternberg (Ed.), *Human abilities: An information processing approach* (pp. 127–150). San Francisco: Freeman.

Meyer, K., Rasch, T., & Schnotz, W. (2010). Effects of animation's speed of presentation on perceptual processing and learning. *Learning and Instruction, 20*(2), 136–145. doi:10.1016/j.learninstruc.2009.02.016

Molich, R., & Nielsen, J. (1990). Improving a human-computer dialogue. Computing Practices, Communications of the ACM, 33(3).

Myers, B. A. (1996). *A brief history of human computer interaction technology.* Human Computer Interaction Institute, School of Computer Science, Carnegie Mellon University.

Noble, Z. (2015). How fog computing makes the internet of thing run. *The Business of Federal Technology.* Retrieved July 19, 2018 from: https://fcw.com/articles/2015/06/30/hiw_fog_computing.aspx

Schmidt-Weigand, F., Kohnert, A., & Glowalla, U. (2010). A closer look at split visual attention in system- and self-paced instruction in multimedia learning. *Learning and Instruction, 20*(2), 100–110. doi:10.1016/j.learninstruc.2009.02.011

Shackel, B. (1960). Note on mobile eye viewpoint recording. *Journal of the Optical Society of America, 59*(8), 763–768. doi:10.1364/JOSA.50.000763 PMID:14445350

Sibert, L. E., & Jacob, R. J. K. (2000). Evaluation of eye gaze interaction. *Proceedings of the SIGCHI conference on Human Factors in Computing Systems.* 10.1145/332040.332445

Sinclair, B. (2017). *IoT Inc. How your company can use the internet of things to win in the outcome economy.* New York, NY: McGraw-Hill Education.

Stankovic, J. A. (2014). Research directions for the Internet of things. *IEEE.* Retrieved March 11, 2018 from https://www.cs.virginia.edu/~stankovic/psfiles/IOT.pdf

Starker, I., & Bolt, R. A. (1990). A gaze-responsive self-disclosing display. In *Proceedings of the ACM CHI'90 Human Factors in Computing Systems Conference* (pp. 3-9). Addison-Wesley/ACM Press.

Swan, M. (2012). Sensor mania! The internet of things, wearable, computing, objective metrics, and the quantified self 2.0. *Journal of Sensor and Actuator Networks,* (1), 217-253. doi:10.3390/jsan1030217

Tinker, M. A. (1963). *Legibility of Print.* Ames, IA: Iowa State University Press.

Tobii. (2018). *Tobii is the world leader in eye tracking.* Retrieved March 5, 2018 from: https://www.tobii.com

Tong, H. M., & Fisher, R. A. (1984). *Progress Report on an Eye-Slaved Area-of-interest Visual Display.* Report No. AFHRL-TR-84-36, Air Force Human Resources Laboratory, Brooks Air Force Base, Texas.

Vertegaal, R. (1999). The GAZE groupware system: Mediating joint attention in multiparty communication and collaboration. In *Proceedings of the ACM CHI'99 Human Factors in Computing Systems Conference* (pp. 294-301). Addison-Wesley/ACM Press. 10.1145/302979.303065

Ware, C., & Mikaelian, H. T. (1987). An evaluation of an eye tracker as a device for computer input. In *Proceedings of the ACM CHI+GI'87 Human Factors in Computing Systems Conference* (pp. 183-188). New York: ACM Press.

YouTube. (2018). Introduction to the Internet of Everything. *Eli the Computer Guy.* Retrieved July 26, 2018 from: https://youtu.be/iCzQNTL4-Rs

Zhai, S., Morimoto, C., & Ihde, S. (1999). Manual and gaze input cascaded (MAGIC) pointing. In *Proceedings of the ACM CHI'99 Human Factors in Computing Systems Conference* (pp. 246-253). Addison-Wesley/ACM Press. 10.1145/302979.303053

ADDITIONAL READING

Bergstrom, J. R., & Schall, A. J. (2014). Eye tracking in user experience design. Morgan Kaufmann, imprint of Elsevier Inc. Waltham: MA.

Bojko, A. (2013). *Eye tracking the user experience.* Brooklyn, NY: Rosenfeld Media, LLC.

Di Martino, B., Li, K. C., Yang, L. T., & Esposito, A. (2018). *Internet of everything: Algorithms, methodologies, technologies and perspectives (Internet of Things)* (1st ed.). Singapore: Springer imprint of Springer Nature Singapore Pte Ltd. doi:10.1007/978-981-10-5861-5

Duchowski, A. T. (2003). *Eye tracking methodology: theory and practice.* London: Springer. doi:10.1007/978-1-4471-3750-4

Holmqvist, K., & Andersson, R. (2017). *Eye tracking: A comprehensive guide to methods, paradigms and measures.* Lund, Sweden: Lund Eye-Tracking Research Institute.

Hyönä, J. (2010). The use of eye movements in the study of multimedia learning. *Learning and Instruction, 20*(2), 172–176. doi:10.1016/j.learninstruc.2009.02.013

Jacob, R. J., & Karn, K. S. (2003). Eye tracking in human-computer interaction and usability research: Ready to deliver the promises. In The mind's eye (pp. 573-605).

Just, M. A., & Carpenter, P. A. (1980). A theory of reading: From eye fixations to comprehension. *Psychological Review, 87*(4), 329–354. doi:10.1037/0033-295X.87.4.329 PMID:7413885

Nielsen, J., & Pernice, K. (2010). Eyetracking web usability. New Riders imprint of Peachpit, division of Pearson Education. Berkeley: CA.

Rowland, C., Goodman, E., Charlier, M., Light, A., & Lui, A. (2015). *Designing connected products.* Sebastopol, CA: O'Reilly Media, Inc.

KEY TERMS AND DEFINITIONS

Area of Interest (AOI): An area of interest refers to the select sub-regions of the displayed stimuli, to extract metrics.

Fixation: A fixation is a series of gaze points very close in time and in space. The gaze cluster constitutes a fixation, where the eyes are looking at an object.

Fixation Count: The fixation count is the amount of fixation points within the area of interest.

Fixation Sequence: A fixation sequence is based on fixation positions and timing to generate a fixation sequence representing the order of attention.

Fixation Time: The fixation time indicates the amount of time it takes a respondent (or all respondents on average) to look at a specific AOI from stimulus onset.

Gaze Points: Gaze points show the elements of a stimulus the eyes are looking at.

Heat Map: A heat map is a visualization showing the general distribution of fixations and gaze points indicating attention. Red areas represent the highest number of gaze points, followed by yellow and green.

Internet of Everything (IoE): Bringing together people, processes, data, and things using networked connections to increase knowledge and understanding for product and service innovations. In addition, two-way communications become possible and more complex with programmed actions as a result of the data collected and analyzed.

Internet of Things (IoT): Refers to the things/devices connected to the Internet and each other.

Ratio: The ratio allows extracting information about how many respondents guided their gaze towards a specific area of interest.

Saccades: Saccades are the eye movements between fixations.

Time to First Fixation (TFF): The time to first fixation indicates the amount of time it takes a respondent to look at a specific area of interest from stimulus onset.

Chapter 11
Ultra–Low–Power Strategy for Reliable IoE Nanoscale Integrated Circuits

Jorge Semião
(iD) https://orcid.org/0000-0002-7667-7910
University of Algarve, Portugal

Marcelino Santos
(iD) https://orcid.org/0000-0002-2091-1165
University of Algarve, Portugal

Ruben Cabral
University of Algarve, Portugal

Isabel C. Teixeira
University of Algarve, Portugal

Hugo Cavalaria
University of Algarve, Portugal

J. Paulo Teixeira
University of Algarve, Portugal

ABSTRACT

Ultra-low-power strategies have a huge importance in today's integrated circuits designed for internet of everything (IoE) applications, as all portable devices quest for the never-ending battery life. Dynamic voltage and frequency scaling techniques can be rewarding, and the drastic power savings obtained in subthreshold voltage operation makes this an important technique to be used in battery-operated devices. However, unpredictability in nanoscale chips is high, and working at reduced supply voltages makes circuits more vulnerable to operational-induced delay-faults and transient-faults. The goal is to implement an adaptive voltage scaling (AVS) strategy, which can work at subthreshold voltages to considerably reduce power consumption. The proposed strategy uses aging-aware local and global performance sensors to enhance reliability and fault-tolerance and allows circuits to be dynamically optimized during their lifetime while prevents error occurrence. Spice simulations in 65nm CMOS technology demonstrate the results.

DOI: 10.4018/978-1-5225-7332-6.ch011

INTRODUCTION

In today's Integrated Circuits (IC) two important requirements are size and power consumption, which optimally should be the lowest possible. Particularly in IC and cyber-physical systems developed for Internet-of-Everything (IoE) applications, size and power impose the use of state-of-the-art CMOS nanotechnologies. Moreover, the IoE paradigm is enabling the interaction with a wide variety of devices, which tend to be self-powered and equipped with complex digital systems, including microcontrollers, sensors and sensor networks. Therefore, power consumption in CMOS integrated circuits, as never before, has a huge importance in today's chips for IoE applications, as all self-powered devices quest for the never-ending battery life, but also with smaller and smaller dimensions every day, in order to be used widely. However, the use of reduced CMOS technology with reduced power budgets imposes additional reliability challenges for such hardware, which must be considered earlier since the design stage, to guarantee that circuits will operate with no errors. Therefore, reliability and power consumption are two key concerns in the development of today's IoE chips.

Several low-power techniques are available to reduce consumption in today's chips. In energy savings techniques, the bottom line is to use power only when needed. In this way, aggressive techniques like power-gating are gaining ways in several application levels of abstraction. Not only at transistor level, where the classical power-gating is used, but also at system-level, where programmable RTC (Real-Time-Clocks) are being widely used to power-off the circuit to the minimum operation, in order to reduce power consumption when it is not needed. Then, periodically and sparsely in time, the RTC will wake-up the system and allow the minimum operation time to perform the required operation, so it can put the system back to sleep again.

In addition, Adaptive Voltage and Frequency Scaling (AVS) techniques and Dynamic Voltage and Frequency Scaling (DVFS) techniques can be very important to reduce performance and power consumption when it is not needed. The future requirements of IoE devices tend strongly towards the reduction of power consumption even at the expense of some performance reduction, as the energy efficiency paradigm becomes increasingly important. IoE applications require the use of nearly-zero power consumption sensors, to be available while gathering data from everywhere using nearly-zero energy, and sparsely can transmit these data to the web. These never-ending battery achievements can only be achieved with more than one technique, and working at different power supply voltage (VDD) and clock frequency levels.

However, in order to further increase energy savings, the DVFS techniques can be taken to the limit, by reducing the supply voltage to subthreshold voltage levels in the power-supply. In this case, clock frequency must also be drastically reduced, to guarantee a fail-safe operation. Subthreshold operation has already been studied in the past, and the work of Calhoun, Benton H. et al. (2005), Keller, Sean et al. (2011) Radfar, Mohsen et al. (2012), Hanson, S. et al. (2008), Giustolisi, G. et al. (2003), Kim, Jae-Joon et al. (2004), Li, Ming-Zhong et al. (2013), and Sahu, Alok et al. (2014), are several examples of previous works dealing with subthreshold voltage operation. However, working at subthreshold voltage levels puts digital CMOS circuits in a very vulnerable and unreliable situation. The reduced energy available in the circuit considerably reduces performance and considerably increases variability. Errors are more prone to happen, especially due to: transient faults, operation induced delay-faults, process variations, power-supply variations, temperature variations, electromagnetic interference (EMI), single-event upsets (SEU), radiation, etc... Fortunately, aging degradations caused by effects such as Bias Temperature Instability (BTI) are reduced, due to the reduced voltages applied to transistors' gates.

On the other hand, reliability techniques can be used to reduce and minimize the risks of using subthreshold voltages. For example, carefully controlling the operational conditions of the circuit by sensing performance deviations may allow to identify operationally induced variations. We refer the sensing devices (which can be implemented on-chip) as Performance Sensors (PS). Moreover, appropriate design techniques can also minimize external induced errors (e.g., by improving shielding in circuit design), or process variation effects. Yet, considering IoE applications, some soft-errors in the hardware may even be acceptable, and/or can also be detected and eventually corrected at higher abstraction levels, for instance by using statistical techniques to identify outliers in a data set collected from IoE sensors, or using machine learning techniques as done by Sharma, Vishal Chandra et al. (2015). Nevertheless, in the development of chips and sensors for IoE applications, power is probably the most critical factor. Previous works such as Cabral, Ruben et al. (2017) and Semião, J. et al. (2018) present different performance sensors to work at subthreshold voltage levels and increase circuit reliability. These on-chip sensors can be used to, simultaneously, control power-supply voltage reduction in AVFS schemes and avoid error occurrence, when working at subthreshold power-supply voltages.

The purpose of this work is to propose a new ultra-low-power strategy for reliable operation of ICs, focused on IoE applications. Power consumption is drastically reduced by working at subthreshold power-supply voltages, and reliability is guaranteed by using a cooperative work of local and global performance sensors, to adapt dynamically the supply voltage and clock frequency, which are carefully chosen with values to obtain a considerable power reduction, but without jeopardizing performance.

The reminder of the paper is as follows. The background work on subthreshold voltage operation, reliability and DVFS techniques for subthreshold voltage levels is presented on the next section. The following section presents the proposed Local Performance Sensor (LPS), its architecture and functionality, while the Global Performance Sensor (GPS) is described in its own section. After, the proposed Adaptive Voltage and Frequency Scaling strategy is described, namely how the GPS and the LPS allow to work at subthreshold voltages with a reliable operation. Finally, before the summary of future works and conclusions at the end of the chapter, the implementation tests and results are presented and analyzed.

BACKGROUND

In today's IoE chips, energy consumption optimization is mandatory, and in it one very important research topic is the subthreshold voltage operation. Especially for circuits where performance is not a critical factor, this topic became increasingly important and is now a key feature to reduce power consumption. It can be applied to digital circuits, like in the works of Li, Ming-Zhong, et al., 2013, and Sahu, Alok, et al., 2014, or to analog circuits, like in the works of Do, Aaron V. et al. (2008) and Giustolisi, G. et al. (2003), or to mixed-signal applications, like in the work of Chakraborty, Saurav, et al. (2008), or even at memory applications, like in the works of Yoo, H.J. (1998), and Hanson, S. et al. (2008). And, to work at subthreshold power-supply voltages, circuit design and cell design should be carefully analyzed. To understand the trend concerning the evolution of subthreshold design techniques, the work of Radfar, Mohsen et al. (2012) must be considered, as it presents a complete review of several studies on the field and explores the major aspects of subthreshold design methodology.

As energy reduction and circuit optimization are top priorities, some works are focused on the modeling and characterization of new devices designed specifically for operation at subthreshold levels, like the work of Kim, Jae-Joon et al. (2004) and the work of Numata, Toshinori & Takagi, Shinichi (2004).

The goal is to achieve more efficient designs and to optimize the required energy for a correct circuit operation. Other works established ground rules and methods to design logic gates to operate on minimum and optimum energy points at subthreshold power-supply levels, like in the works of Calhoun, Benton H. et al. (2005), and Calhoun, Benton H. et al. (2004). In Calhoun, Benton H. et al. (2005), the authors define the concept of energy minimization, and present analytical methods to allow calculating the Optimum Supply Voltage (optimum VDD) and MOS Threshold Voltage (Vth), minimizing power consumption for a specific operating frequency. As denoted by Calhoun, Benton H. et al. (2004), transistors' sizing is extremely important to optimize energy reduction in subthreshold circuits. Nevertheless, the work of Keller, Sean et al. (2011) uses adaptive body biasing, as well as body dimensions' adjustments, to achieve a reliable minimum energy operation. These techniques allow minimizing operational errors by introducing new fault tolerant methods, as well as new and more robust cell design techniques to significantly improve reliability.

The investigation of the minimum energy operating point or a single gate has been the focus of previous works such as Calhoun, Benton H. et al. (2004), and Calhoun, Benton H. et al. (2005). However, as denoted by Cavalaria, Hugo et al. (2017), to determine the optimal operating conditions to reduce energy in a complete circuit is not an easy task, as the minimum-energy VDD value for a certain gate will not certainly be the same for all circuit gates. Moreover, the minimum energy point may lead to an extreme low energy situation where error rate is above limits and reliability methods used can no longer guarantee a safe operation. Instead of the minimum energy VDD point, a tradeoff among several operational parameters should be considered, when defining the optimal VDD value for an ultra-low-power operation, considering all the gates in the circuit. Some works authors like Gonzalez, R. et al. (1997), or Burr, J. et al. (1991), consider the Energy-Delay Product (EDP, i.e., Power*Delay^2) to establish a balance between performance and power consumption, or the Energy-Delay^n metric (i.e., Power*Delay^m with m greater than 2), if more weight is needed on the delay. Minimizing the EDP of a circuit results in a particular design point where 1% of energy can be traded off for 1% of delay. However, as denoted by Markovic, Dejan et al. (2004), although the EDP metric is useful for comparison of different implementations of a design, the design optimization points targeting EDP may not correspond to an optimum solution under desired operating conditions. Therefore, other metrics have been used in the past, like in the work from Markovic, Dejan et al. (2004), which uses sensitivity metrics to achieve an optimum VDD, or the work from Cavalaria, Hugo et al. (2017), which analyzes all the gates in a circuit to obtain a weighted VDD value identified as the best tradeoff between Power and Performance, reducing considerably power still not jeopardizing performance, neither the correct operation with an increased vulnerability to errors.

Regarding reliability and fault tolerant methods, various sensors were proposed in the past and can be used to measure performance, although not all were proposed as performance sensors. Changes in performance, in signal transitions or in circuit delays, correspond to changes in performance. Therefore, previous works on delay-fault sensors, soft-error sensors, or even aging sensors, may be also classified as performance sensors, as referred by Semião, J. et al. (2014).

Regarding on-chip sensor location and sensor use in the circuit, generally there are two approaches: a global sensor or a local sensor. Global sensors normally monitor key critical paths, critical paths' replicas, or key parameters, to detect circuit's performance degradation. For instance, that is the case of works from Gauthier, C. R. et al. (2006), Tschanz, J. et al. (2007), Keane, J. et al. (2007), and Kim, D. et al. (2009). Their usage in a circuit is very easy and straightforward, because performance monitoring, normally, is independent from circuit operation, which is why they are easily adopted by industry. However, they do not monitor circuit at the actual locations where errors occur, and, because of that, their estimated Process, Voltage, Temperature and Aging (PVTA) variations may differ from the ones that in the real circuit can produce an error.

On the other hand, Local sensors normally monitor performance degradations locally, in the actual circuit implementing the mission functionality, in key locations in the circuit where errors are more prone to occur. Therefore, when used correctly, they can give a real measure of circuits' performance status. Several examples of local sensors can be found in the works of Martins, C. V. et al. (2011), Ernst, D. et al. (2003), Vazquez, J.C. et al. (2010) and Semião, J. et al. (2014), and Cabral, Ruben et al. (2017). However, unlike Global sensors, their use and implementation in a circuit is more complex. Moreover, performance monitoring can only be done on-line if, and when, the critical paths they monitor are activated, which depends on circuit operation.

Interestingly, Semião, J. et al. (2012) presented an improved solution to monitor performance degradation with both Global and Local sensors. In this work, both sensors work cooperatively to minimize error occurrence. Unfortunately, in this work neither GPS nor LPS sensors can work at subthreshold power supply voltages. However, recently the same authors have published new performance sensors, especially developed to work at subthreshold voltage levels. In Cabral, Ruben et al. (2017), the performance Local sensor for subthreshold operation is presented and explained, and its use in key locations in the circuit can provide a good performance evaluation of the circuit. More recently, in Semião, J. et al. (2018), the performance Global sensor for subthreshold operation was presented, and in this work the Global sensor is proposed as a good solution for industry adoption. However, a better solution would be to reuse Local and Global sensors in the same implementation, because they can complement each other, providing a more reliable sensor solution. Most of all, the concurrent use of GPS and LPS in the same circuit can further optimize circuit operation by reducing safety margins and allowing to achieve highest energy savings.

The purpose of this chapter is to present the complete performance sensor solution for subthreshold operation, including both Local and Global sensors and allowing an ultra-low-power strategy for reliable IoE nanoscale digital circuits. The sensors' main goal is to avoid errors, monitoring PVTA variations by sensing circuit's performance limits at each operational conditions (PVTA status). By acting preventively, i.e., before the errors actually occur, these sensors allow to automatically control circuit operation, namely clock frequency and power-supply voltage, to implement an AVS (Adaptive Voltage Scaling) and work at the minimum power-supply voltage (reducing energy consumption), for the circuit's real operational and environmental conditions.

LOCAL PERFORMANCE SENSOR (LPS)

In this section, the Local Performance Sensor (LPS) for subthreshold operation is presented. This sensor architecture was previously presented in Cabral, Ruben et al. (2017) as the Low-Power Scout-Flip-Flop (LP Scout-FF), to increase tolerance and preventive fault-detection of delay-faults. The purpose of this Local sensor is to monitor data transitions at key Flip-flops (FF), in order to identify the occurrence of unsafe transitions. The unsafe transitions are, in fact, signal transitions at the data input of the FF that were correctly captured, but in the eminence of an error. To determine locally these unsafe transitions, delays are used inside the FF to create virtual windows and detect these unsafe transitions (i.e., data transitions which are in the eminence of causing a delay-fault). A delay fault at the input of a memory element (FF) induces a logic error, that can easily propagate throughout the digital circuit. Moreover, to increase error-tolerance and allow the capture of late transients at the data input of the FF, the clock signal of the master latch in the FF is also delayed, creating an additional tolerance margin. Both features, the detection of unsafe transitions and the capture of late transients, allow to monitor and control circuit operation when working with a high variability in circuit performance (namely, using reduced VDD voltages, or using AVS techniques), even though operating with limited slack margins in the circuit, which corresponds to an optimized energy and performance operation.

Architecture and Functionalities

Local sensor architecture is presented in Figure 1. This sensor comprises three functionalities, as depicted in Figure 1: (i) typical D-type flip-flop functionality; (ii) delay-fault tolerance functionality; and (iii) functionality of detecting unsafe data transitions. The typical D-type flip-flop functionality is implemented with the light-blue components in Figure 1, which include a common master-slave D FF with a data input D, a Clock input C, and the data outputs Q and $\bar{Q}$. The delay-fault tolerance functionality is implemented with the light orange components in Figure 1, which include two additional internal signals, $Ctrl$ and $\overline{Ctrl}$, to generate a delayed clock signal in the master latch and to provide an additional time to capture late transients in the FF. The functionality of detecting unsafe data transitions is implemented with the light green components in Figure 1, which include an Activity Sensor block, to signalize transitions in the eminence of an error in the internal data signal H, an additional Sensor Output signal, SO, and an additional Sensor Reset signal, $\overline{SR}$ (an active-low reset signal).

It is important to note that the detection of unsafe transitions at the FF's data input is, in fact, the main purpose of the Local sensor functionality. By acting preventively, the detection of unsafe transitions during online operation can trigger corrective actions to avoid errors. In this work, as the purpose is to reduce power consumption by implementing an Adaptive Voltage and Frequency Scaling (AVFS) scheme, the corrective action is to increase the power-supply voltage to reduce propagation delays in the critical path and avoid errors.

For better understanding these three functionalities in the Local sensor, Figure 2 presents the timings and delay margins in key signals in the Local Sensor, in respect to the clock period. In a typical flip-flop, the allowed delay in a data path is, utterly, the clock period. However, considering a safety margin to avoid errors and to account the FF setup time and some additional variability, all the data signals should arrive at FF's input during the safe margin (indicated with green color in Figure 2). The unsafe margin in a typical FF is indicated in Figure 2 with the yellow color. However, in the proposed Local Performance Sensor, an additional tolerance margin is added (the orange area in Figure 2), to avoid errors and capture late transients at FF's data input. Therefore, the unsafe margin in this sensor-FF, i.e., the margin where FF captures data correctly but in the eminence of an error, is indicated in Figure 2 with the yellow and orange areas. If a signal arrives at FF's input during this unsafe margin, the sensor signalizes it, indicating that corrective measures should be taken to avoid errors. If late transients occur beyond the unsafe margin (the red area in Figure 2), an error data signal is captured in the FF.

Improved Reliability and Sensor Functionality

The use of a sensor to detect unsafe data transitions improves the reliability of the circuit. In this work, sensor functionality, i.e., the detection of unsafe data transitions at the FF input, is based on the Activity-

Figure 1. Local performance sensor architecture

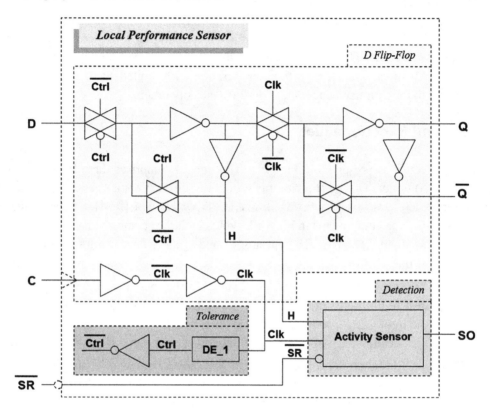

Figure 2. Path-delay margins identified in the LPS within the clock period

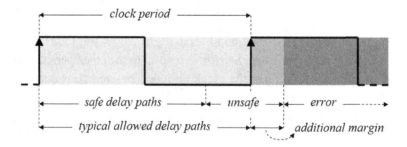

Sensor block (in Figure 1). As all circuits in this work, this Activity Sensor block was designed to work at reduced VDD voltage levels, down to subthreshold levels.

Figure 3 presents the detailed architecture of the Activity Sensor block. From Figure 1 we can see that signal *H* is obtained inside the FF, at the internal output of the master Latch. In the Activity Sensor, this *H* signal is delayed by a Delay Element (DE_2), which feds an XOR gate to generate a pulse (*det* signal) for every transition in this *H* signal, with its pulse duration being proportional to the propagation delay of the DE_2 block. This pulse is created for every correct capture of a new signal in the FF. The sensor output (*SO* signal) is signalized (output high) when the generated pulse (*det* signal) and the clock signal (*Clk*) are simultaneously active (high). Therefore, transistors Q1 – Q4 and the inverter gate implement a logic AND functionality. As the DE_2 block delays the captured signal in the FF (the *H* signal), if the generated pulse (*det* signal) and the new clock pulse occurs simultaneously, it means that the FF captured an unsafe new data. If the propagation delays increase due to adverse PVTA variations, the delay margin to start signalizing unsafe captures in the FF will also increase (due to the increased delay of the DE_2 block), which is a good result for the sensor functionality, as the sensor becomes more sensitive when operating conditions worsen.

Transistors Q_5 and Q_6 implement an on-retention logic feature, to avoid the use of an additional latch to hold an active sensor output signal (SO). Therefore, to reset the sensor output and re-initiate the sensing functionality, an active-low reset signal (the $\overline{SR}$ input signal) is used to activate transistor Q_7 and force *SO* signal to the low state.

It is important to note that the XOR gate should be implemented using a pass-transistor logic, to allow VDD to be reduced to subthreshold voltage levels, as referred in Cabral, Ruben et al. (2017).

In addition, regarding the Delay Element block, it is a simple buffer (two inverters). However, multiple buffers can be used to provide higher delays in the DE block and provide different sensitivities to the sensor. The number of buffers used should be chosen according with: the τ_{slack}/T_{CLK} ratio (where τ_{slack} is the time slack, i.e., the difference between the clock period and the longest path delay or critical path delay, and T_{CLK} is the clock period), the clock frequency, the technology, and the sensor's sensitivity needed for a chosen worst case PVTA conditions. More detailed information can be found in Cabral, Ruben et al. (2017).

Figure 3. Activity sensor architecture

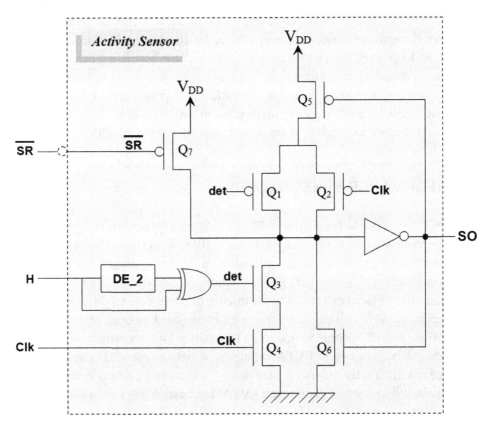

Delay-Fault Tolerance Functionality

The purpose of the delay-fault tolerance functionality is to add an additional tolerance to delay-faults. The circuitry used to implement this feature is identified in Figure 1 as the Tolerance part, with the light orange color. This feature is implemented with an additional Delay Element block (DE_1), and an inverter cell. These two components create a delayed clock signal inside the FF, accessed in signals *Ctrl* and $\overline{Ctrl}$, to control the capture of data signals in the FF. In fact, these *Ctrl* and $\overline{Ctrl}$ signals are the clock signals connected to the FF's master latch (the slave latch is connected to the non-delayed, typical, clock signal). Therefore, by delaying the clock only in the master latch, it puts the FF in a transparent mode during this time delay, and allows the FF to capture late arrivals during this added tolerance margin, increasing tolerance to delay-faults. During this transparent mode, a new input data will be automatically transferred to the output. Therefore, the tolerance margin is equal to the delay between the two clocks of the FF, the Clk and the Ctrl signals.

Nevertheless, the proposed additional tolerance implementation may introduce two constraints: the presence of short-delay paths, and the impact of delayed captures in subsequent FF stages. Regarding the presence of short-delay paths in the FF's input combinational logic cone, if a short path arrives at the FF during the transparent mode, it will cause an erroneous data capture. To overcome this limitation, a minimum-path length constraint must be added at the input of each Local Sensor FFs, and additional Delay Element cells (similar to DE_1 and DE_2) should be added in the short paths to slow down fast paths (as done in other previously published solutions, like Semião, J. et al. (2008)).

Regarding the impact of delayed captures in subsequent FF stages, this is the typical problem of time borrowing. By delaying the capture in one FF, this delay should be recovered in subsequent FF stages. If consecutive critical paths exist in consecutive stages, an extra DE_1 cell can be used in the following FF stages to accommodate the extra delay time, or a DE cell with additional buffers and delay capability. However, if feedback loops exist in FFs with critical paths, no time borrowing can be used. In this case, the design must be modified (or re-synthesized), to avoid feedback loops in critical paths.

Nevertheless, as the detection and signalizing of unsafe data captures in the FF start prior to the clock period, if corrective measures are then taken, no time borrowing will occur. Still, this feature gives the circuit an additional tolerance to errors to account with unpredictable variability.

GLOBAL PERFORMANCE SENSOR (GPS)

In this section, the Global Performance Sensor (GPS) for subthreshold operation is presented. This sensor architecture was previously presented in Semião, J. et al. (2018) as the Low-Power Global Performance Sensor, i.e., a non-intrusive global sensor that guarantees a reliable operation even with the use of aggressive low-power techniques (such as DVFS or subthreshold operation). The GPS is based on two dummy critical paths (CP) placed externally to the circuit, to create several different delay paths along the two dummy critical paths. Two distinct dummy paths are used, instead of only one, because one path is highly sensitive to NBTI degradations, while the other is highly sensitive to PBTI aging effects. This way, the GPS will be sensitive to PVTA variations, which are typically the main variations that affect performance in a circuit. By monitoring the delays in these two dummy critical paths, according with the available clock frequency and estimated PVTA degradation, we can evaluate the performance of the GPS under the working conditions and extrapolate for the main circuit, implementing the mission functionality of the chip. Moreover, by registering the correct output of the GPS evaluation of the dummy paths, it is possible to know if the performance is relaxed for the available clock frequency and PVTA degradations, or if it is stressed and error occurrence is eminent.

In our Ultra-Low-Power AVS strategy, power-supply voltage can be automatically adjusted according with the GPS evaluation without interfering with the main circuit operation.

Architecture and Functionality

The main architecture for the GPS is presented in Figure 4. As shown, it includes a controller block, two dummy critical paths, and two groups of Sensor Latches. The controller block launches two consecutive signal transitions (Low-to-High and High-to-Low) in each dummy signal path, to trigger two different signal propagations in each dummy path. The Sensor Latches, placed and distributed along both dummy paths, will capture the signals along the paths for the available clock period. These Sensor Latches, as it will be explained later on, have activity sensor blocks (Figure 3) to detect and signalize unsafe data captures in the latch. Therefore, the number of flagged Sensor Latches allows to evaluate the performance of the GPS dummy paths according with the available clock frequency and PVTA degradation. For a relaxed (low) clock frequency, no Sensor Latch will be signalized (or detect an unsafe data capture); however, for a stressed (high) clock frequency, the first Sensor Latches in the paths will be activated (detecting unsafe data captures). As we do not know which dummy critical path ages more, OR gates are used to connect the Sensor Latches from both dummy paths, to obtain one final Sensor Latch output (and GPS output).

In Figure 5, the dummy Critical Paths are presented in more detail. One dummy path is implemented with NOR gates (dummy critical path 1 in Figure 5), creating a critical path that, presumably, will have a higher aging degradation, when compared to the critical paths of the circuit, if the NBTI effect is considered (which strongly influences the degradation of PMOS transistors' threshold voltage, V_{th}). The second dummy path is implemented with NAND gates (dummy critical path 2 in Figure 5), creating a second critical path that, presumably, will have a higher aging degradation, when compared to the

Figure 4. Global performance sensor architecture

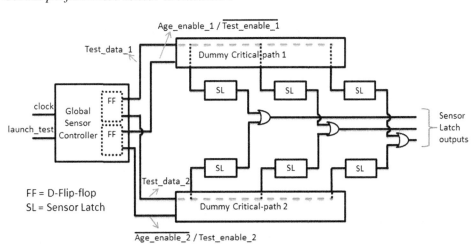

Figure 5. Detail of the dummy critical paths in the GPS

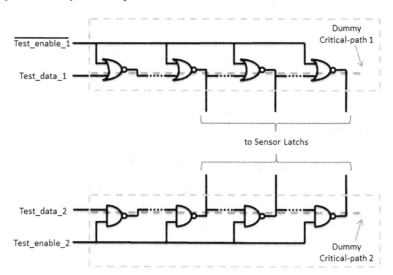

critical paths of the circuit, if the PBTI effect is relevant (which strongly influences the degradation of the V_{th} in NMOS transistors).

As the Global sensor monitors signal delays in paths that are not the actual Critical Path (CP) in the main circuit, it is important to impose an extreme aging degradation to these dummy CP in the GPS. This is because we want to extrapolate for the main circuit the performance evaluation of the GPS. Hence, it is important that the main circuit does not age more than the GPS. This way, a safety margin will be used, to account for differences among the main circuit's CP and the GPS dummy paths. Also, as aging degradations are cumulative, the GPS will become more sensitive when degradations worsen, and in the proposed sensor architecture, the existing safety margin always work in favor of error avoidance and not the opposite. That is also the reason for using two dummy CP, one sensitive to NBTI aging and the other sensitive to PBTI aging. Nevertheless, as it will be seen later on, the use of both GPS and LPS allows to constantly tune the GPS evaluation according with LPS activation.

The NORs and the NANDs input port-map are equally important for the high aging degradation of the PMOS and NMOS transistors in the dummy paths. Figure 6 presents the internal architecture for NOR and NAND gates used in the dummy paths. For the NOR gate, the probability for transistor P1 to be in stress mode (NBTI induced degradation) is equal to the probability of having its NOR_chain input at logic value 0. If the Global sensor is activated periodically, this signal will most likely be at low logic value most of the time, making a high degradation probability for transistor P1. However, the probability to put P2 in stress mode is equivalent to the probability of having both P1 and P2 transistors on, in other words,

$$\mathrm{P}\left(\left[\mathrm{NOR\_chain}\right]_{input} = 0\right) \times \mathrm{P}\left(\left[\mathrm{Age\_enable\_1}\right]_{input} = 0\right).$$

Considering that the Global sensor is activated periodically, Age_enable_1 signal has low probability to be at 0 logic value. Henceforth, P2 will have negligible degradation. Yet, a high degradation probability of dummy CP 1 is guaranteed with the high degradation probability of all the P1 transistors from the

NOR chain, due to the NBTI effect. Moreover, if a higher degradation is needed in the dummy critical path, a 3-input NOR gate can also be used, with two of its inputs connected to the same NOR_chain input and having now two PMOS transistors in a high aging state. However, if subthreshold voltages are to be used, 3-input gates that use a classic CMOS and implementation should be avoided, as may restrict VDD reduction.

Regarding the NAND gates, a similar analysis can be drawn. For the NAND gate in Figure 6, the probability for transistor N1 to be in stress mode (due to PBTI effects) is equal to the probability of having its NAND_chain input at logic value 1. As the Global sensor is activated periodically, this signal will most likely be at low logic value most of the time, making a high degradation probability for transistor N1. However, the probability to put N2 in stress mode is equivalent to the probability of having both N1 and N2 transistors on, i.e.,

$$P\left(\left[\text{NAND\_chain}\right]_{input} = 1\right) \times P\left(\left[\overline{\text{Age\_enable\_2}}\right]_{input} = 1\right).$$

Considering that the Global sensor is activated periodically, $\overline{\text{Age\_enable\_2}}$ signal has low probability to be at 1 logic value. Henceforth, N2 will have negligible degradation. Yet, a high degradation probability of dummy CP 2 is guaranteed with the high degradation probability of all the N1 transistors in the NAND's path due to PBTI effect.

Sensor Latch

As explained and observed in Figure 4, Sensor Latches are used to capture the signals along the dummy paths. The architecture of these Sensor Latches is presented in Figure 7. The Sensor Latches are composed by a common D-Latch, to implement the Latch functionality, and an Activity Sensor (as presented in Figure 3), to implement the sensor functionality. The existence of a D-Latch functionality allows to capture signals with the existing clock, which allows to compare the delays of the dummy paths with the existing clock period. The latches are enabled when the clock signal is logical low, i.e., they are in transparent mode when the clock is logical low, and in the non-transparent mode (opaque) when the clock is logical high. Regarding the activity sensor, it's the same block used for the LPS (Figure 3). The

Figure 6. Internal structure and port map for NOR gates and NAND gates

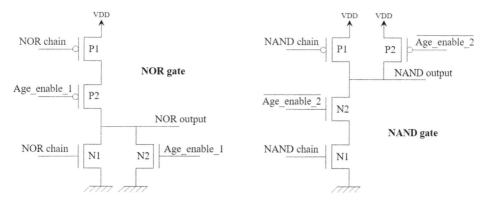

purpose of its use here is to signalize when unsafe captures occur in the Sensor Latch. As the Sensor Latches are placed along the dummy paths, for a given clock period it is expected that the Sensor Latches connected at the end of the dummy paths are signalized, and the Sensor Latches connected earlier in the dummy paths are not signalized. This way we can have a measure of the comparison made between the delays along the dummy CP and the clock period, having a rate for the performance level of the circuit. Moreover, the activity sensor implements an on-retention logic, to keep sensor output (SO) active once it is activated, and until the sensor reset $\overline{SR}$ is activated (logical low).

ADAPTIVE VOLTAGE SCALING FOR ULTRA-LOW-POWER

Dynamic Voltage and Frequency Scaling (DVFS) techniques are usually implemented with a discrete number of voltage and frequency pairs, initially defined and dynamically selected during different workload conditions. Therefore, there is no feedback from the circuit about the performance at the given operational and environmental conditions (it's an open loop approach). The pre-defined voltage and frequency pairs are chosen to keep sufficient margin to allow circuit operation and to guarantee a reliable operation across the range of best and worst case PVTA variations. Consequently, this conservative approach imposes wide margins to secure reliable operation, resulting in efficiency loss and denoting that the energy reduction achieved with this approach can be improved. Adaptive Voltage Scaling (AVS) techniques, applied in combination with DVFS, or isolated, can be a solution to optimize this energy efficiency problem.

Figure 7. Sensor Latch architecture

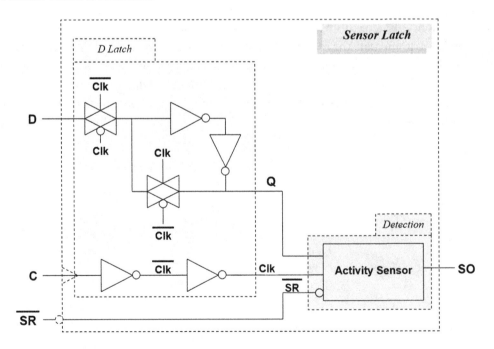

AVS techniques can effectively overcome limitations of DVFS, thru the use of an efficient feedback loop approach, by measuring workload directly at runtime and immediately acting, defining output of a high accuracy variable power supply. Wilcox, K. et al. (2015) reported that vendors like AMD, already apply AVFS techniques in their CPUs, like the 'Excavator' CPUs cores, incorporating 10 AVFS modules with energy savings.

The ultra-low-power strategy for reliable integrated circuits proposed in this chapter is, in fact, an AVS strategy. It should be used in combination with DVFS, to use several modes of operation, each mode corresponding to an initial pair of supply voltage and clock frequency, but using AVS to optimize operation and energy consumption for each clock frequency. The purpose of the proposed AVS approach is to use GPS and LPSs to monitor circuit delays and sense performance versus the workload requirements, to act directly by controlling and changing the power-supply voltage. Whenever GPS and LPSs sense slowness and performance loss under high workload requirements, the controller acts by increasing supply voltage provided by the power supply unit; whenever sensors sense high performance under low workload requirements, controller acts by slowly decreasing supply voltage, until the edge of detection. This way the circuit supply voltage is regularly (continuously) and permanently adjusted to its optimum value. Moreover, one important feature of the proposed AVS scheme, which is not available in existing AVS or DVFS techniques, is that the power-supply voltage level can be reduced drastically to work at subthreshold voltage levels, boosting enormously the energy savings. Another important feature, also not available in traditional AVS and DVFS standard techniques, is the simultaneous use of Local and Global sensors. GPS can monitor regularly circuit operation and tune power-supply voltage accordingly, to obtain an efficient power consumption for the required circuit performance and workload. LPS can also trigger power-supply voltage changes, but most importantly it monitors circuit performance locally, where functional errors may occur, and triggers GPS tuning. All the sensors work with a minimum security margin, defined by design. This way, it is possible to guarantee that the performance of the system is exactly enough as required by the user. It is also possible to guarantee that the system performs reliably. And mainly, it is possible to guarantee that the supply voltage defined is exactly the minimum voltage required for operation at each PVTA existing degradations and operational conditions, during circuit's lifetime.

AVS Strategy Implementation and Use

The typical implementation and use of the proposed AVS strategy is as follows.

During project development, main circuit's CPs should be identified, preferably using an aging aware static timing analysis tool to characterize and define the worst case circuit's CPs. With this information, the GPS is designed (or selected from a list of different pre-defined GPS implementations), namely the dummy critical paths created with the NAND and NOR gates, so that the delays in the dummy paths exceed (in time response) the main circuit's CPs. The designer must choose how many NAND/NOR gates to use, according with the circuit's CP, how many Sensor Latches are used and how sparsely/densely placed in the dummy CP outputs (depending on the required sensitivity).

During manufacturing, an initial calibration procedure is mandatory, to tune GPS with LPSs' outputs. In this calibration procedure, off-line tests are performed by applying, to the main circuit, deterministic delay fault test patterns (e.g., using scan-based delay-fault oriented tests) at different VDD and frequency values. This allows to characterize and define, for each chip, voltage and frequency pairs where LPS are in the eminence of detecting unsafe transitions, and the corresponding GPS output (number of Sensor Latches detecting unsafe transitions that occurred in their data input) for no LPS unsafe detection. These voltage and frequency pairs are, with a small safety margin, the minimum operational supply voltage values for each clock frequency, i.e., the points for an efficient operation regarding performance and power consumption. Along with this information, it will be also known the code word used for the parametric DC-DC converter to deliver minimum working VDD for each clock frequency (identified as the optimal VDD values, or VDD_{OPT}), and the code word for the GPS output (identified as the optimal GPS output, or GPS_{OPT}). These corresponding codes will be stored in memory (in two registers), to initiate the on-field operation.

During the on-field operation, the circuit will run online with no direct interference from the sensors. However, sensors are used to measure key parameters that allow to characterize performance, and this information is used by the AVS controller to change the power-supply voltage when PVTA degradations occur. Throughout normal operation and circuit lifetime, aging degradations are constantly happening and, because these degradations are cumulative in time, the path-delay fingerprint is slowly changing. Therefore, sensors are crucial to: (1) increase VDD to accommodate increased delays for the available clock period, guaranteeing an error free operation; (2) reduce VDD to the minimum value that guarantees an error free operation, when PVTA and operational conditions causes a non-optimized operation; and (3) tune GPS using the LPSs unsafe detections, to maintain an error-free operation with a minimum safety margin. Note that, according with circuit application and on-field use, the GPS off-line tuning performed during manufacturing can also be repeated sparsely later on during lifetime, to guarantee an efficient tuning of the GPS.

Figure 8 summarizes a typical optimized circuit operation and how sensors (GPS and LPSs) are used to keep the circuit running with the smallest VDD value for each clock frequency. The selected outputs of the dummy critical paths, connected to Sensor Latches in the GPS, must guarantee that main circuit's CP has its delay between the maximum and minimum value of the dummy paths connected to Sensor Latches. Moreover, the Sensor Latch detection margin and the use of several Sensor Latches, along the dummy paths in the GPS, will create a performance measure by signalizing progressively more unsafe data captures in the Sensor Latch outputs when VDD is reduced (or aging degradations increase), for a given clock frequency. When the detection margins of each Sensor Latch in the GPS, or each LPS, are reached during the active phase of the clock, their Activity Sensor signalizes an unsafe data capture. In a typical situation, as illustrated in Figure 8, circuit's CP delay is placed somewhere in the middle of Global Sensor's dummy paths delays, and the most sensitive Sensor Latches (connected to the high-delay dummy paths) are signalizing error detections (S1-S4), while the less sensitive Sensor Latches (connected to the low-delay dummy paths) do not signalize error detections (S5-S7).

The control mechanism of the AVS strategy is done by storing the code word for the GPS output for the optimized operation (in Figure 8 it would be GPS_{OPT}= "*100*", which represents the number 4, for the first 4 Sensor Latches detecting unsafe data captures), and the power-supply voltage value is changed accordingly (changing VDD_{OPT}), to maintain the GPS output equal to the stored GPS that represents the optimized operation (note that by increasing VDD, fewer Sensor Latches are signalized; and by reducing VDD, more Sensor Latches are signalized).

Considering aging effects, during product lifetime, it is expected that aging degradations are higher in the dummy paths than in the main circuit's CPs. This is because dummy paths are activated sparsely in time, being most of the time in a high aging degradation condition (as explained before). However, if unpredicted PVTA variability occurs and the LPSs detect unsafe transitions in the main circuit, with no new unsafe transitions in the GPS (that is, no need to change VDD), it means that higher aging degrada-

Figure 8. Typical optimized circuit operation and sensor use

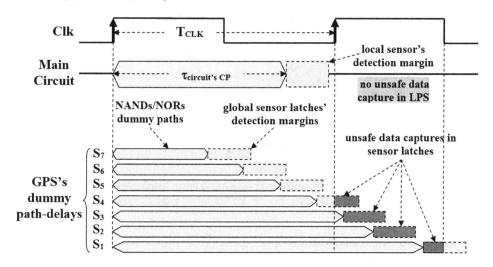

tions occur in the main circuit and not in the GPS dummy paths, and the GPS needs to be tuned again. In this case, the stored GPS output (GPS_{OPT}) is updated with a decreased value (in Figure 8 example, it means storing the number 3 word, $GPS_{OPT}="011"$), and the VDD is changed accordingly to a higher step value, to maintain circuit operation with no unsafe transitions in the main circuit. Note that GPS is responsible for the coarse grain performance monitoring, while LPSs are in charge of the fine grain performance monitoring and GPS tuning, and that both GPS and LPSs can trigger VDD changes to guarantee an efficient performance and power consumption.

AVS Controller

Figure 9 shows the state diagram of the AVS controller. The initial state is *LOCAL SENSING*, as LPS are always on-line when the circuit is performing its main function. *GLOBAL SENSING* state is triggered sparsely in time (during power-up or triggered from a timer with a low period), or when LPS detect an unsafe data capture ($LPS = 1$). The global sensing operation triggers the GPS analysis on circuit performance, as explained in the previous section. After global sensing operation, if no local sensor was activated ($LPS = 0$) and if the global sensor output code (GPS_{OUT}) is equal to the stored GPS output for the optimized operation (GPS_{OPT}), it means that the current VDD is the optimum value and no action is needed. If local sensors were not activated ($LPS = 0$) and the GPS output code GPS_{OUT} indicates a higher activation level when compared to the stored GPS_{OPT} code ($GPS_{OUT} > GPS_{OPT}$), it means that VDD must be increased, and the register that contains the VDD code (VDD_{OPT}) that will control the DC-DC converter module is changed during the *CHANGE VDD* state. Moreover, if local sensors were not activated and the global sensor output GPS_{OUT} indicates a lower activation level when compared to the stored GPS_{OPT} code ($GPS_{OUT} < GPS_{OPT}$), it means that the current VDD could be lowered to improve power savings, and the register with the current VDD code (VDD_{OPT}) is changed during *CHANGE VDD* state, to optimize circuit operation. However, if local sensors flag an unsafe data capture ($LPS = 1$) and GPS indicates no need to increase VDD ($GPS_{OUT} \leq GPS_{OPT}$), it means that at least one of the circuit's critical path aged faster than the dummy CP, and thus, GPS is no longer tuned with the circuit for a minimum safety margin. In this case, the controller enters the *CHANGE VDD & UPDATE GPS$_{OPT}$* state, the register that contains the VDD code (*VDD$_{OPT}$*) is changed to so that VDD is increased one step through the DC-DC converter, and the stored GPS output for the optimized operation (*GPS$_{OPT}$*) is updated to a safer *GPS$_{OPT}$* value (*GPS$_{OPT}$ = GPS$_{OPT}$ – 1*). Note that if local sensors are flagged (*LPS = 1*) but GPS also indicates that VDD should be increased (*GPS$_{OUT}$ > GPS$_{OPT}$*), the controller enters the *CHANGE VDD* state and only VDD is changed, because it means that GPS is still tuned with the main circuit and the LPS.

IMPLEMENTATION, TESTS, AND RESULTS

In this section, a test circuit will be used to explain and analyze the implementation requirements, restrictions, tests, and to analyze results. The test circuit, or circuit under test (CUT), is named PM4-2, which is a Pipeline Multiplier, with 4 bits (4 bits in each input word), 2 balanced pipeline stages, 9 inputs (8 data, from two input words, and 1 clock), 8 data outputs (one 8-bit output word), 24 Flip-Flops (3 of them were replaced with LPS), and 234 combinational gates. The circuit, sensors and AVS circuitry, are implemented in a proprietary 65nm CMOS technology library, using PTM (Predictive Technology Model) transistors obtained from Arizona State University (2011). Typical nominal conditions for this technology include VDD =1.1V, with T=27°C, and the minimum working power-supply voltage is 0.16V in VDD. Circuit simulations were performed with Synopsys HSPICE simulator, and results are presented in this section.

For complete methodology demonstration, the proposed AVS strategy was implemented in the CUT. The complete implemented test circuit is presented in Figure 10, with its main blocks. Before the circuit was implemented, an aging-aware Static Timing Analysis was performed over the CUT, to identify which of the memory cells are considered critical, i.e., the flip-flops that capture critical paths. In this regard, 3 flip-flops were identified and, therefore, replaced by LPS flip-flops (with their sensor output connected through an OR gate to the AVS controller module). Also, a digitally controlled parametric DC-DC converter was used, with a 3-bit word data input which allows us to define 8 different VDD values, achieving a voltage range from 0.3V to 0.4V (later we will explain why this voltage range has been used). Moreover, in the GPS, 7 Sensor Latches were used in each dummy path. Therefore, a

Figure 9. AVS controller state diagram

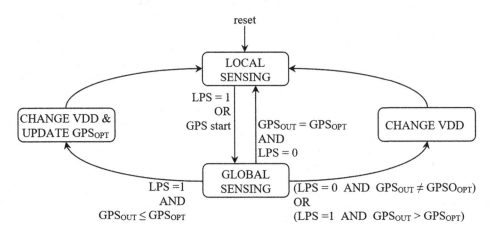

3-word data was used to code the AVS controller registers, both for sensors' safe output and for storing the optimum VDD value.

Implementation Requirements

The implementation of a circuit to work at subthreshold voltages imposes additional requirements. In this case, complex logic gates like Flip-flops, Latches and XOR gates were implemented with pass-transistor logic gates, to allow working at subthreshold voltages. Moreover, for typical combinational logic gates, only 2-input logic gates were used, to avoid gates with more than 2 stacked transistors and, again, allow the circuit to work at subthreshold voltages.

The problem of reducing too much the power-supply voltage is that it may put the circuits in a very vulnerable situation. The sensitivity to several different external and internal factors is huge, due to the very low energy available in the circuit, and especially any small change in VDD, imposed by the AVS controller or induced by external causes (like electromagnetic interference (EMI), or temperature variations), can cause a significant change in circuit delays. Fortunately, aging effects like BTI (Bias Temperature Instability) are reduced, due to the lowered voltages applied to transistors' gates. Because

Figure 10. Block diagram for the Circuit Under Test (CUT)

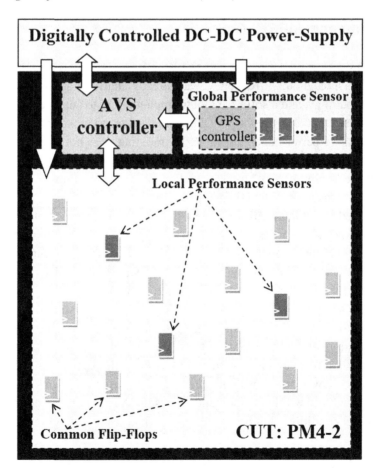

of this, frequency of operation has to be considerably reduced, to accommodate all of the possible delay variations. However, some studies on subthreshold voltage operation (Zhai, Bo et al. (2004)) indicate that working deep in subthreshold operation is energy inefficient. This is because when the clock frequency is hugely reduced, the leakage power consumption becomes dominant. In fact, the time over which a circuit is leaking (delay) grows exponentially in this region, while leakage current itself does not drop as rapidly with reduced VDD, as explained in Zhai, Bo et al. (2004). Therefore, it is important to operate in a very low energy point, to reduce considerably power consumption, but not reducing considerably performance (clock frequency); otherwise, it will be energy inefficient.

Moreover, being aware of the increase on operational risks for subthreshold circuits, care must be taken to contain and minimize the increased negative effects, for example improving shielding around the circuit to minimize external induced delay-faults, and closely controlling the operational conditions of the circuit to minimize operational induced errors. In this regard, the use of both Local and Global performance sensors, and also the increased delay-fault tolerance implemented in LPS (which are used in the critical memory cells of the circuit), as done in the proposed AVS strategy, avoids (or minimizes) delay-fault error occurrence. Nevertheless, it is important to note that, typical IoE applications and IoE sensor applications are not critical, i.e., they do not deal with human lives, and some errors may be acceptable and even corrected at higher abstraction levels (for example, by statistically identifying outliers in a data set collected from IoT sensors). Therefore, it is important to identify a tradeoff between power consumption (to be drastically reduced), and error avoidance and/or prevention.

Power vs. Performance: MERIT Tool

In an authors' previous work (Cavalaria, Hugo et al. (2017)), this optimum balance between power and performance, that is, VDD and clock frequency, was already analyzed and studied. In fact, it was already proposed a methodology, and a software tool to implement it, to analyze automatically circuits at subthreshold operation and to define the best VDD voltage values to maximize power savings, but also working with an acceptable performance (clock frequency) that does not jeopardize circuit operation. The proposed MERIT (cMos EneRgy sImulaTor) tool automatically determines for a circuit, and for each individual gate, the minimum VDD for a correct operation, and the optimal VDD obtained from a tradeoff between power consumption and delay operation.

MERIT was designed to automatically analyze a digital circuit or logic gate, and to characterize it for power dissipation, energy and propagation delays, in respect to the power-supply voltage (VDD). It is based on HSPICE simulations, which are invoked automatically to allow automated multiple circuit simulations and results' analysis. The main purpose of this software tool is to determine the optimum VDD for which the best tradeoff between power and performance is obtained for a given circuit or gate. Whether the analysis is done for a gate, or for a complete circuit, the operation is almost the same, performing multiple parameter simulation testing on a single gate, or on circuits and sub-circuits, by automatically and sequentially simulating all the logic gates of the circuit for multiple parameters. The overall results for the complete circuit are thus obtained, gathered from multiple partial simulations. These multiple and sequential simulations over different logic gates and parameter variations allows to obtain results that are automatically analyzed within the tool, and the results deliver conclusions regarding energy and delay for different initial conditions and parameters. As a final result, the optimum VDD is obtained.

The algorithm used in MERIT to obtain the optimum VDD is based on analyzing the variations in power consumption and delay obtained when VDD is reduced. As power decreases when VDD is reduced, and propagation delays increase, the optimal VDD is obtained by determining the minimum VDD for which the propagation delays are not drastically increased. In more detail, as power and delay have opposite growth trends along VDD variation, the growth trends are normalized and the optimum VDD value is obtained when the distance between these two slopes is minimum, resulting an optimum VDD value, where power is considerably reduced, and the delay is not considerably enhanced.

The MERIT tool was applied to the CUT and all the AVS circuitry included (main circuit in Figure 10, excluding the DC-DC converter) and the results obtained indicated that the optimum VDD is, approximately 0.36V, while the minimum working VDD to guarantee operation in all the cells in the circuit is 0.16V.

Tests and Results

After circuit implementation with the target library, and considering the requirements presented in the previous sections, a series of simulation tests were performed. The first one was to define the voltage and frequency pairs (VDD and clock frequency, f_{CLK}) that puts the circuit, LPS and GPS, always in the same workload, that is: (1) no LPS signalizing (*LPS=0*), but in the eminence of a critical transition detection; and (2) obtaining in the GPS output the code word of "100" (number 4), which indicates that 4 Sensor Latches are signalized (the high sensitive ones), 3 Sensor Latches are not signalized (the less sensitive ones), thus making $GPS_{OPT} = GPS_{OUT} = $ *"100"*. Figure 11 presents all the voltage and frequency pairs when VDD is changed from 0.3V to the nominal VDD of 1.1V. As the clock frequency variation range is high, the frequencies' axis is displayed in logarithmic scale in Figure 11. If we consider the optimum VDD obtained before, 0.36V, the corresponding frequency value for the $GPS_{OPT} = GPS_{OUT} = $ *"100"* is approximately 50 MHz. In contrast, the voltage-frequency pair for the nominal power-supply voltage is VDD = 1.1V / f_{CLK} = 2.1 GHz.

For the voltage and frequency pairs obtained in Figure 11, the power dissipation was also obtained by simulation. Figure 12 represents the power dissipation for each VDD value starting from 0.3V to 1.1V. To help the reader and to allow an easier understanding of the graph, power dissipation is shown

Figure 11. VDD voltage and clock frequency pairs for LPS = 0 and $GPS_{OPT} = GPS_{OUT} = $ "100"

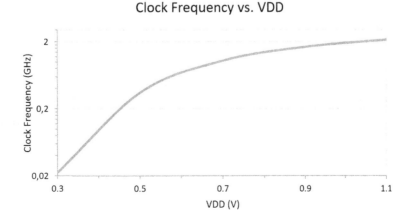

Figure 12. Power Dissipation in respect to VDD, for different voltage and frequency pairs that define $GPS_{OPT} = GPS_{OUT} = \text{"}100\text{"}$

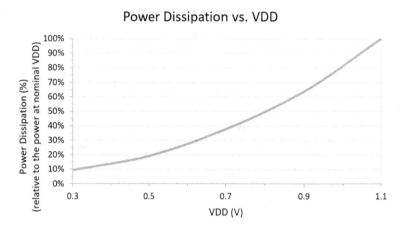

in percentage values, as compared to the power dissipation value obtained for nominal VDD of 1.1V. Therefore, for the highest VDD value, power dissipation is 100%. However, working at a reduced voltage and frequency pair with VDD = 0.3V (and f_{CLK} = 22.2 MHz), circuit is consuming less than 10% of the initial power budget, which is a very interesting result.

Finally, in the last test result presented, it is important to show that the AVS strategy is working correctly, optimizing operation and power consumption and, simultaneously, guaranteeing an error free operation. Figure 13 shows an operation for f_{CLK} = 22.2 MHz, and continuing to use $GPS_{OPT} = \text{"}100\text{"}$. For this test, the DC-DC converter was selected to allow operating in a voltage range from 0.3 to 0.4V, to allow 8 different VDD steps for the AVS controller to control and adjust the power-supply voltage (note that it is out of the scope of this chapter to present the DC-DC converter circuit). The initial VDD value used in the simulation was 0.378V, which corresponds to an initial code word of $VDD_{OPT} = \text{"}100\text{"}$ for the DC-DC converter (note that in Figure 11, for f_{CLK} = 22.2 MHz the corresponding voltage pair is 0.3V, which means that this initial VDD is not the optimum and the AVS controller should detect it). With the starting clock frequency pair of VDD = 0.378V / f_{CLK} = 22.2 MHz, the GPS output word is $GPS_{OUT} = \text{"}100\text{"}$, which means that $GPS_{OPT} \neq GPS_{OUT}$, and circuit operation is not optimized. Therefore, when GPS is activated, the AVS system identifies this non-optimized operation and changes VDD by decreasing the VDD code used, and correspondingly the VDD output value of the DC-DC converter. As we can see in Figure 13, VDD value is being consecutively decreased, starting from 0.378V, then 0.358V, 0.339V, 0.319V, until it reaches the final 0.3V value. With this last VDD value and with the clock frequency of the second 22.2 MHz, we reached the voltage and frequency pair presented in Figure 11, and therefore, $GPS_{OPT} = GPS_{OUT} = \text{"}100\text{"}$, obtained for $VDD_{OPT} = \text{"}000\text{"}$. Finally, as the optimum operation point was reached, unless working and environmental conditions changes, or circuit ages, the AVS system will remain operational in this low energy and optimized operation point. Note that in Figure 13, LPS is always zero, which indicates that no unsafe data transition occurred in the LPS critical flip-flops.

Figure 13. Power Dissipation for VDD reduction

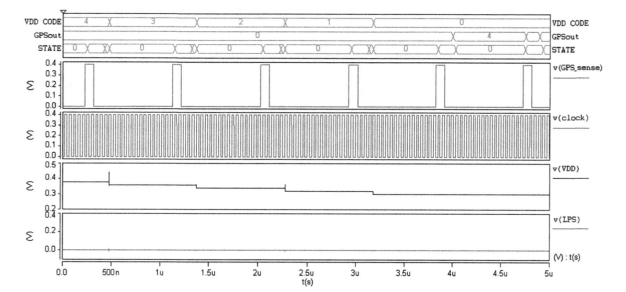

FUTURE RESEARCH DIRECTIONS

Future work includes obtaining silicon data from a test chip already manufactured, to allow characterize LPS and GPS in a real physical implementation. Also, it is important to validate circuit operation at subthreshold voltage levels, and to characterize real power savings obtained from this AVS strategy.

Considering a long-term future research, it is the authors' purpose to implement the proposed AVS strategy and performance sensors in a small general purpose processor, to be used in IoE hardware circuits especially made for IoT sensors and sensor networks. This prospective work also includes an on-going research work on performance sensors for memory circuits, namely, for SRAM and DRAM circuits. As memory usage is increasing in today's chips, occupying the greatest part of a System-on-Chip (SoC) silicon area with figures of around 90% of SoC density, SRAM's robustness and power consumption is considered crucial today. Consequently, semiconductor memory has become the main responsible of the overall SoC area, and also for the active and leakage power in embedded systems. Therefore, the simultaneous use of performance sensors both for logic and memory parts is very important in any AVS strategy. Therefore, the final goal is to produce state-of-the-art sensors and circuits for IoE applications, which can consume nearly zero power while guaranteeing reliable operation.

CONCLUSION

In this chapter, an ultra-low power Adaptive Voltage Scaling (AVS) strategy for subthreshold voltage operation of CMOS digital circuits was presented. The control mechanism of the AVS strategy is based on aging-aware local and global performance sensors, which allow to implement an ultra-low-power strategy for reliable IoE nanoscale integrated circuits. One important result is that all the circuits were especially designed to work at subthreshold power-supply voltage levels, while maintaining a reliable operation in the presence of PVTA variations. Another important aspect of this AVS strategy is that the local and global performance sensors can monitor performance not only in the main circuit but also in the added AVS circuitry (for instance, if a critical path is identified in the GPS controller, a LPS can be used to monitor unsafe transitions in this critical path). Spice simulations for a 65nm CMOS technology show that VDD reductions increase sensors' sensitivity, which shows that sensors are more cautious when errors are more prone to happen due to the reduced voltages used. In addition, by allowing to reduce to subthreshold voltage levels, less than 10% power budget used for nominal conditions is required, by operating in an optimum voltage and frequency pair operation point that allows to highly reduce power consumption but not jeopardizing performance and circuit operation.

REFERENCES

Arizona State University. (2011). *Predictive Technology Model*. Retrieved March 8, 2018, from http://ptm.asu.edu/

Burr, J., & Peterson, A. M. (1991). Ultra low power CMOS technology. *Proceedings of NASA VLSI Design Symposium*, 4.2.1–4.2.13.

Cabral, R., Cavalaria, H., Semião, J., Santos, M., Teixeira, I., & Teixeira, J. P. (2017). Performance Sensor For Subthreshold Voltage Operation. *Proceedings of the 1st INternational CongRess on Engineering and Sustainability in the XXI cEntury - INCREaSE 2017*. DOI: 10.1007/978-3-319-70272-8_31

Calhoun, B. H., Wang, A., & Chandrakasan, A. (2004). Device Sizing for Minimum Operation in Subthreshold Circuits. *Proceedings of the IEEE Custom Integrated Circuits Conference*. 10.1109/CICC.2004.1358745

Calhoun, B. H., Wang, A., & Chandrakasan, A. (2005). Modeling and sizing for minimum energy operation in subthreshold circuits. *IEEE Journal of Solid-State Circuits*, *40*(9), 1778–1786. doi:10.1109/JSSC.2005.852162

Cavalaria, H., Cabral, R., Semião, J., Santos, M., Teixeira, I., & Teixeira, J. P. (2017). Power-Delay Analysis For Subthreshold Voltage Operation. *Proceedings of the 1st INternational CongRess on Engineering and Sustainability in the XXI cEntury - INCREaSE 2017*. DOI: 10.1007/978-3-319-70272-8_30

Chakraborty, S., Mallik, A., & Sarkar, C. K. (2008). Subthreshold performance of dual-material gate CMOS devices and circuits for ultra-low power analog/mixed-signal applications. *IEEE Transactions on Electron Devices*, *55*(3), 827–832. doi:10.1109/TED.2007.914842

Do, A. V., Boon, C. C., Anh, M., Yeo, K. S., & Cabuk, A. (2008). A sub-threshold low-noise amplifier optimized for ultra-low-power applications in the ISM band. *IEEE Transactions on Microwave Theory and Techniques*, *56*(2), 286–292. doi:10.1109/TMTT.2007.913366

Ernst, D., Kim, N. S., Das, S., Pant, S., Rao, R., Pham, T., . . . Mudge, T. (2003). Razor: A Low-Power Pipeline Based on Circuit-Level Timing Speculation. *Proceedings of the 36th Annual IEEE/ACM International Symposium on Microarchitecture (MICRO-36)*. 10.1109/MICRO.2003.1253179

Gauthier, C. R., Trivedi, P. R., & Yee, G. S. (2006). *Embedded Integrated Circuit Aging Sensor System.* Sun Microsystems, US Patent 7054787.

Giustolisi, G., Palumbo, G., Criscione, M., & Cutri, F. (2003). A low-voltage low-power voltage reference based on subthreshold MOSFETs. *IEEE Journal of Solid-State Circuits, 38*(1), 151–154. doi:10.1109/JSSC.2002.806266

Gonzalez, R., Gordon, B., & Horowitz, M. A. (1997). Supply and threshold voltage scaling for low power CMOS. *IEEE Journal of Solid-State Circuits, 32*(8), 1210–1216. doi:10.1109/4.604077

Hanson, S., Seok, M., Sylvester, D., & Blaauw, D. (2008). Nanometer device scaling in sub-threshold logic and SRAM. *IEEE Transactions on Electron Devices, 55*(1), 175–185. doi:10.1109/TED.2007.911033

Keane, J., Kim, T., & Kim, C. (2007). An on-chip NBTI sensor for measuring PMOS threshold volt-age degradation. *Proc. Int. Symp. on Low Power Electronics and Design (ISLPED)*, 189-194.

Keller, S., Bhargav, S., Moore, C., & Martin, A. J. (2011). Reliable Minimum Energy CMOS Circuit Design. *Vari'11: 2nd European Workshop on CMOS Variability.*

Kim, D., Kim, J., Kim, M., Moulic, J., & Song, H. (2009). *System and Method for Monitoring Reliability of a Digital System.* IBM Corp., US Patent 7495519.

Kim, J.-J., & Roy, K. (2004). Double gate MOSFET subthreshold circuit for ultralow power applications. *IEEE Transactions on Electron Devices, 51*(9), 1468–1474. doi:10.1109/TED.2004.833965

Li, M.-Z., Ieong, C.-I., Law, M.-K., Mak, P.-I., Vai, M.-I., & Martins, R. P. (2013). Sub-threshold standard cell library design for ultra-low power biomedical applications. *Engineering in Medicine and Biology Society (EMBC) 2013 35th Annual International Conference of the IEEE*, 1454.

Markovic, D., Stojanovic, V., Nikolic, B., Horowitz, M. A., & Brodersen, R. W. (2004). Methods for True Energy-Performance Optimization. *IEEE Journal of Solid-State Circuits, 39*(8), 1282–1293. doi:10.1109/JSSC.2004.831796

Martins, C. V., Semião, J., Vazquez, J. C., Champaq, V., Santos, M., Teixeira, I. C., & Teixeira, J. P. (2011). Adaptive Error-Prediction Flip-flop for Performance Failure Prediction with Aging Sensors. *Proceedings of the 29th IEEE VLSI Test Symposium 2011 (VTS'11)*. 10.1109/VTS.2011.5783784

Numata, T., & Takagi, S. (2004). Device design for subthreshold slope and threshold voltage control in sub-100-nm fully depleted SOI MOSFETs. *IEEE Transactions on Electron Devices, 51*(12), 2161–2167. doi:10.1109/TED.2004.839760

Radfar, Shah, & Singh. (2012). Recent Subthreshold Design Techniques. *Active and Passive Electronic Components*. doi:. doi:10.1155/2012/926753

Sahu & Eappen Sahu. (2014). Sub-Threshold Logic and Standard Cell Library. *International Journal of Innovative Research in Science, Engineering and Technology, 3*(1).

Semião, J., Cabral, R., Santos, M., Teixeira, I., & Teixeira, P. (2018). Performance Sensor for Reliable Operation. *Proceedings of the 12th International Conference on Universal Access in Human-Computer Interaction (UAHCI), integrated in the 20th HCII*. 10.1007/978-3-319-92052-8_28

Semião, J., Freijedo, J., Rodriguez-Andina, J., Vargas, F., Santos, M. B., Teixeira, I. C., & Teixeira, J. P. (2008). Time Management for Low-Power Design of Digital Systems. Journal of Low Power Electronics. *Special Issue on LPonTR, 4*(3). doi:10.1166/jolpe.2008.194

Semião, J., Pachito, J., Martins, C., Jacinto, B., Vazquez, J., Champac, V., ... Teixeira, J. (2012). Aging-aware Power or Frequency Tuning with Predictive Fault Detection. *IEEE Design & Test of Computers, 29*(5). doi:10.1109/MDT.2012.2206009

Semião, J., Romão, A., Saraiva, D., Leong, C., Santos, M., Teixeira, I., & Teixeira, P. (2014). Performance Sensor for Tolerance and Predictive Detection of Delay-Faults. *Proceedings of the International Symposium on Defect and Fault Tolerance in VLSI and Nanotechnology Systems Symposium 2014 (DFT'14).* DOI: 10.1109/DFT.2014.6962092

Sharma, V. C., Gopalakrishnan, G., & Bronevetsky, G. (2015). Detecting Soft Errors in Stencil based Computations. *11th Workshop on Silicon Errors in Logic - System Effects (SELSE).*

Tschanz, J. (2007). Adaptive Frequency and Biasing Techniques for Tolerance to Dynamic Temperature-voltage Variations and Aging. *Proc. IEEE Int. Solid-State Circ. Conf. (ISSCC)*, 292-293. 10.1109/ISSCC.2007.373409

Vazquez, J. C. (2010). Predictive Error Detection by On-line Aging Monitoring. *Proc. IEEE Int. On-Line Test Symp. (IOLTS)*. 10.1109/IOLTS.2010.5560241

Wilcox, K., Akeson, D., Fair, H. R., Farrell, J., Johnson, D., Krishnan, G., ... White, J. (2015). *4.8 A 28nm x86 APU optimized for power and area efficiency.* IEEE International Solid-State Circuits Conference - (ISSCC) Digest of Technical Papers, San Francisco, CA. 10.1109/ISSCC.2015.7062937

Yoo, H. J. (1998). Dual vt self-timed CMOS logic for low subthreshold current multigigabit syn-chronous DRAM. *IEEE Transactions on Circuits and Systems. 2, Analog and Digital Signal Processing, 45*(9), 1263–1271. doi:10.1109/82.718594

Zhai, B., Blaauw, D., Sylvester, D., & Flautner, K. (2004). *Theoretical and Practical Limits of Dynamic Voltage Scaling.* DAC2004, San Diego, CA. 10.1145/996566.996798

ADDITIONAL READING

Agarwal, M., Paul, B. C., Zhang, M., & Mitra, S. (2007). Circuit Failure Prediction and Its Application to Transistor Aging. *Proceedings of the VLSI Test Symposium (VTS'2007)*, pp. 277-286, Berkeley, CA, USA. 10.1109/VTS.2007.22

Bhardwaj, S., Wang, W., Vattikonda, R., Cao, Y., & Vrudhula, S. (2006). Predictive Modeling of the NBTI Effect for Reliable Design. *Proceedings of the IEEE Custom Integrated Circuits Conference (CICC)*, September 2006. 10.1109/CICC.2006.320885

Grasser, T., Stampfer, B., Waltl, M., Rzepa, G., Rupp, K., Schanovsky, F., ... Kaczer, B. (2018). Characterization and physical modeling of the temporal evolution of near-interfacial states resulting from NBTI/PBTI stress in nMOS/pMOS transistors. *IEEE International Reliability Physics Symposium (IRPS)*. Burlingame, CA, USA, 11-15 March, 2018. DOI: 10.1109/IRPS.2018.8353540

Semião, J., Pachito, J., Martins, C., Santos, M., Teixeira, I., & Teixeira, P. (2012). The Influence of Clock-Gating On NBTI-Induced Delay Degradation. 18th IEEE International On-Line Testing Symposium – IOLTS'12, Sitges, Spain, June 27-29, 2012, DOI: 10.1109/IOLTS.2012.6313842

Semião, J., Romão, A., Leong, C., Santos, M., Teixeira, I., & Teixeira, P. (2014). Aging-Aware Dynamic Voltage or Frequency Scaling. *Proceedings of the XXIX Conference on Design of Circuits and Integrated Systems (DCIS'14)*. Madrid, Spain, November 26-28, 2014. DOI: 10.1109/DCIS.2014.7035599

Vazquez, J.; Champac, V.; Semião, J.; Santos, M.; Teixeira, I. C.; Teixeira, J. P. (2013). Process Variations-aware Statistical Analysis Framework for Aging Sensors Insertion. Journal of Electronic Testing: Theory and Applications (JETTA). On-line first in March, 3, 2013. DOI: . doi:10.100710836-013-5358-z

Wang, W., Yang, S., Bhardwaj, S., Vrudhula, S., Liu, F., & Cao, Y. (2010, February). The Impact of NBTI Effect on Combinational Circuit: Modeling, Simulation, and Analysis. [VLSI]. *IEEE Trans. on Very Large Scale Integration*, *18*(Issue: 2), 173–183. doi:10.1109/TVLSI.2008.2008810

KEY TERMS AND DEFINITIONS

Adaptive Voltage Scaling: A power reduction technique that allows to change the power-supply voltage in a circuit with a high precision parametric variation, and using an efficient feedback loop approach, by measuring workload directly at runtime and immediately act. This technique uses a close loop approach to control the voltage and maintain a low-power operation.

Critical Path: A critical path is the longest combinational path in a circuit, or is the signal path that has the highest delay from the excitation of the path to the path output, or until all the variables in the path are stable.

Dynamic Voltage and Frequency Scaling: A power reduction technique that uses pre-defined voltage and frequency pairs that allow changing power-supply voltage and clock frequency simultaneously, to impose different power consumption and performance operation modes.

Time Slack: Time slack, or slack margin, or just slack, is an available time margin left unused in a clock period, that is, the difference between the clock period and the longest path delay, or critical path delay, in a sequential circuit.

Unsafe Data Capture: Unsafe Data Capture is a data capture in a memory cell (a flip-flop (FF), or a latch, for example) that is in the eminence of a delay-fault error. When signal transitions occur in the data input of an FF that were correctly captured, but in the eminence of an error, we consider that it was an unsafe data capture.

Chapter 12
Security Awareness in the Internet of Everything

Viacheslav Izosimov
Semcon Sweden AB, Sweden

Martin Törngren
iD https://orcid.org/0000-0002-4300-885X
KTH Royal Institute of Technology, Sweden

ABSTRACT

Our societal infrastructure is transforming into a connected cyber-physical system of systems, providing numerous opportunities and new capabilities, yet also posing new and reinforced risks that require explicit consideration. This chapter addresses risks specifically related to cyber-security. One contributing factor, often neglected, is the level of security education of the users. Another factor, often overlooked, concerns security-awareness of the engineers developing cyber-physical systems. Authors present results of interviews with developers and surveys showing that increase in security-awareness and understanding of security risks, evaluated as low, are the first steps to mitigate the risks. Authors also conducted practical evaluation investigating system connectivity and vulnerabilities in complex multi-step attack scenarios. This chapter advocates that security awareness of users and developers is the foundation to deployment of interconnected system of systems, and provides recommendations for steps forward highlighting the roles of people, organizations and authorities.

INTRODUCTION

Joe[1] was driving a long-hauler on his way to Michigan. Suddenly, the truck electronics started acting crazy showing speeds above 90 mph, lots of failures on the display, beeping all over. He pulls off the truck onto the sideway. That day most of the trucks stopped all over the country, not possible to fix or repair on a short notice... This led to goods not being delivered, with empty supermarkets, empty gas stations, stopped production plants, and other economically negative consequences. What was the reason for these events? A good friend recommended installing a great app for fuel consumption monitoring.

DOI: 10.4018/978-1-5225-7332-6.ch012

Joe did and so did many drivers. The app was helpful until the very last update... Luckily, some trucks were still operational and the reserve vehicles were put to help.

The system will not be more secure than the knowledge in security of its creators. Security knowledge and awareness of engineers that implement or install a system can be as critical as the choice of a crypto algorithm and a proper key management infrastructure. Security-awareness of system users and operators are critical to ensure that the system is not compromised. Irrespective of the technical quality, any solution becomes effectively unsecure if the user leaks out passwords or blindly accepts installation of malicious software.

The focus of this chapter will be on smart cyber-physical systems (CPS) in Internet of Things (IoT) that provide services critical for society. Examples of these smart systems include connected passenger cars, intelligent transportation systems, smart household appliances and alike. This chapter considers them together with their drivers, operators, installation engineers and other persons directly and indirectly involved into their creation and during operation. These systems live in the Internet or exist as part of an era of connectivity and dependencies represented by infrastructures such as 3G/4G/5G, global navigation and positioning systems, providing and requesting services. The IoTs are nowadays part of infrastructures in healthcare, energy, transportation and many others. The level of interaction in these infrastructures has increased substantially with advances in development and enhancement of "clouding", connecting to and making use of cloud computing services. This type of connectivity nowadays raises concerns for robustness and trustworthiness. A fault or a malicious attack on one of system's components, even the least critical at first glance, may affect other, critical, ones. A trend is, thus, emerging towards "edge computing", as a way to decentralize the cloud and reduce some of the risks associated with the clouding. For example, Satyanarayanan et al. (2013) advocate for cloudlets as a viable connectivity alternative to clouds in hostile environment, ultimately considering the whole Internet or its parts as possibly hostile, e.g. in the event of a cyberwar, natural disaster or during military operations.

The chapter will also look into examples of "not yet smart" systems and will advocate that they must be designed with the same level of security requirements as those connected to the Internet. Otherwise, these "not yet smart" systems pose potential serious threats to society when they unintentionally find their ways to the connected world, in situations often unexpected. In a modern society, it is nearly impossible to avoid these connections, due to actions of users, due to system complexity and sometimes due to security negligence of system developers.

According to the Roundtable on Cyber-Physical Security, Peisert et al. (2014), developers and users are responsible for security of an embedded product. Tariq, Brynielsson & Artman (2014) studied the problem of users' security awareness in where they conducted a number of semi-structured interviews in a large telecommunication organization.

The authors of this chapter decided to use a similar approach to evaluate security-awareness of developers, engineers and academics, by conducting a number of interviews and surveys. The chapter will give some insight into the study of user awareness in a user-centric survey.

To evaluate state of practice in security of existing systems, authors conducted two practical attacks feasible, in particular, due to security-unawareness of system developers and users. The attacks involve a connected smart product, a modern commercial vehicle, e.g. Joe's truck, and an off-line critical facility.

The objectives of this chapter are to:

- Present background and relevant literature on cyber-physical security and security awareness;

- Present and discuss results of the authors' interview study with developers and security experts (with the short version published in Izosimov & Törngren (2016));
- Present and discuss results of the authors' survey study with developers and users (with the short version published in Izosimov & Törngren (2016));
- Present and evaluate two practical attack scenarios, for a smart connected car and for an offline facility (more detailed version is published in Izosimov et al. (2016));
- Discuss a possible course of action for organizations and authorities, with focus on development and usage of embedded smart products and connected services;
- In addition, tell stories to give some insights to educational effort towards developers and to the development environments in large- and medium-size companies;
- And, finally, list examples of the attacks matched against the security-awareness and roles of developers and users (operators).

BACKGROUND

Evolving of Internet of Things (IoTs) pose substantial security challenges both technically and with respect to the users and developers. For example, Elkhodr, Shahrestani & Cheung (2013) discussed several possible attacks in IoTs, considering such specific IoT aspects as object naming, interoperability and identity management. Roman, Najera & Lopez (2011) highlighted challenges for dealing with security in IoTs, in particular, those related to scalability of solutions and dramatically increased amount of interactions. In some special cases of IoTs, for example, in smart power grids, security was considered on a physical connectivity level, Lee, Gerla & Oh (2012), and at a system level, Mo et al. (2012) and Cui et al. (2012). Mo et al. (2012) presented an interesting attack model for smart power grid systems. In Cui et al. (2012), a particular case for coordinated data-injection attack on power grid was discussed. Authors suggested a detection mechanism for this attack and pointed out the fact that the attack detection can be computationally sophisticated for a large grid. This is, in fact, one of the greatest challenges in any IoT infrastructure. IoT complexity makes it hard to have full technical understanding of smart product and services. MSB (2014) presented guidelines on security processes in industrial automation, where people played a great role. This report is a good reference to practical implementation of IoTs for industrial automation domain.

In IoT systems, "software security" plays an important role. In particular, risks related to software, Peisert et al. (2014), Sobel & McGraw (2010), Li et al. (2014), are seen as one of the largest contributing factors to lack of security in the overall system. Complexity, heterogeneity and complex software frameworks make software essentially critical for system security. At the same time, software tools drastically reduce threshold and minimize time needed for an attacker to prepare an efficient attack on a software level. In recent past, however, hardware security started to gain a momentum, not least due to increased hardware complexity, largely distributed development and manufacturing chains. For example, a whole variety of hardware manipulation methods were established, from a simple hardware counterfeit, Leest & Tuyls (2013) to highly sophisticated Hardware Trojans, Mitra, Wong & Wong (2015), Tehranipoor & Koushanfar (2010), Tsoutsos & Maniatakos (2014). This triggered US Government to react and to establish new trade policies for hardware, Mitra, Wong & Wong (2015). The third one, communication security was always a great concern for research community. Researchers documented and studied attacks on various communication protocols, network infrastructures and interfaces, on military communications, Stillman & DeFiore (1980), mobile networks, Zhang & Fang (2005), wireless, Sakarindr & Ansari (2007), peer-to-peer interfaces such as Bluetooth, Carettoni, Merloni & Zanero (2007), Dunning (2010) and attacks on supporting functions such as GPS, Larcom & Liu (2013).

However, a majority of attacks in IoTs and cyber-physical systems (CPS) involve more than a single attack "type", are often very sophisticated and done in several steps. Complexity of attacks was outlined in, for example, Kwon, Liu & Hwang (2013), where a tight connection to physical environment in a stealthy deception attack on CPS systems was pointed out. In the cyber-world, a related example is a distributed denial-of-service (DDoS) attack or flooding attack, Eom et al. (2008), where attackers follow an "attack tree" structure, trying different attack paths until either an attack is successful or is detected. In cyber-physical and IoT worlds, attacks are not only complex but they are also very heterogeneous, often with high involvement of human actors in a number of different roles.

In this chapter, security evaluation is based on Anderson (2008) book, which provides insights into both cyber and embedded aspects of security. The book contains a number of inspiring examples interesting for both researchers and practitioners. Further, the security understanding is complemented with the latest publications on a number of hackers' forums, BlackHat conference outlines and the Escar conference recent publications on security in automobiles.

A governmental organization in the UK conducted a study similar to the study presented in this book chapter. The UK study covers the cyber-security domain (at a country level) targeting the security awareness of the organizations and their management, GOV.UK (2018). However, the UK study does not cover embedded and cyber-physical systems, nor IoT systems. This book chapter uses a similar approach from the research point of view but applies it to embedded systems domain, e.g. interviews and surveys, further extending the scope with the practical evaluation of attack scenarios. Note, however, that the statistical methods used in the UK cyber-security study are not applicable to the work presented in this book chapter due to small population sizes. Authors of this book chapter did not have comparable resources to the governmental organizations for covering all the organizations across the country. The study presented in this book chapter provides motivation why these studies are necessary and should be sponsored and initiated by the governmental authorities to evaluate security awareness of both users and developers of IoT systems. The present study advocates for the need of regular (on a yearly basis) representative public studies within the IoT embedded and cyber-physical system domain, similar in size to the UK cyber-security study, because the study information is critical for planning prioritized measures on a country level towards overall national cyber-security resilience. Political decisions and budget spending must be motivated by the objective facts and not by the subjective and often bias guesses.

Back to 2006, Manjak (2006) conducted a study on using social engineering to increase cyber-security awareness of users of personal computers and the university computer network. In this study, the University at Albany, the State University of New York (SUNY), put a lot of effort into reducing security incidents by informing and "engineering" students and employees to adapt proper computer usage, to learn computer ethics and to comply with basic principles of cyber-security hygiene. The first attempt failed, with barely no effect demonstrated. The users tend not to accept the guilt and blamed the IT department and computers' software for permitting infections. However, the first failed attempt played a critical role in enabling the second attempt, a lot more successful. In the second attempt to increase security-awareness, SUNY decided to use more interactive methods and even involved basketball players of the local team to propagate the important information to students. The effort also propagated to the employees of the campus. The measurement of the second attempt revealed drastically reduced number of cyber-security incidents, at students' personal computers, employees' computers and for the overall computer network. Further, users demonstrated a lot less risky network behavior that contributed to the overall positive outcome. Hence, the education of users played a significant role in the increase of their security-awareness. As human beings do not change whether they work with the personal computer or an IoT device, the findings should re-apply onto the domain of embedded and cyber-physical systems. The increase in security-awareness requires education and an overall information strategy, in the case of this book chapter, the education and the strategy at the national level.

While a (limited) number of security-awareness studies for IT cyber-security are available for general public and researchers, e.g. GOV.UK (2018), Manjak (2006), authors could not find studies on security-awareness of developers and users of embedded and cyber-physical systems in IoT. To the best of the authors' knowledge, the study in this book chapter appears to be one of the first of its kind targeting embedded and cyber-physical IoT systems.

The authors have, however, found evidences for the existence of similar studies. For example, the ENISA (2017) report provides evidences of a study on security-awareness in the IoT domain while omitting the study details directly summarizing the conclusions. The ENISA report conclusions confirm findings of the authors of this book chapter, and will be matched against authors' findings in Conclusions. Another example is the study from Japan, IPA (2010), proving recommendations for developers and users of IoT systems, where the awareness is in focus. Similar examples are the more recent recommendations such as ACEA (2017). ACEA (2017) guidelines dedicate the whole section to training of security-awareness. National Institute of Standards and Technology (NIST) at the US Department of Commerce has an extensive program for IoT security, NIST (2018). The Draft NISTIR 8228, for example, states, "Many organizations are not necessarily aware of the large number of IoT devices they are already using and how IoT devices may affect cybersecurity and privacy risks differently than conventional information technology (IT) devices do." The source of this statement is not provided. However, it may point to the publically-unavailable security-awareness studies within the NIST. In 2017, in Sweden, Swedish Civil Contingencies Agency (MSB) organized a seminar on security awareness, partly considering security awareness in the IoT systems (the material is available online in MSB (2017)). Thus, the importance of security-awareness of developers and users of IoT systems is clearly perceived as an issue, yet very little detailed information is available about the level of security awareness. Further, a number of organizations offer a great chunk of programs for security trainings to increase security-awareness as, for example, in the healthcare sector with many of these programs targeting IoT and embedded systems. Hence, the authors dedicate this book chapter to bridge this information gap on security awareness even if the study in this book chapter as such is limited to a small portion of population.

Examples of attacks against embedded and cyber-physical IoT systems are highlighted in Appendix 3, with awareness of developers and users helping to prevent these attacks.

INTERVIEWS

This section presents interview study on developers' understanding of embedded security, evaluating responses from security experts in the area since they are the ones who spread the security knowledge and setup directions of future development in the security domain. The interview study is limited to 15 individuals and serve as an introduction to the topic of security awareness. 15 respondents is a too small portion of the population to make statistically significant conclusions.

At first, the goal of the interview study was to see the present status of embedded security understanding in industry, by managers and developers responsible for development of products and services. Second, the interview study compared understanding of embedded security between respondents from industry and academia. In the interviews, the authors use two questionnaires for academic and non-academic (industry, service organizations, authorities, etc.) audience with 8 questions. In total, the authors interviewed 10 non-academic respondents (from transportation, telecom, healthcare and machine industry) and 5 academic (from universities and a research institute), sending out more than 50 questionnaires. In general, the questionnaire triggered a large interest in the organizations.

The interviews were conducted in the period from October to December 2014. The questions were sent out in advance and most of the respondents had time to prepare their answers (and even ask for permissions from managers). The interviews were performed anonymous with the direct textual transcription of the answers such that the answers could not be linked to a particular respondent or their organization, via the voice, pictures, or by any other means. Most of the interviews were performed face-to-face; authors had two respondents together in one of the interviews (counted as a single respondent in the study); and one interview was conducted over telephone. Each interview took about one hour, with some, however, lasting for as much as 3 hours and with some as short as 20 minutes.

Question 1: What Do You Consider as Main Security Threats for Your Products / Services? How Have You Identified These Threats?

The rationale behind this question was to trigger discussion with the respondent and to evaluate in an "open" fashion relation of the respondent to security in general and to embedded security in particular. The question was complemented during discussion with requests for confirmation on importance of system-level, software-level and hardware-level security. The relation to the actual product or services was important in case of a non-academic respondent. Many of the respondents took the question with a bit of uncertainty on what the actual answer can be, that is, what is "between the lines". However, after some clarification, the discussion could start and usually respondents felt more comfortable closer to the end of the interview.

Most of the respondents considered computer security important for products and services, except the only one who claimed that, because his/her products are not connected to the Internet, considering embedded or computer security is not necessary.

In total, 14 respondents out of 15 considered computer security important. Several of respondents pointed out advanced persistent threat (APT) as one of the main threats to their products and organizations. In particular, not because of the APT as such but because other attackers (for example, criminal organizations) can utilize holes and backdoors identified or created by APT. One respondent claimed that one large APT has a record of about 2000 unreported holes in common operating systems such as Windows or Linux. Another respondent claimed that another APT had installed a similar amount of backdoors into embedded systems as a measure to counterbalance the first APT in case of a potential cyber-war.

Respondents pointed out "usual criminals" and criminal organizations are one of the most common attackers even for embedded systems. According to respondents, the organizations themselves and employees can also act intentionally or unintentionally as attackers on products of their customers. One respondent pointed out that, in general, individuals with the ability to create dangerous software, both intentionally and unintentionally, can become part of an attack if they themselves use the software (or someone else uses their software to conduct an attack). These individuals that "play" can become a source of an attack, often unintentionally. The respondent provided curious scanning of ports on a PLC (Programmable Logic Controller) of a power station as an example. It can lead to overload of that PLC and cause a failure of that station with substantial economic consequences.

To the surprise, terrorists were not named as one of the major attack sources. Respondents claimed that the physical terrorist attack is still scarier to general public than an online attack from an unknown source. According to the respondents, the terrorists are the only ones who want to happily risk or even miss their lives during an attack. The online terrorist attack does not offer this possibility, or, at least, this is not possible directly.

With respect to attacks on individuals and their privacy, a variety of home services were named as one of the main attack sources expected to grow in future.

Some of the respondents claimed that basically everyone is a potential source of an attack, intentionally or unintentionally. The source of this attack will be exceptionally hard to trace and link to this particular teenager.

With respect to a technical "attack level", the majority of respondents see system-level, software-level or communications as the ones responsible for the most of security violations. Hardware related security problems, however, were claimed as "exotic" and "an academic exercise", not connected to real-life.

The following citation can summarize the discussion on Question 1:

"If we, Europeans, are afraid of external attacks, in North America, they are afraid of own employees and, in India, they are afraid of their suppliers."

Thus, the subjective factor of fear and social and national background play often an important role in naming a potential source of attack, which should be accounted for in constructing a globally balanced attack vector for embedded systems in IoTs.

With regard to the second part of the question "How have you identified these threats?" respondents had difficulty to point out direct sources. Among identifications of the threats, respondents used public sources, incident reporting within their organizations, conducted their own reasoning, information from red alert teams, information obtained from public incident databases. Some used "stomach feeling" and some did not provide information about sources of their conclusions at all.

Question 2: How Does Your Organization Handle Security Threats?

With respect to this question, 9 out of 15 respondents had a clear strategy on acting upon identified security threats. However, only 5 out of 15 suggested suitable efficient methods to react quickly upon the detected threat. In particular, respondents from telecom were the best, with clear examples on acting and defeating threats that could affect their products. Many organizations, however, had it difficult to imagine the necessary steps to prioritize critical threats and run escalation procedures.

One of the best answers included dedicated response teams and mechanisms for triggering alert sequences, clear routings for incident response and corporate policies. Some had even a dedicated security competence centrum, which permanently works with the security threats and ensures a proper education of organization personnel to be able to react quickly and efficiently. One of the answers also suggested securing intrusion information for tracing and identification of attackers.

Other answers included suggestions of stopping writing code in C and using Java instead. Some suggested that corporate management should take clear security responsibility and it is important to stop "placing data on people" who cannot be trusted. Some respondents suggested regular updates as a primary measure to deal with security issues, some wanted to build-in security from the beginning such that "things would run smoothly on their own" without any intervention.

This citation can summarize the results obtained on Question 2: "The worst that can happen. If nothing happens for a while and suddenly everything collapses and you don't know why." That recalls Joe's story with his truck.

Question 3: How Do You Identify and Follow Up on New Security Attacks? Perform Analysis of Their Criticality?

Question 3 is related to Question 2 and was supposed to support the discussion arisen from the previous question. According to authors' evaluation, 10 of 15 respondents work to classify and identify new threats, which is somewhat better than in the case of Question 2. Answers included dedicated response teams that work on scanning for identification of potentially related attacks and doing prioritization. Some have dedicated processes in the organization that are regularly executed to identify new relevant threats and propagate the information throughout the organization. Some do "hacking" of the own software. Some acquire (or even buy) attack software and develop it further to perform assessment of their own products. Many respondents participate in forums and conferences, dedicated security societies and communities, read research articles and online forum publications. Some have a number of research projects on security and supply M.Sc. thesis students with security evaluation assignments. Many (but not all) perform risk analysis and do cost estimations, that is, to react or not on the attack. However, 5 out of 15 respondents (including the one who does not consider security important) do not do much for following up on the new threats.

With respect to the second part of the question "Perform analysis of their criticality?" answers of the respondents were rather limited. In some more advanced cases, e.g. from telecom, the red alert team dictated the criticality and set deadlines to fix the breach identified. Several respondents answered "everything is critical". Other respondents pointed out incident databases for criticality levels. In general, the majority of the respondents had difficulty to answer on this part of the question.

Question 4: How Important Embedded Security for Your Organization Compared to IT Security / Cybersecurity?

With this question, the idea was to clarify relationship between embedded security and cyber-/IT-security. Discussion also included evaluation whether respondents differentiate between these two "securities". 3 out of 15 thought that IT security is the same as embedded security (including the one who did not consider security important). 5 out of 15 were sure that embedded security is different from IT security. 7 out of 15 were not sure about the relationship.

With respect to importance of embedded security versus cyber-security, 3 out of 15 considered that cyber-security is the most important and, the same, 3 out of 15, considered that embedded security is, instead, the most important. Other, 9 out of 15 considered that both "securities" are equally important (or unimportant according to that one respondent that did not consider security important for his/her product because of no connectivity).

To summarize the answer, "there is no border line" any longer as one of the respondents stated.

Question 5: Which Security Attributes Are the Most Important for Your Product / Service? How Do You Ensure "Traceability" of This Attribute in Development, Operation and Maintenance?

With this question authors wanted to identify which attributes are the most important to the respondents, in particular, according to CIA (Confidentiality, Integrity and Availability) classification. Most of the respondents had a clear idea about these attributes. 9 out of 15 stated that all three attributes are equally important. Other, remaining answers, included:

- Integrity alone was the most critical for one respondent and availability was the most critical for another one.
- Intellectual property was named once.
- Reliability was critical for the one that considered security as not important.
- One respondent pointed out "trademark" as the most critical.
- Importance of accountability was also emphasized.

One respondent had an interesting perspective with respect to customers' view on security attributes. According to him/her "customers do not have a foggiest idea what is important for security – it is important to them that things should run smoothly".

Majority of respondents were united on importance of classification of all the threat vectors according to CIA, performing CIA ranking. A few respondents also stated that for individual applications, CIA weights could be different.

With respect to the second part of the question "How do you ensure "traceability" of this attribute in development, operation and maintenance?" again respondents found it difficult to answer. Internal processes were pointed out as one possible answer and to integrate security from the beginning into the development process was another "good" answer. The majority of the respondent again could not provide a clear answer on the second part of the question.

Question 6: If Relevant, What Is the Relation Between Security and Safety for Your Products / Services?

Purpose of this question was to study interrelation between safety and security. Majority of respondents (9 out of 15) see a clear connection between security and safety, especially for embedded systems. 6 out of 15, however, either do not work with safety-critical products (for example, in case of telecom) or do not see a clear connection (including the one that does not consider security important). In particular, some of these answers included "all is safety – no security", "we have not seen safety issues due to security problems" and "for our system, the relation is not very clear". To summarize the majority of answers, an interesting statement was provided from a healthcare domain: "huge risk when you put this thing into a human body" when talking about embedded systems used in transplants and connected automated insulin injectors.

Question 7: Which Security Standards Exist in Your Application Domain? And Question 8: Which of These Standards Do You Use for Your Products / Services?

The purpose with these questions was to identify important security standards (including safety standards that contain security-related clauses). Originally, authors' separated these questions in the discussion, for the standards that exist in the domain and for the standards that are, actually, in use by the respondents. It turned out that these two questions could be merged into a single question. For those who did not use security standards, existence of them was not important. Those who knew about standards existence were, actually, using the standards that they knew about. The lists of existing standard and standards in use were almost identical. In addition, academic respondents were not interested in standards at all. On contrary, industry respondents were very much interested in standards. Even the one who did not consider security important for his/her product (see the discussion in Question 1) was clear that, if the security standard existed in his/her domain, then it would be used.

To summarize, 9 out of 15 use standards at least on a "business level". Of those 9, 7 use "technical" security standards. 5 out 15 do not use any security standard and do not consider them important (4 out of those 5 were, in fact, academics). The remaining 1 respondent was the one who considered security standards important but did not have them in his/her domain and that is why was not using them. The majority of respondents were using ISO 27000 family of standards (on a "business level"). From technical standards, respondents named encryption standards, NIST standards, common criteria, CWE (Common Weakness Enumeration), IEC 61508 (with a clause on security for safety), IEC 62443, ISO 17799, SS-3492, FDA "thresholds" (that include even security aspects), security protocols from the suppliers and few other alternatives.

INTERVIEW SUMMARY AND SURVEY STUDY

The overall summary of the interview study is presented in the "Interviews" column in Table 1. In particular, only 33% consider valid security methods and, respectively, follow up on new threats. Less than 50% use security standards during technical work (it can be attributed to lack of security standards in many areas). Respondents did not consider hardware-based attacks seriously despite evidences and US export regulations.

During the work in the interview study, it became clear that industry is attracted to questions of embedded security, while more work is necessary to distribute the security knowledge. Hence, it was proposed to organize a larger industrial event. Academic and industry speakers, knowledgeable in security, were invited. In particular, speakers were invited who could give introduction into hardware security topic. About 100 participants registered, with the majority coming from industry and some from academia and other organizations. Authors summarized talks of the event, discussed with the speakers, asked questions of interest and conducted the survey study presented in this section.

During introduction to the conference, main outcomes from the interview study were presented and conference participants were requested to complete survey to re-validate the findings. In columns "Survey" in Table 1, authors outline results obtained. The greatest differences are in questions (2), (9) and (10). The respondents of the survey were more uncertain about their security strategies and considered less security standards in business and technical levels. The reason for lower numbers of security standards

Table 1. Summary of interviews (15 respondents) and survey (55 respondents – all, academic and industry), % yes answers

Topic	Interviews	Survey (All)	Survey (Acad.)	Survey (Ind.)
1. Security is important	93	95	100	98
2. Use a valid and clear security strategy	60	29	13	27
3. Consider valid security methods	33	44	38	42
4. Classify and identify new threats	66	45	50	35
5. Follow up on new threats	33	46	63	35
6. Embedded and IT security are equally important	60	96	100	98
7. CIA attributes are all important	60	63	63	60
8. Safety can be affected by security threats	60	98	100	98
9. Use security standards: business level	60	17	25	13
10. Use security standards: technical level	47	12	13	13

can be that, during interviews, respondents could clarify what it was meant with the security standards and could elaborate more, which could have effect. The final survey result is, nevertheless, alarming, especially for use of the standards.

Interestingly, 96% considered embedded and IT security equally important and 98% that safety can be affected by security threats. It was only 60% for both in the interview study. This case can be attributed to way the interviews were conducted, when, during discussion, respondents could bring up their multi-grained view of the problem. Usage of valid security methods was slightly increased to 44% (from 33% in the interview study). Still the number is rather low. With respect to threats, for threat classification and following new threats, 45 and 46% were obtained, respectively, which can be considered somewhat similar to the interview study with 66 and 33% (considering similarity of the questions, 66 and 33% would effectively produce average of 50%). Thus, about 50% do not work with the security threats, which is alarming, considering that this is an independent outcome from the interviews and the survey.

Authors were interested to compare relationship between academic and industrial respondents. The comparison is shown in Table 1, "Survey (Acad.)" against "Survey (Ind.)". The results match well except two questions related to classification and following on new threats. For academic respondents, 50 and 63% identify and follow new threats, while for industry, this is only 35%. This makes findings even more alarming, e.g. only 1/3 of industry respondents work with security threats. This means that, to transfer to Joe's example, his truck may well be one of the trucks without functionality to withstand new types of security attacks, and can easily fall a victim to an emerging attack category!

With respect to a technical "attack level", the majority of interview respondents see system-level, software-level or communications as the ones responsible for the most of security violations. Hardware related security problems, however, were claimed as "exotic" and "an academic exercise", not connected to real-life. This is not true since a number of issues were reported with respect to hardware counterfeits Leest & Tuyls (2013), hardware backdoors, Tsoutsos & Maniatakos (2014), and alike, and import regulations were even introduced by the United States against counterfeited hardware components Mitra, Wong & Wong (2015).

Authors also wanted to study views on the attackers. Initially, the categories of attackers were obtained from the interview study. Several of respondents pointed out advanced persistent threat (APT), e.g. attackers with large resources like countries, as one of the main threats to their products and organizations. In particular, not because of the APT as such but because other attackers (for example, criminal organizations) can utilize holes and backdoors identified or created by APT. APTs are not interested to close these holes since they use the holes for their own purposes. Criminals and criminal organizations were named as one of the most common attackers even for embedded systems according to the respondents. They have relatively large resources and courage to conduct variety of attacks with the purpose to make money out of it. The organizations themselves and employees can also act intentionally or unintentionally as attackers on products of their customers. An employee can attack his/her organization for one reason or another due to, for example, conflict at work or urgent need of money. Individuals with the ability to create dangerous software (e.g. hackers or crackers), both intentionally and unintentionally, can become part of an attack if they themselves use the software (or someone else uses their software to conduct an attack). For example, curious scanning of ports on a PLC (Programmable Logic Controller) of a power station can lead to overload of that PLC and cause a failure of that station with substantial economic consequences.

Similar to the interview study, terrorists were not named as one of the major attack sources. The general claim here was that the physical terrorist attack is still scarier to general public than an online attack from an unknown source. Another reason is also that terrorists are the only attackers who want to happily risk or even miss their lives during an attack, while the online terrorist attack does not offer this possibility, at least, not directly.

The list of attackers was extended with competitors and users, who might potentially either initiate the attacks or become a part of the attack scenario.

Authors systematized list of attackers and formed survey questions for evaluation. The results from the survey study are presented in Table 2, columns "Acad." and "Ind.". As can be seen, "hackers" are leading with 63% for industry and 88% academia. The second place is competitors, 46 and 50%, respectively. The third place is users, with 44 and 38%. This finding is rather controversial. Organizations consider their main users as a threat to their businesses and products! Academic respondents also consider more of other types of attacks (38%) than industry (17%). Advanced Persistent Threat (APT) is considered

Table 2. Considered attackers by survey respondents (academic, industry and users), %

Attackers	Acad.	Ind.	Users
1. Advanced Persistent Threat (APT)	13	7	14
2. Terrorists	25	20	7
3. Hackers	88	63	68
4. Users	38	44	14 (21)
5. Employees (in case of users "Colleagues")	25	17	7
6. Competitors	50	46	-
7. Others	38	17	11
Criminals were pointed out as the most common type of attackers in the interview study (while were purposely omitted in the survey). They were, for example, more "popular" than the "Others" category in the survey. 57% of users also consider that criminals are a common type of attackers. Survey and interview studies are complementary.			

as rather lower priority attacker category for both academic and industry respondents, while is ranked high for other organizations (second highest after hackers). Note also that authors purposely omitted criminals, which were pointed out as the main category of attackers in the interview study, to study the level of influence on the audience in the survey. Interestingly, criminals were not pointed out by any of the respondents (there was a possibility to write additional information) and the "others" is still 22% (considering all 55 respondents). 22% is less than the level of "popularity" of criminals in the interview study. This shows that surveys should be used carefully and results from the survey are necessary to complement with the detailed interviews, highlighting fine-grained aspects in the answers.

Finally, authors were interested to know opinion about inclusion of security-related information into user manuals, since according to the opinion of the authors, users must be aware of security implications due to smart products that they use. 89% of respondents in the survey study considered that manuals must include security-related information. According to check on the present manuals, however, manufacturers and service providers, for some reason, do not provide sufficient security related information to the users. This is clearly an indication that possible security risks can arise due to users' unawareness of the fact that the products that they use can be maliciously manipulated or due to resulting lack of knowledge on possible countermeasures. To follow up this question, authors have conducted additional survey study targeting users of smart systems.

The user-related survey included 28 respondents from the younger generation that use smart products every day. The following results were obtained (in % Yes answers) as shown in Table 3.

Authors could conclude that users are aware about security. However, very small fraction of users is aware of security recommendations for their smart products (32%) and, as the result, only 29% consider these recommendations sufficient and only 14% follow the recommendations. 96% of respondents consider essential providing of security information into the user manuals. To transfer to Joe's example, only few of the truck drivers would follow security recommendations!

Finally, a common misconception is that users are the most concern about their privacy. As this survey illustrates, this is not true. Only 46% consider privacy attacks more critical than integrity attacks. A quested was also added about attackers into the survey. Part of the results is depicted in Table 2, column "Users". Hackers are on top of the list. Then, in fact, criminals have received 57% (criminals are omitted in Table 2). This matches well the interview study outcome. Users consider themselves as attacker as well but only 14% (compare to 44% as perceived by the industry). 21% of respondents consider also that other users are attackers. Advanced Persistent Threat (APT) has obtained 14%. Colleagues and terrorists obtained the same value of 7% each. Further, 11% of users consider relatives as potential attackers.

Table 3. Users survey, %

Do you consider security important for your personal devices and all systems that you use at home and while in public?	96%
Are you aware of security recommendations for these devices?	32%
Do you consider these security recommendations sufficient?	29%
Do you follow these security recommendations?	14%
Do you agree that product user manuals (guides) should provide security information to you?	96%
In your devices, do you consider attacks against privacy more critical than against integrity? (**integrity:** absence of improper system alterations – potentially hazardous)	46%

In the interviews and survey, due to very limited population base, authors could not find it possible to differentiate between different industries without disclosure of the anonymity of the respondents or without falling into a trap of making generalizations from too small samples. However, authors would like to point out telecommunication industry that clearly demonstrated superiority in the security-awareness; authors could trace this superiority in the survey exercise as well. Not only telecommunication industry, most industries will contribute to the IoT products and, consequently, to their security. Engineers with security background in telecommunication are presently hot on the job market and attractive due to their understanding of the cyber-security. New upcoming regulations, customer requests or attacks faced force IoT companies, both new start-ups and traditional, to obtain staff competences in the security for IoT systems.

Authors wrote two small stories on how security knowledge and awareness can propagate between industries in Appendix 1 and Appendix 2. The story in Appendix 1 tells about inter-industrial knowledge exchange and security awareness training activity organized by the governmental agency. In that story, governmental agency contributed to establishing the knowledge transfer and enabling the education effort for security-awareness. The story is Appendix 2 tells about security knowledge transfers between industries and successive increase of security-awareness within a given industry (with automotive as an example) once started. The story in Appendix 2 also outlines the environment that many developers face in their companies with lack of resources and support for security activities. Security awareness at all levels, starting from the top management, play an important role for making a reasonably secure product or providing a service with a good security level. In that story both media and research contributed to success and knowledge transfers from other industries and academia.

TWO EXAMPLES OF PRACTICAL ATTACKS

To evaluate practical aspects of attacking embedded systems, the authors studied an app attack on a modern smart car and an attack on an offline critical facility.

App Attack on a Modern Car

In this section, an app attack on a modern smart car will be presented (authors have studied this attack in collaboration with one large automotive manufacturer).[2] First, the attacker creates a malicious app that bypasses security mechanisms of Google App Store or Apple App Store. Second, through social engineering the attacker encourages users to download the app on their mobile phones, using ads, twits and similar. Third, mobile phone, when it is connected via a wireless interface to a car (via Bluetooth, for example), performs scanning of connection profiles, looking for possible backdoors. When one or more backdoors are identified, the app is updated with the new functionality (to explore that backdoor) across multiple mobile phones.

The next step now is to perform modifications of the infotainment cluster. Since a limited number of suppliers provide implementation of the cluster and standard solutions are often used (Linux, Android, iOS or QNX), the already known "attack portfolio" can be re-used. When the infotainment cluster is hijacked and software is updated, there will be a number of interesting options available by showing incorrect fuel level, incorrect speed, motor temperature, activating microphone to listen to communication inside the car, creating a number of sounds (for example, a crash sound, which will force the driver to act dangerously), etc. Indeed, the attacker can stop here. However, more options will be available if the attack continues. The attacker can exercise gateway functionality to a CAN bus. Once the gateway is bypassed, a full control of the car can be taken.

The app can then establish communication via a network of proxies, using mobile phones of users that no nothing about presence of malicious functionality on their phones. Thus, a fleet of cars can be compromised at once, at virtually no cost. The attackers themselves may not be interested to deal with the fleet of compromised vehicles, but they can sell it further on to interested groups and organizations.

A simplified version of a car attack can be also executed via workshops, thus, without the need to compromise drivers' mobile phones. In this case, a workshop network is compromised at first and then an attack is executed directly via workshop tools.

One interesting version of attack on a passenger car was reported in US, where one insurance company installed an Internet-connected monitoring tool on the internal OBDII contact to monitor drivers' behavior in exchange of the reduced insurance fee. (OBDII is a physical interface inside the car used for car diagnostics at the workshops and assessment of the vehicle by authorities.) Virtually no security was provided at this tool and it was easily compromised, Brewster (2015).

Attack on an Offline Facility

This section presents a second attack example, a facility that, due to security reasons, is not connected to the Internet.[3] Four ways to get in are possible.

- **The First Case:** Facilities are served with people. Their mobile phones, in particular, private phones, can be utilized in a similar fashion as above (e.g. by installing a malicious app). Mobile phones can use a variety of interfaces to explore the facility (maybe, someone will want to charge a mobile phone via a USB port, for example?). In this case, innocent users will become victims of an attacker and will act on attacker's behalf similar to the automotive case above.
- **The Second Case:** The attack is performed in a more technical fashion. Equipment used in these facilities needs to undergo updates, software fixes, upgrades, or new equipment should be installed. It is often taken away from the facilities and then it gets connected to the Internet, in one way or another, and can be, hence, compromised. In this case, the attacker will have to identify suppliers of equipment to facilities first. They will, then, compromise network of the supplier(s) and, introduce malicious functionality into supplier's development chain. This variant of attack scenario is more like a cyber-attack, even though the facility is not connected to the Internet. Embedded systems of this facility are an attack target, which makes it an embedded system attack at the end.
- **The Third Case:** The attacker will go further on into the "supply chain" and will install backdoors either in software that can be potentially used in these facilities or in hardware (also known as "Hardware Trojans"). This attack requires, however, substantial resources and direct access to development and manufacturing chain.

However, it will allow to compromise not one but many facilities at once. Alternatively, instead of creating backdoors themselves, the attacker will use already existing backdoors, purposely or not purposely created by others, for example, by an Advanced Persistent Threat (APT), which will save a lot of time and effort. This attack variant is more of an emerging trend than a current state of practice.

However, such attacks were already reported where attackers were, for example, using existing hardware backdoors Mitra, Wong & Wong (2015).

- **The Last, Fourth Case:** the attacker will try to explore unknown and unintentional bridges from non-critical system elements to a critical one. It can happen that the air conditioning or ventilation system is connected to the Internet (since it was considered as non-critical, and excluded from the security work). The attacker will first compromise this system and then try to exploit potential bridges between the system and the critical off-line systems at the facility. If the ventilation system is not connected to the Internet, installation of a malicious component inside the system during, for example, routine maintenance is another possible option for an attacker.

Comparison

The traditional concept with drawing "borders" or "circles" does not work any longer in the IoT world due to enormous complexity, super-connectivity and unlimited computational capabilities to anyone. Thresholds to execute the above attacks are constantly reduced, both in terms of time and knowledge.

Table 4 illustrates the automotive app attack and the off-line critical facility attack (with the second variant of this attack focusing on the supplier's network). As it can be seen, the attack on a critical off-line facility takes 7 steps to perform compared to the automotive app attack that takes 10 steps. Moreover, off-line facility's assets can be more interesting for the attacker. The app attack on a modern car is complex and can be difficult to perform, which, however, according to the case study on this attack, is fully feasible. By far, not all the attackers will be interested to accomplish all 10 steps. Some attackers will stop at the info-cluster level (at 8 steps). For some attackers, installation of a malicious app on the driver's mobile phone can be already sufficient (with only 4 steps necessary). The hypothesis of the authors is that attacks with fewer steps are, in general, more common since they take less effort and less time.

Note that, in the automotive scenario, the attacker used users' unawareness of mobile phone security and smart car security. Insufficient security awareness of developers (both of the info-cluster and the internal CAN network) contributed to susceptibility to the attacks. In the off-line facility scenario, suppliers are unaware of connection between security of the facility and security of their network. Maintenance personnel of the facility are unaware of security implication of outsourcing of the maintenance work to the external suppliers. In turn, operators of the facility are not aware that the equipment of the facility has been compromised. They consider the facility as "fully secure" due to disconnection from the Internet and will not be ready, hence, to react in the event of unleashed attack.

DISCUSSION

In Joe's example, some of the truck manufacturers obviously did not consider possible security threats, of those "less secure" trucks not all drivers followed security recommendations and the attack, if executed, is quite likely to be successful for those truck drivers and their trucks…

How can we stop attacks at people's homes and critical IoT (and offline) facilities? Indeed, proposing technically sound security solutions is one possible way forward. However, these security solutions should acknowledge responsibilities of developers and service provides as well as the level of security education of users and operators. Otherwise, even a super-smart security solution can fail due to that

Table 4. Attack steps

	Smart Car Attack	**Offline Facility Attack**
# Steps	1. Create app 2. Place app to an app store 3. Social engineering 4. App installation 5. Scanning Bluetooth 6. Update app 7. Enable "right" profile 8. Hijacking info-cluster 9. Scanning gateways 10. Opening CAN bus	1. Identify suppliers 2. Get into suppliers net 3. Development chain modification 4. Wait until update 5. Update equipment 6. Activate code inside 7. Unleash attack
Severity	Vehicles fleet in danger, society-critical	Critical facility in danger, society-critical

classical case of "a password exchanged to a muffin" or unsecure implementations. A number of steps are necessary. At first, a proper attack vector for a product should be determined within, for example, a manual exercise. Security risks and countermeasures should be suggested and integrated into development. It is beneficial if the independent reviews can be conducted on both the security evaluation and the level of implementation of countermeasures. Such approaches, as the recently suggested SAHARA approach for automotive systems, Macher et al. (2015), can be used to provide a systematic analysis and ranking of security risks, including their relation to safety properties of a system. Companies and organizations should strive for security culture with security education of personnel, security monitoring and alert response teams. Standards on both technical and business levels should be facilitated and demanded. Manuals and guides for customers should include sufficient information on the product security and actions that must be undertaken in case of security breaching. Products that are imported to the country should be subjected to security evaluation on compliance to basic security principles both technically and in form of proper manuals and installation guides. Users and operators should be regularly updated on the subject of embedded security, by facilitating reporting on embedded and IoT security "issues" and publishing information on security violations. In general, education on embedded security should be taken to each high school classroom, where pupils can learn about embedded security and their own responsibilities as members of the society. Emerging IoT society will not leave any member unattended and everyone can become a victim. The whole society must be prepared to act in the IoT world, with security thinking in mind.

Some of the interview respondents claimed that basically everyone is a potential source of an attack, intentionally or unintentionally. This brings us to the example of using victim's mobile phone to perform an attack, without victim being aware of that (as discussed in the attack scenarios presented in the previous section). Moreover, since, in IoT, unlimited connectivity and computational capacity will be available to everyone, it means that anyone can potentially become an attacker. For example, any unhappy teenager will be soon potentially able to run a DDoS on public services (similar to MSB2 (2014)) to ensure that the qualification exam after high school will be cancelled. The source of this attack will be exceptionally hard to trace and link to this particular teenager.

These changes will not happen by themselves and it is a responsibility of authorities to facilitate them. Authorities can impose rules and create facilitating regulations. However, they cannot make any single product secure and make each user or operator aware of security issues in that product. Therefore, acting on the educational level and launching security investigations to demonstrate susceptibility of infrastructural components and certain products can be a possible solution. Another possible solution is to establish a voluntary country-level embedded and IoT security standard and voluntary security marking for smart products and services that comply with this standard.

The majority of interview respondents (of those who use security standards) seems to be relying on their own adaptations of the standards, often derived from one or several "common" sources. As one respondent has stated "own requirements are best". The reflection to this is that "own requirements" can be a dangerous path because, in security, it is often good to use something that has been thoroughly validated by the experts on presence of security flaws. A good example here is the "open" encryption standards that can be scrutinized by the security community before deployment. Own "custom-made" solutions become often easily compromised due to lack of independent reviews.

Lack of proper security standards is clearly present, in particular, those standards that are domain-specific. Academia is not interested in helping in standardization work, while industry is very much interested in standardization. Academic respondents focus more on research and education aspects in security, studying new threats and security methods. This is, however, not a very healthy trend because standards are one of possible ways for researchers to influence development of embedded products and incorporate their knowledge into multiples of IoT products. A dialog here can benefit both researchers and industry, facilitating information exchange and development.

With issues happening in the security domain and constant reporting on security implications, users' security awareness should increase and, at some turning point, embedded security will become a competitive feature of a product or an infrastructure. In this case, manufacturers and operators will be interested themselves to ensure that they receive this voluntary "security marking" to increase sales, which, in turn, will initiate a positive feedback-loop leading to the overall security increase. However, it has been warned that security marking alone may not work, Peisert et al. (2014), and may create a "false sense of security".

With new threats constantly emerging, the evaluation must include a "dynamic" security aspect with organizations constantly reacting and taking actions to secure products and services against these new threats. This is what some of the interview respondents have proposed. In addition, voluntary security assessments on smart products and evaluations of manuals and guidelines can be effective. Penetration testing of critical infrastructures and evaluation of processes in development organization can be beneficial to ensure that defects are detected before they are utilized in malicious purposes or cause safety-critical faulty behavior.

When all around is smart and connected, it is ultimately users' or operators' responsibility to ensure own security, which demands a good level of understanding of embedded security by practically everyone. Each person will become responsible for his smart vacuum cleaner at home, for her smart car, smart watch and alike – but users must be informed about security (and related safety) risks and ways of reducing them. This is ultimately a duty of developers, which is, unfortunately, not the case today, at least with respect to consumer products as the study indicated.

Authors wrote two fictional stories, in Appendix 1 and Appendix 2, on how security-awareness and security knowledge can propagate between the developers, between industries and within the same industry domain. The role of governmental authorities and research are essential to make those stories a success story.

FUTURE RESEARCH DIRECTIONS

Similar to "classic" IT cyber-security, the authors consider apparent that the focus in embedded/cyber-physical security will eventually shift to security-awareness. The emphasis will shift from technical or algorithmic paradigms to socio-technical, giving people back their important role. Deployment of Internet of Things (IoT) applications has accelerated in past few years, with research boosting around Cloud Computing, Systems of Systems and Cyber-Physical Systems. Due to lack of security-awareness, security related aspects have not been addressed so far. But security-awareness is strongly emphasized now in many research agendas in related areas, for example, the ECSEL SRA, AENEAS, ARTEMIS & EPoSS (2018). Until the proposed research and industry agenda in IoT security is achieved, many of currently deployed solutions will lack systematic approaches to reliability and security. This makes current deployment of Internet-based solutions susceptible for massive attacks and makes them highly non-resilient. Despite the fact that many of critical entities, such as factories, aircraft, critical country infrastructures, commercial vehicles, etc. are nowadays connected, the approaches used so far cannot protect them. This results in an increased trend of failures in these infrastructural components, *seldom with consequences*, e.g. leading to "blackouts" discussed in newspapers, and *mostly without consequences*, e.g. leading to, at glance, non-critical service disruptions, with the latter ones, in fact, potentially more severe. The successful multi-step attacks may manifest themselves in those slight deviations from the normal, eventually resulting in accomplishment of the goals set by the attacker, without noticing.

Addressing security is also central for achieving safety of future connected systems such as automated transportation systems, where lacking availability, compromised integrity and unintended functions, can cause direct harm to human lives, AENEAS, ARTEMIS & EPoSS (2018).

This book chapter opens up a "door" towards possible solutions at the level of society as such, motivating for the need of security research towards human phycology and sociology as a corner-stone to the truly viable IoT security solutions. The present research in this direction of security awareness, for embedded and cyber-physical systems, is not extensive by any means, thus, opening up for great opportunities and discoveries. The book chapter can serve as a first aid in future steps to be taken.

The following can be examples of future research opportunities:

- Establish and conduct national-wise studies in the IoT domain, accounting for statistically significant portion of the population.
- Formalize and classify boundaries of systems of interests and systems of influence in the IoT domain, and define their dynamic behavior for both defenders and attackers as the roles, interfaces, windows and circles change.
- Establish game theories to enable behavioral studies of developers' and users' security-awareness vs. attackers' maturity and effort in the complex IoT environment.
- Create viable economic models of incentives on both "defense" and "attack" sides in IoT.
- Define the proper function of law in IoT and what acts can influence the "game" and support the model of incentives, what should be the legal sanctions, and what punishment to permit.

CONCLUSION

There is clearly a gap in security understanding of developers. Security standards are also lacking, and those that are available are not used. Nearly all respondents (including users), however, consider security important which can drive development of embedded security and help with introduction of appropriate methods and standards. However, there is presently a gap in security "education" of the users of smart products and services, with security information often lacking in the manuals, which are supposed to be the main source of users' product and service information. Security-aware developers and users can directly or indirectly prevent or reduce the risk of attacks on embedded and cyber-physical IoT systems. Appendix 3 lists examples of the attacks matched against the security-awareness and roles of developers and users (operators) in prevention of these attacks.

Note that the study presented in this book chapter is limited due to small population size. Authors did not have the possibility to perform a study similar to GOV.UK (2018). For that, a similar effort, supported and authorized on a ministry level, is required. Authors' ambition is that the study in its current form will motivate the effort of a large-scale investigation. The results are alarming and pose the risks to national security. Hence, authors would recommend statistically significant investigations on a yearly basis, similar to the GOV.UK (2018) study, to be able to measure and control security-awareness of both developers and users. When performing large scale statistical study, it is important to construct questions in different ways to address categories of respondents in the most appropriate manner. Recall also from Manjak (2006) that a decent information strategy is necessary to "outreach" both developers and users, with the "winning team" showing the lead.

ENISA (2017) report comes to a similar conclusion as in this book chapter, specifying Gap 2: "Lack of awareness and knowledge", stating namely "There is an overall lack of awareness regarding the need of security in IoT devices", which leads to measure 4.2.4: "Human Resources Security Training and Awareness" and recommendation 6.2: "Raise awareness for the need for IoT security". The recommendation is intended for IoT industry, providers, manufacturers, associations, academia, consumer groups and even regulators. ENISA (2017) states "Many security incidents could be avoided if developers and manufacturers were aware of the risks they face on a daily basis" and recommends 3 steps:

- "Security education and training needs to be established in industries"
- "End users and consumers have to be educated"
- "Among the developer community, awareness needs to be raised to adopt fundamental security principles"

In this book chapter, the recommendations, as derived from the discussion, are somewhat more extensive:

- Companies and organizations should strive for security culture with security education of personnel, security monitoring and alert response teams
- Standards on both technical and business levels should be facilitated and demanded
- Manuals and guides for customers should include sufficient information on the product security and actions that must be undertaken in case of security breaching
- Products that are imported to the country should be subjected to security evaluation on compliance

- Users and operators should be regularly updated on the subject of embedded security, e.g. facilitate mandatory publishing of information on security violations
- Education on embedded security should be taken to each high school classroom
- Authorities should impose rules of the "game" and create security facilitating regulations

DISCLAIMER

The opinion and views contained in this book chapter are those of the authors and do not represent the official opinion of Swedish Civil Contingencies Agency (MSB).

ACKNOWLEDGMENT

This research was supported by the Swedish Civil Contingencies Agency (MSB).

REFERENCES

ACEA. (2017). *ACEA principles of automobile cybersecurity*. Retrieved from https://www.acea.be/publications/article/acea-principles-of-automobile-cybersecurity

AENEAS, ARTEMIS, & EPoSS. (2018). *Strategic Research Agenda for Electronic Components and Systems*. Retrieved from https://efecs.eu/publication/download/ecs-sra-2018.pdf

Anderson, R. J. (2008). *Security engineering: A guide to building dependable distributed systems* (2nd ed.). Hoboken, NJ: John Wiley & Sons.

Brewster, T. (2015). *Security: Hacker says attacks on 'insecure' progressive insurance dongle in 2 million US cars could spawn road carnage*. Retrieved from https://www.forbes.com/sites/thomasbrewster/2015/01/15/researcher-says-progressive-insurance-dongle-totally-insecure

Carettoni, L., Merloni, C., & Zanero, S. (2007). Studying Bluetooth malware propagation: The BlueBag project. *IEEE Security and Privacy*, *5*(2), 17–25. doi:10.1109/MSP.2007.43

Cui, S., Han, Z., Kar, S., Kim, T. T., Poor, H. V., & Tajer, A. (2012). Coordinated data-injection attack and detection in the smart grid: A detailed look at enriching detection solutions. *IEEE Signal Processing Magazine*, *29*(5), 106–115. doi:10.1109/MSP.2012.2185911

Dunning, J. P. (2010). Taming the Blue Beast: A survey of Bluetooth based threats. *IEEE Security and Privacy*, *8*(2), 20–27. doi:10.1109/MSP.2010.3

Elkhodr, M., Shahrestani, S., & Cheung, H. (2013). The Internet of Things: Vision & challenges. In *Proceedings of the IEEE TENCON Spring Conference* (pp. 218-222). Washington, DC: IEEE Computer Society.

ENISA. (2017). *Baseline security recommendations for IoT in the context of critical information infrastructures*. Heraklion, Greece: European Union Agency for Network and Information Security.

Eom, J.-H., Han, Y.-J., Park, S.-H., & Chung, T.-M. (2008). Active cyber attack model for network system's vulnerability assessment. In *Proceedings of International Conference on Information Science and Security* (pp. 153-158). Washington, DC: IEEE Computer Society. 10.1109/ICISS.2008.36

GOV.UK. (2018). *Cyber security breaches survey 2018.* Retrieved from https://www.gov.uk/government/statistics/cyber-security-breaches-survey-2018

IPA. (2010). *Approaches for embedded system information security (2010 revised edition): Know your organization's security level by checking 16 points.* Retrieved from https://www.ipa.go.jp/files/000014118.pdf

Izosimov, V., Asvestopoulos, A., Blomkvist, O., & Törngren, M. (2016). Security-aware development of cyber-physical systems illustrated with automotive case study. In *Proceedings of 2016 Design, Automation & Test in Europe Conference & Exhibition* (pp. 818–821). San Jose, CA: EDA Consortium. doi:10.3850/9783981537079_0756

Izosimov, V., & Törngren, M. (2016). Security Evaluation of Cyber-Physical Systems in Society Critical Internet of Things. In *Proceedings of the Final Conference on Trustworthy Manufacturing and Utilization of Secure Devices TRUDEVICE 2016.* Barcelona: UPCommons.

Kwon, C., Liu, W., & Hwang, I. (2013). Security analysis for cyber-physical systems against stealthy deception attacks. In *Proceedings of American Control Conference* (pp. 3344–3349). Washington, DC: IEEE Computer Society.

Larcom, J. A., & Liu, H. (2013). Modeling and characterization of GPS spoofing, In *Proceedings of IEEE International Conference on Technologies for Homeland Security* (pp. 729-734). Washington, DC: IEEE Computer Society.

Lee, E.-K., Gerla, M., & Oh, S. Y. (2012). Physical layer security in wireless smart grid. *IEEE Communications Magazine, 50*(8), 46–52. doi:10.1109/MCOM.2012.6257526

Leest van der, V., & Tuyls, P. (2013). Anti-counterfeiting with hardware intrinsic security, In Proceedings of 2013 Design, Automation & Test in Europe Conference & Exhibition (pp. 1137-1142). San Jose, CA: EDA Consortium.

Li, Y., Hui, P., Jin, D., Su, L., & Zeng, L. (2014). Optimal distributed malware defense in mobile networks with heterogeneous devices. *IEEE Transactions on Mobile Computing, 13*(2), 377–391. doi:10.1109/TMC.2012.255

Macher, G., Sporer, H., Berlach, R., Armengaud, E., & Kreiner, C. (2015). SAHARA: A security-aware hazard and risk analysis method. In *Proceedings of 2015 Design, Automation & Test in Europe Conference & Exhibition* (pp. 621–624). San Jose, CA: EDA Consortium. doi:10.7873/DATE.2015.0622

Manjak, M. (2006). Social engineering your employees to Information Security. In *Global Information Assurance Certification Gold Papers for Security Essentials.* Swansea, UK: SANS Institute.

Mitra, S., Wong, H.-S. P., & Wong, S. (2015). *Stopping hardware Trojans in their tracks.* Retrieved from https://spectrum.ieee.org/semiconductors/design/stopping-hardware-trojans-in-their-tracks

Mo, Y., Kim, T. H.-H., Brancik, K., Dickinson, D., Lee, H., Perrig, A., & Sinopoli, B. (2012). Cyber-physical security of a smart grid infrastructure. *Proceedings of the IEEE, 100*(1), 195-209.

MSB2. (2014). *International case report on cyber security incidents: Reflections on three cyber incidents in the Netherlands, Germany and Sweden.* Retrieved from https://www.msb.se/RibData/Filer/pdf/27482.pdf

MSB. (2014). *Guide to increased security in industrial information and control systems.* Karlstad, Sweden: Swedish Civil Contingencies Agency.

MSB. (2017). *Informationssäkerhet och bedrägerier.* Retrieved from https://www.msb.se/sv/Forebyggande/Informationssakerhet/Stod-inom-informationssakerhet/Informationssakerhet-och-bedragerier/

NIST. (2018). *NIST Cybersecurity for IoT Program.* Retrieved from https://www.nist.gov/programs-projects/nist-cybersecurity-iot-program

Peisert, S., Margulies, J., Nicol, D. M., Khurana, H., & Sawall, C. (2014). Designed-in security for cyber-physical systems. *IEEE Security and Privacy, 12*(5), 9–12. doi:10.1109/MSP.2014.90

Roman, R., Najera, P., & Lopez, J. (2011). Securing the Internet of Things. *Computer, 44*(9), 51–58. doi:10.1109/MC.2011.291

Sakarindr, P., & Ansari, N. (2007). Security services in group communications over wireless infrastructure, mobile ad hoc, and wireless sensor networks. *IEEE Transactions on Wireless Communications, 14*(5), 8–20. doi:10.1109/MWC.2007.4396938

Satyanarayanan, M., Lewis, G., Morris, E., Simanta, S., Boleng, J., & Ha, K. (2013). The role of cloudlets in hostile environments. *IEEE Pervasive Computing, 12*(4), 40–49. doi:10.1109/MPRV.2013.77

Sobel, A. E. K., & McGraw, G. (2010). Interview: Software security in the real world. *Computer, 43*(9), 47–53. doi:10.1109/MC.2010.256

Stillman, R., & DeFiore, C.R. (1980). Computer security and networking protocols: Technical issues in military data communications networks. *IEEE Transactions on Communications, 28*(9), 1472-1477.

Tariq, M. A., Brynielsson, J., & Artman, H. (2014). The security awareness paradox: A case study, In *Proceedings of the IEEE/ACM International Conference on Advances in Social Networks Analysis and Mining* (pp. 704-711). Piscataway, NJ: IEEE Press. 10.1109/ASONAM.2014.6921663

Tehranipoor, M., & Koushanfar, F. (2010). A Survey of Hardware Trojan Taxonomy and Detection. *IEEE Design & Test of Computers, 27*(1), 10–25. doi:10.1109/MDT.2010.7

Tsoutsos, N. G., & Maniatakos, M. (2014). Fabrication attacks: Zero-overhead malicious modifications enabling modern microprocessor privilege escalation. *IEEE Transactions on Emerging Topics in Computing, 2*(1), 81–93. doi:10.1109/TETC.2013.2287186

Zhang, M., & Fang, Y. (2005). Security analysis and enhancements of 3GPP authentication and key agreement protocol. *IEEE Transactions on Wireless Communications, 4*(2), 734–742. doi:10.1109/TWC.2004.842941

KEY TERMS AND DEFINITIONS

Advanced Persistent Threat: A malicious threat by a well-organized group, often government, with virtually unlimited resources, to target persistently and effectively the assets of the selected attack target with highly sophisticated stealthy attacking measures over an unlimited period of time.

Asset: The artefact with a distinct value (monetary, information, service) in the system of interest.

Attack Scenario: A scenario that describes steps and ways the attacker may use vulnerability (deficiency in the system design or services).

Breach: A security-related incident, often caused by exploited vulnerability, potentially resulting in theft and damage to the system and its services.

Cyber-Physical Systems: The system controlled by computers (or so-called embedded computing systems), tightly integrated with the external surrounding environment, including their users, Internet, physical environment, where its physical components are deeply intertwined with hardware and software components, often acting in different temporal and spatial scales, interacting in multiple ways internally and with the external environment, exhibiting multiple modes and distinct behaviors.

Cybersecurity: The protection of computer systems from theft and damage to their assets and from manipulation and distraction of their services.

Red Alert Team: The team of people in an organization dedicated to identify vulnerabilities, follow-up on the security threats and issue security alerts across the organization, suggesting counter-measures to balance the security threats and enforcing procedures and methods to fix vulnerabilities.

Safety: The protection from harm to health of people (or, in some cases, also economic damage).

Security Awareness: Knowledge and attitude of an individual, a group of people, an organization to protection of assets (physical, information, economic) of the individual, the group of people, the organization.

Threat: An intent to cause harm to an individual, a group of people, to steal or to damage property, to manipulate the system, to disrupt or to halt services, motivated by a value of the assets in question.

ENDNOTES

[1]   Joe is a fictional character. Any resemblance to actual persons, living or dead, or actual events is purely coincidental.

[2]   Note that the detailed technical information on the attack is omitted in this chapter, and details can be found in Izosimov et al. (2016).

[3]   Note that authors have not executed this attack, only empirically studied possibilities of execution of the attack steps. The practical evaluation of this attack was left to the responsible organizations.

APPENDIX 1: THE WORKSHOP STORY

This appendix gives insights to possible positive effect of the educational effort for developers. Simon is a developer who is invited to the educational effort, a workshop, together with other developers. Simon is a fictional character. Any resemblance to actual persons, living or dead, or actual events is purely coincidental.

Simon was invited to participate in a security workshop after he took part in the interview security study done at one university. The study was initiated by the governmental agency who was also hosting the workshop. Workshop was attended in part by interview respondents, in part by other security experts and in part by employees interested in embedded security questions, like Simon. In general, workshop participants took the outcome of the interview study positively. In particular, that one respondent who did not consider security important got a lot of attention from the audience, Simon was also surprised. Audience was united about difficulties in separation between embedded security and cyber security and acknowledged cyber-embedded interrelation within complex CPS systems. The need for standardization in security domain was also discussed. The workshop involved several other presentations, on security of industrial control systems (SCADA), security in telecommunications and a number of presentations on security research work on securing energy systems, IT security challenges, information security, cryptography and security in healthcare.

During the lunch break, Simon participated in an exercise on prioritization of attack vectors for society-critical IoT systems. As an attack target, his team chose a railroad and an air traffic control. Workshop participants received 4 attackers' portraits, "kidz" (somewhat lost teenagers who want to show off), "security researcher" (who want to show that his/her security principles works), "terrorists" (who want to force society to accept the "proper truth") and "advance persistent threat (APT)" (who want to cause substantial economic damage without being detected). Simon's team managed to create attack vectors within the lunch break with respect to these 4 attackers and constructed 4 multi-step attack scenarios with various numbers of steps. In one of them (the APT), the scenario would run over a longer period of time to "compromise" the entire railroad infrastructure with, for example, forcing train delays and causing a number of small but visible accidents. In case of terrorists, the attack target was changed to the emergency phone number system. Workshop participants from other team than Simon's considered this target more attractive for terrorists with a possibility of more direct personal involvement. A complex attack scenario composed of physical, cyber and embedded attack steps was suggested. It involved blocking ambulances and other emergency vehicles for a long period of time by remote braking in into the alarm system, smart sensors, cameras and alike combined with distributed physical attacks, using weapons and bombing, and massive DDoS on respective online emergency services and service phone numbers. In general, Simon and his team could quickly identify main attack components, estimate probability of attacks and construct attack scenarios, and all within less than an hour. Simon had always troubles in understanding of security and often felt hopeless to execute commands of the red alert team. This exercise helped him to gain self-confidence and demonstrated that people like him have the ability to construct, analyze and document complex attack scenarios in a tight time frame, at a good level of details, and suggest possible countermeasures to effectively stop the attacker. Jointly, during the follow-up 30-minute workshop slot, workshop organizers provided feedback (in audience discussion), prioritized attacks and selected countermeasures of those suggested by the workshop participants.

This type of exercise helped Simon and other developers to gain security understanding. Designers like Simon themselves should become a backbone of the society for prevention of attacks and their creativity can become a good support for creating proper mechanisms for securing complex IoT systems. People are naturally capable of dealing with complex and loosely defined problems and, if certain training is provided, are able to efficiently manage security threats, perform prioritization and selection of countermeasures. Attackers are themselves humans (or, at least, virtual human instantiations) and it is reasonable to quest them with human defenders. At the workshop, the term "apprenticeship" was also named with the suggestion that designers experienced in security should train "apprentices" to ensure development of security knowledge and methods within the respective organizations. Simon decided to talk to his manager and to request a mentor from the red alert team, who could meet him every second week and talk about embedded security.

On a technical side, tool support is, as well, necessary for defenders to act efficiently and resolve quickly computation-intensive and data search-intensive tasks, by using, for example, cloud computational capacity, as the attacker would do. However, absence of tools should not be used as a motivation of not doing exercises on constructing attack vectors for individual organizations, products and services. About 20 people, including Simon, could easily organize themselves and conduct exercise within less than an hour using only a pen and a paper.

After the workshop, Simon confronted his top management on the need of security training within his company. The management did not accept his proposition and declined to invest into security education of the employees. Simon decided to quit his work after confronting the management and went on to increase his knowledge in the area, which he apparently liked the most, embedded security for IoT systems. Simon is now a well-paid consultant delivering security advice and security training to a broad range of companies within his industry sector with his old company as one of the primary clients.

Thanks to the governmental agency that enabled this possibility for training and knowledge exchange and thanks to Simon who confronted his management and took that difficult decision. According to Simon, the interest for his training and consultancy is drastically increasing and he is again hiring more security consultants in his privately-owned company.

APPENDIX 2: THE TRAVELLING MAN STORY

This appendix gives insights to the development environment of large and medium-sized organizations. The story is created to provide support on the question of why security awareness can propagate between the developers and within and in-between development organizations. Mike, Ben, Laura, Alexander, Michael, Kim and Peter are fictional characters. Any resemblance to actual persons, living or dead, or actual events is purely coincidental. Choose of automotive industry is of pure coincidence and the story is imagination of the authors of this book chapter.

Mike worked at a large automotive manufacturer in a Board of Directors trying to figure out how to take the company out of the crises after the Lehman Brothers crash in 2008. Two years later still the order intake was low and the company was bleeding money, cache flow was never near to the pre-crisis level. One morning Mike found on his desk the so-called Oakland article about researchers hacking an unknown passenger car. Mike had no idea who put it on his desk.

Mike was not in mood going over the financial numbers again, that seemed to be hopeless, and he started reading the article. "Gosh! Do we do anything about security in our company except the IT security?" That seemed to be a problem different from that cash flow what he was trying to solve in the last two years, he really needed a break. He called in Ben, a research director, asking whether anyone is doing research on the vehicle security.

Apparently of more than 100 research projects, there was only one targeting automotive security and that one was about to be closed as most of other research projects, to save the precious cash flow, according to directive. Ben was rather eager to close the security project quicker than planned as a research overspending and that project seemed to be not bringing any value to the customers, comparted to, for example, HMI projects or the diesel engine software optimization projects. Research projects were rather difficult to close as there are always more than one party involved and some obligations and promises were made to the funding agencies. Still Ben was doing his best to prevent starting new research projects and closing down existing or simply reducing the company's participation to nearly 0 man-hours; the diesel project he would, of course, keep.

Cash flow was not at all good, Ben as many other didn't get any extra bonus that year. The security project had already no company's engineers involved, only a part-time project manager, Laura, who was about to go on maternity leave and that was a perfect time to finally close the project. Still the project was for some reason backed by Aftersales, and they were the guys with a strong influence. "Mike, I promise I close this deem project tomorrow!" said Ben to Mike in a phone call, "Anyway, our customers don't care about security! This is not important for them! We all know!" "In fact, Ben, I've just read a research article this morning and I want to give you a different order." "What? Mike, do you read research articles?" "I did spend some time at university doing my PhD as you know." Mike proudly replied and smiled. That was clearly not Ben's case, who got to his Research position after many years working in a factory directly after College, slowly advancing in his career. In the job interview, Ben promised to do only "industrial" research that would help to sell more and cheaper cars, particularly focusing on diesel engines and cheaper production processes. That was a real selling point to the top management, as diesel engines were the most popular among the customers who also wanted to have vehicles at as low cost as possible, and Ben got the Research Director position a bit more than a year ago.

"Ben, yes, we have cash flow problems but I also see that in case we survive, security may become one of the priorities. Give the guys what they need. Put them also in contact with the IT department. Our vehicles are connected but we have done some savings on security as you know. Just connect and drive, that may be too risky. No security regulation whatsoever that demand any security but still… Better we change it." Ben replied "OK, as you like. Anyhow, Aftersales for some reason do not want to close the security project. I had like 10 meetings with them already trying to explain the situation. They are the only ones who put engineering resources." Mike got some rather awful stomach feeling "Add engineers from other projects, ensure that this security project has resources!" Ben replied "Sure, you are the boss!" Ben closed down some other projects this day, including his favorite diesel project, and moved engineers to the security project. Laura was choked about the news and so was Alexander who kept working on the project from a partner organization. Alexander was a research engineer from university's telecom department (or what was left from that department after the IT crash in early 2000s) and was adapting telecommunication knowledge in cyber-security to automotive domain. Laura kept good track of the backlog and all got to work directly, the company demo was just in a month ahead. She first thought to escape the shame when the baby is born…

Several years later, Alexander worked in a completely different project, in a completely different place. Yes, many years have passed, with some large-scale recalls due to security breaches as, for example, the Jeep re-call. The automotive manufacturer where he worked years ago did not face recalls due to security. Mike helped to establish a proper security policy based on Alexander's input, IT department took responsibility even for the vehicle security (Alexander could find a good connection there as many of the staff members worked previously in telecommunication), they made changes to the Telematics unit and Alexander's research ideas went straight into production. One idea that Alexander liked the most was to ensure that only the vehicle itself can establish external connections and to limit the connectivity window to the minimum. This approach was applied even to older vehicles, already in operation, thus, improving their security virtually at no cost.

Alexander was now at Tier-1, doing some system engineering. Security was not all a priority as the customers, large automotive manufacturers, did not previously require any work for security despite all the directives and regulations that were approved world-wide this summer, in Europe, in the US and in China. That was frustrating. Alexander knew that it would change one day. This morning his project received an updated compliance matrix to fill in. "Wow!" was Alexander's first impression when he looked at it. He could see all his 190 security policy points. "Hmm. Apparently, it becomes an industry-wide standard." To reply for the compliance was an easy task and no one had doubts since the management was aware of the new security regulations in place after the summer. Media run a large campaign to inform about oncoming changes and nearly everyone got affected at a personal level, even top management and their family members.

However, none really worked with security in the Tier-1 company, except one crypto-guy who was encrypting the software images. The customer wanted a quick delivery just in 3 weeks of initial security work products. Alexander run around to see whether anyone had competence at security, e.g. from a previous job or research at university. And he could find. Michael, Kim and Peter. Michael worked in a telecommunication company before and was equally puzzled as Alexander why security was not a priority in automotive industry; he also watched Jeep and other hacking films. Kim did research on security some years ago at university, published well-cited articles at highly renowned conferences and highly-ranked security journals. Kim thought that she would work with security after employment but quickly found herself doing some other "more important" work tasks. Kim wanted to come back to university, which turned out to be quite impossible, and she stayed. Peter worked in the aero-space domain with security aspects and was at some point head-hunted by the HR department as an expert. His security work was mostly on the shelves and he was unsure why the company wanted to keep him at all.

Michael took the cyber-security manager role. Kim was appointed to Security Expert. Peter assumed the role of Cyber-security Line Manager. The integration of security into the product started from an early concept phase for the first time ever... Thanks to both media with their public effort that helped to get easy acceptance from the top management and thanks to the automotive manufacturer customer who required the cyber-security in their products. And thanks to Mike who spent one morning off the cash flow problem. (We still don't know who put the Oakland research article on his desk that morning.) As Ben has retired, the research projects are again flourishing. Mike has taken the Research Director role after finally solving the cash flow problem, supported the company's transition to electrical vehicles and the autonomous driving is a next target. Mike already promoted several security research projects on AI within the organization and more to come, thanks to NHTSA and other organizations requiring security in automotive domain.

APPENDIX 3: SECURITY-AWARENESS AND ATTACK TYPES

This appendix lists possible examples of attack scenarios against IoT infrastructures in Table 5. For each example, the role of users and developers is considered, e.g. a security-aware developer and/or user (operator) can prevent or reduce the risk of the attack when considering design or operational measures. Note that the list of attack scenarios is not complete and is provided for illustrative purposes.

Table 5. Attack scenarios and security-awareness

Attack Scenario or Category	Human involvement (e.g. user)	Possibility for prevention via security-awareness
Attacks on object naming, interoperability and identity	Modification of the identity of the IoT components, performing "theft" of this identity and using of this identity for masquerading. The attack can as well target user (operator) identity.	Designers aware of this type of attack can consider measures to prevent the attack or make it impractical. Users (operators) if aware of this attack scenario can take actions to protect own identify and identity of the IoT elements.
Scalability attacks	Attacks that explore multiple interfaces and multiple components of the IoT infrastructure with overload measures using the internal properties (sources) of the IoT infrastructure.	Designers aware of this type attack can investigate scalability properties of the IoT infrastructure, thus, making this attack impossible. Users (operators) if aware may observe the attack and take specified preventive actions.
Coordinated data-injection attacks	Attack against measurement support (sensors) of the IoT infrastructure to provoke the desired state in the infrastructure and trigger the desired action from the operator (users).	Developers if aware can consider data-injection attacks within the analysis of the system. Users (operators) if aware of the attack can decide not trigger the "desired" operation and use reporting channel to get confirmation of the action before undertaking it.
Heterogeneous complex software frameworks attacks	The attack that targets deficiencies of software frameworks, platforms used in IoT infrastructures (for example, it can target operating system, communication stack software)	Developers if aware can take actions to "design away" deficiencies of framework and platforms or to enable dedicated mechanisms. Users may decide not to expose their elements to risky conditions to avoid the "entry point"
Hardware-level attack on largely distributed development and manufacturing chains	The attack targets the supply chain of hardware components enabling the attacker to install desired functionality into the hardware (e.g. Hardware Trojans).	Developers may build it mechanisms in the design to indicate modifications and the organizations may introduce dedicated assessment and testing mechanisms to the supply chain. User (operator) if aware may examine the hardware component before using it whether the component may look suspicions, as well trace supply sources of that component.
Attacks on communication protocols, network infrastructures and interfaces	General attack type that attempts to explore weaknesses of communication protocols (at different levels), systematic deficiencies of network infrastructures or known issues with the interfaces used.	Developers if aware may decide not to use communication protocols or interfaces with known security risks, or may correct deficiencies or close the backdoors before deployment. Users (operators) may decide not to use IoT devices that deploy risky mechanisms or protocols, or ensure that the connectivity is limited to the minimum necessary level.
Mobile network attacks	The attack that takes over mobile communication parts of the IoT infrastructure, for example, with rogue base stations.	Developers can consider this possibility in their designs and "harden" the designs against the attack, e.g. using application measures. Users if aware can observe suspicious switching between the base stations in IoT components.
Wireless network attacks	The attack that takes over wireless network (or networks) of the IoT infrastructure, with for example, faked or hijacked access points.	Developers can consider this possibility in their designs and "harden" the designs against the attack, e.g. using additional dedicated wireless security protocols. Users if aware can observe suspicious switching between the access points in IoT components, and regularly examine the connections.
Peer-to-peer interface attacks (incl. Bluetooth attack)	The attack that penetrates (and explores) peer-to-peer interface attempting to enable or introduce functionality desired by the attacker.	Developers can consider this possibility in their designs and restrict the designs against the attack, e.g. by disabling unnecessary access modes. Users if aware can observe on-going attack when the attacker explores the interface, and switch-off the connectivity, report the case.
Navigation attacks (incl. GPS attack)	The attack that takes over navigation capability of the system.	Designers can build in complementary redundancy measures for navigation (e.g. based on wireless connectivity). Users if informed may rely less on the navigation capability, double-checking the actual position.
Sophisticated multi-step attacks	Combined attack that involves multiple steps, many of the steps are often related to social engineering of users	Designers can build in resilience against this type of attack performing system analysis, conducting penetration testing and clearly defining the role of the users and operators in the system. Users can resist social engineering better if informed about possibility exposure to this kind of attack, thus, making virtually impossible for an attacker to advance the attack.
Stealthy deception attacks	The attack that establishes a coherent (but fake) system view to users of the system when overtaking the system	Designers can build in resilience against this type of attack performing system analysis, defining manual steps for operators and users. Users can look for suspicious patters and "freezing" of system information.
Distributed multi-choice denial-of-service (DDoS) attacks (incl. multi-choice flooding attack)	Attack type that systematically explores weak links throughout large infrastructure (several infrastructures), users that have access to the infrastructure are also systematically explored	Designers can build in mechanisms for identification, cut down and blocking sources of the attack in early attack phases. Users can take measures not to reduce the risk of exploitation of themselves and their devices as a "weak link" during advancement of the attack via the attack tree.
Heterogeneous multi-role social engineering attacks	Attack type that directly targets users or a whole organization (even several organizations e.g. over the supply chain), sometime involving identity thief of top management (even CEO).	Organizations can build in protection mechanisms into their organizations to prevent this type of attack. Employees can trigger an alarm in case the social engineering attack has taken place (e.g. if team members, their management, purchase department are affected).

Chapter 13
Securing Over-the-Air Code Updates in Wireless Sensor Networks

Christian Wittke
Leibniz-Institut für innovative Mikroelektronik, Germany

Kai Lehniger
Leibniz-Institut für innovative Mikroelektronik, Germany

Stefan Weidling
Leibniz-Institut für innovative Mikroelektronik, Germany

Mario Schoelzel
Leibniz-Institut für innovative Mikroelektronik, Germany

ABSTRACT

With the growing number of wireless devices in the internet of things (IoT), maintenance and management of these devices has become a key issue. In particular, the ability to wirelessly update devices is a must in order to fix security issues and software bugs, or to extend firmware functionality. Code update mechanisms in wireless sensor networks (WSNs), a subset of IoT networks, must handle limited resources and strict constraints. Also, over-the-air (OTA) code updates in the context of an IoT ecosystem may open new security vulnerabilities. An IoT security framework should therefore be extended with additional mechanisms to secure the OTA code update functionality. The chapter presents an overview of various OTA code update techniques for WSNs and their security flaws along with some existing attacks and possible countermeasures. It is discussed which attacks can be used more easily with the code update functionality. Countermeasures are compared as to whether they secure the weakened security objectives, giving a guideline to choose the right combination of countermeasures.

DOI: 10.4018/978-1-5225-7332-6.ch013

INTRODUCTION

With the growing number of wireless devices in the Internet of Things (IoT), maintaining and managing these devices has become a key issue. In particular, the ability to wirelessly update devices is a must in order to fix security issues and software bugs, or to extend firmware functionality. Recent attacks, such as the Mirai Distributed-Denial-of-Service (DDoS) attack (Kolias, Kambourakis, Stavrou, & Voas, 2017), where IoT devices were used as a botnet, have shown that IoT can be used very easily to cause serious damage.

Thereby, code update mechanisms in these devices must cope with limited computational resources, power constraints, and limited bandwidth for communication. On top of that, the capability of wireless code updates also opens new security vulnerabilities in these systems.

Wireless Sensor Networks (WSNs) are a subset of IoT networks that are suited for long time operations without any human interaction. The elements of the network, called nodes, are mostly battery powered. For this reason, the resource restriction in terms of power consumption is even more critical than in classical IoT applications. Classical security measures may be impractical because of these restrictions. Focusing on WSNs is therefore useful because they represent an edge case for IoT applications.

When the over-the-air (OTA) code update feature for devices is placed in the context of an IoT ecosystem (Rahman, Daud, & Mohamad, 2016), it becomes clear that additional measures are needed to prevent the opening of new security holes. An IoT ecosystem typically identifies four layers, as shown in Figure 1.

The code update initially affects all layers, as it passes from the users/devices/applications via the IoT fog and network to the addressed IoT devices/sensor nodes. However, potential new security vulnerabilities only affect the wireless communication between the network's gateway and IoT devices, assuming that security mechanisms of an IoT security framework are already in place. The code update feature may allow already existing security mechanisms to be bypassed. This means that an IoT security framework (Babar, Stango, Prasad, Sen, & Prasad, 2011; Pacheco & Hariri, 2016; Rahman, Daud, & Mohamad, 2016) needs to be extended with additional mechanisms to secure the OTA code update functionality.

Figure 1. OTA code update in the context of an IoT ecosystem

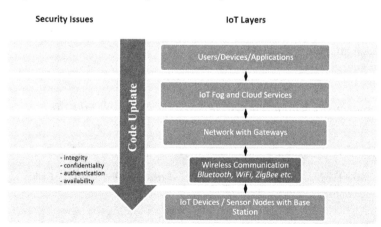

This chapter first presents a general overview of various OTA code update techniques for WSNs. This ranges from interpreter-based systems, over modularized systems that allow exchanging particular modules to systems where the full binary image can be replaced. Distribution protocols and techniques for improving the reliability of these updates are also presented. In particular, the authors discuss important techniques for reducing the size of the code update that must be transmitted wirelessly, taking into account some practical limitations. The authors focus on two main techniques: first, a differencing algorithm to find reusable data, or the optimal combination of instructions; second, preprocessing the binary files to increase their similarity. Examples are provided for both techniques.

Based on this overview of existing OTA code update techniques, their security flaws as well as some existing attacks and possible countermeasures are presented. Although the code update feature has several benefits, it also comes with new scopes from the attacker's point of view. For this reason, securing the code update is a very important issue. Therefore, the authors will present a classification of security threats and discuss which of them can be used more easily with code update functionality. In particular, the authors will show which of the basic security objectives confidentiality, integrity, and availability are weakened and to what extent. Finally, the authors present state-of-the-art countermeasures and clearly compare them to whether they are securing the above-mentioned weakened security objectives.

BACKGROUND

Update functionality for WSNs has been an intensive research topic since WSNs themselves were introduced. The benefits are obvious: once deployed in the field, a WSN can be debugged, maintained, extended in its function, or completely re-tasked without being physically accessible. While the complexity of WSN scenarios can range from dozens to several hundred or thousand nodes, the importance of OTA code updates is increasing. The general procedure for updating wireless sensor nodes over the air is shown in Figure 2.

First, the update itself needs to be generated. To avoid having to disseminate the entire image in the form in which it is usually stored in the internal flash memory of the sensor node, it is therefore first preprocessed in various approaches, for example, converted into control commands, compressed, or converted into a delta with the aid of the old image.

The next step is the dissemination of the code update. This can be divided into two general cases: providing the update for all nodes or a subset of the network. In both cases, the dissemination requires a management to reach all addressed nodes.

Figure 2. General procedure for updating wireless sensor nodes over the air

The execution of the update on each participating node is one of the last steps. This phase depends on the execution environment on the node or, more specifically, its integration of the update functionality. It can be integrated as an independent application, as part of the operating system (OS) or a middleware, or as a device specific firmware (Brown & Sreenan, 2006).

After the update is executed, the fault detection phase is used to check the installation progress of the new image and to initiate a repair in case of a fault to avoid the loss of nodes. Nevertheless, a check should be made or feedback should be given in each step of the process within the WSN or to the administration to be able to react to faulty conditions (Brown & Sreenan, 2013).

Next, an overview of different update approaches will be presented. The dissemination and execution of the code update will be discussed in sections Update Dissemination and Executing the Update. Techniques for reducing the cost of reprogramming WSNs, including delta file generation, will be presented in the Reducing the Costs for Dissemination section.

Different Update Approaches

One of the main reasons for designing a code update in a modular fashion is that in a system statically linked at compile time, code updates become more expensive, since a whole system image must be distributed (Han, Kumar, Shea, Kohler, & Srivastava, 2005, p. 1). Instead, modular designs allow updating only parts of the image and leaving the rest unchanged. Examples of modules that could be dynamically loaded are routing protocols, sensor drivers, and application programs (Han, Rengaswamy, Shea, Kohler, & Srivastava, 2005). There are different approaches to implementing these concepts.

OS-Based Approaches

A typical sensor node consists of resources such as a microcontroller, external memory, transceiver, power source, and, of course, sensors (Vieira, Coelho, Da Silva, & da Mata, 2003). An OS has to *manage the allocation of these resources to users in an orderly and controlled manner* (Farooq & Kunz, 2011, p. 2). Strict resource constraints of sensor nodes have led to new approaches to design an OS for use in WSNs. An overview of challenges and approaches is given by Dong, Chen, Liu, & Bu (2010).

Table 1. Comparison of operating systems for WSNs with respect to their wireless reprogrammability

	Tiny OS	FlexCup	Contiki	SOS	RETOS	LiteOS	SenSpire OS	Enix OS
Linking type	static	dynamic	dynamic	dynamic	dynamic	dynamic	dynamic	dynamic
Dynamic Loading approach	-	runtime relocation	runtime relocation	loadable modules	runtime relocation	runtime relocation	loadable modules	kernel-supported PIC
Reprogrammable	■	■	■	■	■	■	■	■
Application	✓	✓	✓	✓	✓	✓	✓	✓
Drivers	✓	✓	✓	✓	✗	✗	n/a	✗
Kernel	✓	✓	✗ ✗	✗	(✓)	✗	✓	✗

The focus of this chapter is on OSs for WSNs that are already known to support network reprogramming. An overview of this is given in Table 1 and described in the following paragraphs.

Static Linking vs. Dynamic Linking and Loading

Linking can be performed statically or dynamically at runtime on the sensor node. Therefore, the type of linking mechanism has a significant impact on the reprogramming cost because it determines what needs to be transmitted to the sensor node. Since statically linked code no longer contains symbolic information, because all the library routines used in the application are copied to the image by the linker, it is difficult to update or move parts of the application. For example, TinyOS (Hill, et al., 2000), a widely used OS for sensor networks, provides support for efficient modularity through components. However, since the components are statically linked to the kernel to form a complete image, it is not possible to modify the system after linking (Levis & Culler, 2002). Therefore, for a wireless code update, entire binary files have to be distributed at high cost, e.g. with Deluge (Hui & Culler, 2004).

Meanwhile, there are approaches such as FlexCup (Marron, et al., 2006) that introduce a dynamic linking mechanism where the actual linking is performed at runtime on the sensor node, enabling dynamic loading of TinyOS components.

It allows drivers, protocols, etc. to be independent of the actual application. Components that are already stored in the memory of the sensor node and are not affected by the code update need not be disseminated. Only the new symbol and relocation tables are sent to the nodes along with the compiled image of the changed components. But this approach uses the flash memory extensively and the symbol and relocation tables can lead to major updates.

Runtime relocation and position-independent code (PIC) are orthogonal approaches to dynamic linking/loading. For approaches such as Contiki (Dunkels, Gronvall, & Voigt, 2004), RETOS (Cha, et al., 2007), and LiteOS (Cao, Abdelzaher, Stankovic, & He, 2008), which use runtime relocation, the application binary must be relocated at runtime before loading into the program memory, while static relocation occurs, for example, through the linker. During the relocation, data is moved or addresses are changed. To avoid the overhead of relocating addresses at runtime on the wireless sensor node, other approaches such as Enix OS (Chen, Chien, & Chou, 2010) generate PIC using the compiler. With dynamically loaded modules, approaches such as SOS (Han, Rengaswamy, Shea, Kohler, & Srivastava, 2005) and SenSpire OS (Dong, Chen, Liu, Bu, & Liu, 2009) allow network reprogramming at module granularity. This is realized by modules being PIC binaries that implement specific tasks and use relative relocatable addresses instead of absolute addresses. It means that entire modules can be updated after the deployment of the sensor nodes.

VM-Based Approaches

The need for flexible systems has inspired the use of virtual machines (VMs) in WSNs (Han, Rengaswamy, Shea, Kohler, & Srivastava, 2005). For example, a virtual address space provided by the VM could allow suspended programs to swap to a backing store by using a sensor node's non-volatile memory to enable a low-power sleep mode.

In addition, virtual machines can also take over the code update functionality. As shown, e.g. by Maté (Levis & Culler, 2002), an energy cost reduction can be achieved for transmitting updates through its high-level interface, which allows complex programs to be very short and to encode updates into instructions. However, Maté can only change VM applications after deployment. Updates to the system software (OS, VM or middleware) are possible with VMStar (Koshy & Pandey, 2005), for example.

Update Dissemination

To remotely reconfigure sensor nodes without physical access after they have been deployed in the field, the generated program update must be disseminated over a wireless network. Important concepts for the dissemination of code updates include the dissemination strategy and the nature of the sensor nodes. Techniques for reducing the dissemination costs of reprogramming WSNs will be presented later. A survey of data dissemination in WSNs is given for example by Zheng & Wan (2014). Dissemination protocols can be compared based on the number of hops and the dissemination strategy. An overview is given in Table 2.

The basic network reprogramming functionality can be provided by the entire program code dissemination. In principle, a distinction can be made in the dissemination between single-hop and multi-hop approaches.

In a single-hop approach such as XNP (Crossbow Network Programming) (Crossbow Technology, Inc., 2003), the update is broadcasted by the source node, in this case the base station, to all the nodes in range within a single hop. This implies that the sensor nodes to be updated need to be within the communication range of the base station. However, due to the single hop boundary, such an approach does not scale to large sensor networks. Sensor nodes that are not within range of the base station cannot be updated.

To solve the problem, multi-hop network programming is needed in which code updates are disseminated, hop by hop, from the base station to the destination node via other nodes. One of the main challenges of multi-hop network programming is to propagate program code without saturating the network.

Protocols like MOAP (Multihop Over-the-Air Protocol) (Stathopoulos, Heidemann, & Estrin, 2003) and Trickle (Levis, Patel, Culler, & Shenker, 2004) try to avoid flooding the network by disseminating packets to a selective number of nodes, using a simple publish-subscribe mechanism or by periodically broadcasting information to local neighbors.

Table 2. Comparison of dissemination protocols

	XNP	**MOAP**	**Trickle**	**Deluge**	**MNP**	**Freshet**
Hops	Single	Multi	Multi	Multi	Multi	Multi
Dissemination strategy						
Broadcast	Yes	Yes	Yes	Yes	Yes	Yes
Pages	No	No	No	Yes	Yes	Yes
Number of sources	Single	Single	Single	Single	Single	Multi

However, in previous approaches, a node must first receive the complete update before it is able to provide it to other nodes. To allow portions of the update to be forwarded to the requesting nodes before the update has been fully received, the code update can be split into pages, as done by Deluge (Hui & Culler, 2004) and MNP (Multihop Network Reprogramming Protocol) (Kulkarni & Wang, 2005). In this way, each page can be made available to other nodes upon receipt.

To further accelerate dissemination, multiple sources (gateways) of code can be used to start the update as suggested by the Freshet protocol (Krasniewski, Panta, Bagchi, Yang, & Chappell, 2008). Multiple sources are handled by providing a loose coupling of nodes to a source and disseminating the code in waves. It also handles collisions when waves meet.

Executing the Update

A common approach to wired programming a sensor node is to load the new image into the node's program memory with a bootloader that has permission to write data to the user application section. However, since this would require the dissemination of the entire image, a simple bootloader approach is not suitable for the most wireless reprogramming techniques. A virtual machine-based approach like Maté *is not efficient to execute in the long-term* (Dong, Chen, Liu, Bu, & Liu, 2009). Most *OSs* for sensor nodes adopt the dynamic linking and loading approach to address this dissemination and execution issue, as discussed earlier.

When a sensor node is updated, components such as the program (flash) memory, Random-Access (RAM), and external memory (e.g., EEPROM) are usually involved, as shown in Figure 3.

In the case of network reprogramming, the program binary to be loaded can be obtained either by using the communication stack or directly attached storage (Abrach, et al., 2003). The general procedure for executing a code update on the sensor node is shown in Figure 4.

Figure 3. Actors and components involved in over-the-air programming

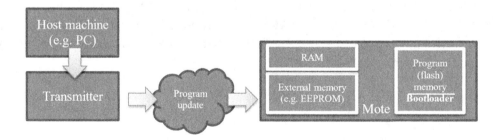

Figure 4. General procedure for executing the code update on the sensor node

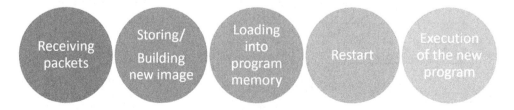

After receiving a code update that is disassembled into network packets, the new image to be loaded is typically either stored in the sensor node's (external) memory or reassembled before it is loaded into the program flash memory. Marron et al. (2006) are giving two reasons for using flash memory as an external memory component for storing and processing code updates:

1.   The size of a code image is usually much larger than the available RAM, so that the code image cannot be completely prepared in RAM.
2.   Program code can only be written to program memory from a special bootloader section. The code image must first be prepared externally before it is written.

Under certain circumstances it may be necessary to reset the sensor node after loading the new program image into the internal program flash, because *without a reboot, pointer variables might point to locations in memory that are no longer valid* (Marron, et al., 2006). After the reboot, the new code takes effect and execution of the new program begins.

Reducing the Costs for Dissemination

As noted by Harte, Rollo, Popovici, & O'flynn (2010), a major issue with network reprogramming is *how to efficiently propagate the updates through the network* (p. 503). The transmission during code update dissemination has a significant impact on the energy efficiency and the lifetime of wireless sensor nodes. To reduce the cost of distributing the code updates, there are a variety of approaches in the literature.

For example, the compression of native code modules may reduce the size of the update, and therefore the dissemination time and power consumption, but it must be noted that the decompression on the sensor nodes requires processing time and power (Tsiftes, Dunkels, & Voigt, 2008).

As the size and density of a network grows and the packet loss is high, the performance of network reprogramming deteriorates. Approaches like MC-Deluge (Xiao & Starobinski, 2005) and Rateless Deluge (Hagedorn, Starobinski, & Trachtenberg, 2008) are using network coding to transmit data to prevent the lack of scalability.

While most dissemination protocols require the radio to be always on during reprogramming, MNP turns off the radio of a node if it is not supposed to transmit or receive *since the energy spent on idle listening is the major source of energy consumption* (Kulkarni & Wang, 2005).

Incremental Reprogramming

There are significant developments in the field of incremental reprogramming. In order to reduce the dissemination costs, incremental code updates only propagate changes to the affected nodes of the WSN. The available current program image is used to build the new version. So-called delta files may consist of data and commands to build the new image on the node itself, e.g. as described by Reijers & Langendoen (2003). Delta files encode the differences between the current and the new image and can therefore be significantly smaller than the new image. Therefore, delta files are transmitted instead of the new image.

There are several incremental approaches to improve the efficiency of reprogramming wireless sensor nodes, but the idea of incremental changes is not new. Rsync (Tridgell, 1999) introduced a remote data update algorithm, which forms the basis of later works. It was originally developed for binary file exchange over a low bandwidth link. This algorithm operates by splitting the files into blocks of fixed size and exchanging block signature information, followed by a simple hash search algorithm for block matching at arbitrary byte boundaries, and transmitting only blocks that have been recognized as being different.

This algorithm is used for block-based algorithms (Jeong, 2003; Jeong & Culler, Incremental network programming for wireless sensors, 2004). It has been adapted because fixed-block comparison cannot find shared blocks when the program code image is shifted, which happens, for example, when inserting some lines of code. Since the diff algorithm is unaware of the program code structure, the sizes of diff scripts do not necessarily match the sizes of the updates. For example, minor changes can lead to code shifts. It does not mitigate the effects of function and global variable shifts, which causes the delta to be large.

Byte-level algorithms (Hu, Xue, He, & Sha, 2009; Mo, Dong, Chen, Bu, & Wang, 2012; Dong, Mo, Huang, Liu, & Chen, 2013; Mazumder & Hallstrom, 2013) are a further development of the block-based algorithms. Since both program images are available on the host system, no block signatures need to be exchanged between the host and the sensor node, and finer granularity is possible. These algorithms try to find the optimal combination of bytes copied from the old code image.

After initial attempts had been made to find the best delta encoding, other approaches attempted to increase the program similarity instead, to keep the delta small. Koshy & Pandey (2005) introduced slop regions to reduce the effects of code shifts. Changes to functions are contained within a slop region after each function.

Zephyr (Panta, Bagchi, & Midkiff, 2009) and Hermes (Panta & Bagchi, 2009) use an indirection table for function calls to reduce the effects of function shifts. As a result, only the entries of the indirection table have to be changed in case of shifts. Indirect calls, however, lead to additional runtime costs. For this reason, Hermes uses the indirection table to patch the call instructions by removing the indirection.

Kachman & Balaz (2016) try to further reduce the delta size by not rebuilding the full image on the sensor node. Instead, changes are patched directly. In this way, only the changed parts of the image have to be encoded as a delta file. The problem with this approach is the extensive use of the flash memory. Lehniger, Weidling, & Schoelzel (2018) propose a page-based approach, where each page of the image is written only once in the flash memory, and it is important to find a good sequence for the pages to be updated.

In this section, an overview of existing strategies for updating WSNs over the air was given. Typical mechanisms for the generation, compaction, and distribution of code updates and required properties of the execution environment on the nodes were discussed. The next section will discuss related security issues. An existing classification of WSN attacks from the literature is further structured to show which classes of attacks could possibly be simplified by improperly secured code update functionality. Various ways for using the attack classes to alter the code update will be presented. Available countermeasures will be presented as well.

SECURITY PROBLEMS IN OTA CODE UPDATES

As presented in the previous section, a lot of research has been done on code updates for WSNs. Various techniques and principles have been presented for the distribution of the code updates in the network, the size and traffic reduction to minimize resource consumption, and the execution environment for performing the update on the node. The OTA update can restore an entire network, e.g., if there is a bug in the software and the WSN is already distributed in the field. However, such an OTA code update may also create new potential security flaws, as the code update provides the adversary with an infrastructure to install new code on a sensor node and execute the code there. Many attacks in WSNs that aim to install malicious code in a sensor node may be simplified in this way, because the most common way to inject malicious code onto a sensor node is to use a security flaw in the protocol stack of the WSN. If code update functionality is available, an adversary could, in the simplest case, use an unprotected code update function to install his own code, because this is what the code update is meant to do. Moreover, the distribution mechanism of a code update can be used to propagate the malicious code to nodes that cannot be physically reached by the attacker, or to nodes that are even out of the reach of an attacker's device. For example, this creates significant security flaws for factories in the age of industry 4.0. These potential risks must be taken into account when developing the code update functionality. Although many code update surveys exist (Brown & Sreenan, 2013; Han, Kumar, Shea, & Srivastava, Sensor network software update management: a survey, 2005; Brown & Sreenan, 2006), they do not explicitly address the security issues associated with these update techniques. While some papers consider specific security aspects such as authentication or secrecy associated with code updates, the authors discuss all fundamental security principles such as confidentiality, integrity, and availability (Padmavathi & Shanmugapriya, 2009; Federal Office for Information Security (BSI), 2007), and show how they are affected by the presented OTA code update mechanisms. These security principles extend IoT security aspects (encryption, trust management and secure routing protocols), as they should guarantee security against attacks on IoT devices beyond the gateway (see Figure 1), i.e. to counteract attacks using the code update as an instrument to attack nodes directly through the wireless communication channel. For this reason, the authors present a classification of possible attacks and discuss how they can be used to attack a code update, as well as how they can be simplified if an attacker can use available code update mechanisms. Typical countermeasures for these threats are presented and the consequences of using these countermeasures along with the described code update strategies will be discussed.

Goals of an Attack and Security Objectives

Security is one of the most important non-functional properties for OTA updates in WSNs. An attack usually affects at least one of the classical security objectives, i.e. integrity, confidentiality, authenticity, and availability. Which of them is violated depends on the goal of the attacker. The goal is usually either to retrieve information from the WSN or to manipulate its function. As a result, the attacker may not want his activity being detected, or he does not care to be detected. This results in four general goals of an attacker, which are classified along with the affected security objectives, as shown in Figure 5.

If the attacker wants to change the behavior of the WSN, it primarily violates the integrity and/or availability objective. Integrity of a WSN means that neither information nor functionality can be altered by unauthorized persons. Availability is the property that the WSN is able to provide the service when requested. Both availability and integrity may be affected by an attack that targets the behavior of the WSN. However, it may be the goal of the attacker to change the behavior unnoticed. This is of particular interest when information should be modified or the system should discontinue providing the service without the suspicion that it was caused by an attacker. This may avoid countermeasures by the operator of the WSN. On the other hand, the goal of the attack may only be to interrupt the service of the WSN, whereby it is not important for the attacker to increase the operator's attention.

Figure 5. Classification of the goals of an attacker

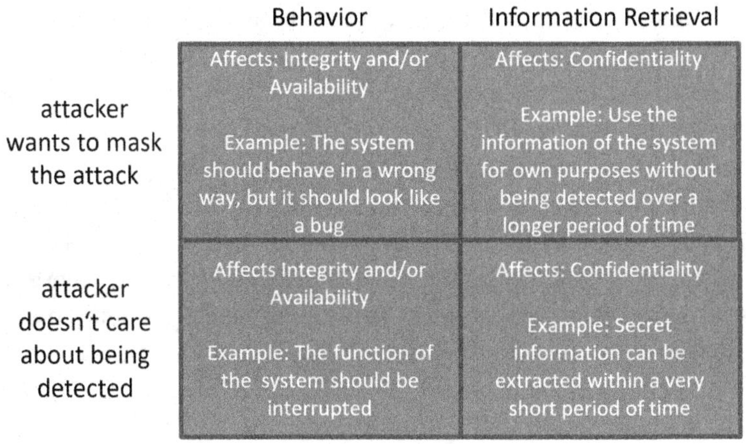

	Behavior	Information Retrieval
attacker wants to mask the attack	Affects: Integrity and/or Availability Example: The system should behave in a wrong way, but it should look like a bug	Affects: Confidentiality Example: Use the information of the system for own purposes without being detected over a longer period of time
attacker doesn't care about being detected	Affects Integrity and/or Availability Example: The function of the system should be interrupted	Affects: Confidentiality Example: Secret information can be extracted within a very short period of time

Another goal of an attacker may be to retrieve information from the WSN. This directly affects the security objective confidentiality. Confidentiality ensures the secrecy of information transmitted in the WSN. After all, retrieving data should happen without being discovered. This allows an attacker to use the WSN infrastructure for its own purposes over a long period of time. In some other situations, an attacker may want to retrieve only specific data. In this case, the attacker does not care about being detected unless the data can be used even if the operator of a WSN becomes aware of the attack. Keeping these goals of an attacker in mind, this section shows how classical attacks can be used to accomplish these goals, and how to use unsecured code update functionality to simplify attacks.

Classification of WSN Attacks and Mechanisms

Attacks aim to achieve at least one of the goals outlined by violating the classical security objectives. In many cases they use the radio interface to achieve the desired security breach, but of course there is also the possibility of directly attacking the node hardware if physical access is possible. The authors will focus on attacks using the radio interface, and how an insecure code update can support or simplify these attacks. First, the authors want to classify known attack mechanisms because there are many ways to attack WSNs.

Classical attack mechanisms can generally be divided into two categories: passive and active attacks. A systematic classification that covers and extends the classifications from (Padmavathi & Shanmugapriya, 2009; Tomic & McCann, 2017) is shown in Figure 6. This overview highlights the mechanisms that can benefit from code update functionality.

Passive Attacks

Passive attacks do neither influence nor tamper the WSN behavior, i.e., there is no modification of sensor nodes or transmitted data. Passive attacks can be used by an attacker to gain knowledge of the WSN's behavior or transmit sensitive information without being detected. There are several ways to passively attack WSNs (Kadri, Feham, & M'hamed, 2010).

By eavesdropping the data transmission the WSN can be monitored by an adversary using a separate receiver outside the deployment area of the WSN. When eavesdropping is done during code update transmission, an attacker may get access to the complete code executed on the sensor node, including the code update execution environment and the protocol stack. Both can give hints for further attacks. It is impossible to prevent eavesdropping by an attacker, but by encrypting the transmitted data it may become useless for him. Advantages and disadvantages of encrypting the code image are discussed in section Encryption and Confidentiality.

But even if the code image is encrypted, an adversary can analyze the traffic on the network. The activity and communication behavior of the nodes may contain information for an attacker. In this way, an attacker may also analyze the distribution mechanism for a code update in a WSN, which may later allow him to disrupt the distribution of a code update. Both attacks – eavesdropping and traffic analysis – will harm the confidentiality of the data transmitted. (Padmavathi & Shanmugapriya, 2009).

A more sophisticated, but also passive attack against the privacy is camouflage an adversary, i.e. to add a sensor node to the WSN pretending to be a normal node. All traffic routed through this node can be monitored and analyzed (Padmavathi & Shanmugapriya, 2009; Sharma & Diwakar, 2012). This may be of particular interest if such a node should record a code image. But if a code update is spread very rarely, the adversary does not want be constantly present with special equipment. Camouflage may be supported by preceding traffic analysis to trigger a code update.

Active Attacks

The counterpart to passive attacks are active attacks. These attacks are used to influence the WSN, e.g., by altering information and data, sending (unauthorized) data within the network, or tampering sensor nodes. Some of these attacks can be simplified if a code update function is available and allows modifying code on the nodes. But also the traffic for the code update functionality itself can be altered by these attacks, for example, to inject malicious code into the nodes. The authors will discuss the latter point first.

Figure 6. Classification of security threats in WSNs. Marked threats can benefit from code update functionality.

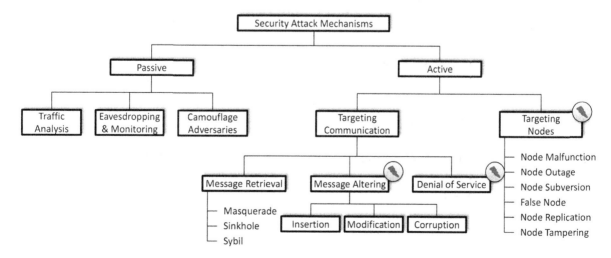

Using Code Update to Simplify Active Attacks

According to Figure 6, the authors further classify active attacks into attacks aimed at manipulating the node itself and attacks aimed at manipulating the communication between the nodes. Attacks on communication often seek to obtain information from the WSN (message retrieval attack), but unlike passive attacks, this happens through interaction with the existing network. With a sinkhole attack, a node attempts to attract traffic to retrieve the information collected by other nodes. In WSNs this can be achieved at the routing layer by manipulating parameters that control the routing decision, such as the use of a high transmission power. Another popular example is the HELLO flood attack (Pal Singh, Sweta, & Jyoti, 2010), in which an adversary advertises a high quality route to the sink by sending out manipulated HELLO-beacons. As an extension, a Sybil attack is a variant of a sinkhole attack in which a single node imitates multiple identities to even force fault-tolerant routing schemes to route all the data through this node (Pathan, Lee, & Hong, 2006).

Another way of retrieving confidential information is a Masquerade attack in which an attacker-controlled node pretends to be part of the network by using the credentials of a privileged node. This requires that these credentials have been previously obtained, e.g., by reverse engineering an original node.

This class of active message retrieval attacks is performed without manipulating original nodes in the network. Since existing nodes in this class of attacks will not be affected, their OTA functionality does not matter and does not contribute to supporting this type of attack. However, such an attack may be easily detected if the retrieved data is missing from the original sink.

Message Altering can be used by an attacker to force security vulnerabilities in the protocol stack of a WSN by injecting wrong messages. Traffic can be altered by inserting new message, modifying, or corrupting messages. Message Insertion can be done simply by sending a new message with hazardous content. Accepting only messages that have a correct signature may prevent this attack, but then simple replay attacks are still feasible. The modification of messages has the same goal, i.e. causing forbidden effects inside the WSN by modifying parts of a specific message (Kiyomoto & Miyake, 2014). However, message modification is difficult without manipulating existing nodes. First, a message sent by a regular node must not reach the intended recipient, and second, must be received by an attacker to be modified and retransmitted. Malicious code on the regular sender can be used to directly modify the message there and therefore simplify this attack. This allows messages to be modified without the risk of detecting the change. Hence, OTA update can be used to support these attacks by introducing malicious code into particular nodes. Message corruption can be used to suppress the reception of important messages or to force the retransmission of messages by provoking collisions. This can easily be achieved by jamming, with two drawbacks: jamming with high transmission power can be easily detected, and secondly, the whole deployment area may be not covered by the jamming signal. Because of this, a code update can support an attacker inject malicious code that can send out a jamming signal using an already existing node.

A denial-of-services (DOS) attack is designed to put the network (or any part of it) in an inoperative state which is an attack on availability. It destroys performance by exhausting the resources of the network. In that case, the WSN is not able to provide its intended service (Sharma & Diwakar, 2012). This attack could be the sum of many node outage attacks when at least too many nodes are disabled, so that the redundancy of the entire network is exhausted. This kind of attack is potentially executed at any network layer: Jamming at physical layer, forcing collisions at link layer, etc. If physical access to the network is not possible, OTA update can help inject malicious code that creates the intended behavior in any node of the network. This is of particular interest if the DOS attack should have a permanent effect, e.g. by battery depletion, or the WSN is distributed over a wide area. In such a case, a DOS attack with external instruments may require a significant effort, which can be reduced by modifying the code of the WSN.

Another large class of attacks is based on techniques for manipulating the behavior of nodes. These attacks either introduce new nodes in the network with altered behavior, or they use existing nodes whose behavior is altered.

Classical attacks that introduce new nodes on the network for an attack are called false node and node replication. False node is adding a malicious node to the WSN which disseminates malicious data into the network. Node replication is similar to false node attacks. The main difference is that the replicated node is not an additional node in the sensor network, but mimics an existing node.

Typically, these techniques require the knowledge of the software running on these nodes. In both cases, Node Subversion may be used to support these attacks. Node subversion can be considered to reverse engineer a sensor node (software and possibly hardware) when the attacker has physical access to the devices. This can be used to reveal information as well as the secret key of the device. If no physical access to nodes is possible, the code update functionality may be used to leak the software running on the nodes through eavesdropping or sinkhole attacks.

Classical attacks for modifying the behavior of existing nodes are called Node Malfunction and Node Outage. Node malfunction attacks the integrity of data. The code update can be used to induce code which tampers, for example, the data aggregation within the WSN, thus forming the basis to support other attacks such as message modification, message corruption, and so forth. Node outage can be provoked using the code update. The attacker could trigger a code update without finishing or clearing all the code on the node. In this state, the sensor node is unable to fulfill the intended function within the network. Hence, these attacks can benefit a lot of code update functionality if the update is not secure and allows modified binary files to be uploaded.

Using Classical Mechanisms for Attacking the Code Update

Conversely, these classical attacks may be applied in an OTA code update system to provide the prerequisite for the abovementioned attacks, i.e. the code update function may be used abusively by an adversary to induce its own code with added functions or to manipulate the update mechanism to do this.

Figure **7** shows a classification for attacking the code update, which may be the preparation for further attacks. On the one hand, an adversary can use passive techniques to attack the code update. The OTA code update introduces the risk of losing intellectual property if an adversary records the update while it is spread to all nodes in the sensor network. On the other hand, update manipulation, prevention and insertion are active attacks with different intentions or means. Update manipulation can be used to inject

Figure 7. Classification for attacking the code update

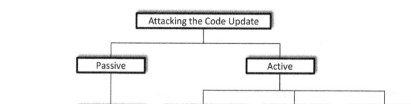

code into an update by manipulating a regular code update. The intent is to add additional code to the update to tamper the nodes in a WSN. This can be achieved by message modification if the update is not properly secured. The same intent, but with a different meaning, is achieved by update insertion. In contrast to update manipulation, update insertion creates a new code update to inject additional code. This requires at least some knowledge of the distribution mechanism, the preparation of the image for the execution environment on the nodes, and the required credentials. This information may be retrieved by message retrieval attacks. Camouflage attacks, node malfunction and/or node replication may be used to initiate a malicious code update attack by an adversary.

The third active attack is update prevention. Its intention is to keep certain nodes at the current software version. In this case, regular updates will not be installed with the intention that ongoing attacks could be circumvented after a code update. This attack can be carried out by a denial of service attack or message destruction.

In either case, altering the binary image or preventing the WSN from being updated will result in a compromised node or a node that is executing an old binary image.

SOLUTIONS AND RECOMMENDATIONS

This section examines the various attacks enumerated in the previous section and presents state-of-the-art countermeasures to counteract the individual attacks and to achieve the fundamental security objectives. With regard to these security objectives, the countermeasures are grouped into areas: code attestation and secure erasure, authentication and integrity and encryption and confidentiality.

The security issues can be viewed from several angles: First, use the code update to remove malicious code. Here, the code attestation can help to find compromised nodes, and secure erasure can remove the malicious code from the node. Second, make the code update itself so secure that it cannot be used to inject malicious code. Here, methods for ensuring authenticity and integrity can prevent the exploitation of code updates over the air. Third, the code update can be encrypted so that it cannot be analyzed or used without permission.

Each of the following subsections summarizes the functionality and goal of the three areas and gives examples of countermeasures.

Code Attestation and Secure Erasure

Code attestation is used to determine whether a node is compromised or not. If a node is compromised, secure erasure can be used to delete malicious code on the node. After that, a code update can be used to reinstall the software and restore the node. After reinstalling the software, the node has again to be verified by code attestation to ensure that there is no longer any malicious code that has compromised the new installation. Code attestation and secure erasure can counteract attacks that target the sensor node (see Figure 6) and lead to unscheduled behavior and code modifications, e.g., node malfunction and node outage. However, code attestation and secure erasure are reactive countermeasures and cannot prevent these attacks, but can restore the node if an attack has occurred. Both approaches are implemented and discussed in different techniques to secure code updates. First, the authors will describe code attestation and then secure erasure in detail.

A correct code attestation means to verify the code for its intended state and functionality, i.e., without any modified malicious parts and functions in the code. In general, code attestation can be distinguished in software-based attestation and hardware-based attestation.

Hardware-based attestation uses dedicated, tamper-resistant hardware or physical access to the device. A Trusted Platform Module (TPM) provides such a hardware-based attestation as signed evidence that provides feedback on the state of the system. In addition, the TPM can test the system in which it is integrated. However, this approach requires a dedicated TPM chip in the system, which is not suitable for low-cost devices in WSNs. Also, physical access for testing the device (e.g., reading the memory) is not possible for attestation, especially for OTA code updates that should fill in the gap to reach all nodes in a WSN without requiring physical access to all nodes.

In contrast to hardware-based attestation, software-based attestation differs in that nodes no longer check themselves, but rather that the sensor nodes check each other or are checked by the base station. In this way, in the case of hardware-based attestation, the other nodes or the base station act as a trusted entity such as a TPM. This is the reason why software-based attestation is typically based on a challenge-response interaction (Kiyomoto & Miyake, 2014). The challenge is sent by a node of the neighborhood or base station, and the response from the device under test needs to have a specific value and arrive at the verifier within a defined time frame. The timeframe is chosen as small as possible so that the attacker does not have enough time to manipulate the response computation. An example of a challenge-response approach is the computation of a checksum consisting of different memory parts or the internal state of the device, e.g., the code memory, registers and program counter (Perito & Tsudik, 2010). However, software-based attestation is more vulnerable to attacks (Castelluccia, Francillon, Perito, & Soriente, 2009). For example, when the code attestation is executed, the adversary can hide the additional code during attestation. The malicious code can be moved between different memories or hidden by using compression. Also time-based attestation can be exploited as described by Shankar, Chew, & Tygar (2004). Kiyomoto & Miyake (2014) also mention other attacks against memory-based attestation, such as replay attack (sending the correct value from the previous attestation) or computation attack (computing the value on the fly or paralyzing the execution to increase the speed).

Kiyomoto & Miyake (2014) introduce a distributed remote attestation protocol to find malfunction of nodes. It does not require any secret information on the node, precise timing measurements, or a tamper-resistant device. The nodes test each other with a value that applies to the attestation of other nodes. Thus, each node checks the integrity of the other nodes data. The scheme consists of an initialization and an attestation phase. If there are unexpected changes in program or data on a node, the protocol stops that particular node by sending a termination request. The verifying node and sender of the request also terminates itself because the reason for the request could be a compromising of the verifying node. In this case, a secure erasure and code update could be used to restore the node. However, stopping the node should prevent the spread of malicious code on the network. In addition, the scheme of Kiyomoto and Miyake is based on the divided local storage of the sensor node. On the one hand the program area and on the other hand the memory area. The program area contains values of the different nodes themselves and the memory area holds calculated hash values and is based on the program area values of the other nodes. This setup and the the creation of values takes place in the initialization phase. In the attestation phase, the nodes randomly select registers for two cases. When selecting a register from program area, the node computes the hash value and compares it to the received value from another node that has saved that value in the respective memory area. Otherwise, the node gets the corresponding value from the program area of the other node, computes its hash values, and compares it to the stored hash value from the randomly selected register in the memory area. By receiving and comparing these values, the nodes can test each other for compromise.

As previously described, code attestation can verify if a node is compromised. If code attestation reveals compromising, there are two ways to handle it. The first one is to exclude the node from the network, and second one is to recover the node. However, before the node can be recovered, all the malicious code must be removed. This is done by secure erasure. A secure erasure mechanism can remove all code in the rewritable memories, which means that the malicious code is also removed. This removal can be done by a secure erasure function stored in a read-only memory. Writing random code to all other memory can erase the malicious code. In Addition, the function is protected in the read-only memory and cannot be manipulated.

Perito & Tsudik (2010) propose an approach to combat the latter attacks, i.e. *node malfunction* and *node outage*, with a new primitive Proofs of Secure Erasure (PoSE) and take advantage of the bounded memory model for embedded devices. The small ROM of a device is needed to store two functions: read-and-send and receive-and-write. One is used to receive random bits from the verifier to clear all memory and the other to send it to the prover, respectively. Both functions can be used to verify and update nodes. Because of saving the two functions in the ROM, they cannot be manipulated and are used for erasing the memory in the case of compromise. This should guarantee that there is no malicious code left after erasing the memory and before sending the update to restore the node.

There are several other works aiming at attestation and secure erasure, for example by Wagner (Wagner, 2011), Karame & Li (Karame & Li, 2015), and Kohnhaeuser & Katzenbeisser (Kohnhaeuser & Katzenbeisser, 2016). Wagner (Wagner, 2011) is also using PoSE.

The above countermeasures can be used for code attestation and secure erasure in WSNs. However, they are also related to the code update type supported by the code update mechanism. Table 3 summarizes the conditions for different code update strategies for the execution environment and their dependencies for code attestation and secure erasure. Code Attestation (in software, but also in hardware) can be used for different types of code update strategies. So it does not matter if the strategy used supports module updates, delta image updates, or full replacements. As long as the state of the node to be verified is known, code attestation can be used for verification. However, there are limitations to secure erasure for repairing a malicious node. Secure erasure is only useful if there is the possibility to update/repair the node with a full replacement of the image. The reason for this is obvious, since all rewritable memory must be cleared to ensure that the malicious code has been removed before a code update can recover the node. Module replacement and delta image code updates can be used under untampered conditions, but the restoration of a compromised node requires the ability to completely replace the image.

Table 3. Code attestation and secure erasure dependencies on execution environment

Code Update Type	Code Attestation HW	Code Attestation SW	Secure Erasure
Full replacement	✓	✓	✓
Module replacement	✓	✓	✗
Delta image	✓	✓	✗

Encryption and Confidentiality

This subsection introduces techniques for providing confidentiality for OTA code updates. Confidentiality can be achieved by encrypting the image prior to its dissemination in the network. The encrypted image is protected against eavesdropping and cannot be analyzed for weaknesses. Furthermore, the image is inaccessible to build a false node or theft of intellectual property, when it is disseminated over the air.

There are several algorithms for encrypting data, one symmetric and the other asymmetric. The main difference is the keys used for encryption and decryption. Symmetric approaches use the same key, while asymmetric approaches use key pairs. The key pair of an asymmetric algorithm consists of a public key for encryption and a private key for decryption. However, cryptographic secrecy is associated with a high demand for energy and computational power because most algorithms are not implemented for resource-constrained devices. This is the main reason why standardized and common algorithms are not suitable for WSN and explains the rare use in the area of updating WSNs. In this case, however, the operator of a WSN must consider that an attacker always has the ability to save the entire image when a full update is disseminated in the network. This means that an attacker can use the image for different attacking scenarios. One could be a node replication attack in which the attacker builds a node that behaves like the original node, but with additional capabilities. This scenario can be used to gain initial access to the network and drive further attacks, e.g. to disable security checks.

Another mentioned scenario is not directly attacking the WSN, but the intellectual property used to maintain the network, that is the software and images of the nodes. The stored image can be used for node subversion, for own purposes to gain knowledge or to analyze weaknesses for the preparation of attacks.

Some approaches have been published in research to implement confidentiality for WSN applications. Kadri, Feham, & M'hamed (2010) generally state that public key encryption in WSNs is not supported because the battery and computational power is limited. The development of new sensor node technologies and energy-efficient public key encryption, such as elliptic curve cryptography gives the possibility to use public-key approaches in WSNs. The authors propose a new lightweight implementation of a public key infrastructure (PKI), called μPKI. The basic concept is to use public key operations only for some steps, e.g., for session key computation, to guarantee authentication and confidentiality. To send messages and packages within the network, the node is capable to use the generated session key and encrypt the data with a symmetric approach. The benefit is that symmetric approaches require less computational power than asymmetric approaches. However, each node must be able to perform an asymmetric algorithm for key generation and a symmetric algorithm for message encryption and decryption. This approach was not developed for confidentiality in the dissemination of code updates in WSN. But since the update is also divided into packages, it can be used to encrypt the data from a code update.

Nirmala & Manjunath (2010) suggest a solution for a network program update protocol for clustered WSNs. The scheme is confidential to securely broadcast the program image, uses mobile agents for the update distribution, and is implemented in two phases: the key computation phase and the network program update phase. Before deployment, each node is assigned a unique random string. This string is used in the key computation phase to secure the individual keys and the computation of three different keys. The first key is used between base stations and cluster heads (mobile agents), the second key is used in clusters, and there are also individual keys between the cluster head and sensor nodes. In the phase of a network program update based on Deluge, the image is hashed (i.e. packets of an image), the hash is added, and the keys of the key computation phase are used to encrypt the update between base station and cluster head and between cluster head and sensor node respectively. This guarantees a confidential dissemination of the code update in a WSN.

Nirmala & Manjunath (2015) propose a solution without the need for mobile agents who move to the defined place, but uses so-called multicast group heads for multicast groups. For each of the groups, a key is computed involving the head and all the members of the multi cast group in a key agreement protocol.

As it is still a complex and difficult task to provide confidentiality in a WSN for code updates, there is another possible solution. The approach provides the use of delta image updates instead of encryption for an update. The advantage is that no encryption is required if the delta image consists only of instructions and operations that are sent to update the node. However, this approach has the disadvantage that it is not allowed to send a full image for an update, which would be necessary if a compromised node needs to be repaired over the air. But in this case the update could be encrypted since it is better to invest some resources for the decryption to recover the node than to exclude the node from the WSN.

Authentication and Integrity

As described in section Code Attestation and Secure Erasure, code attestation and secure erasure are powerful and important mechanisms for recovering compromised nodes. But they are reactive counter-measures and can only detect an attack once it has happened. One way to prevent node compromise is to use authentication and integrity mechanisms for an update that is provided in a WSN. On the one hand, these mechanisms can provide authentication, that is, the update comes from an authorized entity. On the other hand, this update is not manipulated by providing an integrity verification that can guarantee that the update is not being manipulated by an attacker. Thus, both techniques, authentication and integrity, can counteract attacks that target the communication in a network (see Figure 6), e.g., message modification and message corruption. The simplest and most common solution to achieve integrity and authenticity is to use a combination of hash functions and public-key algorithms to sign the hash value. Furthermore, it is common to use a hash chain for the packets when the update is sent, i.e. for all update strategies and dissemination protocols.

Authenticity can secure that updates are installed only by the WSN administrator, which means that no third party can insert new code into the WSN by using the interface of the code update mechanism. In the case of WSNs, this means that some entities can have access to the network, while others can only get information from the sensor nodes. However, the administrator can also trigger a code update for the WSN. An adversary should not be able to do either one or the other. Public key algorithms can be used to achieve authenticated code updates. This is done by using the private key of the network administrator. The private key is used to sign the image with a chosen algorithm before spreading it on the network. When the node receives the data, it can verify the image using the public key of the administrator and the respective algorithm. This approach is simple but not efficient due to the limited computational power and energy resources of sensor nodes in WSNs. This approach requires a full sign of the update, which is secure but too exhausting due to many public key operations. But authenticity can ensure integrity of secure code updates when combined with integrity mechanisms. Therefore, fast and energy-efficient hash algorithms are used to compute a hash value from the message. This value is signed with a public-key algorithm instead of signing the entire image. Because of less public key operations, energy is saved because the part of the messages that need to be signed is smaller than the whole image.

Providing authentication and integrity when using code update in WSNs can counter many attack scenarios when over-the-air updates occur. Message modification is one of those that can be counteracted. The modification may induce new code for further tampering or authorization. This kind of attack can be counteracted by using integrity checksums in combination with authentication methods as mentioned above. In detail, the checksum is used to detect changes in the code update. If an attacker changes the update, he must also change the checksum. Otherwise, the computed checksum of the data would not match, and changing the checksum is really easy since the computation can be done quickly. However, the attacker also needs to sign the checksum with the administrator's private key, which is unknown to the attacker. So, when checking and correcting the checksum, integrity is given on the condition that the attacker cannot manipulate the integrity check. This can be achieved by signing the integrity checksum with a private key. This technique is the reason for using authentication along with integrity verification and can be applied to all distribution and code update techniques.

Deng, Han, & Mishra (2006) also introduce a hybrid scheme based on the above-mentioned principle. The goal is to prevent false or malicious code updates, and each node must authenticate the received image before using or propagating it. Therefore, the authors introduce a hybrid combination of hash value computation and authentication. The scheme needs only a small overhead compared to a non-secure update scheme like Deluge. This makes the scheme suitable for WSNs. The difference in the hybrid combination is based on a tree with a root signature and a spanning tree below with hashes of the following code packets. Each packet thus contains the hash values for all underlying child packages of the built tree. This supports unsorted receiving of packets that can be caused by transmission errors in the WSN and require only little overhead. Deng, Han, & Mishra (2006a) present two additional schemes for building a hash chain with authentication for their scheme described in the previous text section.

Another attack aimed at data integrity is message corruption. The goal of this attack is to prevent the node from being updated and to disrupt the update process. By using integrity verification, the manipulated data can be recognized before the update is started. This means that the update process on the node will not start because the verification can be easily computed and corrupted messages can be recognized. In this case, the node cannot be updated but will work with the last setup.

Lanigan, Gandhi, & Narasimhan (2006) propose a protocol to ensure that only trusted updates are disseminated in the sensor network, combining authentication and integrity. In fact, this should protect the sensor network from nodes that are compromised by updates and discovered later, so the update is checked for integrity before being forwarded.

Seshadri, Luk, Perrig, van Doom, & Khosla (2006) present a protocol for detecting and recovering compromised sensor nodes. The protocol SCUBA strongly guarantees the correct patching of sensor nodes or at least the detection, if the update failed. The protocol uses Indisputable Code Execution (ICE) for the untampered execution of code, even if the sensor node is compromised. Thus, this work can be used for both, i.e. a secure code update in untampered environments and also for the recovery of compromised sensor nodes. The integrity of code updates is ensured by the atomic execution of ICE verification functions, i.e. no interrupts are allowed and any malicious code on the node cannot affect the node's recovery. The verification function of SCUBA uses CPU states for the checksum computation, which in case of compromised nodes leads to two possible effects. Either the checksum is false or the computation takes too long if the attacker tries to manipulate the checksum computation.

The advantage over attestation is that compromised nodes cannot infect other nodes and, ideally, nodes cannot be compromised from the beginning. Because this kind of solution is reactive, it offers two benefits. First, no energy is wasted on detecting malicious code, that is, attestation, and second, the malicious node has no time to propagate that code.

Furthermore, it is advantageous if the update can be verified as each packet is received, rather than first receiving the complete update, followed by the verification, for example to send the update to the next node.

FUTURE RESEARCH DIRECTIONS

This book chapter has shown that there are several approaches to the general procedure of code updates. Generation, dissemination, and execution are widely explored and there are also concepts and solutions to gain security for wireless code updates. However, there are still some open issues in providing the full security package for IoE. Especially the area of WSNs presents challenges for providing confidentiality due to the demand for resources for cryptographic algorithms.

Intrusion Detection Systems and Intrusion Prevention Systems are used in computer networks to detect and prevent a large variety of attacks. Through the constant evaluation of certain machine states and network communication, attacks can be identified by treacherous behavior. However, collecting and analyzing the necessary amount of data without generating too much overhead in the network is yet an unsolved problem for WSNs.

CONCLUSION

In this book chapter, an overview of existing strategies for updating WSNs over the air was given and related security issues were discussed. WSNs as a subset of IoT networks are subject to hardware restrictions and therefore complicate the application of security measures. Typical mechanisms for the generation, compaction, and distribution of code updates and required properties of the execution environment on the nodes were discussed. Subsequently, an existing classification of WSN attacks from the literature was further structured to show which classes of attacks could possibly be simplified by improperly secured code update functionality. It turned out that especially attacks aimed at changing messages and nodes could benefit. In particular, if no physical access to the WSN is possible or the attack should be hidden from the WSN operator. Various ways for using the attack classes to alter the code update were presented. This shows that if the wireless update functionality is placed in the context of an IoT ecosystem, additional measures may be required to prevent the opening of new vulnerabilities. An IoT security framework would need to be extended with additional mechanisms to secure the OTA code update functionality. Available countermeasures were presented and it was shown that not all countermeasures could be used together with all possible mechanisms for providing code updates. This means that the choice of well suited countermeasures depends on the security objectives and the used code update mechanism. By discussing interdependencies, this book chapter provided a guideline to choosing the right combination of countermeasures.

REFERENCES

Abrach, H., Bhatti, S., Carlson, J., Dai, H., Rose, J., Sheth, A., ... Han, R. (2003). MANTIS: System support for multimodal networks of in-situ sensors. In *Proceedings of the 2nd ACM international conference on Wireless sensor networks and applications* (pp. 50-59). ACM. 10.1145/941350.941358

Babar, S., Stango, A., Prasad, N., Sen, J., & Prasad, R. (2011). Proposed embedded security framework for internet of things (iot). In *2nd International Conference on Wireless Communication, Vehicular Technology, Information Theory and Aerospace & Electronic Systems Technology (Wireless VITAE)* (pp. 1-5). IEEE. 10.1109/WIRELESSVITAE.2011.5940923

Brown, S., & Sreenan, C. (2006). *Updating software in wireless sensor networks: A survey*. Citeseer.

Brown, S., & Sreenan, C. J. (2013). Software updating in wireless sensor networks: A survey and lacunae. *Journal of Sensor and Actuator Networks*, 717-760.

Cao, Q., Abdelzaher, T., Stankovic, J., & He, T. (2008). The liteos operating system: Towards unix-like abstractions for wireless sensor networks. *International Conference On Information Processing in Sensor Networks*, 233-244. 10.1109/IPSN.2008.54

Castelluccia, C., Francillon, A., Perito, D., & Soriente, C. (2009). On the difficulty of software-based attestation of embedded devices. *Proceedings of the 16th ACM conference on Computer and communications security*, 400-409. 10.1145/1653662.1653711

Cha, H., Choi, S., Jung, I., Kim, H., Shin, H., Yoo, J., & Yoon, C. (2007). RETOS: resilient, expandable, and threaded operating system for wireless sensor networks. *Proceedings of the 6th international conference on Information processing in sensor networks*, 148-157. 10.1145/1236360.1236381

Chen, Y.-T., Chien, T.-C., & Chou, P. H. (2010). Enix: a lightweight dynamic operating system for tightly constrained wireless sensor platforms. *Proceedings of the 8th ACM Conference on Embedded Networked Sensor Systems*, 183-196. 10.1145/1869983.1870002

Crossbow Technology, Inc. (2003). *Mote In-Network Programming User Reference Version 20030315*. Retrieved from https://www.eol.ucar.edu/isf/facilities/isa/internal/TinyOSdoc/Xnp.pdf

Deng, J., Han, R., & Mishra, S. (2006). Efficiently authenticating code images in dynamically reprogrammed wireless sensor networks. *Fourth Annual IEEE International Conference on Pervasive Computing and Communications Workshops*.

Deng, J., Han, R., & Mishra, S. (2006a). Secure code distribution in dynamically programmable wireless sensor networks. *The Fifth International Conference on Information Processing in Sensor Networks*, 292-300. 10.1145/1127777.1127822

Dong, W., Chen, C., Liu, X., & Bu, J. (2010). Providing OS support for wireless sensor networks: Challenges and approaches. *IEEE Communications Surveys and Tutorials*, *12*(4), 519–530. doi:10.1109/SURV.2010.032610.00045

Dong, W., Chen, C., Liu, X., Bu, J., & Liu, Y. (2009). Dynamic linking and loading in networked embedded systems. *IEEE 6th International Conference on Mobile Adhoc and Sensor Systems*, 554-562.

Dong, W., Mo, B., Huang, C., Liu, Y., & Chen, C. (2013). *R3: Optimizing relocatable code for efficient reprogramming in networked embedded systems*. IEEE INFOCOM.

Dunkels, A., Gronvall, B., & Voigt, T. (2004). Contiki - a lightweight and flexible operating system for tiny networked sensors. *29th Annual IEEE International Conference on Local Computer Networks*, 455-462. 10.1109/LCN.2004.38

Farooq, M. O., & Kunz, T. (2011). Operating systems for wireless sensor networks: A survey. *Sensors (Basel)*, *11*(6), 5900–5930. doi:10.3390110605900 PMID:22163934

Federal Office for Information Security (BSI). (2007). *IT-Security Guidelines*. BSI.

Hagedorn, A., Starobinski, D., & Trachtenberg, A. (2008). Rateless Deluge: Over-the-Air Programming of Wireless Sensor Networks Using Random Linear Codes. Academic Press.

Han, C.-C., Kumar, R., Shea, R., Kohler, E., & Srivastava, M. (2005). A dynamic operating system for sensor nodes. In *Proceedings of the 3rd international conference on Mobile systems, applications, and services* (pp. 163-176). ACM. 10.1145/1067170.1067188

Han, C.-C., Kumar, R., Shea, R., & Srivastava, M. (2005). Sensor network software update management: A survey. *International Journal of Network Management*, *15*(4), 283–294. doi:10.1002/nem.574

Han, C.-C., Rengaswamy, R. K., Shea, R., Kohler, E., & Srivastava, M. (2005). SOS: A dynamic operating system for sensor networks. *Proceedings of the Third International Conference on Mobile Systems, Applications, And Services (Mobisys)*, 1-2.

Harte, S., Rollo, S., Popovici, E., & O'flynn, B. (2010). *Energy-efficient reprogramming of heterogeneous wireless sensor networks*. InTech.

Hill, J., Szewczyk, R., Woo, A., Hollar, S., Culler, D., & Pister, K. (2000). System Architecture Directions for Networked Sensors. In *Proceedings of the Ninth International Conference on Architectural Support for Programming Languages and Operating Systems* (pp. 93-104). Cambridge, MA: ACM. 10.1145/378993.379006

Hu, J., Xue, C. J., He, Y., & Sha, E. H.-M. (2009). Reprogramming with minimal transferred data on wireless sensor network. *IEEE 6th International Conference on Mobile Adhoc and Sensor Systems*, 160-167.

Hui, J. W., & Culler, D. (2004). The dynamic behavior of a data dissemination protocol for network programming at scale. In *Proceedings of the 2nd international conference on Embedded networked sensor systems* (pp. 81-94). ACM. 10.1145/1031495.1031506

Jeong, J. (2003). *Node-level representation and system support for network programming*. Academic Press.

Jeong, J., & Culler, D. (2004). Incremental network programming for wireless sensors. *First Annual IEEE Communications Society Conference on Sensor and Ad Hoc Communications and Networks*, 25-33.

Kachman, O., & Balaz, M. (2016). Optimized differencing algorithm for firmware updates of low-power devices. *IEEE 19th International Symposium on Design and Diagnostics of Electronic Circuits & Systems*, 1-4.

Kadri, B., Feham, M., & M'hamed, A. (2010). Lightweight PKI for WSN uPKI. *The Journal of Security and Communication Networks*, 135-141.

Karame, G. O., & Li, W. (2015). Secure Erasure and Code Update in Legacy Sensors. In M. Conti, M. Schunter, & I. Askoxylakis (Eds.), Trust and Trustworthy Computing (pp. 283-299). Springer International Publishing. doi:10.1007/978-3-319-22846-4_17

Kiyomoto, S., & Miyake, Y. (2014). Lightweight attestation scheme for wireless sensor network. *International Journal of Security and Its Applications*, 25-40.

Kohnhaeuser, F., & Katzenbeisser, S. (2016). Secure Code Updates for Mesh Networked Commodity Low-End Embedded Devices. In I. Askoxylakis, S. Ioannidis, S. Katsikas, & C. Meadows (Eds.), Computer Security -- ESORICS 2016 (pp. 320-338). Springer International Publishing. doi:10.1007/978-3-319-45741-3_17

Kolias, C., Kambourakis, G., Stavrou, A., & Voas, J. (2017). DDoS in the IoT: Mirai and other botnets. *Computer*, *50*(7), 80–84. doi:10.1109/MC.2017.201

Koshy, J., & Pandey, R. (2005). Remote incremental linking for energy-efficient reprogramming of sensor networks. *Proceedings of the Second European Workshop on Wireless Sensor Networks*, 354-365.

Koshy, J., & Pandey, R. (2005). VMSTAR: Synthesizing Scalable Runtime Environments for Sensor Networks. *Proceedings of the 3rd International Conference on Embedded Networked Sensor Systems* (pp. 243-254). San Diego, CA: ACM. 10.1145/1098918.1098945

Krasniewski, M. D., Panta, R. K., Bagchi, S., Yang, C.-L., & Chappell, W. J. (2008). Energy-efficient on-demand reprogramming of large-scale sensor networks. *ACM Transactions on Sensor Networks*, *4*(1), 1–38. doi:10.1145/1325651.1325653

Kulkarni, S. S., & Wang, L. (2005). MNP: Multihop network reprogramming service for sensor networks. *Proceedings of the 25th IEEE International Conference on Distributed Computing Systems*, 7-16. 10.1109/ICDCS.2005.50

Lanigan, P. E., Gandhi, R., & Narasimhan, P. (2006). Sluice: Secure dissemination of code updates in sensor networks. *26th IEEE International Conference on Distributed Computing Systems*, 53-53. 10.1109/ICDCS.2006.77

Lehniger, K., Weidling, S., & Schoelzel, M. (2018). Heuristic for Page-based Incremental. *Proc. of the 21st IEEE International Symposium on Design and Diagnostics of Electronic Circuits and Systems*.

Levis, P., & Culler, D. E. (2002). Maté: a tiny virtual machine for sensor networks. In *Proceedings of the 10th International Conference on Architectural Support for Programming Languages and Operating Systems* (pp. 85-95). San Jose, CA: ACM. 10.1145/605397.605407

Levis, P., Patel, N., Culler, D., & Shenker, S. (2004). Trickle: A self-regulating algorithm for code propagation and maintenance in wireless sensor networks. *Proc. of the 1st USENIX/ACM Symp. on Networked Systems Design and Implementation*.

Marron, P. J., Gauger, M., Lachenmann, A., Minder, D., Saukh, O., & Rothermel, K. (2006). FlexCup: A flexible and efficient code update mechanism for sensor networks. *European Workshop on Wireless Sensor Networks*, 212-227. 10.1007/11669463_17

Mazumder, B., & Hallstrom, J. O. (2013). An efficient code update solution for wireless sensor network reprogramming. *Proceedings of the International Conference on Embedded Software (EMSOFT)*, 1-10. 10.1109/EMSOFT.2013.6658582

Mo, B., Dong, W., Chen, C., Bu, J., & Wang, Q. (2012). An efficient differencing algorithm based on suffix array for reprogramming wireless sensor networks. *IEEE International Conference on Communications (ICC)*, 773-777. 10.1109/ICC.2012.6364214

Nirmala, M., & Manjunath, A. (2010). Secure program update using broadcast encryption for clustered wireless sensor networks. *Sixth International Conference on Wireless Communication and Sensor Networks (WCSN)*, 1-6. 10.1109/WCSN.2010.5712303

Nirmala, M., & Manjunath, A. (2015). SCUMG: Secure Code Update for Multicast Group in Wireless Sensor Networks. *12th International Conference on Information Technology-New Generations (ITNG)*, 249-254. 10.1109/ITNG.2015.46

Pacheco, J., & Hariri, S. (2016). IoT security framework for smart cyber infrastructures. IEEE International Workshops on Foundations and Applications of Self* Systems, 242-247.

Padmavathi, G., & Shanmugapriya, A. (2009). A survey of attacks, security mechanisms and challenges in wireless sensor networks. *International Journal of Computer Science and Information Security, 4*(1-2).

Pal Singh, V., Sweta, J., & Jyoti, S. (2010). Hello Flood Attack and its Countermeasures in Wireless Sensor Networks. *International Journal of Computer Science Issues, 7*.

Panta, R. K., & Bagchi, S. (2009). *Hermes: Fast and energy efficient incremental code updates for wireless sensor networks*. IEEE INFOCOM.

Panta, R. K., Bagchi, S., & Midkiff, S. P. (2009). Zephyr: Efficient incremental reprogramming of sensor nodes using function call indirections and difference computation. *Proc. of USENIX Annual Technical Conference*.

Pathan, A.-S. K., Lee, H.-W., & Hong, C. S. (2006). Security in wireless sensor networks: issues and challenges. *The 8th International Conference Advanced Communication Technology, 6*.

Perito, D., & Tsudik, G. (2010). Secure Code Update for Embedded Devices via Proofs of Secure Erasure. In D. Gritzalis, B. Preneel, & M. Theoharidou (Eds.), Computer Security -- ESORICS 2010 (pp. 643-662). Springer Berlin Heidelberg. doi:10.1007/978-3-642-15497-3_39

Rahman, A. F., Daud, M., & Mohamad, M. Z. (2016). Securing sensor to cloud ecosystem using internet of things (iot) security framework. *Proceedings of the International Conference on Internet of things and Cloud Computing*, 79. 10.1145/2896387.2906198

Reijers, N., & Langendoen, K. (2003). Efficient code distribution in wireless sensor networks. In *Proceedings of the 2nd ACM international conference on Wireless sensor networks and applications* (pp. 60-67). ACM. 10.1145/941350.941359

Seshadri, A., Luk, M., Perrig, A., van Doorn, L., & Khosla, P. (2006). SCUBA: Secure code update by attestation in sensor networks. *Proceedings of the 5th ACM workshop on Wireless security*, 85-94. 10.1145/1161289.1161306

Shankar, U., Chew, M., & Tygar, J. D. (2004). Side effects are not sufficient to authenticate software. *USENIX Security Symposium*.

Sharma, R., & Diwakar, C. (2012). *Security Analysis of Wireless Sensor Networks. International Journal of Research in Engineering & Applied Sciences*, 774–786.

Stathopoulos, T., Heidemann, J., & Estrin, D. (2003). *A remote code update mechanism for wireless sensor networks*. UCLA, Center for Embedded Networked Computing. doi:10.21236/ADA482630

Tomic, I., & McCann, J. (2017). *A Survey of Potential Security Issues in Existing Wireless Sensor Protocols. IEEE Internet of Things Journal*. doi:10.1109/JIOT.2017.2749883

Tridgell, A. (1999). *Efficient algorithms for sorting and synchronizatio*. Australian National University Canberra.

Tsiftes, N., Dunkels, A., & Voigt, T. (2008). Efficient Sensor Network Reprogramming through Compression of Executable Modules. *5th Annual IEEE Communications Society Conference on Sensor, Mesh and Ad Hoc Communications and Networks*, 359-367. 10.1109/SAHCN.2008.51

Vieira, M. A., Coelho, C. N., Da Silva, D., & da Mata, J. M. (2003). Survey on wireless sensor network devices. *Proceedings IEEE Conference Emerging Technologies and Factory Automation*, 537-544. 10.1109/ETFA.2003.1247753

Wagner, S. (2011). *Attestation and Secure Code Update for Trusted Sensor Nodes* (Master's thesis). Technical University of Munich.

Xiao, W., & Starobinski, D. (2005). Exploiting multi-Channel diversity to speed up over-the-air programming of wireless sensor networks. In *Proceedings of the 3rd international conference on Embedded networked sensor systems* (pp. 292-293). ACM. 10.1145/1098918.1098960

Zheng, X.-L., & Wan, M. (2014). A survey on data dissemination in wireless sensor networks. *Journal of Computer Science and Technology*, *29*(3), 470–486. doi:10.100711390-014-1443-8

ADDITIONAL READING

Brown, S., & Sreenan, C. (2006). *Updating software in wireless sensor networks: A survey*. Citeseer.

Brown, S., & Sreenan, C. J. (2013). Software updating in wireless sensor networks: A survey and lacunae. *Journal of Sensor and Actuator Networks*, pp. 717-760.

Dong, W., Chen, C., Liu, X., & Bu, J. (2010). Providing OS support for wireless sensor networks: Challenges and approaches. *IEEE Communications Surveys and Tutorials*, *12*(4), 519–530. doi:10.1109/SURV.2010.032610.00045

Farooq, M. O., & Kunz, T. (2011). Operating systems for wireless sensor networks: A survey. *Sensors (Basel)*, *11*(6), 5900–5930. doi:10.3390110605900 PMID:22163934

Han, C.-C., Kumar, R., Shea, R., & Srivastava, M. (2005). Sensor network software update management: A survey. *International Journal of Network Management*, *15*(4), 283–294. doi:10.1002/nem.574

Padmavathi, G., & Shanmugapriya, A. (2009). A survey of attacks, security mechanisms and challenges in wireless sensor networks. *International Journal of Computer Science and Information Security, IJCSIS, Vol. 4, No. 1 & 2*.

Tomic, I., & McCann, J. (2017). *A Survey of Potential Security Issues in Existing Wireless Sensor Protocols*. IEEE Internet of Things Journal. doi:10.1109/JIOT.2017.2749883

Zheng, X.-L., & Wan, M. (2014). A survey on data dissemination in wireless sensor networks. *Journal of Computer Science and Technology*, *29*(3), 470–486. doi:10.100711390-014-1443-8

KEY TERMS AND DEFINITIONS

Asymmetric Cryptography: Asymmetric cryptography or public-key cryptography is based on key pairs. It consists of a public key for encryption, known to everyone, and a private key for decryption, known only to the owner. Public-key algorithms can be used for encryption and authentication. Common algorithms are ECC (elliptic curve cryptography) and RSA (Rivest, Shamir, and Adleman cryptosystem).

Authenticity: Authenticity is a property that confirms the identity of an entity.

Code Attestation: Code attestation is a process used to validate the integrity of a device.

Heterogeneity: With regard to wireless sensor networks, the term heterogeneity refers to the property of a network to have nodes with different characteristics.

Integrity: Integrity of a WSN means that neither information nor functionality can be altered by unauthorized persons, and if they are altered, it can be detected.

Internet of Things (IoT): This widely used term refers to the idea that all physical objects are connected to the Internet and have the ability to communicate or interact with each other.

Over-the-Air (OTA) Programming: Methods of distributing software updates to devices using wireless communication can be taken under the term of over-the-air programming.

Secure Erasure: Secure erasure is a process that clears all memory to remove the code on a device, including malicious code.

Symmetric Cryptography: Symmetric cryptography is based on the use of just one key. This key is used for both encryption and decryption and is shared with all entities. Common algorithms are AES (advanced encryption standard), DES (data encryption standard), and triple-DES.

Wireless Sensor Network (WSN): A group of spatially dispersed and wirelessly communicating devices that use sensors to monitor environmental conditions such as temperature or humidity can be called wireless sensor networks. The data can be collected centrally.

Compilation of References

3. GPP. (2016). *Low Power Wide Area Technologies*. Whitepaper. Retrieved from https://www.gsma.com/iot/3gpp-low-power-wide-area-technologies-white-paper/

Abadi, M., Agarwal, A., Barham, P., Brevdo, E., Chen, Z., Citro, C., … Zheng, X. (2016). *Tensorflow: Large-scale machine learning on heterogeneous distributed systems.* ArXiv Preprint ArXiv:1603.04467

ABI Research. (2016). *Best fit use Cases for LPWANs*. Whitepaper. Retrieved from https://www.ingenu.com/portfolio/best-fit-use-cases-for-lpwans/

Abomhara, M., & Koien, G. M. (2014). Security and privacy in the Internet of Things: Current status and open issues. *International Conference on Privacy and Security in Mobile Systems (PRISMS)*, 1-8. 10.1109/PRISMS.2014.6970594

Abrach, H., Bhatti, S., Carlson, J., Dai, H., Rose, J., Sheth, A., ... Han, R. (2003). MANTIS: System support for multimodal networks of in-situ sensors. In *Proceedings of the 2nd ACM international conference on Wireless sensor networks and applications* (pp. 50-59). ACM. 10.1145/941350.941358

Abuzainab, N., & Saad, W. (2017). *Dynamic Connectivity Game for Adversarial Internet of Battlefield Things Systems.* arXiv:1708.05741v2 [cs.IT]

Acampora, G., Cook, D. J., Rashidi, P., & Vasilakos, A. V. (2013). A Survey on Ambient Intelligence in Health Care. *Proceedings of the IEEE, 101*(12), 2470–2494. 10.1109/JPROC.2013.2262913

ACEA. (2017). *ACEA principles of automobile cybersecurity*. Retrieved from https://www.acea.be/publications/article/acea-principles-of-automobile-cybersecurity

Aced López, S., Corno, F., & De Russis, L. (2015). Supporting caregivers in assisted living facilities for persons with disabilities: A user study. *Universal Access in the Information Society, 14*(1), 133–144. doi:10.100710209-014-0400-1

Adib, F., Mao, H., Kabelac, Z., Katabi, D., & Miller, R. C. (2015). Smart Homes that Monitor Breathing and Heart Rate. In *Proceedings of the 33rd Annual ACM Conference on Human Factors in Computing Systems* (pp. 837–846). Seoul, Republic of Korea: ACM. 10.1145/2702123.2702200

Adiono, T., Marthensa, R., Muttaqin, R., Fuada, S., Harimurti, S., & Adijarto, W. (2017). Design of database and secure communication protocols for Internet-of-things-based smart home system. In TENCON 2017 - 2017 IEEE Region 10 Conference (pp. 1273–1278). IEEE. doi:10.1109/TENCON.2017.8228053

AENEAS, ARTEMIS, & EPoSS. (2018). *Strategic Research Agenda for Electronic Components and Systems*. Retrieved from https://efecs.eu/publication/download/ecs-sra-2018.pdf

AGERAR Project. (2018). *Armazenamento e gestão de Energia renovável em aplicações comerciais e residenciais.* Retrieved from http://institucional.us.es/agerar/pt

Aggarwal, C. C., & Abdelzaher, T. (2013). Social sensing. *Managing and mining sensor data*, 237-297.

Agha, K., Pujolle, G., & Yahiha, T. (2015). *Mobile and Wireless Networks*. Somerset: Wiley.

Agiwal, M., Saxena, N., & Roy, A. (2018). Towards Connected Living: 5G Enabled Internet of Things (IoT). *IETE Technical Review*, 1–13. doi:10.1080/02564602.2018.1444516

Ahmed, E., Yaqoob, I., Hashem, I. A. T., Khan, I., Ahmed, A. I. A., Imran, M., & Vasilakos, A. V. (2017). The role of big data analytics in Internet of Things. *Computer Networks*, *129*, 459–471. doi:10.1016/j.comnet.2017.06.013

Ahmed, N., Rahman, H., & Hussain, M. I. (2016). A comparison of 802.11 AH and 802.15. 4 for IoT. *ICT Express*, *2*(3), 100–102. doi:10.1016/j.icte.2016.07.003

Aijaz, A., Dohler, M., Aghvami, A. H., Friderikos, V., & Frodigh, M. (2017). Realizing the tactile internet: Haptic communications over next generation 5G cellular networks. *IEEE Wireless Communications*, *24*(2), 82–89. doi:10.1109/MWC.2016.1500157RP

Aiminho.pt. (2018). *Guia de Orientação para a utilização das Energias Renováveis*. Retrieved from http://www.aiminho.pt/imgAll/file/Sustentar/Guia_de_Orientacao_para_a_utilizacao_das_Energias_Renovaveis.pdf in 6 Jun. 2018.

Akan, O. B., Cetinkaya, O., Koca, C., & Ozger, M. (2018). Internet of Hybrid Energy Harvesting Things. *IEEE Internet of Things Journal*, *5*(2), 736–746. doi:10.1109/JIOT.2017.2742663

Akan, O. B., Fang, H., & Akyildiz, I. F. (2002). Performance of TCP protocols in deep space communication networks. *IEEE Communications Letters*, *11*(11), 478–480. doi:10.1109/LCOMM.2002.805549

Akan, O. B., Isik, M. T., & Baykal, B. (2009). Wireless Passive Sensor Networks. *IEEE Communications Magazine*, *47*(8), 92–99. doi:10.1109/MCOM.2009.5181898

Akan, O. B., Karli, O. B., & Ergul, O. (2009). Cognitive Radio Sensor Networks. *IEEE Network*, *23*(4), 34–40. doi:10.1109/MNET.2009.5191144

Akan, O. B., Ramezani, H., Khan, T., Abbasi, N. A., & Kuscu, M. (2017). Fundamentals of molecular information and communication science. *Proceedings of the IEEE*, *105*(2), 306–318. doi:10.1109/JPROC.2016.2537306

Akan, O., Fang, J., & Akyildiz, I. (2004). TP-Planet: A reliable transport protocol for interplanetary internet. *IEEE Journal on Selected Areas in Communications*, *22*(2), 348–361. doi:10.1109/JSAC.2003.819985

Aktas, M., Kuscu, M., Dinc, E., & Akan, O. (2018). D-DSC: Decoding Delay-based Distributed Source Coding for Internet of Sensing Things. *PLoS One*, *13*(3), e0193154. doi:10.1371/journal.pone.0193154 PMID:29538405

Akyildiz, I. F., & Jornet, J. M. (2010). The Internet of nano-things. *IEEE Wireless Communications*, *17*(6), 58–63. doi:10.1109/MWC.2010.5675779

Akyildiz, I. F., Pierobon, M., Balasubramaniam, S., & Koucheryavy, Y. (2015). The internet of bio-nano things. *IEEE Communications Magazine*, *53*(3), 32–40. doi:10.1109/MCOM.2015.7060516

Alam, F., Mehmood, R., Katib, I., & Albeshri, A. (2016). Analysis of Eight Data Mining Algorithms for Smarter Internet of Things (IoT). *Procedia Computer Science*, *98*, 437–442. doi:10.1016/j.procs.2016.09.068

Alcaraz, C., Najera, P., Lopez, J., & Roman, R. (2010). Wireless sensor networks and the internet of things: Do we need a complete integration? *1st International Workshop on the Security of the Internet of Things (SecIoT'10)*.

Al-Fuqaha, A., Guizani, M., Mohammadi, M., Aledhari, M., & Ayyash, M. (2015). Internet of Things: A survey on enabling technologies, protocols, and applications. *IEEE Communications Surveys and Tutorials*, *17*(4), 2347–2376. doi:10.1109/COMST.2015.2444095

Ali, W., Dustgeer, G., Awais, M., & Shah, M. A. (2017). IoT based smart home: Security challenges, security requirements and solutions. In *2017 23rd International Conference on Automation and Computing (ICAC)* (pp. 1–6). Huddersfield, UK: IEEE. 10.23919/IConAC.2017.8082057

Ali, A., Shah, G. A., Farooq, M. O., & Ghani, U. (2017). Technologies and challenges in developing Machine-to-Machine applications: A survey. *Journal of Network and Computer Applications*, *83*, 124–139. doi:10.1016/j.jnca.2017.02.002

Aloi, G., Caliciuri, G., Fortino, G., Gravina, R., Pace, P., Russo, W., & Savaglio, C. (n.d.). Enabling IoT interoperability through opportunistic smartphone-based mobile gateways. *Journal of Network and Computer Applications, 81*, 74-84.

Alpaydin, E. (2016). *Machine Learning: the New AI*. The MIT press.

AML. (2018). *Amazon Machine Learning*. Retrieved May 11, 2018, from http://aws.amazon.com/aml/

Anderson, R. J. (2008). *Security engineering: A guide to building dependable distributed systems* (2nd ed.). Hoboken, NJ: John Wiley & Sons.

Antonopoulos, A. M. (2016). *The Internet of Money*. Merkle Bloom LLC.

Apache Zookeeper. (2018). Retrieved from https://zookeeper.apache.org/

Arizona State University. (2011). *Predictive Technology Model*. Retrieved March 8, 2018, from http://ptm.asu.edu/

ARM. (2018). *ARM mbed*. Retrieved at October 24 2018, from http://www.mbed.com/en/platform/

Arndt, J., Krause, F., Wunderlich, R., & Heinen, S. (2017). *Development of a 6LoWPAN sensor node for IoT based home automation networks*. Paper presented at the Research and Education in Mechatronics (REM), 2017 International Conference on. 10.1109/REM.2017.8075226

Assaf, W., West, R., Aelterman, S., & Curnutt, M. (2018). *SQL Server 2017 Administration Inside Out*. Microsoft.

Associação Portuguesa de Energias Renováveis. (2017). Retrieved from http://www.apren.pt/pt/dadostecnicos/index.php?id=1147&cat=266

Aste, T., Tasca, P., & Di Matteo, T. (2017). Blockchain Technologies: The Foreseeable Impact on Society and Industry. *IEEE Computer Magazin*, *50*(9), 18–28. doi:10.1109/MC.2017.3571064

Atzori, L., Iera, A., & Morabito, G. (2010). The Internet of Things: A survey. *Computer Networks, 54*(15), 2787-2805.

Atzori, L., Iera, A., & Morabito, G. (2010). The Internet of Things: A survey. *Computer Networks*, *54*(15), 2787–2805. doi:10.1016/j.comnet.2010.05.010

Augustin, A., Yi, J., Clausen, T., & Townsley, W. (2016). A Study of LoRa: Long Range & Low Power Networks for the Internet of Things. *Sensors (Basel)*, *16*(9), 1466. doi:10.339016091466 PMID:27618064

Azuma, R. T. (1997). A survey of augmented reality. *Presence (Cambridge, Mass.)*, *6*(4), 355–385. doi:10.1162/pres.1997.6.4.355

Babar, S., Stango, A., Prasad, N., Sen, J., & Prasad, R. (2011). Proposed embedded security framework for internet of things (iot). In *2nd International Conference on Wireless Communication, Vehicular Technology, Information Theory and Aerospace & Electronic Systems Technology (Wireless VITAE)* (pp. 1-5). IEEE. 10.1109/WIRELESSVITAE.2011.5940923

Bacciu, D., Barsocchi, P., Chessa, S., Gallicchio, C., & Micheli, A. (2014). An experimental characterization of reservoir computing in ambient assisted living applications. *Neural Computing & Applications*, *24*(6), 1451–1464. doi:10.100700521-013-1364-4

Balasubramaniam, S., & Kangasharju, J. (2012). Realizing the internet of nano things: Challenges, solutions, and applications. *IEEE Computer*, *46*(2), 62–68. doi:10.1109/MC.2012.389

Balsamo, D., Merrett, G. V., Zaghari, B., Wei, Y., Ramchurn, S., Stein, S., ... Beeby, S. (2017). Wearable and autonomous computing for future smart cities: Open challenges. In *2017 25th International Conference on Software, Telecommunications and Computer Networks (SoftCOM)* (pp. 1–5). IEEE. 10.23919/SOFTCOM.2017.8115596

Bandodkar, A. J., & Wang, J. (2014). Non-invasive wearable electrochemical sensors: A review. *Trends in Biotechnology*, *32*(7), 363–371. doi:10.1016/j.tibtech.2014.04.005 PMID:24853270

Bandyopadhyay, D., & Sen, J. (2011). Internet of things: Applications and challenges in technology and standardization. *Wireless Personal Communications*, *58*(1), 49–69. doi:10.100711277-011-0288-5

Baños-Gonzalez, V., Afaqui, M., Lopez-Aguilera, E., & Garcia-Villegas, E. (2016). IEEE 802.11ah: A Technology to Face the IoT Challenge. *Sensors (Basel)*, *16*(11), 1960. doi:10.339016111960 PMID:27879688

Banos, V., Afaqui, M. S., Lopez, E., & Garcia, E. (2017). Throughput and Range Characterization of IEEE 802.11 ah. *IEEE Latin America Transactions*, *15*(9), 1621–1628. doi:10.1109/TLA.2017.8015044

Barcelo-Ordinas, J. M., Chanet, J. P., Hou, K. M., & García-Vidal, J. (2013). A survey of wireless sensor technologies applied to precision agriculture. *Precision Agriculture*, 801–808.

Basak, D., Pal, S., & Patranabis, D. C. (2007). Support vector regression. *Neural Information Processing-Letters and Reviews*, *11*(10), 203–224.

Bassett, L. (2015). *Introduction to JavaScript Object Notation: A To-the-Point Guide to JSON* (1st ed.). O'Reilly Media.

Beal, V. (2018). *The 7 layers of the OSI model.* Retrieved July 19, 2018 from: https://www.webopedia.com/quick_ref/OSI_Layers.asp

Bedogni, L., Bononi, L., Di Felice, M., D'Elia, A., Mock, R., Montori, F., & Vergari, F. (2013). *An interoperable architecture for mobile smart services over the internet of energy. In World of Wireless, Mobile and Multimedia Networks (WoWMoM)* (pp. 1–6). IEEE.

Belhi, A., Bouras, A., & Foufou, S. (2017). Digitization and preservation of cultural heritage: The CEPROQHA approach. *2017 11th International Conference on Software, Knowledge, Information Management and Applications (SKIMA)*, 1-7. 10.1109/SKIMA.2017.8294117

Bell, C. (2016). MySQL for the Internet of Things (W. Spahr, Ed.). Apress. doi:10.1007/978-1-4842-1293-6

Ben Hmida, H., & Braun, A. (2017). Enabling an Internet of Things Framework for Ambient Assisted Living. In R. Wichert & B. Mand (Eds.), *Ambient Assisted Living* (pp. 181–196). Cham: Springer International Publishing. doi:10.1007/978-3-319-52322-4_13

Benel, D. C. R., Ottens, D., & Horst, R. (1991). Use of an eye tracking system in the usability laboratory. In *Proceedings of the Human Factors Society 35th Annual Meeting (pp. 461-465).* Santa Monica, CA: Human Factors and Ergonomics Society.

Benford, S., Greenhalgh, C., Reynard, G., Brown, C., & Koleva, B. (1998). Understanding and constructing shared spaces with mixed-reality boundaries. *ACM Transactions on Computer-Human Interaction, 5*(3), 185-223.

Berthold, M. R., Cebron, N., Dill, F., Gabriel, T. R., Kötter, T., Meinl, T., ... Wiswedel, B. (2009). KNIME: The Konstanz Information Miner. *AcM SIGKDD Explorations Newsletter, 11*(1), 26–31. doi:10.1145/1656274.1656280

Bevan N. (2001). International standards for hci and usability. *Int. J. Human-Computer Studies, 55,* 533-552. doi:10:1006/ijhc.2001.0483

Bicen, A. O., & Akan, O. B. (2012). Cognitive Radio Sensor Networks in Industrial Applications. In V. C. Gungor & G. P. Hancke (Eds.), *Industrial Wireless Sensor Networks: Applications, Protocols, and Standards.* CRC Press.

Bicen, A. O., Gungor, V. C., & Akan, O. B. (2012). Spectrum-Aware and Cognitive Sensor Networks for Smart Grid Applications. *IEEE Communications Magazine, 50*(5), 158–165. doi:10.1109/MCOM.2012.6194397

Billinghurst, M., Poupyrev, I., Kato, H., & May, R. (2000). *Mixing realities in shared space: An augmented reality interface for collaborative computing.* Paper presented at the Multimedia and Expo, 2000. ICME 2000. 2000 IEEE International Conference on. 10.1109/ICME.2000.871085

Bimber, O., & Raskar, R. (2005). *Spatial augmented reality: merging real and virtual worlds.* CRC Press. doi:10.1201/b10624

Bluetooth SIG. (2016). *Master Table of Contents & Compliance Requirements: Bluetooth core specification V5.0.* Author.

Bluetooth SIG. (2017). *Bluetooth technology.* Retrieved from https://www.bluetooth.com/bluetooth-technology

Bolaji, A. Q., Kamaldeen, R. A., Samson, O. F., Abdullahi, A. T., & Abubakar, S. K. (2017). A Digitalized Smart Mobile Home Automation and Security System via Bluetooth/Wi-Fi Using Android Platform. *International Journal of Information and Communication Sciences, 2*(6), 93. doi:10.11648/j.ijics.20170206.11

Bolt, R. A. (1981). Gaze-orchestrated dynamic windows. *Computer Graphics, 15*(3), 109–199. doi:10.1145/965161.806796

Bolt, R. A. (1982). Eyes at the interface. In *Proceedings of the ACM Human Factors in Computer Systems Conference* (pp. 360-362). ACM.

Bonetti, F., Warnaby, G., & Quinn, L. (2018). *Augmented Reality and Virtual Reality in Physical and Online Retailing: A Review, Synthesis and Research Agenda. In Augmented Reality and Virtual Reality* (pp. 119–132). Springer. doi:10.1007/978-3-319-64027-3_9

Borlase, S. (2017). *Smart Grids: Advanced Technologies and Solutions* (2nd ed.). Taylor & Francis Group. doi:10.1201/9781351228480

Bosch. (2018). *IoT Platform,* Retrieved at October 24 2018, from http://www.bosch-si.com/iot-platform/iot-platform/iot-platform.html

Botia, J. A., Villa, A., & Palma, J. (2012). Ambient Assisted Living system for in-home monitoring of healthy independent elders. *Expert Systems with Applications, 39*(9), 8136–8148. doi:10.1016/j.eswa.2012.01.153

Botta, A., de Donato, W., Persico, V., & Pescap, A. (2016). Integration of Cloud computing and Internet of Things: A survey. Future Generation Computer Systems, 56, 684-700.

Boucheix, J. M., & Lowe, R. K. (2010). An eye tracking comparison of external pointing cues and internal continuous cues in learning with complex animations. *Learning and Instruction, 20*(2), 123–135. doi:10.1016/j.learninstruc.2009.02.015

Bray, T. (2013). *The JSON Data Interchange Standard.* IETF.

Brewster, T. (2015). *Security: Hacker says attacks on 'insecure' progressive insurance dongle in 2 million US cars could spawn road carnage*. Retrieved from https://www.forbes.com/sites/thomasbrewster/2015/01/15/researcher-says-progressive-insurance-dongle-totally-insecure

Brown, S., & Sreenan, C. J. (2013). Software updating in wireless sensor networks: A survey and lacunae. *Journal of Sensor and Actuator Networks*, 717-760.

Brown, S., & Sreenan, C. (2006). *Updating software in wireless sensor networks: A survey*. Citeseer.

Brush, A., Lee, B., Mahajan, R., Agarwal, S., Saroiu, S., & Dixon, C. (2011). Home automation in the wild: challenges and opportunities. *Proceedings of the SIGCHI Conference on Human Factors in Computing Systems*. 10.1145/1978942.1979249

Buchen, E. (2015). Small satellite market observations. *Small Satellite Conference*.

Bulling, A., & Gellersen, H. (2010, October). *Toward mobile eye-based human-computer interaction. IEEE Pervasive Computing*.

Burgess, J., Mitchell, P., & Highfield, T. (2018). Automating the digital everyday: An introduction. *Media International Australia*, *166*(1), 6–10. doi:10.1177/1329878X17739020

Burleigh, S., Cerf, V. G., Crowcroft, J., & Tsaoussidis, V. (2014). Space for Internet and Internet for space. *Ad Hoc Networks*, *23*, 80–86. doi:10.1016/j.adhoc.2014.06.005

Burr, J., & Peterson, A. M. (1991). Ultra low power CMOS technology. *Proceedings of NASA VLSI Design Symposium*, 4.2.1–4.2.13.

Bush, S. F., Paluh, J. L., Piro, G., Rao, V., Prasad, R. V., & Eckford, A. (2015). Defining communication at the bottom. *IEEE Transactions on Molecular. Biological and Multi-Scale Communications*, *1*(1), 90–96.

Cabral, R., Cavalaria, H., Semião, J., Santos, M., Teixeira, I., & Teixeira, J. P. (2017). Performance Sensor For Sub-threshold Voltage Operation. *Proceedings of the 1st INternational CongRess on Engineering and Sustainability in the XXI cEntury - INCREaSE 2017*. DOI: 10.1007/978-3-319-70272-8_31

Caffe2. (2018). *Caffe2*. Retrieved October 7, 2018, from https://caffe2.ai/

Cai, H., Xu, B., Jiang, L., & Vasilakos, A. V. (2017). IoT-based big data storage systems in cloud computing: Perspectives and challenges. *IEEE Internet of Things Journal*, *4*(1), 75–87.

Calhoun, B. H., Wang, A., & Chandrakasan, A. (2004). Device Sizing for Minimum Operation in Subthreshold Circuits. *Proceedings of the IEEE Custom Integrated Circuits Conference*. 10.1109/CICC.2004.1358745

Calhoun, B. H., Wang, A., & Chandrakasan, A. (2005). Modeling and sizing for minimum energy operation in subthreshold circuits. *IEEE Journal of Solid-State Circuits*, *40*(9), 1778–1786. doi:10.1109/JSSC.2005.852162

Campbell, A. T., Eisenman, S. B., Lane, N. D., Miluzzo, E., Peterson, R. A., Lu, H., & Ahn, G. S. (2008). The rise of people-centric sensing. *IEEE Internet Computing*, *12*(4), 12–21. doi:10.1109/MIC.2008.90

Campbell, C., & Ying, Y. (2011). *Learning with Support Vector Machines* (R. J. Brachman & T. Dietterich, Eds.). Morgan & Claypool. doi:10.2200/S00324ED1V01Y201102AIM010

Canham, M., & Hegarty, M. (2010). Effects of knowledge and display design on comprehension of complex graphics. *Learning and Instruction*, *20*(2), 155–166. doi:10.1016/j.learninstruc.2009.02.014

Cao, Q., Abdelzaher, T., Stankovic, J., & He, T. (2008). The liteos operating system: Towards unix-like abstractions for wireless sensor networks. *International Conference On Information Processing in Sensor Networks*, 233-244. 10.1109/IPSN.2008.54

Cardoso, P. J. S., Guerreiro, P., Monteiro, J., & Rodrigues, J. (2018). Applying an Implicit Recommender System in the Preparation of Visits to Cultural Heritage Places. In M. Antona & C. Stephanidis (Eds.), *Universal Access in Human--Computer Interaction. Design and Development Approaches and Methods: 12th International Conference, UAHCI 2018, Held as Part of HCI International 2018, Las Vegas, USA, July 15--20, 2018.* Springer International Publishing. 10.1007/978-3-319-92052-8_33

Carettoni, L., Merloni, C., & Zanero, S. (2007). Studying Bluetooth malware propagation: The BlueBag project. *IEEE Security and Privacy*, *5*(2), 17–25. doi:10.1109/MSP.2007.43

Cartwright, H. (Ed.). (2015). *Artificial Neural Networks* (Vol. 1260). New York, NY: Springer New York; doi:10.1007/978-1-4939-2239-0

Casas, S., Morillo, P., Gimeno, J., & Fernández, M. (2009). *SUED: An extensible framework for the development of low-cost DVE systems.* Paper presented at the In Proceedings of the IEEE Virtual Reality 2009 (IEEE-VR'09). Workshop on Software Engineering and Architectures for Realtime Interactive Systems (SEARIS).

Casas, S., Rueda, S., Riera, J. V., & Fernández, M. (2012). *On the Real-time Physics Simulation of a Speed-boat Motion.* Paper presented at the GRAPP/IVAPP.

Casas, S., Fernández, M., & Riera, J. V. (2017). Four Different Multimodal Setups for Non-Aerial Vehicle Simulations—A Case Study with a Speedboat Simulator. *Multimodal Technologies and Interaction*, *1*(2), 10. doi:10.3390/mti1020010

Casas, S., Portalés, C., García-Pereira, I., & Fernández, M. (2017). On a First Evaluation of ROMOT—A RObotic 3D MOvie Theatre—For Driving Safety Awareness. *Multimodal Technologies and Interaction*, *1*(2), 6. doi:10.3390/mti1020006

Cassandra. (2018). *Cassandra.* Retrieved October 7, 2018, from http://cassandra.apache.org/

Castelluccia, C., Francillon, A., Perito, D., & Soriente, C. (2009). On the difficulty of software-based attestation of embedded devices. *Proceedings of the 16th ACM conference on Computer and communications security*, 400-409. 10.1145/1653662.1653711

Caudell, T. P., & Mizell, D. W. (1992). Augmented reality: An application of heads-up display technology to manual manufacturing processes. *Proceedings of the Twenty-Fifth Hawaii International Conference.* 10.1109/HICSS.1992.183317

Cavalaria, H., Cabral, R., Semião, J., Santos, M., Teixeira, I., & Teixeira, J. P. (2017). Power-Delay Analysis For Sub-threshold Voltage Operation. *Proceedings of the 1st INternational CongRess on Engineering and Sustainability in the XXI cEntury - INCREaSE 2017.* DOI: 10.1007/978-3-319-70272-8_30

Celebi, M. E., & Aydin, K. (Eds.). (2016). *Unsupervised Learning Algorithms* (1st ed.). Springer International Publishing. doi:10.1007/978-3-319-24211-8

Centenaro, M., Vangelista, L., Zanella, A., & Zorzi, M. (2016). Long-range communications in unlicensed bands: The rising stars in the IoT and smart city scenarios. *IEEE Wireless Communications*, *23*(5), 60–67. doi:10.1109/MWC.2016.7721743

Centers for Disease Control and Prevention. (n.d.). *The state of aging and health in America 2007.* Available: https://www.cdc.gov/aging/pdf/saha_2007.pdf

Cepni, K., Ozger, M., & Akan, O. B. (2017). Vehicular Social Sensor Networks. In Vehicular Social Networks. CRC Press.

Cha, H., Choi, S., Jung, I., Kim, H., Shin, H., Yoo, J., & Yoon, C. (2007). RETOS: resilient, expandable, and threaded operating system for wireless sensor networks. *Proceedings of the 6th international conference on Information processing in sensor networks*, 148-157. 10.1145/1236360.1236381

Chakraborty, S., Mallik, A., & Sarkar, C. K. (2008). Subthreshold performance of dual-material gate CMOS devices and circuits for ultra-low power analog/mixed-signal applications. *IEEE Transactions on Electron Devices*, *55*(3), 827–832. doi:10.1109/TED.2007.914842

Chandramohan, J., Nagarajan, R., Satheeshkumar, K., Ajithkumar, N., Gopinath, P., & Ranjithkumar, S. (2017). Intelligent Smart Home Automation and Security System Using Arduino and Wi-fi. *International Journal of Engineering And Computer Science*, *6*(3), 20694–20698.

Chang, Y. S., Nuernberger, B., Luan, B., & Höllerer, T. (2017). *Evaluating gesture-based augmented reality annotation.* Paper presented at the 3D User Interfaces (3DUI), 2017 IEEE Symposium on. 10.1109/3DUI.2017.7893337

Chavan, J., Patil, P., & Naik, P. (2017). Advanced Control Web Based Home Automation with Raspberry Pi. *International Journal of Advance Research*. Ideas and Innovations in Technology, *3*(2), 221–223.

Chen F., Deng P., Wan J., Zhang D., Vasilakos A, & Rong X., (2015). Data mining for the internet of things: Literature review and challenges. *International Journal of Distributed Sensor Networks*.

Chen, F., Deng, P., Wan, J., Zhang, D., Vasilakos, A. V., & Rong, X. (2015). Data Mining for the Internet of Things: Literature Review and Challenges. *International Journal of Distributed Sensor Networks*, *11*(8), 431047. doi:10.1155/2015/431047

Chen, M., Mao, S., & Liu, Y. (2014). Big data: A survey. *Mobile Networks and Applications*, *19*(2), 171–209. doi:10.100711036-013-0489-0

Chen, Y.-T., Chien, T.-C., & Chou, P. H. (2010). Enix: a lightweight dynamic operating system for tightly constrained wireless sensor platforms. *Proceedings of the 8th ACM Conference on Embedded Networked Sensor Systems*, 183-196. 10.1145/1869983.1870002

Chianese, A., Marulli, F., Moscato, V., & Piccialli, F. (2013). Smartweet: A location-based smart application for exhibits and museums. *International Conference on Signal Image Technology and Internet Based Systems*, 408–415. 10.1109/SITIS.2013.73

Chianese, A., & Piccialli, F. (2015). Improving User Experience of Cultural Environment Through IoT: The Beauty or the Truth Case Study. In *Intelligent Interactive Multimedia Systems and Services. Smart Innovation, Systems and Technologies* (Vol. 40). Cham: Springer. doi:10.1007/978-3-319-19830-9_2

Chianese, A., Piccialli, F., & Jung, J. E. (2016). The Internet of Cultural Things: Towards a Smart Cultural Heritage. *12th International Conference on Signal-Image Technology & Internet-Based Systems (SITIS)*. 10.1109/SITIS.2016.83

Chodorow, K. (2013). *MongoDB: The Definitive Guide*. O'Reilly Media.

Cisco Newsroom. (2018). *Cisco's technology news site*. Retrieved July 26, 2018 from: https://newsroom.cisco.com/ioe

Cisco. (2012). *The Internet of everything: How more relevant and valuable connections will change the world*. Retrieved July 27, 2018 from: https://www.cisco.com/c/dam/global/en_my/assets/ciscoinnovate/pdfs/IoE.pdf

Cisco. (2015). *Fog computing and the internet of things: Extend the cloud to where the things are*. Retrieved July 21, 2018 from: https://www.cisco.com/c/dam/en_us/solutions/trends/iot/docs/computing-overview.pdf

Cisco. (2018). *Jasper*. Retrieved at October 24 2018, from http://www.jasper.com/

Clifton, L., Clifton, D. A., Pimentel, M. A. F., Watkinson, P. J., & Tarassenko, L. (2014). Predictive Monitoring of Mobile Patients by Combining Clinical Observations With Data From Wearable Sensors. *Biomedical and Health Informatics. IEEE Journal of, 18*(3), 722–730. doi:10.1109/JBHI.2013.2293059 PMID:24808218

Coinmarketcap.com. (2015, May 25). *Cryptocurrencies by Market Capitalization.* Retrieved from https://coinmarketcap.com

Collobert, R., Kavukcuoglu, K., & Farabet, C. (2011). Torch7: A Matlab-like Environment for Machine Learning. *BigLearn, NIPS Workshop.*

Costa, P. A. S. (2004). *Atlas do potencial eólico para Portugal continental.* Lisbon: Faculdade de Ciências da Universidade de Lisboa.

Coulouris, G., & Dollimore, J. (2011). *Distributed Systems: Concepts and Design.* Addison-Wesley.

Cowen, L. (2001). *An eye movement analysis of web-page usability* (Unpublished Masters' thesis). Lancaster University, UK.

Crossbow Technology, Inc. (2003). *Mote In-Network Programming User Reference Version 20030315.* Retrieved from https://www.eol.ucar.edu/isf/facilities/isa/internal/TinyOSdoc/Xnp.pdf

Cubo, J., Nieto, A., & Pimentel, E. (2014). A Cloud-Based Internet of Things Platform for Ambient Assisted Living. *Sensors (Basel), 14*(8), 14070–14105. doi:10.3390140814070 PMID:25093343

Cui, S., Han, Z., Kar, S., Kim, T. T., Poor, H. V., & Tajer, A. (2012). Coordinated data-injection attack and detection in the smart grid: A detailed look at enriching detection solutions. *IEEE Signal Processing Magazine, 29*(5), 106–115. doi:10.1109/MSP.2012.2185911

Cunha, M., & Fuks, H. (2014). AmbLEDs para ambientes de moradia assistidos em cidades inteligentes. In *Proceedings of the 13th Brazilian Symposium on Human Factors in Computing Systems* (pp. 409–412). Foz do Iguaçu, Brazil: Sociedade Brasileira de Computação.

Curtin, R. R., Cline, J. R., Slagle, N. P., March, W. B., Ram, P., Mehta, N. A., & Gray, A. G. (2013). MLPACK: A Scalable C++ Machine Learning Library. *Journal of Machine Learning Research, 14*, 801–805.

Dandala, T. T., Krishnamurthy, V., & Alwan, R. (2017). Internet of Vehicles (IoV) for traffic management. In *International Conference on Communication and Signal Processing (ICCCSP)* (pp. 1-4). IEEE. 10.1109/ICCCSP.2017.7944096

Dankberg, M., & Hudson, E. (2016). VIASAT: On a Mission to Deliver the World's Lowest-Cost Satellite Bandwidth. *Recent Successful Satellite Systems: Visions of the Future.*

Danzi, P., Kalør, A. E., Stefanović, Č., & Popovski, P. (2017). *Analysis of the communication traffic for blockchain synchronization of IoT devices.* Retrieved from http://arxiv.org/abs/1711.00540

Darby, S. J. (2018). Smart technology in the home: Time for more clarity. *Building Research and Information, 46*(1), 140–147. doi:10.1080/09613218.2017.1301707

Das, B., & Jain, P. C. (2017). Real-time water quality monitoring system using Internet of Things. *2017 International Conference on Computer, Communications and Electronics (COMPTELIX)*, 78–82. 10.1109/COMPTELIX.2017.8003942

Dash7 Alliance. (2017). *DASH7 Alliance Protocol Specification v1.1.* Retrieved from http://www.dash7-alliance.org/product/d7ap1-1/

Dawaliby, S., Bradai, A., & Pousset, Y. (2016). In depth performance evaluation of LTE-M for M2M communications. In *2016 IEEE 12th International Conference on Wireless and Mobile Computing, Networking and Communications (WiMob).* IEEE.

Da, X. L., He, W., & Li, S. (2014). Internet of things in industries: A survey. *IEEE Transactions on Industrial Informatics*, *10*(4), 2233–2243. doi:10.1109/TII.2014.2300753

DB-Engines. (2018). *DB-Engines*. Retrieved October 7, 2018, from https://db-engines.com

De Koning, B. B., Tabbers, H. K., Rikers, R. M. J. P., & Paas, F. (2010). Attention guidance in learning from a complex animation: Seeing is understanding? *Learning and Instruction*, *20*(2), 111–122. doi:10.1016/j.learninstruc.2009.02.010

de Podestá Gaspar, R., Bonacin, R., & Gonçalves, V. P. (2018). Designing IoT Solutions for Elderly Home Care: A Systematic Study of Participatory Design, Personas and Semiotics. In M. Antona & C. Stephanidis (Eds.), *Universal Access in Human-Computer Interaction. Virtual, Augmented, and Intelligent Environments* (Vol. 10908, pp. 226–245). Cham: Springer International Publishing; doi:10.1007/978-3-319-92052-8_18

de Saint-Exupery, A. (2009). Internet of things: Strategic research roadmap. *IERC-European*. Retrieved March 11, 2018 from: http://www.internet-of-things-research.eu/pdf/IoT_Cluster_Strategic_Research_Agenda_2009.pdf

De Silva, L. C., Morikawa, C., & Petra, I. M. (2012). State of the art of smart homes. *Advanced Issues in Artificial Intelligence and Pattern Recognition for Intelligent Surveillance System in Smart Home Environment*, *25*(7), 1313–1321. doi:10.1016/j.engappai.2012.05.002

Decuir, J. (2015). The Story of the Internet of Things: Issues in utility, connectivity, and security. *IEEE Consumer Electronics Magazine*, *4*(4), 54–61. doi:10.1109/MCE.2015.2463292

Del Carpio, L. F., Di Marco, P., Skillermark, P., Chirikov, R., Lagergren, K., & Amin, P. (2016). *Comparison of 802.11 ah and BLE for a home automation use case.* Paper presented at the Personal, Indoor, and Mobile Radio Communications (PIMRC), 2016 IEEE 27th Annual International Symposium on.

Del Carpio, L. F., Di Marco, P., Skillermark, P., Chirikov, R., & Lagergren, K. (2017). Comparison of 802.11ah, BLE and 802.15.4 for a Home Automation Use Case. *International Journal of Wireless Information Networks*, *24*(3), 243–253. doi:10.100710776-017-0355-2

Deng, J., Han, R., & Mishra, S. (2006). Efficiently authenticating code images in dynamically reprogrammed wireless sensor networks. *Fourth Annual IEEE International Conference on Pervasive Computing and Communications Workshops.*

Deng, J., Han, R., & Mishra, S. (2006a). Secure code distribution in dynamically programmable wireless sensor networks. *The Fifth International Conference on Information Processing in Sensor Networks*, 292-300. 10.1145/1127777.1127822

Derhamy, H., Eliasson, J., & Delsing, J. (2017). IoT Interoperability - On-Demand and Low Latency Transparent Multiprotocol Translator. *IEEE Internet of Things Journal*, *4*(5), 1754–1763. doi:10.1109/JIOT.2017.2697718

Deterding, S., Khaled, R., Nacke, L.E., & Dixon, D. (2011). *Gamification: Toward a Definition.* In CHI 2011 Gamification Workshop Proceedings, Vancouver, BC, Canada.

Dickey, R. M., Srikishen, N., Lipshultz, L. I., Spiess, P. E., Carrion, R. E., & Hakky, T. S. (2016). Augmented reality assisted surgery: A urologic training tool. *Asian Journal of Andrology*, *18*(5), 732. doi:10.4103/1008-682X.166436 PMID:26620455

Dinc, E., & Akan, O. B. (2014). Beyond-Line-of-Sight Communications with Ducting Layer. *IEEE Communications Magazine*, *52*(10), 37–43. doi:10.1109/MCOM.2014.6917399

Dinc, E., & Akan, O. B. (2015). More than the eye can see: Coherence time and coherence bandwidth of troposcatter links for mobile receivers. *IEEE Vehicular Technology Magazine*, *10*(2), 86–92. doi:10.1109/MVT.2015.2410786

Dinc, E., Vondra, M., & Cavdar, C. (2017). Multi-user Beamforming and Ground Station Deployment Problem for 5G Direct Air-to-Ground Communications. *Proceedings of IEEE GLOBECOM.*

Dinc, E., Vondra, M., Hofmann, S., Schupke, D., Prytz, M., Bovelli, S., ... Cavdar, C. (2017). In-flight Broadband Connectivity: Architectures and Business Models for High Capacity Air-to-Ground Communications. *IEEE Communications Magazine, 55*(9), 142–149. doi:10.1109/MCOM.2017.1601181

Disk91.com. (2015). *One day at Sigfox.* Retrieved from https://www.disk91.com/2015/news/technologies/one-day-at-sigfox/

Do, A. V., Boon, C. C., Anh, M., Yeo, K. S., & Cabuk, A. (2008). A sub-threshold low-noise amplifier optimized for ultra-low-power applications in the ISM band. *IEEE Transactions on Microwave Theory and Techniques, 56*(2), 286–292. doi:10.1109/TMTT.2007.913366

Dodge, R., & Cline, T. S. (1901). The angle velocity of eye movements. *Psychological Review, 8*(2), 145–167. doi:10.1037/h0076100

Domazetovic, B., Kocan, E., & Mihovska, A. (2016). Performance evaluation of IEEE 802.11ah systems. In *2016 24th Telecommunications Forum (TELFOR).* IEEE.

Domingos, P. (2015). *The master algorithm: How the quest for the ultimate learning machine will remake our world.* Basic Books.

Dong, W., Chen, C., Liu, X., Bu, J., & Liu, Y. (2009). Dynamic linking and loading in networked embedded systems. *IEEE 6th International Conference on Mobile Adhoc and Sensor Systems,* 554-562.

Dong, W., Chen, C., Liu, X., & Bu, J. (2010). Providing OS support for wireless sensor networks: Challenges and approaches. *IEEE Communications Surveys and Tutorials, 12*(4), 519–530. doi:10.1109/SURV.2010.032610.00045

Dong, W., Mo, B., Huang, C., Liu, Y., & Chen, C. (2013). *R3: Optimizing relocatable code for efficient reprogramming in networked embedded systems.* IEEE INFOCOM.

Dorge, B. M., & Scheffler, T. (2011). *Using IPv6 and 6LoWPAN for home automation networks.* Paper presented at the Consumer Electronics-Berlin (ICCE-Berlin), 2011 IEEE International Conference on.

Dorri, A., Kanhere, S. S., & Jurdak, R. (2017). Towards an optimized blockchain for IoT. *2017 IEEE/ACM Second International Conference on Internet-of-Things design and implementation (IoTDI),* 173–178. doi:10.1145/3054977.3055003

Dorri, A., Kanhere, S. S., Jurdak, R., & Gauravaram, P. (2017). Blockchain for IoT security and privacy: The case study of a smart home. In *2017 IEEE International Conference on Pervasive Computing and Communications Workshops (PerCom Workshops)* (pp. 618–623). Kona, HI: IEEE. 10.1109/PERCOMW.2017.7917634

Draim, J. E. (1987). A common-period four-satellite continuous global coverage constellation. *Journal of Guidance, Control, and Dynamics, 10*(5), 492–499. doi:10.2514/3.20244

Drath, R., & Horch, A. (2014). Industrie 4.0: Hit or hype? *IEEE Industrial Electronics Magazine, 8*(2), 56–58. doi:10.1109/MIE.2014.2312079

Dressler, F., & Fischer, S. (2015). Connecting in-body nano communication with body area networks: Challenges and opportunities of the internet of nano things. *Nano Communication Networks Journal, 6*(2), 29–38. doi:10.1016/j.nancom.2015.01.006

Duchowski, A. T. (2003). *Eye tracking methodology: theory and practice.* London: Springer. doi:10.1007/978-1-4471-3750-4

Dunkels, A., Gronvall, B., & Voigt, T. (2004). Contiki - a lightweight and flexible operating system for tiny networked sensors. *29th Annual IEEE International Conference on Local Computer Networks*, 455-462. 10.1109/LCN.2004.38

Dunleavy, M., & Dede, C. (2014). *Augmented reality teaching and learning. In Handbook of research on educational communications and technology* (pp. 735–745). Springer. doi:10.1007/978-1-4614-3185-5_59

Dunning, J. P. (2010). Taming the Blue Beast: A survey of Bluetooth based threats. *IEEE Security and Privacy*, *8*(2), 20–27. doi:10.1109/MSP.2010.3

Duval, T., Nguyen, T. T. H., Fleury, C., Chauffaut, A., Dumont, G., & Gouranton, V. (2014). Improving awareness for 3D virtual collaboration by embedding the features of users' physical environments and by augmenting interaction tools with cognitive feedback cues. *Journal on Multimodal User Interfaces*, *8*(2), 187–197. doi:10.100712193-013-0134-z

Dynastream. (2017). *Ant Blaze Product Brief*. Retrieved from https://www.dynastream.com/assets/D52/Dynastream.ANT_BLAZE.Product.Brief.pdf

Elkhodr, M., Shahrestani, S., & Cheung, H. (2013). The Internet of Things: Vision & challenges. In *Proceedings of the IEEE TENCON Spring Conference* (pp. 218-222). Washington, DC: IEEE Computer Society.

Ellis, S., Candrea, R., Misner, J., Craig, C. S., Lankford, C. P., & Hutshinson, T. E. 1998). Windows to the soul? What eye movements tell us about software usability. In *Proceedings of the Usability Professionals' Association Conference 1998* (pp. 151-178). Academic Press.

ElShafee, A., & Hamed, K. A. (2012). Design and implementation of a WIFI based home automation system. *World Academy of Science, Engineering and Technology*, *68*, 2177–2180.

Elston, S. F. (2015). *Data Science in the Cloud: with Microsoft Azure Machine Learning and R*. O'Reilly Media.

Elvezio, C., Sukan, M., Oda, O., Feiner, S., & Tversky, B. (2017). *Remote collaboration in AR and VR using virtual replicas*. Paper presented at the ACM SIGGRAPH 2017 VR Village. 10.1145/3089269.3089281

Emoncms. (n.d.). *Emoncms platform*. Retrieved from emoncms.org

ENISA. (2017). *Baseline security recommendations for IoT in the context of critical information infrastructures*. Heraklion, Greece: European Union Agency for Network and Information Security.

EnOcean Alliance. (2016). *Introducing the EnOcean Eco-System*. Retrieved from https://www.enocean-alliance.org/wp-content/uploads/2016/11/Whitepaper_Introducing_the_EnOcean_Ecosystem.pdf

EnOcean. (2013). *EnOcean Radio Protocol 1*. Retrieved from https://www.enocean.com/fileadmin/redaktion/pdf/tec_docs/EnOceanRadioProtocol1.pdf, in 13/06/2018.

EnOcean. (2017). *EnOcean Radio Protocol 2*. Retrieved from https://www.enocean.com/fileadmin/redaktion/pdf/tec_docs/EnOcean_Radio_Protocol_2.pdf, in 13/06/2018.

EnOcean. (n.d.). *868 MHz EnOCean for Europe*. Retrieved from https://www.enocean.com/en/enocean_modules/

Eom, J.-H., Han, Y.-J., Park, S.-H., & Chung, T.-M. (2008). Active cyber attack model for network system's vulnerability assessment. In *Proceedings of International Conference on Information Science and Security* (pp. 153-158). Washington, DC: IEEE Computer Society. 10.1109/ICISS.2008.36

Ergul, O., Dinc, E., & Akan, O. B. (2015). Communicate to Illuminate: State-of-the-art and Research Challenges for Visible Light Communications. Physical Communication Journal, 72-85.

Ergul, O., Shah, G. A., Canberk, B., & Akan, O. B. (2016). Adaptive and Cognitive Communication Architecture for Next-generation PPDR Systems. *IEEE Communications Magazine*, *54*(4), 92–100. doi:10.1109/MCOM.2016.7452272

Ericsson. (2017). *Bluetooth mesh networking*. Whitepaper. Retrieved from https://www.ericsson.com/en/publications/white-papers/bluetooth-mesh-networking

Ernst, D., Kim, N. S., Das, S., Pant, S., Rao, R., Pham, T., . . . Mudge, T. (2003). Razor: A Low-Power Pipeline Based on Circuit-Level Timing Speculation. *Proceedings of the 36th Annual IEEE/ACM International Symposium on Micro-architecture (MICRO-36)*. 10.1109/MICRO.2003.1253179

European SmartGrids Technology Platform. (2016). *Vision and Strategy for Europe's Electricity Networks of the future*. European Commission.

Evans, D. (2012). The Internet of everything: How more relevant and valuable connections will change the world. *Cisco*. Retrieved July 19, 2018 from: https://www.cisco.com/c/dam/global/en_my/assets/ciscoinnovate/pdfs/IoE.pdf

Fabbro, A., Scaini, D., León, V., Vázquez, E., Cellot, G., Privitera, G., ... Bosi, S. (2016). Graphene-based interfaces do not alter target nerve cells. *ACS Nano*, *10*(1), 615–623. doi:10.1021/acsnano.5b05647 PMID:26700626

Fangchun, Y., Shangguang, W., Jinglin, L., Zhihan, L., & Qibo, S. (2014). An overview of Internet of Vehicles. *China Communications*, *11*(10), 1–15. doi:10.1109/CC.2014.6969789

Farooq, M. O., & Kunz, T. (2011). Operating systems for wireless sensor networks: A survey. *Sensors (Basel)*, *11*(6), 5900–5930. doi:10.3390110605900 PMID:22163934

Federal Office for Information Security (BSI). (2007). *IT-Security Guidelines*. BSI.

Felicetti, L., Femminella, M., Reali, G., & Liò, P. (2016). Applications of molecular communications to medicine: A survey. *Nano Communication Networks*, *7*, 27–45. doi:10.1016/j.nancom.2015.08.004

Felnhofer, A., Kothgassner, O. D., Hauk, N., Beutl, L., Hlavacs, H., & Kryspin-Exner, I. (2014). Physical and social presence in collaborative virtual environments: Exploring age and gender differences with respect to empathy. *Computers in Human Behavior*, *31*, 272–279. doi:10.1016/j.chb.2013.10.045

Felzmann, H., Murphy, K., Casey, D., & Beyan, O. (2015). *Robot-assisted care for elderly with dementia: is there a potential for genuine end-user empowerment?* Academic Press. doi:10.130258sg6q

Feng, S., Setoodeh, P., & Haykin, S. (2017). Smart Home: Cognitive Interactive People-Centric Internet of Things. *IEEE Communications Magazine*, *55*(2), 34–39. doi:10.1109/MCOM.2017.1600682CM

Ferrari, A. C., Bonaccorso, F., Fal'ko, V., Novoselov, K. S., Roche, S., Bøggild, P., ... Kinaret, J. (2005). Science and technology roadmap for graphene, related two-dimensional crystals, and hybrid systems. *Nanoscale*, *7*(11), 4598–4810. doi:10.1039/C4NR01600A PMID:25707682

Fibar Group S.A. (2018). *Fibaro*. Retrieved 02/03/2018, 2018, from http://www.fibaro.com

Filho, H. G. S., Filho, J. P., & Moreli, V. L. (2016). The adequacy of LoRaWAN on smart grids: A comparison with RF mesh technology. In *2016 IEEE International Smart Cities Conference* (ISC2). IEEE. 10.1109/ISC2.2016.7580783

Fitts, P. M., Jones, R. E., & Milton, J. L. (1950). Eye movements of aircraft pilots during instrument-landing approaches. *Aeronautical Engineering Review*, *9*(2), 24–29.

Flore, D. (2016). *3GPP Standards for the Internet-of-Things*. 3GPP. Retrieved from http://www.3gpp.org/images/presentations/3GPP_Standards_for_IoT.pdf

Friedewald, M., Da Costa, O., Punie, Y., Alahuhta, P., & Heinonen, S. (2005). Perspectives of ambient intelligence in the home environment. *Telematics and Informatics, 22*(3), 221–238. doi:10.1016/j.tele.2004.11.001

Friedli, M., Kaufmann, L., Paganini, F., & Kyburz, R. (2016). *Energy efficiency of the Internet of Things. Technology and Energy Assessment Report prepared for IEA 4E EDNA*. Lucerne University of Applied Sciences.

Fuchsberger, V. (2008). Ambient assisted living: elderly people's needs and how to face them. In *Proceeding of the 1st ACM international workshop on Semantic ambient media experiences - SAME '08* (p. 21). Vancouver, Canada: ACM Press. 10.1145/1461912.1461917

Ganti, R. K., Ye, F., & Lei, H. (2011). Mobile Crowdsensing: Current State and Future Challenges. *IEEE Communications Magazine, 49*(11), 32–39. doi:10.1109/MCOM.2011.6069707

Gantz, J., & Reinsel, D. (2011). Extracting value from chaos. *IDC iview, 19*(1142), 1-12.

García, F., Pedreira, O., Piattini, M., Cerdeira-Pena, A., & Penabad, M. (2017). A framework for gamification in software engineering. *Journal of Systems and Software, 132*, 21–40. doi:10.1016/j.jss.2017.06.021

Gauthier, C. R., Trivedi, P. R., & Yee, G. S. (2006). *Embedded Integrated Circuit Aging Sensor System*. Sun Microsystems, US Patent 7054787.

Geman, O., Sanei, S., Costin, H.-N., Eftaxias, K., Vysata, O., Prochazka, A., & Lhotska, L. (2015). Challenges and trends in Ambient Assisted Living and intelligent tools for disabled and elderly people. *Computational Intelligence for Multimedia Understanding (IWCIM), 2015 International Workshop on*, 1–5. 10.1109/IWCIM.2015.7347088

Gerla, M., Lee, E. K., Pau, G., & Lee, U. (2014). Internet of vehicles: From intelligent grid to autonomous cars and vehicular clouds. In *World Forum on Internet of Things (WF-IoT)*. IEEE.

Gibbs, W. W. (2016). DIY Home Security. Deter Intruders with an Extra Loud Alarm. *IEEE Spectrum*, 20–21.

Gigli, M., & Koo, S. (2011). Internet of things: Services and applications categorization. *Advances in Internet of Things*. Retrieved March 11, 2018 from: https://pdfs.semanticscholar.org/17b6/b29ab2473298315b92d8451d87336472d87f.pdf

Gilchrist, A. (2016). *Industry 4.0: the industrial internet of things*. Apress. doi:10.1007/978-1-4842-2047-4

Gimeno, J., Morillo, P., Casas, S., & Fernández, M. (2011). An augmented reality (AR) CAD system at construction sites. In *Augmented Reality-Some Emerging Application Areas*. InTech.

Giustolisi, G., Palumbo, G., Criscione, M., & Cutri, F. (2003). A low-voltage low-power voltage reference based on subthreshold MOSFETs. *IEEE Journal of Solid-State Circuits, 38*(1), 151–154. doi:10.1109/JSSC.2002.806266

Glenn, F., Lavecchia, H., Ross, L., Stokes, J., Weiland, W., Weiss, D., & Zaklad, A. (1986). Eye-voice controlled interface. In *Proceedings of the 30th Annual Meeting of the Human Factors Society* (pp. 322-326). Santa Monica, CA: Human Factors Society.

Goldberg, J. H., & Wichansky, A. M. (2003). Eye tracking in usability evaluation: A practitioner's guide. In J. Hyona, R. Radach, & H. Deubel (Eds.), *The mind's eye: cognitive and applied aspects of eye movement research* (pp. 493–516). Amsterdam: North-Holland. doi:10.1016/B978-044451020-4/50027-X

Gold, D. R. (1992). Indoor air pollution. *Clinics in Chest Medicine, 13*(2), 215–229. PMID:1511550

Gomez, C., & Paradells, J. (2010). Wireless home automation networks: A survey of architectures and technologies. *IEEE Communications Magazine, 48*(6), 92–101. doi:10.1109/MCOM.2010.5473869

Gonzalez, R., Gordon, B., & Horowitz, M. A. (1997). Supply and threshold voltage scaling for low power CMOS. *IEEE Journal of Solid-State Circuits*, *32*(8), 1210–1216. doi:10.1109/4.604077

Gordon, L., & Chaczko, Z. (2017). Ontological Metamodel for Consistency of Data Heritage Preservation (DHP). *2017 25th International Conference on Systems Engineering (ICSEng)*, 438-442. 10.1109/ICSEng.2017.67

GOV.UK. (2018). *Cyber security breaches survey 2018*. Retrieved from https://www.gov.uk/government/statistics/cyber-security-breaches-survey-2018

Gram-Hanssen, K., & Darby, S. J. (2018). "Home is where the smart is"? Evaluating smart home research and approaches against the concept of home. *Energy Research & Social Science*, *37*, 94–101. doi:10.1016/j.erss.2017.09.037

Grant, S. (2016). *3GPP Low Power Wide Area Technologies - GSMA White Paper*. GSMA.

Grau, C., Ginhoux, R., Riera, A., Nguyen, T. L., Chauvat, H., Berg, M., ... Ruffini, G. (2014). Conscious brain-to-brain communication in humans using non-invasive technologies. *PLoS One*, *9*(8), 105225. doi:10.1371/journal.pone.0105225 PMID:25137064

Greengard, S. (2015). *The internet of things*. MIT Press.

Green, I. (2017). *Digitisation as a preservation strategy of national heritage — A case of the Owela Museum. In 2017 IST-Africa Week Conference* (pp. 1–5). Windhoek: IST-Africa. doi:10.23919/ISTAFRICA.2017.8102283

Grguric, A., Gil, A. M., Huljenic, D., Car, Z., & Podobnik, V. (2016). A Survey on User Interaction Mechanisms for Enhanced Living Environments. In S. Loshkovska & S. Koceski (Eds.), *ICT Innovations 2015* (Vol. 399, pp. 131–141). Springer International Publishing; doi:10.1007/978-3-319-25733-4_14

Grinberg, M. (2018). *Flask Web Development: Developing Web Applications with Python*. O'Reilly Media, Inc.

GSMA. (2017a). *LTE_M Deployment Guide, 2017*. Retrieved from https://www.gsma.com/iot/wp-content/uploads/2017/09/LTE-M-Deployment-Guide-CLP.29-v1.0.pdf

GSMA. (2017b). *NB-IoT Deployment Guide*. Retrieved from https://www.gsma.com/iot/wp-content/uploads/2017/08/CLP.28-v1.0.pdf

Gugenheimer, J., Stemasov, E., Frommel, J., & Rukzio, E. (2017). Sharevr: Enabling co-located experiences for virtual reality between hmd and non-hmd users. *Proceedings of the 2017 CHI Conference on Human Factors in Computing Systems*. 10.1145/3025453.3025683

Guimarães, C. S. S., Henriques, R. V. B., Pereira, C. E., & da Silva Silveira, W. (2018). *Proposal IoT Architecture for Macro and Microscale Applied in Assistive Technology. In Online Engineering & Internet of Things* (pp. 36–43). Springer.

Gurevich, P., Lanir, J., Cohen, B., & Stone, R. (2012). TeleAdvisor: a versatile augmented reality tool for remote assistance. *Proceedings of the SIGCHI Conference on Human Factors in Computing Systems*. 10.1145/2207676.2207763

Guth, J., Breitenbücher, U., Falkenthal, M., Fremantle, P., Kopp, O., Leymann, F., & Reinfurt, L. (2018). A detailed analysis of IoT platform architectures: concepts, similarities, and differences. Internet of Everything: Algorithms, Methodologies, Technologies and Perspectives, 81-101.

Hagedorn, A., Starobinski, D., & Trachtenberg, A. (2008). Rateless Deluge: Over-the-Air Programming of Wireless Sensor Networks Using Random Linear Codes. Academic Press.

Hall, G. (2015). *Internet of everything: The value of connections*. Cisco Systems. Retrieved July 19, 2018 from: http://danto.info/InfoComm2015_Hall.pdf

Han, C.-C., Kumar, R., Shea, R., Kohler, E., & Srivastava, M. (2005). A dynamic operating system for sensor nodes. In *Proceedings of the 3rd international conference on Mobile systems, applications, and services* (pp. 163-176). ACM. 10.1145/1067170.1067188

Han, C.-C., Kumar, R., Shea, R., & Srivastava, M. (2005). Sensor network software update management: A survey. *International Journal of Network Management, 15*(4), 283–294. doi:10.1002/nem.574

Han, C.-C., Rengaswamy, R. K., Shea, R., Kohler, E., & Srivastava, M. (2005). SOS: A dynamic operating system for sensor networks. *Proceedings of the Third International Conference on Mobile Systems, Applications, And Services (Mobisys)*, 1-2.

Han, S. J., Garcia, A. V., Oida, S., Jenkins, K. A., & Haensch, W. (2014). Graphene radio frequency receiver integrated circuit. *Nature Communications, 5*(1), 3086. doi:10.1038/ncomms4086 PMID:24477203

Hanson, S., Seok, M., Sylvester, D., & Blaauw, D. (2008). Nanometer device scaling in sub-threshold logic and SRAM. *IEEE Transactions on Electron Devices, 55*(1), 175–185. doi:10.1109/TED.2007.911033

Hargreaves, T., & Wilson, C. (2017). *Perceived Benefits and Risks of Smart Home Technologies. In Smart Homes and Their Users* (pp. 35–53). Springer. doi:10.1007/978-3-319-68018-7_3

Hargreaves, T., Wilson, C., & Hauxwell-Baldwin, R. (2018). Learning to live in a smart home. *Building Research and Information, 46*(1), 127–139. doi:10.1080/09613218.2017.1286882

Harrison, G. (2015). *Next Generation Databases: NoSQL, NewSQL, and Big Data*. Apress. doi:10.1007/978-1-4842-1329-2

Hartenstein, H., & Laberteaux, L. P. (2008). A tutorial survey on vehicular ad hoc networks. *IEEE Communications Magazine, 46*(6), 164–171. doi:10.1109/MCOM.2008.4539481

Harte, S., Rollo, S., Popovici, E., & O'flynn, B. (2010). *Energy-efficient reprogramming of heterogeneous wireless sensor networks*. InTech.

Hartridge, H., & Thompson, L. C. (1948). Methods of investigating eye movements. *The British Journal of Ophthalmology, 32*(9), 581–591. doi:10.1136/bjo.32.9.581 PMID:18170495

Hartshorn, S. (2016). *Machine Learning With Random Forests And Decision Trees: A Visual Guide For Beginners*. Amazon Digital Services LLC.

Heimgaertner, F., Hettich, S., Kohlbacher, O., & Menth, M. (2017). *Scaling home automation to public buildings: A distributed multiuser setup for OpenHAB 2*. Paper presented at the Global Internet of Things Summit (GIoTS). 10.1109/GIOTS.2017.8016235

Henkemans, O. B., Caine, K. E., Rogers, W. A., & Fisk, A. D. (2007). Medical monitoring for independent living: user-centered design of smart home technologies for older adults. *Proc. Med-e-Tel Conf. eHealth, Telemedicine and Health Information and Communication Technologies*, 18–20.

Hernandez, D. M., Peralta, G., Manero, L., Gomez, R., Bilbao, J., & Zubia, C. (2017). Energy and coverage study of LPWAN schemes for Industry 4.0. In *2017 IEEE International Workshop of Electronics, Control, Measurement, Signals and their Application to Mechatronics* (ECMSM). IEEE. 10.1109/ecmsm.2017.7945893

Hill, E. W., Vijayaragahvan, A., & Novoselov, K. (2011). Graphene sensors. *IEEE Sensors Journal, 11*(12), 3161–3170. doi:10.1109/JSEN.2011.2167608

Hill, J., Szewczyk, R., Woo, A., Hollar, S., Culler, D., & Pister, K. (2000). System Architecture Directions for Networked Sensors. In *Proceedings of the Ninth International Conference on Architectural Support for Programming Languages and Operating Systems* (pp. 93-104). Cambridge, MA: ACM. 10.1145/378993.379006

Holland, J., & Lee, S. (2018). *Internet of everything (IoE): Eye tracking data analysis. In Harnessing the Internet of Everything (IoE) for Accelerated Innovation Opportunities*. Hershey, PA: IGI Global.

Hosmer, D., Lemeshow, S., & Sturdivant, R. (2013). *Applied logistic regression*. Wiley. doi:10.1002/9781118548387

Hu, J., Xue, C. J., He, Y., & Sha, E. H.-M. (2009). Reprogramming with minimal transferred data on wireless sensor network. *IEEE 6th International Conference on Mobile Adhoc and Sensor Systems*, 160-167.

Huang, W., Alem, L., & Albasri, J. (2011). *HandsInAir: a wearable system for remote collaboration*. arXiv preprint arXiv:1112.1742

Huang, W., Alem, L., & Tecchia, F. (2013a). *HandsIn3d: augmenting the shared 3d visual space with unmediated hand gestures*. Paper presented at the SIGGRAPH Asia 2013 Emerging Technologies. 10.1145/2542284.2542294

Huang, W., Alem, L., & Tecchia, F. (2013b). *HandsIn3D: supporting remote guidance with immersive virtual environments*. Paper presented at the IFIP Conference on Human-Computer Interaction. 10.1007/978-3-642-40483-2_5

Huang, W., & Alem, L. (2013). HandsinAir: a wearable system for remote collaboration on physical tasks. *Proceedings of the 2013 conference on Computer supported cooperative work companion*. 10.1145/2441955.2441994

Huang, X., Leng, T., Zhu, M., Zhang, X., Chen, J., Chang, K., ... Hu, Z. (2015). Highly flexible and conductive printed graphene for wireless wearable communications applications. *Scientific Reports*, *5*(1), 18298. doi:10.1038rep18298 PMID:26673395

Huang, Z., & Yuan, F. (2015). Implementation of 6LoWPAN and its application in smart lighting. *Journal of Computer and Communications*, *3*(03), 80–85. doi:10.4236/jcc.2015.33014

Huh, S., Cho, S., & Kim, S. (2017). Managing IoT devices using blockchain platform. *2017 19th International Conference on Advanced Communication Technology (ICACT) IEEE*. doi:10.23919/icact.2017.7890132

Hui, J. W., & Culler, D. (2004). The dynamic behavior of a data dissemination protocol for network programming at scale. In *Proceedings of the 2nd international conference on Embedded networked sensor systems* (pp. 81-94). ACM. 10.1145/1031495.1031506

Hutchinson, T. E., White, K. P., Martin, W. N., Reichert, K. C., & Frey, L. A. (1989). Human-computer interaction using eye-gaze input. *IEEE Transactions on Systems, Man, and Cybernetics*, *19*(6), 1527–1534. doi:10.1109/21.44068

IEEE. (1998). *IEEE Std 830: Recommended Practice for Software Requirements Specifications*. IEEE.

IMOTIONS. (2015). *7 most used eye tracking metrics and terms*. Retrieved September 25, 2017 from: https://imotions.com/blog/7-terms-metrics-eye-tracking/

IMOTIONS. (2017). *Eye tracking: The complete pocket guide*. Retrieved Dec. 2, 2017 from: https://imotions.com/blog/eye-tracking/

Ingenu. (2016). *Ingenu webinar: How RPMA works*. Retrieved from https://www.youtube.com/watch?v=4beoZapuBXw

Ingenu. (n.d.). *How RPMA works: an educational guide*. Whitepaper. Retrieved from https://www.ingenu.com/portfolio/how-rpma-works-white-paper/

Instituto Nacional de Técnica Aeroespacial. (2018). *INTA Web site*. Retrieved from http://www.inta.es

Intel. (2018). *Intel IoT*. Retrieved at October 24 2018, from http://www.intel.com/content/www/us/en/internet-of-things/overview.html

Internet of Things Research – European Union (2016). *Report on IoT Platform Activity*. Author.

Internet Society. (2001). *The Internet of Things: An Overview*. Retrieved at January 1, 2016, from https://www.internet-society.org/resources/doc/2015/iot-overview

IoT Analytics. (2015). *IoT platforms: The central backbone for the Internet of Things*. Retrieved at October 24 2018, from http://www.iot-analytics.com

IPA. (2010). *Approaches for embedded system information security (2010 revised edition): Know your organization's security level by checking 16 points*. Retrieved from https://www.ipa.go.jp/files/000014118.pdf

iScoop. (2018). *What the Internet of everything really is – a deep dive*. Retrieved July 25, 2018 from: https://www.i-scoop.eu/internet-of-things-guide/internet-of-everything/

Ishii, H., & Kobayashi, M. (1992). ClearBoard: a seamless medium for shared drawing and conversation with eye contact. *Proceedings of the SIGCHI conference on Human factors in computing systems*. 10.1145/142750.142977

Ishii, H., Kobayashi, M., & Arita, K. (1994). Iterative design of seamless collaboration media. *Communications of the ACM*, *37*(8), 83–97. doi:10.1145/179606.179687

ITU-R. (2010). *Technical characteristics and operational objectives for wireless avionics intra-communications (WAIC)*. REPORT ITU-R M.2197.

Izosimov, V., & Törngren, M. (2016). Security Evaluation of Cyber-Physical Systems in Society Critical Internet of Things. In *Proceedings of the Final Conference on Trustworthy Manufacturing and Utilization of Secure Devices TRUDEVICE 2016*. Barcelona: UPCommons.

Izosimov, V., Asvestopoulos, A., Blomkvist, O., & Törngren, M. (2016). Security-aware development of cyber-physical systems illustrated with automotive case study. In *Proceedings of 2016 Design, Automation & Test in Europe Conference & Exhibition* (pp. 818–821). San Jose, CA: EDA Consortium. doi:10.3850/9783981537079_0756

Jacob, R. J., & Karn, K. S. (2003). Eye tracking in human-computer interaction and usability research: Ready to deliver the promises. In The Mind's Eye: Cognitive and Applied Aspects of Eye Movement Research. Academic Press.

Jacob, R. J. K. (1990). *What you look at is what you get: Eye movement-based interaction techniques*. Washington, DC: Naval Research Laboratory.

Jacob, R. J. K. (1991). The use of eye movement in human-computer interaction techniques: What you look at is what you get. *ACM Transactions on Information Systems*, *9*(2), 152–169. doi:10.1145/123078.128728

Jacob, R. J. K. (1995). Eye tracking in advanced interface design. In W. Barfield & T. A. Furness (Eds.), *Virtual environments and advanced interface design* (pp. 258–288). New York, NY: Oxford University Press.

Jacobsson, A., Boldt, M., & Carlsson, B. (2016). A risk analysis of a smart home automation system. *Future Generation Computer Systems*, *56*, 719–733. doi:10.1016/j.future.2015.09.003

Jahn, M., Jentsch, M., Prause, C. R., Pramudianto, F., Al-Akkad, A., & Reiners, R. (2010). *The energy aware smart home*. Paper presented at the Future Information Technology (FutureTech), 2010 5th International Conference on. 10.1109/FUTURETECH.2010.5482712

Jain, P. C., & Taneeru, S. (2016). Performance Evaluation of IEEE 802.11ah Protocol in Wireless Area Network. In *2016 International Conference on Micro-Electronics and Telecommunication Engineering (ICMETE)*. IEEE. 10.1109/ICMETE.2016.23

Jakovljev, S., Subotić, M., & Papp, I. (2017). *Realisation of a Smart Plug device based on Wi-Fi technology for use in home automation systems.* Paper presented at the Consumer Electronics (ICCE), 2017 IEEE International Conference on. 10.1109/ICCE.2017.7889340

James, G., Witten, D., Hastie, T., & Tibshirani, R. (2013). *An Introduction to Statistical Learning with Applications in R.* Springer. doi:10.1007/978-1-4614-7138-7

Jara, A. J., Zamora, M. A., & Skarmeta, A. F. G. (2011). An internet of things–based personal device for diabetes therapy management in ambient assisted living (AAL). *Personal and Ubiquitous Computing, 15*(4), 431–440. doi:10.100700779-010-0353-1

Jaradat, M., Jarrah, M., Bousselham, A., Jararweh, Y., & Al-Ayyoub, M. (2015). The Internet of Energy: Smart Sensor Networks and Big Data Management for Smart Grid. *Procedia Computer Science, 56*, 592–597. doi:10.1016/j.procs.2015.07.250

Jarodzka, H., Scheiter, K., Gerjets, P., & Van Gog, T. (2010). In the eyes of the beholder: How experts and novices interpret dynamic stimuli. *Learning and Instruction, 20*(2), 146–154. doi:10.1016/j.learninstruc.2009.02.019

Javal, E. (1878). Essai sur la physiologie de la lecture. *Annales d'Oculistique, 79,* 97-117.

Jazdi, N. (2014). Cyber physical systems in the context of Industry 4.0. In *2014 IEEE International Conference on Automation, Quality and Testing, Robotics* (pp. 1-4). IEEE. 10.1109/AQTR.2014.6857843

Jeong, J. (2003). *Node-level representation and system support for network programming.* Academic Press.

Jeong, J., & Culler, D. (2004). Incremental network programming for wireless sensors. *First Annual IEEE Communications Society Conference on Sensor and Ad Hoc Communications and Networks,* 25-33.

Jeschke, S., Brecher, C., Meisen, T., Ozdemir, D., & Eschert, T. (2017). Industrial internet of things and cyber manufacturing systems. *Industrial Internet of Things, 2017,* 3–19. doi:10.1007/978-3-319-42559-7_1

Jetly, C. R., Meakin, L. C., Sinitski, E. H., Blackburn, L., Menard, J., Vincent, M., & Antwi, M. (2017). *Multi-Modal virtual-reality based treatment for members with combat related posttraumatic stress disorder: Canadian Armed Forces pilot study.* Paper presented at the Virtual Rehabilitation (ICVR), 2017 International Conference on. 10.1109/ICVR.2017.8007474

Jia, Y., Shelhamer, E., Donahue, J., Karayev, S., Long, J., Girshick, R., ... Darrell, T. (2014). Caffe. In *Proceedings of the ACM International Conference on Multimedia - MM '14* (pp. 675–678). New York: ACM Press. 10.1145/2647868.2654889

Johari, P., & Jornet, J. M. (2017). Nanoscale optical wireless channel model for intra-body communications: Geometrical, time, and frequency domain analyses. *IEEE Transactions on Communications.*

Jones, M., Bradley, J., & Sakimura, N. (2015). *Introduction to JSON Web Tokens.* IETF.

Jorgenson, L. A., Newsome, W. T., Anderson, D. J., Bargmann, C. I., Brown, E. N., Deisseroth, K., ... Marder, E. (2015). The BRAIN Initiative: developing technology to catalyse neuroscience discovery. *Phil. Trans. R. Soc. B, 370*(1668), 20140164.

Jornet, J. M., & Akyildiz, I. F. (2011). Channel modeling and capacity analysis for electromagnetic wireless nanonetworks in the terahertz band. *IEEE Transactions on Wireless Communications, 10*(10), 3211–3221. doi:10.1109/TWC.2011.081011.100545

Jornet, J. M., & Akyildiz, I. F. (2013). Graphene-based plasmonic nano-antenna for terahertz band communication in nanonetworks. *IEEE Journal on Selected Areas in Communications, 31*(12), 685–694. doi:10.1109/JSAC.2013.SUP2.1213001

Jose, A. C., & Malekian, R. (2015). Smart home automation security. *SmartCR, 5*(4), 269–285.

Jose, A., & Malekian, R. (2017). Improving Smart Home Security; Integrating Logical Sensing into Smart Home. *IEEE Sensors Journal, 17*(13), 4269–4286. doi:10.1109/JSEN.2017.2705045

Judd, C. H., McAllister, C. N., & Steel, W. M. (1905). General introduction to a series of studies of eye movements by means of kinetoscopic photographs. Psychological Review, Monograph Supplements, 7, 1-16.

Just, M. A., & Carpenter, P. A. (1980). A theory of reading: From eye fixations to comprehension. *Psychological Review, 87*(4), 329–354. doi:10.1037/0033-295X.87.4.329 PMID:7413885

Kachman, O., & Balaz, M. (2016). Optimized differencing algorithm for firmware updates of low-power devices. *IEEE 19th International Symposium on Design and Diagnostics of Electronic Circuits & Systems*, 1-4.

Kadri, B., Feham, M., & M'hamed, A. (2010). Lightweight PKI for WSN uPKI. *The Journal of Security and Communication Networks*, 135-141.

Kafka, A. (2018). *Distributed streaming platform*. Retrieved from https://kafka.apache.org/

Kafli, N., & Isa, K. (2017). Internet of Things (IoT) for measuring and monitoring sensors data of water surface platform. *2017 IEEE 7th International Conference on Underwater System Technology: theory and applications (USYS)*, 1–6. doi:10.1109/USYS.2017.8309441

Kang, Y.-S., Park, I.-H., Rhee, J., & Lee, Y.-H. (2016). MongoDB-Based Repository Design for IoT-Generated RFID/Sensor Big Data. *IEEE Sensors Journal, 16*(2), 485–497. doi:10.1109/JSEN.2015.2483499

Kang, Y.-S., Park, I.-H., & Youm, S. (2016). Performance Prediction of a MongoDB-Based Traceability System in Smart Factory Supply Chains. *Sensors (Basel), 16*(12), 2126. doi:10.339016122126 PMID:27983654

Kannapiran, S., & Chakrapani, A. (2017). A Novel Home Automation System using Bluetooth and Arduino. *International Journal of Advances in Computer and Electronics Engineering, 2*(2), 41–44.

Karame, G. O., & Li, W. (2015). Secure Erasure and Code Update in Legacy Sensors. In M. Conti, M. Schunter, & I. Askoxylakis (Eds.), Trust and Trustworthy Computing (pp. 283-299). Springer International Publishing. doi:10.1007/978-3-319-22846-4_17

Karnouskos, S., & Terzidis, O. (2007). Towards an information infrastructure for the future Internet of energy. *ITG-GI Conference Communication in Distributed Systems (KiVS)*, 1-6.

Keane, J., Kim, T., & Kim, C. (2007). An on-chip NBTI sensor for measuring PMOS threshold volt-age degradation. *Proc. Int. Symp. on Low Power Electronics and Design (ISLPED)*, 189-194.

Keller, S., Bhargav, S., Moore, C., & Martin, A. J. (2011). Reliable Minimum Energy CMOS Circuit Design. *Vari'11: 2nd European Workshop on CMOS Variability*.

Keysight. (2017). *NB-Iot Technical Fundamentals*. Whitepaper. Retrieved from http://www.keysight.com/upload/cmc_upload/All/20170612-A4-JianHuaWu-updated.pdf

Khan, M. A., & Salah, K. (2018). IoT security: Review, blockchain solutions, and open challenges. *Future Generation Computer Systems, 82*, 395–411. doi:10.1016/j.future.2017.11.022

Kilinc, D., & Akan, O. B. (2013). Receiver Design for Molecular Communication. *IEEE Journal on Selected Areas in Communications, 31*(12), 705–714. doi:10.1109/JSAC.2013.SUP2.1213003

Kim, D., Kim, J., Kim, M., Moulic, J., & Song, H. (2009). *System and Method for Monitoring Reliability of a Digital System.* IBM Corp., US Patent 7495519.

Kim, J.-J., & Roy, K. (2004). Double gate MOSFET subthreshold circuit for ultralow power applications. *IEEE Transactions on Electron Devices, 51*(9), 1468–1474. doi:10.1109/TED.2004.833965

Kim, P. (2017). *MATLAB Deep Learning: With Machine Learning, Neural Networks and Artificial Intelligence* (1st ed.). Apress. doi:10.1007/978-1-4842-2845-6

Kiraz, G., & Toğay, C. (2017). IoT Data Storage: Relational & Non-Relational Database Management Systems Performance Comparison. In A. Yazici & C. Turhan (Eds.), *34. TBD National Informatics Symposium* (pp. 48–52). Ankara, Turkey: Academic Press.

Kiyokawa, K., Takemura, H., & Yokoya, N. (1999). A collaboration support technique by integrating a shared virtual reality and a shared augmented reality. *Systems, Man, and Cybernetics, 1999. IEEE SMC'99 Conference Proceedings. 1999 IEEE International Conference on.* 10.1109/ICSMC.1999.816444

Kiyomoto, S., & Miyake, Y. (2014). Lightweight attestation scheme for wireless sensor network. *International Journal of Security and Its Applications*, 25-40.

Knight, M. (2006). How safe is Z-Wave? *Computing and Control Engineering, 17*(6), 18–23. doi:10.1049/cce:20060601

KNIME. (2017). *KNIME.* Retrieved October 7, 2018, from https://www.knime.com/

Kohnhaeuser, F., & Katzenbeisser, S. (2016). Secure Code Updates for Mesh Networked Commodity Low-End Embedded Devices. In I. Askoxylakis, S. Ioannidis, S. Katsikas, & C. Meadows (Eds.), Computer Security -- ESORICS 2016 (pp. 320-338). Springer International Publishing. doi:10.1007/978-3-319-45741-3_17

Koleva, P., Tonchev, K., Balabanov, G., Manolova, A., & Poulkov, V. (2015). Challenges in designing and implementation of an effective Ambient Assisted Living system. *Telecommunication in Modern Satellite, Cable and Broadcasting Services (TELSIKS), 2015 12th International Conference on*, 305–308. 10.1109/TELSKS.2015.7357793

Kolias, C., Kambourakis, G., Stavrou, A., & Voas, J. (2017). DDoS in the IoT: Mirai and other botnets. *Computer, 50*(7), 80–84. doi:10.1109/MC.2017.201

Korhonen, I., Parkka, J., & Van Gils, M. (2003). Health monitoring in the home of the future. *IEEE Engineering in Medicine and Biology Magazine, 22*(3), 66–73. doi:10.1109/MEMB.2003.1213628 PMID:12845821

Koshy, J., & Pandey, R. (2005). Remote incremental linking for energy-efficient reprogramming of sensor networks. *Proceedings of the Second European Workshop on Wireless Sensor Networks*, 354-365.

Koshy, J., & Pandey, R. (2005). VMSTAR: Synthesizing Scalable Runtime Environments for Sensor Networks. *Proceedings of the 3rd International Conference on Embedded Networked Sensor Systems* (pp. 243-254). San Diego, CA: ACM. 10.1145/1098918.1098945

Koubaa, A., Alves, M. & Tovar, E. (2018). *IEEE 802.15.4: a Federating Communication Protocol for Time-Sensitive Wireless Sensor Networks.* IEEE.

Krasniewski, M. D., Panta, R. K., Bagchi, S., Yang, C.-L., & Chappell, W. J. (2008). Energy-efficient on-demand reprogramming of large-scale sensor networks. *ACM Transactions on Sensor Networks*, 4(1), 1–38. doi:10.1145/1325651.1325653

Kreuzer, K. (2014). *Privacy in the Smart Home - Why we need an Intranet of Things*. Retrieved 02/03/2018, from http://www.kaikreuzer.de/2014/02/10/privacy-in-smart-home-why-we-need/

Krizhevsky, A., Sutskever, I., & Hinton, G. E. (2012). Imagenet Classification with Deep Convolutional Neural Networks. *Advances in Neural Information Processing Systems*, 1–9.

Krupka, L., Vojtech, L., & Neruda, M. (2016). The issue of LPWAN technology coexistence in IoT environment. *17th International Conference on Mechatronics-Mechatronika*, 1–8.

Kulkarni, B. P., Joshi, A. V., Jadhav, V. V., & Dhamange, A. T. (2017). IoT Based Home Automation Using Raspberry PI. *International Journal of Innovative Studies in Sciences and Engineering Technology*, 3(4), 13–16.

Kulkarni, S. S., & Wang, L. (2005). MNP: Multihop network reprogramming service for sensor networks. *Proceedings of the 25th IEEE International Conference on Distributed Computing Systems*, 7-16. 10.1109/ICDCS.2005.50

Kuscu, M., & Akan, O. (2016). The Internet of Molecular Things Based on FRET. *IEEE Internet of Things Journal*, (1), 4-17.

Kuscu, M., & Akan, O. B. (2016). On the Physical Design of Molecular Communication Receiver Based on Nanoscale Biosensors. *IEEE Sensors Journal*, 16(8), 2228–2243. doi:10.1109/JSEN.2016.2519150

Kuscu, M., Kiraz, A., & Akan, O. B. (2015). Fluorescent molecules as transceiver nanoantennas: The first practical and high-rate information transfer over a nanoscale communication channel based on FRET. *Scientific Reports*, 5(1), 7831. doi:10.1038rep07831 PMID:25591972

Kwon, C., Liu, W., & Hwang, I. (2013). Security analysis for cyber-physical systems against stealthy deception attacks. In *Proceedings of American Control Conference* (pp. 3344–3349). Washington, DC: IEEE Computer Society.

La Scala, M., Bruno, S., Nucci, C. A., Lamonaca, S., & Stecchi, U. (2017). *From Smart Grids to Smart Cities: New Challenges in Optimizing Energy Grids*. John Wiley & Sons.

Laamarti, F., & El Saddik, A. (2017). *Home automation serving a healthier lifestyle*. Paper presented at the Medical Measurements and Applications (MeMeA), 2017 IEEE International Symposium on. 10.1109/MeMeA.2017.7985846

Lanigan, P. E., Gandhi, R., & Narasimhan, P. (2006). Sluice: Secure dissemination of code updates in sensor networks. *26th IEEE International Conference on Distributed Computing Systems*, 53-53. 10.1109/ICDCS.2006.77

Larcom, J. A., & Liu, H. (2013). Modeling and characterization of GPS spoofing, In *Proceedings of IEEE International Conference on Technologies for Homeland Security* (pp. 729-734). Washington, DC: IEEE Computer Society.

Lasi, H., Fettke, P., Kemper, H. G., Feld, T., & Hoffmann, M. (2014). Industry 4.0. *Business & Information Systems Engineering*, 6(4), 239–242. doi:10.100712599-014-0334-4

Lau, H., Chan, L., & Wong, R. (2007). A virtual container terminal simulator for the design of terminal operation. *International Journal on Interactive Design and Manufacturing*, 1(2), 107–113. doi:10.100712008-007-0013-5

Lavrova, D., & Pechenkin, A. (2015). Applying Correlation and Regression Analysis to Detect Security Incidents in the Internet of Things. *International Journal of Communication Networks and Information Security*, 7(3), 131–137.

Le Chénéchal, M., Duval, T., Gouranton, V., Royan, J., & Arnaldi, B. (2016). *Vishnu: virtual immersive support for helping users an interaction paradigm for collaborative remote guiding in mixed reality*. Paper presented at the Collaborative Virtual Environments (3DCVE), 2016 IEEE Third VR International Workshop on. 10.1109/3DCVE.2016.7563559

Lee, G. A., Teo, T., Kim, S., & Billinghurst, M. (2017a). *Mixed reality collaboration through sharing a live panorama.* Paper presented at the SIGGRAPH Asia 2017 Mobile Graphics & Interactive Applications. 10.1145/3132787.3139203

Lee, G. A., Teo, T., Kim, S., & Billinghurst, M. (2017b). *Sharedsphere: MR collaboration through shared live panorama.* Paper presented at the SIGGRAPH Asia 2017 Emerging Technologies. 10.1145/3132818.3132827

Lee, M., Hwang, J., & Yoe, H. (2013). Agricultural Production System Based on IoT. In *2013 IEEE 16th International Conference on Computational Science and Engineering* (pp. 833–837). IEEE. 10.1109/CSE.2013.126

Lee, S., Ryu, J., & Ke, F. (2017). *Effects of Representation Format on Eye Movements in Math Problem Solving: Does Iconic Make a Difference?* Paper presented at the annual meeting of Association for Educational Communication and Technology, Jacksonville, FL.

Lee, E.-K., Gerla, M., & Oh, S. Y. (2012). Physical layer security in wireless smart grid. *IEEE Communications Magazine, 50*(8), 46–52. doi:10.1109/MCOM.2012.6257526

Lee, J., Bagheri, B., & Kao, H. A. (2015). A cyber-physical systems architecture for industry 4.0-based manufacturing systems. *Manufacturing Letters, 3*, 18–23. doi:10.1016/j.mfglet.2014.12.001

Lee, J., Kao, H., & Yang, S. (2014). Service innovation and smart analytics for industry 4.0 and big data environment. *Procedia Cirp, 16*, 3–8. doi:10.1016/j.procir.2014.02.001

Lee, K. C., & Lee, H.-H. (2004). Network-based fire-detection system via controller area network for smart home automation. *IEEE Transactions on Consumer Electronics, 50*(4), 1093–1100. doi:10.1109/TCE.2004.1362504

Leest van der, V., & Tuyls, P. (2013). Anti-counterfeiting with hardware intrinsic security, In Proceedings of 2013 Design, Automation & Test in Europe Conference & Exhibition (pp. 1137-1142). San Jose, CA: EDA Consortium.

Lehniger, K., Weidling, S., & Schoelzel, M. (2018). Heuristic for Page-based Incremental. *Proc. of the 21st IEEE International Symposium on Design and Diagnostics of Electronic Circuits and Systems.*

Lennvall, T., Svensson, S., & Hekland, F. (2008). A comparison of WirelessHART and ZigBee for industrial applications. In *2008 IEEE International Workshop on Factory Communication Systems.* IEEE. 10.1109/WFCS.2008.4638746

Lesmeister, C. (2015). *Mastering Machine Learning with R.* Packt Publishing.

Levine, J. L. (1981). *An eye-controlled computer.* Research Report RC-8857. New York: IBM Thomas J. Watson Research Center.

Levine, J. L. (1984). Performance of an eye tracker for office use. *Computers in Biology and Medicine, 14*(1), 77–89. doi:10.1016/0010-4825(84)90022-2 PMID:6713833

Levis, P., & Culler, D. E. (2002). Maté: a tiny virtual machine for sensor networks. In *Proceedings of the 10th International Conference on Architectural Support for Programming Languages and Operating Systems* (pp. 85-95). San Jose, CA: ACM. 10.1145/605397.605407

Levis, P., Patel, N., Culler, D., & Shenker, S. (2004). Trickle: A self-regulating algorithm for code propagation and maintenance in wireless sensor networks. *Proc. of the 1st USENIX/ACM Symp. on Networked Systems Design and Implementation.*

Li, F., & Xiong, P. (2013). *Practical secure communication for integrating wireless sensor networks into the internet of things.* Academic Press.

Li, M.-Z., Ieong, C.-I., Law, M.-K., Mak, P.-I., Vai, M.-I., & Martins, R. P. (2013). Sub-threshold standard cell library design for ultra-low power biomedical applications. *Engineering in Medicine and Biology Society (EMBC) 2013 35th Annual International Conference of the IEEE*, 1454.

Link-labs.com. (2018). *LoRa is groundbreaking physical layer (PHY) wireless technology*. Retrieved from Link-labs. com: https://www.link-labs.com/lora

Li, R., Lu, B., & McDonald-Maier, K. D. (2015). Cognitive assisted living ambient system: A survey. *Digital Communications and Networks*, *1*(4), 229–252. doi:10.1016/j.dcan.2015.10.003

Li, S., Da Xu, L., & Wang, X. (2013). Compressed sensing signal and data acquisition in wireless sensor networks and internet of things. *IEEE Transactions on Industrial Informatics*, *9*(4), 2177–2186. doi:10.1109/TII.2012.2189222

Li, S., Xu, L. D., & Zhao, S. (2015). The Internet of Things: A survey. *Information Systems Frontiers, Springer Publisher*, *17*(2), 243–259. doi:10.100710796-014-9492-7

Li, T., Xia, M., Chen, J., Zhao, Y., & de Silva, C. (2017). Automated water quality survey and evaluation using an IoT platform with mobile sensor nodes. *Sensors (Basel)*, *17*(8), 1735. doi:10.339017081735 PMID:28788098

Li, Y., Hui, P., Jin, D., Su, L., & Zeng, L. (2014). Optimal distributed malware defense in mobile networks with heterogeneous devices. *IEEE Transactions on Mobile Computing*, *13*(2), 377–391. doi:10.1109/TMC.2012.255

Lobaccaro, G., Carlucci, S., & Löfström, E. (2016). A review of systems and technologies for smart homes and smart grids. *Energies*, *9*(5), 348. doi:10.3390/en9050348

Longbottom, C. (2016). *A reference architecture for the IoE*. Retrieved July 19, 2018 from: https://www.whitepapers. em360tech.com/wp-content/uploads/A-reference-architecture-for-IoE.pdf

Long, T., Ozger, M., Cetinkaya, O., & Akan, O. B. (2018). Energy Neutral Internet of Drones. *IEEE Communications Magazine*, *56*(1), 22–28. doi:10.1109/MCOM.2017.1700454

LoRa Alliance. (2015). *A technical overview of LoRa and LoRaWAN*. White paper. Author.

LoRa Alliance. (2017). *LoRaWAN 101 A technical introduction*. Retrieved from https://eleven-x.com/wp-content/uploads/2018/04/LoRaWAN-101-A-Technical-Introduction.pdf

Louis, J.-N., Caló, A., Leiviskä, K., & Pongrácz, E. (2015). Environmental impacts and benefits of smart home automation: Life cycle assessment of home energy management system. *IFAC-PapersOnLine*, *48*(1), 880–885. doi:10.1016/j.ifacol.2015.05.158

Lueth, K. L. (2015). *IoT basics: Getting started with the Internet of Things*. IoT Analytics (White Paper).

Luigi, A., & Antonio, I. (2010). The Internet of things: A survey. *Computer Networks*. Retrieved March 11, 2018 from https://www.cs.mun.ca/courses/cs6910/IoT-Survey-Atzori-2010.pdf

Macher, G., Sporer, H., Berlach, R., Armengaud, E., & Kreiner, C. (2015). SAHARA: A security-aware hazard and risk analysis method. In *Proceedings of 2015 Design, Automation & Test in Europe Conference & Exhibition* (pp. 621–624). San Jose, CA: EDA Consortium. doi:10.7873/DATE.2015.0622

Mackworth, J. F., & Mackworth, N. H. (1958). Eye fixations recorded on changing visual scenes by the television eye-market. *Journal of the Optical Society of America*, *48*(7), 439–445. doi:10.1364/JOSA.48.000439 PMID:13564324

Mackworth, N. H., & Thomas, E. L. (1962). Head-mounted eye-marker camera. *Journal of the Optical Society of America*, *52*(6), 713–716. doi:10.1364/JOSA.52.000713 PMID:14467994

Maglaras, L. A., Al-Bayatti, A. H., He, Y., Wagner, I., & Janicke, H. (2016). Social Internet of Vehicles for Smart Cities. *Journal of Sensor and Actuator Networks*, *5*(1), 3. doi:10.3390/jsan5010003

Mahmood, A., Javaid, N., & Razzaq, S. (2015). A review of wireless communications for smart grid. *Renewable & Sustainable Energy Reviews*, *41*, 248–260. doi:10.1016/j.rser.2014.08.036

Mainetti, L., Patrono, L., & Vilei, A. (2011). *Evolution of wireless sensor networks towards the internet of things: A survey.* Paper presented at the Software, Telecommunications and Computer Networks (SoftCOM), 2011 19th International Conference on.

Majaranta, P., & Bulling, A. (2014). Advances in physiological computing. In Eye tracking and eye-based human-computer interaction (vol. 3, pp. 39-65). Academic Press.

Majaranta, P., & Raiha, K. J. (2002). Twenty Years of Eye Typing: Systems and Design Issues. *Proc. 2002 Symp. Eye Tracking Research and Applications*, 15-22. 10.1145/507072.507076

Malak, D., & Akan, O. (2014). Communication theoretical understanding of intra-body nervous nanonetworks. *IEEE Communications Magazine*, *52*(4), 129–135. doi:10.1109/MCOM.2014.6807957

Malić, M., Dobrilović, D., & Petrov, I. (2016). Example of IoT platform usage for wireless video surveillance with support of NoSQL and cloud systems. In Proceedings of the ICAIIT2016 (pp. 27–34). University "St. Kliment Ohridski". doi:10.20544/AIIT2016.04

Manjak, M. (2006). Social engineering your employees to Information Security. In *Global Information Assurance Certification Gold Papers for Security Essentials*. Swansea, UK: SANS Institute.

Margelis, G., Piechocki, R., Kaleshi, D., & Thomas, P. (2015). Low Throughput Networks for the IoT: Lessons learned from industrial implementations. In *2015 IEEE 2nd World Forum on Internet of Things (WF-IoT)*. IEEE.

Markovic, D., Stojanovic, V., Nikolic, B., Horowitz, M. A., & Brodersen, R. W. (2004). Methods for True Energy-Performance Optimization. *IEEE Journal of Solid-State Circuits*, *39*(8), 1282–1293. doi:10.1109/JSSC.2004.831796

Markram, H., Meier, K., Lippert, T., Grillner, S., Frackowiak, R., Dehaene, S., ... Grant, S. (2011). Introducing the Human Brain Project. *Procedia Computer Science*, *7*, 39–42. doi:10.1016/j.procs.2011.12.015

Marques, G., & Pitarma, R. (2016b). Health informatics for indoor air quality monitoring. In *Information Systems and Technologies (CISTI), 2016 11th Iberian Conference on* (pp. 1–6). AISTI. 10.1109/CISTI.2016.7521375

Marques, G., & Pitarma, R. (2016a). An indoor monitoring system for ambient assisted living based on internet of things architecture. *International Journal of Environmental Research and Public Health*, *13*(11), 1152. doi:10.3390/ijerph13111152 PMID:27869682

Marques, G., & Pitarma, R. (2017). Monitoring Health Factors in Indoor Living Environments Using Internet of Things. In Á. Rocha, A. M. Correia, H. Adeli, L. P. Reis, & S. Costanzo (Eds.), *Recent Advances in Information Systems and Technologies* (Vol. 570, pp. 785–794). Cham: Springer International Publishing; doi:10.1007/978-3-319-56538-5_79

Marques, G., & Pitarma, R. (2018). IAQ Evaluation Using an IoT CO2 Monitoring System for Enhanced Living Environments. In Á. Rocha, H. Adeli, L. P. Reis, & S. Costanzo (Eds.), *Trends and Advances in Information Systems and Technologies* (Vol. 746, pp. 1169–1177). Cham: Springer International Publishing; doi:10.1007/978-3-319-77712-2_112

Marron, P. J., Gauger, M., Lachenmann, A., Minder, D., Saukh, O., & Rothermel, K. (2006). FlexCup: A flexible and efficient code update mechanism for sensor networks. *European Workshop on Wireless Sensor Networks*, 212-227. 10.1007/11669463_17

Martins, C. V., Semião, J., Vazquez, J. C., Champaq, V., Santos, M., Teixeira, I. C., & Teixeira, J. P. (2011). Adaptive Error-Prediction Flip-flop for Performance Failure Prediction with Aging Sensors. *Proceedings of the 29th IEEE VLSI Test Symposium 2011 (VTS'11).* 10.1109/VTS.2011.5783784

Matiko, J. W., Wei, Y., Torah, R., Grabham, N., Paul, G., Beeby, S., & Tudor, J. (2015). Wearable EEG headband using printed electrodes and powered by energy harvesting for emotion monitoring in ambient assisted living. *Smart Materials and Structures, 24*(12), 125028. doi:10.1088/0964-1726/24/12/125028

Matsatsinis, N. F. (2002). An intelligent decision support system for credit card assessment based on a machine learning technique. *Operations Research, 2*(2), 243–260. doi:10.1007/BF02936329

Mayer, R. E. (1985). Mathematical ability. In R. J. Sternberg (Ed.), *Human abilities: An information processing approach* (pp. 127–150). San Francisco: Freeman.

Mazumder, B., & Hallstrom, J. O. (2013). An efficient code update solution for wireless sensor network reprogramming. *Proceedings of the International Conference on Embedded Software (EMSOFT),* 1-10. 10.1109/EMSOFT.2013.6658582

McDaniel, P., & McLaughlin, S. (2009). Security and Privacy Challenges in the Smart Grid. *IEEE Security and Privacy, 7*(3), 75–77. doi:10.1109/MSP.2009.76

McKinney, W. (2011). Data Structures for Statistical Computing in Python. In *9th Python in Science Conf. (SCIPY 2010)* (pp. 51–56). Academic Press.

Medaglia, C. M., & Serbanati, A. (2010). An overview of privacy and security issues in the internet of things. *The Internet of Things,* 389-395.

Medina, D., Hoffmann, F., Rossetto, F., & Rokitansky, C. H. (2012). *A Geographic Routing Strategy for North Atlantic In-Flight Internet Access Via Airborne Mesh Networking.* Academic Press.

Mehdi, G., & Roshchin, M. (2015). Electricity consumption constraints for smart-home automation: An overview of models and applications. *Energy Procedia, 83,* 60–68. doi:10.1016/j.egypro.2015.12.196

Menascé, D. A., & Nakanishi, T. (1982). Optimistic versus pessimistic concurrency control mechanisms in database management systems. *Information Systems, 7*(1), 13-27.

Meng, X., Bradley, J., Yavuz, B., Sparks, E., Venkataraman, S., Liu, D., ... Talwalkar, A. (2016). MLlib: Machine Learning in Apache Spark. *Journal of Machine Learning Research, 17*(1), 1235–1241.

Menon, G. S., Ramesh, M. V., & Divya, P. (2017). A low cost wireless sensor network for water quality monitoring in natural water bodies. *2017 IEEE Global Humanitarian Technology Conference (GHTC),* 1–8. 10.1109/GHTC.2017.8239341

Meyer, K., Rasch, T., & Schnotz, W. (2010). Effects of animation's speed of presentation on perceptual processing and learning. *Learning and Instruction, 20*(2), 136–145. doi:10.1016/j.learninstruc.2009.02.016

Microchip. (2015). *LoRaWAN 101 Class.* Presentation. Retrieved from http://www.spincraft.com/hackers/wp-content/uploads/2017/01/LoRaWAN-101-Class-v2-MARCOM-1.pdf

Microsoft. (2018). *Azure ML Studio.* Retrieved October 7, 2018, from https://studio.azureml.net

Microsoft. (2018). *Microsoft Azure IoT.* Retrieved at October 24 2018, from http://www.microsoft.com/en-gb/internet-of-things/azure-iot-suite

Microsoft-SQL-Server. (2017). *Microsoft SQL Server.* Retrieved from https://goo.gl/nTzmGr

Mihovska, A., & Sarkar, M. (2018). Smart Connectivity for Internet of Things (IoT) Applications. In R. R. Yager & J. Pascual Espada (Eds.), *New Advances in the Internet of Things* (Vol. 715, pp. 105–118). Cham: Springer International Publishing; doi:10.1007/978-3-319-58190-3_7

Milgram, P., & Colquhoun, H. (1999). A taxonomy of real and virtual world display integration. *Mixed reality: Merging real and virtual worlds, 1,* 1-26.

Minerva, R., Biru, A., & Rotondi, D. (2015). Towards a definition of the Internet of Things (IoT). *IEEE IoT Initiative.* Retrieved from https://iot.ieee.org

Minerva, R. (2014). From Internet of Things to the Virtual Continuum: An architectural view. *IEEE Euro Med Telco Conference (EMTC).* 10.1109/EMTC.2014.6996633

Miori, V., & Russo, D. (2017). *Improving life quality for the elderly through the Social Internet of Things (SIoT). In 2017 Global Internet of Things Summit (GIoTS)* (pp. 1–6). Geneva, Switzerland: IEEE. doi:10.1109/GIOTS.2017.8016215

Mitra, S., Wong, H.-S. P., & Wong, S. (2015). *Stopping hardware Trojans in their tracks.* Retrieved from https://spectrum. ieee.org/semiconductors/design/stopping-hardware-trojans-in-their-tracks

MLJAR. (2017). *MLJAR.* Retrieved October 7, 2018, from https://mljar.com/

Mo, Y., Kim, T. H.-H., Brancik, K., Dickinson, D., Lee, H., Perrig, A., & Sinopoli, B. (2012). Cyber-physical security of a smart grid infrastructure. *Proceedings of the IEEE, 100*(1), 195-209.

Mo, B., Dong, W., Chen, C., Bu, J., & Wang, Q. (2012). An efficient differencing algorithm based on suffix array for reprogramming wireless sensor networks. *IEEE International Conference on Communications (ICC),* 773-777. 10.1109/ICC.2012.6364214

Modbus, I. D. A. (2006). *Modbus Application Protocol Specification, V1.1b, December 28.* Retrieved from http://www. modbus.org/docs/Modbus_Application_Protocol_V1_1b.pdf

Molich, R., & Nielsen, J. (1990). Improving a human-computer dialogue. Computing Practices, Communications of the ACM, 33(3).

Monekosso, D. N., Florez-Revuelta, F., & Remagnino, P. (2015). Guest Editorial Special Issue on Ambient-Assisted Living: Sensors, Methods, and Applications. *Human-Machine Systems. IEEE Transactions On, 45*(5), 545–549. doi:10.1109/THMS.2015.2458019

MongoDB. (2018). *MongoDB.* Retrieved September 1, 2015, from https://www.mongodb.org/

Moraitou, M., Pateli, A., & Fotiou, S. (2017). Smart Health Caring Home: A Systematic Review of Smart Home Care for Elders and Chronic Disease Patients. In P. Vlamos (Ed.), *GeNeDis 2016: Geriatrics* (pp. 255–264). Cham: Springer International Publishing. doi:10.1007/978-3-319-57348-9_22

More, S. S., Gai, A. A., Sardar, V. S., Rupareliya, C. S., & Talole, P. T. (2017). Home Automation on Android Using Arduino. *Journal of Android and IOS Applications and Testing, 2*(1).

Morillo, P., Moncho, W., Orduna, J. M., & Duato, J. (2006). *Providing full awareness to distributed virtual environments based on peer-to-peer architectures. In Advances in Computer Graphics* (pp. 336–347). Springer.

Morin, E., Maman, M., Guizzetti, R., & Duda, A. (2017). Comparison of the Device Lifetime in Wireless Networks for the Internet of Things. *IEEE Access: Practical Innovations, Open Solutions, 5,* 7097–7114. doi:10.1109/ACCESS.2017.2688279

Moser, K., Harder, J., & Koo, S. G. (2014). *Internet of things in home automation and energy efficient smart home technologies.* Paper presented at the Systems, Man and Cybernetics (SMC), 2014 IEEE International Conference on. 10.1109/SMC.2014.6974087

Moukas, A., Zacharia, G., Guttman, R., & Maes, P. (2000). Agent-Mediated Electronic Commerce: An MIT Media Laboratory Perspective. *International Journal of Electronic Commerce, 4*(3), 5–21. doi:10.1080/10864415.2000.11518369

MSB. (2014). *Guide to increased security in industrial information and control systems.* Karlstad, Sweden: Swedish Civil Contingencies Agency.

MSB. (2017). *Informationssäkerhet och bedrägerier.* Retrieved from https://www.msb.se/sv/Forebyggande/Informations-sakerhet/Stod-inom-informationssakerhet/Informationssakerhet-och-bedragerier/

MSB2. (2014). *International case report on cyber security incidents: Reflections on three cyber incidents in the Netherlands, Germany and Sweden.* Retrieved from https://www.msb.se/RibData/Filer/pdf/27482.pdf

Mukherjee, S. (2016). *F# for Machine Learning Essentials: Get up and running with machine learning with F# in a fun and functional way.* Packt Publishing.

Müller, A. C., & Guido, S. (2016). Introduction to machine learning with Python: a guide for data scientists. O'Reilly Media.

Mulligan, G. (2007). The 6LoWPAN architecture. *Proceedings of the 4th workshop on Embedded networked sensors.* 10.1145/1278972.1278992

Muñoz, D., Gutierrez, F., & Ochoa, S. (2015). Introducing Ambient Assisted Living Technology at the Home of the Elderly: Challenges and Lessons Learned. In I. Cleland, L. Guerrero, & J. Bravo (Eds.), Ambient Assisted Living. ICT-based Solutions in Real Life Situations (Vol. 9455, pp. 125–136). Springer International Publishing. Retrieved from doi:10.1007/978-3-319-26410-3_12

Myers, B. A. (1996). *A brief history of human computer interaction technology.* Human Computer Interaction Institute, School of Computer Science, Carnegie Mellon University.

Myint, C. Z., Gopal, L., & Aung, Y. L. (2017). Reconfigurable smart water quality monitoring system in IoT environment. *2017 IEEE/ACIS 16th International Conference on Computer and Information Science (ICIS)*, 435–440. doi:10.1109/ICIS.2017.7960032

MySQL. (2018). *MySQL.* Retrieved October 7, 2018, from https://www.mysql.com/

Nakamoto, S. (2009). *Bitcoin: A Peer-to-Peer Electronic Cash System.* Retrieved from https://bitcoin.org/ bitcoin.pdf

Nakano, T., Moore, M. J., Wei, F., Vasilakos, A. V., & Shuai, J. (2012). Molecular communication and networking: Opportunities and challenges. *IEEE Transactions on Nanobioscience, 11*(2), 135–148. doi:10.1109/TNB.2012.2191570 PMID:22665393

Nath, R. K., Bajpai, R., & Thapliyal, H. (2018). IoT based indoor location detection system for smart home environment. In *2018 IEEE International Conference on Consumer Electronics (ICCE)* (pp. 1–3). Las Vegas, NV: IEEE. 10.1109/ICCE.2018.8326225

Nauerth, S., Moll, F., Rau, M., Fuchs, C., Horwath, J., Frick, S., & Weinfurter, H. (2013). Air-to-ground quantum communication. *Nature Photonics, 7*(5), 382–386. doi:10.1038/nphoton.2013.46

Neo4j. (2018). *Neo4j.* Retrieved October 7, 2018, from https://neo4j.com/

Nirmala, M., & Manjunath, A. (2010). Secure program update using broadcast encryption for clustered wireless sensor networks. *Sixth International Conference on Wireless Communication and Sensor Networks (WCSN)*, 1-6. 10.1109/WCSN.2010.5712303

Nirmala, M., & Manjunath, A. (2015). SCUMG: Secure Code Update for Multicast Group in Wireless Sensor Networks. *12th International Conference on Information Technology-New Generations (ITNG)*, 249-254. 10.1109/ITNG.2015.46

NIST. (2018). *NIST Cybersecurity for IoT Program*. Retrieved from https://www.nist.gov/programs-projects/nist-cybersecurity-iot-program

Noble, Z. (2015). How fog computing makes the internet of thing run. *The Business of Federal Technology*. Retrieved July 19, 2018 from: https://fcw.com/articles/2015/06/30/hiw_fog_computing.aspx

Nokia. (2017). *LTE Evolution for IoT connectivity*. Retrieved from https://resources.ext.nokia.com/asset/200178

Nukala, R., Panduru, K., Shields, A., Riordan, D., Doody, P., & Walsh, J. (2016). Internet of Things: A review from 'Farm to Fork.' *Signals and Systems Conference (ISSC)*, 1-6. 10.1109/ISSC.2016.7528456

Numata, T., & Takagi, S. (2004). Device design for subthreshold slope and threshold voltage control in sub-100-nm fully depleted SOI MOSFETs. *IEEE Transactions on Electron Devices*, *51*(12), 2161–2167. doi:10.1109/TED.2004.839760

O'Grady, M. J., Muldoon, C., Dragone, M., Tynan, R., & O'Hare, G. M. P. (2010). Towards evolutionary ambient assisted living systems. *Journal of Ambient Intelligence and Humanized Computing*, *1*(1), 15–29. doi:10.100712652-009-0003-5

Oda, O., Elvezio, C., Sukan, M., Feiner, S., & Tversky, B. (2015). Virtual replicas for remote assistance in virtual and augmented reality. *Proceedings of the 28th Annual ACM Symposium on User Interface Software & Technology*. 10.1145/2807442.2807497

Ojha, T., Misra, S., & Raghuwanshi, N. S. (2015). Wireless sensor networks for agriculture: The state-of-the-art in practice and future challenges. *Computers and Electronics in Agriculture*, *118*, 66–84. doi:10.1016/j.compag.2015.08.011

Olanda, R., Pérez, M., Morillo, P., Fernández, M., & Casas, S. (2006). Entertainment virtual reality system for simulation of spaceflights over the surface of the planet Mars. *Proceedings of the ACM symposium on Virtual reality software and technology*. 10.1145/1180495.1180522

Olof Liberg, O., Sundberg, M., Eric Wang, Y.-P., Bergman, J., & Sachs, J. (2018). EC-GSM-IoT. In Cellular Internet of Things. Academic Press.

openHAB Foundation e.V. (2018). openHAB - a Vendor and Technology Agnostic Open Source Automation Software for Your Home. Retrieved 02/03/2018, 2018, from https://www.openhab.org

OpenStack. (2018). *OpenStack Installation Guide for Ubuntu*. Retrieved from https://docs.openstack.org/mitaka/install-guide-ubuntu/

Orange. (2017). *Orange*. Retrieved September 1, 2018, from https://orange.biolab.si/

Orpwood, R., Gibbs, C., Adlam, T., Faulkner, R., & Meegahawatte, D. (2004). The Gloucester Smart House for People with Dementia — User-Interface Aspects. In S. Keates, J. Clarkson, P. Langdon, & P. Robinson (Eds.), *Designing a More Inclusive World* (pp. 237–245). Springer London; doi:10.1007/978-0-85729-372-5_24

OSGi Alliance. (2018). *OSGi -The Dynamic Module System for Java*. Retrieved 02/03/2018, 2018, from www.osgi.org

Ott, M., & Pozzi, F. (2011). Towards a new era for Cultural Heritage Education: Discussing the role of ICT. *Computers in Human Behavior*, *27*(4), 1365–1371. doi:10.1016/j.chb.2010.07.031

Ozger, M., Cetinkaya, O., & Akan, O. B. (2017). *Energy Harvesting Cognitive Radio Networking for IoT-enabled Smart Grid. ACM/Springer Mobile Networks and Applications (MONET).*

Pacheco, J., & Hariri, S. (2016). IoT security framework for smart cyber infrastructures. IEEE International Workshops on Foundations and Applications of Self* Systems, 242-247.

Padmavathi, G., & Shanmugapriya, A. (2009). A survey of attacks, security mechanisms and challenges in wireless sensor networks. *International Journal of Computer Science and Information Security, 4*(1-2).

Paethong, P., Sato, M., & Namiki, M. (2016). Low-power distributed NoSQL database for IoT middleware. In *2016 Fifth ICT International Student Project Conference (ICT-ISPC)* (pp. 158–161). IEEE. 10.1109/ICT-ISPC.2016.7519260

Páez, D., de Buenaga Rodríguez, M., Sánz, E., Villalba, M., & Gil, R. (2015). Big Data Processing Using Wearable Devices for Wellbeing and Healthy Activities Promotion. In I. Cleland, L. Guerrero, & J. Bravo (Eds.), Ambient Assisted Living. ICT-based Solutions in Real Life Situations (Vol. 9455, pp. 196–205). Springer International Publishing. Retrieved from doi:10.1007/978-3-319-26410-3_19

Pal Singh, V., Sweta, J., & Jyoti, S. (2010). Hello Flood Attack and its Countermeasures in Wireless Sensor Networks. *International Journal of Computer Science Issues, 7.*

Pampattiwar, K., Lakhani, M., Marar, R., & Menon, R. (2017). Home Automation using Raspberry Pi controlled via an Android Application. *International Journal of Current Engineering and Technology, 7*(3), 962–967.

Panta, R. K., & Bagchi, S. (2009). *Hermes: Fast and energy efficient incremental code updates for wireless sensor networks.* IEEE INFOCOM.

Panta, R. K., Bagchi, S., & Midkiff, S. P. (2009). Zephyr: Efficient incremental reprogramming of sensor nodes using function call indirections and difference computation. *Proc. of USENIX Annual Technical Conference.*

Pappenberger, F., Cloke, H. L., Parker, D. J., Wetterhall, F., Richardson, D. S., & Thielen, J. (2015). The monetary benefit of early flood warnings in europe. *Environmental Science & Policy, 51*, 278–291. doi:10.1016/j.envsci.2015.04.016

Parada, R., Melia-Segui, J., Morenza-Cinos, M., Carreras, A., & Pous, R. (2015). Using RFID to Detect Interactions in Ambient Assisted Living Environments. *IEEE Intelligent Systems, 30*(4), 16–22. doi:10.1109/MIS.2015.43

Parameswari, M., & Moses, M. B. (2017). Online measurement of water quality and reporting system using prominent rule controller based on aqua care-IOT. *Design Automation for Embedded Systems.* doi:10.100710617-017-9187-7

Park, E., Kim, S., Kim, Y., & Kwon, S. J. (2018). Smart home services as the next mainstream of the ICT industry: Determinants of the adoption of smart home services. *Universal Access in the Information Society, 17*(1), 175–190. doi:10.100710209-017-0533-0

Parsons, S., & Cobb, S. (2011). State-of-the-art of virtual reality technologies for children on the autism spectrum. *European Journal of Special Needs Education, 26*(3), 355–366. doi:10.1080/08856257.2011.593831

Passos, C., da Silva, M. H., Mol, A. C., & Carvalho, P. V. (2017). Design of a collaborative virtual environment for training security agents in big events. *Cognition Technology and Work, 19*(2-3), 315–328. doi:10.100710111-017-0407-5

Patel, S. M., & Kanawade, S. Y. (2017). Internet of Things Based Smart Home with Intel Edison. *Proceedings of International Conference on Communication and Networks.* 10.1007/978-981-10-2750-5_40

Pathan, A.-S. K., Lee, H.-W., & Hong, C. S. (2006). Security in wireless sensor networks: issues and challenges. *The 8th International Conference Advanced Communication Technology, 6.*

Patil, A., Shaikh, I. S., Ghorpade, V. P., Pawar, V. D., & Memane, P. S. (2017). Home Automation using Raspberry Pi & Windows 10 IOT. *Imperial Journal of Interdisciplinary Research, 3*(3).

Patil, S. A., & Pinki, V. (2017). Home Automation Using Single Board Computing as an Internet of Things Application. *Proceedings of International Conference on Communication and Networks*. 10.1007/978-981-10-2750-5_26

Patolsky, F., & Lieber, C. M. (2005). Nanowire nanosensors. *Materials Today, 8*(4), 20–28. doi:10.1016/S1369-7021(05)00791-1

Pattar, S., Buyya, R., Venugopal, K. R., Iyengar, S. S., & Patnaik, L. M. (2018). Searching for the IoT Resources: Fundamentals, Requirements, Comprehensive Review and Future Directions. *IEEE Communications Surveys and Tutorials*, 1–1. doi:10.1109/COMST.2018.2825231

Pedregosa, F., Varoquaux, G., Gramfort, A., Michel, V., Thirion, B., Grisel, O., ... Duchesnay, E. (2011). Scikit-learn: Machine Learning in Python. *Journal of Machine Learning Research, 12*, 2825–2830.

Peisert, S., Margulies, J., Nicol, D. M., Khurana, H., & Sawall, C. (2014). Designed-in security for cyber-physical systems. *IEEE Security and Privacy, 12*(5), 9–12. doi:10.1109/MSP.2014.90

Peleg, D. (2000). Distributed computing. *SIAM Monographs on discrete mathematics and applications,* (5).

Perera, C. (2017). *Sensing as a Service for Internet of Things: A Roadmap*. Leanpub Publishers.

Perera, C., Liu, C. H., & Jayawardena, S. (2015). The emerging Internet of Things marketplace from an industrial perspective: A survey. *IEEE Transactions on Emerging Topics in Computing, 3*(4), 585–598. doi:10.1109/TETC.2015.2390034

Perera, C., Liu, C. H., Jayawardena, S., & Chen, M. (2014). A survey on internet of things from industrial market perspective. *IEEE Access: Practical Innovations, Open Solutions, 2*, 1660–1679. doi:10.1109/ACCESS.2015.2389854

Perera, C., Zaslavsky, A., Christen, P., & Georgakopoulos, D. (2014). Context aware computing for the internet of things: A survey. *IEEE Communications Surveys and Tutorials, 16*(1), 414–454. doi:10.1109/SURV.2013.042313.00197

Perito, D., & Tsudik, G. (2010). Secure Code Update for Embedded Devices via Proofs of Secure Erasure. In D. Gritzalis, B. Preneel, & M. Theoharidou (Eds.), Computer Security -- ESORICS 2010 (pp. 643-662). Springer Berlin Heidelberg. doi:10.1007/978-3-642-15497-3_39

Perkins, L., Redmond, E., & Wilson, J. (2018). *Seven Databases in Seven Weeks: A Guide to Modern Databases and the NoSQL Movement*. O'Reilly UK Ltd.

Perles, A., Pérez-Marín, E., Mercado, R., Segrelles, J. D., Blanquer, I., Zarzo, M., & Garcia-Diego, F. J. (2018). An energy-efficient internet of things (IoT) architecture for preventive conservation of cultural heritage. *Future Generation Computer Systems, 81*, 566–581. doi:10.1016/j.future.2017.06.030

Phoenix Contact. (2015). *Getting the Most Out of Your WirelessHART® System*. Whitepaper. Retrieved from https://www.phoenixcontact.com/assets/downloads_ed/global/web_dwl_promotion/EN_Whitepaper_IE_WirelessHART_LoRes.pdf

Piczak, K. J. (2015a). Environmental sound classification with convolutional neural networks. *25th International Workshop on Machine Learning for Signal Processing (MLSP)*, 1–6.

Pister, K. S. (1997). *Smart Dust: BAA97-43 Proposal Abstract*. Retrieved April 19, 2018, from berkeley.edu: http://www.eecs.berkeley.edu/~pister/SmartDust/SmartDustBAA97-43-Abstract.pdf

Pitarma, R., Marques, G., & Ferreira, B. R. (2017). Monitoring Indoor Air Quality for Enhanced Occupational Health. *Journal of Medical Systems, 41*(2), 23. doi:10.100710916-016-0667-2 PMID:28000117

Piumsomboon, T., Day, A., Ens, B., Lee, Y., Lee, G., & Billinghurst, M. (2017). *Exploring enhancements for remote mixed reality collaboration.* Paper presented at the SIGGRAPH Asia 2017 Mobile Graphics & Interactive Applications. 10.1145/3132787.3139200

Piumsomboon, T., Dey, A., Ens, B., Lee, G., & Billinghurst, M. (2017). *CoVAR: Mixed-Platform Remote Collaborative Augmented and Virtual Realities System with Shared Collaboration Cues.* Paper presented at the Mixed and Augmented Reality (ISMAR-Adjunct), 2017 IEEE International Symposium on.

Piyare, R., & Tazil, M. (2011). *Bluetooth based home automation system using cell phone.* Paper presented at the Consumer Electronics (ISCE), 2011 IEEE 15th International Symposium on. 10.1109/ISCE.2011.5973811

Ploennigs, J., Ryssel, U., & Kabitzsch, K. (2010). *Performance analysis of the EnOcean wireless sensor network protocol.* Paper presented at the Emerging Technologies and Factory Automation (ETFA), 2010 IEEE Conference on. 10.1109/ETFA.2010.5641313

Portalés, C., & Perales, C. D. (2009). *Sound and movement visualization in the AR-Jazz scenario.* Paper presented at the International Conference on Entertainment Computing. 10.1007/978-3-642-04052-8_15

PostgreSQL. (2018). *PostgreSQL.* Retrieved September 15, 2018, from https://www.postgresql.org/

Pounds-Cornish, A., & Holmes, A. (2002). The iDorm - A Practical Deployment of Grid Technology. In *Cluster Computing and the Grid, 2002. 2nd IEEE/ACM International Symposium on* (pp. 470–470). IEEE. 10.1109/CCGRID.2002.1017192

Pranata, A. A., Lee, J. M., & Kim, D. S. (2017). Towards an IoT-based water quality monitoring system with brokerless pub/sub architecture. *2017 IEEE International Symposium on Local and Metropolitan Area Networks (LANMAN)*, 1–6. 10.1109/LANMAN.2017.7972166

Prasad, S., Mahalakshmi, P., Sunder, A. J. C., & Swathi, R. (2014). Smart Surveillance Monitoring System Using Raspberry PI and PIR Sensor. *Int. J. Comput. Sci. Inf. Technol, 5*(6), 7107–7109.

Predix, G. E. (2018). *Predix: The World's First Industrial Internet Platform.* Retrieved at October 24 2018, from http://www.ge.com/uk/b2b/digital/predix

Quinnell, R. (2015). *Low power wide-area networking alternatives for the IoT.* Retrieved from https://www.edn.com/design/systems-design/4440343/Low-power-wide-area-networking-alternatives-for-the-IoT

Radfar, Shah, & Singh. (2012). Recent Subthreshold Design Techniques. *Active and Passive Electronic Components.* doi:. doi:10.1155/2012/926753

Rahman, A. F., Daud, M., & Mohamad, M. Z. (2016). Securing sensor to cloud ecosystem using internet of things (iot) security framework. *Proceedings of the International Conference on Internet of things and Cloud Computing*, 79. 10.1145/2896387.2906198

Raman, S., Weigel, R., & Lee, T. (2016, March 8). *The Internet of Space (IoS): A future backbone for the Internet of Things?* Retrieved August 29, 2018, from iot.ieee.org: https://iot.ieee.org/newsletter/march-2016/the-internet-of-space-ios-a-future-backbone-for-the-internet-of-things.html

Ramljak, M. (2017). *Security analysis of Open Home Automation Bus system.* Paper presented at the Information and Communication Technology, Electronics and Microelectronics (MIPRO), 2017 40th International Convention on. 10.23919/MIPRO.2017.7973614

Rao, R. R., & Rao, M. V. (2016). A Survey on Recommender System. *International Journal of Computer Science and Information Security, 14*(5), 265–271.

Rashidi, P., & Mihailidis, A. (2013). A Survey on Ambient-Assisted Living Tools for Older Adults. *Biomedical and Health Informatics. IEEE Journal of, 17*(3), 579–590. doi:10.1109/JBHI.2012.2234129

Rathnayaka, A. D., Potdar, V. M., & Kuruppu, S. J. (2011). Evaluation of wireless home automation technologies. *Digital Ecosystems and Technologies Conference (DEST), 2011 Proceedings of the 5th IEEE International Conference on.* 10.1109/DEST.2011.5936601

Rautmare, S., & Bhalerao, D. M. (2016). MySQL and NoSQL database comparison for IoT application. In *2016 IEEE International Conference on Advances in Computer Applications (ICACA)* (pp. 235–238). IEEE. 10.1109/ICACA.2016.7887957

Rawat, P., Singh, K. D., Chaouchi, H., & Bonnin, J. M. (2014). Wireless sensor networks: A survey on recent developments and potential synergies. *The Journal of Supercomputing, 68*(1), 1–48. doi:10.100711227-013-1021-9

Ray, P. P. (2014). Home Health Hub Internet of Things (H3IoT): An architectural framework for monitoring health of elderly people. In *Science Engineering and Management Research (ICSEMR), 2014 International Conference on* (pp. 1–3). Academic Press. 10.1109/ICSEMR.2014.7043542

Razzaque, M. A., Milojevic-Jevric, M., Palade, A., & Clarke, S. (2016). Middleware for Internet of Things: A survey. *IEEE Internet of Things Journal, 3*(1), 70–95. doi:10.1109/JIOT.2015.2498900

Reijers, N., & Langendoen, K. (2003). Efficient code distribution in wireless sensor networks. In *Proceedings of the 2nd ACM international conference on Wireless sensor networks and applications* (pp. 60-67). ACM. 10.1145/941350.941359

REN. (2018). *Produção renovável suficiente para abastecer o consumo de eletricidade em Portugal durante 63 horas.* Retrieved from https://www.ren.pt/pt-PT/media/comunicados/detalhe/producao_renovavel_suficiente_para_abastecer_o_consumo_de_eletricidade_em_portugal_durante_63_horas_2/

Ren, Z., Liu, X., Ye, R., & Zhang, T. (2017). Security and privacy on internet of things. *7th IEEE International Conference on Electronics Information and Emergency Communication (ICEIEC)*, 140-144. 10.1109/ICEIEC.2017.8076530

Riak-KV. (2018). *Riak KV.* Retrieved from http://basho.com/products/riak-kv/

Ricci, F., Rokach, L., & Shapira, B. (Eds.). (2015). *Recommender Systems Handbook.* Springer-Verlag GmbH. doi:10.1007/978-1-4899-7637-6

Risteska Stojkoska, B., & Trivodaliev, K. (2017). A review of Internet of Things for smart home: Challenges and solutions. *Journal of Cleaner Production, 140*, 1454–1464. doi:10.1016/j.jclepro.2016.10.006

Robert, K., Zhu, D., Huang, W., Alem, L., & Gedeon, T. (2013). *MobileHelper: remote guiding using smart mobile devices, hand gestures and augmented reality.* Paper presented at the SIGGRAPH Asia 2013 Symposium on Mobile Graphics and Interactive Applications. 10.1145/2543651.2543664

Rohde&Schwarze. (2016). *Narrowband Internet of Things.* Whitepaper. Retrieved from https://www.rohde-schwarz.com/pt/applications/narrowband-internet-of-things-white-paper_230854-314242.html

Roman, R., Najera, P., & Lopez, J. (2011). Securing the Internet of Things. *Computer, 44*(9), 51–58. doi:10.1109/MC.2011.291

Roman, R., Zhou, J., & Lopez, J. (2013). On the features and challenges of security and privacy in distributed internet of things. *Computer Networks, 57*(10), 2266–2279. doi:10.1016/j.comnet.2012.12.018

Roy, R., & George, K. T. (2017). Detecting insurance claims fraud using machine learning techniques. In *2017 International Conference on Circuit, Power and Computing Technologies (ICCPCT)* (pp. 1–6). IEEE. 10.1109/ICCPCT.2017.8074258

Rutherglen, C., & Burke, P. (2007). Carbon nanotube radio. *Nano Letters*, 7(11), 3296–3299. doi:10.1021/nl0714839 PMID:17941677

Sadeghi, A. R., Wachsmann, C., & Waidner, M. (2015). Security and privacy challenges in industrial internet of things. *Proceedings of the 52nd annual design automation conference*, 54. 10.1145/2744769.2747942

Sahu & Eappen Sahu. (2014). Sub-Threshold Logic and Standard Cell Library. *International Journal of Innovative Research in Science, Engineering and Technology, 3*(1).

Sakarindr, P., & Ansari, N. (2007). Security services in group communications over wireless infrastructure, mobile ad hoc, and wireless sensor networks. *IEEE Transactions on Wireless Communications*, 14(5), 8–20. doi:10.1109/MWC.2007.4396938

Saleem, Y., Crespi, N., Rehmani, M. H., & Copeland, R. (2017). *Internet of things-aided smart grid: Technologies, architectures, applications, prototypes, and future research directions.* ArXiv.

Salunke, P., & Kate, J. (2017). Advanced smart sensor interface in Internet of Things for water quality monitoring. *2017 International Conference on Data Management, Analytics and Innovation (ICDMAI)*, 298–302. 10.1109/ICDMAI.2017.8073529

Sanchez-Iborra, R., & Cano, M.-D. (2016). State of the Art in LP-WAN Solutions for Industrial IoT Services. *Sensors (Basel)*, 16(5), 708. doi:10.339016050708 PMID:27196909

Sano, A., Phillips, A. J., Yu, A. Z., McHill, A. W., Taylor, S., Jaques, N., ... Picard, R. W. (2015). Recognizing academic performance, sleep quality, stress level, and mental health using personality traits, wearable sensors and mobile phones. In *Wearable and Implantable Body Sensor Networks (BSN), 2015 IEEE 12th International Conference on* (pp. 1–6). IEEE. 10.1109/BSN.2015.7299420

Saracchini, R. F. V., & Catalina, C. A. (2015). An augmented reality platform for wearable assisted living systems. *Journal of Theoretical and Applied Computer Science*, 9(1), 56–79.

Satish, T., Begum, T., & Shameena, B. (2017). Agriculture Productivity Enhancement System using IOT. *International Journal of Theoretical and Applied Mechanics*, 12(3), 543–554.

Satyanarayanan, M., Lewis, G., Morris, E., Simanta, S., Boleng, J., & Ha, K. (2013). The role of cloudlets in hostile environments. *IEEE Pervasive Computing*, 12(4), 40–49. doi:10.1109/MPRV.2013.77

Schalkwyk, J., Beeferman, D., Beaufays, F., Byrne, B., Chelba, C., Cohen, M., ... Strope, B. (2010). "Your Word is my Command": Google Search by Voice: A Case Study. In Advances in Speech Recognition (pp. 61–90). Boston, MA: Springer US. doi:10.1007/978-1-4419-5951-5_4

Schmidt, M., & Obermaisser, R. (2017). Adaptive and technology-independent architecture for fault-tolerant distributed AAL solutions. *Computers in Biology and Medicine*. doi:10.1016/j.compbiomed.2017.11.002 PMID:29157726

Schmidt-Weigand, F., Kohnert, A., & Glowalla, U. (2010). A closer look at split visual attention in system- and self-paced instruction in multimedia learning. *Learning and Instruction*, 20(2), 100–110. doi:10.1016/j.learninstruc.2009.02.011

Semião, J., Cabral, R., Santos, M., Teixeira, I., & Teixeira, P. (2018). Performance Sensor for Reliable Operation. *Proceedings of the 12th International Conference on Universal Access in Human-Computer Interaction (UAHCI), integrated in the 20th HCII*. 10.1007/978-3-319-92052-8_28

Semião, J., Freijedo, J., Rodriguez-Andina, J., Vargas, F., Santos, M. B., Teixeira, I. C., & Teixeira, J. P. (2008). Time Management for Low-Power Design of Digital Systems. Journal of Low Power Electronics. *Special Issue on LPonTR*, 4(3). doi:10.1166/jolpe.2008.194

Semião, J., Pachito, J., Martins, C., Jacinto, B., Vazquez, J., Champac, V., ... Teixeira, J. (2012). Aging-aware Power or Frequency Tuning with Predictive Fault Detection. *IEEE Design & Test of Computers, 29*(5). doi:10.1109/MDT.2012.2206009

Semião, J., Romão, A., Saraiva, D., Leong, C., Santos, M., Teixeira, I., & Teixeira, P. (2014). Performance Sensor for Tolerance and Predictive Detection of Delay-Faults. *Proceedings of the International Symposium on Defect and Fault Tolerance in VLSI and Nanotechnology Systems Symposium 2014 (DFT'14).* DOI: 10.1109/DFT.2014.6962092

Sendin, A., Sanchez-Fornie, M., & Berganza, I. (2016). *Telecommunication networks for the smart grid.* Boston: Artech House.

Seo, J. Y., Lee, D. W., & Lee, H. M. (2017). Performance Comparison of CRUD Operations in IoT based Big Data Computing. *International Journal on Advanced Science. Engineering and Information Technology, 7*(5), 1765. doi:10.18517/ijaseit.7.5.2674

Sequans. (2016). *Narrowband LTE: Which apps need Cat M1 and which need Cat NB1?* Retrieved from http://www.sequans.com/narrowband-lte-which-apps-need-cat-m1-and-which-need-cat-nb1/

Serpanos, D., & Wolf, M. (2018). *Internet-of-Things (IoT) Systems.* Cham: Springer International Publishing. doi:10.1007/978-3-319-69715-4

Seshadri, A., Luk, M., Perrig, A., van Doorn, L., & Khosla, P. (2006). SCUBA: Secure code update by attestation in sensor networks. *Proceedings of the 5th ACM workshop on Wireless security*, 85-94. 10.1145/1161289.1161306

Shackel, B. (1960). Note on mobile eye viewpoint recording. *Journal of the Optical Society of America, 59*(8), 763–768. doi:10.1364/JOSA.50.000763 PMID:14445350

Shakhnarovich, G., Darrell, T., & Indyk, P. (Eds.). (2005). *Nearest-Neighbor Methods in Learning and Vision: Theory and Practice.* The MIT Press.

Shankar, U., Chew, M., & Tygar, J. D. (2004). Side effects are not sufficient to authenticate software. *USENIX Security Symposium.*

Shanthamallu, U. S., Spanias, A., Tepedelenlioglu, C., & Stanley, M. (2017). A brief survey of machine learning methods and their sensor and IoT applications. In *2017 8th International Conference on Information, Intelligence, Systems & Applications (IISA)* (pp. 1–8). IEEE. 10.1109/IISA.2017.8316459

Sharma, V. C., Gopalakrishnan, G., & Bronevetsky, G. (2015). Detecting Soft Errors in Stencil based Computations. *11th Workshop on Silicon Errors in Logic - System Effects (SELSE).*

Sharma, R., & Diwakar, C. (2012). *Security Analysis of Wireless Sensor Networks. International Journal of Research in Engineering & Applied Sciences*, 774–786.

Sheng, Z., Yang, S., Yu, Y., Vasilakos, A., Mccann, J. L., & Leung, K. (2013). A survey on the ietf protocol suite for the internet of things: Standards, challenges, and opportunities. *IEEE Wireless Communications, 20*(6), 91–98. doi:10.1109/MWC.2013.6704479

Shen, J., Wang, C., Li, T., Chen, X., Huang, X., & Zhan, Z.-H. (2018). Secure data uploading scheme for a smart home system. *Information Sciences, 453*, 186–197. doi:10.1016/j.ins.2018.04.048

Shishido, H., Ito, Y., Kawamura, Y., Matsui, T., Morishima, A., & Kitahara, I. (2017). Proactive preservation of world heritage by crowdsourcing and 3D reconstruction technology. *2017 IEEE International Conference on Big Data (Big Data),* 4426-4428. 10.1109/BigData.2017.8258479

Shrouf, F., Ordieres, J., & Miragliotta, G. (2014). Smart factories in Industry 4.0: A review of the concept and of energy management approached in production based on the Internet of Things paradigm. In *2014 IEEE International Conference on Industrial Engineering and Engineering Management (IEEM)* (pp. 697-701). IEEE. 10.1109/IEEM.2014.7058728

Shvachko, K., Kuang, H., Radia, S., & Chansler, R. (2010). The hadoop distributed file system. *IEEE 26th symposium on mass storage systems and technologies*, 1-10.

Sibert, L. E., & Jacob, R. J. K. (2000). Evaluation of eye gaze interaction. *Proceedings of the SIGCHI conference on Human Factors in Computing Systems*. 10.1145/332040.332445

Siegel, C., Hochgatterer, A., & Dorner, T. E. (2014). Contributions of ambient assisted living for health and quality of life in the elderly and care services - a qualitative analysis from the experts' perspective of care service professionals. *BMC Geriatrics*, *14*(1), 112. doi:10.1186/1471-2318-14-112 PMID:25326149

Sigfox. (2017). *SIGFOX - The Global Communications Service provider for the Internet of Things (IoT)*. Retrieved from https://www.sigfox.com/en

Sigfox. (2017a). *Sigfox technical overview*. Retrieved from https://www.disk91.com/wp-content/uploads/2017/05/4967675830228422064.pdf

Sigfox. (2017b). *Sigfox technology overview*. Retrieved from https://www.sigfox.com/en/sigfox-iot-technology-overview in 06/06/2018

Sigfox.com. (2018). *Sigfox, the world's leading IoT services provider*. Retrieved from Sigfox: https://www.sigfox.com/en#!/technology

Silva, A. P., Burleigh, S., Hirata, C. M., & Obraczka, K. (2015). A survey on congestion control for delay and disruption tolerant networks. *Ad Hoc Networks*, *25*, 480–494. doi:10.1016/j.adhoc.2014.07.032

Simsek, M., Aijaz, A., Dohler, M., Sachs, J., & Fettweis, G. (2016). 5G-enabled tactile internet. *IEEE Journal on Selected Areas in Communications*, *34*(3), 460–473. doi:10.1109/JSAC.2016.2525398

Sinclair, B. (2017). *IoT Inc. How your company can use the internet of things to win in the outcome economy*. New York, NY: McGraw-Hill Education.

Sivaraman, V., Chan, D., Earl, D., & Boreli, R. (2016). Smart-phones attacking smart-homes. *Proceedings of the 9th ACM Conference on Security & Privacy in Wireless and Mobile Networks*. 10.1145/2939918.2939925

Smirek, L., Zimmermann, G., & Beigl, M. (2016). Just a Smart Home or Your Smart Home–A Framework for Personalized User Interfaces Based on Eclipse Smart Home and Universal Remote Console. *Procedia Computer Science*, *98*, 107–116. doi:10.1016/j.procs.2016.09.018

Snowdon, D., Churchill, E. F., & Munro, A. J. (2001). *Collaborative virtual environments: Digital spaces and places for CSCW: An introduction.* Paper presented at the Collaborative virtual environments. 10.1007/978-1-4471-0685-2_1

Sobel, A. E. K., & McGraw, G. (2010). Interview: Software security in the real world. *Computer*, *43*(9), 47–53. doi:10.1109/MC.2010.256

Sodhi, R. S., Jones, B. R., Forsyth, D., Bailey, B. P., & Maciocci, G. (2013). BeThere: 3D mobile collaboration with spatial input. *Proceedings of the SIGCHI Conference on Human Factors in Computing Systems*. 10.1145/2470654.2470679

Soliman, M. S., Dwairi, M. O., Sulayman, I. I. A., & Almalki, S. H. (2017). Towards the Design and Implementation a Smart Home Automation System Based on Internet of Things Approach. *International Journal of Applied Engineering Research*, *12*(11), 2731–2737.

Sonnenburg, S., Strathmann, H., Lisitsyn, S., Gal, V., García, F. J. I., Lin, W., … Esser. (2017). *Shogun-Toolbox/Shogun: Shogun 6.1.0.* Zenodo. doi:10.5281/zenodo.1067840

Soylemezgiller, F., Kuscu, M., & Kilinc, D. (2013). A traffic congestion avoidance algorithm with dynamic road pricing for smart cities. In *International Symposium on Personal Indoor and Mobile Radio Communications (PIMRC)* (pp. 2571-2575). IEEE. 10.1109/PIMRC.2013.6666580

SpaceX. (2018). *SpaceX.* Retrieved from SpaceX: http://www.spacex.com/mars

Spence, C., Obrist, M., Velasco, C., & Ranasinghe, N. (2017). Digitizing the chemical senses: Possibilities & pitfalls. *International Journal of Human-Computer Studies, 107*, 62–74. doi:10.1016/j.ijhcs.2017.06.003

SQLite. (2018). *SQLite.* Retrieved October 7, 2018, from http://sqlite.org

Stafford, A., Piekarski, W., & Thomas, B. (2006). Implementation of god-like interaction techniques for supporting collaboration between outdoor AR and indoor tabletop users. *Proceedings of the 5th IEEE and ACM International Symposium on Mixed and Augmented Reality.* 10.1109/ISMAR.2006.297809

Stankovic, J. A. (2014). Research directions for the Internet of things. *IEEE.* Retrieved March 11, 2018 from https://www.cs.virginia.edu/~stankovic/psfiles/IOT.pdf

Stankovic, J. A. (2014). Research Directions for the Internet of Things. *Internet of Things Journal, IEEE, 1*(1), 3–9. doi:10.1109/JIOT.2014.2312291

Starker, I., & Bolt, R. A. (1990). A gaze-responsive self-disclosing display. In *Proceedings of the ACM CHI'90 Human Factors in Computing Systems Conference* (pp. 3-9). Addison-Wesley/ACM Press.

Stathopoulos, T., Heidemann, J., & Estrin, D. (2003). *A remote code update mechanism for wireless sensor networks.* UCLA, Center for Embedded Networked Computing. doi:10.21236/ADA482630

Stavropoulos, T. G., Meditskos, G., Andreadis, S., & Kompatsiaris, I. (2015). Real-time health monitoring and contextualised alerts using wearables. In *Interactive Mobile Communication Technologies and Learning (IMCL), 2015 International Conference on* (pp. 358–363). Academic Press. 10.1109/IMCTL.2015.7359619

Stavrotheodoros, S., Kaklanis, N., Votis, K., & Tzovaras, D. (2018). A Smart-Home IoT Infrastructure for the Support of Independent Living of Older Adults. In L. Iliadis, I. Maglogiannis, & V. Plagianakos (Eds.), *Artificial Intelligence Applications and Innovations* (Vol. 520, pp. 238–249). Cham: Springer International Publishing; doi:10.1007/978-3-319-92016-0_22

Stillman, R., & DeFiore, C.R. (1980). Computer security and networking protocols: Technical issues in military data communications networks. *IEEE Transactions on Communications, 28*(9), 1472-1477.

Stocco, A. P., Losey, D. M., Cronin, J. A., Wu, J., Abernethy, J. A., & Rao, R. P. (2015). Playing 20 questions with the mind: Collaborative problem solving by humans using a brain-to-brain interface. *PLoS One, 10*(9), 137303. doi:10.1371/journal.pone.0137303 PMID:26398267

Stojanovic, M. N., Stefanovic, D., & Rudchenko, S. (2014). Exercises in molecular computing. *Accounts of Chemical Research, 47*(6), 1845–1852. doi:10.1021/ar5000538 PMID:24873234

Strohbach, M., Ziekow, H., Gazis, V., & Akiva, N. (2015). Towards a Big Data Analytics Framework for IoT and Smart City Applications. In Modeling and Optimization in Science and Technologies (pp. 257–282). Academic Press. doi:10.1007/978-3-319-09177-8_11

Sugimoto, M., Hosoi, K., & Hashizume, H. (2004). Caretta: a system for supporting face-to-face collaboration by integrating personal and shared spaces. *Proceedings of the SIGCHI conference on Human factors in computing systems.* 10.1145/985692.985698

Sundmaeker, H., Verdouw, C., Wolfert, S., & Freire, L. P. (2016). Internet of food and farm 2020. *Digitising the Industry-Internet of Things Connecting Physical, Digital and Virtual Worlds*, 129-151.

Sun, H., Florio, V. D., Gui, N., & Blondia, C. (2009). Promises and Challenges of Ambient Assisted Living Systems. In *2009 Sixth International Conference on Information Technology: New Generations* (pp. 1201–1207). Las Vegas, NV: IEEE. 10.1109/ITNG.2009.169

Sun, W., Choi, M., & Choi, S. (2013). IEEE 802.11 ah: A long range 802.11 WLAN at sub 1 GHz. *Journal of ICT Standardization*, *1*(1), 83–108. doi:10.13052/jicts2245-800X.115

Sun, Y., Song, H., Jara, A. J., & Bie, R. (2016). Internet of Things and Big Data Analytics for Smart and Connected Communities. *IEEE Access: Practical Innovations, Open Solutions*, *4*, 766–773. doi:10.1109/ACCESS.2016.2529723

Suri, N., Tortonesi, M., Michaelis, J., Budulas, P., Benincasa, G., Russell, S., ... Winkler, R. (2016). Analyzing the applicability of internet of things to the battlefield environment. In *International Conference on In Military Communications and Information Systems (ICMCIS)* (pp. 1-8). IEEE. 10.1109/ICMCIS.2016.7496574

Suryadevara, N. K., Kelly, S., & Mukhopadhyay, S. C. (2014). Ambient Assisted Living Environment Towards Internet of Things Using Multifarious Sensors Integrated with XBee Platform. In S. C. Mukhopadhyay (Ed.), *Internet of Things* (Vol. 9, pp. 217–231). Springer International Publishing. doi:10.1007/978-3-319-04223-7_9

Suykens, J. A. K., Signoretto, M., & Argyriou, A. (Eds.). (2015). *Regularization, Optimization, Kernels, and Support Vector Machines*. CRC Press.

Svitak, A. (2015). *SpaceX, OneWeb Unveil Rival Broadband Constellation Plans*. Retrieved from Aviation Week & Space Technology: http://aviationweek.com/space/spacex-oneweb-unveil-rival-broadband-constellation-plans

Swan, M. (2012). Sensor mania! the internet of things, wearable computing, objective metrics, and the quantified self 2.0. *Journal of Sensor and Actuator Networks*, *1*(3), 217–253. doi:10.3390/jsan1030217

Tabakov, Y. (2014). *DASH7 Alliance Protocol, DASH7 Alliance*. Retrieved from http://dash7-alliance.org/wp-content/uploads/2014/08/005-Dash7-Alliance-Mode-technical-presentation.pdf

Tabbane, S. (2016). *IoT Network Planning*. ITU. Retrieved from https://www.itu.int/en/ITU-D/Regional-Presence/Asia-Pacific/SiteAssets/Pages/Events/2016/Dec-2016-IoT/IoTtraining/IoT%20network%20planning%20ST%2015122016.pdf in 10/06/2018.

Tan, L., & Wang, N. (2010). Future internet: The Internet of Things. In *2010 3rd International Conference on Advanced Computer Theory and Engineering (ICACTE)* (pp. V5-376-V5-380). IEEE. 10.1109/ICACTE.2010.5579543

Tanenbaum, A. S., & Van Steen, M. (2013). *Distributed Systems: Principles and Paradigms*. Pearson Education Limited.

Tariq, M. A., Brynielsson, J., & Artman, H. (2014). The security awareness paradox: A case study, In *Proceedings of the IEEE/ACM International Conference on Advances in Social Networks Analysis and Mining* (pp. 704-711). Piscataway, NJ: IEEE Press. 10.1109/ASONAM.2014.6921663

Tehranipoor, M., & Koushanfar, F. (2010). A Survey of Hardware Trojan Taxonomy and Detection. *IEEE Design & Test of Computers*, *27*(1), 10–25. doi:10.1109/MDT.2010.7

The Things Network. (n.d.). *LoPy Module*. Retrieved from https://www.thethingsnetwork.org/docs/devices/lopy/

Tinker, M. A. (1963). *Legibility of Print*. Ames, IA: Iowa State University Press.

Tobii. (2018). *Tobii is the world leader in eye tracking*. Retrieved March 5, 2018 from: https://www.tobii.com

Tomic, I., & McCann, J. (2017). *A Survey of Potential Security Issues in Existing Wireless Sensor Protocols*. *IEEE Internet of Things Journal*. doi:10.1109/JIOT.2017.2749883

Tong, H. M., & Fisher, R. A. (1984). *Progress Report on an Eye-Slaved Area-of-interest Visual Display*. Report No. AFHRL-ṬR-84-36, Air Force Human Resources Laboratory, Brooks Air Force Base, Texas.

Torrejon, J., Riou, M., Araujo, F. A., Tsunegi, S., Khalsa, G., Querlioz, D., ... Kubota, H. (2017). Neuromorphic computing with nanoscale spintronic oscillators. *Nature*, *547*(7664), 7664. doi:10.1038/nature23011 PMID:28748930

Toschi, G. M., Campos, L. B., & Cugnasca, C. E. (2017). Home automation networks: A survey. *Computer Standards & Interfaces*, *50*, 42–54. doi:10.1016/j.csi.2016.08.008

Tridgell, A. (1999). *Efficient algorithms for sorting and synchronizatio*. Australian National University Canberra.

Tripicchio, P., Satler, M., Dabisias, G., Ruffaldi, E., & Avizzano, C. A. (2015). Towards smart farming and sustainable agriculture with drones. In *IEEE International Conference on Intelligent Environments*, 140-143. 10.1109/IE.2015.29

Tschanz, J. (2007). Adaptive Frequency and Biasing Techniques for Tolerance to Dynamic Temperature-voltage Variations and Aging. *Proc. IEEE Int. Solid-State Circ. Conf. (ISSCC)*, 292-293. 10.1109/ISSCC.2007.373409

Tscheu, F., & Buhalis, D. (2016). *Augmented reality at cultural heritage sites*. In *Information and Communication Technologies in Tourism 2016* (pp. 607–619). Springer. doi:10.1007/978-3-319-28231-2_44

Tseng, M.-C., Liu, K.-C., Hsieh, C.-Y., Hsu, S. J., & Chan, C.-T. (2018). Gesture spotting algorithm for door opening using single wearable sensor. In *2018 IEEE International Conference on Applied System Invention (ICASI)* (pp. 854–856). Chiba: IEEE. 10.1109/ICASI.2018.8394398

Tsiftes, N., Dunkels, A., & Voigt, T. (2008). Efficient Sensor Network Reprogramming through Compression of Executable Modules. *5th Annual IEEE Communications Society Conference on Sensor, Mesh and Ad Hoc Communications and Networks*, 359-367. 10.1109/SAHCN.2008.51

Tsoutsos, N. G., & Maniatakos, M. (2014). Fabrication attacks: Zero-overhead malicious modifications enabling modern microprocessor privilege escalation. *IEEE Transactions on Emerging Topics in Computing*, *2*(1), 81–93. doi:10.1109/TETC.2013.2287186

Tudose, D. Ş., Voinescu, A., Petrăreanu, M.-T., Bucur, A., Loghin, D., Bostan, A., & Ṭăpuş, N. (2011). *Home automation design using 6LoWPAN wireless sensor networks*. Paper presented at the Distributed Computing in Sensor Systems and Workshops (DCOSS), 2011 International Conference on. 10.1109/DCOSS.2011.5982181

Turner, V., Reinsel, D., Gantz, J., & Minton, S. (2014). *The Digital Universe of Opportunities: Rich Data and the Increasing Value of the Internet of Things*. IDC Whitepaper.

Tzounis, A., Katsoulas, N., Bartzanas, T., & Kittas, C. (2017). *Internet of Things in agriculture, recent advances and future challenges*. Academic Press.

Ullah, A. M., Islam, M. R., Aktar, S. F., & Hossain, S. A. (2012). *Remote-touch: Augmented reality based marker tracking for smart home control*. Paper presented at the Computer and Information Technology (ICCIT), 2012 15th International Conference on. 10.1109/ICCITechn.2012.6509774

UN. (n.d.). *World population ageing: 1950–2050*. UN.

Universal Open Platform and Reference Specification for Ambient Assisted Living. (n.d.). Retrieved from http://www.universaal.org/

van den Dam, R. (2013). Internet of Things: The Foundational Infrastructure for a Smarter Planet. In S. Balandin, S. Andreev, & Y. Koucheryavy (Eds.), *Internet of Things, Smart Spaces, and Next Generation Networking* (Vol. 8121, pp. 1–12). Berlin: Springer Berlin Heidelberg. doi:10.1007/978-3-642-40316-3_1

Vassos, S., Malliaraki, E., Dal Falco, F., Di Maggio, J., Massimetti, M., Giulia Nocentini, M., & Testa, A. (2016). *Art-Bots: Toward Chat-Based Conversational Experiences in Museums.* Academic Press. . doi:10.1007/978-3-319-48279-8_43

Vazquez, J. C. (2010). Predictive Error Detection by On-line Aging Monitoring. *Proc. IEEE Int. On-Line Test Symp. (IOLTS).* 10.1109/IOLTS.2010.5560241

Veiga, A., Garcia, L., Parra, L., Lloret, J., & Augele, V. (2018). An IoT-based smart pillow for sleep quality monitoring in AAL environments. In *2018 Third International Conference on Fog and Mobile Edge Computing (FMEC)* (pp. 175–180). Barcelona: IEEE. 10.1109/FMEC.2018.8364061

VELES. (2018). *VELES.* Retrieved September 16, 2018, from https://velesnet.ml

Vera, L., Gimeno, J., Casas, S., García-Pereira, I., & Portalés, C. (2017). *A Hybrid Virtual-Augmented Serious Game to Improve Driving Safety Awareness.* Paper presented at the 14th International Conference on Advances in Computer Entertainment Technology - ACE 2017, London, UK.

Vermesan, O., & Friess, P. (2011). *Internet of Things - Global Technological and Societal Trends From Smart Environments and Spaces to Green ICT.* River Publishers.

Vertegaal, R. (1999). The GAZE groupware system: Mediating joint attention in multiparty communication and collaboration. In *Proceedings of the ACM CHI'99 Human Factors in Computing Systems Conference* (pp. 294-301). Addison-Wesley/ACM Press. 10.1145/302979.303065

Vieira, M. A., Coelho, C. N., Da Silva, D., & da Mata, J. M. (2003). Survey on wireless sensor network devices. *Proceedings IEEE Conference Emerging Technologies and Factory Automation*, 537-544. 10.1109/ETFA.2003.1247753

Vikram, N., Harish, K., Nihaal, M., Umesh, R., Shetty, A., & Kumar, A. (2017). *A low cost home automation system using wi-fi based wireless sensor network incorporating Internet of Things (IoT).* Paper presented at the Advance Computing Conference (IACC), 2017 IEEE 7th International.

Vondra, M., Dinc, E., Prytz, M., Frodigh, M., Schupke, D., Nilson, M., ... Cavdar, C. (2017). Performance Study on Seamless DA2GC for Aircraft Passengers toward 5G. *IEEE Communications Magazine*, 55(11), 194–201. doi:10.1109/MCOM.2017.1700188

Vullers, R. J., Van Schaijk, R., Visser, H. J., Penders, J., & Van Hoof, C. (2010). Energy harvesting for autonomous wireless sensor networks. *IEEE Solid-State Circuits Magazine*, 2(2), 29–38. doi:10.1109/MSSC.2010.936667

Wagner, S. (2011). *Attestation and Secure Code Update for Trusted Sensor Nodes* (Master's thesis). Technical University of Munich.

Walsh, P. J., Dudney, C. S., & Copenhaver, E. D. (1983). *Indoor air quality.* CRC Press.

Wang, C., Wu, J., Ekanayake, J., & Jenkins, N. (2017). *Smart electricity distribution networks.* CRC Press.

Wang, R., Wang, W., daSilva, A., Huckins, J. F., Kelley, W. M., Heatherton, T. F., & Campbell, A. T. (2018). Tracking Depression Dynamics in College Students Using Mobile Phone and Wearable Sensing. *Proceedings of the ACM on Interactive, Mobile, Wearable and Ubiquitous Technologies, 2*(1), 1–26. 10.1145/3191775

Wang, S., Wan, J., Zhang, D., Li, D., & Zhang, C. (2016). Towards smart factory for industry 4.0: A self-organized multi-agent system with big data based feedback and coordination. *Computer Networks*, *101*, 158–168. doi:10.1016/j.comnet.2015.12.017

Wang, W., Song, Y., Zhang, J., & Deng, H. (2014). Automatic parking of vehicles: A review of literatures. *International Journal of Automotive Technology*, *15*(6), 967–978. doi:10.100712239-014-0102-y

Wang, Z. L., & Wu, W. (2012). Nanotechnology-enabled energy harvesting for self-powered micro-/nanosystems. *Angewandte Chemie International Edition*, *51*(47), 11700–11721. doi:10.1002/anie.201201656 PMID:23124936

Ware, C., & Mikaelian, H. T. (1987). An evaluation of an eye tracker as a device for computer input. In *Proceedings of the ACM CHI+GI'87 Human Factors in Computing Systems Conference* (pp. 183-188). New York: ACM Press.

Webb, W. (2012). *Understanding Weightless: Technology, Equipment, and Network Deployment for M2M Communications in White Space*. Cambridge University Press. doi:10.1017/CBO9781139208857

Weiser, M. (1991). The computer for the 21st century. *Scientific American*, *265*(3), 94–104. doi:10.1038cientificamerican0991-94 PMID:1675486

WEKA. (2017). *WEKA: Waikato Environment for Knowledge Analysis*. Retrieved September 18, 2018, from https://www.cs.waikato.ac.nz/ml/weka/

Weyn, M., Ergeerts, G., Berkvens, R., Wojciechowski, B., & Tabakov, Y. (2015). DASH7 alliance protocol 1.0: Low-power, mid-range sensor and actuator communication. In *2015 IEEE Conference on Standards for Communications and Networking (CSCN)*. IEEE. 10.1109/CSCN.2015.7390420

Whitenack, D. (2017). *Machine learning with Go*. Packt Publishing.

Whitmore, A., Agarwal, A., & Da Xu, L. (2015). The Internet of Things—A survey of topics and trends. *Information Systems Frontiers*, *17*(2), 261–274. doi:10.100710796-014-9489-2

Wilcox, K., Akeson, D., Fair, H. R., Farrell, J., Johnson, D., Krishnan, G., … White, J. (2015). *4.8 A 28nm x86 APU optimized for power and area efficiency*. IEEE International Solid-State Circuits Conference - (ISSCC) Digest of Technical Papers, San Francisco, CA. 10.1109/ISSCC.2015.7062937

Wilson, C., Hargreaves, T., & Hauxwell-Baldwin, R. (2015). Smart homes and their users: A systematic analysis and key challenges. *Personal and Ubiquitous Computing*, *19*(2), 463–476. doi:10.100700779-014-0813-0

Wilson, C., Hargreaves, T., & Hauxwell-Baldwin, R. (2017). Benefits and risks of smart home technologies. *Energy Policy*, *103*, 72–83. doi:10.1016/j.enpol.2016.12.047

Wirdatmadja, S. A., Barros, M. T., Koucheryavy, Y., Jornet, J. M., & Balasubramaniam, S. (2017). Wireless Optogenetic Nanonetworks for Brain Stimulation: Device Model and Charging Protocols. *IEEE Transactions on Nanobioscience*, *16*(8), 859–872. doi:10.1109/TNB.2017.2781150 PMID:29364130

Withanage, C., Ashok, R., Yuen, C., & Otto, K. (2014). *A comparison of the popular home automation technologies*. Paper presented at the Innovative Smart Grid Technologies-Asia (ISGT Asia), 2014 IEEE. 10.1109/ISGT-Asia.2014.6873860

Witten, I. H., Frank, E., Hall, M. A., & Pal, C. J. (2016). *Data Mining: Practical Machine Learning Tools and Techniques*. Morgan Kaufmann.

Wolfert, S., Ge, L., Verdouw, C., & Bogaardt, M. J. (2017). Big data in smart farming–a review. *Agricultural Systems*, *153*, 69–80. doi:10.1016/j.agsy.2017.01.023

Wong, B. P., & Kerkez, B. (2016). Real-time environmental sensor data: An application to water quality using web services. *Environmental Modelling & Software, 84*, 505–517. doi:10.1016/j.envsoft.2016.07.020

Xia, F., Yang, L. T., Wang, L., & Vinel, A. (2012). Internet of Things. *International Journal of Communication Systems, 25*(9), 1101–1102. doi:10.1002/dac.2417

Xiang, D., Wang, X., Jia, C., Lee, T., & Guo, X. (2016). Molecular-scale electronics: From concept to function. *Chemical Reviews, 116*(7), 4318–4440. doi:10.1021/acs.chemrev.5b00680 PMID:26979510

Xiao, Y., & Sun, Y. (2018). *A Dynamic Jamming Game for Real-Time Status Updates.* arXiv:1803.03616 [cs.IT]

Xiao, L., Wan, X., Lu, X., Zhang, Y., & Wu, D. (2018). IoT Security Techniques Based on Machine Learning: How do IoT Devices Use AI to Enhance Security? *IEEE Signal Processing Magazine, 35*(5), 41–49. doi:10.1109/MSP.2018.2825478

Xiao, W., & Starobinski, D. (2005). Exploiting multi-Channel diversity to speed up over-the-air programming of wireless sensor networks. In *Proceedings of the 3rd international conference on Embedded networked sensor systems* (pp. 292-293). ACM. 10.1145/1098918.1098960

Yang, J., Liu, M., Lu, J., Miao, Y., Hossain, M. A., & Alhamid, M. F. (2018). Botanical Internet of Things: Toward Smart Indoor Farming by Connecting People, Plant, Data and Clouds. *Mobile Networks and Applications, 23*(2), 188–202. doi:10.100711036-017-0930-x

Yan, K., Tracie, B., Marie, M., Melanie, H., Jean-Luc, B., Benoit, T., & Marie, L. (2014). Innovation through Wearable Sensors to Collect Real-Life Data among Pediatric Patients with Cardiometabolic Risk Factors. *International Journal of Pediatrics, 2014*, 9. doi:10.1155/2014/328076 PMID:24678323

Ye, X., & Huang, J. (2011). *A framework for cloud-based smart home.* Paper presented at the Computer Science and Network Technology (ICCSNT), 2011 International Conference on.

Yoo, H. J. (1998). Dual vt self-timed CMOS logic for low subthreshold current multigigabit syn-chronous DRAM. *IEEE Transactions on Circuits and Systems. 2, Analog and Digital Signal Processing, 45*(9), 1263–1271. doi:10.1109/82.718594

Younis, S. A., Ijaz, U., Randhawa, I. A., & Ijaz, A. (2018). Speech Recognition Based Home Automation System using Raspberry Pi and Zigbee. *NFC IEFR Journal of Engineering and Scientific Research, 5.*

YouTube. (2018). Introduction to the Internet of Everything. *Eli the Computer Guy.* Retrieved July 26, 2018 from: https://youtu.be/iCzQNTL4-Rs

Yu-Wei, D. C. (2015). *Machine Learning with R Cookbook: Explore over 110 recipes to analyze data and build predictive models with the simple and easy-to-use R code.* Packt Publishing.

Zemede, M. (2015). *Explosion of the Internet of Things: What does it mean for wireless devices.* Keisight. Retrieved from http://www.keysight.com/upload/cmc_upload/All/IoT_Seminar_Session1_Explosion_of_the_Internet_of_Things.pdf, in 18/06/2018.

Zhai, B., Blaauw, D., Sylvester, D., & Flautner, K. (2004). *Theoretical and Practical Limits of Dynamic Voltage Scaling.* DAC2004, San Diego, CA. 10.1145/996566.996798

Zhai, S., Morimoto, C., & Ihde, S. (1999). Manual and gaze input cascaded (MAGIC) pointing. In *Proceedings of the ACM CHI'99 Human Factors in Computing Systems Conference* (pp. 246-253). Addison-Wesley/ACM Press. 10.1145/302979.303053

Zhang, M., & Fang, Y. (2005). Security analysis and enhancements of 3GPP authentication and key agreement protocol. *IEEE Transactions on Wireless Communications, 4*(2), 734–742. doi:10.1109/TWC.2004.842941

Zheng, X.-L., & Wan, M. (2014). A survey on data dissemination in wireless sensor networks. *Journal of Computer Science and Technology*, *29*(3), 470–486. doi:10.100711390-014-1443-8

Zhou, B., Li, W., Chan, K. W., Cao, Y., Kuang, Y., Liu, X., & Wang, X. (2016). Smart home energy management systems: Concept, configurations, and scheduling strategies. *Renewable & Sustainable Energy Reviews*, *61*, 30–40. doi:10.1016/j.rser.2016.03.047

Zhou, K., Liu, T., & Zhou, L. (2015). Industry 4.0: Towards future industrial opportunities and challenges. *12th International Conference on Fuzzy Systems and Knowledge Discovery (FSKD)*, 2147-2152. 10.1109/FSKD.2015.7382284

Zhu, C., Sheng, W., & Liu, M. (2015). Wearable Sensor-Based Behavioral Anomaly Detection in Smart Assisted Living Systems. *Automation Science and Engineering. IEEE Transactions on*, *12*(4), 1225–1234. doi:10.1109/TASE.2015.2474743

Zhu, N., Diethe, T., Camplani, M., Tao, L., Burrows, A., Twomey, N., ... Craddock, I. (2015). Bridging e-Health and the Internet of Things: The SPHERE Project. *IEEE Intelligent Systems*, *30*(4), 39–46. doi:10.1109/MIS.2015.57

Zigbee Alliance. (2014). *Webinar presentation: Introducing ZigBee 3.0*. Retrieved from http://www.zigbee.org/download/introducing-zigbee-3-0-webinar-presentation/

Zigbee Alliance. (2017). *Zigbee 3.0 Base Device Behavior Specification*. Retrieved from http://www.zigbee.org/download/paper-zigbee-3-0-base-device-behavior-specification/

Zwolenski, M., & Weatherill, L. (2014). The digital universe: Rich data and the increasing value of the internet of things. *Australian Journal of Telecommunications and the Digital Economy*, *2*(3), 47. doi:10.7790/ajtde.v2n3.47

About the Contributors

Pedro Cardoso holds a PhD in the field of Operational Research from the University of Seville (Spain), a Master in Computational Mathematics from the University of Minho (Portugal) and a Degree in Mathematics - Computer Science from the University of Coimbra (Portugal). He teaches Computer Science and Mathematics at University the Algarve (UAlg) and is member of LARSyS/UAlg. He has high knowledge in the fields of databases, algorithms and data structures, machine learning, data science, and operational research. Over the past few years he edited 2 books with IGI, has been involved in 8 national and international scientific and development projects and is the co-author of more than 60 scientific publications.

Jânio Monteiro graduated in Electrical and Computers Engineering in 1995 from the University of Porto, and later obtained a Master and PhD degrees respectively in 2003 and 2010, also in Electrical and Computer Engineering from Instituto Superior Técnico, Technical University of Lisbon. Since 2003 is a member INESC-ID in Lisbon, where he participated in several European R&TD projects funded by the Information Society Technologies Programme (IST), of the European Commission, namely: Olympic, My-e-Director and Saracen. As part of the Algarve University he has also participated in an international project called ENERGEIA and several national projects with regional companies. He is co-author of more than three dozen publications, including journal articles, papers in scientific conferences, several book chapters, deliverables of projects and national patents. His main areas of interest involve Communication Networks, Smart Grids, Wireless Sensor Networks, Human Machine Interfaces and Internet of Things.

Jorge Semião graduated in Electrical and Computer Engineering from Instituto Superior Técnico - Technical University of Lisbon in 1996, and obtained the Master, in 2001, and the PhD, in 2010, also in Electrical and Computer Engineering from the same university, with specialization in Microelectronics and Electronic and Computer Systems. He started working in research in 1995 at INESC, and now he is a senior researcher at INESC-ID in Lisbon. His main research interests are the design and optimization of digital integrated circuits, the design for testability and the test of electronic circuits, the project of fault-tolerant circuits and the aging of electronic circuits. He participated in several research projects (12), and is the author and co-author of more than 90 scientific articles published, four national patents and four patents still under patent pending. Also obtained awards for "Best INESC-ID PhD student in 2010," for "Best Internship in Electrical Engineering" (awarded by the Ordem dos Engenheiros in 2001), and "Best Teacher in the Bachelor of Electrical and Electronics Engineering " (EST - University of Algarve, in 1999).

João Rodrigues graduated in Electrical Engineering in 1993, he got his M.Sc. in Computer Systems Engineering in 1998 and Ph.D. Electronics and Computer Engineering in 2008 from University of the Algarve, Portugal. He is Adjunct Professor at Instituto Superior de Engenharia, also in the University of the Algarve, where he lectures Computer Science and Computer Vision since 1994. He is member of associative laboratory LARSyS (ISR-Lisbon), CIAC and the Associations APRP, IAPR and ARTECH. He participated in 15 financed scientific projects, and he is co-author more than 120 scientific publications. His major research interests lie in computer and human vision, assistive technologies and human-computer interaction.

* * *

Ozgur B. Akan received his Ph.D. degree in electrical and computer engineering from the Broadband and Wireless Networking Laboratory, School of Electrical and Computer Engineering, Georgia Institute of Technology, Atlanta in 2004. He is currently with the Electrical Engineering Division, Department of Engineering, University of Cambridge, United Kingdom, and the Head of the Internet of Everything (IoE) Group at University of Cambridge. He is also the director of the Next-Generation and Wireless Communications Laboratory in the Department of Electrical and Electronics Engineering, Koc University. His research interests include wireless, nano, and molecular communications, and the Internet of Everything.

Bilgesu Arif Bilgin received his B.S. degree in electrical and electronics engineering from Middle East Technical University in 2008, M.Sc. and Ph.D. degrees in mathematics from Koc University, in 2011 and 2015, respectively. After completing his PhD, he has worked in Next-generation Wireless Communications Lab (NWCL) at Koc University as a postdoctoral research fellow until 2017. He is currently carrying out his research as a postdoctoral fellow in Internet of Everything (IoE) group at the University of Cambridge.

Ruben Cabral is an electrical engineer who is currently working on power and frequency optimization for long term operation of synchronous digital circuits. His other interests are high-level modelling and wireless communication systems like digital broadcast radio (DAB) and IEEE 802.15.3c On his free time Ruben is an advocate of free software and a GNU/Linux user.

Cristiano Cabrita is a 1998 – Graduate Degree in Systems and Computing Engineering from the University of Algarve 1999 – Joined the Department of Electrical Engineering at the Higher Institute for Engineering (ISE), University of Algarve as an Assistant Professor 2001 – M.Sc in systems and computing Engineering from the University of Algarve, Portugal 2004 – Adjoint Professor at the Department of Electrical Engineering at the ISE, University of Algarve 2014 - PhD in electronics and telecommunication engineer in in the field of intelligent systems. His main research areas of interest relate to Systems Identification based on neural networks and fuzzy systems applying Soft computing based algorithms for Local and Global optimization methodologies, such as but not limited to: Neurofuzzy training algorithms, genetic algorithms, genetic programming - time series prediction. Application of neurofuzzy systems and neural networks as models in machine learning.

Sergio Casas-Yrurzum has a master's degree in Computer Engineering and also a bachelor's degree in Telecommunications Engineering - Telematics Specialty. He received the Spanish National Award on University Studies in 2008. He received his PhD in Computational Mathematics at the University of Valencia in 2014. He works as a senior researcher in the Robotics Institute (IRTIC) of the University of Valencia, where he is also a part-time professor at the School of Engineering (ETSE). His expertise is in the simulation field with special focus on Virtual Reality, Augmented Reality and motion cueing.

Dario Cruz obtained a Bachelor Degree in Computer Engineering and Automation in 2013 at the University of Cape Verde and later, in 2018, a Master degree in Electrical and Electronic Engineering at the University of Algarve. Since 2017, he has been working in several research projects at the University of Algarve. His knowledge fields include algorithms for the scheduling of electric vehicles charging, load of electric vehicles protocols and machine learning algorithms.

Ergin Dinc received his B.Sc. degree in Electrical and Electronics Engineering from Bogazici University, Istanbul, Turkey, in July 2012. He received his Ph.D. degree in Electrical and Electronics Engineering from Koc University, Istanbul, Turkey in June 2016. He was a postdoctoral researcher at The Royal Institute of Technology (KTH), Stockholm, Sweden between September 2016 and July 2017. He is currently a postdoctoral research associate in the Internet of Everything (IoE) Group at The University of Cambridge, Cambridge, UK. He is affiliated with the Christ's College, Cambridge. He is the co-Finance Chair of ACM International Conference on Nanoscale Computing and Communication (NanoCom), 2018, Reykjavik, Iceland. He is TPC member for IEEE Emerging Technologies and Factory Automation (ETFA) 2018, Torino, Italy; ACM International Conference on Modeling, Analysis and Simulation of Wireless and Mobile Systems (MSWiM) 2018; IEEE Vehicular Technology Conference (VTC) 2018-Fall, Chicago, USA. He conducts theoretical and experimental research on molecular communication, neural communication and cyber-physical systems.

Inma García-Pereira received the degrees in Audiovisual Communication (2008) and Computer engineering (2015) from the University of Valencia, Spain. She is part of the research team of the University Research Institute on Robotics and Information and Communication Technologies (IRTIC) at the University of Valencia. In this institute she belongs to the ARTEC group, dedicated to 3D interactive graphics, virtual reality, augmented reality and civil simulation. Currently, she is developing her doctorate in the field of indoor real-time locating systems and its application to augmented reality.

Jesús Gimeno Sancho received the master degree (2008) and PhD in Computer Science from the University of Valencia (2016), with a dissertation about "Contributions to the Authoring of Augmented Reality Contents for Education, Industry and Construction Sectors". Currently he is researcher at the IRTIC Institute and part-time professor at the University of Valencia. His research interests include augmented reality, virtual reality, motion capture, real time simulation, advanced user interfaces and mobile computing. In the last years he has served also as visiting scientist at the Augmented Reality Group at Bauhaus Universitat (Weimar, Germany, 2008) and at VRAC Center at Iowa State University (Ames IO, USA, 2010).

Gabriele Giunta (male) obtained a degree in Computer Science, at the Engineering Department of the University of Palermo (Italy). He is head of the "Smart Transport and Infrastructure" Unit within the R&D Laboratory of "Intelligent Systems and Social Software (IS3) for Security, Enterprises, Transport, Infrastructure" at ENGINEERING. He has participated in several Italian Ministry and EC co-funded research projects, such as MAIS (Multichannel Adaptive Information System), DISCoRSO (Distributed Information Systems for CooRdinated Service Oriented interoperability) and NEXOF-RA (Reference Architecture for NESSI Open Framework). In the filed of Smart Transport and Critical Infrastructure Protection, he has coordianted two national projects: Easy Rider (Enhancement of sustAinability and Safety of mobility by integRating Intelligent roaDs, vEhicles and service) and SECURE! (http://secure.eng.it). At the present time, he is involved in STORM (Safeguarding Cultural Heritage through Technical and Organisational Resources Management), an H2020 EU project for design, developing and assessing a technological integrated framework, providing eco-innovative, cost-effective and collaborative methodologies to support all the involved stakeholders to better act in the CH prevention and intervention phases. He is also involved in the H2020 EU DEFENDER (Defending the European Energy Infrastructures) project for developing an adaptable framework for Critical Energy Infrastructure (CEI) security and resilience. Main areas of interest and relevant expertise include Software Engineering, Software Architecture Design, System Integration, Complex Event Processing, Data Mining, Information Fusion, Human-Computer Interaction, Semantic Web Technologies, Knowledge Modeling and Representation, Business Process Modeling and Management, Service Oriented Computing. He has been co-author of several scientific papers in International Conferences and Journals.

Janet Holland completed a Ph.D. in Instructional Design and Technology, with a minor in Communications from the University of Kansas. Dr. Holland currently serves as a Professor at Emporia State University in Emporia, Kansas, teaching graduate students in Instructional Design and Technology. She has served as president of the Kansas Association for Educational and Communications Technology, and conference chair. Research and publication interests include instructional design and technology, human computer interaction design, biometric research including eye tracking, augmented reality, wearable technologies, mobile learning, online learning, and globalization. Dr. Holland has published many book chapters and journal articles, with presentations at many conferences across the US and internationally in Paris, London, Rome. She has won awards for both teaching and research at Emporia State University. As an instructional designer, new technologies are continually examined in an effort to inspire innovative teaching and learning practices.

Viacheslav Izosimov particular areas of my research interest include smart safety-critical embedded systems, mechatronics, robotics, systems of systems, cyber-physical systems and Internet of Things (IoT). I look into dependability, fault tolerance, security and safety aspects of these systems, in connection to hardware level, operating systems, systems architectures and development processes, as well as self-awareness and artificial intelligence of these systems.

José Jasnau Caeiro born the 15th of March 1963. B.Sc. Physics Engineering and Materials Science, Faculdade de Ciências e Tecnolo- gia/Universidade Nova de Lisboa, 1986; MSc. in Electrical and Computer Engineering, Instituto Superior Técnico/Universidade de Lisboa, 1993; PhD. in Electrical and Computer Engineering, Instituto Superior Técnico/Universidade de Lisboa, 2010. Assistant professor of computer science at the Instituto Politécnico de Beja, and invited researcher at INESC-ID Lisboa.

Panagiotis Kasnesis holds a Ph.D degree in computer science from the Department of Electrical and Computer Engineering at the National Technical University of Athens (NTUA). Moreover, he received his Diploma degree in chemical engineering and his M.Sc. in techno-economic systems from the NTUA, in 2008 and 2013 respectively. He has participated as a researcher in several EU research projects and has an expertise in machine learning, Semantic Web technologies and the Internet of Things. He has more than ten publications in international journals, conferences and book chapters.

Dimitrios G. Kogias received his diploma in Physics from the National and Kapodistrian University of Athens in 2001. In December 2004 he received his M.Sc. in Electronics and Radioelectrology and in May 2010 his Ph.D degree from the National and Kapodistrian University of Athens. Currently, he works as an Adjunct Professor in the Department of Electronics at the Piraeus University of Applied Sciences (PUAS). He has, also, participated in various Research projects (e.g., most recently on TRILLION and STORM at HORIZON 2020) funded from National and/or European resources. His current research interests include security in the Internet of Things (IoT), Machine-to-Machine (M2M) communications, privacy issues in these environments and Cloud integration. His works have been published in international Journals and Conferences, while he has, also, co-authored scientific book chapters.

Kai Kreuzer holds a diploma in Mathematics from the Technical University of Darmstadt and is an alumni of the Imperial College London, UK. He works as a Developer Evangelist in the Consumer IoT department of Deutsche Telekom and is a regular speaker at international conferences. In an honorary capacity he is founder of the openHAB project, president of the openHAB Foundation, project lead of Eclipse SmartHome and co-lead of the Eclipse IoT top-level project.

Murat Kuscu received the B.Sc. degree in electrical and electronics engineering from Middle East Technical University (METU), Turkey, in 2011, and the M.Sc. and Ph.D. degrees in Electrical and Electronics Engineering Department of Koc University, Turkey, in 2013 and 2017, respectively. He was a research assistant at Next-generation and Wireless Communications Laboratory (NWCL) between 2011-2017. He is currently a research assistant in the Internet of Everything (IoE) Group, Department of Engineering, University of Cambridge, UK. His current research interests include nanoscale and molecular communications, graphene biosensors, and Internet of Everything.

Sungwoong Lee is an Assistant Professor in the Department of Instructional Design at Emporia State University. He is a broadly trained researcher in Game Studies, with a specialization in scaffolding game-based learning and virtual world design. His dissertation addressed how educational games, combined with various types of learning supports, promoted the acquisition and application of conceptual understanding in order to enhance mathematical problem-solving in the formal educational context. Specifically, he investigated the effects of representation format (i.e., pictorial vs. text representation) on math problem-solving skills in the domain of conceptual understanding. Dr. Lee has conducted design-based research in two areas: scaffolding learning in virtual worlds such as simulation and game environments, and applying new technologies to the classroom setting. He explored the applications and effects of the virtual world on learning with diverse subjects, including students who met normal developmental milestones as well as special-needs students such as children with autism. He is contributing to two research projects on: Earthquake Rebuild - Mathematical Thinking and Learning via Architectural Design and Modeling and Virtual-Reality-Based Social Skills Training for Children with

Asperger's Syndrome. Currently, he has started a new research project to enhance preservice teachers' computational thinking in a makerspace environment.

Kai Lehniger received his M.Sc. degree in computer science from the Brandenburg University of Technology Cottbus - Senftenberg, in 2017. Since 2017 he is member of the sensor networks and mobile middleware group at IHP in Frankfurt (Oder), Germany. His current research interests include energy efficient code updates for wireless sensor networks.

Giuseppe Li Calsi is a Software Engineer with a bachelor's degree in Computer Science. He is skilled in software systems architecture and development and has over ten years of experience on this sector. He has participated in several Italian Ministry and EC co-funded research projects such as Secure, Easy Rider, SeNSori and STORM, contributing to the definition of the software system architecture and to the development of the related software platforms.

Gonçalo Marques is a PhD student in Computer Science Engineering, UBI (University of Beira Interior), thesis title "Internet of Things Architecture for Enhanced Living Environments". He has M.Sc. in Mobile Computing from the Polytechnic Institute of Guarda, Portugal and an Engineering degree in Computer Science also from the same institution. His research interests include software architecture, Internet of Things, intelligent systems, health informatics and ambient assisted living.

João Carlos da Silva Martins born the 3rd of June 1969. B.Sc. Physics Engineering, Faculdade de Ciências e Tecnologia/Universidade Nova de Lisboa, 1994; MSc. in Electrical and Computer Engineering, Instituto Superior Técnico/Universidade de Lisboa, 2008; Ph.D. in Electrical and Computer Engineering, Instituto Superior Técnico/Universidade de Lisboa, 2013. Assistant professor of computer science at the Instituto Politécnico de Beja, and invited researcher at INESC-ID Lisboa.

Luís M. R. Oliveira received the Electrical Engineering diploma, the MSc degree in Electrical Engineering and the PhD degree in Electrical Engineering from the University of Coimbra, Coimbra, Portugal, in 1995, 2001 and 2014, respectively. In 1996 he joined the University of Algarve, Portugal, where he is currently an Adjunct Professor. He is also a researcher in CISE – Electromechatronic Systems Research Centre, Covilhã, Portugal. His research interests include modelling and simulation, fault diagnostics, and protection of electric power systems components.

Charalampos Z. Patrikakis is an Associate Professor at the Dept. of Electronics Engineering of Piraeus University of Applied Sciences. He has participated in more than 32 National, European and International programs, in 16 of which he has been involved as technical coordinator or principal researcher. He has more than 100 publications in chapters of books, international journals and conferences, and has 2 contributions in national legislation. He is a member of the editorial committee of more than 50 international journals and conferences, and has acted as editor in the publication of special issues of international journals, conference proceedings volumes and coedited three books. He is a senior member of IEEE, Assistant Editor In Chief (Special Issues) of IEEE IT Pro Magazine, member of the Technical Chamber of Greece, the European Association for Theoretical Computer Science, ACM, and counselor of the IEEE student department of Piraeus University of Applied Sciences.

Nelson Pinto graduated in Electronic and Telecommunications Engineering Sciences in 2016 from the University of Algarve, and he is currently finishing in the same university, a Master in Electrical Engineering. He is an researcher in European funded project Agerar, focusing in "Renewable Energies", "Energy Management and Efficiency" and "Micro and Smart Grids". His main areas of interest are telecommunications, wireless sensor networks and microelectronics.

Cristina Portalés (PhD in Surveying and Geoinformation, with specialization in Augmented Reality, 2008; IEEE Computer Society member) has been recently (2012-2015) a Juan de la Cierva post-doc fellow at the Institute of Robotics and Information and Communication Technology (IRTIC) at Universitat de València (Spain), where she currently works as full PhD senior researcher. She was formerly graduated with a double degree: Engineer in Geodesy and Cartography from the Universidad Politécnica de Valencia (Spain) and MSc in Surveying and Geoinformation from the Technische Universität Wien (Austria), with the specialization in photogrammetry/computer vision. She obtained her first diploma degree (Bachelor) with honours, for having the best academic record, being awarded with the San Isidoro prize. She was an ERASMUS, PROMOE and Leonardo da Vinci research fellow at the Institute of Photogrammetry and Remote Sensing (Vienna, 1999-2002), a PhD research fellow at the Mixed Reality Laboratory of the University of Nottingham (UK, 2005) and at the Interaction and Entertainment Research Centre of the Nanyang University of Singapore (2006). She received an outstanding PhD. Award by the UPV. First woman receiving the EH Thompson Award (best paper), given by the Remote Sensing and Photogrammetry Society (2010). During 2008-2010 she worked at the Photogrammetry and Laser Scanning Research Group (GIFLE) of the UPV, and during 2011-2012 she at the Technological Institute of Optics, Colour and Imaging (AIDO), being primarily involved in computer-vision related projects and in the project FP7-SYDDARTA, coordinating the technical work of the WP dedicated to software implementation and carrying out managerial tasks. She has been designed (since 2014) as the proposal coordinator for her research group (ARTEC). She is author of more than 60 scientific publications including international conferences, high impact journals, books and book chapters. She has been invited speaker by Univ. Granada, Aula Natura, UNITEC (Honduras), RUVID & Univ. Gjøvik (Norway). She is S&T program committee of diverse international conferences (e.g. ACM SIGCHI ACE, GECCO), highlighting her involvement in the IEEE ISMAR (CORE A*) for taking decisions on the selected papers. She is also reviewer of scientific journals with impact factors (e.g. MDPI Sensors, Springer Journal of Digital Imaging, Elsevier Computers in Industry). Cristina has co-organized the successful ACM Advances in Computer Entertainment Technology Conference 2005. Expert evaluator of FP7 and H2020 proposals. She is Deputy Editor-in-Chief of the scientific journal Multimodal Technologies and Interaction (MTI), and Editor-in-Chief of the International Journal of Virtual and Augmented Reality.

Amany Sarhan received the B.Sc degree in Electronics Engineering, and M.Sc. in Computer Engineering from the Faculty of Engineering, Mansoura University, in 1990, and 1997, respectively. She awarded the Ph.D. degree as a joint research between Tanta Univ., Egypt and Univ. of Connecticut, USA. She is working now as a Full Prof. and head Computers and Control Dept., Tanta Univ., Egypt. Her interests are in the area of: Distributed Systems, Software Restructuring, Object-oriented Databases, and Image and video processing, GPU and Distributed Computations.

Mario Schölzel received a diploma degree in computer science in 2001 from the Brandenburg University of Technology (BTU) in Cottbus. From 2001 to 2006 he worked in the compiler construction group at BTU and received his doctoral degree in 2006. Starting in 2007, he was with the computer engineering group at BTU and worked in the field of fault tolerant computing. In 2014 he received his habilitation degree and became a Professor for Dependable and Energy Efficient Sensor Networks at the Institute of Computational Science at the University of Potsdam. Since 2014 he is also the leader of a junior scientists group at the Leibniz Institute for Innovative Microelectronics (IHP) in Frankfurt (Oder).

Martin Törngren has been a Professor in Embedded Control Systems at the Mechatronics division of the KTH Department of Machine Design since 2002. He has particular interest in Cyber-Physical Systems, model based engineering, architectural design, systems integration, and co-design of control applications and embedded systems. He has authored/co-authored more than 100 peer reviewed publications, and also been in charge of developing and leading graduate and continued education courses. He spent time as a post-doc at the EU-JRC, and did a 10 month sabbatical 2011/12 at UC Berkeley. In 1996 he co-founded the company Fengco Real-time Control AB, specializing in advanced tools for developers of embedded control systems and related consultancy. In 1994 he received the SAAB-Scania award for qualified contributions in distributed control systems, and in 2004 the ITEA achievement award 2004 for contributions in the EAST-EEA project. He served as the technical coordinator of the international iFEST ARTEMIS project with 21 partners (2010-2013). Networking and multidisciplinary research have been characteristic throughout his career. From 1999-2004 he served as the Chairman of the Swedish real-time systems association, and he has represented KTH as a core partner in the EU networks of excellence in Embedded systems design, Artist2 and ArtistDesign, and in the Artemis industrial association. He is moreover the principal initiator and Director

Lazaros Toumanidis was born on 1983 in Thessaloniki, Greece. He received his Electronics Engineering degree from the Piraeus University of Applied Sciences in 2014 (first in his class). Since then, he has been working in National and EU research projects. He is a research associate of the CONSERT team of the Communications & Networks Lab of the Electrical & Electronics Engineering Department of University of West Attica.

Stefan Weidling received his Diploma in Computer Science (2012) and the Dr. rer. nat. degree in the field of fault-tolerant system design (2016) from the University of Potsdam, Germany. Currently, he is working as a postdoctoral researcher in the sensor networks and middleware platforms group at IHP in Frankfurt (Oder), Germany. His current research focuses on new methods for improving the energy efficiency, reliability, and maintenance of wireless sensor networks as resource-constrained computing systems.

Christian Wittke received his M.Sc. degree in information and media technology from the Brandenburg University of Technology Cottbus - Senftenberg, in 2013. Since 2013 he is member of the sensor networks and mobile middleware group at the Leibniz Institute for Innovative Microelectronics (IHP) in Frankfurt (Oder), Germany. He is currently pursuing the Ph.D. degree in computer science. His research interests include the development of hardware implementations for elliptic curve cryptography and their resistance to side channel analysis attacks.

Michael G. Xevgenis is a junior researcher at the Dept of Electronics Engineering of TEI of Piraeus and holds the MSc in Networking and Data Communications of Kingston University of London in collaboration with TEI of Piraeus. He has participated in the cloud federation project in association with researchers of the NTUA. He has experience in troubleshooting telephony problems, internet connectivity problems and satellite TV problems, skills that he acquired when he worked at Forthnet S.A in the first level technical support dept. In addition, he has worked at O.T.E in the second level technical support department as network administrator in matters of troubleshooting network problems for ADSL, VDSL and OTETV IPTV users. He participates in the EU projects STORM and TRILLION, as is the cloud administrator of PUAS' OpenStack Infrastructure.

Index

A

B

C

D

E

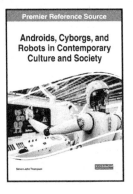

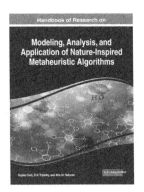

Ensure Quality Research is Introduced to the Academic Community

Become an IGI Global Reviewer for Authored Book Projects

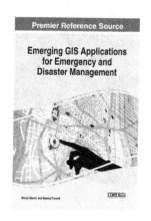

The overall success of an authored book project is dependent on quality and timely reviews.

In this competitive age of scholarly publishing, constructive and timely feedback significantly expedites the turnaround time of manuscripts from submission to acceptance, allowing the publication and discovery of forward-thinking research at a much more expeditious rate. Several IGI Global authored book projects are currently seeking highly qualified experts in the field to fill vacancies on their respective editorial review boards:

Applications may be sent to:
development@igi-global.com

Applicants must have a doctorate (or an equivalent degree) as well as publishing and reviewing experience. Reviewers are asked to write reviews in a timely, collegial, and constructive manner. All reviewers will begin their role on an ad-hoc basis for a period of one year, and upon successful completion of this term can be considered for full editorial review board status, with the potential for a subsequent promotion to Associate Editor.

If you have a colleague that may be interested in this opportunity, we encourage you to share this information with them.

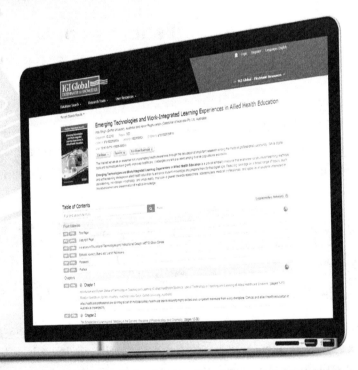

Printed in the United States
By Bookmasters